Quests for Freedom

Quests for Freedom

Biblical, Historical, Contemporary

SECOND EDITION

Edited by
Michael Welker

CASCADE Books · Eugene, Oregon

QUESTS FOR FREEDOM
Biblical, Historical, Contemporary
Second edition

Copyright © 2019 Wipf and Stock Publishers. All rights reserved. Except for brief quotations in critical publications or reviews, no part of this book may be reproduced in any manner without prior written permission from the publisher. Write: Permissions, Wipf and Stock Publishers, 199 W. 8th Ave., Suite 3, Eugene, OR 97401.

The first edition of this volume was published by Neukirchener Verlagsgesellschaft mbH.

Cascade Books
An Imprint of Wipf and Stock Publishers
199 W. 8th Ave., Suite 3
Eugene, OR 97401

www.wipfandstock.com

PAPERBACK ISBN: 978-1-5326-5397-1
HARDCOVER ISBN: 978-1-5326-5398-8
EBOOK ISBN: 978-1-5326-5399-5

Cataloguing-in-Publication data:

Names: Welker, Michael, 1947–, editor.
Title: Quests for freedom : biblical, historical, contemporary, 2nd ed. / edited by Michael Welker.
Description: Eugene, OR: Cascade Books, 2019. | Includes bibliographical references and indexes.
Identifiers: ISBN: 978-1-5326-5397-1 (paperback). | ISBN: 978-1-5326-5398-8 (hardcover). | ISBN: 978-1-5326-5399-5 (ebook).
Subjects: LCSH: Liberty—Congresses. | Liberty—Religious aspects—Christianity—Congresses. | Liberty—Biblical teaching—Congresses. | Political theology.
Classification: JC585 Q478 2019 (print). | JC585 (ebook).

Manufactured in the U.S.A.

Contents

Acknowledgments / ix
Preface to the Second Edition / xi
List of Contributors / xiii
Abbreviations / xv

Introduction: Concepts and Practices of Freedom in the Biblical Traditions and in Contemporary Contexts / *Michael Welker* / 1

PART 1: Freedom and Domination

Introduction / *Elisabeth Schüssler Fiorenza* / 7

1. A Blight on the Nation: Slavery in Today's America / Ron Soodalter / 14

2. "To Be a Free Nation": Myth, Ritual, and Ethics of Freedom in the Old Testament as Political Encouragement / *Manfred Oeming* / 26

3. Slave Wo/men and Freedom in the Pauline Tradition: Some Methodological Reflections / *Elisabeth Schüssler Fiorenza* / 46

4. The Paradox of Freedom: Mary, the Manhattan Declaration and Women's Submission to Childbearing / *Katharina von Kellenbach* / 72

PART 2: Self-Determination and Concepts of Freedom

Introduction / *Peter Lampe* / 95

5. What It Is to Be Free / *Rüdiger Bittner* / 98

6. Concepts of Freedom in Antiquity: Pagan Philosophical Traditions in the Greco-Roman World / *Peter Lampe* / 116

7. Two Meanings of Freedom in the Eastern Patristic Tradition / *Cyril Hovorun* / 134

8. Freedom, Sin, and Evil: Lutheran Meditations / *Risto Saarinen* / 147

9. Protestant Concepts of Freedom and Their Foundations in Biblical Traditions / *Friederike Nüssel* / 164

PART 3: Freedom as Given and Shaped by God

Introduction / *Larry W. Hurtado* / 183

10. God's Work for Human Freedom / *Patrick D. Miller* / 185

11. Freedom in Apocalyptic Perspective: A Reflection on Paul's Letter to the Romans / *Beverly Roberts Gaventa* / 199

12. Freed by Love and for Love: Freedom in the New Testament / *Larry W. Hurtado* / 214

13. The Innovative Concept of Freedom in Paul / *Hans-Joachim Eckstein* / 235

PART 4: Freedom as Ethos of Belonging

Introduction / *Dirk J. Smit* / 251

14. Concepts of Freedom in Deuteronomy / *Jan Christian Gertz* / 254

15. Potentials for Freedom in Concepts of Order: Transformations of Wisdom and Political Theology in the Hebrew Bible / *Jürgen van Oorschot* / 267

16. Freedom in Community: "Surprising Discovery" and "Paradoxical Connection"? / *Dirk J. Smit* / 278

17. Concepts of Freedom in the Czech Reformation / *Jindřich Halama* / 315

PART 5: The Dialectics of Freedom and Modernity

Introduction / *Michael Welker* / 339

18. Freedom and Commitment: Christian Tradition and Liberal Humanism / *Carver T. Yu* / 343

19. Freedom in Postcolonial Perspective / *Susan Abraham* / 360

20. Freedom and Human Rights: The Cosmopolitan Context of the Justification of Rights in Roman Catholicism / *Francis Schüssler Fiorenza* / 384

21. Divine Spirit and Human Freedom / *Michael Welker* / 413

Scripture Index / 427
Names Index / 438

Acknowledgments

This book documents the results of an extended interdisciplinary and international dialogue about concepts and practices of freedom in the biblical traditions and contemporary contexts. We brought together theologians, professors of religious studies and philosophy, historians and biblical scholars. They came from the USA, Scotland, Germany, Finland, Czech Republic, South Africa, and Hong Kong.

The multi-year dialogue was made possible by the generosity of the RAG Aktiengesellschaft and its former member of the Managing Board, Ulrich Weber (now Managing Board of the DB). We are very grateful to him and to the Evangelische Kirche im Rheinland, which brought us into contact with the RAG and also opened its Film Funk Fernseh Zentrum (FFFZ) in Düsseldorf with special rates for some of our meetings. In particular, we thank the former Präses Dr. Nikolaus Schneider, former Vizepräses Petra Bosse-Huber, Vizepräses Christian Drägert and Prof. Dr. Bernd Wander. We also thank the wonderful staff of the FFFZ.

We are most grateful to Sabine Wagner who was a perfect organizer of our meetings in Düsseldorf, Berlin, and Heidelberg over several years. We thank Dr. Nina Mützlitz, Elisabeth Deutscher, and Hajo Kenkel for perfect cooperation in preparing the manuscript for publication. Finally, we are very grateful to the Neukirchener Verlag and Ekkehard Starke.

Michael Welker
Heidelberg, Spring 2014

Preface to the Second Edition

This book explores a very wide range of theological, philosophical, psychological, social, and political concepts and practices of freedom. In several years of collaboration and many fruitful discussions, it has been developed by scholars from eight countries and four continents. Only one year after its publication in Germany, it was out of print, although its international distribution left much to be desired. We are therefore delighted that the Cascade Books, an imprint of Wipf and Stock Publishing, has prepared and launched a new edition, which now includes bibliographies for each essay as well as indexes for Scripture and names.

May this book continue to promote international and interdisciplinary reflection on freedom, its framework conditions, its powers of radiation, and creativity—and its numerous endangerments.

Michael Welker
Heidelberg, January 2019

Contributors

Susan Abraham is Assistant Professor of Theological Studies at Loyola Marymount University Los Angeles, USA.

Rüdiger Bittner is Professor emeritus of Philosophy at the University in Bielefeld, Germany.

Hans-Joachim Eckstein is Professor of New Testament Studies at the University of Tübingen, Germany.

Beverly Roberts Gaventa is Distinguished Professor of New Testament in the Department of Religion at Baylor University, USA.

Jan Christian Gertz is Professor of Old Testament Studies at the University of Heidelberg, Germany.

Jindřich Halama is Professor of the Department of Theological Ethics at the University of Prague, Czech Republic.

Cyril Hovorun is Lecturer at the faculty of the Theological Academy of Kiev, Ukraine, and visiting professor at Yale Divinity School.

Larry W. Hurtado is Professor emeritus of New Testament Language, Literature and Theology at the University of Edinburgh, Scotland.

Katharina von Kellenbach is Professor of Religious Studies and former Chair of the Department of Philosophy and Religious Studies at St. Mary's College of Maryland, the Honors College of the State of Maryland, USA.

Peter Lampe is Professor of New Testament Studies at the University of Heidelberg, Germany.

Patrick D. Miller is Professor emeritus of Old Testament Theology at Princeton Theological Seminary, USA.

Friederike Nüssel is Professor of Systematic Theology at the Heidelberg University, Germany.

Manfred Oeming is Professor of Old Testament Studies at the University in Heidelberg, Germany.

Jürgen van Oorschot is Professor of Old Testament Studies at the Friedrich-Alexander-University in Erlangen-Nürnberg, Germany.

Risto Saarinen is Professor of Ecumenical Theology at the University of Helsinki, Finland.

Elisabeth Schüssler Fiorenza is Professor of New Testament Studies at Harvard Divinity School in Cambride, USA.

Francis Schüssler Fiorenza is Professor of Roman Catholic Theological Studies at Harvard Divinity School in Cambridge, USA.

Dirk J. Smit is Professor for Systematic Theology at Stellenbosch University, South Africa.

Ron Soodalter serves on the Board of Directors of the Abraham Lincoln Institute, Maryland, USA.

Michael Welker is Senior Professor of Systematic Theology at the University of Heidelberg, Germany.

Carver T. Yu is President and Professor in Dogmatic Theology at the China Graduate School of Theology in Hong Kong.

Abbreviations

BZAW	Beiträge zur Zeitschrift für die alttestamentliche Wissenschaft
FRLANT	Forschungen zur Religion und Literatur des Alten und Neuen Testaments
HUT	Hermeneutische Untersuchungen zur Theologie
LCL	Loeb Classical Library
TDNT	*Theological Dictionary of the New Testament.* 10 vols. Edited by Gerhard Kittel and Gerhard Friedrich. Translated by Geoffrey W. Bromiley. Grand Rapids: Eerdmans, 1964–76
TDOT	*Theological Dictionary of the Old Testament.* 16 vols. Edited by G. Johannes Botterweck, Helmer Ringgren, and Heinz-Josef Fabray. Grand Rapids: Eerdmans, 1974–2018
TRE	*Theologische Realenzyklopädie.* 40 vols. Edited by Gerhard Müller et al. Berlin: de Gruyter, 1977–
TWNT	*Theologische Wörterbuch zum Neuen Testament.* 10 vols. Edited by Gerhard Kittel and Gerhard Friedrich. Stuttgart: Kohlhammer, 1932–79
WUNT	Wissenschaftliche Untersuchungen zum Neuen Testament
ZAW	*Zeitschrift für die alttestamentliche Wissenschaft*
ZNW	*Zeitschrift für die neutestamentliche Wissenschaft*

Introduction

Concepts and Practices of Freedom in the Biblical Traditions and in Contemporary Contexts

Michael Welker

In his contribution "What It Is to Be Free," the philosopher Rüdiger Bittner argues that freedom is marked by a degree, by a caliber. "Your freedom is nothing but your world's unhostility"—and our world can be more or less hostile or unhostile towards us. He warns against "high-minded statements both of individual and political freedom." We should rather ask where we are "held back, where we are oppressed, and what to do about it," where we can avoid, circumvent or overcome barriers. Thus, we should understand freedom as "a direction of some of our endeavors." With this proposal, Bittner's proposal fits in with those contributions that have suggested focusing our attention on "concepts of freedom" with a concentration on "practices and contexts of freedom."

I

Several of the chapters presented deal with the topic of freedom as liberation from slavery, mainly in the biblical traditions, but with perspectives on contemporary contexts (Manfred Oeming and Elisabeth Schüssler Fiorenza); in one case a whole people is concerned (Old Testament), in the other case one of the weakest groups in society, the female slaves (New Testament). Ron Sodalter and Katharina von Kellenbach explore exemplary contemporary situations of slavery and oppression.

In the following parts several chapters consider political and legal attempts to identify directions in which not only individual but also communal endeavors work against existing or potential limitations and barriers or try to prevent the establishment of barriers that hinder or limit individuals and communities "to do this or that." They focus on the ancient Greek notions of the freedom of speech in the assembly (*parrhesia*), the equal right to speak publicly (*isegoria*), equality before the law (*isonomia*) and the equality of polis leadership (*isokratia*) as elements of the ability of individuals or groups in the society to govern themselves (*eleutheria*) (Jan Gertz, Jürgen van Oorschot, Larry Hurtado, Peter Lampe).

II

Important attempts to transcend the oligarchic limitations of these strivings are explored in the Old Testaments traditions: The remembrance of the successful emancipation and liberation of the people from foreign oppression and from captivity becomes the basis for a pathos of release and emancipation from foreign rulership in general (Patrick D. Miller). Various attempts to limit the situation of individual slavery on the one hand and the introduction of a neighborhood ethos, a fraternal ethos and even an ethos of love on the other aim at the establishment of morals that support mutual respect and care. Some contributions also reflect on religious attempts to limit political power over individuals, groups or a whole society by understanding and respecting God as the source and guarantee of freedom (Jürgen van Oorschot, Jan Gertz, Beverly Gaventa, Hans-Joachim Eckstein, and others).

This religious claim tries to relativize the barriers between social classes, even between the king and the (full) citizens. It can go hand in hand with an ambivalent rhetoric of "slavery" with respect to the human relation to God (Jan Gertz, Elisabeth Schüssler Fiorenza, Hans-Joachim Eckstein), but also with "covenantal" reflections that see God in a perspective of kenosis and partnership. Religious thought also tries to deal with the topic of individual and communal self-jeopardizing, which even uses religious, legal and moral means (sin). It even tries to deal with the barriers erected by powers such as death, which seem to set ultimate limits to freedom (Patrick Miller, Jan Gertz, Hans-Joachim Eckstein, Beverly Gaventa).

III

Several chapters show that some of the aspects and directions mentioned above are more or less dominant or weakened in specific biblical contexts and traditions, depending on situations and contexts. With regard to the topic of slavery these tendencies were partly criticized and partly justified as strategies to stimulate emergent processes of transformation (Elisabeth Schüssler Fiorenza, Larry Hurtado, Hans-Joachim Eckstein). Several contributions explore biblical attempts to develop exemplary patterns of thought, behavior and action that enhance the sensitivity toward typical forms of mutual hindrance, impediment, and subordination. These prohibitive and defensive strategies can move towards (or can be generated by) the development of forms of mutual honoring and care that enhance the other person's freedom. The interest in the development of these patterns of thought and behavior is characteristic of many biblical traditions and contexts. Paul can connect an ethos of creative self-limitation in favor of others with the recommendation "to become slave to one another through love" (Gal 5:13). Several biblical traditions correlate these ethical patterns with an appreciation of attempts to understand and respect the freedom of God (in doxology) as a source of human freedom (Beverly Gaventa).

Over against these observations, a warning against texts centered on a male elite with an imperial rhetoric of enslavement to God brought the challenge to discern imperial rhetoric or anti-imperial discourse in the Pauline corpus. In what forms and under which conditions do religious strategies to support emergent transformations of social and moral traditions tend to serve appeasement and camouflage (Elisabeth Schüssler Fiorenza) and turn into sterile forms of mere moral appeal?

IV

Another tradition of thought, introduced with respect to Patristic texts, centers on the differentiation of freedom as *autexousia*, as self-control, "innate to all human beings," and as *eleutheria*, the search for and the ability to enjoy beatitude (Cyril Hovorun). Both dimensions are seen in the "inner realm" of the human person. This stimulates challenges to differentiate and, in the line with Reformation thought, to relate "natural capacity" and "spiritual dignity" (Risto Saarinen) and directs attention to the potentials of "free will" and the individual moral and religious experience.

Several chapters indicate that the anthropological discourse correlated with these interests should on the one hand not lose the differentiated field of experience and insight described above and on the other hand should rise to the challenge of contemporary scientific anthropological research (Friederike Nüssel). Reformation thought anticipates modern ideas such as "freedom as a matter of individual fulfillment in individual identity and distinctiveness" versus "individual and communal fulfillment in the context of communal fulfillment and sacrifice" or in "changing political and economic conditions of life and institutions" (Dirk Smit). This leads to the questions how Christian symbols, rhetoric and practices have been able to shape and will continue to shape a multidimensional "ethos of belonging" (Dirk Smit), an "ethos of commitment" (Carver Yu) or an "ethos of tolerance" (Jindrich Halama), a tolerance that leaves room for the appreciation of radically different types of Christianity and different religious and moral traditions.

V

These directions of thought can be correlated with the question of how dominant religious traditions such as Roman Catholicism are able to relate today to human rights ethics and policies and a cosmopolitanism that tries to mobilize against political and religious "imbalances" in the name of freedom (Francis Fiorenza, Susan Abraham). Of interest is the compatibility of religious thought with legal and political evolutions that we connect with the notion of freedom. Legal and political dynamics are expected to work against a mere rhetoric of moral appeals and Sunday speech declarations. In the opposite direction, how and on what basis can insights of the biblical traditions illuminate and overcome shortcomings in political and moral visions of leading contemporary voices (Michael Welker)? Can we make the "Spirit" plausible as a religious and cultural reality and as a measure of freedom?

Part 1

Freedom and Domination

Introduction

Elisabeth Schüssler Fiorenza

According to the *Collins English Dictionary*, freedom is defined as "personal liberty, as freedom from slavery, bondage serfdom etc., as liberation or deliverance, as freedom from confinement and bondage, as the quality or state of being free, esp. to enjoy political and civil liberties."[1] Freedom entails self-determination, choice, independence, autonomy, liberty or lack of restrictions. Freedom entails the absence of poverty, starvation, disease and oppression. To be free means *not to be a slave wo/man*. This first section of the book opens *Quests for Freedom* with the intention of contextualizing its reflections on freedom with respect to the reality of slavery.

In 1791, when the Bill of Rights was adopted and thousands of Africans continued to live in slavery, a free African American by the name of Benjamin Banneker wrote to Thomas Jefferson.[2] Banneker appeals to the idea that G*d created all equal, an idea that tied together religious faith and political liberty in a democracy:

> That one universal Father hath given being to us all, and that he has not only made us all of one flesh, but that he hath also, without partiality, . . . endowed us all with the same faculties, and that however variable we may be in society or religion, however diversified in situation of color, we all are the same family and stand in relation to him.

He reminds Jefferson of the time when the British crown sought to curtail the freedom of their colony, the time when Jefferson clearly saw "the injustice of a state of slavery" and "the horrors of its condition" and "publicly held forth this true and invaluable doctrine":

1. *Collins English Dictionary*.
2. Copy of a letter from Benjamin Banneker to the secretary of state with his answer, Electronic Text Center, University of Virginia Library.

> We hold these truths to be self-evident, that all are created equal; that they are endowed by their Creator with certain unalienable rights, and that among these are life, liberty and the pursuit of happiness.

However, Banneker also points out that Jefferson has not acted upon these words but has continued the inhuman practices of slavery despite his proclamation of the unalienable rights of liberty, happiness, and justice for all:

> But, Sir, how pitiable it is to reflect, that although you were so fully convinced of the benevolence of the Father of Mankind, and of his equal and impartial distribution of these rights and privileges, which he has conferred upon them, that you should at the same time counteract his mercies, in detaining by fraud and violence so numerous a part of my brethren, under groaning captivity and cruel oppression, that you should at the same time to be found guilty of that most criminal act, which you professedly detested in others, with respect to yourselves.

However, this contradiction is not peculiar to Jefferson. It has its roots in Athenian democracy, in Christian Scriptures and theological traditions, and it is still characterizing our own times when freedom is proclaimed for a few while there are more slaves on the planet as at any other time in human history.[3] On June 27, 2011, the US State Department released its Trafficking in Persons (TIP) report, an annual ranking of how well—or how badly—countries around the world are doing to fight modern forms of slavery. Yet, slavery remains one of the most invisible reality. The report is a sobering litany of horrific abuses and the faltering efforts of many governments to stop these crimes. Being forced into domestic servitude is one of the most common forms of human trafficking. Hence, any theological reflection on freedom needs to take into account this historical and contemporary context of slavery and servitude. Any intellectual and theological discussion of freedom that spiritualizes freedom in the face of slavery or restricts freedom to a few by denying the equality of all contributes ideologically to this global situation of enslavement.

Hannah Arendt traces the origins of the concept of freedom to the ancient Greek *polis*, the Greek city-state, from which our word politics derives. Politics could only be practiced by those elite gentlemen, the *kyrioi*, who had freed themselves from the necessities of life. It rests on the distinction between the *household*, the realm of necessity, and the public space of the *polis*, where free men discovered who they were and established their

---

3. See Skinner, "A World Enslaved." See also Brooten, ed., *Beyond Slavery*.

individuality with the assistance of others. In contrast to the household, which was given over to necessity and economics, the politics was the realm of freedom.[4]

However, Arendt does not spell out that the individuals who could engage in the political realm were only freeborn propertied male citizens, the *kyrioi*, whereas the household as the realm of necessity was the domain of freeborn and slave wo/men.[5] To lift this into consciousness, I have coined the term *kyriarchy* to characterize such a system of domination. *Kyriarchy* is derived from Greek *kyrios* (*Latin dominus*)—the lord, slave master, father, husband, propertied free male to whom all the members of the household were subordinated and by whom they were controlled—and the Greek verb *archein*—to rule, dominate, control. The household as the realm of necessity was also the realm of domination. Freedom in this classical and western political sense was the property of freeborn propertied men only. It was the *kyrios/dominus* who was the free citizen. Western democracy has been built on the subordination and enslavement of the subordinated members of household and state. The perspective of slave wo/men on freedom has not been transmitted but it rings through the centuries claiming freedom and wellbeing for all without exceptions.

Utilizing this concept of democratic kyriarchy for elaborating Paul's understanding of freedom, Rick F. Talbott has introduced the notion of *kyridoularchy*, which is a composite of three terms: *kyrios*, *doulos* (slave), and *archein*. According to Talbott, kyridoularchy was a central strategy of Paul that "required power to be used to empower or honor those with less status in his communities. In this case, power remained a strategy towards community solidarity and cohesion aligned with Paul's ideology."[6] Paul's ideology and strategy, however, remained kyriarchal and therefore bifurcated. Hence, Talbott concludes that Paul's strategy was to control his communities through the rhetoric of kyridoularchy: "To justify Paul's use (of) power because it served to empower others . . . obscures the central and complex role power played (Rom 15:1–3; 1 Cor 12:7; Phil 2:1–7). *Kyridoularchy* was an idealized model for Paul that he required others to imitate . . . But again, Paul's demand for such obedient submission to kyridoularchy was ironically a form of kyriarchy."[7]

Whereas according to Hannah Arendt, in the fifth century the concept of freedom became associated with the Christian notion of inner freedom

---

4. Arendt, "What Is Freedom?"
5. See duBois, *Slaves and Other Objects*.
6. Talbott, *Jesus, Paul, and Power*, 93n1.
7. Talbott, *Jesus, Paul, and Power*, 109.

and the freedom of the will, Talbott (among others) locates the beginning of this development in Paul's writings. Since it is impossible to trace here the Christian history of this bifurcation of freedom, I will just mention one incident that has become crucial in the framing of the discussion of freedom in Christian modernity.

The *Twelve Articles of the Peasant Revolt* were formulated on March 6, 1525, by a representative of the Upper Swabian Peasant League in the German Peasant's war. Article 3 states: "Christ freed us from all bondage ... According to the Scriptures we are free people and we wish to be free."[8] The peasants asked for the abolition of feudal bondage, which they argued was against the gospel of freedom. Both Luther and Melanchthon objected that the serf can participate in inner freedom. Equality does not exist in the profane realm but only in the spiritual realm where the distinction between Lord and serf is abolished.[9] Christian freedom is inner freedom and means to no longer be subjected to the power of sin. Such an understanding of freedom legitimated the enslavement of whole continents through colonialism and still today enables the practices of slavery.

With "A Blight on the Nation: Slavery in Today's America," Ron Soodalter opens this section on slavery and freedom. He details how slavery is at work, not only in the USA, but across the globe, traces the history of slavery in order to contextualize *human trafficking* in an unbroken legacy of bondage, elaborates "equal opportunity slavery," and details how modern-day slavery has become a big business that touches all of our lives in different ways. Soodalter concludes: "Slavery is legal nowhere in the world, and yet it is practiced everywhere. It is estimated that approximately 27 million people are in bondage worldwide" (p. 15).

In "To be a Free Nation in Our Land," Manfred Oeming in turn discusses the myth, ritual, and ethics of freedom in the Hebrew Bible, or the Christian Old Testament. The myth of freedom tells the story of the transformation of an enslaved people to a free nation. The story of the Exodus is one of the foundational myths of the people of Israel. The rituals of freedom are the Sabbath, circumcision, and especially Passover. Thus the whole Jewish liturgical calendar celebrates Jewish liberation from bondage into freedom.

Oeming's elaboration of the "Ethics of Freedom" discusses first the legal status of slaves, to which many passages allude but do not clearly spell out, reviews the value and work of slaves, and compares Israelite slaveholding with that of the Near East. In the final section, Oeming discusses three

---

8. Carpentier et al., *The Emergence of Human Rights in Europe*, 61. The original text of the Twelve Articles in German by the city of Memmingen: http://stadtarchiv.memmingen.de/918.html.

9. Brecht, "Die Menschenrechte in der Geschichte der Kirche," 54–55.

narratives of liberation: Neh 5; Jer 34; and 2 Chr 28—three texts that illustrate his conclusion: "The biblical traditions are telling a long story of liberation of Israel—yet the texts hardly talk about the rights of slaves and don't develop a ongoing religious pressure to release them. In legal writings and in daily live, biblical Israel's ethics often fell way behind its mythic narratives. Measured by its own criteria, Israel was living in a sinful state" (p. 48).

Oeming's elaboration makes it clear that Scriptural and the*logical discourses on freedom call for a hermeneutics of suspicion and an ethics of interpretation in the face of the sufferings of slavery. My own contribution, "Slave Wo/men and Freedom in the Pauline Tradition" discusses the methodological shifts necessary to understand freedom both in the ancient and in the contemporary contexts of slavery. The paper seeks to shift the focus of our attention from Paul's kyridoularchal understanding of freedom (which is elaborated in the articles of the 3rd section) to an understanding of freedom in Christ, i.e. the messianic corporation, which inspired the struggles of slave wo/men for freedom.

Whereas the genuine Pauline letters are unclear with respect to slavery, the so-called post-Pauline letters argue for an acceptance of slavery. While in the Pauline letters freedom seems to be understood as belonging to all the members of the *ekklēsia*, the Post-Pauline household codes clearly articulate rules of subordination for those who remain caught up in the realm of necessity, the household. These injunctions to accept slavery must not only be seen in the context of the discourses and practices of manumission in Roman antiquity, but they must also be understood to sustain a slave mentality of subordination. An ethics of interpretation recognizes the ongoing power of the Scriptural language of freedom to shape our socio-political symbolic universes and religious-theological capabilities for imagining and advocating a different world free of slavery and domination.

Finally, in "The Paradox of Freedom," Katharina von Kellenbach discusses the ethos of submission transmitted through the household code texts, but focuses on wo/men and heterosexual marriage rather than on slavery. She seeks to challenge "theological discourses that ground freedom in submission and obedience," and points out that in the U.S. "the rallying cry for Christian freedom has become a potent weapon in the battle to curtail women's control over conception and childbearing" (p. 72).

After critically discussing the Protestant theological reception of Paul's message as "the paradox of freedom," she turns to the *Manhattan Declaration* and its political arguments, which call on Christians to engage in "civil disobedience" in order to defend "the sanctity of human life" and the "dignity" of heterosexual marriage. These discourses assert that "the family can never be a democracy of free equals but must remain a sacred hierarchy, in which women (and children) are to submit, by divine design and degree, to male authority. This inherently contradictory position among Christian proponents of liberty, democracy and equality is reconciled by dressing it up as "paradox" and "by advertising it as in the best interest of women" (p. 81).

In the second half of her paper, von Kellenbach explores the "paradox of freedom" in and through a careful reading of the annunciation story in Luke. Mary is seen as an "exemplar of obedience" and has been used to inculcate the subjugation of women. Von Kellenbach seeks to understand her as "talking back" to the angel and as acting to assure her own safety and that of her child. Mary becomes the paradigm of "freedom understood as response-ability to God."

Von Kellenbach concludes: "The religious and political impulse to force a woman into submission in order to endure a pregnancy against her will and better judgment serves no discernible moral or theological value. The desire to curtail women's ability to respond is inherently abusive and will not lead to the kind of freedom that has traditionally been expressed as obedience and submission to the will of God" (p. 90).

In sum, the contributions of this section explore the implications and ideological effects of Scriptural and the*logical discourses on freedom in a world still characterized by the ongoing brutality of slavery. They reject the pacifying notion of "inner freedom" and the ethics of submission as sin and as the ideological legitimization of unfreedom. Thereby they seek to ground our theoretical and practical reflections on freedom in the brutal reality of slavery and sex-trafficking.

Bibliography

Arendt, Hannah. "What Is Freedom?" In *Between Past and Future: Eight Exercises in Political Thought*, 142–69. New York: Penguin, 1993.

Brecht, Martin. "Die Menschenrechte in der Geschichte der Kirche." In *Zum Thema Menschenrechte: Theologische Versuche und Entwürfe*, edited by Jörg Bauer, 39–96. Stuttgart: Calwer, 1977.

Brooten, Bernadette, ed. *Beyond Slavery: Overcoming Its Religious and Sexual Legacies*. Black Women, Womanist Thought, Social Justice. New York: Palgrave, 2010.

Carpentier, Jean et al. *The Emergence of Human Rights in Europe: An Anthology*. Education File. Strasbourg: Council of Europe Publishing, 2001.

Collins English Dictionary. 10th ed. New York: HarperCollins, 2009.

DuBois, Page. *Slaves and Other Objects*. Chicago: University of Chicago Press, 2003.

Skinner, E. Benjamin. "A World Enslaved." *Foreign Policy* 165 (Mar/Apr 2008) 62–67. https://foreignpolicy.com/2009/10/08/a-world-enslaved.

Talbott, Rick F. *Jesus, Paul and Power: Rhetoric, Ritual and Metaphor in Ancient Mediterranean Christianity.* Eugene, OR: Cascade Books, 2010.

1

A Blight on the Nation
Slavery in Today's America

Ron Soodalter

For two years, twelve Mexican and Guatemalan field workers in South Florida were enslaved by the Navarretes, a family of traffickers. The family beat them, chained them to a pole, and at night, locked them in boxes and truck trailers with little food and no plumbing, while keeping them in ever-increasing debt. During the day, they were taken to work in the tomato fields of two of the state's biggest growers—Six Ls and Pacific. When their day's work was done, they were taken back to their prison. Finally, one of the workers pounded a hole through the trailer and crawled out; he got a ladder, and helped the others to escape. The Navarretes were arrested and indicted on trafficking charges. They pled guilty, were sentenced to jail, and ordered to pay their victims $240,000 in restitution. Officials at Six Ls and Pacific could not be reached for comment. Assistant U.S. Attorney Doug Molloy called it one of Southwest Florida's "ugliest slavery cases ever," and added, "We have a number of similar—and ongoing—investigations." And yet, despite the successful prosecution of seven slavery cases involving over 1,000 workers, and despite pressure from such organizations as Amnesty International USA, until recently, Governor Crist refused to acknowledge the presence of slavery in Florida's fields.

An American humorist named Will Rogers once said, "It's not that we're so dumb, it's just that what we know ain't so."

Certain things Americans know to be true. We know that the South kept slaves, and the North fought a righteous war of liberation. We know that the slave trade was legal until the Civil War. We know that the Emancipation Proclamation freed all the slaves, and that the United States has been slavery-free ever since. These things we know—and none of it is true.

On the other hand, most Americans do *not* know that slavery not only exists throughout the world today; it flourishes. Slavery is legal nowhere in the world, and yet it is practiced everywhere. It is estimated that approximately 27 million people are in bondage worldwide; that's more than twice as many people as were taken in chains during the entire 350 years of the African slave trade. Human trafficking is one of the most profitable criminal enterprises of our time, along with drugs and guns, and is responsible for tens of billions of dollars in revenues worldwide. You might point to all those backward emerging nations—what we used to call "Third World" countries—and you'd be partly right. But it's also such "civilized" countries as England, France, Spain, Italy, Israel, Scotland, Ireland, Greece, Sweden, Denmark, Japan, and China. I have been invited here to Düsseldorf, to discuss the concept and reality of modern-day slavery. Yet, even as I speak, instances of human trafficking are occurring right here in Germany. According to the U.S. State Department Trafficking in Persons Report,

> Germany is a transit and destination country for men and women trafficked for the purposes of commercial sexual exploitation and forced labor. Victims were trafficked to Germany from other parts of Europe, Africa (primarily Nigeria), Asia, and the Western Hemisphere. Approximately one-quarter of sex trafficking victims were German nationals trafficked within the country.
>
> Twelve percent of trafficking victims were younger than 18 years old. The majority of identified sex trafficking victims were exploited in bars and brothels. Reported incidents of forced labor occurred mainly in restaurants, catering, and the domestic work and agriculture sectors.[1]

The record of successful prosecutions in Germany has declined from 193 in 2006, to 168 in 2007—the most recent year for which data is available in the face of our research. A number of these convictions have resulted in suspended sentences for the convicted traffickers.

Most Americans express relatively little surprise when made aware of trafficking abroad. They are, however, shocked to discover that modern-day slavery is occurring in the United States. Most Americans do *not* know that

---

1. *U.S. State Dept. Trafficking in Persons Report*, June, 2009.

slavery is alive and more than well in our own country, thriving in the dark, and practiced in many forms in places you'd least expect.

The simple truth is, humans keep slaves; we always have. Historically, we Americans see ourselves as the world's foremost messengers and practitioners of personal freedom. And yet, there has always been bondage in our land. Always. There has never been a single day without slavery on the North American continent, from its European discovery right up to the present moment.

An Unbroken Legacy of Bondage

In 1493, on his second voyage across the Atlantic, and before even establishing a colony, Christopher Columbus enslaved hundreds of Taino Indians and shipped them home to Spain. The wave of armed and armored conquistadores that followed brought a plague of butchery and enslavement upon the Indians that destroyed entire cultures. With the age-old rationale that any foreign society is inferior to one's own, the Spaniards, in their quest for treasure, used the "God-told-me-to-do-it" argument to justify a policy of rape, slaughter, and enslavement. They called it, *la guerra de sangre y fuego*—the war of blood and fire; sometimes they simply called it, "pacification."

And when the Spaniards found that the Indians were dying in droves from brutality and European diseases, their king gave his consent to sail to *Africa* for slaves—*bozales*, as they were called—beginning what would become the three-and-a-half century-long trans-Atlantic trade. Ultimately, every European power claiming land in the New World followed Spain's example. French, Dutch, Portuguese, and English settlers from Canada to the bottom tip of South America owned slaves. Slave labor became an accepted social and economic reality.

It's a safe bet that the majority of Americans believe the curse of slavery ended with the Civil War and the laws that presumably banished it forever from our shores; nothing could be further from the truth. It continued more quietly and on a smaller scale, but without pause. While legal emancipation might have come with the 13th Amendment, that didn't stop the southern planters from *re*-enslaving countless thousands of African Americans. Crops in the South still needed planting, cultivating, and harvesting, and there was a vast population of unemployed former slaves. Planters instituted a system that was as close to the old slavery as possible, but with some new wrinkles.

This time, it was called "peonage," and it was simply a form of debt bondage slavery. Thousands of Blacks—and poor Whites—were duped or coerced into signing contracts as field workers or sharecroppers. Farm owners would hold their pay, and the workers were often obligated to make all their purchases from the "company store," using tickets rather than money. When their annual contracts expired, they found that the crops they raised never paid the debts they owed. Although these "debts" were often fraudulent or impossibly inflated, the penalty for non-payment was jail or worse. The law was on the planters' side. The only alternative was to stay on the land and try to work off the debt, which never seemed to lessen or disappear. Worst of all, the debt passed from parent to child, binding families to the land with no hope of advancement or escape. Each year became a frustrating, spirit-crushing effort to break even. Peonage was practiced across the South and upheld for decades by local and national government. A full federal ban on peonage slavery was not passed until 1948, and still it persisted across much of the South into the Civil Rights era of the 1960s.

Guests of the Nation

On a much broader national scale, whenever there weren't enough willing or available native sons to do the nation's work, we imported our labor force. During World War I, when our boys were off fighting in France, we welcomed thousands of Mexican workers—often right into forced labor situations—only to throw them out after the war ended. The pattern repeated itself prior to the Depression, and during World War II.

In 1943, the government formalized its approach to foreign labor by creating the H2, or Guestworker, program to aid in providing temporary jobs in the Southern fields. The concept was not new; bring them in when we need them, oust them when we don't. From its beginning, the program was characterized by inequity and brutality; as recently as 1986 in Florida, Jamaican cane cutters who attempted a work stoppage over poor conditions were set upon by armed police with attack dogs, acting at the employers' behest. The workers were brutalized, loaded onto planes and sent home. The incident became known as the "Dog Wars."

The mostly Asian and Latin American immigrants who come here every year for farm and field work under the Guestworker program number in the tens of thousands, and one thing has become clear: it provides a splendid opportunity for mistreatment and enslavement. Through contractor misrepresentation and a stunningly lax government program of monitoring, the worker is often indentured before he even leaves home.

Slavery in America hit its lowest ebb by the 1960s, due largely to the nation's new outlook on Civil Rights. But beginning in the 1980s, and then exploding in the 1990s, slavery came back with a vengeance. With the end of the Cold War, and the tripling of the global population from two to over six billion, borders collapsed around the world. Countless displaced people were caught up in the fight for survival and became easy targets for traffickers. Human trafficking grew exponentially; and America, once again, became a prime destination for slavers.

Equal Opportunity Slavery

Most Americans' concept of slavery comes right out of *Uncle Tom's Cabin* and *Gone with the Wind*—the chains, the whip in the overseer's hand, the crack of the auctioneer's gavel. That was one form of bondage. The slavery plaguing America today takes different forms, but make no mistake, it's the real deal. Where the law sanctioned the slavery of the 1800s, today it's illegal. Where masters once took pride in the ownership of slaves as a sign of status, today's slaves are kept hidden, making it all the more difficult to locate the victims and punish the offenders. Where the slaves in America were once mostly African and African American, today we have "equal opportunity" slavery; modern-day slaves come in all races, all types, and all ethnicities. We are, if anything, totally democratic when it comes to owning and abusing our fellow man. All that's required is the chance of a profit and a person weak enough and vulnerable enough to enslave.

This is capitalism at its worst. Before the American Civil War, slaves were expensive. In the 1850s, a slave sold for around $1,200. In today's currency, that comes to somewhere between $40,000 and $50,000. This level of investment predisposed the owners to take care of their human property, at least to the extent that their longevity and their productivity were ensured. We're talking economics here, not kindness or humanitarianism. You would no more destroy property of such worth than you would cripple a good plow horse or neuter a seed bull.

Today's slave can be bought for as little as a hundred dollars. This makes the modern slave not only affordable, but also disposable. In the event of serious illness or injury, it's often cheaper—and less likely to arouse suspicion—to let a slave die than it is to buy medicine and services. All forms of slavery are horrific; however, today's slavery is one of the more diabolical strains to emerge in the thousands of years in which we've been enslaving our fellows, especially when you consider that it doesn't exist without a "bundle" of other crimes, including kidnapping, document fraud, assault, torture, rape, and sometimes homicide, to name just a handful.

So How Many Slaves Are We Talking About?

According to a U.S. State Department study, somewhere around 17,000 foreign nationals are trafficked into the United States from at least 35 countries and enslaved *each year*. Some victims are smuggled into the United States across the Mexican and Canadian borders; others arrive at our major airports daily, carrying either real or forged papers. The old slave ship of the 1800s has been replaced by the 747. Victims come to the United States from Africa, Asia, India, Latin America, and the former Soviet Republics. Overwhelmingly, they come on the promise of a better life, with the opportunity to work and prosper in America. Many come in the hope of earning enough money to support or send for their families. In order to afford the journey, they fork over their life savings and go into debt to people who make promises they have no intention of keeping; and instead of opportunity, when they arrive they find bondage. They can be found—or more accurately, *not* found—in all fifty states, working as farmhands, domestics, sweatshop and factory laborers, gardeners, restaurant and construction workers, and victims of sexual exploitation. These people do not represent a class of poorly paid employees, working at jobs they might not like. They exist specifically to work, they are unable to leave, and are forced to live under the constant threat and reality of violence. They no longer control their own lives. By both historical and legal definition, they are slaves. Today, we may call it human trafficking, but make no mistake: it is the slave trade.

Nor are native-born Americans immune from slavers; many are stolen or enticed from the streets of their own cities and towns. I recently attended the trial of a man who was accused—and ultimately convicted—of forcing minors into prostitution and keeping them there through violence. This is not a rare occurrence. Some sources, including the federal government, estimate in the hundreds of thousands the number of U.S. citizens—primarily children and adolescents—at risk of being caught in slavery annually.

What is particularly infuriating is the fact that this is a crime that, as a rule, goes unpunished. For the moment, let's accept the government's estimate of about 17,000 foreign nationals trafficked into slavery in the United States per year; coincidentally there are also about 17,000 people murdered in the U.S. each year. The national success rate in solving murder cases is about 70%; around 11,000 murders are "cleared" annually. But according to the U.S. government's own numbers, the annual percentage of successful trafficking and slavery prosecutions is less than 1% of the number of cases estimated to occur within a given year. In 2007, for example, the Department of Justice's Civil Rights Division obtained only 103 convictions for human trafficking.

And to further complicate matters, when they *are* rescued, survivors often deny their situation. There are several reasons for this: the language barrier, a deep sense of shame, fear for their lives and those of their families in their country of origin, and a sense of obligation to pay their debt. In addition, traffickers program them to fear the police and immigration officials. And in some instances, they come to identify with their keepers.

We don't yet know how President Obama will respond to the human trafficking crisis; it's too soon to tell. Both he and Secretary of State Clinton have been saying all the right things. But we do know that the response under the Bush Administration was inadequate on any number of levels.

Slavery Comes in Many Guises

When the U.S. government addresses the subject of human trafficking, it has tended to focus primarily on the area of sexual exploitation. More sensational than most other forms of slavery, its victims are subjected to serial rape, physical injury, psychological damage, and constant exposure to sexually transmitted diseases, including HIV.

But terrible though forced prostitution is, there are many other forms of slavery thriving right under our noses. If most of us don't see them, we're in good company; neither do most of our police or public officials. The plight of enslaved domestics factors large and accounts for a significant number of America's slaves. In one instance, the Justice Department announced the conviction of a Wisconsin couple for human trafficking. According to the charges, they had "held the victim in a condition of servitude for 19 years, requiring her to work long hours, seven days a week . . . they threatened her with deportation and imprisonment if she disobeyed them," and forced her to hide in the basement when people entered the house. The government convicted the couple on forced labor charges and of harboring an undocumented alien; they were each sentenced to serve four years in prison. Meanwhile, where does this woman go to reclaim nineteen lost years?

Agriculture is another major area of human trafficking. There is an unknown number of victims of forced labor growing and picking our fruit and vegetables. They come to America looking for a decent wage. Instead, they are enslaved by crime syndicates and families—and sometimes, inadvertently, by our own government—in such states as Florida, North Carolina, South Carolina, and Georgia.

The good news is, there have actually been some recent inroads made in the area of agricultural servitude. When Taco Bell refused to stop buying tomatoes picked by slaves, the South Florida-based Coalition of Immokalee

Workers organized a march, boycott, and hunger strike, and at one point sponsored a camp-out on the front lawn of Taco Bell's corporate headquarters. College students across the nation responded to a "Ban the Bell" campaign, and drove the fast food operation from their campuses. After stonewalling for four years, Taco Bell met with workers at the bargaining table, and—among other concessions—swore never again to purchase produce derived from slave labor. They were followed, one by one, by such major purchasers as McDonald's, A&W, Long John Silver, Pizza Hut, Whole Foods, Chipotle, and Burger King. And recently, Compass Group—the world's largest foodservice organization—came aboard with all 10,000 of its companies. There are hold-outs, such as Wendy's, Wal-Mart, and Quiznos, but that little workers' coalition, with the support of the public, will bring them around as well. Their message is clear: slavery and worker abuse simply will not be tolerated.

New Business Models

In researching our book, *The Slave Next Door,* Kevin Bales and I were stunned to discover the many and varied ways in which traffickers ply their trade and make their living. While the greatest number of slaves in America today falls into three categories—agricultural slavery, sexual exploitation, and domestic servitude—there is no lack of ingenuity on the part of traffickers in exploiting their victims. Slave traffickers are imaginative and innovative businessmen. Where an opportunity exists for exploitation, however strange or unlikely, there's a good chance there is a hidden slave. Here's one for you: What do deaf Mexicans and an African boys' choir have in common? In a word, slavery.

An attractive young Mexican woman named Adriana Paoletti was a major player in a particularly vicious family-run human trafficking ring. It came to be referred to as the Deaf Mexicans Case. For ten years, Adriana traveled to the poor neighborhoods of her native Mexico and enticed their deaf young people with tales of a better life in "el Norte." The vision she painted for them was a lie. The Paolettis, themselves a deaf family from Mexico, made a thriving business of illegally importing deaf and hearing-impaired men and women into California, transporting them to Chicago and New York City, and enslaving them there as street peddlers. In New York City, fifty-seven of the deaf Mexicans were crammed into two small, rundown apartments, and forced to sleep on the floor or on bare mattresses. They were threatened, abused, and beaten as a matter of course. Some of the women were systematically raped. Every day, seven days a week, they were each given one hundred cheap trinkets and sent out to sell them for a dollar apiece. Some of the men were given two hundred trinkets a day. They were all told not to return until every trinket was sold. For twelve to eighteen hours, they would walk the city's streets or stand on corners staring at the sidewalk and holding out their trinkets; or they would ride the subways, eyes cast down, leaving with the riders a pen or a key chain and a small, worn card reading, "I am deaf," and returning to collect either the trinket or a dollar. If they came home at night with any trinkets left, they were beaten, shocked with stun guns, denied food and water, or locked out.

The Paoletti family made a fortune. Just do the math: With most of the fifty-seven victims bringing home at least $100 a day, the family was taking in a minimum of $5,000 daily in New York City alone.

So why didn't the victims simply leave? After all, their knowledge of the city's streets and subway routes was staggering; and yet, their freedom to roam at will was an illusion. The victims couldn't communicate with the world outside their group. They didn't speak, write, or sign English—and in many cases, couldn't read or write at all. And they were living under the constant threat of violence. Neighbors later told the authorities of "a nightly horror show of barefoot women, clad only in nightgowns, fleeing from the houses with men in pursuit; of babies crying . . . unattended; of walls vibrating from slamming doors and pounding fists."

When the trafficking ring was finally broken, it was not because of the various public servants who had witnessed the conditions in which these people lived and done nothing. It was because the victims finally decided they'd had enough. After several unsuccessful attempts to make themselves understood to the local police, four of the men were befriended by an older deaf American—a good Samaritan. Although he spoke no Spanish, he helped them write a letter describing their enslavement. At four in the morning, they walked into a local police station and handed the letter to the desk sergeant.

What followed was a pre-dawn police raid, the arrest of the Paolettis—or at least, those who could be found—and a long difficult path towards mental and physical healing for the victims. As a senior member of the Justice Department observed, "They will need a support network all their lives." It's been over eleven years, and they see themselves as having been enslaved, as victims of fraud, and now, as survivors. No doubt they still have nightmares, still remember what it was to be slaves; and although they're free, they will always carry the scars.

Trafficking, more often than not, entails a betrayal of trust. When the betrayer is a minister of the church and the victims are children the crime is particularly egregious. In the 1990s, a Texas minister, traveling in Zambia, heard a local boys' choir, and he asked their parents if he might take them back to Texas, where he would stage concerts for them. The money they earned, he promised, would be used to build schools and provide living essentials for members of the village. The boys went with him, and their concerts were, indeed, successful, filling churches and halls, and the money poured in. Little of it ever reached Zambia; no schools were built, and each of the boys' families received only around $20 a month. The minister kept nearly every dollar the choir earned. He also forced the boys to sing as many as seven concerts daily, and locked them in a trailer when they weren't singing. He denied them medicine when sick and food if they dared to complain or refused to sing. He forced them to dig him a swimming pool by hand, in the hot Texas sun. And he told them that if they tried to escape, they would be severely punished. When any of the boys rebelled, they were deported in shame to Zambia, where—on the minister's word—their families disowned them.

Finally, Immigration officials questioned some of the boys, and when they found out what had been occurring at the minister's house, they were incredulous. A church choir, enslaved by a man of God . . . Such things simply don't happen, and certainly not here! The facts were borne out, however, and the group was rescued. Of the eleven boys in the choir, ten elected to remain in the United States. Most of them have not done well. Shame and alcoholism are a common thread, and there is little or no contact with their families in Zambia.

One of the boys, Given Kachepa, is a rare exception. Only eleven and an orphan when trafficked by the minister, he lived in slavery for two years. After his liberation in 2000, he was adopted by a Texas family and introduced to a new life as a middle-class American. Since then, he has graduated college and is studying to be a dentist. Given also travels throughout the country with his adoptive mother, sharing his experience and lecturing on the realities of slavery in America.

In those early days of trafficking awareness, unless there were the physical marks and scars most officials associated with slavery, they were reluctant to pursue a case. Members of the minister's own congregation, once their suspicions were aroused, were frustrated in their repeated efforts to involve members of law enforcement. Their attempts to connect with the FBI, the Attorney General, and various senators and congressmen, as well as such high-profile media figures as Oprah Winfrey, brought no response. Neither the minister nor his family, who shared control of the boys, was ever punished or held accountable for their actions.

I used to think that this issue of modern-day slavery didn't touch me personally; I was mistaken. There's a chance that the clothes I wear and the food I eat have been tainted by slavery. Cotton, that symbol of bondage in the pre-Civil War South, is now being picked by slave labor on three continents. The orange juice and tomato I have with my burger at lunch could very well have come from a Mexican or Guatemalan immigrant working under coercion. The rug we walk on at home could have been woven in India, Pakistan or Nepal by one of a hundred thousand child slaves, seven, eight, nine years old. Cell phones and lap tops require an element called tantalum; it comes from an ore that is mined in the Congo, often by slaves. Does this mean that all tomatoes, all oranges, rugs, cotton shirts, cell phones and lap tops are the products of slave labor? Certainly not; but some are, and we just never know. It's that insidious.

So Who's Doing What to Free America's Slaves?

Of the relatively few cases in which slaves are rescued, only around one-third result from government action. Another third comes from the victim escaping on his or her own. And the last third is as a result of the efforts of what we call "good Samaritans"—in other words, us. As often as not, a concerned citizen will notice that something isn't quite right about that housekeeper next door; she cries a lot, keeps to herself, and rarely leaves the house. A call to the authorities can bring about an investigation, but generally, sadly, we don't know what clues to look for. We're not alone; usually, the authorities don't have any idea what slavery looks like, either. According to federal law, a minor who is working in prostitution is automatically categorized as a victim of human trafficking. Yet, unless he has received the proper training, a policeman can look at an underage prostitute, and he sees only a prostitute. The possibility doesn't occur to him that she is in a coercive situation. He arrests her, and out of fear, she says nothing. And so she's victimized three times: first by the trafficker, then by the johns who rape her daily, and finally by members of the system that should be structured to rescue and support her, but instead, ensure that the cycle continues.

There *is* major federal legislation in place; it's called the Trafficking Victims Protection Act—the TVPA—and it was passed in 2000. Every two or three years, it undergoes a congressional reauthorization; this occurred in November 2008. Many significant improvements were made to the original law, but much remains to be done. Clearly, what is needed is greater awareness, organized training programs for law enforcement and for the average citizen, better cooperation among and between government agencies and non-governmental organizations, a lot more money, and a more equitable system of allocating the funding.

Thus far, forty-six out of fifty states have passed their own anti-human trafficking laws, but most of them focus mainly, if not entirely, on the issue of prostitution and sex slavery. However, no one form of slavery is more horrific than another, and we simply can't afford to ignore the other types of bondage. Also, the state laws usually concentrate on catching and punishing the traffickers, and ignore the vital issue of long-term support and counseling for the survivors.

It's essential that Americans are made aware that this blight exists in our country today. Without an educated public, there is no hope of eliminating slavery. Every day, newspapers print stories of human trafficking here and abroad. Just this week, for example, a trafficker from Mexico was sentenced in Georgia for forcing young Mexican women into prostitution when they arrived in America. An ex-serviceman in Maryland confessed to forcing a sixteen-year-old girl into prostitution in his apartment. A police raid on a Pennsylvania spa resulted in the trafficking arrest of three South Korean women. And a New Jersey pimp pled guilty to running a human trafficking ring in which he used drugs and violence to control his victims. The amount of material is impressive, yet we remain oblivious. We simply cannot solve a problem we don't understand.

So certain things we know to be true: we know the crimes of human trafficking and slavery exist in our country, our city, and sometimes the house next door; we know there is a past-due need to train and sensitize both civilians and law enforcement to find and approach it with skill and sensitivity; and we know that without pressure from us, it will not get done. Albert Einstein said, "The world is a dangerous place, not because of those who *do* harm, but because of those who look at it without doing anything." As a society, we Americans tend to look—trusting and childlike—to our institutions and our leaders for guidance and for salvation. Yet, if history has taught us anything, it's that the only hope of forward movement derives from whatever pressure for change we place upon our leaders and our institutions.

America was born with the congenital disease of slavery, and, legal or not, it has never left us. Today we are still conflicted about our ante-bellum slave past and its ugly aftermath. We study it, lament it, and argue it as a haunting presence from our dark history. Yet while we were looking the other way, slavery in America evolved into a whole new beast that lives in darkness among us and feeds on ignorance and misery. Only through our awareness, our concern, and our commitment can it be driven out. This problem is not covered with the dust of the past, and is clearly within our power to address and to resolve. I find it both challenging and exhilarating to think that we can be the generation to end this nation-long affliction.

2

"To Be a Free Nation"

Myth, Ritual, and Ethics of Freedom in the Old Testament as Political Encouragement

MANFRED OEMING

Israel's national anthem contains the following text:

> As long as deep in the heart,
> The soul of a Jew yearns,
> And forward to the East
> To Zion, an eye looks
> Our hope will not be lost,
> The hope of two thousand years,
> To be a free nation in our land,
> The land of Zion and Jerusalem

This text by Naftali Herz Imber summarizes central elements of Israel's self-image.[1] The author deliberately takes up old traditions when composing this

---

1. Imber (1856–1909) moved to Palestine in 1882 from Galicia. His text has many political implications: "Hatikva" means "The Hope" and expresses the expectation of the Jewish people that they would someday return to the land of their forefathers as prophesied in the Hebrew Bible. Exiled from the land of Israel in 70 CE by the Roman army led by Titus, who destroyed the Temple in Jerusalem, the people of Israel lived for two thousand years in exile and said special daily prayers for return to the land while facing the East in the direction of Jerusalem. The melody was arranged by Samuel

anthem. The hope of freedom and national autonomy in an independent "land of Zion and Jerusalem" breathes a great deal of the spirit of biblical theology. In the following I would like to show how much this sentence "to be a free nation" (להיות עם חופשי *lihjot 'am chofschi*) incorporates a vast river of Old Testament religion.

In his description and analysis of the religion of the first Christians, Gerd Theissen used a wide concept of "religion" that is also useful for our context: religion is a cognitive and emotional relationship to the transcendent that is articulated in a organized system of signs. This complex semiotic system contains at least four elements:[2]

A. *Myth*: A myth explains in narrative form what determines the foundations of reality. These include the foundational narratives in the Bible, such as the creation narratives, the stories about the patriarchs Abraham, Isaac, Jacob, and Josef, the exodus from Egypt under Moses as well as the conquest of the land under Joshua and the Judges, the establishment of the state under Saul, David, and Solomon, the complex history of Israel and Judah up to its destruction and revival during the Persian era. In absolute numbers a history spanning about 3,500 years,[3] from the creation of the world to the rededication of the wall by Nehemiah, a history full of signs and wonders.

B. *Ritual*: Rituals are repeated behavioral patterns that interrupt daily human activity in order to cultically portray and experience the divine reality, as told in mythic narratives.

C. *Ethics*: In reference to the nature of God, his history with his creation and his commandments, ethics creates a framework for human activity, in which human action becomes a symbolic indication of the divine example.

D. *Political encouragement*. The ancient biblical traditions have many implications for changing the modern realities of slavery.

Cohen, an immigrant from Moldavia, from a musical theme in Smetana's "Moldau" (1874), which is partly based on a Scandinavian folk song.

2. For a semiotic interpretation of religion, see Theissen, *Die Religion der ersten Christen* (ET = *The Religion of the Earliest Christians*).

3. The Jewish calendar counts as follows: from the creation of the world until today (2012) there are 5,773 years according to biblical chronology. This number can be understood in radical opposition to scientific idea of an almost infinite period of time in which the universe developed. This opposition is found especially in American creationism, which condemns Darwinism by stating that the earth was only created about 6000 years ago (see the differentiated [**AQ: nuanced?**] discussion in Numbers, *The Creationists*). It is also possible to understand this number symbolically as mythic expression for the fact that creation is a well-ordered system, see Oeming, "Weltbild im Alten Testament."

According to this model I will unfold my thoughts about freedom in the Old Testament in four directions.

The Myth of Freedom

Myth provides us with the view of history and reality that is determined by the current relation to a specific god. Old Testament myths are fundamentally determined by narratives about the search for one's own land and independent political existence under the guidance of YHWH, the God of Israel. Biblical historiography finds its organizing principle in the divine promise of the land and the gradual fulfillment of this promise (also including the loss of the Promised Land). The Hexateuch is carried by the tension between slavery and liberation. Shaped by the charismatic leadership of Moses and the miracles of God, the transformation of a people of slaves to a free nation plays an all-important role.

With Gerhard von Rad, I doubt whether we can refer to the exodus as "Israel's primary confession," as the central kerygma of the Old Testament, the center of scripture; the Old Testament contains too many other "centers" (such as the revelation at Sinai, a priestly Zion–temple theology, a prophetic vision for the future, or the wisdom teachings of action and consequence). Yet, without a doubt, the spirit of the exodus is one of the foundational pillars of Old Testament tradition history. The exodus is one of Israel's fundamental myths (alongside the creation and patriarchal narratives, as well as the genealogical lists of true Israel in 1 Chr 1–11, in which the Chronicler deliberately pushes the exodus tradition into the background).

The exodus from Egypt, the symbolic place of bondage and slavery, is so central for the Pentateuch that Israel's God introduces himself with reference to this event:

> I am the LORD your God, who has brought you out of the land
> of Egypt, out of the house of bondage.

In his acceptance speech for the his honorary doctorate, awarded by the theological faculty of the University of Heidelberg, Patrick Miller advocates that we should incorporate this introductory formula into Christian confession, as it is constitutive for the biblical image of God. Our credo should state:

> I believe in God the almighty, creator of heaven and earth, who
> brought Israel from Egypt from the house of bondage . . .

With this courageous (but hardly enforceable) suggestions, Pat Miller has correctly emphasized the fact that Old Testament message of political liberation should indeed be an important part of Christian confession.

Genesis 12 introduces Egypt almost as a "mythic" place of remembering: here one must fear for one's life when married to a beautiful woman; this woman will be led into Pharaoh's harem—by force, if need be. Abraham's and Sarah's exodus from Egypt, made possible by YHWH's opposition to Pharaoh ("But the LORD afflicted Pharaoh and his household with mighty plagues"—Gen 12:17) is a departure into the promised land of Canaan, a haven of freedom. This first exodus already shows how God's help enables escape from life-threatening slavery. This short episode is a precursor of national history. Under the leadership of Moses, this individual foreshadowing becomes the experience of the entire nation and thus a central confession of faith. The many-layered myth of the exodus from Egypt is a complex myth of a *religion of freedom*; the land flowing of milk and honey is a counter-location to the land of slavery.

Sandro Botticelli's painting "The Story of Moses" (1481–1482), which was created in the Sistine Chapel in Rome, is a case example of this rich heritage based on the exodus from slavery—even in the Apostolic Palace, the official residence of the Pope in the Vatican City. A "royal" Moses, clothed in gold, is portrayed in seven different ways: as a murderer (which points to the tragic connection between liberation and violence!), as a fugitive, as a chivalrous hero defending Jethro's daughter (which points to the importance of military heroism), as a contemplative shepherd, as a mystical recipient of divine revelation, and as the military leader of the exodus community.

There is heated debate over the historical truth of the Hebrew slaves in Egypt.[4] Extrabiblical sources provide us with little information, almost with nothing. Recent publications have shown once again that Israel's existence as slaves in Egypt cannot be substantiated by archaeological, iconographic or epigraphic means.[5] There are, indeed, very few archaeological witnesses regarding slave life in Egypt. Archaeology cannot illuminate this issue. The existing images all serve the purpose of glorifying the rich and the victorious. Pharaoh vanquishes his enemies and the high officials command their servants who dote on their every need.

In our reconstruction of the religious world, we are entirely dependent on the biblical texts. This is why the term "myth" is particularly appropriate: the lexeme μυθος is defined as "fanciful story full of wonders and fantasy."

---

4. Brockmeyer, *Antike Sklaverei*.
5. E.g., Finkelstein and Silberman, *The Bible Unearthed*, 48–71.

It is not highly important, however, whether Israel's slavery was fictional or not, because the message that God's people are freed slaves retains its validity in any case. These mythical texts love to portray their reality in stark black and white contrast (as a pedagogical tool): Israel's existence as lowly construction slaves for Pharaoh's magnificent buildings in a Ghetto is the ultimate symbol of bondage. The most emotional and disturbing symbol of Israel's oppression is the systematic killing of all newborn Israelite boys. It is questionable whether such an action actually was part of Pharaoh's disciplinary measures against his subjects. Extrabiblical sources cannot verify this point.

Whether the road to freedom was only taken by a small "Egypt-group" of Israelites, whether it led them along the Sirbonic Sea or along the southern edge of the Sinai peninsula can hardly be confirmed today—not to mention whether this road was a secret escape or a consequence of powerful plagues. In any case: the narrative myth of the liberation from Egyptian oppression as a sign of the power of Israel's God has become a powerful comfort of the centuries and one of the favorite texts of liberation theology.

Rituals of Freedom

The events narrated by the mythic texts are internalized in systematic fashion. Israel develops a very intensive program of repetition and memorization in order to keep the memory of the exodus alive. The admonitions "remember" (זכר) and "do not forget" (אל־תשכח) are the backbone of religious practice. The texts develop an incredible power for shaping culture as they are regularly read, memorized and recited. All this influences the interpretation of ritual actions. I will mention three: Sabbath, circumcision, and Passover.

The Sabbath refreshes the memory of liberation on a weekly basis. It interrupts the dictatorship of daily routine:

> Observe the Sabbath day and keep it holy, as the LORD your God has commanded you. Six days you shall labor and do all your work, but the seventh day is a Sabbath of the LORD your God; you shall not do any work—you, your son or your daughter, your male or female slave, your ox or your ass, or any of your cattle, or the stranger in your settlements, so that your male and female slave may rest as you do. Remember that you were a slave in the land of Egypt and the LORD your God freed you from there with a mighty hand and an outstretched arm; therefore the

> LORD your God has commanded you to observe the Sabbath day. (Deut 5:12–15)

The permission to incorporate strangers by means of circumcision into the covenant between YHWH and his people is also important:

> And throughout the generations, every male among you shall be circumcised at the age of eight days. As for the homeborn slave and the one bought from an outsider who is not of your offspring. (Gen 17:12)

The primary aspects of God's liberation shape the Jewish calendar. As a kind of "catechism", the Jewish liturgical year symbolizes and actualizes the various stages of the divine liberation: *Rosh-hashana* initiates the large festivities in the fall. The *Day of Atonement* as the liberation from sin, *Sukkoth* as the celebration of human beings on their path from slavery to freedom, *Simchat Torah* as a joyful celebration of the commandments of freedom, *Chanukkah* as the celebration of the liberation from the Tyrant Antiochus IV Epiphanes, *Purim* as the celebration of the liberation from Haman's genocidal plans, *Pesach* as the high point of the liturgical calendar celebrates the liberation out of Egypt, and *Shavuot* as the final celebration rejoicing in the revelation of the Torah.

Even if *Pesach* is thus not the only ritual in the Jewish liturgical calendar with a connection to the topic of freedom, it is the most important one. Whoever has celebrated this feast in the context of a Jewish family knows of the joy that fills the celebrants on this night more than any other night of the year.[6] For my purposes here, I do not need to go into all of the individual elements that make up the Pesach celebration. It has long been recognized that Pesach—just as also *Shavuoth* and *Sukkoth*—has shifted its original agrarian focus by "historizing" the remembrance of the one event that occasioned all other gifts of freedom (revelation at Sinai, desert wanderings).

The ritual text in Exod 12 describes the night in which the angel of the God went through Egypt and killed all first-born of the Egyptians. Only those who had smeared the blood of the *Pesach* lamb on their door were spared this death. Israel knows of this high price of freedom. Every first-born Jewish boy has to fast on the evening before *Pesach* to remind himself and all others that the first-born of Egypt had to die so that Israel could be free.

---

6. In 2002 und 2007 I was given the opportunity to celebrate the entire ritual with my friend Oded Lipschits in Alon Hagalil/Israel. Aside from the many family related aspects, these occasions also provided insight into the multi-perspectival symbolism of this ritual. It is entirely possible to read the entire *Pesach Haggada* as a manifest of freedom.

And Moses said to the people, "Remember this day, on which you went free (יְצָאתֶם) from Egypt, the house of bondage, how the LORD freed you from it with a mighty hand: no leavened bread shall be eaten. You go free on this day, in the month of Abib. So, when the LORD has brought you into the land of the Canaanites, the Hittites, the Amorites, the Hivites, and the Jebusites, which He swore to your fathers to give you, a land flowing with milk and honey, you shall observe in this month the following practice: "Seven days you shall eat unleavened bread, and on the seventh day there shall be a festival of the LORD. Throughout the seven days unleavened bread shall be eaten; no leavened bread shall be found with you, and no leaven shall be found in all your territory. And you shall explain to your son on that day, 'It is because of what the LORD did for me when I went free from Egypt.' "And this shall serve you as a sign on your hand and as a reminder on your forehead—in order that the Teaching of the LORD may be in your mouth—that with a mighty hand the LORD freed you from Egypt. You shall keep this institution at its set time from year to year." (Exod 13:3–10)

We must take notice of the inner connection between exodus and eisodus, between the liberation from foreign oppression and the gift of a new land as a place of freedom. The fact that Josiah celebrated this day as a central festival in Jerusalem (2 Kgs 23:21ff.) was probably a clever political move that turned *Pesach* into the central nation celebration of Jewish freedom.

The Ethics of Freedom

In Legal Texts

The legal status of slaves (female and male) is—as so often in the Old Testament—nowhere presented in a clear systematic fashion; instead, many passages only imply criteria that lead to much vagueness and great debate and speculation among scholars.[7]

According to Exod 21:32, the value of a slave was thirty shekels of silver (see the thirty shekels awarded to Judas for the betrayal of Jesus?).

---

7. Boer, *Erlösung aus der Sklaverei*; Briggs, "Slavery and Gender"; Cardellini, *Die biblischen "Sklaven"-Gesetze im Lichte des keilschriftlichen Sklavenrechts*; Carmichael, "The Three Laws on the Release of Slaves"; Chirichigno, *Debt-Slavery in Israel and the Ancient Near East*; I. Fischer, "Was kostet der Exodus?"; Levinson, "The Manumission of Hermeneutics"; Osumi, "Brandmal für Brandmal"; Schenker, "Die Freilassung der hebräischen Sklaven"; Van Seters, "Law of the Hebrew Slave"; Veijola, "Du sollst daran denken, dass du Sklave gewesen bist im Lande Ägypten."

Leviticus 27:3–8 provides us with a price list, according to which the value of slave fluctuated between ten and fifty shekels, depending on age, gender, and condition.[8] The texts differentiate between various different kinds of slaves:[9] individuals that potentially can be released from slavery as a kind of temporary slave (mainly due to financial debt or forced labor, compare 1 Sam 8 or 1 Kgs 9:15–21). These individuals would work as slaves until their debt was paid or the forced labor was accomplished. Such slaves could continue to shape their own family life autonomously and even live on their own property. Other types of slavery were permanent—these included those who forfeited all their individual rights and became the property of their owner into whose household they were incorporated. Robbed of all his personal freedom, such a full slave has the legal status of an object, which can be used, abused, bought, sold, or traded by his owner. Slaves often do not have a name, a family, or a genealogy. Aside from slaves of war (see Num 21:26ff.; Judg 5:30; 1 Sam 4:9; Joel 3:3ff.; also the young Israelite women in Aram (2 Kgs 5), who seems to be treated with respect), individuals could also become slaves due to kidnapping or organized slave trade (see the story of Joseph and his brothers; in this context: the commandment not to steal is primarily intended to stop human slave trade, see Deut 24:7!).[10] Slavery was also used as a punishment for thieves who were not able to restore what they had stolen (Exod 22:3). In extreme situations we encounter the selling of one's own life (Lev 25:39–54) or the life of one's children (2 Kgs 4:1; Neh 5) into slavery. The slaves had to do the "dirty work" on the fields, in the quarries, mines, or on the galleys. Women were subject to slightly different rules than men. According to the Book of the Covenant, women always were permanent slaves. Even if the details are not clear in all aspects, we find no explicit mentioning of sexual slavery, several texts explicitly condemn rape (Jer 22:3). It did occur in early times that female slaves bore children that were then counted as the children of her mistress (Gen 16:1–2; 30:3–12), but the main task of female slaves was household work. Female slaves could become married wives; in this case they could no longer be sold. Either the husband had to perform his marital duties (food, clothing, intercourse), or he had to let her go free without recompense (Exod 21:7–11). We encounter

---

8. Since thirty pieces of silver was equivalent to the salary for 3,000 working days, this means it is the value of eight years of work. (Compared to the present-day situation, it would be approximately 200,000 Euros.) In any case, a healthy slave was an object of high value.

9. Cf. Dietrich, "Sklaverei AT"; Grieser and Hilpert, "Sklave/Sklaverei"; Kreuzer and Schottroff, "Sklaverei."

10. See the contribution by Gertz in this volume.

a variation in Deuteronomy, where both genders are treated equally, and women are also released in the seventh year (Deut 15:12).

The Hebrew language does not differentiate precisely between all of these groups of slaves; it refers to male slaves as עֶבֶד or מְשָׁרֵת [11] and female slaves as שִׁפְחָה or אָמָה.[12] There were several ways to attain freedom; either by financial redemption, by grant, by means of *seisachtie*,[13] or other special circumstances (see Jer 34 and Neh 5). Each slave could thus hold the justified hope that someday he or she would be free; perhaps just a small hope but nonetheless real. (Israelite wisdom traditions, however, point out that true freedom cannot be realized in this life; instead, it shifts its hope to the realm of the dead. Job's longing prayer [Job 3] paints post mortal existence as the long-awaited realization of freedom.) Israel's (assumed) experience of slavery and exodus play an important role in the validation of many of these legal statutes. Israel's laws and conventions try to reflect what the myth conveys.

Legal texts in the Bible often have parallels in the ancient Near East.[14] When comparing legal statutes on slavery, we can clearly see the comparatively kind approach of the biblical texts: perhaps it is coincidence that the first legal matter addressed by the Book of the Covenant is the rights of slaves (Exod 21:1–12). Slavery (at least due to debt, the most common type) is limited to a time of six years. After this time, the slave has the opportunity to buy his freedom again.

> When you acquire a Hebrew slave, he shall serve six years; in the seventh year he shall go free, without payment. If he came single, he shall leave single; if he had a wife, his wife shall leave with him. If his master gave him a wife, and she has borne him children, the wife and her children shall belong to the master, and he shall leave alone. But if the slave declares, "I love my

---

11. It is especially remarkable that these terms are also elements of the language of the court; they regulate the relationship of the king to his subjects, and they are also used especially as a religious honorific title denoting the relation of a pious to his God!

12. Mirguet, "Les titres שפחה et אמה."

13. A "decree by government decision freeing slaves"; it was used as a political means to obtain popular favor since Solon of Athens, but even among the Kassites in the seventeenth century BCE, used again and again especially at the start or during times of emergency rule. See the excursus in G. Fischer, *Jeremiah 26–52*, 252–53, with a list of all seisachties mentioned in the ancient.

14. The most important book on this subject was written by Innocenzo Cardellini: *Die biblischen "Sklaven"-Gesetze im Lichte des keilschriftlichen Sklavenrechts*; see also Dandamayev, "The Economic and Legal Character of the Slaves' Peculium in the Neo-Babylonian and Achaemenid Periods"; and Mendelsohn, *Slavery in the Ancient Near East*.

master, and my wife and children: I do not wish to go free," his
master shall take him before God. He shall be brought to the
door or the doorpost, and his master shall pierce his ear with an
awl; and he shall then remain his slave for life. When a man sells
his daughter as a slave, she shall not be freed as male slaves are.
If she proves to be displeasing to her master, who designated her
for himself, he must let her be redeemed; he shall not have the
right to sell her to outsiders, since he broke faith with her. And
if he designated her for his son, he shall deal with her as is the
practice with free maidens. If he marries another, he must not
withhold from this one her food, her clothing, or her conjugal
rights. If he fails her in these three ways, she shall go free, without payment. (Exod 21:2–11)

Biblical laws protect even slaves from bodily harm (*ius talionis* Exod 21:23–25; Lev 24:20; Deut 19:21), guarantee a fair process before a court of law (Job 31:13–15). The *ius talionis* (in contrast to the Codex Hammurabi) does not distinguish between slaves and free men in terms of property laws (this is at least one possible interpretation).[15] On the other hand, we should not overemphasize the difference between Israel and the rest of the ancient Near East. Slavery existed also in Israel.

In conclusion, I would like to briefly analyze three texts that talk of the freedom that Israel owes itself: Neh 5; Jer 34; and 2 Chr 28. All three texts deal with releasing slaves into freedom.

Nehemiah 5

There was a great outcry by the common folk and their wives
against their brother Jews. Some said, "Our sons and daughters
are numerous; we must get grain to eat in order that we may
live!" Others said, "We must pawn our fields, our vineyards,
and our homes to get grain to stave off hunger." Yet others said,
"We have borrowed money against our fields and vineyards to
pay the king's tax. Now we are as good as our brothers, and our
children as good as theirs; yet here we are subjecting our sons
and daughters to slavery—some of our daughters are already
subjected - and we are powerless, while our fields and vineyards
belong to others." It angered me very much to hear their outcry
and these complaints. After pondering the matter carefully, I
censured the nobles and the prefects, saying, "Are you pressing

---

15. Cf. Oeming, "Wisdom as a Central Category in the Book of the Chronicler."

claims on loans made to your brothers?" Then I raised a large crowd against them and said to them, "We have done our best to buy back our Jewish brothers who were sold to the nations; will you now sell your brothers so that they must be sold back to us?" They kept silent, for they found nothing to answer. So I continued, "What you are doing is not right. You ought to act in a God-fearing way so as not to give our enemies, the nations, room to reproach us. I, my brothers, and my servants also have claims of money and grain against them; let us now abandon those claims! Give back at once their fields, their vineyards, their olive trees, and their homes, and abandon the claims for the hundred pieces of silver, the grain, the wine, and the oil that you have been pressing against them!" They replied, "We shall give them back, and not demand anything of them; we shall do just as you say." Summoning the priests, I put them under oath to keep this promise. I also shook out the bosom of my garment and said, "So may God shake free of his household and property any man who fails to keep this promise; may he be thus shaken out and stripped." All the assembled answered, "Amen," and praised the LORD. The people kept this promise.

A scandalous story: the Jews are not acting according to their foundational myth. A difficulty appears in the middle of the report on the reconstruction of the wall;[16] women come pleading to Nehemiah as if he were the king. Nehemiah takes these laments on the consequences of debt slavery very seriously. His project of reconstructing the wall is highly dependent on the solidarity of all those involved. The inner order of the society is highly important to a successful conclusion of his project. Nehemiah's first person report is a document of a theological controversy in post exilic times. The political organization of the community, the shape of social justice and daily life in Judah are called into question. Reinmuth assumes a clear Torah-centered redaction that collated and reworked Nehemiah's report. He believes that the redactional layer shows clearly how priestly and scribal circles, not prophetic groups, carried and continued Nehemiah's reforms. I believe that this report is the work of a theological school associated with the Chronicler. Such a narrative on an exemplary Torah-observant life could very well

---

16. Reinmuth differentiates two different reports; cf. Kratz: "Mit dem Mauerbau hat der Schuldenerlass gar nichts zu tun, um so mehr mit der Rolle Nehemias als Statthalter Judas wie Neh 13; er dürfte also nachgetragen sein" (*Die Komposition der erzählenden Bücher des Alten Testaments*, 70). To which one of the different waves of redactions Kratz is reckoning Neh 5:1–13 is not clear, but somewhere between 450 and 300 it will have taken place. Completely different is Hieke (*Nehemia*), who is—rightly—reading the text as an original unit.

have been idealistic historiography of the Chronistic school. Especially the quick answer of the creditor that they will stand back from all of their claims seems highly unrealistic: "They replied: We shall give them back, and not demand anything of them; we shall do just as you say." Where did a call to repentance ever have such immediate results? Nehemiah's success seems miraculous. In all of this, we cannot point to clear indications of Chronistic language; I tend towards the interpretation that these texts are indeed part of the original report of Nehemiah. I find the answer to the controversial question, what function this report had, in the area of kerygmatic intention. I find it hard to believe that this is a document in which Nehemiah defends himself against suspicions brought forward by the Persian authorities; instead, I think we are dealing with a justification in the face of God. This "theopolitical" writing is saturated with prayers and serves the purpose of mediating ethical ideals, not historiography. We are dealing with a fictious "ideal situation"[17] that intends to speak to the conscience of all creditors. Nehemiah is the ideal political leader, because he is an ideal spiritual leader.[18] "Whoever does not reckon with miracles is no realist"—this classic statement by David Ben Gurion is also embodied with Nehemiah. Liberation from external enemies can only succeed if miraculous acts of solidarity—as demanded by Torah—occur on the inside.

The second story is even more interesting and more characteristic for Israel's self-understanding.

Jeremiah 34[19]

> [8] The word which came to Jeremiah from the LORD after King Zedekiah had made a covenant with all the people in Jerusalem to proclaim a release among them—[9] that everyone should set free his Hebrew slaves, both male and female, and that no one

---

17. This or similar terms (like "idealized scene" or just "scene") are used by Würthwein in order to describe the nature and function of the many "history like" stories in the Old Testament "historiography," e.g., Würthwein, *Studien zum Deuteronomistischen Geschichtswerk*, 156 (Naboth's vineyard), 199 (Josiah's reform).

18. In more evangelical or fundmentalistic circles Nehemiah is received as an ideal leader of the community, e.g., in Willow Creek the Book of Nehemiah enjoys the status of "one of the most important books of the Bible"; cf., e.g., Sanders, *Spiritual Leadership*, 155–60.

19. See Kessler, "The Law of Manumission in Jer 34"; Schenker, "Die Freilassung der hebräischen Sklaven nach Dtn 15,12 und Jer 34,8–2,"; Maier, *Jeremia als Lehrer der Tora*; G. Fischer, *Jeremia 26–52*, 242ff.; Otto, "Der Pentateuch im Jeremiabuch"; G. Fischer, *Jeremia*.

should keep his fellow Judean enslaved. [10] Everyone, officials and people, who had entered into the covenant agreed to set their male and female slaves free and not keep them enslaved any longer; they complied and let them go. [11] But afterward they turned about and brought back the men and women they had set free, and forced them into slavery again. [12] Then it was that the word of the LORD came to Jeremiah from the LORD: [13] Thus said the LORD, the God of Israel: I made a covenant with your fathers when I brought them out of the land of Egypt, the house of bondage, saying: [14] "In the seventh year each of you must let go any fellow Hebrew who may be sold to you; when he has served you six years, you must set him free." But your fathers would not obey Me or give ear. [15] Lately you turned about and did what is proper in My sight, and each of you proclaimed a release to his countrymen; and you made a covenant accordingly before Me in the House which bears My name. [16] But now you have turned back and have profaned My name; each of you has brought back the men and women whom you had given their freedom, and forced them to be your slaves again. [17] Assuredly, thus said the LORD: You would not obey Me and proclaim a release, each to his kinsman and countryman. Lo! I proclaim your release—declares the LORD—to the sword, to pestilence, and to famine; and I will make you a horror to all the kingdoms of the earth. [18] I will make the men who violated My covenant, who did not fulfill the terms of the covenant which they made before Me, take the calf which they cut in two so as to pass between the halves: [19] The officers of Judah and Jerusalem, the officials, the priests, and all the people of the land who passed between the halves of the calf [20] shall be handed over to their enemies, to those who seek to kill them. Their carcasses shall become food for the birds of the sky and the beasts of the earth. [21] I will hand over King Zedekiah of Judah and his officers to their enemies, who seek to kill them—to the army of the king of Babylon which has withdrawn from you. [22] I hereby give the command - declares the LORD—by which I will bring them back against this city. They shall attack it and capture it, and burn it down. I will make the towns of Judah a desolation, without inhabitant.

This is an absolutely scandalous story. Its inner logic proceeds as follows:

vv. 8–11 Description of the human events
    vv. 8, 10 Freeing of the slaves initiated by Zedekiah
        v. 11 renewed enslaving of the freed slaves

vv. 12–22 God's reaction
> vv. 13–14 historical review with a quote from Deut 15:12–13, 18
>> vv. 15–16 repetition of the description in vv. 8–11
>>> vv. 17–20 judgment on those who have broken the covenant
>>> vv. 21–22 judgment on Zedekiah

The story describes Judah in great distress; the Babylonians besiege the city Jerusalem for the second time. Jeremiah had preached for thirty years that the Babylonians are God's tool of judgment because Israel has sinned against the Torah. Now the enemy stands at the gates once again and the immanent catastrophe is clear even to those who so far have trusted in God's grace. In this time of greatest need, Zedekiah has an idea, which he proclaims in a publicity stunt (v. 15):

> Lately you turned about and did what is proper in My sight, and each of you proclaimed a release to his countrymen; and you made a covenant accordingly before Me in the House which bears My name.

It seems as if a great gathering at the temple had occurred, during which all committed themselves in sacred oath to observe God's law and release the indebted slaves. As a result, the Babylonians departed from the city. The historical background may have been a campaign of Pharaoh Hofra (= Apries), who ruled Egypt since 588 and who, like Necho before him, tried to expand his influence against weak Babylon to the north. Trusting in Egypt, Zedekiah broke his vassal treaty with Nebuchadnezzar. Nebuchadnezzar's retribution was horrible; he conquered the entire country except for Lachish, Aseka, and Jerusalem. When Hofra moved north, the Babylonians briefly interrupted their siege and temporarily gathered their forces against the Egyptians. The inhabitants of Jerusalem misinterpreted these events and believed that YHWH would now permanently spare them from the Babylonians. In order to repair the destroyed areas of Jerusalem, they once again bound the former slaves into slavery. Nebuchadnezzar, however, returned soon after and conquered and destroyed the "holy" city.[20] Should this text be historical, we may differentiate three different motivations for the initial release of the slaves: *economic*: in a besieged city each additional person in a house hold was a burden to the head of the house; *military*: the city needed every last person to man the defenses; *theological*: the inhabitants of Jerusalem actually realized that it was against God's will to hold slaves. Its YHWH's will and Israel's identity not to suppress people. Releasing the slaves would

---

20. See, e.g., Volz, *Jeremia*, 317.

pacify God's anger and defer the conquest at the last moment. Shortly after this repentance, however, the people seemed to repent from the repentance (indicated by a word play on the root שוב). The "historic" reasons are not very clear, but the author of the text makes his intentions quite clear by inserting a divine speech: This speech clearly shows God's flagrant anger at the cynical behavior of Judah and its king. This theological-ethical scandal explains why God allowed the Babylonians to conquer Jerusalem.

If this were the true story, it would be hard to understand why the DtrG does not mention it. This episode would have been an ideal explanation for Dtr, especially its nomistic wing, as to how and why Judah brought destruction upon itself: Israel and Judah were punished for massively breaking their covenant with God enslaving there brothers and sisters. I believe that the author of 2 Kgs 24 did not know of these "events" because they were not added until later. With R. P. Carroll (*Jeremiah*) and Georg Fischer (*Jeremiah 26–52*), whose radical skepticism in regards to the historicity of Jeremiah I do not share in general, I do believe that this special episode is a secondary bit of fiction created by a "Chronistic theologian" that was inspired by Neh 5 and intended as a kind of negative counterpart to it. Just as Nehemiah's contemporaries created the conditions for reconstructing the wall by an act of solidarity (d^eror), Zedekiah's contemporaries created the condition for the destruction of the wall by undoing their d^eror. The king himself thus becomes a string puppet whose commands could be readily overturned by anyone.

2 Chronicles 28

Second Chronicles 28:8–15 tells of a prophet with the name Oded, who protests in the name of God that the Israelites take 200,000 individuals as slaves of war after Ahaz has vanquished the Judeans.

> The Israelites captured 200,000 of their kinsmen, women, boys, and girls; they also took a large amount of booty from them and brought the booty to Samaria. A prophet of YHWH by the name of Oded was there, who went out to meet the army on its return to Samaria. He said to them, "Because of the fury of YHWH God of your fathers against Judah, He delivered them over to you, and you killed them in a rage that reached heaven. Do you now intend to subjugate the men and women of Judah and Jerusalem to be your slaves? As it is, you have nothing but offenses against YHWH your God. Now then, listen to me, and send back the captives you have taken from your kinsmen, for

the wrath of YHWH is upon you!" Some of the chief men of the Ephraimites—Azariah son of Jehohanan, Berechiah son of Meshillemoth, Jehizkiah son of Shallum, and Amasa son of Hadlai - confronted those returning from the campaign and said to them, "Do not bring these captives here, for it would mean our offending YHWH, adding to our sins and our offenses; for our offense is grave enough, and there is already wrath upon Israel." So the soldiers released the captives and the booty in the presence of the officers and the entire congregation. Then the men named above proceeded to take the captives in hand, and with the booty they clothed all the naked among them - they clothed them and shod them and gave them to eat and drink and anointed them and provided donkeys for all who were failing and brought them to Jericho, the city of palms, back to their kinsmen. Then they returned to Samaria.

Although the Israelites were the instruments of God's judgments, they now have gone too far, as the prophet Oded states in vv. 9–11. Brothers may not make slaves out of brothers! It would be a grave sin incurring God's wrath against Israel (although justified according to the standards of the ancient Near East) to turn the Judeans into slaves. "Do not bring these captives here, for it would mean our offending YHWH, adding to our sins and our offenses; for our offense is grave enough, and there is already wrath upon Israel." In vv. 14–15 the story reaches a dramatic turning point: the prisoners are not only released, they also receive all of the booty as their property and are given recompense: those who were naked (by this means the defeated are publicly humiliated and dishonored) are clothed and released close to Jericho. There has been much discussion on the historicity of this narrative.

With reference to Hos 9:9 and 10:9, Patrick Arnold believes this episode to be historical and even assumes the prophet Hosea behind the pseudonym Oded.[21] Sara Japhet assumes a limited regional episode that may have provided the basis for a story in which the Chronicler elevated a regional conflict onto a national level.[22] I believe that this story is completely fictitious. The Chronistic school wanted to articulate its ideal of *one* people of God and reinforce their ethos of brotherly solidarity. F. Scott Spencer is quite correct in emphasizing the parallels between this "report" and the parable of the Good Samaritan in Luke 10.[23]

I believe that these three stories (Neh 5; Jer 34; and 2 Chr 28) about releasing slaves are important because they emphasize how Israel's nature, its

---

21. Arnold, "Hosea and the Sin of Gibeah."
22. Japhet, *I & II Chronicles*, 354.
23. Spencer, "2 Chronicles 28:5–15 and the Parable of the Good Samaritan."

covenant with YHWH, its political, economic and ethical wellbeing (and its demise) are completely connected with the issue of slavery. *Releasing* slaves is a central aspect of this religion. This is true for its mythic narratives, its ritual practice, and its specific ethics. The importance of God's covenant with his people is clearly emphasized in the self-curse in Jer 34:16–20:

> I will make the men who violated My covenant, who did not fulfill the terms of the covenant which they made before Me, like the calf which they cut in two so as to pass between the halves: The officers of Judah and Jerusalem, the officials, the priests, and all the people of the land who passed between the halves of the calf shall be handed over to their enemies, to those who seek to kill them. Their carcasses shall become food for the birds of the sky and the beasts of the earth.

These three narratives of liberation show clearly that the final goal of God's story with his people is "to be a free nation in its own land."

The Biblical Message of Freedom as a Political Encouragement

Israel went out of Egypt, out of its own slavery—and conquered a land that was not free; they have had to fight against the population of Canaan and during this foundational war they killed many of them. They created an independent state—but with slaves. The prize of freedom was a horrific war, was a kind of genocide—and slavery. This is the "bitter pill" in history: freeing the slave is connected to violence. The biblical traditions are telling a long story of liberation of Israel—yet the texts hardly talk about the rights of slaves and don't develop a ongoing religious pressure to release them. In legal writings and in daily live, biblical Israel's ethics often fell way behind its mythic narratives. Measured by its own criteria, Israel was living in a sinful state. As we have seen there were only few times in which Israel was very aware that this was wrong. The reality and the power of the biblical ideas of freedom and liberation have still to come—even in Israel.

Sadly, the issue of slavery and slave liberation is not only a historical phenomenon. Buying and selling human beings occurs all over the planet. The "source markets" are found mostly in third world countries and also, following the collapse of the Soviet Union, also in Eastern countries. The buyers are found in all areas of the so-called first world. The increase of globalization also means increase in human slavery. The Internationale Organisation für Migration (IOM) estimates that 500,000 women and children a year are sold from Eastern Europe to Western Europe. Other estimates speak of 120,000 to 200,000.[24] It's not at all an easy task to free enslaved peoples because the "business" offers high profit and has low risk![25] As Ron Soodalter impressively showed in this volume, human trade is a very current reality. He concludes: "Slavery is legal nowhere in the world, and yet it is practiced everywhere. It is estimated that approximately 27 million people are in bondage worldwide" (p. 15 above)

Bibliography

Arnold, Patrick. "Hosea and the Sin of Gibeah." *Catholic Biblical Quarterly* 51 (1989) 447–60.
Boer, Dick. *Erlösung aus der Sklaverei: Versuch einer biblischen Theologie im Dienst der Befreiung*. Münster: ITP-Kompass, 2008. [ET = *Deliverance from Slavery: Attempting a Biblical Theology in the Service of Liberation*. Historical Materialism Book Series 110. Leiden: Brill, 2016.]
Briggs, Sheila. "Slavery and Gender." In *On the Cutting Edge: The Study of Women in Biblical Worlds. Essays in Honor of Elisabeth Schüssler Fiorenza*, edited by Jane Schaberg, Alice Bach, and Esther Fuchs, 171–92. New York: Continuum, 2004.
Brockmeyer, Norbert. *Antike Sklaverei*. Erträge der Forschung 116. Darmstadt: Wissenschaftliche Buchgesellschaft, 1987.
Cardellini, Innocenzo. *Die biblischen "Sklaven"-Gesetze im Lichte des keilschriftlichen Sklavenrechts: Ein Beitrag zur Tradition, Überlieferung und Redaktion der alttestamentlichen Rechtstexte*. Bonner Biblische Beiträge 55. Königstein: Hanstein 1981.
Carmichael, Calum M. "The Three Laws on the Release of Slaves (Ex 21,2–11; Dtn 15,12–18; Lev 25,39–46)." *Zeitschrift für alttestamentliche Wissenschaft* 112 (2000) 509–25.
Carroll, Robert P. *Jeremiah*. OTL. Louisville: Westminster John Knox, 1986.
Chirichigno, G. *Debt-Slavery in Israel and the Ancient Near East*. JSOTSup 141. Sheffield: JSOT Press, 1993.
Dandamayev, M. A. "The Economic and Legal Character of the Slaves' Peculium in the Neo-Babylonian and Achaemenid Periods." In *Gesellschaftsklassen im Alten Zweistromland und in den angrenzenden Gebieten*, edited by D. Otto Edzard, 35–40. Internationaler assyriologischer Kongress 18. Munich: Beck, 1972.
Dietrich, Walter. "Sklaverei AT." In *TRE* 31 (2000) 367–73.
Finkelstein, Israel, and Neil A. Silberman. *The Bible Unearthed: Archaeology's New Vision of Ancient Israel and the Origin of Its Sacred Texts*. New York: Free Press, 2001.
Fischer, Georg. *Jeremia 26–52*. Herders theologischer Kommentar zum Alten Testament. Freiburg: Herder 2005.
———. *Jeremia: Der Stand der theologischen Diskussion*. Darmstadt: Wissenschaftliche Buchgesellschaft, 2007.

---

24. See, e.g., Kreutzer and Milborn, *Ware Frau*.
25. See the movie "Trade" by Marco Kreuzpaintner.

Fischer, Irmtraud. "Was kostet der Exodus? Monetäre Metaphern für die zentrale Rettungserfahrung Israels in einer Welt der Sklaverei." *JBTh* 21 (2006) 25–44.
Grieser, Heike, and Konrad Hilpert. "Sklave/Sklaverei." *Lexikon Theologie und Kirche*³ 9 (2000) 656–57.
Hieke, Thomas. *Die Bücher Esra und Nehemia*. Neuer Stuttgarter Kommentar. Altes Testament 9/2. Stuttgart: Verlag Katholisches Bibelwerk, 2005.
Japhet, Sara. *I & II Chronicles: A Commentary*. Old Testament Literature. Louisville: Westminster John Knox, 1993.
Kessler, Martin. "The Law of Manumission in Jer 34." *Biblische Zeitschrift* 15 (1971) 105–8.
Kratz, Reinhard G. *Die Komposition der erzählenden Bücher des Alten Testaments: Grundwissen der Bibelkritik*. UTB 2157. Göttingen: Vandenhoeck & Ruprecht, 2000.
Kreutzer, Mary, and Corinna Milborn. *Ware Frau: Auf den Spuren moderner Sklaverei von Afrika nach Europa*. Salzburg: Ecowin, 2008.
Kreuzer, S., and Luise Schottroff. "Sklaverei." In *Sozialgeschichtliches Wörterbuch zur Bibel*, edited by Frank Crüsemann et al., 524–30. Gütersloh: Gütersloher, 2009.
Levinson, Bernard M. "The Manumission of Hermeneutics: The Slave Laws of the Pentateuch as a Challenge to Contemporary Pentateuch Theory." In *Congress Volume: Leiden*, edited by André Lemaire, 281–324. Vetus Testamentum Supplements 109. Leiden: Brill, 2006.
Maier, Christl M. *Jeremia als Lehrer der Tora: Soziale Gebote des Deuteronomiums in Fortschreibungen des Jeremiabuches*. FRLANT 196. Göttingen: Vandenhoeck & Ruprecht, 2002.
Mendelsohn, I. *Slavery in the Ancient Near East: A Comparative Study of Slavery in Babylonia, Assyria, Syria, and Palestine, from the Middle of the Third Millennium to the End of the First Millennium*. New York: Oxford University Press, 1949.
Mirguet, Françoise. "Les titres שפחה et אמה: Recherche de lexicographie biblique." *Zeitschrift für die alttestamentliche Wissenschaft* 116 (2004) 242–50.
Numbers, Ronald L. *The Creationists: The Evolution of Scientific Creationism*. New York: Knopf, 1992.
Oeming, Manfred. "Weltbild im Alten Testament." In *TRE* 35 (2003) 569–81.
———. "Wisdom as a Central Category in the Book of the Chronicler: Considerations on the Significance of the Talio-Principle in a Sapiental Construction of History." In *Shai le-Sara Japhet: Studies in the Bible, Its Exegesis and Its Language*, edited by M. Bar-Asher, D. Rom-Shiloni, E. Tov et al., 125*–41*. Jerusalem: Bialik Institute, 2007.
Osumi, Y. "Brandmal für Brandmal: Eine Erwägung zum Talionsgesetz im Rahmen der Sklavenschutzbestimmungen." *Annual of the Japanese Biblical Institute* 18 (1992) 3–30.
Otto, E. "Der Pentateuch im Jeremiabuch: Überlegungen zur Pentateuchrezeption im Jeremiabuch anhand neuerer Jeremia-Literatur." *Zeitschrift für Altorientalische und Biblische Rechtsgeschichte* 12 (2006) 245–306
Schenker, A. "Die Freilassung der hebräischen Sklaven nach Dtn 15,12 und Jer 34,8–22." In *Recht und Kult im Alten Testament: Achtzehn Studien*, 150–57. Orbis Biblicus et Orientalis 172. Göttingen: Vandenhoeck & Ruprecht, 2000.
Sanders, J. O. *Spiritual Leadership: Principles of Excellence for Every Believer*. Chicago: Moody, 2007.

Spencer, F. Scott. "2 Chronicles 28:5-15 and the Parable of the Good Samaritan." *Westminster Theological Journal* 46 (1984) 317-49.
Theissen, Gerd. *Die Religion der ersten Christen*. Gütersloh: Gütersloher, 2002. [ET = *The Religion of the Earliest Churches: Creating a Symbolic World*. Translated by John Bowden. Minneapolis: Fortress, 2003.]
Van Seters, John. "Law of the Hebrew Slave: A Continuing Debate." *Zeitschrift für die alttestamentliche Wissenschaft* 119 (2007) 169-83.
Veijola, Timoo. "'Du sollst daran denken, dass du Sklave gewesen bist im Lande Ägypten': Zur literarischen Stellung und theologischen Bedeutung einer Kernaussage des Deuteronomiums." In *Gott und Mensch im Dialog: Festschrift für Otto Kaiser zum 80. Geburtstag*, edited by Markus Witte, 1:353-73. 2 vols. BZAW 345. Berlin: de Gruyter, 2004.
Würthwein, Ernst. *Studien zum Deuteronomistischen Geschichtswerk*. BZAW 224. Berlin: de Gruyter 1994.

3

Slave Wo/men and Freedom in the Pauline Tradition

Some Methodological Reflections

ELISABETH SCHÜSSLER FIORENZA

"So then, friends, we are children not of the slave but of the free woman. For freedom Christ has set us free. Stand firm, therefore, and do not submit again to a yoke of slavery." Gal 4:31—5:1 NRSV

The topic of "Freedom in the Pauline Tradition" can be approached from different theoretical directions and with different hermeneutical lenses. By placing the freedom of slave wo/men in the center of attention—and I use here slave wo/men in the generic sense to include men[1]—I seek to bring to the fore that freedom can only be fully understood as an actual social reality when juxtaposed and measured with respect to slavery.[2] To be free means not to be a slave wo/man.

---

1. Such a use seeks to bring to awareness the fact that the generic masculine "slaves" erases slave wo/men from consciousness and reduces the category of "woman" to elite, free wo/men.

2. The neo-liberal gospel of freedom is preached in a world, in which slavery exists on an unprecedented scale. However most of us are not conscious that millions of people in Europe, Africa, Asia and the Americas have been forced by traffickers into prostitution or debt bondage, because we believe that slavery was abolished in the 19th

Just like slavery, freedom is to be understood first and foremost, I argue, not just as a metaphorical but as a socio-political expression that applies to real people and not just to ideas and ideals, religious or political. Hence, the rhetorical deployment of "freedom" in the Pauline tradition needs to be adjudicated in light of the institution of slavery and the effects of its ideology on slave wo/men. In other words, the context of slavery is constitutive for the rhetorical function of freedom-language.

It must not be overlooked, however, that my methodological approach is a minority approach among Pauline interpreters. It does not only eschew a literalist "one-to-one meaning" of the text but also recognizes the multiplicity of textual meanings and interpretations. Hence, it calls for an ethics of interpretation. It does not inquire so much as to what freedom *means* but what work the rhetoric of freedom does in a context of slavery. Studies on freedom tend to focus on the ideological-conceptual level[3] of the term but generally do not take the institution of "slavery" as a reference point of meaning, whereas those on slavery tend to focus on the institution and ideology of slavery without explicating the significance of their interpretations for the understanding of freedom in the Pauline tradition.

If one juxtaposes freedom and slavery as socio-political-religious realities rather than metaphorizing them, then the question immediately arises as to whether the Pauline tradition has anything to say about actual freedom—that is, freedom from force, violence and dehumanization; freedom to move, act and decide according to one's own judgment and desire. Do they speak about the actual freedom of slave wo/men, or do they only speak about the idea or concept of freedom? Do they use freedom only in a metaphorical but not in a material sense? Does this mean that Christian freedom is not actual or social freedom but only conceptual and metaphorical? Many would argue that the latter is the case and that freedom in the Pauline tradition means only spiritual freedom, not freedom from domination in the material sense. Such an argument is usually based on the assumption that "real freedom" and the critique of slavery is only conceivable in a post-Enlightenment society. To quote James Dunn in place of many: "Hindsight and the superior Wisdom of the post-Enlightenment European is not a very

---

century. For most people "slavery" has become just a metaphor for undue hardship. This metaphorization of slavery and freedom makes global exploitation acceptable. See Skinner, *A Crime So Monstrous*; Bales, *Disposable People*; Miers, *Slavery in the Twentieth Century*; and Andrew Cockburn, "21st-Century Slaves."

3. For the discussion of freedom from various perspectives, see Wirszubski, *Libertas as A Political Ideal at Rome*; Harris, ed., *Freedom as a Political Ideal*; Nestle, "Freiheit"; Jones, *Freiheit in den Briefen des Apostels Paulus*; Vollenweider, *Freiheit als neue Schöpfung*; Dunn, *Christian Liberty*; Galloway, *Freedom in the Gospel*.

good base for criticism which attempts to censure first-century ethics. Slavery became a moral issue only with the Slave Trade ... The fact that our moral sensibilities have been sharpened over a span of two millenia should not give us license to find fault with those who, two millenia earlier, did not share our Enlightenment."[4]

Charting the Problem

While the concept or ideal of freedom in the Pauline tradition has been much studied,[5] its meaning is not generally determined in relation to slavery understood not in a conceptual or metaphorical but in a socio-political sense. Whereas it is debated whether Paul himself condoned slavery, the so-called *Haustafel* texts of the Pauline tradition[6] clearly speak about the proper behavior of Christian slave wo/men in actual bondage. The works of Balch,[7] Elliott,[8] Niederwimmer,[9] Crouch,[10] and Thraede[11] have convincingly argued for such a socio-political understanding of slavery. Hence, these texts are a primary site on which the rhetoric of freedom and slavery in the Pauline tradition has to be negotiated.[12]

The texts classified as *Haustafel*—a label derived from Lutheran teaching on social status and roles (*Ständelehre*)—are concerned with a threefold relationship to the *kyrios* of the household:[13] that of wife, slave wo/man, and sons/children to the head of the household—the husband, slave-master,

---

4. Dunn, "The Household Rules of the New Testament," 60.

5. See, e.g., Anshen, *Freedom*; Harris, ed., *Freedom as a Political Ideal*; Niederwimmer, *Der Begriff der Freiheit im Neuen Testament*; Adler, *The Idea of Freedom*; Betz, *Paul's Concept of Freedom*; and Vogt, *Ancient Slavery and the Ideal of Man*.

6. For the key role of these texts in the reconstruction of early Christian beginnings, see my book, *In Memory of Her*.

7. Balch, *Let Wives Be Submissive*.

8. Elliott, *A Home for the Homeless*.

9. Niederwimmer, *Askese und Mysterium*.

10. Crouch, *The Origins and Intention of the Colossian Haustafel*.

11. Thraede, "Frau."

12. For the discussion of different historians' reconstruction of the lives of slave wo/men in antiquity, see the book by McKeown, *The Invention of Ancient Slavery*.

13. For the Roman household and "family," cf. Dixon, *The Roman Family*; Garnsey and Saller, *The Roman Empire*; D. B. Martin, "The Construction of the Ancient Family"; Bradley, *Discovering the Roman Family*; Saller, *Patriarchy, Property, and Death in the Roman Family*; Saller, "Women, Slaves, and the Economy of the Roman Household"; Balch and Osiek, *Families in the New Testament World*; Lassen, "The Roman Family"; Gardner, *Family and Familia in Roman Law and Life*, 93–104.

father, lord. Each member of this kyriarchal[14] relationship receives different admonitions. The central interest of these texts is to enforce the submission and obedience of the socially weaker group—wives, slaves, and children—on the one hand, and the authority of the head of the household, the *pater familias and kyrios*, on the other hand.[15]

The complete form of the *Haustafel* is found only in Col 3:18—4:1,[16] which focuses on the admonition of slave wo/men, and Eph 5:22—6:9, which focuses on the marriage relationship. The full form of the *Haustafel* is not found in the remaining passages: 1 Pet 2:18—3:7; 1 Tim 2:11-15; 5:3-8; 6:1-2; Titus 2:2-10; 3:1-2; *1 Clement* 21:6-8; Ignatius, *To Polycarp* 4:1—6:2; Polycarp 4:2—6:1; *Didache* 4:9-11; *Barnabas* 19:5-7. One must therefore ask whether it is the three pairs of admonitions found only in Colossians and Ephesians that are characteristic of the form, or whether the pattern of submission/obedience is the most significant element.[17] It seems, in fact, that the pattern of kyriarchal submission need not always include all four social status groups addressed in Colossians and Ephesians. The pattern sometimes mentions only some of the subordinate groups; it may also include obedience to the political powers of the state or address the governance of the Christian community.[18] The injunction to obedience and submissiveness occurs already in the authentic Pauline letters,[19] for example, in Rom 13 and 1 Cor 14. It therefore cannot be attributed solely to what exegetes have called "early Catholicism."[20] While this pattern of kyriarchal submission functions differently in the different early Christian documents and their social-ekklesial-historical contexts, the "socio-political dimension" of this pattern is constant.

---

14. This neologism is derived from Greek *kyrios* = emperor, slave master, father, husband—the elite, propertied, male head of household. I suggest that this term is more appropriate than the commonly used "hierarchical," since not all dominance relations are sacred.

15. Cf. C. J. Martin, "The Haustafeln (Household Codes) in African American Biblical Interpretation."

16. See the excellent dissertation of Bugg, "Baptism, Bodies, and Bonds."

17. Lillie, "The Pauline House-Tables," pointed to the "pattern of submission" as characteristic for the *Haustafel* texts. For a christological justification of this pattern of subordination, see Kähler, *Die Frau in den Paulinischen Briefen*. For a feminist evangelical interpretation of the pattern as a pattern of "mutual submission," see Mollenkott, *Women, Men, and the Bible*; and Scanzoni and Hardesty, *All We're Meant to Be*.

18. Lührmann, "Wo man nicht mehr Sklave und Freier ist."

19. See the work of Kittredge, *Community and Authority*.

20. For a review of the discussion see Luz, "Erwägungen zur Entstehung des 'Frühkatholizismus.'"

Much of the discussion of the "household code" texts has focused on their historical-religious origin, as well as on their the*logical meaning and authority or their "Christian" character. Research of the past twenty years or so, however, has raised significant questions as to their philosophical derivation and their social function, especially in view of emancipatory tendencies in the first century. Independently of each other, the classicist Thraede and the "New" Testament scholars Lührmann, Balch, and Elliott have concluded that the household code texts share in the Aristotelian philosophical trajectory concerning household management (*oikonomia*) and political ethics (*politeia*). A political, philosophical tradition quite different from the Stoic code of duties is present, one concerned with the relationships between rulers and ruled in household and state.

Previously, some exegetes had maintained that the *Haustafel* was uniquely Christian[21] because it addressed the subordinate groups as moral agents, whereas the majority of scholars believed that it was patterned after the Stoic code of duty[22] and probably mediated by Hellenistic Jewish propaganda.[23] This scholarly consensus seems to have given way to a sociopolitical interpretation which does not exclude the Stoic parallel but has the added virtue of accounting for the three structural sets of subordinate relationships and admonitions.

Thus the discussions of the last two decades seem to have made a significant breakthrough regarding the philosophical provenance of the "code." Such research has documented a growing interest among diverse philosophical directions and schools in the first century to reassert the Aristotelian political ethos—albeit often in a modified, milder form.[24] The "household code" ethic of the New Testament shares in this stabilizing reception of Aristotelian ethics and politics.

Aristotle, in contrast to the Sophists, stressed that the kyriarchal relationships in household and city, as well as their concomitant social differences, are based not on social convention but on "nature." He therefore insisted that the discussion of political ethics and household management begin with "the smallest parts; and the primary and smallest parts of the

---

21. Among others, see Schroeder, "Die Haustafeln des Neuen Testaments," whose thesis was popularized in English by John H. Yoder.

22. For a review of this position and its main representatives see the works of Crouch, Balch, and Elliott. See also Weidinger, *Die Haustafeln*, who argued that the Stoic concept of duty is the basis for the *Haustafeln*.

23. Daube, *The New Testament and Rabbinic Judaism*, 90–105, argued for the Jewish provenance of the *Haustafeln*.

24. See Thraede, "Zum historischen Hintergrund der 'Haustafeln' des NT"; Wicker, "First Century Marriage Ethics"; Balch, "Household Ethical Codes."

household are master and slave, husband and wife, father and children" (*Politics* 1253b). According to Page DuBois, Aristotle takes the domination of the master over the slave as paradigmatic for all forms of rule and authority.[25]

Hence, I submit that the *Haustafel* is best understood as "pattern of kyriarchal submission" which inculcates and legitimates the power of the *kyrios*—the free head of household and citizen—over his slaves, wife and children who are subject to his power. That is, they are not free. The kyriarchal household and state are the points of reference for the meaning of the pattern of kyriarchal submission. The kyriarchal household pattern conceives not only of family, but also of church and state in terms of the kyriarchal household. The Christian community soon comes to be called "the household of G*d," whereby G*d is understood in analogy to the Roman emperor who, from the time of Augustus, is understood as the *pater patriae*[26] and *dominus dominorum*.

In light of the scholarly consensus on the *Haustafel* as a part of political philosophy, the question of whether it was already Paul or the post-Pauline tradition that introduced and advocated this Greco-Roman "pattern of kyriarchal submission" has become even more pressing. Scholars usually try to address this problem by arguing that, in his letter to Philemon[27] and in 1 Cor 7: 21–24,[28] Paul advocates that slave wo/men should become free and be treated as "beloved." However, both texts are so ambiguous that equally as many scholars argue that Paul insists that they must remain in slavery. Yet, the undecidability of Paul's meaning and the ambiguity of the Pauline texts on slave-wo/men's behavior make it possible to argue that the post-Pauline tradition could plausibly claim the teaching of Paul on slavery for its legitimization of slave wo/men's unfreedom.

This textual situation—Pauline ambiguity about slavery and post-Pauline advocacy of the ethos of slavery—has constituted a serious hermeneutical and the*logical problem not only for abolitionists in the American slave controversy of the nineteenth century,[29] but also still does so for progressive exegetes, theologians and churches today. Whereas it is debated whether

---

25. Du Bois, *Slaves and Other Objects*, 189–205.

26. Syme, *The Roman Revolution*, 509–24; see also my book *The Power of the Word*.

27. It is debated whether Onesimus was a runaway slave, a slave sent to Paul by Philemon, or no slave at all. Cf. Callahan, "Paul's Epistle to Philemon"; Callahan, *Embassy of Onesimus*; Lampe, "Keine Sklavenflucht des Onesimus"; Winter, "Philemon."

28. Causing the problem of interpretation is the brachylogy of 1 Cor 7:21b, that is, the omission of an object for the phrase *mallon chrēsai*, which means "rather use," which one can supplement either with freedom or with slavery.

29. Harrill, *Slaves in the New Testament*, 165–92.

Paul opted for the freedom of slave wo/men, there is no doubt that Paul's teaching used the metaphor of slavery to characterize the past and present situation of Christians, the religious realm, and power of sin. Paul's metaphorical use of "slavery" erases the lived brutal realities of slavery as well as the power differences between slave and free wo/men. It seems that slavery as a socio-political institution and its practices are religiously legitimated, while at the same time the metaphorization of slavery by Paul erases the existing differences between slave and free wo/men.

In a similar way, the injunction to husbands to love (Eph 5:25–33; Col 3:19) does not undermine this traditional kyriarchal structure of the code but reinforces it insofar as this love does not constitute wives as equals. Freeborn wives are not called to love, but to subordination, because they do not possess the freedom of the master of the house. Moreover, slave-masters are not required to have *agapē* for their slave wo/men. Finally, in such a kyriarchal structure and mindset, the exhortations to the whole community to love one another meant something different in different contexts of domination. It did mean something different for freeborn men than for slave wo/men—for husbands than for wives—since mutual love requires freedom from domination and the power of choice. If *agapē has as its prerequisite* the freedom to love and is not possible under compulsion and force, then the much-praised Pauline "love ethic" did not apply to the majority of Christians—neither to freeborn women nor to slave wo/men—but only to *kyrioi*, or freeborn elite men.

Rather than to critically analyze and discuss this replacement of freedom with *agapē* in Pauline rhetoric and its socio-political consequences, scholars—as far as I can see—have developed the following arguments in "defense of Paul":

1. Most often, it is argued that Paul and early Christianity could not abolish the all-pervasive legal system of Roman slavery because they did not have the power to do so. Hence, we do not find a direct statement in the Christian Testament that would condemn slavery outright. Paul is a "man of his time" and cannot be blamed for not advocating the abolition of slavery.[30] As Orlando Patterson categorically states: "Paul neither defended nor condemned the system of slavery, for the simple reason that in the first century Roman imperial world in which he lived, the abolition of slavery

---

30. See, for example, Bevere, *Sharing in the Inheritance*, 247n94., who argues, "Christians of the time had little power to change politically. Indeed, given the fact that there was no such thing as representative democracy, it likely would never have occurred to them to try and change the structures."

was intellectually inconceivable, and socially, politically and economically impossible.[31]

This argument, however, avoids the problem posed by the Pauline tradition. It is not a question of whether Paul was able to abolish the *system of slavery*, but a question of whether the proclamation "for freedom Christ has set us free" had any implications for the lives of slave wo/men who joined the messianic *ekklēsia*. In other words, did conversion and baptism involve manumission or being treated as an equal in the early Christian house churches, or did it only pertain to one's soul? This question is an appropriate question since we know that the Synagogue and certain Jewish groups such as the Essenes and the Therapeutae enabled manumission and freedom for slave wo/men. We also know that private associations admitted slave wo/men as full members.

2. Another attempt to save Paul from his critics is to argue that the "opponents" of Paul were libertine enthusiasts and hence Paul had to curb their demands for unlimited freedom. While the "opponent" construction has fallen into disrepair, the "anti-imperial" Paul has been championed by scholars in the past decade or so. It is argued, on the one hand, that Paul thinks in terms of the Roman imperial universe of slavery; on the other hand, that his metaphorical use of slavery does not re-inscribe it, but radically challenges it. Richard Horsley, for example, has argued that Christ, in his resurrection, has become a *counter-emperor* and Paul's mission was "to build a new international society as an alternative to Roman imperial society."[32] It was Paul who built this new society and developed its symbolic universe "from scratch."[33] Although Paul did not explicitly criticize institutionalized slavery, his program was far more radical than to simply point out abusive aspects of the slave system.

Paul, however, could not count on "his" communities to continue his radical anti-imperial program, so the argument goes, because his communities had internalized the dominant symbolic universe of imperial slave society. Thus, a genuine re-socialization into the alternative symbolic universe was difficult. Although a new ideal was articulated in Gal 3:28, and probably baptismally embodied, it was difficult for it to take root in the communities. "Thus it is also not surprising to find in the Deutero-Pauline letters Colossians, Ephesians, and the Pastorals a reversion to the basic hierarchical social relations of the imperial order embodied in the slave-holding

---

31. Patterson, "Paul, Slavery and Freedom," 266.
32. Horsley, "Paul and Slavery," 189.
33. Ibid., 165.

patriarchal household."³⁴ This apology for Paul constructs a deep chasm between the anti-imperial Paul, his failing communities, and the following generation. It seeks to downplay the metaphorical inscription of the slavery system into the early Christian symbolic universe. Finally, it resorts to Jewish Scriptural language in order to legitimate slavery.

3. A third way to explain away the defense and inculcation of the ethos of slavery in the Pauline tradition is to question the appropriateness of the thesis of those who understand the pre-Pauline baptismal formula Gal 3:28 not just as articulating an ideal but also as having been realized in practice. In a spirited reply to Horsley, Stanley K. Stowers insists that the understanding of slavery as evil comes not from the bible, but stems from modern Enlightenment thinking which understands the person as "autonomous and self-governing."³⁵ In Paul's Bible, Stowers argues, "slavery is pervasive, brutal, and sanctioned by God." The Hebrew Bible not only allows slavery, but also speaks of the Israelites as slaves of G*d. Hence, Stowers concludes: "It seems that those who have seen Paul as an opponent of slavery have not come to terms with the scripture that Paul held as authoritative."³⁶

Moreover, those who understand Gal 3:28 as claiming that the status differences between Jewish and Greek wo/men, slave and free wo/men, and between husband and wife are no longer valid in Christ operate allegedly with the modern assumption that social roles and attributes can be peeled away. However, if one were to peel away socially-imposed roles in Mediterranean society—so the argument goes—one would find nothing. In such a society, the self is not "trapped behind social roles" but is "constituted in social interaction."³⁷ Stowers maintains, therefore, that Gal 3:28 does not mean that social status, ethnicity or the sexes have "been eliminated, even if the importance of such roles has been relativized, because the form of this world is passing away."³⁸

Stowers seems not to recognize, however, that it is he who construes the interpretation of Gal 3:28 in terms of a modern understanding of the person as autonomous from social roles. Slavery is not a "social role," I would argue, but a kyriarchal institution that robs people of their humanity and personhood. Stowers also falls prey to the same modern fallacy of which he accuses others when he assumes that only modern persons—but not ancient Mediterraneans—could envision a life in freedom. This overlooks

34. Ibid., 191.
35. Stowers, "Paul and Slavery."
36. Ibid., 306.
37. Ibid.
38. Ibid., 307.

the information we have on slave wo/men's uprisings. Fugitive slave wo/men constituted a serious problem and massive slave wo/men revolts took place between 140 and 70 BCE.[39] These uprisings, which "assumed the scale of a war with thousands of armed men on both sides and pitched battles between armies, sieges, and occupation of cities,"[40] were not fought in order to become free of "slave roles" and find one's "true self," but were fought for freedom from the dehumanizing bondage of slavery. To suggest that ancient Mediterranean slave wo/men could not envision being free is tantamount to modernist prejudice.

4. The fourth strategy in defense of Paul's and the whole Christian Testament's ambivalent stance toward slavery and the Pauline tradition's advocacy of slavery is the scholarly recourse to "eschatology"[41] or "apocalypticism." However, it is rarely acknowledged that both the terms "apocalypticism" and eschatology are "modern" terms created by scholars in the 19th century. The term eschatology, designating the teaching about the "last things" and about the "end of the world," is a dogmatic creation of the*logical scholarship.

Paul, so it is argued, expected the end of the world and Jesus' return in glory very soon, and hence he did not develop a "social program" of political equality and freedom. Since the end of the world was at hand, one should not expect Paul to be concerned with the abolition of slavery or with building an egalitarian society. Rather, Paul expected the "Day of the Lord" and the *parousia* of Christ in the imminent future. Like the parables of Jesus, he envisioned G*d as a Lord and slave-master[42] whose judgment and wrath would destroy all dehumanizing powers in the very near future.

This argument overlooks, however, that the Pauline correspondence also knows of a different kind of eschatology which scholars have dubbed "realized eschatology." This is the conviction that G*d's alternative world and society have already begun, here and now. The proclamation "for freedom Christ has set us free" speaks of the past, not the future. The central image of salvation is that of "being bought free from slavery at a high price." The power of *hamartia*, from which the baptized were set free, is the power to enslave. The proclamation "for freedom Christ has set us free" does not speak about our soul but about *us*, that is, about people, about those baptized into the messianic corporation—at least that is how it could have

---

39. Cf. also Bradley, *Slavery and Rebellion in the Roman World*.
40. Callahan, "Slave Resistance in Classical Antiquity," 143.
41. See, e.g., Larry Hurtado's conference paper on "Freed by Love and for Love."
42. See Beavis, "Ancient Slavery as an Interpretive Context for the New Testament Servant Parables"; Glancy, *Slavery in Early Christianity*, 102–29.

been heard by slave wo/men in the community. Whereas Paul might have understood the "yoke of slavery" metaphorically, slave wo/men would have understood and identified it as unfreedom and bondage, as slavery itself.

To summarize: The understanding that emerges if one reads Paul in an idealistic fashion which emphasizes the conceptual-metaphorical meanings of his teaching about freedom is different than if one reads texts as rhetorical arguments, arguments which engage actual problems and disagreements. While an analysis in terms of Paul's concepts and thought focuses on the great apostle who teaches with authority and has the power to enforce his teachings, a rhetorical approach sees Paul as one voice among many within a rhetorical debate. Rhetoric does not just focus on the author but also on the audience, the rhetorical situation and the socio-political-religious location of the speaker and the argument. It does not just focus on *logos* but also on *pathos* and *ethos*.[43] It does not *identify with* or take the *standpoint* of Paul but those of slave wo/men.

By "defending the teaching of Paul," however, scholars avoid both asking whether Paul's teaching was accepted and exploring the consequences of his metaphorical use of slavery for the practice of freedom. Hence, they are able not to address the violence of unfreedom legitimated by pro-slavery Scriptural texts or to ask whether such kyriarchal violence becomes intrinsic to Christian self-understanding and the*logy if it is not critically deconstructed. Moreover, by identifying Paul's teaching conceptually with early Christian beliefs and practices, interpreters overlook not only that his "teaching and conceptuality" is argumentative rhetoric, but also that there were alternative voices and options that sought to maintain slave wo/men's freedom.

Instead, the "defense of Paul" resorts to a spiritualizing and moralizing approach to freedom in terms of love, i.e. to an antiquarian understanding which maintains that the desire for freedom and equality is a modern post-Enlightenment projection and that slave wo/men in antiquity were not capable of such a desire—although the Roman slave wars and slave resistances document the opposite. When scholarly arguments neglect the "other" voices in the debate which are also inscribed in the Pauline tradition, or when they do not engage in a discussion as to why slave wo/men and their desires for freedom don't come into view, they re-inscribe familiar prejudices against slave wo/men as "things without voice." If we instead assume that slave wo/men took the baptismal confession "neither slave nor free wo/men" in the "messianic corporation" at face value and insisted on their socio-religious equality, we then must carefully examine assumptions

---

43. See my book, *Rhetoric and Ethic*.

and methods which allow scholars to rule out such an argument on grounds of their theoretical frameworks. Instead they tend to hide behind the apologetic argument that the abolition of the institution of slavery was not possible or thinkable at the time.

Methodological–Hermeneutical Reflections

Placing slave wo/men and their struggles in early Christianity at the center of hermeneutical attention rather than the concept of freedom will require several shifts in methodological and hermeneutical approach. First of all, it asks for a methodological shift from a philosophical idealist tendency which emphasizes concepts to an understanding of text as rhetorical construction and persuasive communication. Understanding texts as arguments requires that one not only ask what the text means, but also whom it seeks to persuade, whose interests it articulates, and to what ends.

The result is different if one reads the Pauline tradition as rhetorical argument rather than as "teaching," or a collection of concepts and ideas. Rhetoric does not just focus on the author but also on the audience, the rhetorical situation and the socio-political-religious location of the speaker, the audience and the argument. It does not just focus on *logos* but also on *pathos* and *ethos*. In the following, I would like to sketch four such methodological shifts:

First, approaching the topic of freedom in the Pauline Tradition in and through a focus on slave wo/men raises three key methodological issues:

1. How should we read grammatically kyriocentric, i.e. elite male (*kyrios* = slavemaster) centered texts? In the kyriocentric text, slave wo/men are doubly invisible. On one hand, the masculine form of *doulos* is usually not translated as male slave but as the generic *slave*, while the feminine form always is translated as female slave. However, slave wo/men as historical agents are generally not mentioned in the Pauline corpus, the one exception being an allegorical reference. On the other hand, the gendered generic term *gynē* or "woman" seems to refer only to freeborn wo/men. Hence, studies on "women" in the Pauline tradition tend to focus on freeborn wo/men. To keep slave wo/men in the center of hermeneutical attention requires a re-theoretization not only of gender but also of class/status, ethnicity, race and imperial power.[44] For instance, texts such as 1 Cor 6 and 7 raise quite different issues if one keeps in mind that slave wo/men were the sexual property of their male and female masters, that they often could not marry or keep

---

44. See the collection of essays in Nasrallah and Schüssler Fiorenza, eds., *Prejudice and Christian Beginnings*.

their children, and that they were frequently forced into prostitution. It raises the foundational question as to whether freedom was the pre-condition, the *sine qua non*, for being a morally accountable member of the *ekklēsia*.

2. Placing slave wo/men in the center of attention also requires that one move from a hermeneutical or descriptive analysis of the text to a rhetorical analysis—one that pays attention not only to the author and his statements, but also to the audience to whom the text is addressed, the rhetorical problem it seeks to overcome, and the socio-political situation and symbolic universe shared by author and audience. Generally, the label rhetoric/rhetorical is understood to refer to speech as stylistic ornament, technical means or linguistic manipulation—as discourse utilizing irrational, emotional devices that are contrary to critical thinking and reasoning. However, this negative popular and academic understanding of rhetoric must be carefully distinguished from rhetoric understood as a communicative intellectual practice involving contexts, interests, values, and visions. The revival of rhetoric as critical, cultural, and intellectual discourse has both rediscovered the significance of rhetoric in the production of knowledge in general and underscored the "rhetoricity" or "rhetoricality" of texts and interpretations in particular. The *rhetoric of inquiry* focuses on epistemological and disciplinary questions such as the following: How is knowledge constructed? What counts as interesting research question? What kind of knowledge gets privileged? How is disciplinary authority constructed? What kind of socio-political or cultural religious interests are served? There are many more. Hence, I suggest that one needs to adopt a critical rhetorical analysis of the whole Pauline tradition, including the letters that scholars deem to be post-Pauline, in order to adequately approach the problem of slave wo/men and freedom.

3. A rhetorical approach calls for an ethics of interpretation and a hermeneutics of critical evaluation to be applied to biblical texts that either function as authoritative Scripture in Christian communities today or as cultural classics in the public square. Two examples may suffice:

The Hagar-Sarah allegory in Gal 4:21–31 contrasts the slave woman and the free woman in order to illustrate enslavement to the law and freedom in Christ.[45] Although Paul is not addressing the social institution of slavery here, he re-inscribes the dichotomies between slaves and free in the interest of Christian superiority. He probably does so in order to theologically divest non-messianic Judaism of its claim to religious identity as descended from Abraham. "Christian"[46] freedom's identity and superiority is

---

45. Briggs, "Paul on Bondage and Freedom in Imperial Roman Society"; Briggs, "Slavery and Gender."

46. For the discussion as to whether the categories "Christian" and "Jewish" are

purchased in and through "the casting out" of the son of the slave woman. A bloody history of Christian anti-Judaism has been the consequence of this rhetoric. As Sheila Briggs observes, without question the rhetoric of this text "depends on metaphors taken from the institution of slavery and the sexual use of women in slavery. One may argue that Paul's use of the language of slavery in figurative speech did not constitute an endorsement of slavery in the social realm; however, one cannot simply sever the rhetorical strategy from the content of the discourse."[47]

To give another example, Paul's discussion of freedom in the letter to the Romans which also theologically re-inscribes the Roman imperial discourse of slavery[48] and freedom. With the collapse of the Roman Republic, Patterson claims that civic political freedom was replaced with the absolutist, sovereign freedom of the divine emperor who embodied the imperial state and guaranteed the collective security and honor of Roman citizens. In Romans, freedom is a free gift bestowed by G*d who is characterized as *kyrios*—slave-master. The free gift of freedom requires obedience and subjection to the master. Now that the baptized have been set free from the power of sin, they have "become enslaved to G*d" (Rom 6:20–23). By becoming "slaves of G*d,"[49] Christians become exactly what slaves are to their master. Patterson diagnoses this Pauline rhetoric as the "power language of the imperial ruling elite."[50] According to Patterson, "Paul boldly turns the contemptuous Roman view of the Christians on its head, arguing that in their endurance and suffering they build just the kind of character which the elite Roman idealized. Gone, it seems, is the reversal of status, the sublation of powerlessness into power."[51] This characterized the rhetoric of the baptismal formula in Gal 3:28. Hence, a hermeneutics of suspicion and critical evaluation for proclamation is required if Christians do not want to continue the imperial rhetoric of enslavement to G*d. The task of a critical ethics of evaluation is not simply to validate the original meaning of the text (if that can be had), but also to assess its inscriptions of meaning and their function in our own contemporary contexts. It seeks to engender a different constellation of the the*logical discourses, cultural visions

---

appropriate for the first century see, e.g., Denise Kimber Buell, Johnson Hodge, Daniel Boyarin, Judith Lieu, and others.

47. Briggs, "Galatians," 224.
48. See Castelli, "Romans," 293–95.
49. Cf. D. B. Martin, *Slavery as Salvation*; Peterson, *Rediscovering Paul*.
50. Patterson, *Freedom*, 341.
51. Ibid., 342.

and social worlds evoked by sacred texts along with the contemporary struggles against slavery and for freedom. Attention to the the*logical re-inscription of freedom in terms of the imperial slave system would allow us to formulate an alternative understanding of freedom fashioned in and through the *ekklēsia*, understood as the radically democratic decision-making assembly for whose existence freedom is a *sine qua non* condition.[52]

Second, the focus on slave wo/men engenders a critical rhetoric of inquiry that is able to facilitate a shift from a philosophical-the*logical focus on *concepts* of freedom to the exploration of the *intersection* of freedom in the *ekklēsia* and the impact of the imperial institution of slavery on it. This entails a shift from text to context. Paul's rhetoric of freedom and slavery can only be assessed if it is analyzed as a persuasive communication in a particular historical–rhetorical situation, constructing a symbolic universe that is shared by the people to whom he writes. Hence, one cannot be content to simply outline the the*logical "concepts" of the Pauline tradition; one also needs to examine how its the*logical language relates to social structures and ekklesial conflicts, as well as how it is shaped by its particular socio-political historical situation. The conflicts in Galatia or Corinth were not debates about abstract the*logical concepts but about different ways of viewing the world and about rhetorical struggles to define the self-understanding and life of the *ekklēsia*. Paul is one, but not the *sole* authoritative voice in these debates. For instance, Gal 3:28—which declares the socio-political status divisions between Jews and Greeks, slave and free wo/men, male and female as no longer existing in Christ, i.e. in the *ekklēsia*—is in this view not understood as a peak formulation of Paul, but as a pre-Pauline baptismal tradition shared by Paul and the Galatian, Corinthian, Ephesian or Roman Christians, and possibly understood differently by different groups of people. It presupposes that Christian slaves were full members of the community, partook in the common meals and received the gifts of the Spirit. Hence they expected to be treated as equal "brothers and sisters" and no longer as slaves. The so-called *Haustafel* texts are arguments seeking theologically to intervene on behalf of the established slave-masters and the imperial Roman order because of the revolutionary potential of the *ekklēsia*.

Third, a shift of theoretical attention from Paul to slave wo/men as historical agents requires a shift from a history of ideas to a history of struggles, from text to context. For instance, in his magisterial work *Freedom. Freedom in the Making of Western Culture*, Orlando Paterson argues that

---

52. To stress the radical democratic roots of *ekklēsia* does not require to limit it to its Greek classical heritage. Rather, it can also take into account the radical democratic traditions of Israel, the assembly of the people of G*d. It necessitates that we cease to construct a sharp dichotomy between Greek and Jewish thought.

"freedom was socially constructed—not discovered . . . in a specific pair of struggles generated by slavery."[53] Kurt Raaflaub also shows that the political notion of freedom was articulated in the context of the Persian wars when the isonomic Greek *polis* resisted occupation and domination by a authoritarian monarchic empire that had quite different value-systems and social-political structures. This confrontation and conflict was then and is now understood in terms of freedom and slavery, a conflict that strengthened the ethos of the isonomic *polis* as the assembly of free and equal citizens.[54] Both explorations of the concept of freedom stress that it needs to be understood in terms of the struggles against subjection and slavery.

The re-construction of a radical egalitarian *ekklēsia* discourse as an alternative to the discourse of empire is necessary in order to understand and evaluate Pauline the*logy in terms of the struggles submerged in historical texts. Attention to the democratic language of *ekklēsia* and the subordination discourses of empire in the Pauline tradition will break open and expand the resources for the the*logical discussion of freedom. It will caution us against understanding freedom too quickly in terms of relationality and self-giving love. Articulating biblical theology in terms of the rhetoric and ethos of the conflict between empire and *ekklēsia*, i.e. the radical egalitarian assembly of full citizens, allows one to trace the interaction of multiple perspectives and makes possible a discourse that can bring those who are historically silenced and marginalized, such as slave wo/men, into view. In the current moment, when the rhetoric of president Bush's "agenda of freedom" which legitimates torture, surveillance, and wars of occupation as liberation, the rhetoric of the "free world" versus the "empires of evil," the rhetoric of winners and losers, of good and evil, orthodoxy and heresy threatens to exclude and to do violence, such a the*logical discourse is urgently needed.

However, the significant work done on Paul and Empire[55] in recent years has persisted in understanding itself as uncovering the "real" anti-imperial Paul, rather than critically analyzing the impact of his rhetoric. The desire to have Paul represent "anti-imperial" discourse has prevented direct confrontation with the manner in which Paul's language and practice is shaped by empire. Because scholars have not explicitly acknowledged the constructive and rhetorical dimension of their work, its impact has not been as effective as it might be in bringing into dialogue the ancient and contemporary contexts. The desire to have Paul represent "anti-imperial discourse" for Christians today, has prevented direct confrontation with the manner

---

53. Ibid., 3.
54. Raaflaub, *Die Entdeckung der Freiheit*, 320ff.
55. See my book *The Power of the Word*, for the literature and its discussion.

in which Paul's language and practice is shaped by empire. Recovery and reconstruction of the conflict inscribed in Pauline discourses between the rhetoric of *ekklēsia* and that of empire, both of which are present within the breadth of early Christian communities, would advance the discussion of "Paul and politics" or "freedom in the Pauline tradition" in a necessary and important direction.

The *fourth* shift is a shift from legitimating the Pauline the*logical re-inscription of freedom in terms of the imperial slave system to the articulation of an alternative rhetoric and practice of freedom, one to which the Pauline and post-Pauline discourse of freedom can be understood as a rhetorical response. This presupposes that we seek to listen to the voices to whom the extant Pauline tradition responds and with whom it argues. This means that first of all we have to relinquish our understanding of Paul as the sole founder and authoritative leader of the communities to whom he writes. Rather than to see Paul, in a modernist fashion, as the authoritative leader and charismatic individual, one needs to think of him as one of many voices that have shaped the symbolic universe and social practices of early Christian communities.

Envisioning the Struggles of Slave Wo/men for Freedom

The assertion "for freedom Christ has set us free from slavery" can be understood as a common confession to which Paul appeals in Galatians and which he uses toward his own argumentative ends. But if early Christians did not have the power to abolish the system of slavery, as many scholars have pointed out, what kind of historical-rhetorical situation could one construct to which this rhetoric can be seen as a fitting response? Two characteristics of Roman slavery in distinction to Athenian slavery seem to be significant.

First, although slavery was a brutal institution, there were not only ideological but also practical tendencies in the Roman Empire to mitigate at least urban slavery. Law and literature of the time sought to curb physical cruelty and emphasized that slaves were human beings and should be allowed a level of independence as well as certain rights and freedoms. It was in the interest of masters and slaves, for example, that slave wo/men could accumulate wealth (*peculium*) for doing business. Moreover, since all masters invested money in their slave wo/men, reasonable treatment of them was in their masters' own interests.

However, most important is the religious ethos that demanded equality. In his description of the "contemplative" or "philosophical" life of the

Therapeutae and Therapeutrides,[56] Philo stresses that this ascetic community "has no slaves to wait upon them as they consider that the ownership of servants is entirely against nature. For nature has borne all to be free, but the wrongful and covetous acts of some who pursued that source of inequality have imposed their yoke and invested the stronger with power over the weaker."[57] Instead of slave wo/men, young freeborn men served at table at their communal meals.

Philo speaks in a similar fashion about the Essenes, a Jewish community that is often identified with the Qumran community:

> Not a single slave is found among them, but all are free, exchanging services with each other and they denounce the owners of slaves, not merely for their injustice in outraging the law of equality, but also for their impiety in annulling the stature of Nature, who, mother-like, has born and reared all alike, and created them genuine brothers, not in mere names but in very reality . . . (Philo, *Quod omnis probus liber sit*, 79).[58]

Second, in distinction to classical slavery, Roman slavery condoned manumission by individuals and corporate manumission. Formal manumission reintegrated slave wo/men into society by making them Roman citizens. Although the system of slavery was entrenched in the Roman Empire, the manumission of individual slave wo/men as well as corporate manumission was widespread. This willingness to free slaves may not have been for humanitarian reasons, but it indicates that Roman slavery was not automatically a life-long state.[59]

In light of these two discourses of manumission, the ethical and the legal, two scenarios can be envisioned to have been in play in the messianic *ekklēsiai*. One is the ethos of equality and freedom in the house-church, the other is the practice of buying the freedom of slave wo/men who belonged to non-Christian households either by individual patrons or with the funds of the congregation. The fact that this dual possibility existed in the *ekklēsia* is apparent, for instance, in the injunction of 1 Tim 6:1-2, a text that is dated around the same time as Ignatius, *ad Polycarp*, and which distinguishes between two groups of slave wo/men. The first verse tells slave wo/men to "regard their masters as worthy of all honor, so that the name of G*d and the teaching may not be blasphemed," whereas verse two is addressed to those who have "believing masters." In both cases the ethos of slavery is

---

56. Cf. Taylor, "The Women 'Priests' of Philo's *De Vita Contemplativa*.
57. Philo, *De Vita Contemplativa* 70, in *Philo: On the Contemplative Life*.
58. Quoted by Garnsey, *Ideas of Slavery*, 78.
59. Cf. Harrill, *The Manumission of Slaves in Early Christianity*.

rhetorically re-enforced. On the one hand, slave wo/men who complained about and called for the repentance of their Christian masters who had fallen back into the sin of the kyriarchal practices of slavery are told "not to be disrespectful" to them on the grounds that they are "brothers," members of the church. On the other hand, slave wo/men who may have pleaded to be bought free from pagan slave masters are told to respect them.

The first scenario of slave wo/men asking to be treated as equals in the house-church is similar to that of the Therapeutae. This demand would have made sense both in cases where the whole household was baptized and became Christian and in house-churches whose members were all coming from Christian households. Hence, they did not need to undergo a formal manumission because the baptismal affirmation "for freedom Christ has set us free" had given them equal standing in the *ekklēsia*. In this case, the social-status differences between slave master/mistress and slave wo/men would have been replaced by the notion that all the baptized are "siblings"[60] and "beloved" children of G*d. Hence, on the basis of the ethos of equality and freedom, mutuality and respect among the different members of the household was to be practiced. However, the exhortation of 1 Timothy admonishes slave wo/men and not masters. It does not rebuke the masters for failing to live the Christian ethos of equality and freedom, but rather uses this ethos to reinforce the submissive behavior of Christian slave wo/men.

The second scenario is referred to by Ignatius of Antioch. Writing to the bishop Polycarp in Smyrna, Asia Minor, he testifies to the early Christian practice of corporate manumission, albeit he is against it.

> Do not behave arrogantly towards slaves, either male or female. But let them not be puffed up. Rather let them be enslaved all the more to the glory of G*d. Let them not desire to be manumitted out of the money in the common chest, so that they may not be found slaves of desire. (Ignatius, *Ad Polycarp* 4.3)

It seems that early Christian *ekklēsiai* had adopted the Roman practice of manumission to enact the second scenario, which required the formal manumission of slave wo/men who belonged to non-Christian masters. Slave wo/men could be and regularly were given their freedom in the Roman Empire. The widespread manumission of slaves was a distinctive feature of the Roman institution of slavery.[61] Moreover, corporate manumission seems to have been practiced by private associations, in cultic places such as Delphi, and by Jewish synagogues.

---

60. Cf. Aasgard, *'My Beloved Brothers and Sisters!'*; Schäfer, *Gemeinde als "Bruderschaft."*

61. Hope, "Status and Identity in the Roman World," 129.

According to Harrill, evidence for this practice is found among Jewish communities all over the ancient world, from Egypt to the north shores of the Black Sea. Jewish synagogues had common chests. "These chests functioned institutionally in ways similar to those in a Roman *collegium* (*arca collegii, arca communis, arca publica, ratio publica, respublica collegii*) which one or more officers of the association managed. Hellenistic private associations also operated a common fund (*tameion, koinon*)."[62] Harrill suggests that Ignatius saw three dangers in the corporate practice of manumission by Christians which he seeks to avoid with this exhortation. Firstly, there was the fear that some would join the Christian community only for the sake of money, expecting that the *ekklēsia* would buy their freedom; secondly, there was the danger of pagan slander against Christians for subverting slavery; and thirdly, there was the potential problem of rivalry and competition among the different house churches in a Metropolitan area which Ignatius sought to unify under the authority of one bishop.[63] E. A. Judge has pointed to a fourth possible reason why such practices of manumission were curtailed or rejected by the writers of the so-called household code tradition:

> With regard to the household obligation, the NT writers are unanimous; its bonds and conventions must at all costs be maintained ... There is of course ... the interest of the patronal class ... but the primary reason, no doubt, is that the entrenched rights of the household as a religious and social unit offered the Christians the best possible security for their existence as a group. Any weakening here would thus be a potentially devastating blow to their own cohesion, as well as having revolutionary implications from the point of view of the public authorities.[64]

Judge sees correctly that the rhetoric of the "household code" is due to the interest of the "patronal," or, better, the "master" class. He plays down this insight, however, by arguing instead with the *Haustafel* tradition in the interest of masters rather than slave wo/men. Yet, his argument nevertheless presupposes that the house-church was governed by the "principles of fraternity" and that it presented a threat only "if enthusiastic members failed to contain their principles within the privacy of the association and thus were led into political indiscretions or offenses against the hierarchy

---

62. Harrill, "Ignatius, Ad Polycarp. 4.3 and the Corporate Manumission of Christian Slaves," 122 with references.

63. Ibid., 136.

64. Judge, *The Social Patterns of Christian Groups in the First Century*, 75ff.

of the household."⁶⁵ Such an argument overlooks the fact that the conversion of free wo/men, slave wo/men and young people who belonged to the household of an unconverted *pater familias* already constituted a potential political offense against the kyriarchal order. This had to have been considered an infringement of the political order, for the kyriarchal order of the house was considered the paradigm of the state. Since the kyriarchal *familia* was the nucleus of the state, conversion of the subordinated members of the household who were expected to share in the religion of the *pater familias* already constituted a subversive act. Buying them free from their masters, however, would not have undermined, but would rather have followed the Roman order.

The prescriptive *Haustafel* trajectory attempted to play down this subversive potential by asserting the congruence of the Christian ethos with that of kyriarchal house and state, rather than by purchasing free slave wo/men who had converted. This trajectory did not continue the ethos of the house-church, with its egalitarian and collegial structures, but sought to modify this ethos and bring it in line with the structures of kyriarchal family and society.⁶⁶ In doing so, the *Haustafel* trajectory sought to kyriarchalize not only the early Christian ethos of "fraternity," or, better, of "the discipleship of equals," but also the very structures of the Christian community. However, the prescriptive character of the *Haustafel* texts indicates that such a process of kyriarchalization was still not in force in subsequent centuries, and it has never been completely accomplished.

In both scenarios of reconstruction, the early Christian assertion "for freedom Christ has set us free" would have engendered a concrete practice of actual freedom from slavery. As I have argued in *In Memory of Her*, slave wo/men who joined the messianic community expected to be treated as free persons. Such expectations were engendered by the Christian proclamation that all members of the community were "set free by Christ." Such formulas occur again and again in the Pauline letters: "You were bought with a price, do not become human slaves" (1 Cor 6:20; 7:23). The goal of Christian calling is freedom: "You were called to freedom" (Gal 5:13), because "where the Spirit of the Lord is there is freedom" (2 Cor 3:17). To argue that Christian freed-wo/men who insisted on their call to freedom had only "a superficial understanding of the gospel"⁶⁷ is to minimize the effects of this the*logical

---

65. Ibid., 76.

66. For the distinction between ethos and ethics, see Keck, "Ethos and Ethics in the New Testament." For the interrelation between house church and *collegia*, see Malherbe, *Social Aspects of Early Christianity* and the work of Klauck.

67. Crouch, *The Origin and Intention of the Colossian Haustafel*, 127.

rhetoric of freedom in a Greco-Roman context where both slavery and manumission were commonly-accepted institutional practices.

Liberation from the slavery of the dehumanizing powers of sin, slave law, and death—from the conditions of the present "evil age"—has "freedom" as its goal and purpose. "As a result, *eleutheria* (freedom) can be understood as the central the*logical concept which sums up the Christian situation before God as well as in this world."[68] Therefore, slave wo/men who became Christians must have heard this proclamation of freedom as performative rhetoric asserting that among those baptized "there were neither slave nor free wo/men" (Gal 3:28).

Thus, the re-activation of the Aristotelian ethos which maintains sociopolitical differences of gender, ethnicity, and slavery as *natural and therefore unchangeable* differences between women and men, as well as between slaves and freeborn, has to be seen within the context of cultural-political and ekklesial debates and struggles. In this context of struggle, the household-code trajectory can be seen not only as "Christianizing" the kyriarchal Aristotelian ethos of inequality, but also as humanizing and modifying it by obliging the *pater familias* to exercise love, consideration, and responsibility. From the perspective of freeborn and slave wo/men, however, the *Haustafel* ethos is a serious setback, since it does not strengthen Roman cultural tendencies to manumission and religious claims to equality and mutuality between free and slave wo/men.

By reinforcing the kyriarchal submission of those who, according to Aristotle, must be ruled, and by abandoning their claim to freedom, the early Christian ethos of co-equal discipleship loses its capacity to structurally transform the kyriarchal order of family and state. By adapting the Christian community to its kyriarchal society without taking into account the Roman practice of manumission, the *Haustafel* ethos opens up the *ekklēsia* to political co-optation by the Roman Empire and, in the process, sacrifices the freedom of slave wo/men. That such a process of co-optation required centuries to complete—and was never fully achieved—speaks for the vitality of the early Christian ethos of coequal discipleship and freedom. In this kyriarchalizing process, the vision of *agapē* and freedom, mutuality, and solidarity among Christians gradually becomes transformed from a "new reality" to mere moral appeal. Submission and obedience—not freedom, equality, and justice—are institutionalized by this kyriarchal scriptural ethos. Since this ethos was not restricted to the household but was also adopted by the *ekklēsia*, Christian faith and praxis ceased to provide a structural-political-religious alternative to the dominant kyriarchal culture

68. Betz, *Galatians*, 255.

of slavery and imperial ethos. The Christian preaching of the gospel and the churches' hierarchical-kyriarchal structures became a contradiction that stripped from the gospel of freedom its transforming power in history.

Bibliography

Aasgard, Reidar. *'My Beloved Brothers and Sisters!' Christian Siblingship in Paul*. Studies of the New Testament and Its World. London: T. & T. Clark, 2004.

Adler, Mortimer J. *The Idea of Freedom: A Dialectical Examination of the Conceptions of Freedom*. Garden City, NY: Doubleday, 1968.

Anshen, Ruth Nanda, ed. *Freedom: Its Meaning*. New York: Harcourt Brace, 1940.

Balch, David L. "Household Ethical Codes in Peripatetic, Neopythagorean, and Early Christian Moralists." In *Society of Biblical Literature Seminar Papers*, edited by Paul J. Achtemeier, 2:397–404. Missoula, MT: Scholars, 1977.

———. *Let Wives Be Submissive: The Domestic Code in 1 Peter*. Society of Biblical Literature Monograph Series 36. Chico, CA: Scholars, 1981.

Balch, David L., and Carolyn Osiek. *Families in the New Testament World: Households and House Churches*. The Family, Religion, and Culture. Louisville: Westminster John Knox, 1997.

Bales, Kevin. *Disposable People: New Slavery in the Global Economy*. Berkeley: University of California Press, 1999.

Beavis, Mary Ann. "Ancient Slavery as an Interpretive Context for the New Testament Servant Parables with Special Reference to the Unjust Steward (Lk 16:1–8)." *Journal of Biblical Literature* 111 (1992) 37–54.

Betz, Hans Dieter. *Galatians*. Hermeneia. Philadelphia: Fortress, 1979.

———. *Paul's Concept of Freedom in the Context of Hellenistic Discussions about the Possibilities of Human Freedom*. Berkeley: Center for Hermeneutical Studies, 1977.

Bevere, Allan R. *Sharing in the Inheritance: Identity and the Moral Life in Colossians*. Journal for the Study of the New Testament Supplement Series 226. Sheffield: Sheffield Academic, 2003.

Bradley, Keith R. *Discovering the Roman Family: Studies in Roman Social History*. New York: Oxford University Press, 1991.

———. *Slavery and Rebellion in the Roman World, 140 BC–70 BC*. Bloomington: Indiana University Press, 1989.

Briggs, Sheila. "Galatians." In *Searching the Scriptures: A Feminist Commentary*, edited by Elisabeth Schüssler Fiorenza, 2:218–36. New York: Crossroad, 1994.

———. "Paul on Bondage and Freedom in Imperial Roman Society." In *Paul and Politics: Ekklesia, Israel and Imperium*, edited by Richard A. Horsley, 110–23. Harrisburg, PA: Trinity, 2000.

———. "Slavery and Gender." In *On the Cutting Edge: The Study of Women in Biblical Worlds. Essays in Honor of Elisabeth Schüssler Fiorenza*, edited by Jane Schaberg, Alice Bach, and Esther Fuchs, 171–92. New York: Continuum, 2003.

Bugg, Laura Elizabeth. "Baptism, Bodies, and Bonds: The Rhetoric of Empire in Colossians." Th.D. diss., Harvard University, 2006.

Callahan, Allen Dwight. *Embassy of Onesimus: The Letter of Paul to Philemon*. New Testament in Context. Valley Forge, PA: Trinity, 1997.

———. "Paul's Epistle to Philemon: Towards and Alternative Interpretation." *Harvard Theological Review* 86 (1993) 357–76.
———. "Slave Resistance in Classical Antiquity." *Semeia* 83/84 (1998) 133–51.
Castelli, Elizabeth. "Romans." In *Searching the Scriptures: A Feminist Commentary*, edited by Elisabeth Schüssler Fiorenza, 2:272–300. New York: Crossroad, 1994.
Cockburn, Andrew. "21st-Century Slaves." *National Geographic* 204 (September 2003).
Crouch, James E. *The Origins and Intention of the Colossian Haustafel*. FRLANT 109. Göttingen: Vandenhoeck & Ruprecht, 1972.
Daube, David. *The New Testament and Rabbinic Judaism*. 1956. Reprint, Eugene, OR: Wipf & Stock, 2011.
Dixon, Suzanne. *The Roman Family*. Ancient Society and History. Baltimore: Johns Hopkins University Press, 1992.
du Bois, Page. *Slaves and Other Objects*. Chicago: University of Chicago Press, 2008.
Dunn, James D. G. *Christian Liberty: A New Testament Perspective*. Carlisle, UK: Paternoster, 1999.
———. "The Household Rules of the New Testament." In *The Family in Theological Perspective*, edited by Stephen C. Barton, 43–64. Edinburgh: T. & T. Clark, 1996.
Elliott, John H. *A Home for the Homeless: A Social-Scientific Exegesis of 1 Peter, Its Situation and Strategy*. 1981. Reprint, Eugene, OR: Wipf & Stock, 2005.
Galloway, Lincoln E. *Freedom in the Gospel: Paul's Exemplum in 1 Cor 9 in Conversation with the Discourses of Epictetus and Philo*. Contributions to Biblical Exegesis and Theology 38. Leuven: Peeters 2004.
Gardner, Jane. *Family and Familia in Roman Law and Life*. Oxford: Clarendon, 1998.
Garnsey Peter. *Ideas of Slavery from Aristotle to Augustine*. W. B. Stanford Memorial Lectures. Cambridge: Cambridge University Press, 1996.
Garnsey Peter, and Richard P. Saller. *The Roman Empire: Economy, Society and Culture*. Berkeley: University of California Press, 1987.
Glancy, Jennifer A. *Slavery in Early Christianity*. Oxford: Oxford University Press, 2002.
Harrill, J. Albert. "Ignatius, Ad Polycarp. 4.3 and the Corporate Manumission of Christian Slaves." *Journal of Early Christian Studies* 1/2 (1993) 103–42.
———. *The Manumission of Slaves in Early Christianity*. Hermeneutische Untersuchungen zur Theologie 32. Tübingen: Mohr/Siebeck, 1995.
———. *Slaves in the New Testament: Literary, Social and Moral Dimensions*. Minneapolis: Fortress, 2006.
Harris, B. F., ed. *Freedom as a Political Ideal*. Sydney: McQuarrie University, 1964.
Hope, Valerie. "Status and Identity in the Roman World." In *Experiencing Rome: Culture, Identity and Power in the Roman Empire*, edited by Janet Huskinson, 125–52. New York: Routledge, 2000.
Horsley, Richard A. "Paul and Slavery: A Critical Alternative to Recent Readings." *Semeia* 83/84 (1998) 153–200.
Jones, F. Stanley. *Freiheit in den Briefen des Apostels Paulus*. Göttinger theologische Arbeiten 34. Göttingen: Vandenhoeck & Ruprecht, 1987.
Judge, E. A. *The Social Patterns of Christian Groups in the First Century: Some Prolegomena to the Study of New Testament Ideas of Social Organization*. Christ and Culture Collection. London: Tyndale, 1960.
Kähler, Else. *Die Frau in den Paulinischen Briefen: Unter besonderer Berücksichtegung des Begriffes der Unterordnung*. Zurich: Gotthelf, 1960.

Keck, Leander E. "Ethos and Ethics in the New Testament." In *Essays in Morality and Ethics: The Annual Publication of the College Theology Society*, edited by James Gaffney, 29–49. New York: Paulist, 1980.

Kittredge, Cynthia Briggs. *Community and Authority: The Rhetoric of Obedience in the Pauline Tradition*. Harvard Theological Studies. Harrisburg, PA: Trinity, 1998.

Lampe, Peter. "Keine Sklavenflucht des Onesimus." ZNW 76 (1985) 135–37.

Lassen, Eva. "The Roman Family: Ideal and Metaphor." In *Constructing Early Christian Families: Family as Social Reality and Metaphor*, edited by Halvor Moxnes, 103–20. London: Routledge, 1997.

Lillie, William. "The Pauline House-Tables." *Expository Times* 86 (1975) 179–82

Lührmann, Dieter. "Wo man nicht mehr Sklave und Freier ist: Uberlegungen zur Struktur frühchristlicher Gemeinden." *Wort und Dienst* 13 (1975) 53–83.

Luz, Ulrich. "Erwägungen zur Entstehung des 'Frühkatholizismus.'" ZNW 65 (1974) 88–111.

Malherbe, Abraham. *Social Aspects of Early Christianity*. 1977. Reprint, Eugene, OR: Wipf & Stock, 2003.

Martin, Clarice J. "The Haustafeln (Household Codes) in African American Biblical Interpretation: 'Free Slaves' and 'Subordinate Women.'" In *Stony the Road We Trod: African American Biblical Interpretation*, edited by Cain Hope Felder, 206–31. Minneapolis: Fortress, 1991.

Martin, Dale B. "The Construction of the Ancient Family: Methodological Considerations." *Journal of Roman Studies* 86 (1996) 40–60.

———. *Slavery as Salvation: The Metaphor of Slavery in Pauline Christianity*. New Haven: Yale University Press, 1990.

McKeown, Niall. *The Invention of Ancient Slavery*. London: Duckworth, 2007.

Miers, Suzanne. *Slavery in the Twentieth Century: The Evolution of a Global Problem*. Lanham, MD: AltaMira, 2003.

Mollenkott, Virginia Ramey. *Women, Men, and the Bible*. Nashville: Abingdon, 1977.

Nasrallah, Laura, and Elisabeth Schüssler Fiorenza, eds. *Prejudice and Christian Beginnings: Investigating, Race, Gender, and Ethnicity in Early Christian Studies*. Minneapolis: Fortress, 2009.

Nestle, Dieter. "*Freiheit.*" In *Reallexikon für Antike und Christentum*, edited by Theodore Klauser, 18:269–306. Stuttgart: Hiersmann, 1972.

Niederwimmer, Kurt. *Askese und Mysterium*. FRLANT 113. Göttingen: Vandenhoeck & Ruprecht, 1975.

———. *Der Begriff der Freiheit im Neuen Testament*. Theologische Bibliothek Töpelmann 11. Berlin: Töpelmann, 1966.

Patterson, Orlando. *Freedom: Freedom in the Making of Western Culture*. New York: HarperCollins, 1991.

———. "Paul, Slavery and Freedom: Personal and Socio-Historical Reflections." *Semeia* 83/84 (1998) 263–79.

Peterson, Norman. *Rediscovering Paul: Philemon and the Sociology of Paul's Narrative World*. 1983. Reprint, Eugene, OR: Wipf & Stock, 2008.

Philo. *Philo: On the Contemplative Life*. Edited and translated by F. H. Colson. Loeb Classical Library. Cambridge: Harvard University Press, 1941.

Raaflaub, Kurt. *Die Entdeckung der Freiheit: Zur historischen Semantik und Gesellschaftsgeschichte eines politischen Grundbegriffes der Griechen*. Vestigia 37. Munich: Beck, 1985.

Saller, Richard P. *Patriarchy, Property, and Death in the Roman Family.* Cambridge Studies in Population, Economy, and Society in Past Time 25. Cambridge: Cambridge University Press, 1994.

———. "Women, Slaves, and the Economy of the Roman Household." In *Early Christian Families in Context: An Interdisciplinary Dialogue,* edited by David L. Balch and Carolyn Osiek, 185–204. Grand Rapids: Eerdmans, 2003.

Scanzoni, Letha, and Nancy Hardesty. *All We're Meant to Be: A Biblical Approach to Women's Liberation.* Waco: Word, 1975.

Schäfer, Klaus. *Gemeinde als "Bruderschaft": Ein Beitrag zum Kirchenverständnis des Paulus.* Europäische Hochschulschriften. Reihe XXIII, Theologie 333. Frankfurt: Lang, 1989.

Schroeder, David. "Die Haustafeln des Neuen Testaments." Ph.D. diss., University of Hamburg, 1959.

Schüssler Fiorenza, Elisabeth. *In Memory of Her. A Feminist Reconstruction of Christian Origins.* 10th ann. ed. New York: Crossroad, 1983/1994.

———. *The Power of the Word: Scripture and the Rhetoric of Empire.* Minneapolis: Fortress, 2007.

———. *Rhetoric and Ethic: The Politics of Biblical Studies.* Minneapolis: Fortress, 1999.

Skinner, E. Benjamin. *A Crime So Monstrous: Face-to-Face with Modern-Day Slavery.* New York: Free Press, 2008.

Stowers, Stanley K. "Paul and Slavery: A Response." *Semeia* 83/84 (1998) 295–311.

Syme, Ronald. *The Roman Revolution.* Oxford: Oxford University Press, 1939.

Taylor, Joan E. "The Women 'Priests' of Philo's *De Vita Contemplativa*: Reconstructing the Therapeutae." In *On the Cutting Edge: The Study of Women in Biblical Worlds,* edited by Jane Schaberg, Alice Bach, and Esther Fuchs, 102–22. New York: Continuum, 2003.

Thraede, Klaus. "Frau." *Antike und Christentum* 6 (1970) 197–267.

———. "Zum historischen Hintergrund der 'Haustafeln' des NT." *Jahrbuch für Antike und Christentum, Ergänzungsband* 8 (1981) 359–68.

Vogt, Joseph. *Ancient Slavery and the Ideal of Man.* Translated by Thomas Wiedemann. Cambridge: Harvard University Press, 1975.

Vollenweider, Samuel. *Freiheit als neue Schöpfung: Eine Untersuchung zur Eleutheria bei Paulus und in seiner Umwelt.* FRLANT 148. Göttingen: Vandenhoeck & Ruprecht 1989.

Weidinger, Karl. *Die Haustafeln: Ein Stück urchristlicher Paränese.* Untersuchungen zum Neuen Testament 14. Leipzig: Hinrichs, 1928.

Wicker, Kathleen O'Brien. "First Century Marriage Ethics: A Comparative Study of the Haustafels and Plutarch's Conjugal Precepts." In *No Famine in the Land: Studies in Honor of John L. McKenzie,* edited by James W. Flanagan and Anita Weisbrod Robinson, 141–53. Homage Series 2. Missoula, MT: Scholars, 1975.

Winter, Sarah C. "Philemon." In *Searching the Scriptures: A Commentary,* edited by Elisabeth Schüssler Fiorenza, 2:301–12. New York: Crossroads, 1994.

Wirszubski, Chaim. *Libertas as a Political Idea at Rome during the Late Republic and Early Principate.* Cambridge: Cambridge University Press, 1950.

4

The Paradox of Freedom

Mary, the Manhattan Declaration, and Women's Submission to Childbearing

KATHARINA VON KELLENBACH

This paper challenges theological discourses that ground freedom in submission and obedience to God's will, particularly as that relates to women. Scholars of theology and biblical studies not infrequently sideline issues of gender and sexuality because they appear to belong to the subfield of feminist theology. But in the contemporary world, no item on the theological agenda is more embattled and divisive than marriage, reproduction and sexuality. In the context of the "culture wars" in the United States, the rallying cry of Christian freedom has become a potent weapon in the battle to curtail women's control over conception and childbearing. This paper will place biblical and doctrinal teachings of Christian freedom within the context of the politics of reproductive choice and of heterosexual marriage. I will begin with the Protestant theological reception of Paul, then examine the Manhattan Declaration (November 2009), and end with some reflections on the reduction of faith to obedience in Luke's Annunciation to Mary.

The Paradox of Freedom

The theological affirmation that Christian freedom is found in unconditional submission to God's will is referred to as the "paradox of freedom." I will argue that the theological rhetoric of "paradox" should be heard within political and economic contexts that buttress the *empowerment* of (free propertied) Christian men who understand themselves as moral subjects endowed with inalienable rights of agency, political freedom and personal autonomy while at the same time legitimating the *disempowerment* of women and slaves, whose autonomy and agency are structurally denied. In a moment we will see how contemporary US American Christian leaders use the rhetoric of "paradox" to persuade women to choose submission under the headship of their husbands as proper path towards Christian salvation. The theological seeds of such Christian politics are contained in Protestant interpretations of Paul that locate the freedom of the Christian believer in self-effacing service to the neighbor. Paul's teachings are presented as an invitation to the autonomous individual believer to forgo willful assertions of independence, selfhood and individuality because they constitute separation from God, and hence sin:

> Since they do not belong to themselves, but to God and to one another, they are being freed to love God and one another, together and concretely, indeed confidently…They are being freed to gratefully and willingly obey God's will. They are being freed to perform all the duties of love.[1]

Such submission to service as the primary or exclusive path towards Christian freedom is a problematic theological prescription in light of women's bondage to male authority and family control. Since women's "grateful and willing" obedience has been enforced by structures of violence, women's surrender of personal autonomy is often involuntary. Freedom is, more often than not, the prerogative of men who may be persuaded to embrace "belonging" in a free act of faith, while women's submission to the "duties of love" is already presupposed. Women's compliance can be, has been, and is being compelled by law, harsh economic reality and domestic violence. The term "belonging" hides the reality of such enforced dependency. "For Paul," argues Hans-Joachim Eckstein in "The Innovative Concept of Freedom in Paul," "liberation from sin, from the condemnation of the law and from the impending death is not aimed at the absolute 'autonomy' and

---

1. Smit, "Freedom in Community"—chap. 16 below.

'self-sufficiency of the person. On the contrary, it is intended as an enabling for a life of relationship that is of community and mutual acceptance."[2]

While some feminists share the disillusionment over the promises of liberalism and individual rights, we must ask: whose "autonomy" and "self-sufficiency is the primary concern in such statements?" For most women across time and cultures, the autonomous assertion of individuality was not within (sinful) reach. The Bible is not known for its robust defense of women's personhood and autonomy: women's moral agency is not presupposed in the economic, religious and political realm nor protected in the personal and sexual domain. Women's bodily autonomy, in particular, was firmly committed to male control. Female sexuality and reproductive potential are managed by fathers and/or husbands. Rape and adultery are defined with respect to male ownership of women's sexuality rather than as a violation of women's bodily autonomy. Sexual misconduct is considered an offense against the proprietary interests of men (Leviticus). Restitution is owed to the father of a virgin (rape, seduction) and the husband of a wife (adultery), while men are allowed multiple wives, concubines and access to prostitutes. In rare cases where women are seen as initiating (and thereby responsible for) sexual intercourse, such instances involve animals (Leviticus) or the incestuous assault of a drunken father (Genesis; e.g., Lot after the destruction of Sodom). In the Gospels, we hear about adulterous women (John 4:17; 8; Luke 7) but not about adulterous men. While biblical scriptures do not deny the personhood of women altogether, the sexuality of women required male control and supervision.[3] Women's bodily autonomy and right to make decisions over their own bodies receives little, if any, biblical mandate. By nature, divine law, and/or social convention, women are supposed to submit to male authority in the area of sexuality and reproduction.

In light of the weight of patriarchy embedded in the biblical traditions, how can Paul's exhortations to submit to God's will retain any liberating meaning? Joachim Eckstein maintains that freedom is not constituted by "freedom from" external rule and coercive control but rather by "freedom for" "relationship not experienced as limitation but as the realm of unfolding."[4] But for women and slaves, household relationships are the site of restriction of self-possession, autonomy and self-sufficiency. For women, whose bodily autonomy and "freedom from" coercion have not been robustly established, giving up claims to "freedom from" oppression is not liberating. Eckstein

---

2. Eckstein, "The Innovative Concept of Freedom in Paul"—chap. 13 below.

3. See Judith Romney Wegner's insightful legal discussion of men ownership of women's reproduction in *Chattel or Person?*

4. Eckstein "The Innovative Concept of Freedom in Paul."

argues that "the innovative concept of freedom in Paul consists precisely in the definition of freedom as the ability for community and for service in reciprocal awareness and personal acceptance."[5] For many women, the most intimate relationships are also the most ambivalent because of the ways in which love and service, degradation and exploitation are intertwined. Exegetical analyses of biblical texts that maintain gender-blindness mask the political implications of theological terms such as freedom and submission. It is striking that several contributors to this volume endorse "service" as the pinnacle of Christian freedom in the midst of a global economic system that consigns women to the service sector of the workforce as well as in private households. While one can only hope that more men discover the benefits of service and the career potentials in the service industry, women ought to beware of such gender-blind prescriptions.

In her essay Elisabeth Schüssler Fiorenza points towards the sociopolitical implications of the theological terminology of freedom. In her contribution on "Slave Wo/men and Freedom in the Pauline tradition," Schüssler Fiorenza insists that the "rhetorical deployment of 'freedom' . . . needs to be adjudicated in light of socio-political and economic realities." As a New Testament scholar she demands that the discussion move from the text into the context, from Paul's eventual incorporation of imperial, kyriarchical *Haustafeln* to the resistance and struggle for liberation among Greco-Roman slaves, male and female. Heeding her call, I would like to shift attention from the biblical text and its theological reception into the political context of the contemporary American culture wars involving the Christian concept of freedom.

For many right-wing American Christians, the term "freedom" functions as a sacred value that encapsulates the birthright of American Christian citizen. The historical reality that freedom was, for a long time, restricted to white, male, propertied heads of household, may not be entirely lost on some neoconservative Christian intellectuals. But in the contemporary context, the "paradox of freedom" serves to safeguard the freedom of individuals to engage in economic pursuit, political decision making and religious service while at the same time advocating for patriarchal marriage and against reproductive choice. Contraception, abortion and gay marriage have become the preferred battleground to debate individual freedom, selfish desire and faithful submission to God's will. American Christian women, in particular, are admonished to relinquish control over fertility and to abandon self-interested ambitions. Women's access to birth control, abortion and reproductive health services have moved into the center of political

---

5. Eckstein "The Innovative Concept of Freedom in Paul."

debate ranging from health care coverage, to the appointment of Supreme Court justices, and the electability of political and presidential candidates.

The Manhattan Declaration

The *Manhattan Declaration*, released November 20, 2009, calls on Christian communities to engage in "civil disobedience" in defense of "the sanctity of human life, the dignity of marriage as a union of husband and wife, and the freedom of conscience and religion."[6] Originally signed by 168 Roman Catholic, Protestant and Orthodox religious leaders, including seventeen Roman Catholic bishops and seven women, two of whom co-signed as wives of pastors, the document cites Dietrich Bonhoeffer and Martin Luther King to announce Christian resistance in order to "roll back the license to kill that began with the abandonment of the unborn to abortion" and to uphold a "healthy marriage culture" rooted in the "sexual complementarity of man and woman." The Manhattan Declaration is divided into three parts: the first, titled "Life" maintains that the Supreme Court's legalization of abortion thirty six years ago implemented a "culture of death" and stripped legal protection from the "weak and vulnerable against violent attack." In the second part, the authors demand the restoration of "Marriage" understood as a complementary unit of man and woman in keeping with God's sexual script established in Gen 2:23 and Eph 5:32 (*Haustafel*). Under the heading of "Religious Liberty," "the right to religious freedom" buttresses a Christian platform for "civil disobedience" that refuses to "comply with any edict that purport to compel our institutions to participate" in abortions or accept immoral sexual partnerships. The Manhattan Declaration received wide public attention, not least because the Roman Catholic Archbishop of Washington DC, Bishop Wuerl was among the original co-signers. He proceeded to threaten the Washington DC city council with immediate closure of all Catholic social services if the council dared to enact legislation legalizing gay marriage (which it did in December 2009). The Manhattan Declaration is an ecumenical document that received support from a wide spectrum of religious leaders. It allows insight into the thinking of the reinvigorated Christian patriarchy movement in the United States.

I want to begin with the second item of the Manhattan Declaration which ostensibly opposes gay marriage but really advances an understanding of heterosexuality that entrenches the submission of women. Proponents of Christian patriarchy are retrieving the concept of the "complementarity" of man and woman as "ordained by God and blessed by Christ." "Human

---

6. http://www.Manhattandeclaration.org.

beings" the authors write, "are not merely centers of consciousness or emotions, or minds, or spirits, inhabiting non-personal bodies" but rather form a "dynamic unity of body, mind and spirit." As particular female and male bodies, heterosexuality is seen as "a commitment that is sealed, completed and actualized by loving sexual intercourse in which the spouses become one flesh" and share life "at every level of being—the biological, the emotional, the dispositional, the rational, the spiritual." The alleged complementarity of the male and female body, of penetrator and penetrated, of active and passive, of rational and emotional, of leader and follower, of head and body, is thereby resurrected as the "crowning achievement of God's creation."

> The Bible teaches us that marriage is a central part of God's creation covenant. Indeed the union of husband and wife mirrors the bond between Christ and the church. And so just as Christ was willing, out of love, to give himself up for the church in complete sacrifice, we are willing, lovingly, to make whatever sacrifices are required of us for the sake of the inestimable treasure that is marriage.

The framers of the Manhattan Declaration are quite aware that this marriage metaphor demands the full subjugation of women as spelled out in Eph 5:22–24:

> Wives, be subject to your husbands, as to the Lord. For the husband is the head of the wife as Christ is the head of the church, his body, and is himself its Savior. As the church is subject to Christ, so let wives also be subject in everything to their husbands.

As men are to follow the headship of Christ, women are called to submit modeling the role of the church as subordinated partner in this covenant. The "thriving marriage culture" envisioned by the Manhattan Declaration is built upon women's voluntary (?) acceptance of male headship. Women are called to become "helpmeets" as spelled out in Genesis and to enable men to fulfill their roles as husbands in order to grow into their responsibilities as Christ-like leaders of their households. While the framers of the Manhattan Declaration leave the precise patriarchal arrangements of male headship to the imagination, other proponents invoke Paul to argue that women ought to submit to their husbands irrespective of male character or merit. One of the more unabashed illustrations of this unconditional principle of male headship comes from British Reformed Baptist pastor Geoff Thomas who is a prolific contributor to *Banner of Truth,* an extensive Christian website and publishing house for books and sermons promoting "Biblical Christianity through Literature":

In other words, the reason why wives are to submit to their husbands is not because they are wonderful guys who deserve it. Sometimes husbands deserve very little from their wives. The reason why you submit is because your Lord Jesus Christ deserves it. Out of gratitude to him, for all that he has done for you, you submit. It is not because you love your husband that much, but it is because you love the Lord Jesus more. That is the key. I obey the one I love; I do whatever he tells me to do. A wife's submission to her husband is "*as to the Lord*" Paul tells us in our text. I am willing to do whatever it is he tells me to do. My reverence for Christ motivates me to obey him in everything he says. I am in his Word, and I am doing his Word day by day. I am doing it in my home, in the daily chores of life.[7]

And, Geoff Thomas continues, "According to the apostle there is no possibility of a married woman's surrender to a heavenly Lord which is not made visible and actual by submission to her husband." The complementarity of the sexes prescribes marital submission as a woman's only path to submit to God's will in Christ. For women, Christian freedom boils down to obedience to their husband. While such teachings seem to contradict core ideals of American democracy and Protestant Christianity, their appeal among white Protestant Christians is growing. Fringe movements, such as the Quiverfull Movement are developing a potent Christian subculture, spawning Christian publication outlets, bookstores, radio stations, websites and are embraced by many families in the burgeoning homeschooling movement, that is estimated by the US Department of Education to enroll a million school-age US children.[8] Several of the signatories to the Manhattan Declaration are activists in this movement and/or represent organizations that subscribe to its ideology.[9]

The Quiverfull Movement, in particular, has turned pronatalism into a central Biblical mandate and has popularized women's submission to unlimited fertility into a Christian calling. Fertility rates in white Protestant families have outpaced Catholic families as women have turned unlimited reproduction into their Christian calling.[10] The poster child family of this

---

7. Geoff Thomas, "Wives Submit to Their Husbands," released on 9/27/2005; http://www.banneroftruth.org/pages/articles/article_detail.php?885.

8. Joyce, *Quiverfull*, ix.

9. Signers include: James Dobson's "Focus on the Family"; Tony Perkins for Family Research Council; David Neff, *Christianity Today*; Maggie Gallagher, National Organization for Marriage; Gary Bauer, Campaign for Working Families; Brian Brown, National Organization for Marriage.

10. The name is based on Ps 127:3–5: "Lo, sons are a heritage from the LORD, the fruit of the womb a reward. Like arrows in the hand of a warrior are the sons of one's

movement is the Duggar family, and Ms. Duggar has recently given birth to her 19th child, an event announced in major news organizations, including National Public Radio.[11] Since the Bible considers children a blessing, more children must be an even greater blessing. The movement's name and inspiration are based on Ps 127:3–5, which declares that "sons are a heritage from the LORD, the fruit of the womb a reward. Like arrows in the hand of a warrior are the sons of one's youth. Happy is the man who has his quiver full of them! He shall not be put to shame when he speaks with his enemies in the gate." According to the Quiverfull Movement, any reproductive control is contrary to God's will. Complete submission to "life," reduced to its sexual and reproductive biological component, is promoted as women's path towards Christian freedom.

> We exalt Jesus Christ as Lord, and acknowledge His headship in all areas of our lives, including fertility. We exist to serve those believers who trust the Lord for family size, and to answer the questions of those seeking truth in this critical area of marriage.[12]

Nancy Campbell, the post-feminist prophetess of this movement, elevates submission to God in the area of fertility to a gospel truth.

> ... Scripture passage after Scripture passage which extol the virtue of trusting the Lord to control the womb and the necessity that believers be fruitful and multiply. For six-thousand years, believers viewed children as a blessing and reward of the Lord greatly to be desired ... Does the Bible address the question of child prevention? Is cutting off the godly seed ever an act of "good stewardship?" Are economic considerations a valid biblical ground for closing the womb?[13]

The answer is a resounding "No." The relinquishment of bodily autonomy and control over fertility is promoted as female vocation set out in the Bible. The woman who chooses "child prevention" is selfish. Adherents of the Quiverfull movement purport to be in the mainstream of the biblical interpretation. Charles D. Provan, another spokesman of the Protestant anti-contraception movement, asserts in *The Bible and Birth Control*, that by examining

---

youth. Happy is the man who has his quiver full of them! He shall not be put to shame when he speaks with his enemies in the gate."

11. http://www.duggarfamily.com/.
12. http://www.quiverfull.com/.
13. http://www.quiverfull.com/resources.php; Campbell, *Be Fruitful and Multiply*.

> all the Biblical bases for refusing contraception, and the teachings of Martin Luther, John Calvin, Cotton Mather, and others ... contraception is shown to be strongly against God's plan for family life.[14]

Contraception is understood to be an assertion of the selfish will, equivalent to disobedience to God's (pronatalist) will. But this submission in matters of sexuality does not, in the minds of Quiverfull adherents, contradict the sacred value of freedom. On the contrary, women's sexual receptivity and obedience constitutes the biblically mandated precondition of freedom. The freedom of the Christian faithful, understood as "freedom from" control and coercion, remains a unifying rallying cry of American Christian conservatives. In the words of the Manhattan Declaration:

> The right of religious freedom has its foundation in the example of Christ himself and in the very dignity of the human person (sic!) created in the image of God ... Immunity from religious coercion is the cornerstone of an unconstrained conscience. No one should be compelled to embrace any religion against his (sic!) will.

The "unconstrained conscience," however, does not extend to the Christian wife. In an analysis of neoconservative intellectuals on the American Right, Claire Snyder, a professor of political theory at George Mason University, argues that the current assault on women's reproductive rights and personal autonomy employs the notion of "freedom" in a profoundly contradictory manner. In "Paradox or Contradiction: The Marriage Mythos in Neoconservative Ideology," Snyder shows that both secular and religious neoconservative thinkers restrict liberal principles of freedom to the public sphere while denying their applicability in the realm of the family and thus to women.

> The other way in which neoconservatives claim to solve the 'paradox of freedom' is by arguing that the traditional family—particularly heterosexual marriage and fatherhood—forms the 'seedbed of virtue' that undergirds democratic self-government. This is in itself paradoxical: how can patriarchal marriage, which reinforces male dominance, provide the foundation for democracy since democracy requires equality for all its citizens, including women? The neoconservative position directly contests the feminist argument that the patriarchal family undermines rather than undergirds democracy by directly contributing to the inequality of women ...[15]

14. http://www.quiverfull.com/resources.php.
15. Snyder, "Paradox or Contradiction," 152.

Already in 2000, the infamous Southern Baptist Convention endorsed such a hierarchical understanding of the family when it declared that the "conjugal union of man and woman, ordained by God from creation," calls on women to "submit graciously."[16] The family can never be a democracy of free equals but must remain a sacred hierarchy, in which women (and children) are to submit, by divine design and degree, to male authority. This inherently contradictory position among Christian proponents of liberty, democracy and equality is reconciled by dressing it up as "paradox" and by advertising it as being in the best interest of women. In fact, advocates of patriarchal heterosexual marriage maintain that it is "feminist" in so far as it protects women from male violence, self-centeredness and indifference towards their offspring. Claire Snyder explains:

> This move hinges on the idea that patriarchal marriage protects women by domesticating men who would otherwise pose a threat and by forcing them to take responsibility for the children they father. In return, of course, the father must be recognized as head of the household—a position explicitly endorsed by the Christian Right.[17]

Her analysis is corroborated in the Manhattan Declaration which blames "social pathologies of every sort," including delinquency, drug abuse, crime, incarceration, hopelessness and despair on the erosion of patriarchal marriage.[18] Feminism's fatal flaw, in the eyes of conservative Christian leaders, is that women's demand for equality leads directly to the disintegration of the family, raising divorce rates, male violence in and outside the fam-

---

16. Southern Baptist Convention: http://www.sbc.net/bfm/bfm2000.asp. "A husband is to love his wife as Christ loved the church. He has the God-given responsibility to provide for, to protect, and to lead his family. A wife is to submit herself graciously to the servant leadership of her husband even as the church willingly submits to the headship of Christ. She, being in the image of God as is her husband and thus equal to him, has the God-given responsibility to respect her husband and to serve as his helper in managing the household and nurturing the next generation."

17. Snyder, "Paradox or Contradiction," 149.

18. This new politics is a continuation of the church's opposition to the early stirring of women's movement: In the words of Pope John XXIII: "But even if the economic independence of women brings certain advantages, it also results in many, many problems with regards to their fundamental mission of forming new creatures! Hence we have new situations that are serious and urgent . . . These arise in the area of family life: in the care and education of youngsters, in homes that are left without the presence of someone that they need so much; in the loss of disturbance of rest resulting from the assumption of new responsibilities; and above all in keeping feast days holy, and in general, in fulfilling those religious duties which are the only thing that can make a mother's work of training her children really fruitful." quoted in Gudorf, "Contraception and Abortion in Roman Catholicism," 65.

ily, child abuse, sexual promiscuity, and the delinquency of children. Even "genocide and 'ethnic cleansing'" are seen as "flowing from the same loss of the sense of the dignity of the human person and the sanctity of human life that drives the abortion industry." The stakes could not be higher. Women's acceptance of "complementarity" and submission to childbearing becomes the cornerstone for a "truly consistent ethic of love and life for all humans in all circumstances." The Manhattan Declaration promises that complementary heterosexuality will restore "the profound beauty, mystery, and holiness of faithful marital love" and that men will once again accept "the behavioral conditions of procreation" and enter into "life-long commitment" that is beneficial for the raising their offspring. The flourishing of men in faith and family depends on women's surrender of freedom, autonomy and agency.

The Annunciation and Women's Submission to Childbearing

There is no better place to consider the "paradox of freedom" than Luke's Annunciation of Mary's pregnancy. The interpretive tradition has called Luke 2 the *Annunciation* and not the *Proposal*. The possibility of Mary's "No" appears to have been unthinkable. Luke's story of Mary's "choice" has traditionally supported pronatalist Christians positions and is routinely invoked to encourage women to accept "crisis pregnancies" as manifestations of divine will. The Vatican, for instance, upholds Mary as "the Theotokos, in whose motherhood the *vocation to motherhood bestowed by God on every woman* is raised to its highest level."[19] The story of Mary's reaction to this unplanned pregnancy serves to delegitimize any woman's "No" to motherhood, irrespective of circumstance or reasoning, because it can be presented as a woman's denial of God's intention for a "culture of life," and therefore as murder. This interpretation of Mary unites significant sectors in the Roman Catholic, Protestant and Orthodox pro-life movements despite significant Mariological differences. I want to challenge this reading of the Annunciation as an unqualified mandate for childbearing.

Mary's faith has been condensed to her unquestioning obedience to God's will. Her response to the angel's Annunciation: "Here am I, the servant/slave (*doulē*) of the Lord; let it be done to me according to your word" (Luke 2:38) expresses her unconditional obedience as the central constituent of faith. It is Mary's lack of contention, her restraint of doubt, the absence of argument, the tranquility of her acceptance that turns Mary

---

19. http://www.vatican.va/holy_father/john_paul_ii/encyclicals/documents/hf_jp-ii_enc_25031995_evangelium-vitae_ge.html.

into an "exemplar of obedience or a model of faith."[20] But, I will argue, such a reduction of faith to obedience is problematic for both gendered and general political reasons. First, it enforces patriarchal expectations of women's silence. Women and slaves are not supposed to "talk back," to question or object to the will of their superiors. Although Mary's self-designation as a *doulē kyriou* can be interpreted as empowerment since her enslavement to God proclaims independence from any earthly owner,[21] her identification as a slave raises the specter of "service that is not a matter of choice but subjection to the alien will of an owner." For centuries, Mary's line has been used to justify the subjugation of women, as Schaberg rightly notes in *The Illegitimacy of Jesus*:

> [Mary's] person and fate have been regarded as subsumed into that of her son, her own will, autonomy, and initiative abdicated. She is seen as subordinated to God, his representatives, and her own son. Is Mary's consent Luke's way of setting her up as a model, *the* model, for submissive feminine behavior, and of articulating an acceptance of patriarchal belief in female inferiority, dependency, and helplessness?[22]

A slave is not supposed to challenge orders given by her owner. Throughout history, women and slaves were denied response-ability. Only their husbands and/or legal owners were considered moral agents, charged with authority of decision-making. Patriarchy has curtailed women's ability to say "No" on the basis of the law, by force of custom or by compulsion backed by physical violence. In fact, women's "yes" is often already presupposed. Few courts of law, even in the contemporary world, are willing to respect and enforce a woman's "No." Mary's "do unto me according to thy will" sounds suspiciously like a woman's resigned compliance with a sexual assault. Once the romantic halo of holiness is removed, we are faced with a frightened teenager who is given little control over her initiation into reproductive sexuality, a fate she shares with a shocking number of young girls.[23]

For Christian interpreters, the possibility of Mary's hesitation, challenge, or objection is normatively predetermined as sinful rebellion. According to Paul, the wages of saying "No" to God is death (Rom 6:23) and

---

20. Gaventa, "Nothing will be impossible with God," 32.

21. Gaventa points our correctly, "if Mary is God's slave, then she cannot at the same time be the slave of human beings." *Mary*, 54.

22. Schaberg, *Illegitimacy of Jesus*, 135–36.

23. "An Oregon Social Learning Center study of chronically delinquent girls found that the median age of the first sexual encounter among detained girls was 7." DeSaar, "Precious Girls without a Happy End."

the "'free' act of refusing to honor God as God" constitutes "false human freedom" that "produces the disaster that follows . . . Because of this refusal of worship and glory to God, God 'handed them over'"[24] to sin and death. In Pauline language, "you are slaves of the one whom you obey, either of sin, which leads to *death*, or of obedience, which leads to righteousness (Rom 6:16). Once one has become "obedient from the heart" (Rom 6:17) and turned oneself into "slaves of righteousness" (6:19), there won't be any hesitation or doubt. This language of unconditional obedience, I submit, once applied to women's reproductive lives, misconstrues the intricate process of weighing risks and benefits, of negotiating alternatives, of assessing different options, and eventually, at arriving at what bioethicists call, "informed consent" or peace of heart with one's choice. Must we consider such a process of reproductive decision-making a willful disobedience against God?

Talking Back—Freedom as Response-Ability

One could object that Mary's pregnancy was different from all other pregnancies because it occurred after an angelic announcement and direct communication with God. Since God spoke directly, human doubt and hesitation should be anathema. But such unhesitating reaction in faith is not the only message of the Bible. There is a rich tradition of negotiation with God in the Bible that tells stories of faithful servants who respond with reservation, objection and protest to God's directly communicated command. Particularly in the Hebrew Scriptures, faith is not identified with unconditional submission. *Arguing with God*,[25] is Anton Laytner's summation of the Jewish tradition's practice of perceiving argument not as the opposite of faith but as its very medium. The faithful servant is characterized by response-ability and the willingness to respond. Dialogue with God is not only a right but the obligation of the believer. Critical engagement with God and *God-wrestling* are at the core of Israel's identity, as well as the literal meaning of its name:[26] Jacob battles the angel of God/God at the river Jabbok (Gen 32:22) and is renamed *Isra-el* = God-wrestler.[27] Abraham bargains with God

---

24. Gaventa, "Freedom in Apocalyptic Perspective"; chap. 11 below.
25. Laytner, *Arguing with God*.
26. Waskow, *God-Wrestling*.
27. In Genesis Rabbah (70:3), the rabbis ask why Jacob would set conditions after he received a direct revelation from God standing next to a ladder reaching into the heavens: "If God will be with me, and will keep me in this way that I go, and will give me bread to eat and clothing to wear, so that I come again to my father's house in peace, then the LORD shall be my God . . ." (Gen 28:21). According to Rabbi Yohanan this is the correct sequence: "The text requires no rearrangement. For this is what Jacob

over the number of righteous in Sodom required to avert divine judgment (Gen 18); Moses negotiates the terms of his engagement and continuously mediates between God and the people of Israel (Exod 6–7); Jeremiah retorts to God's proclamation that he has been appointed from the womb to serve as God's spokesman with "Ah, Lord God! Truly I do not know how to speak, for I am only a boy" (Jer 1:5–6). His pleas to be excused are only abated when God promises "I am with you to deliver you" (1:8). Jonah hurls his anger at God once his prophecy of Nineveh's imminent destruction is reversed (Jonah 4:1–11) and receives an individual tutorial in God's anguish over destruction and punishment. Job demands a hearing in order to charge God with injustice inflicted on him (Job). "From the wellspring of the book of Job," asserts Alicia Suskin Ostriker poetically, "there flows a river of living waters of opposition to authority within Judaism that has affected all of Western history ... Is there another major religion in which human beings habitually argue with God? In attempting to understand this combination of intimacy and resistance, we may remember that historical Judaism originates in a slave rebellion and an advocacy of freedom that continue to resound in the aspirations and rhetoric of oppressed people throughout the world."[28] The biblical role models who argue with God are not chastised for rebelliousness. Although Jacob-Israel is wounded in the hip, and Job is terrified, their active engagement and debate is considered praiseworthy. Their "insubordination" is not tagged as lack of faith. Argument is part of the covenantal theology.

Human response-ability constitutes freedom in the biblical tradition. The Hebrew Bible illustrates the drama of human freedom that unfolds in dialogue with God. God is both moved by and reactive to the ingenuity (i.e. creativity and chaos) of human responses to God's plan for creation in general and for Israel in particular. The rabbinic tradition has further elaborated on the mutuality of covenantal obligations that requires human response and allows human challenge of God. In some cases, human beings may even prevail against God as when "the rabbis commission Abraham to bring a case against God, whereby Abraham refutes and shames all the witnesses God brings against Israel ... into silence"[29] God may be shamed into repentance, as Carleen Mandolfo argues in *Daughter Zion Talks Back to the Prophets*. God is also reported to be delighted by the halakhic prowess and resourcefulness of the rabbis and acquiesces to Rabbi Eliezer's superior

---

meant: 'If all the conditions that God promised me—to be with me and to protect me—are fulfilled: then I will keep my vow'" (*Genesis Rabbah* 70:3, quoted in Laytner, *Arguing with God*, XIV).

28. Ostriker, *For the Love of God*, 134.
29. Mandolfo, *Daughter Zion Talks Back to the Prophets*, 124.

halakhic reasoning in the Talmud by exclaiming: "my sons have defeated me, my sons have defeated me" (Baba Mezia 59a–59b).[30] Far from demanding unquestioning submission, God is portrayed as savoring critical engagement and dialogue as part of the covenantal relationship. The individual believer (albeit usually male) and the community of Israel (represented by male heads of household) are called to negotiate covenantal obligations and to respond vigorously to divine commissions.[31] For Abraham Joshua Heschel, the relational engagement with God is the very center of the Jewish faith experience as expressed in the prophetic "theology of pathos."

At the risk of overgeneralization, one could say that the Christian theological tradition draws more heavily on Biblical models of faith as individual acts of obedience while the Jewish tradition expands on the covenant as a dynamic relationship negotiated between God, prophetic mediators, and the covenanted community. While the rabbis appreciate that Abraham bargains vigorously on behalf of the doomed Sodomites, Christian commentators locate Abraham's faithfulness primarily in his unquestioning willingness to obey God's command to sacrifice his son.[32] It has long puzzled commentators, Jewish and Christian alike, that Abraham would question God's moral judgment in the case of the Sodomites but not in the case of the command to sacrifice his son. In any case, Abraham's unconditional submission tends to overshadow his bargaining skills in the Christian tradition's definition of faith.

In the New Testament, and particularly in Paul, "talking back" is closely associated with defiance and rebellion against God flowing from Adam's Original Sin. Few stories in the New Testament would commend a disciple for "talking back." There is the exception of Jesus in the Garden of Gethsemane who asks of his father, "if you are willing, remove this cup

---

30. *Hebrew-English Edition of the Talmud*, edited by I. Epstein, translated by Salis Daiches and H. Freedman, London: Soncino, 1986.

31. Biblical women are less likely to "talk back" without being reprimanded. For instance, Sarah's laughter is censored in the rabbinic commentaries (while Abraham's laughter is not); Miriam's questioning of Moses' marriage is punished by leprosy. Female characters seem to be more readily reproached and chastised for insubordination (Jezebel).

32. Why Abraham objected to God's intended destruction of Sodom but not to God's command to sacrifice his Son in the *Akedah* is the subject of many interpreters. In the Midrash, Sarah dies alone after hearing from Satan who tells her (falsely, as it turned out) that Isaac has been sacrificed by his father. Ginzberg relates: "Thus Abraham returned home alone, and when Sarah beheld him, she exclaimed, "Satan spoke truth when he said that Isaac was sacrificed," and so grieved was her soul that it fled from her body (Ginzberg, *Legends of the Jews*, 286). The sound of the Shofar blown on New Year is brought in relation to the sound emitted by Sarah at the moment of her demise." (Ginzberg, *Legends of the Jews*, n.256).

from me," (NRSV, Luke 22:42) But the scene concludes with his compliance: "yet, not my will but yours be done," thereby reaffirming faith as complete submission to the father's will. Mary, as well, questions the "how" ("how can this be, since I am a virgin?" Luke 1:34), but she does not demand to know the "why" ("why me?," "why now?," "why this way?"). For Jane Schaberg, these two Lukan scenes are connected. She argues that Luke's settings in the Annunciation and Gethsemane capture the strain and tension in Jesus' and Mary's struggle to come to terms with the divine will:

> If Luke does intend the scene of Jesus' agony to evoke the scene of the annunciation to Mary, it can be argued that we have another indication that in spite of the joy and calm of this annunciation scene (recognized by artists down through the centuries), there is an underlying note of struggle. Joy and calm do not come cheaply in Luke, even here.[33]

It is noteworthy, that while Jesus bargains with God and asks explicitly to be spared the cup of violence, Mary merely "ponders these things in her heart" (Luke 2:19; 2:51). Her struggle remains speechless and internalized. That there might have been protest and negotiation on Mary's part can be inferred from the angel's last line: "For nothing is impossible with God" (Luke 1:37). As Beverly Gaventa has pointed out:

> Gabriel's closing words have received relatively little study in recent scholarship on Luke. By and large, treatments . . . attend to the final statement of Mary (her self-identification as *doulē* of the Lord) in relation to the question of Mary's faith, her consent, her cooperation with God.[34]

Intertextual parallels to the angel's affirmation of God's power point towards stories in the Hebrew Scriptures that involve objection. There are three instances in which God feels similarly pressured to assert unlimited divine power: Sarah laughs over the prospect of post-menopausal pregnancy and is told "Is anything too wonderful for the Lord?" (Gen 18:14). Moses threatens his resignation ("if this is the way you are going to treat me, put me to death at once" [Num 11:15]) in order to avert God's wrath towards the people. He then doubts God's ability to provide meat for disgruntled Israelites for an entire month while they are camped out in the desert. Moses' frustration and disbelief is met by: "Is the Lord's power limited?" (Num 11:23). Last, there is Job's acknowledgment, "I know you can do all things" (42:2–3) when God meets him in the whirlwind to answer his challenge.

33. Schaberg, *Illegitimacy of Jesus*, 135.
34. Gaventa, "Nothing will be impossible with God," 28.

Given these parallels, one may infer that Mary talked back. The angel's forceful affirmation of divine power can be seen as a response to Mary's objection and doubt. Her fear extracted additional divine promise of protection and assurance for her own safety and that of her child. Luke fails to give voice to Mary's *response-ability* as a mother-to-be. But as every mother knows, a child is not (only) a miraculous gift but also a colossal responsibility that requires provision, protection and persistent care. As a future mother, Mary *had to* negotiate for protection as this Proposal exposed her to the vagaries of a teenage pregnancy out of wedlock.

Contrary to patriarchy's long literary misrepresentation and legal confinement of women as passive vessels of male seed, women have always plotted to ensure their own and the survival and well-being of their children. Matthew introduces Mary's pregnancy after the genealogy of Jesus, an all-male line of descent that is broken up by references to four women. These four women are: *Tamar*, a widow who conceived a child for her deceased husband by disguising herself as a prostitute who is frequented by her father-in-law (Gen 38); *Rahab*, called "the harlot," who protected Joshua's spies in her house in Jericho, for which services she was saved and rewarded with her family (Josh 6:17); the Moabite *Ruth*, who seduced Naomi's elder relative Boaz into marriage (Ruth 3:9) and bore the grandfather of David; *Bathsheba* who was coerced into adultery by King David (2 Sam 11) as "the wife of Uriah" and later became the mother of Solomon. Each of these women conceived under irregular and questionable circumstances. Two engaged in prostitution, one seduced her redeemer, while Bathsheba was raped and/or engaged willingly in an adulterous affair with King David. Each gave birth to a favored son. Each woman was forced to engage in ruses and to manipulate powerful men in order to secure the legitimacy and survival of their sons in the shadow of patriarchal marriage laws. These four women prepare the context in which Mary confronts an unintended "crisis pregnancy." Like her, the women of the genealogy were not passive vessels of legitimate children or paragons of virtue of a "healthy marriage culture," as envisioned in the Manhattan Declaration. Rather, as Beverly Gaventa summarizes "none of them fits in with the way things are 'supposed' to be. Each of these women is presented as threatening the status quo in some way, and each is in turn threatened."[35]

The women of Matthew's genealogy act, at least temporarily, without protection from male heads of household. While ultimately loyal to patriarchal values of family lineage and the birth of sons, they "resort to wiles

---

35. Gaventa, *Mary*, 38.

and guiles in their selfless struggle for what is regarded as right and noble."[36] These women do not act straightforwardly but deceptively as they make their way around the rules of male-dominated society.[37] It is striking how many stories involving biblical women unfold without clear divine commandment, instruction or intervention.[38] While God commands Abraham, instructs Moses and entrusts the prophets with a particular message, their wives (with the exception of Hagar), prophetic sisters, and fellow fighters (Ruth, Esther) often act without explicit divine direction and guidance. One may attribute the paucity of God's direct dialogue with Biblical women to (male) authorial disinterest or wish to draw inferences about women's different experiences with God. In either case, women's lives in the Bible unfold, as Schaberg notes for Matthew's foremothers, with a "significant lack of intervention on the part of God. There has been no miraculous, direct intervention to right the wrongs, or remove the shame, or illuminate the consciousness, or shatter structures. The references to divine activity are strikingly spare. God does not intrude by speech or miracle, but overrules without interfering with natural causation."[39]

Freedom, Response-ability, and Reproduction

Christian conceptions of freedom should move beyond the language of unconditional submission to God's will towards an understanding of faith that is searching, flexible and responsive to individuals' concrete personal and political circumstances. Patriarchal notions of women as passive vessels of male seed, whose compliance with God's "pro-life" command can be enforced by state law and community coercion, must be rejected as misappropriations of the Christian language of the "paradox of freedom." Beverly Harrison called "any society that incorporates a perdurable structure of coercion, even violence, against women as morally appropriate to its functioning but claims that it upholds the sanctity of or respect for human life . . . deluded."[40] To assume that Jesus had a "right to life" apart from his mother's response-ability is incompatible with the central message of Christian freedom.

36. Fuchs, "Status and Role," 79.

37. Fuchs, "Status and Role," 79.

38. Trible notes this difference between the sacrifice of Isaac and the sacrifice of Jephthah's daughter. See Trible, *Texts of Terror*, 95. Books that focus on the faith adventures of women, as for instance the Books of Ruth and Esther, feature no appearance of or instruction by God.

39. Schaberg, *Illegitimacy of Jesus*, 33.

40. Harrison, *Our Right to Choose*, 197–98.

Freedom, understood as response-ability to God, anchors human moral agency. Mary's acceptance of an extraordinary and dangerous pregnancy constituted an act of reproductive response-ability. The same pregnancy would have to be considered irresponse-able, if she had submitted to fatalism and powerlessness. The difference between responsible and irresponsible pregnancies is determined by a woman's empowerment rather than any successful outcome and the likely survival of her child. For instance: In April of 1942, four months after the Wannsee Conference, a German Jewish woman, Ruth Cronheim decided that she would embark on another pregnancy which she interpreted as a sign of God's providential presence, in a letter to Rabbi Regina Jonas. For this woman, the prospect of giving birth to another Jewish child constituted an act of faith in defiance of the genocidal machinery of the Nazis. She gave birth to a son on December 11, 1942 and was deported to Auschwitz on March 2, 1943, where the presence of a three month old baby likely sealed her fate upon arrival.[41] She is listed as "missing," as is her newborn son. I consider this pregnancy an act of response-able resistance, although it was ultimately doomed and was condemned by many of her contemporaries in Berlin. While her pregnancy was response-able despite its tragic ending, other pregnancies imposed on women in the midst of war, or as a result of contraceptive failure, rape, or bad luck should be considered irresponse-able. Any pregnancy that unfolds without a woman's consent and without her reasoned consideration of her ability to deliver and care for a child in the throes of natural or man-made disaster, marital discord, economic, social or political upheaval is disempowering and profoundly irresponsible. The religious and political impulse to force a woman into submission in order to endure a pregnancy against her will and better judgment serves no discernible moral or theological value. The desire to curtail women's ability to respond is inherently abusive and will not lead to the kind of freedom that has traditionally been expressed as obedience and submission to the will of God.

We may not be able wrench the figure of Mary from her textual and dogmatic restraints in order to access her reproductive choice as empowerment.[42] The Magnificat certainly portrays an intensely empowered speaker

41. Von Kellenbach, "Reproduction and Resistance during the Holocaust."

42. Esther Fuchs concludes her overview of the "Literary Characterization of Mothers and Sexual Politics in the Hebrew Bible" with some resignation: "The fact is that the annunciation type-scene, in its many variations, drives home the opposite message: that woman has no control over her reproductive potential. YHWH has control and he is often anthropomorphized in the biblical narrative. Furthermore, all the divine messengers, dispatched to proclaim the imminent miraculous conception, are male figures. The literary constellation of male characters surrounding and determining the fate of the potential mother dramatizes the idea that woman's reproductive potential should be

who affirms: "from now on all generations will call me blessed" (Luke 1:48). This is not a speaker who abdicates responsibility to God, husband or biological vicissitudes. Instead, by embracing her freedom to choose, Mary experiences an empowerment that surpasses social respectability and the restraints of heterosexual morality. Instead of describing her faith with the vocabulary of submission and obedience, Mary's choice is better illustrated as a step into an unknown and unknowable future that requires unconditional trust. It is a faith that is cognizant of the odds, respectful of the doubts, and considerate of the fears engendered by a mysterious and inscrutable future. Such an act of response-able faith overcomes the fear of the future.

The faith embraced by the framers of the Manhattan Declaration, on the other hand, is rooted in fear of the future. Deep anxiety over the loss of control over women, and profound worries over the loosening of (hetero) sexual constraints make the return to patriarchal law and order so appealing. For the signers of the Manhattan Declaration God's will is manifested in the biology of genetic cell divisions (i.e. conception), as well as in the culturally correct use of body parts for the purpose of "heterosexual union." But such biologically reductionist definitions of "life" and "gender" do not resonate with the biblical message of God's will for human response-ability that calls forth the courage to move beyond the old ways of the world and to dare the unconventional and the unknown.[43]

---

and can be controlled only by men. It is true that the presence of the potential husbands progressively decreases in the annunciation-type scene, but his presence is, nevertheless, essential" (135).

43. Hannah Arendt (*The Human Condition*) locates the concept of freedom in the Christian doctrine of forgiveness that anchors the possibility of open future. Without forgiveness, she argues, there could be no unpredictable new beginnings and the world would run in karmic cycles, an endless chain of cause and effect. She develops the concept of *natality* from the "the Gospels' 'glad tidings:' A child has been born to us" (247). Christianity's message" that only love can forgive because only love is fully receptive to *who* somebody is" (242) is not located in Christ's sacrificial willingness to die for the forgiveness of sinners but in "love's own product. The child ... is an indication that they [the lovers] will insert a new world into the existing world." (242) To Arendt, the good news of Christianity is signified by the Madonna with Child, not Christ on the cross. "The miracle that saves the world ... is, in other words, the birth of new men and the new beginning, the action they are capable of by virtue of being born. Only the full experience of this capacity can bestow upon human affairs faith and hope, those two essential characteristics of human existence which Greek antiquity ignored altogether ..." (247).

Bibliography

Arendt, Hannah. *The Human Condition*. Chicago: University of Chicago Press, 1998.

Campbell, Nancy. *Be Fruitful and Multiply: What the Bible Says about Having Children*. San Antonio, TX: Vision Forum Ministries, 2003.

DeSaar, Malia Saada. "Precious Girls without a Happy End." *Washington Post*, November 14, 2009.

Epstein, I., ed. *Hebrew–English Edition of the Talmud*. Translated by Salis Daiches and H. Freedman. London: Soncino, 1986.

Fuchs, Esther. "The Literary Characterization of Mothers and Sexual Politics in the Hebrew Bible." In *Women in the Hebrew Bible: A Reader*, edited by Alice Bach, 127–41. New York: Routledge, 1999.

———. "Status and Role of Female Heroines in the Biblical Narrative." In *Women in the Hebrew Bible: A Reader*, edited by Alice Bach, 77–84. New York: Routledge, 1999.

Gaventa, Beverly Roberts. *Mary: Glimpses of the Mother of Jesus*. Studies on Personalities of the New Testament. Columbia: University of South Carolina Press, 1995.

———. "'Nothing will be impossible with God': Mary as Mother of Believers." In *Mary, Mother of God*, edited by Carl E. Braaten and Robert W. Jensen, 19–36. Grand Rapids: Eerdmans, 2004.

Ginzberg, Louis. *The Legends of the Jews*. Vol. 5. Philadelphia: Jewish Publication Society, 1925.

Gudorf, Christine. "Contraception and Abortion in Roman Catholicism." In *Sacred Rights: The Case for Contraception and Abortion in World Religions*, edited by Daniel Maguire, 55–78. Oxford University Press, 2003.

Harrison, Beverly Wildung. *Our Right to Choose: Toward a New Ethic of Abortion*. Boston: Beacon, 1983.

Joyce, Kathryn. *Quiverfull: Inside the Christian Patriarchy Movement*. Boston: Beacon, 2009.

Kellenbach, Katharina von. "Reproduction and Resistance during the Holocaust." In *Women and the Holocaust*, edited by Esther Fuchs, 19–33. Lanham, MD: University Press of America, 1999.

Laytner, Anson. *Arguing with God: A Jewish Tradition*. Northvale, NJ: Aronson, 1990.

Mandolfo, Carleen. *Daughter Zion Talks Back to the Prophets: A Dialogic Theology of the Book of Lamentations*. Semeia Studies 58. Atlanta: Society of Biblical Literature, 2007.

Ostriker, Alicia Suskin. *For the Love of God: The Bible as an Open Book*. New Brunswick, NJ: Rutgers University Press, 2007.

Schaberg, Jane. *The Illegitimacy of Jesus: A Feminist Theological Interpretation of the Infancy Narratives*. San Francisco: Harper & Row, 1987.

Snyder, R. Claire. "Paradox or Contradiction." In *Confronting the New Conservatism: The Rise of the Right in America*, edited by Michael J. Thompson, 144–63. New York: New York University Press, 2007.

Trible, Phyllis. *Texts of Terror: Literary-Feminist Readings of Biblical Narratives*. Overtures to Biblical Theology. Philadelphia: Fortress, 1984.

Waskow, Arthur. *God-Wrestling*. New York: Schocken, 1978.

Wegner, Judith Romney. *Chattel or Person? The Status of Women in the Mishnah*. Oxford: Oxford University Press, 1992.

Part 2

Self-Determination and Concepts of Freedom

Introduction

Peter Lampe

The essays explore various concepts of freedom from philosophical, systematic-theological as well as historical perspectives. From a philosophical perspective, *Rüdiger Bittner* attempts a definition of freedom by analyzing its relationship to terms such as unimpeded, unresisted, uncoerced, not enslaved, not subjected to norms or to the laws of nature, or having no master. He checks the compatibility of determinism and freedom, and discusses various other relationships, such as between freedom of action and freedom of the will, between freedom and Kantian autonomy as well as "ordinary" autonomy, between negative freedom ("free from") and positive freedom ("free to"), and between political and individual freedom. As nobody is free in the sense of "without barriers that make one's doing or becoming difficult or impossible," it makes sense to talk about different degrees of freedom that distinguish humans. The essay holds that freedom does not mean to be exempt from natural or moral laws. Furthermore, free will is irrelevant for freedom. Autonomy—no matter whether Kantian or "ordinary"—and freedom are not essentially connected, and no distinction should be made between negative and positive freedom.

Risto Saarinen in his essay on freedom, sin, and evil discusses the Lutheran doctrine of *simul iustus et peccator,* its relationship to freedom and its potential connection with the anthropology of modern evolutionary theory, linking Christian anthropology with the sciences and modern problems of evil. Contrary to the shift in Luther studies in the early twentieth century, whereby *simul iustus et pecator* would mean a permanent failure to do good and a lack of freedom, the essay argues that this does not reflect Luther's own view. *Simul iustus et peccator* cannot be reduced to its twentiethth-century outlook that gave rise to exaggerated interpretations. The essay moves on by considering "righteous and sinner" and human freedom in view of modern anthropology. The modern dualism present in the distinction between genotype and individual phenotype bears some resemblance with the theological tradition, with the notion of "flesh" resembling the genotype and the phenotypic person being a parallel to the somatic *oikos* (*ego*). In this biological perspective, freedom is reflected in the fight against diseases, which is a permanent struggle. The article presents various strategies for coping with suffering. Whereas *simil iustus et peccator* expresses the permanent struggle of a Christian, the *simul* of "suffering and virtue" embodied in these strategies describes the existence of many people and their continuous struggle with suprapersonal forces. Such struggles testify to human freedom because an intentional effort is required when encountering adversity.

Friederike Nüssel discusses Protestant concepts of freedom and their biblical foundations. Following a brief overview of Luther's ideas, the freedom concepts in the theologies especially of Karl Barth and Wolfhart Pannenberg are addressed. While freedom plays a key role in Barth's theology, particularly in the doctrine of revelation (the sovereign God's revelation is the realization of divine freedom, which thereby enables human freedom; perfect freedom and love are the substrates of the biblical attributes of God), Pannenberg focuses on God's freedom particularly actualized within history. For his theology, freedom is less foundational, with solely love being the substrate of God's attributes. Both theologians also diverge in their assessment of Biblical interpretation. While for Pannenberg historical critical exegesis is substantial for his theology, Barth holds that the members of the Church exercise the freedom given to the Church in interpreting Scripture in a way that is determined by the flow of Scripture rather than general methods of interpretation. For Barth, human freedom occurs in the fellowship of the Church. Despite the divergences, Nüssel highlights the points on which the two approaches converge. The article holds that the exercise of human freedom involves an independent opinion on questions of faith through individual evaluation of Scripture, with the support of the Church. This requires adequate argumentation, without which simplistic biblical interpretation does not serve the freedom of faith.

Peter Lampe presents various concepts of freedom from Greco-Roman times. The expansion of the eastern powers of Lydia and Persia in the sixth and early fifth centuries gave reason to conceptualize *external, political freedom* in classical Greek times, both collective (the independence of the polis) and individual political freedom, with the latter, however, being limited to the exclusive circle of free male citizens within the Greek polis. In Hellenistic and Roman times, the importance of the polis as frame of reference faded, the individual's inner self as one horizon of thought became important and correspondingly the concept of *internal freedom*, with the Cynics and Stoics being at the forefront of this line of thought. A third part of the essay focuses on *free will*, with the caveat, however, that in antiquity will and determination were closely connected to intellectual functions and not considered an independent function of the human psyche as in modern times. Freedom of choice and decision-making, based in rational thinking, and the corresponding responsibility for one's own acts, were widely accepted, even by deterministic Stoics—a tension they had to solve. In the last part, the essay comments on the historical material, not only on the discriminatory character of the concepts, but also on the potentials and downsides of the shift of emphasis from external to internal freedom. Furthermore, the idea of freedom of decision is confronted with modern neurobiological insights.

Cyril Hovorun explores concepts of freedom in the eastern patristic tradition, focusing on τὸ αὐτεξούσιον (self-control, allowing non-determined behavior) and ἐλευθερία. The former is innate to everybody's human nature, while ἐλευθερία, freedom from sin and death, is a gift of God that needs to be struggled for—by choosing good by means of the free will given to everybody together with the αὐτεξούσιον. Thus, αὐτεξούσιον and ἐλευθερία cannot be separated. The teleological purpose of αὐτεξούσιον is ἐλευθερία, which in turn is only possible because of the αὐτεξούσιον and the free choice to become free in Christ. At the same time, the two freedoms interact through the mediation of the will, whereby the decision to do good and achieve ἐλευθερία requires the assistance of God's grace. Such co-activity is crucial to the Eastern Fathers' understanding of salvation. Thus, human freedom plays a key role in the salvation process, being a partner of the Divine in this respect.

5

What It Is to Be Free

Rüdiger Bittner

Various things are said to be free. There is free will, but there is also free beer, free speech, free fall, a free society and many other things. I will focus on human beings who are free, justifying this choice as I go along by explaining those other uses as derived in various ways from this one. So the question in what follows is, what is it for human beings to be free?[1]

Constructive Part

Being no Slave

In antiquity and the middle ages, people were considered free when they were not slaves or serfs, i.e. when they were not, as a matter of social and legal status, subject to others' making them do, omit or become this or that. This may well be the oldest sense of "free" or of corresponding words in ancient languages. It bears only historical interest today, because slavery and serfdom as legal institutes no longer exist. There are people who are exploited or suppressed, but even if they are therefore unfree, that unfreedom is not a legally enshrined social status.

---

1. Thanks to the members of our research group and to Andrew Escobedo (Athens, Ohio) for helpful discussions of earlier versions of this text.

Being Unimpeded

In modern understanding, people are free when they are not fettered, imprisoned or the like. Witness Hobbes: "Liberty, or Freedome, signifieth (properly) the absence of Opposition; (by Opposition, I mean externall Impediments of motion)."[2] Witness Goethe, who has Mephisto invite Faust to leave his study:

> Damit du losgebunden, frei,
> Erfahrest, was das Leben sei[3]

where surely "losgebunden" (untied) is a synonym of "frei" (free)—and throughout I shall take German "frei" as a synonym of English "free." Witness above all the fact that the word "free" when on holiday, i.e. when there are no theoretical aspirations in the offing, is very often used in the sense of "unimpeded." Thus a free kick in football is a kick that the other team is supposed not to obstruct, and if your boat gets stuck in the reeds you may well find it difficult to free it again. Or think of the lovely German expressions "im Freien" and "unter freiem Himmel," literally "in the free" and "under free sky," which both just mean "outdoors." So to be free is, basically, to be unfettered or unrestricted in movement.

Not Being Subject to the Laws of Nature

Whether somebody is to be considered free or not depends, then, on what counts as a fetter. One suggestion here is that nature in general is a fetter of humans. The argument runs as follows. Everything in nature, we suppose, happens according to causal laws. Now what humans do is a part of nature and hence subject to these laws as well. Thus what humans do is determined by laws of nature rather than by the agents themselves. Therefore, agents are not free, they are fettered by the laws of nature. Conversely, freedom would be, specifically, the capacity of producing effects other than in accordance with the causal laws of nature.

Freedom so understood, "indeterministic freedom," as it may be called, is what is at issue in the classical dispute over freedom and determinism (this expression being, strictly, a misnomer, since freedom is a quality people have or lack, whereas determinism is a view about the general character of things happening). In this dispute some have argued that, since determinism is true, no-one is free, and others have argued that, since we

---

2. Hobbes, *Leviathan* (1651), chap. 21, first paragraph.
3. Goethe, *Faust* v. 1542f.

know that we are free, determinism is false. Thus both these parties agree that determinism's truth is incompatible with anyone's being free, a view called incompatibilism. However, this view appears mistaken, and compatibilism, holding that even if determinism is true, humans may be free, seems correct. For if it is assumed, as it should, that humans and their doings are part of nature, then the fact that these doings are governed by laws of nature is no ground for inferring that they are not in the hands of the agents themselves. If humans are part of nature, then the laws of nature are not their fetters: you are not fettered by what you are and by the way you yourself work. Defenders of indeterministic freedom are therefore bound either to abandon nature's being governed by laws, which is an uncomfortable option to take, given what we know about nature, or to hold that human agents are not parts of nature entirely, the part of them that is exempt from nature's laws being called their will, which is supposed to be free. This is certainly the more popular, but hardly a less desperate option. We have no grounds for assuming such a non-natural enclave within nature other than the fact that it would give us indeterministic freedom. This understanding of freedom, then, should better go. Nature which runs through you is not a restriction on you. As only the assumption of indeterministic freedom was attacked by neuroscientists in recent debates, these debates may safely be disregarded here.

Not Being Subject to Norms

A second line of thought for determining what is to count as a fetter focusses on laws which, in contrast to laws of nature, are sometimes disobeyed, norms, as I shall call them. Thus we speak of linguistic norms, legal norms, moral norms, and all these are sometimes not obeyed. On the present proposal, norms restrict those subject to them, for the norm bars them from doing or omitting certain things. This idea underlies many locutions we use in speaking of norms. Thus when we say that somebody is legally "bound" to appear in court, the law requiring this is evidently understood as a fetter; and though the ordinary speaker of English may not be aware of the fact, the Latin root of the word "obligation" carries the same idea of something binding. Conversely, people are often said to be free to do something when there is no norm requiring that they refrain from doing it.

In fact, norms do not bind people. Subject to a norm, or to a valid norm, you are not thereby barred from doing what the norm prohibits. You only ought not to do it. Whether you do do it is a different matter. Since fetters are instruments barring you from doing certain things, and norms do not do that, but only make it the case that you ought not to do something, norms are no fetters, and people are not free by virtue of not being subject to a norm.

To be sure, when you are subject to a norm, you may also be barred from doing what the norm prohibits, by the police for instance, and so you may, in addition, not be free to do what you ought not to do. Indeed, if the police reliably act in accordance with what you ought and ought not to do, it could even be said that you are not free to do something because you ought not to do it. This would be a coincidence, though. Even then you are restricted in what you do by the police, not by the norm, however reliable the link between the two, and so the norm does not diminish your freedom.

Admittedly, to say that one is no less free for being subject to a norm goes against current usage. We do say that you are not free to enter that house when you are not permitted to, though no locks and no police are there to stop you. However, usage must yield to a systematic understanding of a term; and as the fundamental sense of "free" in its modern use does seem to be "being unfettered", the notion of norms curtailing freedom must go. It may be dismissed all the more easily on seeing the source of the confusion. Ever since the Stoics formed the idea of a rational order of the world to which we are to adjust our conduct, it remained attractive to assume that what we ought to do is anchored in how the world really is. Even Kant, bent on separating what happens and what ought to happen, on occasion appeals to the order of things in justifying the authority of moral norms.[4] This assumption, that what we ought to do is laid down in the way things are, makes it natural to think, conversely, that a norm to which we are subject is some sort of resistance to our doing what the norm prohibits, that the norm channels us into the right path, even though it does not make impossible our going wrong. In fact, however, the Stoic link is broken. There are things that we ought to do and then there are things that it is difficult or impossible for us not to do, and the first quality is different from the second, though occasionally they hold of the same thing.

It may also be this confusion of what we can with what we may do which underlies that tenet in the philosophy of law, especially that inspired by Kant, which says that the function of law is to make one individual's freedom compatible with that of another.[5] First of all, one freedom cannot be incompatible with another, only statements can. Leaving that aside, though, there is still no incompatibility between the statement that you are

---

4. Kant, *Grundlegung zur Metaphysik der Sitten* (1785), Academy edition IV, 453–54.

5. See for instance Böckenförde and Enders, "Freiheit und Recht, Freiheit und Staat," 43.

free, i.e. unhindered, to grab some thing and the statement that I am free to grab it. To be sure, once you have grabbed it, I am no longer free to do so since probably you hinder me, but that fails to show an incompatibility between the statements that you are free, and that I am free, to grab it in the first place. An incompatibility emerges only once we turn from what either of us can to what either of us may do. Saying that I own this thing and so alone may do with it as I please does contradict saying that you own it and alone may do with it as you please. However, these statements no longer concern what you and I are unhindered, but only what you and I are permitted to do, and with this shift the attraction of the formula that law is to make individuals' freedom compatible is lost. It looked as if humans, by means of law, could and should heal an incompatibility in the order of things, the incompatibility consisting of everyone's being free. In fact, there is no incompatibility in that. Thus that tenet about the function of law boils down to saying that law determines what individuals may and may not do, and that is hardly news.

Being Unresisted

So you are no less free either because what you do is in accordance with the laws of nature or because you are subject to norms. Only impediments, with Hobbes' phrase, diminish your freedom. The word "impediment," however, is ambiguous. It can be understood in a narrow sense, as referring to something that excludes, or in a wide sense, as referring to something that only resists or stands in the way of, something else. Thus on the one hand the classical doctrine of *impedimenta matrimonii* lists conditions each of which makes void from the start a supposed marriage contract,[6] and the expression "marriage impediment" is still used in just this sense in the law of various English speaking countries. On the other, when in *Richard III*, Act V, Richmond declares that they have "thus far ... march'd on without impediment,"[7] he is evidently not saying that their march was not quelled, which is trivial, seeing that they have arrived. He is saying that so far they have met with no resistance. So the English word can be used in either way. The same holds for "Hindernis" in German: an "Ehehindernis" is the same thing as a marriage impediment, but a "Hindernislauf", an obstacle-race, is a race not suppressed, but only made more difficult, by hurdles and ditches.

It appears that Hobbes is using "impediment" in the wide sense, since "opposition," the word explicated by "impediments," is naturally understood

---

6. Thomas Aquinas, *Summa theologiae*, suppl. qu. 50, a. 1.
7. Shakespeare, *Richard III*, Act V, scene 2.

as something only standing in one's way, not as something forestalling one's movement entirely. And he is in accord with ordinary usage here. Taking freedom to be the absence of external impediments, we consider impediments not only what stops, but also what resists movement. This becomes evident, once again, in non-philosophical uses of "free," like "free fall." For this is a fall completing its course not just without the body falling being intercepted, but also without its being resisted or deflected by other forces.

Indeed, there is a material reason so to understand "impediment" in an account of freedom, which is finitude. Your resources, in time, money, strength or whatever, are limited. So if you find something resisting you on your way, you may not be halted in your progress, you may overcome it thanks to whatever resources you spend on overcoming it. You will, however, be stymied somewhere else, since whatever you spend here will no longer be available there. You will be stymied disjunctively: either a or b or c ... will no longer be feasible, given what you put into overcoming this impediment. Being stymied disjunctively, however, should for finite creatures count as being stymied, period, and so as being unfree. For even if no particular thing is categorically withheld from you, the fact that by going for one you are barred from others is a restriction. It is a restriction even if it is up to you which thing you take and which therefore you let go, possibly not even being aware of letting it go. For though in that setting no one thing is altogether inaccessible, some combinations are, and that should count no less as a fetter than being denied access to some things entirely. Think of a restaurant offering set menus only. Here there is no dish from which you are barred from the start, but having chosen one you are denied others. This is a fetter. You are restricted, not just after the first course, but right from the start, hindered as you are to eat across the menu. Thus impediments in the narrow sense strike particular options from your list of feasibles and are therefore fetters. Impediments in the wide sense strike options disjunctively from your list of feasibles and are therefore fetters no less.

It follows that whatever you encounter that makes your life difficult abridges your freedom. For either you are denied something outright, by an impediment in the narrow sense, then clearly you are constrained. Or you merely find yourself resisted, by an impediment in the wide sense, then you have to pay for overcoming the resistance, in whatever currency, and so you foreclose yourself one or the other from a range of further things, since your funds in any case are limited. Thus when the price of bread rises, your freedom suffers, for that change deprives you, if not of bread, then of something else that you give up for the sake of bread. Consequently, even the morose faces of your colleagues in the morning take away some of your freedom, since you need an extra coffee, or an extra bit of patience, to get started under such circumstances. It is true, we normally do not speak this way. Such things we consider mere adversities, and we only say that you are deprived of your freedom when you are put into prison or something of the sort. However, if to be free is to be unfettered, there is in this respect no good reason to speak as we normally do and to find a loss of freedom only in the glaring cases of one's getting locked up and similar things. Anything should count as a fetter that constrains you in doing things, and the rise in the price of bread does. Also, we sometimes do speak this way. Remember free beer: that is clearly beer the consumption of which is not burdened by the demand for money in exchange. Ordinary beer, then, beer that you are charged for, is unfree beer; which is to say that it is beer in consuming which you are not free. So talk of free beer (and free entrance etc.) supposes that adversities like prices charged do affect people's freedom.

Not Being Probably Resisted

Actually, not only difficulties you do encounter, but also those likely to get in your way diminish your freedom. If the beer is only half free, every other pint being charged for, then, not knowing whether your place in the line is odd or even, you are right now constrained in your pursuit of beer by the probability of 0.5 of having to pay for it. Never mind how much you are constrained (Bayesians say you are as constrained as you would be by the prospect of definitely having to pay half the price), the point is that you are. The mere likelihood of your running into difficulty over this beer is itself, as of now, a difficulty you encounter.

Having no Master

That probable resistance suffices to make you less free accounts for the fact that sometimes your freedom is abridged by someone's being your master. One is another's master when the former, by whatever means, can make the latter do or forbear doing things at his or her discretion. The former is in that case, equivalently, lord over the other, the latter is subject, and the relation between them is domination. (*Herrschaft* in German. The explication just given essentially follows Max Weber's account of *Herrschaft*,[8] deviating from it in more or less important details which I omit to discuss here.) So somebody is your master not by being able to do you harm, as for instance

---

8. Weber, *Wirtschaft und Gesellschaft*, 28–29.

by killing you, but by being able to get you to do things as he or she thinks fit, for instance by threatening to kill you if you don't.

Practically always nowadays, people can make others do things at their discretion only within limited domains, limited in space, time and matter, and this is one difference between slavery and wage-labour.[9] Furthermore, very often nowadays people acquire the position of being able to make others do things at their discretion by these others' consent. This is another difference between slavery and wage-labor: domination over the wage-laborer is based on a contract with him or her. Thus considering my credible promise of giving you a certain amount of money at the end of the day, you make me your master for this day, putting me in a position of being able today to get you to do things at my discretion.

The mere fact, though, that I *can* make you do things at my discretion does not diminish your freedom, for you meet with no resistance to your endeavors in my bare ability to make you do this or that. In fact, however, once I am able, I am also likely, to get you to do things you do not yourself want to do and so to prevent you from doing what you do want to do, and as just argued, the probability of my resisting you is itself a resistance you face. So being subject to a master does not by itself make you less free, for a master omitting to exert the ability to make you do things does not constrain you. The relevance of this point is only theoretical, though. In actual cases of domination you are indeed less free, for masters are likely to obstruct the paths of their subjects.

This also serves to explain the expression "free speech." As Hobbes noted,[10] not the speech is free, but the speaker; and speakers are free as long as there is no one likely to get them by whatever means to forbear speaking, generally or at some time and place or on some set of topics.

Nor is your freedom any less diminished if it was you who by a contract made me your master: you are no less locked in somewhere for having locked in yourself. And in contrast to ordinary cases of locking oneself in, you may be wise in entering such a contract. Indeed, depending on what I give you in exchange, you may even achieve a net gain in freedom through the deal: the bread becoming affordable for you thanks to what I pay you may count for more than my obstructing your path with commands.

---

9. "A slave is a wage-labourer in perpetuity," said Chrysippos in the third century BCE, as reported by Seneca, *de beneficiis* III, 22.

10. Hobbes, *Leviathan* chap. 21, second paragraph.

Being Unresisted in What One Wants

Do you have positively to want to do something for a resistance to your doing it to count as an impediment, or is something already an impediment which makes more difficult some course of action, whether you want to pursue it or not? Hobbes, defining a free man as one "that in those things, which by his strength and wit he is able to do, is not hindred to doe what he has a will to,"[11] chooses the former understanding: only to be hindered in doing what one has a will to do is a case of being unfree. The difficulty with this line is well known, however: of two people equally situated the one who wants more things turns out to be less free, so that one way to increase one's freedom would be to cut down on one's desires, and that does not appear plausible.[12] The extent of the two people's freedom should rather depend only on their situation and therefore be equal. True, you may more keenly perceive your being constrained in what you want to do than in other things, but that does not touch the question of how free you are in fact. Anything, then, which makes some line of activity, desired or not, harder to pursue for you should count as an impediment diminishing your freedom. While some find it hard to accept that the opening of a route one does not have the slightest reason or desire to pursue should enhance one's freedom, such resistance may only stem from the assumption that a gain, or loss, in freedom is always a good, or bad, thing, and this assumption is easy to give up. There are many routes about the accessibility or inaccessibility of which we rightly do not care in the least.

Conclusion

If any obstacle encountered diminishes one's freedom, we are never just free, but only freer or less free, since as long as we live we meet with resistance, or the probability of resistance, on our paths. We are only at one time freer than at another time, here freer than there, and some of us are freer than others. Admittedly, we sometimes use the word "free" absolutely, saying things like "Charles is free," but in such cases it is understood from the context which restriction he escaped, be it prison or the opposite defender's coverage. When, however, somebody is said to be free without implicit reference to some particular restriction, then that statement is false, for it could only be taken as saying that the person is free throughout, and nobody is.

---

11. Hobbes, *Leviathan*, chap. 21, second paragraph.
12. This is the objection of the contented slave. See for instance Berlin, *Four Essays on Liberty*, 139–40.

So it is a mistake to ask, as I have been doing, what it is for humans to be free, since this suggests that freedom is a quality people either have or lack. The right question to ask is what makes one freer than another, and the answer is that one's facing less resistance on one's ways does. Figuratively, we could set up a relief map for each person, showing the steepness of all the paths in front of him or her: this would be the person's freedom map. So talk of one's being free is misleading in yet another way, for it suggests that it is something about you we are indicating when we call you free or unfree. Formally it is something about you, no doubt, for it is you to whom we ascribe this quality, but actually it is the situation you are facing that makes our statement true or false. Your freedom is just your world's unhostility.

Critical Part

Freedom of the Will

The foregoing account of what it is for humans to be free is, in traditional terminology, an account of freedom of action, since it makes one's freedom depend on the extent to which one is not impeded by external resistance in what one does. Freedom of action, however, was traditionally distinguished from freedom of the will. Free will is, according to an ancient explication, the faculty of choosing what one does and so in particular the faculty of choosing doing good or evil.[13] This faculty, part of human nature and not given to animals, serves to explain the existence of evil: having the choice, humans chose wrongly and brought evil into a good, because well-ordered world.[14] On the other hand, according to a contemporary explication, the one due to Harry Frankfurt, one has free will if one wills this or that because one wills to have this will.[15] On this account, humans do not invariably have free will. The addict who wishes to be rid of the craving for the drug does not.

As for the ancient conception, it is difficult to see what earns the capacity of choice, or its possessor, the attribute "free". The paths divide in front of you, so you can go left and you can go right. You have free will, so it is for you to decide, whether first weighing the pros and cons or not. Yet in what sense is the choice you come up with a free choice? Answer: it is free in the sense that what you choose is not fixed by natural conditions, as it would be in the case of an animal. This must be the answer, for otherwise

---

13. See for instance Basilius of Caesarea, *Adversus Eunomium* 29.660.51–52.
14. Basilius of Caesarea, *Quod deus non est auctor malorum* 31.332.44–45.
15. Frankfurt, "Freedom of the Will and the Concept of a Person," 20–21.

the explanation of evil fails. If what you choose is determined by natural conditions, then it is not you who brings evil into the world when choosing wrongly, but evil is due to these conditions, and that leaves us with the uncomfortable choice between an infinite regress in the explanation of evil and the assumption of evil being inherent in the natural order.[16] That answer, however, is unsatisfactory. As argued above (1 c), not to be determined by natural conditions is not required for a decision or action to be free. If you are a part of nature, then what you do cannot but flow from natural conditions, and laws of nature are no fetters for you, but just describe the way you work. So even if it is true that you take one path by mere unconditioned will, this does not show you to be unfettered and thus free. Had your decision depended on natural conditions instead, you could have been free no less. Hence, free will in the ancient sense seems to be irrelevant to the question when one is free.

With regard to Frankfurt's contemporary explication of free will it is even harder to see why the condition there described should be relevant for one's being free. Those who want things because they want to want them may be happier than those who find wants in themselves which they disapprove, but cannot extirpate. For one thing, though, there seems to be a large area between these extremes. There may be wants people just acquiesce in having without either approving or disapproving them, and in such cases there is no worrisome inner division. Granting for now, however, that people are somehow not in good standing if they want things without wanting to want them, why should that defect be a lack of freedom? It would rather seem that they lack some kind of unity, self-control or, with an expression Frankfurt later used, wholeheartedness.[17] Given that freedom is a matter of the paths in front of you being open, agreement within oneself as described by Frankfurt again seems to be irrelevant for freedom.

Negative and Positive Freedom

Little needs to be said about Isaiah Berlin's influential distinction between a negative and a positive concept of freedom,[18] or as he puts it occasionally, between freedom from . . . and freedom to . . .[19] As Gerald MacCallum has shown, this is a non-distinction, for a full statement of someone's being free needs to specify which impediment to doing what does not stand in that

---

16. The argument here is Augustine's, *de civitate dei* XII, 6.
17. Frankfurt, "Identification and Wholeheartedness."
18. Berlin, *Four Essays*, 121–22.
19. Berlin, *Four Essays*, 131.

person's way. "free" is a three-place predicate: you need somebody who is free, an impediment from which the person is free, and something which the person is therefore free to do (or to be, to experience etc.).[20] Hence any freedom is someone's freedom both from ... and to ...

Political Freedom

Individual freedom is commonly distinguished from political freedom.[21] Indeed, discussions of the two have so far drifted apart that political freedom has come to seem a different kind of freedom from that which is ascribed to individuals.

This impression is misleading. In fact, there is just freedom,[22] and it is the same sort of thing everywhere, with only the fillers of MacCallum's three variable positions varying. To see this, it is helpful to distinguish between two ways of speaking of political freedom which differ in who or what is described as free. On the one hand, the expression "political freedom" refers to the freedom *of* a city or state. On the other, it refers to the freedom of citizens *within* a city or state.[23]

An example of the first usage can be found in Herodotus:

> After 520 years of Assyrian rule, the Medeans first began to secede; and in the fight for freedom they got the better of the Assyrians, shook off the servitude and became free.[24]

There is no suggestion here that the individual Medean was freer when Assyrian rule came to an end. For all we are told the opposite may be true. The idea is, rather, that the Medean people as a whole was freer when it was no longer dominated by the Assyrians. And presumably it was freer in just the sense described earlier, namely, that impediments on its way, like tributes extracted, privileges withheld etc., came to be removed. So political freedom in this sense does not require a different understanding of freedom. It merely requires accepting collective subjects like the Medean people as

---

20. MacCallum, "Negative and Positive Freedom." MacCallum's point has been widely accepted, for instance by John Rawls, *A Theory of Justice*, 202, and by van Parijs, *Real Freedom for All*, 17–18.

21. For instance, John Stuart Mill opens *On Liberty* by declaring that his topic is not "the so-called Liberty of the Will ... ; but Civil, or Social Liberty."

22. Pettit, *A Theory of Freedom*, attempts as well to bring together the different perspectives on freedom, though on another basis than the one proposed here.

23. Hobbes similarly distinguishes between "the Libertie of Particular men" and "the Libertie of the Common-wealth": *Leviathan*, chap. 21, paragraph 8.

24. Herodotus, *Historiae* I, 95.

bearers of the attribute "free." Whether this extension is justified is not the issue here. Important is only that "political freedom" in this usage does not leave behind the general understanding of freedom outlined so far.

Euripides in his *Supplices* provides an example of the second usage. The Theban herald enters the scene asking who the lord of the country is, and Theseus corrects him:

> The city is not ruled by one man, it is free. The people holds power, sharing it in yearly rotation. Nor does the rich man get the largest part, but the poor man's part is equal.[25]

Here, by contrast, there is no suggestion that the city is free because it is not ruled by foreigners. Rather, the city is free because power in the city is divided equally between citizens. Not, to be sure, between all the city's inhabitants: citizens form a subgroup of these. The interesting question, though, is why city or citizens should be considered free on the grounds that political power is shared? The answer seems to be: individual citizens are, if not free, then at any rate freer, when they have access to political power and so to shaping the restrictions under which they otherwise operate. Materially, the decrees of a monarch may be no more restrictive than the regulations set up by a citizens' committee with rotating membership. However, each citizen has a chance under the latter regime, but not under the former, to see to it that the regulations are what he wants them to be. That makes them less of a restriction: you are freer where you have a chance to do something about your fetters. Certainly, everything taken together you may be freer under a monarch than under the citizens' rule.[26] Thus Theseus is exaggerating when he claims that the city is free because it is not ruled by one man. Yet keeping other things constant, it is freer. When you get a hand in shaping the restrictions to which you are subject, this is a gain in freedom.

It is a gain in *your* freedom: political freedom in this second usage does not refer to the city's, but to the individuals' being free. However, enjoying political freedom in this sense the individuals are free in the same sense as explained before, namely, unfettered, only that political freedom is in particular the absence of political fetters Political fetters in turn, according to the argument above (1 d X-ref), are not the norms of the city. They are the threats by means of which political agents press individuals into doing what otherwise they would not do (1 g X-ref). Political freedom in neither usage, then, is a different kind of freedom. In the former, it is a collective subject's being free in the sense expounded before, and in the latter it is

---

25. Euripides, *Supplices* 404–408.
26. Hayek, *Constitution of Liberty*, 15, stresses this point.

part of an individual's being free, again in the sense already expounded, that part which is constituted by the absence of political hindrances to his or her doing things.

Being Uncoerced

On the argument above, any difficulty you encounter, whether surmountable or not, makes you less free. There is, however, a much narrower understanding of what diminishes your freedom, allowing as freedom-relevant fetters only those intentionally imposed by other people. This is, correspondingly, a more generous understanding of freedom: you are free already when others do not make you do or forbear doing something. Others' making you do or forbear doing something might be called coercion: freedom on this line of thought amounts to being uncoerced.[27] Note the difference here between being forced and being coerced: heavy rain may force you to stay in, but it does not coerce you, and so on the present proposal it leaves you as free as before. On the proposal advocated in the first part, by contrast, both the rain and the people who coerce you or are likely to do so make you less free.

Regarding this dispute ordinary usage is divided again. We do not speak of an infringement of your freedom when you cannot go out because of the weather. On the other hand, suppose you visit a prison and, the guard accompanying you having just been called away, a gust of wind closes the cell door behind you and you are locked in. On the present proposal we have to say that you spend the next quarter of an hour, until they find you, in perfect freedom, and we definitely do not want to say that. While discrepancies between theory and usage cannot be avoided completely, this one appears pretty devastating. Still, there are those who are ready to live with it, and not much can be said to convince them otherwise. Ordinary usage, then, does not decide the issue between those who take a free human being as someone unresisted and those who take a free human being as someone uncoerced.

So the question becomes which of the two concepts is better at tracking differences important in our experience. Which boundary line is crucial, that between what makes life difficult and what does not, or that between what others make you do or omit and whatever else happens in your life? Clearly the first, for two reasons. First, making our way against resistances is a pervasive phenomenon of our life. True, at times we stop rowing and let the boat drift, but only at times: most of us for most of the day are struggling, one way or the other. For such creatures the difference between what

---

27. Hayek, *Constitution of Liberty*, 12; Berlin, *Four Essays*, 122.

makes things difficult and what does not, between fighting uphill and fighting on level ground, is all-important. The difference between those things in one's life which do, and those which do not, come about through coercion pales in comparison.

Nor is it evident, secondly, why other people's making you do or omit doing things, by contrast to anything whatever, be it people or nature, making you do or omit doing things, should be so significant as to determine the extent of your freedom . Hiking in the Alps I once found my path blocked by a landslip and was forced to take an unpleasant detour. Had a group of people, for the sheer fun of it, made me turn back, I would certainly have been far more annoyed and outraged. This difference in reactions, though, fails to support the notion that only the latter incident made me less free: outrage can, but certainly need not, be caused by a loss in freedom. Rather, it is very natural to think that, with regard to freedom, the two incidents, the real and the imagined one, are on a par.

Kantian Autonomy

For Kant, autonomy is an individual's being subject to laws of his or her own making, and only to such laws.[28] Autonomy, as Kant uses the term, is thus closely related to the ancient, political notion of autonomy, which is a city's making itself its laws, rather than receiving them from a foreign power.[29] Indeed, Kant occasionally employs the term himself in this traditional sense.[30] "Law" in the explanation just given needs to be understood narrowly, however: kings perhaps aside, nobody is subject only to self-given laws. So "law" is to be understood as "moral law," and autonomy is moral autonomy, i.e. one's being subject to moral laws of one's own making, and to no other moral laws. Kant holds that every human being, indeed every rational agent, enjoys autonomy in this sense.

However, Kantian autonomy is not a viable understanding of one's being free. As just argued, Kantian autonomy is moral autonomy, and the idea of moral autonomy itself is untenable. The reason is that there is no giving of moral laws, whether to yourself or to others. If you are subject to a moral law, then it is the case that you ought to do or not to do certain things. However, you did not make that the case, nor did anyone else, God included. After all, what could anyone do to bring it about that, say, lying

---

28. The present reading is based primarily on Kant, *Grundlegung zur Metaphysik der Sitten*, 432–47.

29. See for instance Thucydides, *History of the Peloponnesian War* V, 18.

30. See Kant, *Zum ewigen Frieden*, 346.

is wrong? If law got made on Mount Sinai, it was not a moral law, but the law of a theocratic state. If on the other hand it was a moral law that was proclaimed there, it was not made, but only brought to people's attention. The idea of giving a moral law, of making a type of action right that was not right before, makes no sense, and so the idea of giving a moral law to yourself doesn't either.[31]

No doubt, it was the task of Kantian autonomy to obviate the need for any moral Mount Sinai: the fundamental rules for our conduct we need not receive from on high. However, in declaring that we rather give them to ourselves Kant shows himself still wedded to that mountain. He asks us to take over the job that used to be God's, whereas he should have scratched it.

What makes moral autonomy untenable, however, also makes it unnecessary. If lying is wrong, it was not made so, and so in particular its wrongness is not like a barrier put in your path by anyone. Neither then do you need for your freedom's sake to do the barrier-putting yourself. As argued above (1 d), the wrongness of lying only speaks against lying, it does not restrict you in what you do. You are no less free for lying being wrong.

Ordinary Autonomy

When we ordinarily speak of autonomy, we do not have in mind a person's being subject to her own and only to her own moral laws. We understand autonomy as self-determination,[32] i.e. as a person's herself determining what she does, undergoes, or becomes, either in general or in particular areas of her life. Note that in this understanding the "-nomy" part of autonomy, i.e. the idea that what the person imposes on herself has the form of law, is not preserved:[33] self-determination may be erratic.

Autonomy so conceived is a matter of degree: one can be in control of more or less of what concerns oneself. And nobody has full autonomy: what we become is never completely up to us. Still, the important question for present purposes is whether more autonomy also brings more freedom.

Not always. What suggests that freedom and autonomy always grow together are cases of the following sort. Your well-meaning parents decide for you where and with whom you spend your time, thus making it difficult or impossible for you to come to appreciate good things beyond their purview. Here self-determination would help to enlarge the range of things

---

31. These doubts about Kantian autonomy are developed in my article: Bittner, "Autonomy and Then."

32. See for instance Baumann, *Die Autonomie der Person*, 9.

33. Frankfurt explicitly rejects this idea: "Autonomy, Necessity, and Love," 131.

open to you. Yet there is also the opposite story. Exercising your autonomy, i.e. self-determination, you get yourself into a rut, you erect barriers around you that again make it difficult or impossible for you to appreciate good things outside your circle, and the world will only open to you once you lose some of your control. Autonomy as self-determination being about who is in charge and freedom being about what is open, the two may diverge. Hence autonomy as it is ordinarily understood does not offer a viable account of freedom, as little as Kantian autonomy did.

Conclusion

So what is it to be free? It is to be without barriers that make difficult or impossible one's doing or becoming this or that. No-one, however, is simply without such barriers. Only some face more or higher ones than others. So while no-one is free, some are freer than others.

This is the positive thesis, here are the negative ones. To be free is not to be exempt from either natural or moral law. Freedom of the will, whether in the ancient or the modern version, is irrelevant for freedom. A distinction between negative and positive freedom cannot be drawn. Freedom and autonomy are not essentially connected, no matter whether autonomy is understood in Kant's way or in accordance with current usage. Not only coercion by others makes one less free. Political freedom is not a different kind of freedom: while sometimes this expression refers to a collective subject's being unhindered, in most cases it refers to that part of individuals' freedom that consists in their being unhindered by political obstacles.

Given this understanding of freedom, the high-minded statements both of individual and of political freedom[34] can go. Freedom is not a human predicament or privilege. Surely one hen may be freer than another, for example if her cage is larger. Rather than declaring that humans as such are free we should care about people's profile of unfreedom and understand what the important resistances are under which they labor. "Freedom", in fact, may not be a particularly useful concept, whether in individual or in political contexts. It does mark an important and pervasive dimension of our experience, the dimension of being subdued, caught up in things and hindered as against having open space ahead. Yet with regard to your individual or our collective situation it is little use to say that you need freedom

---

34. Friedrich Schiller:
"Der Mensch ist frei geschaffen, ist frei,
Und würd er in Ketten geboren."
in: "Die Worte des Glaubens" (1798).

or that we want more freedom in this country. The real question is where you are held back, where we are oppressed, and what to do about it. Liberals, i.e. friends of freedom, should worry about where life becomes difficult for someone.

Individually or politically, then, there is no state, and hence no aim, of being simply free. Freedom is a direction of a variety of our endeavors—true, of endeavors that are often close to our hearts.

Bibliography

Baumann, Peter. *Die Autonomie der Person.* Perspektiven der analytischen Philosophie. Paderborn: Mentis, 2000.

Berlin, Isaiah. *Four Essays on Liberty.* Oxford: Oxford University Press, 1969.

Bittner, Rüdiger. "Autonomy and Then." *Philosophical Explorations* 5 (2002) 217–28.

Böckenförde, Ernst-Wolfgang, and Christoph Enders, "Freiheit und Recht, Freiheit und Staat" (1985). In Böckenförde, *Recht, Staat, Freiheit.* Enlarged ed. Frankfurt: Suhrkamp, 2006.

Frankfurt, Harry G. "Autonomy, Necessity, and Love." In *Necessity, Volition, and Love.* 129–41. Cambridge: Cambridge University Press, 1999.

———. "Freedom of the Will and the Concept of a Person" (1971). In *The Importance of What We Care About: Philosophical Essays,* 11–25. Cambridge: Cambridge University Press, 1988.

———. "Identification and Wholeheartedness" (1987). In *The Importance of What We Care About,* 159–76. Cambridge: Cambridge University Press, 1988.

Goethe, Johann Wolfgang. *Faust.* 1828–29.

Hobbes, Thomas. *Leviathan.* 1651.

Hayek, Friedrich A. von. *The Constitution of Liberty.* London: Routledge, 1960.

Kant, Immanuel. *Grundlegung zur Metaphysik der Sitten* (1785). Academy ed. IV.

———. *Zum ewigen Frieden* (1795). AA VIII.

Parijs, Philippe van. *Real Freedom for All.* Oxford: Oxford University Press, 1995.

Pettit, Philip. *A Theory of Freedom: From the Psychology to the Politics of Agency.* Cambridge: Polity, 2001.

Rawls, John. *A Theory of Justice.* Oxford: Oxford University Press, 1972.

Schiller, Friedrich. "Die Worte des Glaubens." 1880.

Thomas Aquinas. *Summa Theologica.*

Weber, Max. *Wirtschaft und Gesellschaft.* Grundriss der verstehenden Soziologie. 5th ed. Tübingen: Mohr/Siebeck, 1972.

6

Concepts of Freedom in Antiquity
Pagan Philosophical Traditions in the Greco-Roman World

Peter Lampe

Any attempt to tackle this broad subject in an essay cannot be more than sketchy. It shoots a multitude of rays through the focus of a few lenses and ends up projecting handy outlines—that is, simplifications. A detailed differentiation between individual ancient authors is hardly possible.[1]

A second warning flag needs to be raised. This paper will focus on thoughts that were exchanged within the discourse of an elite group of ancient intellectuals, on nothing more. Even when the thoughts of a slave about freedom were "quoted," as Dio Chrysostom, in the first century C.E.,

---

1. For still useful overviews, see von Arnim, "Die stoische Lehre von Fatum und Willensfreiheit"; Schmitz, *Der Freiheitsgedanke bei Epiktet und das Freiheitszeugnis bei Paulus*; Schlier, "ἐλεύθερος"; Pohlenz, *Griechische Freiheit*; Mayr, "Das Freiheitsproblem in Platons Staatsschriften"; Nestle, *Eleutheria*; Wirszubski, *Libertas als Politische Idee im Rom der Späten Republik und des Frühen Prinzipats* (for Stoicism and *libertas*, see 177–81); Klein, ed., *Prinzipat und Freiheit* (for *libertas* in Tacitus, see 391–420); J. Bleicken, *Staatliche Ordnung und Freiheit in der römischen Republik*; Shotter, "Principatus ac Libertas"; Raaflaub, "Freiheit in Athen und Rom"; Raaflaub, *Die Entdeckung der Freiheit*; Bobzien, *Determinism and Freedom in Stoic Philosophy*; Bobzien, "The Inadvertent Conception and Late Birth of the Free-Will Problem"; R. Sorabji, *Emotion and Peace of Mind*; Knuuttila, *Emotions in Ancient and Medieval Philosophy*; A. Hahmann, *Was ist Willensfreiheit*.

did in his *Oratio* 15, this slave is still a literary figure made up by Dio and not a real slave. The paper cannot reflect all views, not the sexually abused slave girls' feelings about slavery, for example. It cannot reflect the views on freedom of underprivileged free persons who did not have enough to eat, while the slaves from across the street were well provided for by their master.² Did these hungry people share Epictetus' Stoic view that "it is better to die of hunger, but in a state of freedom from grief and fear, than to live in plenty, but troubled in mind?"³ Hardly. They probably did not care about inner freedom while they were starving.

Attempting to outline certain dominant tendencies in a discourse of intellectuals, this essay cannot claim to present anything like *the* Greek, Hellenistic or Roman concept of freedom—because such a thing hardly ever existed. One only needs to look at Dio Chrysostom's two speeches about slavery (*Or.* 14–15), where he juxtaposes and most often deconstructs all kinds of views on the terms "free" and "enslaved." He himself comes up with the Stoic concept that the wise person alone is free. Freedom is knowing what is allowable and forbidden (τὰ ἐφειμένα καὶ τὰ κεκωλυμένα); slavery is being ignorant in this respect. In this sense, a "man who is regarded as a slave and is so called and who . . . often has been sold . . . will be more free than the Great King" (*Or.* 14.18).⁴ However, Dio Chrysostom is also aware of the popular view that when one person lawfully possesses another human, in the same way as he or she possesses "goods and cattle," and "has the right to use him as he likes, then this human being is . . . the slave" of the first (*Or.* 15.24). Already in antiquity, different notions of freedom and slavery existed side by side, so that Dio—and the apostle Paul⁵—could engage in dialectical wordplays.

A last word of caution needs to be given, this time in regard to actual *practices* of freedom. When attempting to construct a picture of these practices, immediately methodological problems arise. How representative are our sources? Most of them were written by free, or at least freed, persons—even the sources to which we would turn first, the papyri and the inscriptions. Not only literary sources, but also inscriptions are "rhetorical" in the sense that they do not necessarily mirror actual practices, but mostly

---

2. Cf., e.g., Lampe, *Die stadtrömischen Christen in den ersten beiden Jahrhunderten*, 158–60; ET = *From Paul to Valentinus*, 189–93.

3. *Enchir.* 12.1.

4. Cf. the apostle Paul's dialectical formulation that a slave is a freed person of the Lord, and a free person is enslaved by Christ (1 Cor 7:22). In a similar way, Plato plays with the literal and metaphorical meanings. Free citizens are slaves of the law (*Leg.* 715d; cf. also *Ep.* 354e).

5. See note 4, above.

free persons' *perceptions* of their social relationships. The analysis of the practices of freedom in the Greco-Roman world would again be a different project. This paper can only allow for occasional glimpses of actual practice.

Classical Greek Times: Freedom as External, Political Freedom

Collective External Freedom

"Freedom" is one of the features of the polis.[6] It denotes the political independence of the polis. A polis needs to be free both from tyrants[7] and from external enemies,[8] such as the Persians, that is, independent in interstate relationships, sovereign as a *res publica*. In this sense, the term ἐλευθερία comes close to αὐτονομία,[9] πολιτεία (in the sense of a free commonwealth, an independent polis)[10] and even σωτηρία.[11]

Individual External Freedom[12]

Only citizens of a polis enjoy individual freedom, not slaves, not residents without political rights. Only male citizens participate in the collective freedom of the polis. "Free" in this sense means to be able to govern and to *rule*

---

6. Plato, *Leg.* 693b-d; 694b; 697c-d; Aristotle, *Pol.* 1296b 17ff; Thucydides, *Hist.* 6.20.2; 6.89.6; Pindar, *Pythia* 1.61-63.

7. Herodotus, *Hist.* 5.78.

8. E.g., Aeschylus, *Persae.* 403 (ἐλευθεροῦτε πατρίδα); Plato, *Menex.* 239d; *Ep.* 355e; Thucydides, *Hist.* 3.54; Xenophon, *Hell.* 5.2.12; Homer, *Il.* 6.526ff; Pindar, *Olympia* 12.1; *IG* VII 48, 49, 1711, 1856.

9. E.g., Thucydides, *Hist.* 3.10.5; Xenophon, *Hell.* 3.1.20f; 6.3.7-9; Polybius, *Hist.* 4.27.5; 21.19.9; Isocrates, *Paneg.* 117.

10. Cassius Dio, *Hist. Rom.* 54.25.1 (τήν τε ἐλευθερίαν καὶ τὴν πολιτείαν); cf. 9.31.7; 48.13.6. A free commonwealth ruled by the citizens and not by a monarch or just a few aristocrats (e.g., Aristotle, *Pol.* 1279a 39; 1293b 22).

11. Cf., e.g., Thucydides, *Hist.* 3.59; Xenophon, *Hell.* 2.4.20; Cassius Dio, *Hist. Rom.* 45.31.2. Being liberated is being saved.

12. One particular aspect of "inner" freedom, the voluntary choice and decision, already discussed by Plato and Aristotle, will be treated separately in part 3 below.

oneself (τὸ ἄρχον ἑαυτοῦ);[13] it means to be free from others (ἀπ' ἀλλήλων),[14] which slaves are not.[15]

(a) However, this freedom is only feasible within the framework of a democratic polis, which is understood as a κοινωνία and φιλία of free persons:[16] The free individuals of a polis rule themselves by giving a νόμος to the polis. Individual freedom thus is tied to the *nomos* and limited by it.[17] The *nomos* expresses the free persons' own and common will, and protects their freedom against despotism and arbitrariness of individual tyrants (τύραννος) and mobs (πλῆθος).[18] *Anomia* therefore has nothing to do with the concept of freedom. There is only freedom under the protective law, not from it. The law, guided by reason,[19] creates a sheltered space to breathe and to live—at least for free male citizens.

(b) Secondly, as a free citizen you can only rule yourself if you are willing to have your share in governing (ἄρχειν) the polis. One free person after the other needs to participate in a rotating system of execution of power. In other words, "ruling" (ἄρχειν) and "being ruled" (ἄρχεσθαι) need to alternate in a free individual's life. Only in this way can you "live how you want it" (ζῆν ὡς βούλεταί τις).[20]

---

13. Pseudo-Plato, *Defin.* 415a; cf. 412d: to have the control (ἐξουσία) in life over the things that concern oneself.

14. Plato, *Leg.* 832d 2; cf. *Resp.* 576a 5–6.

15. Slaves do not belong to themselves by nature but to someone else (ὁ γὰρ μὴ αὑτοῦ φύσει ἀλλ' ἄλλου ἄνθρωπος ὤν); they are pieces of property (κτῆμα), according to Aristotle, *Politica* 1254a 14-16. See also Dio Chrysostom, *Or.* 15.24, above. Accordingly, free persons live for the sake of their own, not for the sake of another person whom they serve and who represents their purpose (Aristotle, *Metaph.* 982b 25-26: ἄνθρωπος . . . ἐλεύθερος ὁ αὑτοῦ ἕνεκα καὶ μὴ ἄλλου ὤν).

16. Cf. Aristotle, *Pol.* 1279a 21; 1280b 30–39.

17. Cf. Aristotle, *Pol.* 1287a 18–33; Herodotus, *Hist.* 7.104.16-21; 3.38; Plato, *Ep.* 354e–355d; *Leg.* 715d (δοῦλοι τοῦ νόμου); Euripides, *Supplices* 429–432.

18. Cf., e.g., Aristotle, *Pol.* 1292a 4–32.

19. Aristotle, *Pol.* 1287a 28–33.

20. Aristotle, *Pol.* 1317b 2–3, 11–17; cf. Euripides, *Supplices* 404–408. In Rome, the concept of *libertas populi* was less ambitious. It did not mean the political participation of the citizens, only their equality in front of the law and their protection against caprices of the governing officials. Cf. Livy 3.54.6. This limited political notion of freedom made it possible for manumitted slaves, contrary to the practice in the Greek world, usually to receive Roman citizenship (until the *Lex Aelia Sentia* of the year 4 CE and the *Lex Iunia* of about 19 CE restricted this praxis). For the Romans, it seemed easier to grant citizenship because citizenship did not automatically entail participation in political power. Under the emperors, *libertas* dwindled to nothing more than personal and legal protection of the citizen. And for critical senatorial circles, *libertas* denoted nothing more than a faint memory of the past political power of the senatorial oligarchy in the Roman republic; they used the term *libertas* as a motto for their intellectual

(c) It is obvious that this freedom can be achieved only within a democratic polis[21] where the legislature and jurisdiction (νόμος; see a) and the execution of power (ἄρχειν; see b) are shared by all free citizens[22] who enjoy *equal* (ἰσότης, ἰσονομία) political rights[23] (ἰσοψηφία),[24] equal right to execute *power* (ἰσοκρατία; see b), equal *honor* (ἰσοτιμία),[25] as well as the equal right of *free public speech* in official meetings (ἰσηγορία, παρρησία), which is a basic prerequisite of individual freedom. "Free is the tongue of the free," Sophocles writes.[26] In the private sphere, παρρησία denotes frank and open speech between friends.[27] Because the polis is perceived as a φιλία of free and equal citizens, the same frank speech can take place in the public arena. This illustrates how exclusive the circle of people is for whom freedom is conceptualized.

(d) Freedom is *endangered* whenever the authority of the common *nomos* is questioned. This happens as soon as a free person enjoys his individual rights so excessively[28] that he is estranged (*Entfremdung*) from the common law. Then he no longer perceives the *nomos* of the polis as his own expression of will—which it originally was. This person begins to create his own *nomoi*, which ultimately leads into the same misery as despotism does.[29]

Erosion also sets in as soon as the community as a whole amends and supplements the *nomos* by constantly creating ψηφίσματα, adapting it to

---

resistance against the Principate. Cf., e.g., Tacitus, *Hist.* 1.16.

21. Plato, *Resp.* 562b 11–c 2: Λέγεις δ' αὐτὴν (i.e., δημοκρατίαν) τί ὁρίζεσθαι; Τὴν ἐλευθερίαν, εἶπον. τοῦτο γάρ που ἐν δημοκρατουμένῃ πόλει ἀκούσαις ἂν ὡς ἔχει τε κάλλιστον καὶ διὰ ταῦτα ἐν μόνῃ ταύτῃ ἄξιον οἰκεῖν ὅστις φύσει ἐλεύθερος.

22. Cf. also Aristotle, *Pol.* 1291b 30-38 (... κοινωνούντων ἁπάντων μάλιστα τῆς πολιτείας ὁμοίως); 1275a 22f (πολίτης δ' ἁπλῶς οὐδενὶ τῶν ἄλλων ὁρίζεται μᾶλλον ἢ τῷ μετέχειν κρίσεως καὶ ἀρχῆς); *Eth. Nic.* 1134b 15 (ἰσότης τοῦ ἄρχειν καὶ ἄρχεσθαι).

23. Cf. Aristotle, *Pol.* 1255b 20 (ἐλευθέρων καὶ ἴσων); 1291b 31, 34-35; 1318a 9-10; *Eth. Nic.* 1143b 15; Plato, *Resp.* 557a; 563b; Plutarch, *Dio* 37.5.3-37.6.1; already Herodotus, 3.80.26.

24. For Republican Rome, cf. Tacitus, *Hist.* 1.16.

25. Only at the Saturnalia, the slaves were also allowed this privilege. Cf. Lucian, *Saturnalia* 7.29; 13.5.

26. Sophocles, *Frg.* 927a; cf. Herodotus, *Hist.* 5.78; Demosthenes, *Or.* 21.124.4; *Frg.* 13.21; Polybius, *Hist.* 2.38.6.1; 4.31.4-5; 7.10.1.5; Plato, *Resp.* 557b 4-5 (ἐλευθερίας ἡ πόλις μεστὴ καὶ παρρησίας γίγνεται); Lucian, *Calumniae* 23.7 (ἐλεύθερον καὶ παρρησιαστικόν); Euripides, *Supplices* 438-441; Democritus, *Frg.* 226 (οἰκήιον ἐλευθερίης παρρησίη); Tacitus, *Hist.* 1.1, and *Dial.* 40 (for Republican Rome).

27. See, e.g., Sampley, "Paul and Frank Speech"; and Sampley "Paul's Frank Speech with the Galatians and the Corinthians."

28. Cf. Aristotle, *Pol.* 1316b 24–25.

29. Plato, *Leg.* 699e 4; 701a 5–701c 4; cf. 698a-b: ἡ παντελὴς καὶ ἀπὸ πασῶν ἀρχῶν ἐλευθερία is as bad as despotism; *Resp.* 561d 5–562a 2.

ad hoc desires of the crowds, e.g., by dissolving the borderlines between slaves and free persons[30] or between men and women.[31] Plato and Aristotle frowned on such attempts. The willingness to supplement the *nomos* allegedly opens the door for demagogues and leads to the decay of freedom, to tyranny and arbitrariness. In short, too much freedom allegedly leads back to slavery.[32]

Gender roles and slavery thus were not questioned by either Aristotle or Plato.[33] Aristotle even stated that people are slaves or free persons *by nature* (φύσει).[34] Later the Stoics with their natural law maxim of fundamental equality and freedom of all humans as rational beings—as well as Pauline Christianity (Gal 3:28)—came up with different ontological pictures, without, however, drawing the practical consequence of freeing slaves;[35] neither did some of the fathers of modern democracy, George Washington and Thomas Jefferson.[36]

Hellenistic and Roman Times: Internal Freedom (Cynics, Stoics)

Freedom is still considered a *summum bonum*,[37] although (or because) the external freedom of the polis and the citizen's external freedom within the polis have faded. Since the decline of the Greek polis, the polis and its *nomos* have not been the frame of reference anymore; the *kosmos* and the inner self have become the individual's horizon.[38]

30. Cf. Plato, *Resp.* 563b; Aristotle, *Pol.*, e.g., 1254b 19–1255b 2. For Aristotle, slavery is δίκαιος (1255a 2).

31. Cf. Plato ibid.; Aristotle, *Pol.* 1254b 13–14.

32. Cf., e.g., Plato, *Resp.* 563e–564a (unbridled freedom ultimately leads to slavery and tyranny); *Ep.* 354e–355a; Aristotle, *Pol.* 1292a 4-36; Isocrates, *Areop.* 20.5-8.

33. Cf. Plato, *Resp.* 563b: Equality between the sexes and between slaves and free persons would mean too much "freedom of the crowd" (ἔσχατον, ὦ φίλε, τῆς ἐλευθερίας τοῦ πλήθους); it would be unhealthy for a good state. In reference to slavery, see Aristotle *Pol.*, e.g., 1255a 1ff; 1255b 6ff.

34. Aristotle, *Pol.* 1254a 14.

35. Cf., e.g., Seneca's famous *Ep. ad Lucilium* 47. Before the Stoics, in 366 BCE, the rhetor and sophist Alcidamas stated that nature did not create slaves and that God bestowed freedom to everybody (*Frg.* 1).

36. An exception in this generation of U.S. Southern aristocrats was Robert Carter, who was driven by his newly embraced Baptist faith. See Levy, *The First Emancipator*.

37. E.g., Diog. Laert., *Biogr.* 6.71.11 (about Diogenes); Epict., *Diss.* 4.1.52, 54; 1.12.12; *Ench.* 1.4 (freedom and happiness are tied together); Dio Chrysost., *Or.* 14.1, 3.

38. Cf., e.g., Epict., *Diss.* 4.1.6-10; *Gnom. Stob.* 31, 38f; *Frg.* 35 in Florilegium, Cod. Paris. 1168 [501 E] (οὐδεὶς ἐλεύθερος ἑαυτοῦ μὴ κρατῶν); Diog. Laert., *Biogr.* 7.121f

The Cynics try to maintain an external freedom by emigrating from society, becoming migrant drop outs, enjoying freedom from fear, from any human master (not from God: ἐλεύθερος ὑπὸ τὸν Δία) and using freedom of speech by openly criticizing tyrannical structures of society.[39] The Cynics thus combine their rough external freedom with an internal freedom (freedom from desires for external goods and from painful emotions such as fear, shame, etc.). But for those who dread the filthy existence of a Cynic and do not want to drop out of society, what is mainly left is the cultivation of internal freedom.

The individual person in Hellenistic and Roman times experiences a lack of external freedom when he or she cannot freely control external matters such as their own body,[40] their economic welfare, social relationships and politics.[41] The ultimate "freedom" is to act independently (ἐξουσία αὐτοπραγίας),[42] to live how one wants without being hindered or pushed,[43] thus to command and shape oneself. But this can only be achieved in regard to the inner personal life. The art of living is to distinguish wisely[44] between what we can command (τὰ ἐφ' ἡμῖν)[45] and what we do not have under our control (τὰ ἀλλότρια).[46] Autonomy and sovereignty only exist in regard to the inner self (τὰ ἔσω).[47] Only there are you free to rule yourself.

(about Zenon and the Stoics). At best, smaller communities than the polis become the frame of reference, e.g., the Epicurean community, in which Epicurus is praised as the "liberator of those being in company with him" (Lucian, *Alex.* 61.10f), or the Platonic Academy.

39. Diogenes Sinop., *Ep.* 7.
40. Epictetus, *Diss.* 1.1.11; 4.1.66, 73, 100: the body is an ἀλλότριον.
41. Epictetus, *Diss.* 1.22.9–10.
42. Diogenes Laertius, *Biogr.* 7.121; Philo, *Omn. Prob. Lib.* 21; cf. 41.
43. Epictetus, *Diss.* 1.17.21; 4.1.1, 11, 62, 89–90; 1.12.9; 2.1.23; 2.23.42; cf. Dio Chrysost., *Or.* 14.13. Already Aristotle, *Pol.* 1317b; *Eth Nic.*1110a–1113a 14, used this terminology, but when talking about being "not hindered" he referred to external powers or to the lack of external means, for example. For Epictetus, however, the unimpeded freedom relates to his inner life. As soon as he consentingly subjects his irrational impulses and reasoned choices to God (τὴν ὁρμὴν τῷ θεῷ, *Diss.* 4.1.89), who sends him fever and other unpleasant external things, nothing can rub him the wrong way. As long as he aligns his ὁρμή to God's will and its often unpleasant external manifestations that affect him, nothing obstructs this ὁρμή. In Roman philosophy, Lucretius picks up on these ideas (2.251–293; free from inner constraint and coercion); also Seneca, *Vita Beata* 15.6–7.
44. Cf. Epictetus, *Diss.* 4.1.63; 1.22.9–10.
45. Epictetus, *Diss.* 1.1.17.2; *Enchir.* 1.5.
46. Cf. Epictetus, *Diss.* 2.13.8; 4.1.83, 100–101; 3.24.68; 1.1.21; *Enchir.* 1.5; 5; 19.2. One needs to learn to contempt these matters and to deprive them from any influence on one's emotional life.
47. Epictetus, *Diss.* 2.13.11; *Enchir.* 29.7.

The inner freedom consists of (a) freely developing one's own ideas, opinions and plans, desires and aversions, choices and refusals. It consists of the faculty of choosing what, e.g., you want to consider true and false or morally right and wrong (προαίρεσις). It implies that you can choose in which way you want to deal with the external impressions of the world. You have this power of free decision.[48] Below, we will expand on this latter particular variant of freedom (part 3).

(b) The internal freedom consists of becoming free from all passions and emotions (ἀπάθεια), e.g., from fear, worries, anxieties, wrath, sadness, but also from caring feelings and pity![49] The ultimate, though almost unreachable goal is becoming free from fear of death.[50]

(c) Furthermore, freedom consists of being independent from the admiration of others,[51] and of developing an undemanding nature with a minimum of needs and desires; it means being free from the domination of false desires and yearnings (ἐπιθυμίαι).[52] If all of this is accomplished (at least wise models such as Socrates and Diogenes allegedly showed that it is possible),[53] calmness is gained (ἀταραξία), which is regarded as equivalent to freedom.[54]

A "happy flow of life" (εὔροια) is achieved once we have learned to distinguish between those things we can influence and those we cannot—and once we have learned happily to accept and to be content with those things that we do not have at our disposal. If God wants me to run a fever, I want it too.[55] Already Zenon as well as Chrysippus reportedly used the parable of a dog who happily runs beside the wagon to which it is tied. This dog is "free." The one who is dragged along by the wagon is not.[56]

---

48. Epictetus, *Diss.* 1.17.21–29; 1.1.12; 2.10.1; 2.15.1; 3.1.40; 3.24.69; 4.1.74, 100; 4.5.12; 1.19.8–9; *Enchir.* 6; 9; *Gnom. Stob.* 31.

49. Epictetus, *Enchir.* 16 (and 11–12); *Diss.* 2.1.21, 24; 4.1.82f; Xenophon, *Mem.* 4.5.3.

50. Epictetus, *Diss.* 3.26.38–39; *Enchir.* 5. Epictetus knows that hardly anybody reaches this goal of perfection: 4.1.114ff, 123ff, 151ff; 2.19.24–25.

51. Epictetus, *Enchir.* 19.2.

52. Epictetus, *Enchir.* 15; *Diss.* 4.1.87; *Gnom. Stob.* 38; Xenophon, *Apol.* 16.

53. E.g., Epictetus, *Diss.* 4.1.114ff, 123ff, 151ff.

54. Epictetus, *Diss.* 2.1.21; 1.24.8–9; 4.1.84; 3.13.13; 3.15.12; 1.1.22; 2.16.41; 2.18.28; *Enchir.* 12.2.

55. Epictetus, *Diss.* 4.1.89–90; 1.12.8–9; 2.16.42; 2.23.42; *Enchir.* 53.1.

56. Hippolytos, *Philos.* 21 = SVF 2.975.

Free Will?

The question could mislead us to compare ancient apples and modern oranges. The Greeks connect the concept of βούλεσθαι / βουλή, closely to intellectual functions, whereas "will" in modern philosophical concepts of the last three centuries often is more of an independent function of the human psyche and, for instance in Schopenhauer's thinking, a metaphysical principle.[57] "Free will," in modern terms, therefore cannot be part of the Greek freedom concept; it should not be read into it, not even into Aristotle's deliberations (see below).

Nevertheless, Greek thinkers in general do not question their freedom of choice and decision—a decision-making based on rational thinking. For them, this freedom is self-evident.

Even when a god or a demon influences your thinking, you yourself are considered the author of the decision. No matter how much Athena tries to calm Achilles, he himself decides to be swayed by her (Homer, *Il.* 1.216; for a demon, see Aeschylus, *Agam.* 1505). Contrary to us, these authors do not feel the tension between divine influence and free human decision-making. Or, in other words, divine influence does not diminish the humans' responsibility for their own acts.

The freedom of decision is simply presupposed by the Greek thinkers, by Plato[58] and Carneades, as well as by Aristotle and his school, especially Theophrastus, by Zenon, Chrysippus, Epicurus, and even the Cynic Oinomaos.[59] Zenon and Chrysippus, however, on the basis of their reflections about causality, are the first to seriously expound the problems of the notion of freedom of decision. But they do not shove it from the pedestal as the decisive factor that causes human actions.[60] In Hellenistic-Roman times, freedom of decision is included in terms such as αὐτεξούσιον,[61] freedom of

---

57. For the difference, see, e.g., Pohlenz, *Griechische Freiheit*, 131–41; cf. Dihle, *Die Vorstellung vom Willen in der Antike*. For criticism of Dihle, see Zöller, *Die Vorstellung vom Willen in der Morallehre Senecas*, 7, 38; et al.

58. See below for the ending of the *Resp.*

59. For Aristotle, Zenon, Chrysippus, Epicurus, Arcesilaos, Carneades and Oinomaos, see, e.g., Pohlenz, *Griechische Freiheit*, 135–39. According to Epicurus and his consequent atomism, freedom denotes an event without causes and becomes a metaphysical principle. The individual's free choice between different options is not determined by any causes. For Epicurus' opposition against the Stoic determinism, cf. Diog. Laert., *Biogr.* 10.133f. In reaction to Stoicism, Epicurus and Carneades became radical representatives of indeterminism. Cf. Cicero (*de fato* 19, 23–28, 31–32, 39–46) who himself opposed determinism.

60. Cf., e.g., SVF 2.974, 1000, and see below.

61. Cf. Epictetus, *Diss.* 4.1.62–75.

choice, self-determination and, again, προαίρεσις. προαίρεσις, the choosing of one alternative over another, might be considered a forerunner of the modern concept of free will,[62] but nothing more. The following only briefly and selectively zooms in on the ancient discussion.

Aristotle's juridical distinction between ἑκών and ἄκων (willing versus involuntary) has nothing to do with the modern metaphysical problem of "free will"; it is aimed at solving the legal question of a person's accountability for his or her actions.[63] A starting point of the ancient discussion is the ethical question, already posed by Socrates and picked up by Aristotle,[64] whether our wrongdoing is voluntary or not. Do we voluntarily choose the wrong and therefore are responsible and juristically accountable? For the ancients, the answer is self-evident: yes.

Socrates, however, complicated the discussion by claiming that our choosing is always dependent on our intellectual insights. This connection gave rise to a double notion of voluntariness. (a) Wrongdoing, according to Socrates, has its origin in wrong intellectual insights clouded by desires. The wrongdoer, in this sense, does not have the right knowledge; he is mislead by lack of knowledge and therefore acts involuntarily, because "nobody is willingly bad." Only the wise acts voluntarily; his acts are anchored in proper intellectual insights.[65] This Socratic definition of voluntariness is not to be confused with the psychological notion of freedom of decision espoused by Plato: (b) Even the wrongdoer has the freedom of decision. He, on his own, chooses between different options and is accountable for his action.[66] According to Plato, in our psychological freedom, we can choose to become unfree in the Socratic sense, by choosing to give in to the desires of the body and thus becoming intellectually clouded; we ourselves are responsible for this[67]— a view that combines both freedom notions. Whether or not Socrates himself consented to this notion of psychological freedom is unclear. According to the Peripatetics,[68] he did not.

62. Cf., e.g., Epict., Diss. 2.15.1 (ἡ μὲν προαίρεσις ἐλεύθερον φύσει καὶ ἀνανάγκαστον).

63. See the clear reference to legislature at the beginning of his deliberations about free choice in Nic. Eth. 1109b,34, and cf. further, e.g., Pohlenz, Griechische Freiheit, 134–35.

64. Nic. Eth. 1109b, 30—1115a, 3.

65. Plato, De justo 374.a 7 and Aristotle, Nic. Eth. 1113b, 14f (οὐδεὶς ἑκὼν πονηρός); Xenoph., Mem. 3.9.4 (... νομίζω οὖν τοὺς μὴ ὀρθῶς πράττοντας οὔτε σοφοὺς οὔτε σώφρονας εἶναι).

66. Cf. Plato. Resp. 617ff, esp. 617e: ἀρετὴ δὲ ἀδέσποτον, ἣν τιμῶν καὶ ἀτιμάζων πλέον καὶ ἔλαττον αὐτῆς ἕκαστος ἕξει. αἰτία ἑλομένου· θεὸς ἀναίτιος.

67. Cf. Phaedo 81bff.

68. Ps.-Aristotle, Magna Moralia 1.9.7.3 (Σωκράτης ἔφη, οὐκ ἐφ' ἡμῖν γενέσθαι τὸ

Aristotle underscored the psychological freedom of choice and expressly refuted Socrates' opinion that nobody is willingly bad.[69] According to Aristotle, we act voluntarily (and are thus accountable) if we are not forced or held back by external factors and not ignorant about the circumstances in which we act (βίᾳ καὶ δι' ἄγνοιαν). Our personality then is the sufficient cause of our acts (ἄνθρωπος ... ἀρχὴ τῶν πράξεων).[70] This definition includes both the aspect of external freedom of our acting (not forced and not held back) and the internal aspect of freedom from deception about the circumstances. The προαίρεσις, our voluntary choice between good and bad, qualifies us ethically.[71] Aristotle did not ask any further questions about factors that might determine this προαίρεσις. Only much later did the Peripatetics push on further with the question.[72] Neither Plato nor Aristotle was interested in grand theories of freedom.

Although the Stoics propagated metaphysical monism, they nurtured an ethical dualism: the human being, characterized by the opposition between reason and rationality on the one hand and irrational sensuality and drives on the other, needs to overcome the latter with the aid of virtues. It is therefore important for the Stoics that the individual person has the free choice to do so. However, their pantheistic metaphysical monism, according to which all things in the universe, including human beings, are moved by the divine cosmic force within it, hinders this optimism. Are individual humans with their own personalities still the true cause (ἀρχή) of their own actions? Or are fate (εἱμαρμένη) and providence (πρόνοια) responsible? Is human freedom of choice still compatible with the determinism espoused by Chrysippus? For Chrysippus, nothing happens by chance. Everything is determined by antecedent causes (προηγουμέναις τισὶν αἰτίαις) and therefore necessary (ἀνάγκη).[73]

The Stoics, aware of the tension within their system, tried hard to defend the freedom of choice in light of their metaphysical monism. Contrary to their critics, they asserted that their determinism *is* compatible with the concept that humans cause their actions themselves so that they can be held accountable for them. How could they get away with this assertion?

σπουδαίους εἶναι ἢ φαύλους).

69. ἡ δὲ μοχθηρία ἑκούσιον; Nic. Eth. 1113b, 16–17.

70. Nic. Eth. 1112b, 31, and 1111a, 22–24, reads: "Ὄντος δ' ἀκουσίου τοῦ βίᾳ καὶ δι' ἄγνοιαν, τὸ ἑκούσιον δόξειεν ἂν εἶναι οὗ ἡ ἀρχὴ ἐν αὐτῷ εἰδότι τὰ καθ'ἕκαστα ἐν οἷς ἡ πρᾶξις.

71. τῷ γὰρ προαιρεῖσθαι τἀγαθὰ ἢ τὰ κακὰ ποιοί τινές ἐσμεν, Nic. Eth. 1112a, 1–2.

72. See Alexander of Aphrodisias (about 200 CE) below.

73. Cf. Chrysippus, Stoicus (SVF II-III) 2.264; Plutarch., de fato 572; 574; comm. not. 1076; Cic., de nat. deor. 2.65.164.

Chrysippus distinguished between *main* and *minor* causes, holding that the external circumstances, which are subject to the cosmic causal nexuses, are only ancillary causes, whereas the human personality functions are the main source of a decision. The person therefore voluntarily decides and acts.[74] Thus, we are back to the Stoic distinction between the uncontrollable, determined external things (the ἀλλότρια) and the internal things (τὰ ἔσω) that the individual can control (τὰ ἐφ' ἡμῖν; see above): The ancillary causes of a decision belong to the sphere of the uncontrollable external things (ἀλλότρια), whereas the human personality with its internal life (τὰ ἔσω) functions as the main cause.

For the Peripatetic Alexander of Aphrodisias, this was not enough. He pleaded for the ἀναίτιοι προαιρέσεις, the choices without a cause. Our decisions to behave in this or that way belong to "the things we can control" (τὰ ἐφ' ἡμῖν); they are "uncaused."[75] At the turn from the second to the third century CE, Alexander laid a stepping stone towards the later conceptions of a free will.

The correlate of the ancient presupposition of freedom of decision was pedagogical hopefulness. Quintilian, for example, was driven by an almost unlimited pedagogical optimism[76] behind which the Stoic doctrine of individual progress toward wise perfection can be discerned. Any human being, regardless of age, can become better and strive towards perfection if he or she wants to do so.

Quintilian's passage *Inst.* 12.11.23 appears quite modern: even elderly people can study and grasp what they really desire to learn. Correspondingly, 1.1.16–17, 19 asserts: Mental training and education conveying both *mores* and *litteras* should begin already in the first years of childhood and not as late as at the age of seven. In 12.1.42, Quintilian pleads for a liberal, pedagogically oriented criminal justice system. If culprits, "as commonly conceded," can meliorate their ethos, if they want to do so, then it is in the public's interest not to punish these delinquents.[77] Quintilian admitted that the inborn disposition of a person plays an important role—it is one of the uncontrollable externals—but the enhancements by learning and practice that individuals freely work on are as crucial.[78]

74. Cf. Cic., *de fato* 41ff.
75. E.g., *Mantissa* 171.17–27.
76. E.g. in *Inst.* 12.2.1; 12.11.11–13.
77. Cf. also 7.4.18.
78. E.g., 12.1.32; 12.2.2-4; 10.7.8-9, 24-25, 29; 11.2.1,50; 11.3.11, 19; 10.2.20; similarly, e.g., Chrysippus (see Pohlenz, *Griechische Freiheit*, 138). However, in *Inst.* 10.2.21, even Quintilian gives in to his classroom experience and admits that further labors are useless where the teacher runs "against nature." Not only Quintilian, also Plato, at least

As the flipside of his pedagogical ideas, Quintilian nurtured a perplexingly optimistic, if not naive, image of humankind; for example, in 12.1.4: "Vileness and virtue cannot jointly inhabit in the selfsame heart, and it is as impossible for one and the same mind to harbor good and evil thoughts as it is for one man to be at once both good and evil." Choose the good and try hard—and you will succeed.

Comments

The most problematic points in the ancient concepts of freedom have already been cited above: (a) discriminating gender differences and (b) the institution of slavery were not questioned.

Modern theorists applied the idea of external freedom to all humans. But even in modern times, attempts have always been made to declare certain groups of humanity less human, and therefore less deserving of freedom. In this way, the idea of freedom for all humans could be formally left untouched, but at the same time it was sarcastically eroded by a discriminating rhetorical trick. Modern slavery was justified in this way, and in the twentieth century, the discriminating rhetoric of "subhuman beings" reached its devastating climax in the Nazi propaganda, which led to such horrible manifestations as the concentration camps.[79]

(c) The shift of emphasis from external freedom to inner freedom that we observed had possibilities and downsides.

- Inner freedom could much more easily be universalized than external freedom. *All* humans, even externally enslaved persons, could learn to live the Stoic inner freedom. The concept of inner freedom, developed at a time when the cosmos had replaced the polis as the frame of reference for the individual, comprised a universalistic tendency.

---

at the end of the *Respublica*, admits that our (genetic) predisposition plays a role. But for him, this does not restrict our capability of free decision-making and our responsibility for our acting. How is this possible? Plato uses a trick. He relocates our free decision-making into the pre-existence of our soul; before we enter the earthly life we freely choose which *daimon* will dominate our life (ὑμεῖς δαίμονα αἱρήσεσθε. πρῶτος δ' ὁ λαχὼν πρῶτος αἱρείσθω βίον ᾧ συνέσται ἐξ ἀνάγκης, Resp. 617e). Therefore, our acting is still based on our free decision-making. If our soul chose to get this or that predisposition (*daimon*) that limits or facilitates our acting on earth, this acting is still the result of our free choice. See 617e, 619c.

79. For an atrocious example, see, e.g., the book *The Revolt against Civilization: The Menace of the Under Man* (1925) by the racist anthropologist Lothrop Stoddard, which led to the Nazi's *Untermensch* propaganda. In 1930, Alfred Rosenberg, in *Der Mythos des 20. Jahrhunderts*, promptly quoted Stoddard (214).

- The opposite is true about the Greek concept of external freedom, which was highly particularistic. An exclusive circle of males, with polis citizenship, appropriate education and financial means,[80] enjoyed this privilege.
- The reduction to inner freedom included a resignation: the admission that external freedom for all was unachievable. External freedom for all was not even conceptualized in theory, let alone tried in praxis.
- The concept of external freedom in a polis had a communal aspect. This kind of freedom required the biotope of a community. The individualistic conception of inner freedom, on the contrary, lost this aspect. The loss could yield very tangible consequences:

(d) One of Epictetus' goals was freedom from caring feelings and pity. These feelings should be only superficial, not touching your inner self. Epict., *Enchir.* 16, reads like this:

> Beware that you be not carried away by the impression (φαντασία) that the (suffering) person (in front of you) is in the midst of external ills (ἐν κακοῖς τοῖς ἐκτός) ... Do not, however, hesitate to sympathize with him (συμπεριφέρεσθαι; to go about with him) so far as words go, and, if occasion offers, even to groan (συνεπιστενάξαι) with him, but be careful not to groan also in the center of your being (ἔσωθεν).

Epictetus was a former slave. He would have looked at the external ills of his former colleagues in the same way.

However, the criticism needs to dig deeper. (e) Aristotle was optimistic about being able to make ontological statements about freedom. He thought he could detect freedom in a person as a natural quality: somebody is free by nature (φύσει) or not.

Not only in Alcidamas' or Seneca's eyes[81] is this problematic, also from a postmodern perspective, especially a constructivist point of view. In a constructivist view, ontological statements about freedom, human dignity or the equality of human beings are not possible. There is nothing to *detect* in the ontic reality that could be called freedom. Freedom, dignity and

---

80. See Aristotle's deliberations about freely giving (ἐλευθεριότης) out of one's means as appropriate behavior of a free man (ἐλευθέριος; *Nic. Eth.* 1119b, 22ff). The expression "education fitting for a free man" (ἐλευθέριος παιδεία) can be found in Plutarch, *Non posse suaviter* 1094d, 9; *Consol.* 113a, 2; Diodorus Siculus, *Biblioth.* 13.27.2.2; Lucian, *Anach.* 20.25; Aelius Aristides, *Kata ton exorchoumenon* 414.15. See also Alcaeus, *Frg.* 72.12; Clement of Alexandria, *Strom.* 3.4.30.1.

81. See above n. 35.

equality, on the contrary, need to be *ascribed* and attributed to the human being by means of performative language, and this constructed new reality will give birth to behavioral consequences.[82]

(f) The concept of freedom of decision and its correlate of an almost unlimited pedagogical optimism, combined with an optimistic anthropology, would have caused the apostle Paul to shake his head; it made Augustine frown. For the apostle, followed by Augustine, the natural human being is a sin-dominated old Adam, lost forever, who needs to be changed radically by God into a new human being (e.g., Rom 6). For the Christian apostle, pedagogics was meaningless without this divine "new creation" and the infusion of the divine Spirit. Augustine later taught that hereditary sin burdens humans so heavily that, de facto, their God-given freedom of decision only leads to evil. Only through God's grace can the freedom of choosing the good be regained.

In modern times, the idea of freedom of decision was, of course, problematic for extreme deterministic thinkers such as the Marquis Pierre-Simon Laplace, but also problematic for Kant, whose *Reine Vernunft* was not able to state that the human will is free. Only Kant's *Praktische Vernunft* came up with the solution that a person can feel free once he or she is confronted with an absolute claim of a law or another imperative.

Today's neurobiological results, at least at first glance, seem to question the existence of a free will (experiments by Libet and others):[83] What we *perceive* as our free decision to execute an action actually does not seem to be a free decision, because the brain activity that corresponds to this perception is *preceded* by another brain activity (unnoticed by us) that allegedly generates the action *before* we feel that we decide to perform this action. In other words, decisions are made in an unconscious "readiness potential" of our brain *before* we ourselves think we make a free decision. Who is steering this "readiness potential" in our brain? Athena (Homer, *Il.* 1.216)? A demon (Aeschylus, *Agam.* 1505)? Not the entity that we perceive as our Ego on the level of our consciousness?[84]

However, it is still our brain that makes the decision. At least experiments such as Libet's did not deal a decisive blow to the concept of free will—for several reasons. (a) Libet and his successors were wrong in presupposing that humans are able to exactly state the moment in which they feel

82. Cf. further, e.g., Lampe, *New Testament Theology in a Secular World*, 10, 37–41, 90.

83. Cf. further, e.g., Lampe, *New Testament Theology in a Secular World*, 37–41; Soon et al., "Unconscious Determinants of Free Decisions in the Human Brain."

84. For the Ego as a construct of our brain, see Lampe, *New Testament Theology in a Secular World*.

they make a decision. Experiments by Keller and Heckhausen proved the contrary.[85] (b) Theoretically the conscious perception of making a decision might be simply a delayed feedback of what—as an act of free will—unconsciously goes on earlier. The concepts of "free will" and "consciousness" are not necessarily tied together. (c) But we do not even need this theoretical crutch. More recent experiments refuted that Libet and others succeeded in separating the actual decision-making from the perception of making a decision. An experimental study by C. S. Herrmann and his team demonstrated that the unconscious brain activity in the "readiness potential" does not prepare a *specific* movement; it only *generally* prepares the motoric apparatus for action. Thus, it does not determine which one of two alternative motoric actions a subject chooses.[86] In other words, the actual decision to move my right finger to a spot above my eyebrow is not made in the "readiness potential." Thus, our everyday notion that a volitional act—the "self" feels in this act that it makes a decision—induces a motoric action has not become obsolete. The discussion is not over.

Bibliography

Arnim, Hans von. "Die stoische Lehre von Fatum und Willensfreiheit." Vienna: Phil. Gesellschaft University of Wien, 1905.
Bleicken, Jochen. *Staatliche Ordnung und Freiheit in der römischen Republik*. Frankfurter Althistorische Studien 6. Kallmünz: Lassleben, 1972.
Bobzien, Susanne. *Determinism & Freedom in Stoic Philosophy*. Oxford: Clarendon 1998.
———. "The Inadvertent Conception and Late Birth of the Free-Will Problem." *Phronesis* 43 (1998) 133–75.
Dihle, Albrecht. *Die Vorstellung vom Willen in der Antike*. Sammlung Vandenhoeck. Göttingen: Vandenhoeck & Ruprecht 1985.
Hahmann, Andree. *Was ist Willensfreiheit?: Alexander von Aphrodisias über das Schicksal*. Marburg: Tectum, 2005.
Herrmann, C. S. et al. "Analysis of a Choice-Reaction Task Yields a New Interpretation of Libet's Experiments." *International Journal of Psychophysiology* 67/2 (2008) 151–57.
Keller I., and H. Heckausen. "Readiness Potentials Preceding Spontaneous Motor Acts: Voluntary vs. Involuntary Control." *Electroencephalogrphy and Clinical Neurophysiology* 76 (1990) 351–61.

85. Keller and Heckausen, "Readiness Potentials Preceding Spontaneous Motor Acts." Subjects sometimes even identified the moment of their conscious decision-making as being 800 ms *after* the corresponding movement of the body had begun.

86. Herrmann et al., "Analysis of a Choice-Reaction Task." Differently, however, Soon et al., "Unconscious Determinants," who, on the basis of the brain activity preceding the awareness that a decision is made, claim to be able to predict about 60% of the outcomes of simple choices.

Klein, Richard, ed. *Prinzipat und Freiheit*. Wege der Forschung 135. Darmstadt: Wissenschaftliche Buchgesellschaft, 1969.

Knuuttila, Simo. *Emotions in Ancient and Medieval Philosophy*. Oxford: Clarendon 2004.

Lampe, Peter. *From Paul to Valentinus: Christians at Rome in the First Two Centuries*. Edited by Marshall Johnson. Translated by Michael Steinhauser. Minneapolis: Fortress, 2003.

———. *New Testament Theology in a Secular World: A Constructivist Work in Philosophical Epistemology and Christian Apologetics*. Translated by Robert L. Brawley. London: T. & T. Clark, 2012.

———. *Die stadtrömischen Christen in den ersten beiden Jahrhunderten: Untersuchungen zur Sozialgeschichte*. 2nd ed. WUNT 2/18. Tübingen: Mohr, 1989.

Levy, Andrew. *The First Emancipator: Slavery, Religion, and the Quiet Revolution of Robert Carter*. New York: Random House, 2007.

Mayr, F. "Das Freiheitsproblem in Platons Staatsschriften." PhD diss., University of Vienna, 1960.

Nestle, Dieter. *Eleutheria: Studien zum Wesen der Freiheit bei den Griechen und im Neuen Testament, I: Die Griechen*. HUT 6. Tübingen: Mohr/Siebeck, 1967.

Pohlenz, Max. *Griechische Freiheit: Wesen und Werden eines Lebensideals*. Heidelberg: Quelle & Meyer 1955.

Raaflaub, Kurt. *The Discovery of Freedom in Ancient Greece*. Translated by Renate Franciscono. Chicago: University of Chicago Press, 2004.

———. *Die Entdeckung der Freiheit*. Vestigia 37. Munich: Beck 1985.

———. "Freiheit in Athen und Rom." *Historische Zeitschrift* 238 (1984) 529–67.

Rosenberg, Alfred. *Der Mythos des 20. Jahrhunderts: Eine Wertung der seelisch-geistigen Gestaltenkämpfe unserer Zeit*. Munich: Hoheneichen, 1941.

Sampley, J. Paul. "Paul and Frank Speech." In *Paul in the Greco-Roman World: A Handbook*, edited by J. Paul Sampley, 293–318. Harrisburg, PA: Trinity, 2003.

———. "Paul's Frank Speech with the Galatians and the Corinthians." *Philodemus and the New Testament World*, edited by J. T. Fitzgerald et al., 295–321. Novum Testamentum Supplements 111. Leiden: Brill, 2004.

Schlier, H. "ἐλεύθερος κτλ." In *TWNT* 2 (1935) 484–500

———. "ἐλεύθερος κτλ." In *TDNT* 2 (1964) 487–502.

Schmitz, Otto. *Der Freiheitsgedanke bei Epiktet und das Freiheitszeugnis des Paulus: Ein religionsgeschichtlicher Vergleich*. Neutestamentliche Forschungen, 1. Reihe, Paulsstudien 1. Gütersloh: Bertelsmann, 1923.

Shotter, D. C. A. "Principatus ac Libertas." *Ancient Society* 9 (1978) 235–55.

Soon, C. S. et al. "Unconscious Determinants of Free Decisions in the Human Brain." *Nature Neuroscience* 11 (2008) 543–45.

Sorabji, Richard. *Emotion and Peace of Mind: From Stoic Agitation to Christian Temptation*, Oxford: University Press 2000.

Stoddard, Lothrop. *The Revolt against Civilization: The Menace of the Under Man*. New York, 1923.

Wirszubski, Chaim. *Libertas als Politische Idee im Rom der Späten Republik und des Frühen Prinzipats*. Darmstadt: Wissenschaftliche Buchgesellschaft, 1967.

———. *Libertas as a Political Idea at Rome during the Late Republic and Early Principate*. Cambridge: Cambridge: University Press. 1960.

Zöller, Rainer. *Die Vorstellung vom Willen in der Morallehre Senecas.* Beiträge zur Altertumskunde 173. Munich: Saur, 2003.

7

Two Meanings of Freedom in the Eastern Patristic Tradition

Cyril Hovorun

What in English is called *freedom*, in the eastern Patristic thought had a variety of meanings denoted by different Greek words. The modern concepts of freedom are notably different from the relevant notions developed in the classical or Patristic era. The modern ones largely own to the era of Reformation and Enlightenment. However, their birth dates much earlier than sixteenth–seventeenth centuries. They go back to the times of Augustine who was probably the first who introduced the thematology of freedom to the western intellectual discourse. In parallel to Augustine and the western thought that followed him, the Greek-speaking Christian east developed its own tradition of the idea of freedom. As with Augustine, so with the Greek Fathers, the idea of freedom was not much rooted in the Antiquity. It was elaborated in the contexts of various Christian theological controversies. The Christian east, however, started paying attention to the concept of freedom significantly before Augustine.

Augustine's deliberations on freedom were an extrapolation of his polemics against Manichaeans and Pelagians. In the East, the concept of freedom was developed as a reaction to Gnosticism, Arianism, and, significantly later, Monothelitism. Christianity from its earliest age emphatically operated such categories as sin and evil. In the context of the Greek thought, this provoked discussions on the origins and nature of evil. Some tried to explain why evil is possible, by introducing a dualistic distinction between existent good and supposedly existent evil. They corresponded the former with spirit and the latter, with matter. Both good and evil appeared to be existent on the same ontological level and, according to the popular Gnostic belief, originated from different deities. Christianity, however, did not accept such an interpretation of origins of evil. Instead, Christian theologians found the reason why evil is possible, in freedom. It is because of their freedom that humans sin and therefore give space for evil in the world. Thus, the idea of freedom was developed by the early Christian thought as an alternative to the dualistic idea of evil as a substance which has its own nature and exists equally with the good substances.

In the fourth century, the idea of freedom was developed further. In his polemics against Arius, Athanasius of Alexandria suggested to distinguish between the world created by God Father, and the Son born by the Father, by engaging the idea of God's will. Indeed, although the Father, according to Athanasius, is a beginning for both the Son and the world, he brings them to existence in different ways. The Son was pre-eternally born without mediation of Father's will, while the world was created with mediation of God's will. Thus the concept of will helped Athanasius to distinguish birth from creation, the origins of the Son from the origins of the world. The Cappadocians who faced a more radical version of Arianism represented by Eunomius, had to do with the anthropological issues, including the issue of human freedom and will. They inherited from the Antiquity the idea that freedom and will are integral parts of the human intellect, νοῦς. Therefore, when exploring the intellectual capacities of human nature, they touched on the issues of will and freedom as well.

A clear distinction between the intellect, will, and freedom was made in the course of the theological controversy concerning the number of wills in Christ. This controversy started in the beginning of the seventh century and ended up with the decisions of the sixth ecumenical council convened in Constantinople in 670. The main point of the controversy was whether Christ had one will which belonged to his person, or two wills that should be ascribed to his two natures. The former understanding, which later on would be called Monothelitism, was rejected by the Church. The teaching on two wills in Christ was established as a doctrine of the Church, while the teaching on one will was condemned at the ecumenical council. During the controversy, theologians, among whom the most prominent one was Maximus the Confessor, developed far more advanced concepts of human will and human freedom than they were known in the pre-Christian Antiquity.

As regards the notion of freedom, in the Patristic era it became understood in two ways. Each way was denoted by a specific term. Both terms can be translated into English with the word "freedom." Original Greek words, however, were different from each other and denoted distinct aspects of freedom.

The first Greek term to be considered is τὸ αὐτεξούσιον.¹ This is a composite word consisted of two words: αὐτός—"self," and ἐξουσία—"power," "authority." In the context of the Patristic usage of the word, it can be better translated as 'self-control'. In the Patristic tradition, τὸ αὐτεξούσιον meant a faculty of the human nature that allows humans to behave in a non-determinable way. No one can force a human being to do something which he or she, either consciously or unconsciously, does not decide to do. This kind of freedom also allows a human being to choose between multiple options. This faculty is innate in every human being. It cannot be eliminated from the human nature.² Neither can it be reduced, nor corrupted. It can change only if the human nature changes. This however would mean that human nature ceased to be human. Neither sin nor death can deprive a human being of this faculty. Athanasius of Alexandria asserts that humans never cease to be free, whether they choose for good or for evil.³ A person may have τὸ αὐτεξούσιον as a potentiality, not fully distinguishable or visible. This potentiality, however, can be always activated. Owing to the potentiality of τὸ αὐτεξούσιον, a human being can at any moment choose the way he or she should act. This choice can relate either to the moral issues or to the decisions we make in everyday life, like what apple to pick up, green or red.

In the Greek Patristic thought, there were other terms synonymous to τὸ αὐτεξούσιον. They also express freedom as an ability of the intellect to control human nature and will. Among these terms are τὸ ἑκούσιον (voluntary), τὸ ἡγεμονικὸν (having control, authority over something) etc.

Τὸ αὐτεξούσιον is not a biblical term. A similar, yet not exactly the same word occurs in Paul: "But the man who has settled the matter in his own mind, who is under no compulsion but has control over his own will (ἐξουσίαν δὲ ἔχει περὶ τοῦ ἰδίου θελήματος), and who has made up his mind not to marry the virgin—this man also does the right thing" (1 Cor 7:37). Basil of Caesarea, when explaining what sort of control or power Paul means, uses the word τὸ αὐτεξούσιον: "Each of us has received from God self-control (τὸ αὐτεξούσιον), as saint Paul says in the first [epistle] to

---

1. See Hederich, "αὐτεξούσιος—qui sui juris, sive suae potestatis est 2) de imperio infinito, de regno, cujus potestas nullis limitibus circumscribitur; αὐτεξουσιότης—libera potestas" (*Lexicon Graeco-Latinum et Latino-Graecum*, part I, 155); Sophocles: "free will, freedom of the will" (*Greek Lexicon of the Roman and Byzantine Periods*, 278); Stephanus: "sui potestatem habens, qui sui juris est et suae potestatis"; it is "quod Latini Theologi Liberum arbitrium appellarunt." Corresponding Latin terms are "licentiosus, emancipates" (*Thesaurus Graecae Linguae*, vol. 2, cols. 2502–3).

2. See Basil of Cesarea, *Enarratio in prophetam Isaiam* 1.45.4–5 (all Greek texts hereafter are quoted according to the *Thesaurus Linguae Graecae* [TLG]).

3. *Contra gentes* 4.12-5 [TLG].

Corinthians."[4] Thus Basil tries to connect the concept of τὸ αὐτεξούσιον as it was developed already by the fourth century, with the Scripture and particularly the Paul's ideas about freedom.

At the same time, the term τὸ αὐτεξούσιον had a strong connection with the political and social realities of the Greco-Roman world. It was borrowed from the vocabulary of antiquity. In this vocabulary, it meant power, including an absolute power of gods or political rulers.[5] In this sense, the word is used, for instance, by Philo of Alexandria who speaks of τὸ αὐτεξούσιον as an absolute power of God.[6] In Philo, it is synonymous with the adjective "autocratic."[7] The word also means free in the sense 'not slave' and thus signifies social status of a free person.[8]

From the classical Greek tradition, the word τὸ αὐτεξούσιον was imported to the early Christianity. The Christian authors, however, elevated the meaning of τὸ αὐτεξούσιον to a more personal level. They also linked it to the matters of salvation. Clement of Alexandria, for example, insists that humans are free (αὐτεξούσιος) in a sense that they can be saved only through their free choice (ἑκουσίῳ προαιρέσει). Salvation, thus, can be adopted only in an intelligent way and consciously (ἐμφρόνως, οὐκ ἀφρόνως).[9] To do something which would engage intellect, means for Clement en-activation of freedom, because, following the ancient tradition, he regarded freedom as a feature of the human intellect. According to Clement, we can do good things only when our freedom is involved. As he puts it, the wisdom of the Father persuades our freedom (τὸ αὐτεξούσιον) to do good things.[10] Thus God offers us salvation not without our consent, but always through our freedom. Freedom is an instrument, a conductor, and a mediator for our salvation. Without it, salvation cannot be adopted by an individual. Other Christian authors took up these ideas of Clement. In particular, Irenaeus of Lyon affirms that every human being is free, and God only advises him how to act, without violating his freedom.[11]

---

4. *Homilia de virginitate* 2.40–41 [TLG].

5. See Hederich: "de imperio infinito, de regno, cujus potestas nullis limitibus circumscribitur" (*Lexicon Graeco–Latinum et Latino–Graecum*, part I, 155)

6. *Plant* 46.4 [TLG].

7. Αὐτεξουσίῳ καὶ αὐτοκράτορι βασιλείᾳ (*Heres* 301–302 [TLG]).

8. See in Diodorus Siculus: τούς τε γὰρ αἰχμαλώτους ἀφῆκεν αὐτεξουσίους χωρὶς λύτρων (*Bibliotheca historica* 14.105.4.1–2 [TLG]). Sophocles defines it as "one's own master, free agent" (*Greek Lexicon of the Roman and Byzantine Periods*, 278).

9. *Paedagogus* 1.6.33.3–4 [TLG].

10. *Stromata* 5.13.83.5.1–2 [TLG].

11. *Adversus haereses* 21.17-9 [TLG].

The Fathers considered freedom as a distinctive feature of the human nature. Together with intellect, freedom distinguishes humans among the rest of the created world. For instance, Nemesius of Emessa affirms that the difference between humans and animals is that the former, unlike the latter, act in a rational and free way (ἐλεύθερον καὶ αὐτεξούσιον).[12]

Among the Fathers of the Church, Cappadocians are distinguished for their concern about the issue of freedom. This issue was dear to them and they significantly contributed to its development. Thus, according to Gregory of Nazianzus, human beings have been created free. They cannot be subordinated to nobody and nothing except God and the law of his commandments.[13] Basil of Caesarea develops this idea further. God created us free and not subordinated (ὑπεξούσιος).[14] Freedom is good, therefore, being free is far better than being subordinated (τὸ αὐτεξούσιον τοῦ ὑπεξουσίου βέλτιον).[15] Gregory of Nyssa considers the ability of a person to control himself (τὸ αὐτεξούσιον) as an ultimate kind of freedom (ἀκρότατον τῆς ἐλευθερίας εἶδος).[16] He, thus, recognises that there are different kinds of freedom. He calls one of them τὸ αὐτεξούσιον, and the other, ἐλευθερία.

The Cappadocean Fathers liked to emphasise that freedom is an honour of human beings. For Gregory of Nazianzus, for instance, freedom is something that humans should be proud of. It is their honour (τιμή).[17] According of Basil of Caesarea, freedom is a Godlike part of the human soul (τὸ αὐτεξούσιον τὸ θεοειδὲς τῆς ψυχῆς).[18] To Gregory of Nyssa, man is honoured by freedom, which makes him enjoying beatitude.[19] Gregory goes as far as affirming that human beings, owing to their freedom, are equal to God (ἰσόθεον γάρ ἐστι τὸ αὐτεξούσιον).[20]

As it was mentioned earlier, freedom, for the Fathers, is the only possible solution to the problem of the origins of evil. For them, evil is possible because humans have free will. It is freedom and not God that is the cause of evil, as Gregory of Nyssa explains.[21] For Basil of Caesarea, it is through their

---

12. *De natura hominis* 2.650-6 [TLG].
13. *De pauperum amore* 35.892.10-12 [TLG].
14. *Adversus Eunomium* 29.697.44-5 [TLG].
15. *Adversus Eunomium* 29.697.39-40 [TLG].
16. *Orationes viii de beatitudinibus* 44.1300.34-36 [TLG].
17. *In theophania* 36.324.21 [TLG].
18. *Sermo de contubernalibus* 30.817.2-5 [TLG].
19. *De mortuis non esse dolendum* 9.54.2-3 [TLG].
20. *De mortuis non esse dolendum* 9.54.10 [TLG]; see also *De creatione hominis sermo primus* 29a.6-7 [TLG]: προαίρεσιν ἡμῖν αὐτεξουσίαν ἐμβαλεῖ τὴν δυναμένην ποιῆσαι ἡμᾶς ὁμοιωθῆναι θεῷ.
21. *Oratio catechetica magna* 5.126-30 [TLG].

freedom that humans choose either good or evil.[22] Freedom is like a scale, which can move equally to good and to evil.[23] Freedom by its nature can be a beginning and a root of sin (ἀρχὴ γὰρ καὶ ῥίζα τῆς ἁμαρτίας τὸ ἐφ᾽ ἡμῖν καὶ τὸ αὐτεξούσιον).[24] The Cappadoceans regarded freedom as an instrument. As created by God, freedom cannot be bad *per se*. At the same time, it can be abused and turned into a "weapon of sin" (ἁμαρτίας ὅπλον), using the words of Gregory of Nyssa.[25]

It is common to believe in our days that freedom is closely linked to will. Sometimes people even do not draw distinction between them. They also like to attribute them to the personality of a human being, as person's individual features. In the early patristic era these two concepts were also regarded as similar or even identical. The early Christian theologians, in conformity with what they inherited from the Antiquity, often considered freedom and will as features of the human intellect, νοῦς. At some stage, however, the Fathers started drawing distinction between the two notions, and the distinction of both of them from the intellect. It was distinction and not separation though. The Fathers did not cease to believe that freedom, will, and intellect are closely related to each other and are inseparable features of the human spiritual nature. They started putting emphasis on distinction between the three categories during the controversy over the wills of Christ in the seventh century. In the course of the controversy, they demonstrated that the will is an attribute of nature, and not of *persona* or hypostasis. It should be said here that intellect, νοῦς, was attributed to the human nature, and not *persona*, as well.

The seventh-century controversy was not focused on the human will in general. Its main focus was on the problems of composition of the incarnate God, Christ. It was Christological controversy, and not anthropological. The Fathers were interested in the anthropological agenda as far as it helped them to solve Christological issues. Simultaneously, they made solutions achieved during the Christological debate applicable to anthropology. Therefore, in the course of the Monothelite controversy, it was established first that Christ's human will belongs to his human nature. When applied to the human nature in general, this Christological conclusion meant that in case of humans, their will is an attribute of their nature as well.

In the seventh century, a close association of will and nature was expressed in many ways. Thus, they are linked indissolubly, as it was declared

22. *Adversus Eunomium* 29.660.39–41 [TLG].
23. *Sermones de moribus a Symeone Metaphrasta collecti* 32.1120.12–14 [TLG].
24. *Quod deus non est auctor malorum* 31.332.44–45 [TLG].
25. *In Ecclesiasten* 5.428.1–12 [TLG]; see also *In Ecclesiasten* 5.301–2 [TLG].

in the letter of Pope of Rome Agatho: "The human will is *natural*, and who refuses the human will in Christ, without only the sin, does not recognise that he has a human soul."[26] Will was also regarded a property of the human nature. For instance, Pope Martin affirms: "The *energeia* and will of our essence constituted its (= of the essence) natural property."[27] Similar statement occurs in Maximus the Confessor who refers to Christ: "The Fathers decreed that . . . the same person <of Christ> is visible and invisible, mortal and immortal, corruptible and incorruptible, touchable and untouchable, created and uncreated. And according to the same reverent way of understanding, they also correctly taught that there are two wills of one and the same person."[28] Maximus goes even further in equating will to property. Will, to him, is not only a "natural power" (φυσικὴ δύναμις), but also an "intellectual desire" (λογικὴ ὄρεξις) of soul.[29] Therefore, such faculties of "intellectual soul" as willing, thinking, etc., are indissolubly linked to each other so that "we consider when willing, and in considering, we choose the things which we would. And when willing we also inquire, examine, deliberate, judge, are inclined toward, elect, impel ourselves toward, and make use of a thing."[30]

After having attributed will to the nature, the theologians faced the problem, how then the will could be free, given that the nature is not free. There was a common belief that whatever belongs to the nature is tied by necessity. The person could not choose what would belong to his nature. Therefore, everything natural was associated with necessary; it was not free. The theologians were helped to solve this problem by the idea inherited from the classical thought, that will is closely connected with intellect. Therefore, even though will is a faculty of nature, it remains free, because of its intellectual character. Will is a free movement of human intellect, as it is stated in the definition which Maximus the Confessor ascribes to Clement of Alexandria: "Will is a self-controlled movement (αὐτεξούσιος κίνησις) of the autocratic intellect."[31] John of Damascus repeats this definition in other

---

26. Naturalis est humana voluntas, et qui voluntatem humanam in Christo abnegat absque solo peccato eum nec habere humanam animam confitetur (Riedinger, ed., *Acta Conciliorum Oecumenicorum, series secunda*, [ACO$_2$] II^1 77$^{26-27}$).

27. ACO$_2$ II^1 406$^{12-13}$; 407$^{11-12}$; see also Pope Agatho: Quidquid ad proprietates naturarum pertinet, duplicia omnia confitetur (ACO$_2$ II^1 67^{26}–68^1).

28. *Disputatio* PG 90, 300^b [TLG].

29. *Disputatio* PG 90, 293^b [TLG].

30. *Disputatio* PG 90, 293^{b-c} [TLG].

31. *Fragmentum* 40 [TLG]; this definition does not occur in any of the works of Clement.

words: "Will is a natural, intellectual, self-controlled, and aspiring movement of intellect (νοῦς)."[32]

Although will was attributed to the common human nature, it is an individual that operates it. Therefore, freedom of the natural will is rooted in the freedom of *persona*. It should be noted here that the patristic concept of *persona* must not be confused with the modern ideas of personhood. In the Patristic era, the theologians identified *persona* with a particular and concrete being, hypostasis. The distinction between *persona* and nature was taken from the Aristotelian categories of particular and common essences (οὐσίαι). Therefore, *persona* was believed to be a particular instance of the common human nature. In terms of theology and philosophy of that time, everything that humans share in common, belongs to the human nature. Whatever belongs to a particular individual only, is his hypostatic or personal feature. Therefore, to say that will belongs to the human nature would mean that it is shared by all human beings, and not by only one person.

Although the Fathers drew distinction between nature and hypostasis, they never separated them, as both categories apply to the same human being which always remains one and undivided. Distinction between *natura* and *persona* suggested nothing more but different outlooks at the same human being. The two categories describe the same undivided human being in terms of commonality of all human beings, and particularity of any given person. The category of nature would describe what a single human being has in common with other humans, while the category of *persona* would describe what makes a human being different from others. Maximus the Confessor suggested to understand the two categories as a common meaning of any given human being, and a particular way of existence of the common human nature respectively. He interpreted human nature as λόγος, i.e. nature's principal, meaning, or definition. *Persona* for him was a "mode of existence" (τρόπος τῆς ὑπάρξεως), which is a concrete way of realization of a nature. When applied to the category of will, this distinction would mean that, on the on hand, the human will is common to all people and characterises their λόγος, *i.e.* human nature. On the other hand, a concrete way of actualisation of the will depends on the person. All human beings have will, yet each of them has it personalised. Maximus characterises the common will with expression "to will simply" (ἁπλῶς θέλειν).[33] The way that any concrete person uses his will, corresponds for Maximus to the question "how to will" (πῶς θέλειν).[34] It does not mean that a person has two wills, natural

---

32. *Institutio elementaris* 10.2 [TLG].
33. *Disputatio* 292b.
34. *Disputatio* 292d–293a.

and personal. These characteristics provide two outlooks at the same natural will. They describe how the same will that belongs to the nature, works when operated by any given human being.

The way someone operates his natural will is always free. Freedom secures a unique way of realization of one's natural will. Two persons who share the same will, practice it in each one's personal way. This is possible because they are free. Without freedom, they would exercise their wills in a very similar manner. The freedom to actualize one's will should be described by the term τὸ αὐτεξούσιον. This is the same kind of freedom which was described by the earlier Fathers as the honour of human beings that makes them equal to God.

As it was said, τὸ αὐτεξούσιον is a kind of freedom that is innate in all human beings. This does not mean however that it is always easy for humans to do whatever they decide. They experience tragic difficulties in acting according to their choice, when they choose to do good, as described by apostle Paul: "I don't understand what I am doing. For I don't do what I want to do, but instead do what I hate" (Rom 7:15). Inability to act according to one's decision is caused by sin, as Paul clarifies: "I have the desire to do what is right, but I cannot carry it out. For I don't do the good I want to do, but instead do the evil that I don't want to do. But if I do what I don't want to do, I am no longer the one who is doing it, but it is the sin that lives in me" (Rom 7:18–20). Ability of humans to act without any difficulty according to their decision, especially when they about to choose good, in the Greek Christian tradition is called ἐλευθερία (adjective ἐλεύθερος).

This word has been borrowed from the classical tradition where it was widely spread. Searching through the TLG database returns over 14,000 matches for the root ελευθερ-. The word originates from ἔρχομαι (ἐλεύθω) = "come" and etymologically denotes someone *qui vadit, quo vult*.[35] It means being not slave or dependant on any alien circumstance or force. In the classical world, the word denoted mostly free civil status of a person. It meant someone who is not slave.[36] Apart of its mainly social connotations, in the period of Antiquity the word also had psychological implications. Thus, Euripides speaks of being free of fear: ἐλεύθερος φόβου. Moral implications of the term were furthered in Stoicism. For instance, Epictetus who many

---

35. See Hederich, *Lexicon Graeco-Latinum*, part I, 263. Other correspondent Latin terms are *liber, non servus; liber, immunis, liberatus; liberalis, ingenuus, generosus*.

36. See Liddell, Scott, Jones, *Greek–English Lexicon*, 532; Frisk, *Griechisches etymologisches Wörterbuch*, vol. 1, 490–91; Stephanus, *Thesaurus Graecae Linguae*, vol. IV, 722; Chantraine, *Dictionnaire étimologique de la langue grecque. Histoire des mots*, vol. 1, 336.

believe to be early Christian stoic (AD 55–135) defines ἐλευθερία as person's freedom from sin, fear, sadness, and anxiety.[37]

It is hardly possible to find any moral aspect in the word "freedom" as this word appears in the Septuagint. The word is used here mostly in the political and social senses implying free citizens, free women, etc.: Deut 21:14; Jdt 16:23; 1 Macc 10:33; 2 Macc 9:14; 1 Macc 15:7; 1 Macc 2:11; Lev 19:20; 3 Macc 3:28; 1 Esd 4:53; 1 Macc 14:26; Sir 33:26; 1 Esd 4:49; Sir 7:21; Jas 1:25; 2:12; 1 Kgs 20:11; 3 Macc 7:20; Prov 25:10; Sir 10:25; Neh 13:17; Deut 15:12–13; 1 Macc 12:30; Job 39:5; Jer 41:14; Exod 21:2, 5; Ps 87:5; Exod 21:26–27; 1 Kgs 20:8; Jer 41:9, 16; Deut 15:18; Eccl 10:17; 2 Macc 2:22; 2 Macc 1:27. As an exception may be considered a passage from 4 Macc 14:2: "O reason, more royal than kings and freer than the free (ἐλευθέρων ἐλευθερώτεροι)!" This passage, however, reflects the developments of the notion in the wider hellenistic thought, which enforced the idea of freedom with psychological implications.

The situation changes dramatically in the New Testament. Paul develops a complex theology of freedom and builds it on the traditional meaning "not being a slave": "Scripture says that Abraham had two sons, one by the slave girl and one by the freewoman. The son of the slave girl came to be born in the way of human nature; but the son of the freewoman came to be born through a promise. There is an allegory here: these women stand for the two covenants. The one given on Mount Sinai—that is Hagar, whose children are born into slavery; now Sinai is a mountain in Arabia and represents Jerusalem in its present state, for she is in slavery together with her children. But the Jerusalem above is free (ἐλευθέρα), and that is the one that is our mother" (Gal 4:22–26). He concludes: "So, brothers, we are the children not of the slave girl but of the freewoman" (Gal 4:31). Freedom that Christians may enjoy is a gift both of Christ (Gal 5:1) and the Spirit (2 Cor 3:17). It is applicable not only to humans, but to the entire created world: "The creation itself would also be set free from slavery to decay in order to share the glorious freedom of God's children" (Rom 8:21).

The posterior patristic thought appears to be coherent with the New Testament tradition. Among the first Christian theologians, Ignatius passes from the literal understanding of slavery and freedom to a more profound one, which implies not only the ties he was bound with after his arrest, but also the resurrection in Christ.[38] Ignatius makes it clear that he implies a sort of freedom which is better than freedom from slavery or imprisonment

---

37. *Dissertationes ab Arriano digestae* 2.1.23–25 [TLG].
38. *Epistulae vii genuinae* 4.4.3.1–5 [TLG].

(κρείττονος ἐλευθερίας ἀπὸ Θεοῦ τύχωσιν).³⁹ For Ignatius who was a free Roman citizen, to be arrested and brought from Antioch to Rome under custody, was a striking experience of enslavement. From this experience which was new to him and unknown to many Christian fellows whom he addressed, he developed the idea of inner freedom which is independent from whether a person is slave or enjoys freedom of citizenship, whether he has a wide multiplicity of choices or the range of his choices is dramatically reduced. Justin explains further what sort of freedom it is. It is deliverance from any sort of passion, while submission to the passion, to him, is an ultimate slavery.⁴⁰ Clement of Alexandria associates freedom with ability to see spiritually without any obstacle.⁴¹ This kind of freedom, for the early Christian Fathers, can be achieved only through virtues, when one chooses the way of life. For instance, one of the most popular Christian writers of the early period, Hermas, when addressing the issue of freedom says that freedom in the Christian sense can be achieved only by keeping the commandments of the Lord.⁴²

From the fourth century onward, the issue of freedom in the sense of ἐλευθερία is in the focus of the moral teaching of the Fathers. This kind of freedom, which as it was said earlier means person's liberation from passions and sins, becomes an essential Christian virtue and goal. Gregory of Nyssa, for instance, puts freedom in one line with grace, life, consolation, and immortality.⁴³

The Fathers accentuated that this kind of freedom cannot be achieved through human efforts only. Its ultimate source is the Triune God. A person can be free only in Christ, as John Chrysostomos affirms summarizing both the New Testament and the Patristic traditions: "There is no free <person> but one who lives in Christ" (οὐκ ἔστιν ἐλεύθερος ἀλλ' ἢ μόνος ὁ Χριστῷ ζῶν).⁴⁴ The direct result of Christian faith is freedom from the law of sin. It is also freedom from fear, as Gregory of Nazianzus states (εἴμ' ἐλεύθερος φόβου), apparently recalling Euripides.⁴⁵ The difference here between Gregory and Euripides is that the former puts Christian faith as an obligatory condition of liberation from any sort of fear. Christ is the archetype of any person who is free from his fears, sins, and passions. Humans can be free only through

---

39. *Epistulae vii genuinae* 7.4.3.2–3 [TLG].
40. *Fragmenta operum deperditorum* 15.1–2 [TLG].
41. *Paedagogus* 1.6.28.1.7–8 [TLG].
42. *Pastor* 55.1,2.6 [TLG].
43. *Ad Eustathium de sancta trinitate* 3,1.12.1–4 [TLG].
44. *Ad Theodorum lapsum* 5.16–17 [TLG].
45. *Christus patiens* 1807 [TLG].

participation in the prototypical freedom of Christ who is 'the only free' (ὢν ἐλεύθερος μόνος),⁴⁶ as Gregory of Nazianzus specifies.

The Fathers also acknowledged the role of the Holy Spirit in the liberation of humans from sin and death. It is through the Spirit that people become free in Christ. In the Patristic tradition, the Holy Spirit is often associated with freedom.⁴⁷ In this sense, Gregory of Nazianzus speaks about "freedom of grace" (ἐλευθερία τῆς χάριτος).⁴⁸

In conclusion, the concept of freedom in the eastern Patristic tradition had a variety of meanings, which are, on the one hand, similar and, on the other hand, quite different. There can be distinguished two key meanings, which can be expressed by the words τὸ αὐτεξούσιον and ἐλευθερία. Both terms go back to the antiquity, where they expressed approximately the same thing, freedom as a social status, belonging to the class of citizens and not to the class of slaves. At the same time, already in antiquity the two words had some versatility of use. Τὸ αὐτεξούσιον additionally meant power and control. It is notable also that τὸ αὐτεξούσιον, unlike ἐλευθερία, does not have Biblical roots.

The two words were borrowed by the Fathers who used them to mark two distinct aspects of freedom. Thus, the early Christian theologians assigned τὸ αὐτεξούσιον to a sort freedom which is given to everybody regardless of how unworthy he or she is. On the contrary, ἐλευθερία is a kind of freedom which is to be sought and struggled for. The former is innate into human nature, while the latter is a gift of God.

These two aspects of freedom, however different they may be, should not be separated from each other. The freedom as τὸ αὐτεξούσιον, on the one hand, has its teleological meaning in the freedom as ἐλευθερία. This means that the freedom from sin and death is the purpose of human life. In order to achieve this purpose, a person needs to choose good through the efforts of his or her will which is en-activated by τὸ αὐτεξούσιον. On the other hand, the freedom in a sense of ἐλευθερία is possible only because humans have τὸ αὐτεξούσιον. Someone can become free in Christ only when he or she freely chooses for that.

Freedom in both senses presupposes some control of the human intellect over the nature. In the case of τὸ αὐτεξούσιον, this control is rather potential, while in the case of ἐλευθερία, it is actualized. The two aspects of freedom interact between each other, always with the mediation of will. The power of τὸ αὐτεξούσιον, having been en-activated by the intellect, engages

---

46. *Christus patiens* 1523 [TLG].
47. See, for instance, Basil. *De spiritu sancto* 28.69.24–26 [TLG].
48. *Epistulae* 79.13.5 [TLG].

the will to act. When the will is directed to good, a person may achieve beatitude of freedom from evil. At the same time, this would be impossible through human efforts only. The assistance of God's grace is an obligatory requirement for any human to become truly free. It is with the co-activity of the Holy Spirit that the human intellect chooses for good, the human will finds strength to move to the ultimate Good, which is God, and a person eventually achieves freedom in Christ. This co-activity of a human being and God in the eastern tradition is called "synergy" (συνεργία). This notion is crucial for understanding how the process of salvation was seen by the eastern Fathers. Human freedom in this process plays a key role, being a partner and co-worker of the divine Freedom.

Bibliography

Chantraine, Pierre. *Dictionnaire étimologique de la langue grecque: Histoire des mots.* Vol. 1. Paris: Klincksieck, 1990.

Frisk, Hjalmar. *Griechisches etymologisches Wörterbuch.* Indogermanische Bibliothek. Heidelberg: Winter, 1960.

Hederich, Benjamin. *Lexicon Graeco-Latinum et Latino-Graecum.* Rome: S. Congreg. de Propaganda fide, 1832.

Liddell, Henry George, Robert Scott, and Henry Stuart Jones. *Greek-English Lexicon.* Oxford: Clarendon, 1962.

Riedinger, Rudolf. *Acta Conciliorum Oecumenicorum.* Series secunda. Berlin: de Gruyter, 1984–.

Sophocles, E. A. *Greek Lexicon of the Roman and Byzantine Periods: From B.C. 146 to A.D. 1100.* 3rd ed. New York: Scribner, 1888.

Stephani, Henrici. *Thesaurus Graecae Linguae.* Reprint, Graz: Akademische, 1954.

8

Freedom, Sin, and Evil
Lutheran Meditations

RISTO SAARINEN

Lutheran and Catholic views of freedom stem from Augustine's teaching. Both churches subscribe to the anti-Pelagian views of the church father, but they interpret these views somewhat differently. The standard Catholic teaching holds that all sins are due to the consent of the person. This means that the harmful desire, concupiscence, is not yet in itself sin. Only when the person willingly consents to this desire, he or she becomes a sinner. Lutherans, however, traditionally teach that the presence of harmful desire already qualifies the person as sinner. This means that Christians remain sinners. A Christian is "righteous and sinner at the same time" (*simul iustus et peccator*).[1]

This Lutheran doctrine is ecumenically problematic. Modern branches of Protestantism, such as Methodists and Pentecostals, tend to emphasize sanctification and do not find the view of remaining sinfulness very helpful. The Roman Catholic Church, on the other hand, wants to preserve the view of human freedom present in the idea of consent. The Lutheran doctrine of "righteous and sinner" does not seem to pay attention to human responsibility in avoiding sinfulness. Some progress has, however, been reached in

---

1. For the history and theology of this doctrine, see Schneider and Wenz, eds., *Gerecht und Sünder zugleich?*

ecumenical negotiations. In their *Joint Declaration on the Doctrine of Justification*, Catholics and Lutherans declare that this issue should no longer be regarded as church-dividing. The churches hold together that Christians are "not exempt from a life-long struggle against the contradiction to God within the selfish desires of the old Adam."[2] But this statement does not yet settle the questions of freedom and sin in detail. In order to clarify the issues, the German *Ökumenischer Arbeitskreis* published an in-depth analysis of the doctrine of Christian sinfulness.[3]

Some of the most surprising claims of this analysis are made by Wolf-Dieter Hauschild. His study, "The Formula 'Righteous and Sinner at the Same Time' as Element of the Doctrine of Justification—a Discovery of the Twentieth Century,"[4] investigates the use of this formula from the Reformation to the present day. Hauschild comes to the surprising conclusion that the formula did not play any role before the year 1903. In that year the Catholic scholar Heinrich Denifle published his polemical biography of young Luther, in which he accused the young monk of sexual sins. Denifle considered Luther's view of justification to be an excuse and legitimation of those sins. A person can remain in sin, although he is justified.

Understandably, the Protestant scholars set out to refute Denifle's interpretation. In their defense they developed a new view of young Luther who struggles with his introspective, quilty conscience. The formula *simul iustus et peccator* which could be found in Luther's newly edited monastic texts provided a theological background structure for the Protestant scholars.[5] Their anti-Denifle portrayal of sin-conscious Luther, reminiscent of Kierkegaard and Schopenhauer, contributed to the new identity of Lutheranism.

Hauschild does not, however, pay much attention to the immediate historical impact of the Reformation. He neglects the basic fact that influential figures like Calvin took over Luther's view of remaining sin and made it a standard Protestant view. In spite of this flaw Hauschild's thesis—that *simul iustus et peccator* is a discovery of the twentieth century—remains a productive error which manages to shed light on some puzzles of modern theology and its understanding of freedom and sin.

In the following I will use the historical thesis as a springboard towards contemporary problems regarding human freedom under the condition of

---

2. "Joint Declaration on the Doctrine of Justification," §28.

3. Schneider and Wenz, eds., *Gerecht und Sünder zugleich?* For the critics' view, see 23–24.

4. Hauschild, "Die Formel Gerecht und Sünder zugleich."

5. Ibid., 317–20.

being under sin or bondage. First, I show in which sense Hauschild is right. Second, I also argue that he is wrong insofar as the Reformation period with its immediate historical impact is concerned. Third, I will apply the Reformation discussions to some modern issues, namely, the Darwinist view of human freedom and bondage and the post-Kantian problems of evil. Although the modern world no longer deals with the concept of sin, the problems of natural determinism and natural and unnatural evils continue to haunt people. Does the Lutheran tradition of being righteous and sinner offer any resources in dealing with such modern issues of freedom and bondage? Let it be immediately stated that my reflections are based on family resemblances rather than strict connections. The paper therefore has more the character of meditations than systematic arguments in favor of a given position.

The So-Called Lutheran Paul

Luther studies changed radically in the beginning of the twentieth century. The new generation of scholars of the so-called *Lutherrenaissance* no longer regarded Luther as the father of orthodoxy, but as an individual struggling with his conscience. Karl Holl formulated this turn as follows: "Luther comes to the issues which the great way-opener Paul had foreseen and for which first Søren Kierkegaard in the nineteenth century, as well as Nietzsche, have shown an understanding."[6] While Kierkegaard himself did not regard Luther as capable of true existential dialectics, many eminent scholars of the twentieth century regarded Luther as a soulmate of Kierkegaard.[7]

Because of this individualist and existential paradigm, the permanent struggle with sin and its consequences received new importance for Luther scholars. The new editions of Luther's early lectures coincided with this interest. As these lectures contain Luther's theology of the cross and witness to his personal development in terms of a permanent struggle between flesh and spirit, they provide a great number of suitable prooftexts for Kierkegaard-minded scholars.

One important side-effect of this trend was the emergence of the so-called "Lutheran Paul," an exegetical straw man invented by scholars like W. G. Kümmel and Krister Stendahl for the purpose of arguing that historical Pauline theology deviates considerably from the doctrinal premises of Lutheranism as they are spelled out in the tradition of Lutheran Paul.

6. Holl, *Gesammelte Aufsätze I*, 24–25.

7. See Bornkamm, *Luther im Spiegel der deutschen Geistesgeschichte*, 95–100, 114–17, 156.

Contrary to the alleged conviction of Lutheran scholars, modern exegetes offered a new perspective in which it was claimed that Paul did not teach the permanent sinfulness of the Christian ego in Rom 7. Moreover, Paul had a robust conscience which did not proceed to introspection in a Kierkegaardian manner, as the Lutherans allegedly believed.[8]

The basic problem of this exegetical debate was and still is that the "Lutheran Paul" was to a large extent a product of the early twentieth-century scholarship which connected Lutheran theology with the existential–Kierkegaardian struggle. I have discussed this exegetical debate elsewhere in more detail.[9] The twentieth-century individualist paradigm of the "Lutheran Paul" tends to interpret Rom 7 in terms of complete powerlessness. According to this paradigm, the apostle Paul wants to do good but cannot do it; thus he is "weak-willed" in the classical, Aristotelian (*Nicomachean Ethics*, book 7) sense of repeatedly acting against his own better judgment. If this were true, *simul iustus et peccator* would mean a permanent failure to do good. This was not, however, Luther's own view.

Augustine, Luther, and Calvin

The theological roots of Reformation debates on freedom are found in Augustine's theology, in particular in his diverse statements concerning the relationship between the harmful desires and the state of sinfulness. One can distinguish between different phases in Augustine, depending on how he understands Paul's conflict in Rom 7.[10]

The young Augustine reads Rom 7 as a description of the powerlessness of a worldly person without grace. After 411, however, Augustine revises his view and thinks that the speaker of Rom 7 is the Christian apostle. This speaker cannot do good in a perfect and successful manner, because the repugnancy of remaining sin always effects some impurity. But the apostle can nevertheless achieve good in an external manner. In his late debates with Julian, Augustine increasingly moves towards claiming that the remaining concupiscence almost compulsively causes some sinfulness in the actions of Christians. Although Augustine never quite moves to

---

8. See Westerholm, *Perspectives Old and New on Paul*. The portrayal of the "Lutheran Paul" as a straw man captures my reflections in Saarinen, "The Pauline Luther and the Law."

9. Saarinen, "How Luther Got Paul Right"; and Saarinen, "The Pauline Luther and the Law."

10. I have used Timo Nisula's dissertation: *Augustine and the Functions of Concupiscence*. Elements of this periodization are also found, e.g., in Markschies, "Taufe und Concupiscentia bei Augustinus."

teaching the irresistibility of concupiscence, he nevertheless moves towards claiming that the presence of concupiscence is already in itself sin.

Already in his *Lecture on Romans* (1515/16) Luther comes to the conclusion that the old Augustine who writes against Julian is the definitive doctrinal authority. With respect to the interpretation of Romans 7 and the issue of Christian sinfulness this means that even exemplary Christians like Paul are to be called sinners, since concupiscence contaminates all their actions. The act of consent is, therefore, not an adequate criterion of a person's sinfulness: the mere presence of concupiscence is sufficient to qualify the person as a sinner.[11]

This does not mean, however, that the Christian would be entirely powerless. In Luther's view, apostle Paul is an example of strong-willed Christian. In spite of the remaining sin, he can do good, although not in a perfect and pure manner. The apostle's complaint does not, therefore, pertain to his existential powerlessness, but to the remaining gap between doing good in an externally satisfactory manner and doing good in a perfect and pure manner. At least since Rudolf Hermann, Luther scholars have seen that this is the historical meaning of *simul iustus et peccator*.[12] Luther thus takes over the view of late Augustine, as the church father spells it out especially in his late writings against Julian. The difference to the Roman Catholicism is found in the notion of consent: for Luther, the sin remains in the person even when there is no consent to sin.

Given that this is the correct interpretation of *simul iustus et peccator*, Hauschild's thesis meets serious problems. The Reformation period and later Protestantism received the view expressed in Luther's phrase, taking it to mean that the remaining concupiscence present in all Christians is sufficient to qualify them as sinners, although many good Christians may be able to follow God's will relatively well in their external actions. This result already takes away the edge of Denifle's criticism of Luther: both Lutherans and Catholics can interpret Paul and Augustine as saying that externally good actions are possible. At the same time this view also separates Luther from the existential anguish of Kierkegaard and Schopenhauer as well as from the straw man erected by modern biblical scholars. The justified sinner may have a fairly robust conscience and strong will: he is not perfect, and he is aware that he is therefore sinful, but he may nevertheless trust in God's promises and lead a moderately good life.

Hauschild focuses on the nineteenth century and deals with earlier history only in passing. Although Luther's *Lectures on Romans* were only

---

11. Luther, *Werke, Weimarer Ausgabe*, vol. 56, 339-47.
12. See Hermann, *Luthers These "Gerecht und Sünder zugleich."*

discovered and edited in Karl Holl's times, the description of remaining sinfulness outlined above can be found in other widely distributed treatises, for instance in Luther's writing *Against Latomus*.[13] According to this description, the sinfulness of the justified Christian means that the harmful desire of concupiscence continues to color all his or her actions, leaving them imperfect in some sense. Being righteous and sinner means a permanent struggle, but it does not imply a complete failure in this struggle. The fact of struggle is already sufficient to qualify the person as sinner. Therefore, the demarcation line of sinfulness is not drawn according to the capacity of consent or will-power. Even a person who is relatively free or strong-willed in the sense that she can successfully rule over her own actions nevertheless remains a sinner since sin inevitably in some way colors her actions, keeping her in the struggle. This understanding of "righteous and sinner at the same time" was not only discovered but was also widespread during the Reformation period, as we can see, for instance, from John Calvin's *Institutio*.[14]

In this Protestant anthropology of sin, the root of the problems does not lie in the harmful desire as such, but it is the "flesh" which remains the seat of sinful passions and desires. The harmful emotions cannot be eradicated or moderated in the Stoic manner, because they exemplify the rule of the flesh in the current life. Augustine's fundamental problem with Pelagius and Julian was his growing conviction that the carnal aspect of humanity cannot be abolished in this life. Luther radicalized this feature in his early denials of human freedom; although Melanchthon and Calvin may have moderated this radical view to an extent, later Protestantism basically followed Luther's view of "righteous and sinner at the same time." The twentieth-century Protestantism gave new and exaggerated interpretations of this view, connecting it with introspective conscience, complete powerlessness and Kierkegaardian existentialism. Hauschild is to be commended for seeing this development. But the Protestant theology of *simul iustus et peccator* cannot be reduced to its twentieth-century outlook.

Given this, we nevertheless need to ask a broader systematic question regarding the issue of "righteous and sinner at the same time". Does it really matter whether we understand this doctrine to mean (a) that Christians are powerless but not simply evil or (b) that Christians are strong-willed but not simply virtuous? For both (a) and (b) assume a dualistic anthropology in which two opposing principles, spirit and flesh, remain in the state of struggle. The modern world, however, no longer presupposes such over-personal metaphysical principles which determine both the external

---

13. See Saarinen "The Pauline Luther and the Law."
14. Calvin, *Institutio christianae religionis* (1559), 3, 3, 10–13.

range and internal quality of a person's will-acts. If this is true, the picture of struggle, be it under the guise of (a) or (b), has lost its validity.

In the following it will be argued that the idea of over-personal forces ruling over a person's destiny has not disappeared. The biological worldview employs a complex notion of over-personal forces. Moreover, modern deliberations on the problem of evil continue to ask after the status of various natural forces manifesting themselves in illnesses and catastrophes. A person often remains in constant struggle with such forces. In this struggle the modern person asks, among other things, whether these forces are inevitably to be regarded as being morally neutral, as Immanuel Kant and many others claim. While the natural forces are not produced by an intentional will, they nevertheless seem to contribute to our understanding of goodness, freedom and evil. Although our struggle with natural forces is not essentially a struggle between good and evil, it may, therefore, be connected with it. Given this, there may be some applications of Lutheran theology of evil, sin and freedom to the modern issues.

The Biological World-View

In 1859, Darwin published his *Origin of Species*, a work that has contributed to the modern discussions on human freedom and determinism probably more than any other single book. The twentieth-century breakthroughs in molecular biology have led to the so-called evolutionary synthesis in which Darwin's claims regarding populations and natural selection are connected with the workings of the genes and their DNA.[15]

The evolutionary synthesis contains many anthropological views which continue to challenge theologians and philosophers. One very basic view which does not require deeper scientific details is the distinction between genotype and phenotype. All individuals are permeated by a material dualism in which two principles are operative.

First, the properties of my body represent the phenotype resulting from the random combinations of my genes during the procreation. My life is dependent on this phenotype in a complex manner. I have not chosen this body, but my responsible actions can influence its development and the utilization of its capacities. The phenotypical body is in this sense my *oikos*, the temple in which I can reside and with regard to which I may have some, though limited, freedom.

---

15. The scientific basis of following reflections can be found in any biological textbook; I have used Mayr, *This Is Biology*; and Mayr, *What Evolution Is*.

Second, I carry with me the heritage of my genotype, a complex mess of nuclear acids from which an expert can read not only my personal properties, but also an astonishing variety of more and less successful features of my ancestors since Adam and Eve, maybe even since the earlier days of creation. The duality of genotype and phenotype is in many ways startling and fascinating. All individuals carry within themselves the history of much of the human race. Some inherited features stemming from the distant past may suddenly and dramatically become operative and end the life of the phenotype without any possibility of delay or negotiation.

This means that the phenotype, the somatic body, is also in itself deeply dualistic. On the one hand it is the temple of the spirit: education and cultural progress can take place when the human body works properly. On the other hand, the phenotype is also a body of death: since it constantly manifests the underlying genotype, it remains at the mercy of this broader inheritance. Through this genotype all past generations, dead so long ago, continue to contribute to the present success of the *ego*, the individual here and now.

At the same time it is also true that each genotype is different and unique, since the enormously long, though finite, series of genetic recombinations (in the so-called meiosis) as well as some mutations have made each DNA unique. The gigantic information available in our nuclear acids thus both constitutes our individuality and makes us all children of Adam and Eve. The good works of our ancestors do not, however, help us since their achieved properties cannot be genetically transmitted. Their virtues remain in their proteins which do not have a feedback to the nuclear acids.

One of the doctrines of Darwinism states that neither the species nor the gene but the individual phenotype is the object of natural selection. In this sense the "nature and destiny of man" always remains the nature and destiny of one individual: every nature is different due to its underlying differences in the nuclear acids, and the destiny of each phenotype is unique, given the unique time and place it occupies in its environment. Since the process of natural selection is directed towards individual phenotypes and presupposes a constant production of differences, Darwinism is a highly individualistic world view. At the same time each individual is deeply dependent on the past generations, since they have constituted the genotype on which the properties of this individual depend.

When Paul, Augustine, and Luther describe the human existence as an existence between the flesh and the spirit, these two terms refer to the larger over-personal spheres in which the individual here and now participates. The individual, that is, the bodily phenotype or the somatic *ego*, is something distinct from both of these spheres. Although the body remains deeply dependent on the flesh, an individual body only represents a particular phenotype of the larger anthropic nature. The flesh thus operates like a genotype, a pool of anthropic nature from which the bodily individual becomes differentiated. Reading Rom 7 and 8 from this perspective can lead to meditations which resemble Luther's view of *simul iustus et peccator*, the view of such bondage under larger powers which does not rule out individual particularity, responsibility and freedom. Let me emphasize that the following meditation is strictly systematic, not historical.

Romans 7–8 and Naturalism

In Rom 7:17–18 Paul argues that the lack of goodness in his action is not due to his *ego*, but to the sinful flesh still dwelling in him. He thus experiences a dualism in which a deeper, over-personal power has a hold over Paul's actions. The *ego* may denote either the past or the present Paul (or the typological person discussed); the verses describe, in terms of *a posteriori* reflection, the curious experience that the actions of this *ego* were to a large extent determined by another, over-personal power (sin, flesh) that dwells within the *ego* (*all hê oikousa en emoi*, 7:17). This experience of something bigger influencing the decisions of the somatic *ego* offers a certain parallel to the modern postulate of genotype.

The expression of Rom 7:18: "For I know that nothing good dwells within me, that is, in my flesh" is nevertheless *prima facie* different from the evolutionary anthropology, as the genotype is not merely the source of defects, but also of all useful capacities. In 7:18, the somatic *oikos* is the *ego*, the phenotypic person who experiences that there are other inhabitants within it, and that they are not good. A Darwinist might now remark that the genotype contains a resource of the past which has survived through the millennia of natural selection. How can it be that it contains nothing "good"?

To respond to this remark, a slightly different systematic angle is needed. The so-called "naturalistic fallacy" formulated by G. E. Moore states that we cannot infer the nature of "goodness" from the natural properties of usefulness, economy, or some other beneficial property available for us.[16] If natural selection in the long run favors some genotypic variants (exemplified by certain individual phenotypes) because of their circumstantial adaptive abilities, we cannot infer that they would be "good" in the fundamental

---

16. For Moore's fallacy, see, e.g., Copleston, *A History of Philosophy*, vol. 8, 409–11. Theissen, *Biblischer Glaube in evolutionärer Sicht* (ET = *Biblical Faith*), also offers many noteworthy thoughts belonging to this context.

sense of *agathon*. The favored variants are not selected because of their inherent goodness but because of the adaptive capacity related to their accidental environment. In this—very systematic and ahistorical—sense there is "nothing good... in my flesh." This flesh, the genotypic nature, is a result of long natural selection, but the selection has not made it good. Evolution does not guarantee perfection or even progress; it only brings about a capacity to stay above the threshold of survival.

As Rom 8:6 famously points out, both flesh and spirit have their relative or particular reasons (*phronêma*). The *phronêma* of the flesh is related to death and remains hostile to God (8:5–8) because it focuses on the natural course of things. A naturalist must presuppose the death of all organisms and leave God out of his methodological *phronêma*. Let it be added that Paul's view of naturalism may be too negative in his "flesh discourse"—some other New Testament passages could balance this—but this is mainly because he wants to highlight the nature of sinful bondage as something which is both personal and collective-overpersonal at the same time. Although an individual may have a good phenotype and a strong will, being therefore successful in some undertakings, the over-personal rule of the flesh continues and makes the person sinful in this sense.

In this very peculiar manner there is an argumentative parallelism between Luther's view of permanent bondage under sin and the 20th-century evolutionary synthesis. The twentieth century invented a new anthropological dualism, that of phenotype and genotype. Also the Darwinian dualism has its existential side: even healthy people can today become anxious of their possible genetic disorders which may darken their life or the life of their children. In genetic analysis they also need to deal with their parents and ancestors in new, unprecedented ways.

What is the role of freedom in view of such issues? The propagation of complete powerlessness will not help: we need to fight all diseases, and we must also take care of others who do not have resources to fight them. At the same time, it would be illusory to claim that we could repair the genetic disorders and help the evolution to reach its peak. There is no such peak in evolution, but the struggle continues. A strong will and a certain realism are thus needed. There is, consequently, a certain parallelism to the strong-willed behavior of the apostle Paul in Rom 7–8.

The Experience of *Malum*

Is there a connection between the natural, biological powers which produce health and illness and the deeper philosophical problem of evil? After Kant, the normal answer has been negative. Good and evil are produced by the intentional acts of willing agents; natural forces do not, therefore, relate to the problems of good and evil.

Ingolf Dalferth has, however, argued that evil should not be identified in terms of the agent's intention but in terms of the experience of the patient or recipient. Suffering and illness are for Dalferth examples of evils which lie beyond all evil intention but are nevertheless experienced as evils.[17] In some sense the naturalistic fallacy works in one direction only: there is no natural goodness, but there may well be natural evil. We have seen that the elaboration of sin and human bondage in Paul, Augustine and Luther described above points towards a view in which evil is natural and resides in the over-personal constitution of the flesh, whereas goodness is non-natural and can only be given with the spirit.

Dalferth argues that this Kantian definition of evil in terms of intentional will is much too narrow and much too simple. For him, the most adequate criterion of evil is the experience of the patient, the victim or the person who suffers. If it is the case that the victims of accidents, or cancer patients, or other suffering persons experience that something bad or evil has happened to them, although there is nobody to blame, then the suffering in question is related to evil and raises the problems related to evil.

Both the strength and the weakness of Dalferth's position are obvious. Its strength lies in its realism. When people are facing a serious accident, a fatal illness or a death of their loved one, they feel and experience that something bad has happened to them. Accidents and deaths seldom produce moral elevation. They rather draw people to vicious circles of hopelessness, deprivation and social problems. Although these events do not include evil intentions or wicked persons, they are connected with some inherent *malum*, badness or evil that results from them. It is therefore honest and realistic to say that they are not merely natural processes (which they of course also are, and this should be said), but they involve an experience of evil.

The weakness of this position is that it substantiates the evil in a way which runs contrary to our modern thinking habits. It seems strange to say that, in addition to some evil human intention, there exists evil which encounters us in accidents and illnesses. This sounds dualistic and it may lead to a postulate of the existence of personal evil forces. The following meditation does not want to proceed to that direction, but it argues that the discussion on natural evil resembles the historical problem of remaining

---

17. Dalferth, *Leiden und Böses*. The following description is based on this popular book. For the broader academic treatment, see Dalferth, *Malum*.

sin. There is some *malum* which affects the existence of all people, however strong-willed and good-willed they may be.

Dalferth does not want to claim that all suffering is evil or that suffering and evil are synonymous. Both phenomena are extremely complex and, in addition, our experience of them is complex and individually different. Dalferth underlines the non-dualistic point that evil remains secondary and parasitic to positive creation: illness requires body, accidents presuppose the normal course of things, and so on. What he wants is, however, to take seriously the experience of the one who suffers: this experience of *malum* cannot be taken away by simply saying that nobody intends, or has intended, to harm you.

Coping with Suffering

If this analysis is right, we should ask: how can we cope with the suffering and *malum* that surrounds us even in the relative protection of welfare society? The first option is (1) the project of rationalizing evil by means of writing an intellectual theodicy. My interest here does not, however, proceed to that direction. I am primarily interested in the concrete wrestling of a relatively free and strong-willed person with the powers of sin and evil, including the evil produced by natural forces. I admit that the procedure of writing intellectual theodicy may also serve as a behavioral strategy in this wrestling, but my primary attention is devoted to other strategies.

(2) The catastrophies of nature are often met in terms of progressive optimism, an attitude which aims at upholding the Kantian view of real evil as being always intentional. According to this view, natural adversitites are connected with our ignorance and lack of political good will. When we educate ourselves and next generations, we can overcome all adversities and make the world progressively a better place. Progressive idealism may the most viable political and social strategy of coping with suffering. Education and welfare may not provide the last answers to the problem of suffering, but they may be the adequate political tools at our disposal. In this sense the Enlightenment project of progressive optimism continues to be a successful way to counteract the adversities produced by natural forces. It makes ample use of the available resources of will-power and freedom.

There seems to be, however, a limit beyond which this strategy is no longer helpful. Extreme forms of progressive optimism lead to something like omnipotence delusion. In such extreme form people assume that some intentional agent is behind all problems and adversities and can be held responsible for them. Through naming the responsible persons the society can take care of all kinds of badness. The strategy thus broadens the Kantian idea of evil will lurking behind all kinds of *malum*. Thus one can say that the Foreign Ministry of Finland was responsible for various failures related to the Tsunami catastrophe, or that the American gun laws were responsible for the rampant shooting in the campus. If all guns were prohibited, no shooting could occur. Or, if everybody carried a gun, rampant shooters would be effectively silenced by other gunmen and gunwomen.

The delusion of omnipotence is, of course, a philosophically naive position. It is encouraged by the mass media which wants to personify the responsibilities of all kinds of occurrences that remain beyond human control. According to this line of thought, all adversities, even illnesses and natural catastrophes, are results of human failure and could be controlled by heroic responsibility. If we lived healthily, illnesses could be prevented. If we would take good care of the mother Earth, no natural catastrophes would occur, especially if we could also construct effective warning systems. We often courageously think that we can carry the responsibility of everything in our lives, and in the lives of others. But we are not as omnipotent as we would like to be and progressive optimism does not always work. For this reason, we also need other strategies of coping with pervasive suffering.

(3) A very traditional behavioral strategy of coping with suffering is the act of complaining to God. Amidst of suffering, religious persons (sometimes even less religious persons) doubt God's goodness and omnipotence, complaining: where were you? Why did you let this happen? Philosophically speaking, such complaints to a divine *ombudsman* may sound primitive and strange. If there is a God, God would most likely not be there to satisfy our wishes regarding the course of life. This strategy has, however, been meaningfully and even successfully employed by Christians in various times. The Lutheran bishop of Helsinki, Eero Huovinen, has on two occasions presented such a lament in Finnish mass media. The first time was after the Estonian boat catastrophe, the second time after the tsunami catastrophe. When asked by the journalists to give a religious or theological explanation, Huovinen meditated on the absence and sleep of God and presented critical questions towards God.[18]

Some devout Finnish Christians were irritated and claimed in the public that the bishop should be the advocate of God and not criticize God's purposes. But others were consoled to hear that the bishop sided with other puzzled individuals who lamented and complained. Thus the public complaint became a part of national sorrow enactment, *Trauerarbeit*, and served a therapeutic purpose. It is not the task of human being to explain

---

18. These are collected in a Finnish volume: Huovinen, *Käännä kasvosi, Herra*.

the suffering, but to complain in solidarity with other suffering people. It is therapeutically important that there is an address of this complaint, an *ombudsman* who receives the complaint of suffering consumers. It would have been ridiculous from the bishop to utter quasi-scientist or quasi-philosophical sentences, such as: tsunami results from the movement of continental plateaus, or: suffering is the price we pay of human freedom. The attitude of progressive optimism should also, at least for some proper time, yield to the phenomenon of massive sorrow.

(4) Another behavioral strategy is also therapeutic and Christian, but more sophisticated than the strategy of complaining. This strategy has been called nihilodicy or the questioning of evil by Tuomo Mannermaa. In a very personal book he tells how he survived the crisis caused by his wife's death.[19] The burden of suffering and questions of theodicy surrounded the life of the widower. In the depressive moments he very consciously focused his mind on the remaining good objects and meditated on their lasting value. This meditation evoked the argument of nihilodicy, asking why evil and suffering cannot get hold of all things in life, but some objects remain good and beautiful, staying thus outside of the grasp of *malum*.

Focusing on objects and meditating the argument of nihilodicy slowly helped the widower out of the depression. The argument of nihilodicy has some important rational sides, for instance the idea that evil has no autonomous being but it can only corrupt the good objects in a parasitic manner. Another rational side is given in the observation that the good objects, like the garden, four seasons, streams and other scenes of water, animals, children, good art, starlit night, and the laws of the universe (such lists are a permanent topos in consolation literature), are lasting whereas adversities come and go in a contingent manner.

Fundamentally, however, the force of object therapy does not reside in rational arguments, but in the mediation from the good objects to the suffering soul. The good objects can communicate some of their goodness to the spectator and thus very slowly heal the soul. At the same time, the argumentative side of questioning evil helps the person to continue to focus his or her mind on the good objects. The object therapy need not be religious; the suffering person may simply meditate the good objects of her garden as alternatives to the chaos. Boethius has forcefully elaborated philosophical object therapy in his *Consolation of Philosophy*, a work which combines our first and fourth way of coping with *malum*.

---

19. Mannermaa, *Pieni kirja Jumalasta*.

Suffering and Virtue

It is vitally important to realize that the four strategies outlined above do not manifest complete powerlessness or lack of freedom, but they are accompanied with endurance and strong will in facing the suffering. For the most part, they are no philosophical solutions of the problem of evil, but exemplify the practical opportunities available to a person in a difficult situation. They formulate a particular kind of *simul*, namely, the simultaneity of suffering and virtue. If *simul iustus et peccator* describes the being of a Christian, the simultaneity of suffering and virtue captures the doing of many Christians and other people of good and robust will. It is a doing in which activity stems from passivity and passion.[20]

In sum, the problem of evil and the different ways of coping with suffering exemplify the human encounter with over-personal forces. Philosophers may debate whether such forces are a *malum* or simply natural obstacles, but I have been siding with Dalferth's claim that they are at least experienced as *malum*. The experience we have is an experience of continuous struggle or wrestling. Encountering such force and struggling with it requires a robust will and a strong personal character.

There is thus a certain parallelism between the will-power needed to struggle with sin and the will-power needed to cope with suffering. The struggles of Paul and Luther thus have their non-identical but sufficiently identifiable counterparts in the struggles of modern human beings. Paradoxically, the bondages of sin, obstacles and *malum* give testimony to our personal freedom: in encountering adversities, more intentional effort is needed than in everyday life in general. In this sense personal freedom not only co-exists with the various bondages which shape our lives; it even emerges from the struggle with them. Such coincidences of suffering and virtue in the realm of doing may even point towards deeper theological simultaneities of being.

Summary

Risto Saarinen discusses the historical meaning and contemporary significance of the Reformation doctrine of "righteous and sinner at the same time" in its relationship to freedom. He argues that this doctrine does not mean a permanent inability to do good, but rather a lasting struggle in which good actions can only take place with difficulty. Saarinen regards that the exegetical paradigm of "the Lutheran Paul" often exaggerates the lack of freedom in

---

20. For a broader treatment of similar topics, see Stoellger, *Passivität aus Passion*.

Christian life. After a historical presentation of the views of Paul, Augustine, Luther and Calvin the article looks briefly at the anthropology of modern evolutionary theory. The contemporary distinction between the individual phenotype and the inherited collective pool of genes, the genotype, bears some resemblance to the dualistic anthropologies of the Christian tradition and their understanding of freedom. Saarinen also discusses the various experiences of evil and coping with suffering, arguing that they exemplify a simultaneity of suffering and virtue in which our freedom can be manifested. The picture of struggle between different forces connects Pauline and Lutheran anthropology with the natural sciences and the modern problems of evil.

Bibliography

Bornkamm, Heinrich. *Luther im Spiegel der deutschen Geistesgeschichte: Mit ausgewählten Texten von Lessing bis zur Gegenwart*. 2nd ed. Göttingen: Vandenhoeck & Ruprecht, 1970.
Calvin, John. *Institutio christianae religionis* (1559). Corpus reformatorum 30. Braunschweig: Schwetschke, 1864.
Copleston, Frederick. *A History of Philosophy*. Vol. 8. New York: Image 1985.
Dalferth, Ingolf U. *Leiden und Böses: Vom schwierigem Umgang mit Widersinnigem*. Leipzig: Evangelische Verlagsanstalt 2006.
———. *Malum: Theologische Hermeneutik des Bösen*. Tübingen: Mohr/Siebeck 2008.
Hauschild, Wolf-Dieter. "Die Formel Gerecht und Sünder zugleich als Element der reformatorischen Rechtfertigungslehre—eine Entdeckung des 20. Jahrhunderts." In *Gerecht und Sünder zugleich? Ökumenische Klärungen*, edited by Theodor Schneider and Gunther Wenz, 303–49. Dialog der Kirchen 11. Göttingen: Vandenhoeck & Ruprecht, 2001.
Hermann, Rudolf. *Luthers These: "Gerecht und Sünder zugleich."* Gütersloh: Gütersloher, 1930.
Holl, Karl. *Gesammelte Aufsätze zur Kirchengeschichte I: Luther*. Tübingen: Mohr/Siebeck, 1927.
Huovinen, Eero. *Käännä kasvosi, Herra*. Helsinki: WSOY, 2005.
"Joint Declaration on the Doctrine of Justification." In *Growth in Agreement*, edited by J. Gros et al., 2:566–79. Geneva: World Council of Churches, 2000.
Luther, Martin. *Werke, Weimarer Ausgabe*. Vol. 56. Weimar et al., 1883–.
Mannermaa, Tuomo. *Pieni kirja Jumalasta*. Helsinki: Kirjapaja 1995. (English translation in preparation.)
Markschies, Christopher. "Taufe und Concupiscentia bei Augustinus." In *Gerecht und Sünder zugleich? Ökumenische Klärungen*, edited by Theodor Schneider and Gunther Wenz, 92–108. Dialog der Kirchen 11. Göttingen: Vandenhoeck & Ruprecht, 2001.
Mayr, Ernst. *This Is Biology—The Science of the Living World*. Cambridge, MA: Belknap, 1997.
———. *What Evolution Is*. New York: Basic Books 2002.

Nisula, Timo. *Augustine and the Functions of Concupiscence*. Supplements to Vigiliae Christianae 116. Leiden: Brill, 2012.

Saarinen, Risto. "How Luther Got Paul Right." *Dialog* 46 (2007) 170–73.

———. "The Pauline Luther and the Law: Lutheran Theology Re-engages the Study of Paul." In *The Nordic Paul: Finnish Approaches to Pauline Theology*, edited by Lars Aejmelaeus and Antti Mustakallio, 90–116. Library of New Testament Studies 374. Edinburgh: T. & T. Clark 2008.

Schneider, Theodor, and Gunther Wenz, eds. *Gerecht und Sünder zugleich? Ökumenische Klärungen*. Dialog der Kirchen 11. Göttingen: Vandenhoeck & Ruprecht, 2001.

Stoellger, Philipp. *Passivität aus Passion*. HUT 56. Tübingen: Mohr/Siebeck, 2010.

Theissen, Gerd. *Biblical Faith: An Evolutionary Approach*. Translated by John Bowden. Philadelpia: Fortress, 1985.

———. *Biblischer Glaube in evolutionärer Sicht*. Munich: Kaiser, 1984.

Westerholm, Stephen. *Perspectives Old and New on Paul: The "Lutheran Paul" and His Critics*. Grand Rapids: Eerdmans 2004.

9

Protestant Concepts of Freedom and Their Foundations in Biblical Traditions

Friederike Nüssel

"Church of Freedom"—this is the motto used by the Evangelical Church in Germany for the reform process it has set in motion. The reforms had been considered necessary by several parties for a number of years, to prepare the member churches for the challenges of the next decades in terms of contents and structures.[1] The term "freedom" highlights in a unique manner the specific profile of Evangelical faith and church life, as it has done from its beginnings in the sixteenth-century Reformation movement.

Prerequisites in Reformation Theology

In Martin Luther's theology, which had then and still has today a decisive influence on the essential features and principles of Evangelical theology and church government beyond the borders of Lutheran territory even in Reformed territory, the concept of freedom has a key role to play. Luther defines theology as *scientia libertatis Christiana*.[2] His Evangelical understanding of Christian freedom, which he develops programmatically in "On the Freedom of a Christian" (1520), is grounded in his understanding of the redemption and reconciliation given through Jesus Christ. For it is in Christ's death and resurrection that God revealed his true righteousness, in which he justifies humankind not according to their works, but by faith

---

1. Cf. Rat der EKD, *Kirche der Freiheit*.
2. Luther, "De captivitate Babylonica ecclesiae praeludium (1520)," 538, 30.

alone. According to Luther, the relationship between God and human is established in God's unconditional grace of forgiveness, through which God freely grants us his justification and thereby demonstrates his boundless love to all people. As his justification by faith alone regardless of works frees the human beings from the obligation to justify themselves by their works, they are also liberated to do God's will voluntarily. Since their justification releases them from the condemning power of the law, it sets them free to do good works in faith and thus to follow a Christian way of life. On the basis of this fundamental Reformation insight, fully developed in his main writings of 1520, Luther then explores the anthropological implications of his soteriology in greater depth in his controversy with Erasmus of Rotterdam. For the universal significance of the death and resurrection of Jesus Christ as the reason for humankind's justification by faith alone corresponds to the radicality of human sin, culminating in our inability to believe in God's gospel and to decide for God. In "De servo arbitrio," Luther contradicts Erasmus' hypothesis of free will by demonstrating that the human will is in bondage and not free, as far as the relationship with God is concerned. Left to his own devices, a human being is only able to decide against God.

As the full argumentation in "De servo arbitrio" shows, Luther's essential soteriological and anthropological insights correspond to his essential hermeneutical insight into the authority of Holy Scripture as the only source and guideline for the Christian faith and the teaching of the Church. This realization not only determined Luther's personal attitude towards the Roman Church, but also became, together with the soteriological insight, the hermeneutical principle of the Reformation movement. By its implicit critique of authorities, the so-called scriptural principle liberates from bondage to excessive claims to power made by earthly authorities and at the same time provides the space for reflection on the divine purposes of church and worldly government, and to call on the authorities as institutions of freedom. By gradually bringing this freedom to bear on the public sphere, the Reformation movement became the Protestant movement. While Luther's understanding of Evangelical freedom had immediate repercussions on an institutional level for church proclamation and Evangelical church life and order in the context of church government exercised by regional sovereigns, the idea of Christian freedom was not, or at least not explicitly, established on the level of theological doctrine in its complex significance for the entire interpretation of Christian faith and Christian practice. In the great theological works of Evangelical theologians in the late sixteenth and seventeenth century, the term *libertas* is only mentioned in passing. The *libertas christiana* is not given a whole chapter in material dogmatics, nor in prolegomenas. That the profile of protestantism can be characterized by the concept of freedom on the level of spirituality, of church structures and of theological teaching, is the result of a reflection process undertaken by Evangelical churches and their theologians. This reflection process was triggered by the philosophical and political impact of the Enlightenment, and continued through modernity and secularization into our post-secular present.[3] As the discussion paper on the reform process of the EKD shows, the EKD is determined to face the post-secular challenges expressly as a *Church of Freedom*.

It seems to be relevant that the specific profile of the concept of freedom used in the reform process, has not been connected with a particular theological interpretation and the theological program behind it. This way the inner Evangelical discussion about the understanding of freedom appropriate in an Evangelical perspective is not hindered, but given leeway. The authors of the discussion paper obviously rely on the member churches of the EKD together with the theologians responsible for theological training to support the ministry of a church of freedom—in spite or because of the multiplicity of Evangelical interpretations of freedom and Christian freedom. So can one assume there is a common Evangelical interest in freedom? And is there such a thing as a common Evangelical, basic understanding of freedom? This question cannot be answered in the abstract, but only with reference to concrete concepts of freedom found in the arena of Evangelical theology. In the following section, I will examine the understanding of freedom as presented in two theological conceptions, which have become definitive for Evangelical theology under the conditions of modernity and secularization.

The Concept of Freedom in Karl Barth's Church Dogmatics[4]

In the history of theology, Karl Barth's *Church Dogmatics* is considered one of the first dogmatic theological works in which the concept of freedom and the examination of its biblical foundation has a determining influence on the whole conception of his dogmatics. In contrast to Luther's theology, in which the concept of freedom has a constitutive part to play in his soteriology and anthropology, in Barth's dogmatic it is given a key role in the interpretation of the doctrine of revelation, and thereby in the very foundation of dogmatics, which he develops in the Prolegomena of his Dogmatics

---

3. Cf. Habermas, *Zwischen Naturalismus und Religion*.
4. Barth, *The Church Dogmatics* (CD), vols. I–II.

in the form of his doctrine of the Word of God[5] and carries through in the doctrine of the trinity. Barth's theology offers in a way a meta-theory for the Reformation understanding of Christian freedom, by interpreting God's revelation as the realization of divine freedom, thereby enabling human freedom. This is the basic train of thought Barth follows through in the three parts of his doctrine of revelation. By recurring to the biblical understanding of revelation as the origin of his doctrine of the trinity, he first identifies the immanent trinity as the reason for divine freedom (CD I/1 and I/2, §§8–12). Then, he develops the incarnation of the Word (CD I/2, §§13–15) in his doctrine of the economic trinity as the realization of God's freedom for humankind (CD I/2, §13), which in turn as the outpouring of the Holy Spirit (CD I/2, §§16–18) gives the human being freedom for God (CD I/2, §16).

Barth interprets freedom initially in a general sense as divine potency,[6] through which God decided for this and no other possible way of self-revelation. In implicit discussion of G. W. F. Hegel's concept of the absolute spirit, Barth takes care not to interpret God's revelatory acts as acts necessary for the self-realization of God's divinity. God's Word is God's free act, it is not subject to any requirements. Therefore, God's Word is for Barth "not

---

5. Unlike Reformation or pre-enlightenment protestant dogmatics, Barth can no longer determine God himself and the things of God or the Word of God as the material of dogmatics. According to Barth, the material of dogmatics is rather the talk about God which takes place within the church (CD I/1, 47). The specific task of dogmatics in this respect consists in "the scientific self-examination of the Christian Church with respect to the content of its distinctive talk about God" (CD I/1, 3). Barth claims this kind of self-examination to be necessary, as churchly talk about God remains human talk, even though "in the form of preaching and sacrament it is directed to man with the claim and expectation that in accordance with its commission it has to speak to him the Word of God to be heard in faith" (CD I/1, 47). By permanently being and remaining human talk, especially churchly talk cannot give any guarantee for really being talk about God. Rather, "[i]t is the miracle of revelation and faith . . . when proclamation is for us not just human willing and doing characterised in some way but also and primarily and decisively God's own act, when human talk about God is for us not just that, but also and primarily and decisively God's own speech" (CD I/1, 93). Again, the church's self-examination with respect to its talk about God is only possible on the basis of a criterion which, according to Barth, cannot be anything else than the word of God. Thus, as the word of man the talk about God within the church becomes "the material of dogmatics, i.e., of the investigation of its responsibility as measured by the Word of God which it seeks to proclaim" (CD I/1, 47). For it is the word of God in itself that "makes proclamation proclamation and therewith makes the Church the Church" (CD I/1, 88). This word of God, which the church claims to preach, attests itself according to Barth "in Holy Scripture in the word of the prophets and apostles to whom it was originally and once and for all spoken by God's revelation" (CD I/1, 88). Therefore, the word of God exists in threefold form.

6. Cf. CD I/1, 102.

to be understood as history first and then and as such as decision too. It is to be understood primarily and basically as decision and then and as such as history too."[7] The Word of God is as divine act "also human act, and as such it is also event, but as act and event it is free, as free as God Himself, for indeed God Himself is in the act. God is the Lord. There is no one and nothing above Him and no one and nothing beside him, either on the right hand or the left, to condition Him or to be in a nexus with Him. God is *a se*."[8] It is now constitutive for the understanding of freedom and therefore of God's divinity, that God's aseity is not an empty form of freedom.[9] Rather, it is precisely God's divinity according to Barth, in which all potentiality is included in its actuality and therefore "all freedom in His decision. Decision means choice, exercised freedom. We understand the Word of God very badly in isolation from the unconditional freedom in which it is spoken, but we understand it very badly if we regard it as a mere possibility rather than as freedom exercised, a decision made, a choice taking place."[10] In using his freedom, God is *a se* and therein absolute subject—and this thought contains Barth's whole controversy with German Idealism and with the beginnings of the radical critique of religion in the nineteenth century.

God's being as absolute subject is thus realized in the decision to and performance of the action in which he reveals himself as God the Lord. "God reveals himself as the Lord"[11]—this sentence is the key statement in the Church Dogmatics. It is thereby fundamental for the consistency of Barth's conception that this statement is in no way to be understood as the conclusion of human speculation about the Godhead of God, but solely as the interpretation of God's self-attestation in Holy Scripture.[12] As such, it is an analytical statement for Barth. For one cannot apply the distinction between form and content to the biblical concept of revelation. "When revelation is an event according to the Bible, there is no second question as to what its content may be. Nor could its content be equally well manifested in another event than this."[13] Since according to the biblical concept of revelation, "revelation is . . . in all circumstances the promulgation of the *basileia tou theou*, of the lordship of God,"[14] form and content coincide. "Revelation is

7. Ibid., 156.
8. Ibid., 157.
9. Ibid.
10. Ibid.
11. Ibid., 314.
12. Cf. CD I/2, 505ff.
13. CD I/1, 306.
14. Ibid.

the revelation of lordship and therewith it is the revelation of God. For the Godhead of God, what man does not know and God must reveal to him, and according to the witness of Scripture does reveal to him, is lordship. Lordship is present in revelation because its reality and truth are so fully self-grounded, because it does not need any other actualization or validation than that of its actual occurrence, because it is revelation through itself and not in relation to something else, because it is that self-contained *novum*. Lordship means *freedom*."[15]

Whoever expects at this point to be presented with a broad exegetical digression in evidence of these key statements, will be disappointed. The digression consists of exactly one sentence in small print, pointing out that the Biblical term *exusia* means both: lordship and freedom. The fact that Barth dispenses with evidence in the form of historical critical exegesis in these particularly key points of his dogmatics, is not the result of his ignorance or lack of exegetical competence, but part of his theological program. As his following argumentation shows, Barth proves and substantiates his analysis of the biblical concept of revelation not in philological studies or in historical critical text analysis, but in his interpretation of the biblical speech about God,[16] which is guided by the question *how* God reveals himself as Lord.[17] With reference to Exod 3:13-14,[18] Barth describes this act as self-unveiling, in which God, who by nature cannot be revealed to man, differentiates

15. Ibid.

16. Cf. CD I/1, 307: "Godhead in the Bible means freedom, ontic and noetic autonomy. In the decisions taken in this freedom of God the divinely good becomes event, and truth, righteousness, holiness, and mercy deserve to be called what their names declare because they are real in the freedom of God. It is thus, as One who is free, as the only One who is free, that God has lordship in the Bible. It is thus that He also reveals it. The self-sufficiency or immediacy so characteristic of the biblical revelation is the very thing that characterises it as God's revelation on the one side and as the revelation of lordship on the other."

17. According to Barth, the characteristic feature of the biblical revelation can only be grasped, "when we note that what we have here is not an abstract revelation of lordship but a concrete revelation of the Lord, not Godhead (even Godhead understood as freedom) but God Himself, who in this freedom speaks as an I and addresses by a Thou ... As freedom, lordship and Godhead are real and true in God Himself and only in God Himself, being inaccessible and unknown if God Himself, this I, does not speak and address by a Thou, so, in God Himself, they are the meaning of the event that the Bible calls revelation" (ibid.).

18. For this, cf. the exegesis of the name of God: "'I am that I am' can hardly mean more than that 'I am He whose true name no one can utter.' By its very wording the revealed name is intended to recall the hiddenness even of the revealed God. But under this name, which in itself and as such pronounces His mystery, God does reveal Himself to His people, i.e., He begins, as Ex. 3 instructively shows, to have dealings with Israel through the announcing by Moses of its deliverance out of Egypt" (ibid., 317-18).

himself from himself, becomes unlike himself and thus reveals himself to man. That God can be revealed to man in the event the Bible ascribes to God in its accounts of the events in the times of the patriarchs, of Moses, and the prophets up to Golgotha and the days of Easter and Pentecost,[19] the fact that "he ... can and will and actually does do this," is for Barth a first confirmation of his interpretation of the biblical concept of revelation, according to which "the lordship discernible in biblical revelation consists in the freedom of God."[20] It is the freedom in which he decides to be "not only God the Father, but also—in this direction this is the comprehensive meaning of the whole of the biblical witness—God the Son."[21] The biblical foundation of Barth's doctrine of revelation therefore needs to prove itself in the interpretation of the incarnation of God's Word and outpouring of the Holy Spirit.

Barth presents the corresponding interpretation in §13, by finding the answer to the question about the reality of God's revelation in the New Testament "in the constant reiteration in all its pages of the name Jesus Christ. This name is God's revelation, or to be more exact, the definition of revelation arising out of revelation itself, taken from it and answering to it ... In this and in none other name is there salvation."[22] The interpretation of the event of revelation which took place in the incarnation of the Word in the name Jesus Christ, leads in the perspective of freedom theory in §§13–15 to the following summary: "When it says that the Word became flesh, this becoming took place in the divine freedom of the Word. As it is not to be explained in terms of the world-process, so it does not rest upon any necessity in the divine nature or upon the relation between Father, Son and Spirit, that God becomes man."[23] Since God's aseity is now substantiated in the incarnation of God's Word, one must show in a subsequent step that God in his freedom does not remain on his own, but applies his freedom and thereby makes man's freedom for God possible. Barth demonstrates this in the doctrine of the outpouring of the Holy Spirit. For according to Barth, the Holy Spirit is "God Himself in His freedom exercised in revelation."[24] By exercising his freedom, he is able to be "present to His creature, even to dwell in him personally."[25] Thereby he enables his creature to "achieve

19. Ibid., 320.
20. Ibid.
21. Ibid.
22. CD I/2, 10.
23. Ibid., 135.
24. Ibid., 198.
25. Ibid.

his meeting with Himself in His Word and by this achievement to make it possible . . . Through the Holy Spirit and only through the Holy Spirit does God make His claim on us effective, to be our one Lord."[26]

The reality of God's revealedness for humans and the fact that there is now faith and obedience rendered to God's Word among human beings, "is just as seriously the content of the biblical witness to revelation as is the objective reality of God's revelation"[27] in the incarnation of God's Word. However, Barth does not demonstrate this by referring to biblical accounts on how individuals found faith in Jesus Christ. Rather, Barth proves the understanding of the reality of revelation as God's revealedness for man by referring to the biblical portrayal of the Church as the body of Christ.[28] For "God Himself and God alone turns man into a recipient of His revelation—but He does so in a definite area, and this area, if we may now combine the Old Testament and the New Testament, is the area of the Church."[29] Thus, the freedom opened up by the Spirit, "to be children of God and to know and love and praise Him in His revelation,"[30] is given to the individual only within the sphere of the Church. This means that "the freedom which the Holy Spirit gives us in this understanding and in this sphere—gives, so far as it is His freedom and so far as He gives us nothing else and no less than Himself—is the freedom of the Church, of the children of God."[31] For Barth, this is also the answer to the question so hotly discussed in Reformation times, the question of the human ability to achieve communion with God: "The very possibility of human nature's being adopted into unity with the Son of God is the Holy Ghost."[32]

One would misunderstand Barth's interpretation of the biblical concept of revelation in the prolegomena of the *Church Dogmatics*, if one were to assume that the biblical foundation of his doctrine of revelation were completed in it. Rather, he proves his interpretation of God's revelation as the realization of freedom in all parts of his Church Dogmatics. However, Barth's interpretation of God's reality in the framework of his doctrine of God (chapter 6), is of fundamental importance for the understanding of God's freedom. In his doctrine of God, he substantiates the structure of the concept of freedom by referring to the biblical descriptions of God by his

26. Ibid.
27. Ibid., 206.
28. Ibid., 215–18.
29. Ibid., 210.
30. Ibid., 303.
31. Ibid., 198
32. Ibid., 199.

attributes. Barth interprets the attributes ascribed to God in the biblical scriptures as perfections of divine love and divine freedom,[33] in which God reveals himself as the one who loves in freedom, and who at the same time proves the divinity of his love and the divinity of his freedom. By describing God's being in the dialectic of the concepts freedom and love, Barth verifies the understanding of freedom which determines his doctrine of revelation. On the one side, he verifies that God's freedom is not an empty freedom, because God in his freedom seeks and establishes communion with humans. On the other side, he again emphasizes the aseity of God, in which God as Father, Son and Spirit can exercise his love without human involvement.[34] That this reality of God as freedom of love and love in freedom enables human freedom, and how such human freedom is active in obedience and responsibility towards God's law, is outlined by Barth in his doctrine of God's law within the framework of the doctrine of creation. The biblical foundation to the material interpretation of God's freedom and human freedom presented by Barth in the doctrine of God and of creation, can already be found in the doctrine of Holy Scripture, which I will discuss in conclusion.

In the doctrine of Holy Scripture, we again encounter the basic pattern of Barth's understanding of freedom. Since God has revealed himself to the Church in Holy Scripture, it is only the Scripture that can be claimed to have immediate, absolute authority in the Church as regards content. In its authority as the Word of God, Scripture places the members of the Church under the obligation to listen to each other in the interpretation and application of Scripture.[35] At the same time, however, it calls upon each individual to take on responsibility for the interpretation and application of Scripture in the Church, that is to make use of the freedom of interpretation which Holy Scripture itself opens up as the free Word of God.[36] Here, Barth applies the Reformation interpretation of the priesthood of all believers in his argumentation in a new way. In a subtle analysis, Barth shows that Scripture is witness to the Word of God in that it displays the movement in which the prophets and apostles believed and gave witness. Scripture does this in such a way that we understand this movement as the life and action of the Word of God itself, that we give in to this movement occurring in the Word of God and follow it, that we ourselves are moved and move in

---

33. Barth names as the perfections of the divine loving grace, mercy, patience, holiness, righteousness and wisdom, as the perfections of the divine freedom unity, constancy, eternity, omnipresence, omnipotence and glory (cf. §§30, 31).

34. CD II/1, 257.

35. CD I/2, 598.

36. Ibid., 741, 797.

our own faith and our own witness.[37] Since the interpretation of Scripture is made possible by Holy Scripture itself as the Word of God, then "our self-determination, spontaneity, and activity are engaged in its service."[38]

If the Church is established, sustained and ruled by Scripture, as Barth holds in application of the basic conceptions of creation theology discussed in the traditional doctrine of providence, then the members of the Church are not simply "spectators or even objects"[39] of these actions, but they exercise the freedom given to the Church in responsibility as they interpret Scripture. According to Barth, this is achieved by allowing oneself to be taken into the movement of the Word of Scripture, in obedience and subordination to Scripture,[40] and in the observance and reflection of Scripture.[41] Such subordination to Scripture is not practiced according to Barth, by superordinating general methods of text interpretation to the understanding of Scripture. Rather, the freedom to interpret Scripture enabled by the Word of God as attested in Scripture is exercised in a kind of reflection that allows itself to be determined by the flow of Scripture and puts exegetical methods and insights into the service of the reflection and observance of Scripture. Barth wants his exegesis in the *Church Dogmatics* to be understood as such a kind of reflection. Through his explanation of the biblical understanding of revelation, Barth de facto demands that Scripture should be interpreted responsibly in obedience to Scripture. In his exposition of the biblical understanding of revelation, Barth claims to be exercising the freedom which is constituted by God's free act of revelation.

The Concept of Freedom in Wolfhart Pannenberg's Systematic Theology[42]

In contrast to Karl Barth's *Church Dogmatics*, the idea of freedom does not take on the role of a constructive principle in Wolfhart Pannenberg's *Systematic Theology*. Although of course Pannenberg also discusses God's freedom and human freedom in the material parts of his dogmatics, he does not, like Barth, connect the interpretation of God's revelation as an act of freedom with the challenge to overcome the anthropocentrism of

37. Ibid., 753.
38. Ibid., 701.
39. Ibid., 711.
40. Ibid., 802.
41. For this, cf. CD I/2, 722–23, esp. the short description of the literary side of the exegetical process.
42. Pannenberg, *Systematic Theology* (ST) vols. 1–3.

Neo-Protestantism, thereby responding to the radical critique of religion. For Pannenberg, Barth's conception is one that itself belongs in the line of those that Barth accuses of anthropocentrism because of its subjectivism and decisionism. Not only as part of his discussion of the radical critique of religion, but also as a result of the methodological questions Pannenberg, unlike Barth, puts to theology the task to identify and justify the truth claim of Christian speech about God by understanding God's revelation as a historic event. He argues that the revelatory character of this event can be recognized regardless of faith. This argumentation is presented within the framework of an epistemological foundation, according to which the true meaning of each individual event can only be determined by recurring to the totality of meaning and therefore by considering the end of history. In this way, historic research in general and historical critical exegesis in particular do not only adopt an auxiliary function, but are considered indispensable instruments for the validation of the truth claim of the Christian faith among other disciplines. Thus, the historical critical interpretation of Scripture acquires a constitutive role especially at the key points of *Systematic Theology*. One of the most important of these key points is the question whether and in which sense the story of Jesus and his resurrection can be understood as a historical event and therefore as God's act of revelation.[43]

Similar to Barth, Pannenberg also understands divine actions in the creation, redemption and fulfilment of the world, by which God reveals himself as God and thereby as the Lord of the world, as free, presuppositionless actions of God which are not necessary to God's being. Being the triune God, God "is the free origin of himself and his creatures."[44] However, different to Barth, Pannenberg does not emphasize God's autonomy before all time in his interpretation of God's freedom, but the concept of God's self-actualization in the actions of the economic trinity and thus within history. "God actualizes himself in the world by his coming into it."[45] Though on the one side God's eternal existence in the fellowship of the Father, Son and Holy Spirit is the presupposition for God's coming into the world according to Pannenberg, so that "his eternal essence needs no completion by his coming into the world."[46] But by the creation of a world, God makes himself dependent in his deity and his existence "on the fulfilment of their determination in his present lordship."[47] Pannenberg's theology is not centered

43. Cf. ST 2, 365.
44. ST 1, 410.
45. Ibid., 390.
46. Ibid.
47. Ibid.

around the idea that God could have acted differently, but the fact that God has bound himself to the world in his deity.

This is reflected in the doctrine of God's essence and attributes, as Pannenberg describes God's reality unlike Barth not in the dialectic of freedom and love, but interprets "the attributes of God's essence as they are disclosed in his revelatory action"[48] and "as they are summed up in Exod. 34:6 (cf. Ps 103:8; 145:8) and in the NT witness"[49] altogether as attributes of love. Pannenberg solves the classic problem of the doctrine of God's attributes, which is the question how the multiplicity of biblically attested attributes can provide a real description of God's simplicity, by concluding after an examination of the individual definitions of the attributes that "the difference is not that of the abstract from the concrete. The attributes are concrete aspects of the reality of divine love."[50]

For Pannenberg, the interpretation of the divine attributes leads to the statement found in John 4:8, 16, according to which love is the epitome of the divine essence. He understands the power of love as the "materially concrete form of 'Spirit.'"[51] For the biblical statements "God is Spirit" and "God is love" denote according to Pannenberg "the same unity of essence by which the Father, Son, and Spirit are united in the fellowship of the one God. The statement that "God is Spirit" tells us what kind of Spirit it is whose sound (John 3:8) fills all creation and whose power gives life to all creatures. The Spirit is the power of love that lets the other be."[52] The reason it can give creaturely life its existence, is that "it is already at work in the reciprocity of the trinitarian life of God, as in eternity each of the three persons lets the others be what they are."[53] Therefore, God in himself is the foundation and the origin of life for his creatures. Similar to Barth, the immanent trinity is thus regarded as the presupposition for the economic trinity and the basis for God's free actions in the world. In contrast to Barth, however, Pannenberg emphasizes that God grants his creatures an independent existence. For they can only establish a relationship with God and enter into communion with God if they are independent of him. In the same way he understands the work of the spirit, which actualizes itself in the diverse functions of consciousness, from the awareness of objects via the formation

48. Ibid., 432.
49. Ibid.
50. Ibid.
51. Ibid., 427.
52. Ibid.
53. Ibid.

of self-awareness to an explicit awareness of God, as the basis of the human being's subjective freedom.[54]

The freedom of the human guided by the Spirit realizes itself in the ecstasy of consciousness, through which the human is able to be himself in the other. In this way, as the human being trusts in God in faith, he adequately actualizes the freedom of the creature. "We attain to authentic freedom only where those alienated from God and from themselves let themselves be reconciled to God, so that alienation from our own identity is also overcome."[55] As according to Pannenberg, the proclamation of the gospel can free the human from anxiety about his finite existence and liberate him from the fixation on his own ego, it provides the basis for human independence from the powers of this world and for the freedom "of being able to do this or do that."[56] Similar to Barth, Pannenberg does not believe this is done for the individual as an individual, but in such a way that the tension between the fellowship and the individual is released and reconciled by the work of the Spirit, as the individuals are not only taken into communion with God through their faith, but also into communion with one another. The Spirit thus provides the basis for freedom of faith not only as individual freedom, but as freedom in the fellowship of the Church.

The spirit's gift of authentic freedom in faith is not given apart from the story of Jesus, but rather in such a way that through his faith in Jesus Christ, the believer participates in the relationship to God which determined Jesus' life.[57] However, the believers "are not just taken up into the dynamic of God's work by which they are filled through the Spirit of God."[58] Rather, "with participation in the filial relation they receive their own subjectivity before God that expresses itself as spontaneity in relation to the Father and hence also to all creaturely reality."[59] God's action in creation, granting his creatures their independent being, is completed in the work of the spirit. For the human is now able to recognize the original purpose of his life to have communion with God in Jesus Christ, to actualize it in faith and thereby to exercise his true freedom. According to Pannenberg, this is done in its most concentrated form in the human's act of talking with God, that is in prayer.[60]

---

54. Cf. ST 2, 221.
55. ST 3, 129.
56. Ibid.
57. Cf. ST 3, 217.
58. Ibid., 204.
59. Ibid., 204–5.
60. Ibid.

Part of the true independence the believer gains through faith in Jesus Christ is for Pannenberg finally also the independent appropriation of the Christian witness and thereby the ability to form an independent opinion on questions of one's own faith. Correspondingly, he emphasizes that the Church must support the process of the independent appropriation of the faith in the Church's proclamation of the gospel and confession. Achieving judgmental competence requires a certain degree of inner independence from the communication process, in which the contents of the faith are handed down to the members of the Church. "Precisely that recipients of the tradition should achieve this relation to the substance, and with it this independence of the process of communication and its institutions, ought to be the goal of the process of handing down itself. Christian handing down by proclamation and teaching has reached this goal only when by it recipients achieve their own independent relation to the matter, and hence a relation of immediacy that can cause them to forget the communication process (cf. John 4:42). This immediacy that Christians experience as the work of the Spirit characterizes faith in Jesus, yet not just in the sense of knowledge of Jesus, but as the immediacy of a personal relationship. Believers have immediacy to Jesus because all have individual fellowship with Jesus in faith."[61] The precondition for this immediacy is the independent reading of the Bible.

In these considerations, Pannenberg brings the Reformation interpretation of the priesthood of all believers to bear on the present situation. Like Barth, Pannenberg considers it realized in the independent interpretation and understanding of the Bible. Different to Barth, however, Pannenberg does not connect it with the idea of every Christian's public responsibility for the interpretation of Scripture in the Church. In his view, the freedom of the individual believer is realized and proven in individual appropriation and evaluation. The specific task of theology, which does this in an academic way, is to facilitate this reflection and appropriation on the institutional levels. Since the scriptural principle of the Reformation entered a state of crisis through the Enlightenment's critique of reason and authority, an independent interpretation of Scripture in acknowledgement of this crisis can no longer lay claim to the authority of the biblical Scripture as God's Word without adequate argumentation. The purpose of this is not to deprive the readers of the Bible of their faith in the inspiration of the Bible. Rather, this argumentation is meant to disclose reasons to understand the actions of God as attested in the Bible as actions of *God* to those who do not have this faith. And at the same time, it is meant to instruct the reader how

---

61. Ibid., 124.

to understand the biblical Scriptures in their variety and complexity as testimonies of God's actions of revelation. Referring to individual Bible passages and claiming these as immediate expressions of God's will means asserting a truth claim which does not serve the freedom of faith, which Pannenberg considers rooted in the love of God as attested in the Bible.

Freedom in Acknowledging the Diversity of Christian Interpretations of Scripture

The conceptions put forward by Barth and Pannenberg provide insight into the diversity of modern reflection on Christian freedom in continuity to the Reformation legacy. They show us on the one side the different emphasis one can put on the idea of God's freedom, and how the emphasis in the interpretation of human freedom shifts in consequence. While Barth stresses the absoluteness of God's freedom and interprets human freedom primarily with regard to its limitedness and relativity in relation to God's freedom, Pannenberg understands God's the human true freedom in the form of independence. These different emphases reflect the traditional difference between Reformed and Lutheran thinking. It corresponds with a significant divergence in the way how they refer to the Bible and how they develop their exegetical approach. In his reflection on the biblical concept of revelation, Barth claims the freedom to interpret the talk on revelation in the Bible in the light of the challenges of modern freedom theory. Pannenberg claims the freedom to prove the faith in the revelatory character of the biblical testimony by the application of the historical critique.

In spite of their differences, these two approaches are not mutually exclusive, but can be understood in their diverse perspectives and with their respective insights as fundamental contributions to Evangelical reflection on the foundation and essence of Christian freedom with regard to the Bible. They each bring out central aspects of the biblical testimony, which were also pointed out in the exegetical papers presented in the context of our project. By converging in decisive points in spite of their divergence, they portray the unity of and differences in the Protestant traditions of thought, in which the convergence is greater than the divergence. Both, convergence and divergence, give prominence to God's revelation as a free, that is presuppositionless action of God not necessary to God's being. Both understand God's freedom as the foundation of and precondition for human freedom. Both assume that the human being in his creaturely constitution is free and alienates himself from God in this freedom. Both understand the events of redemption and reconciliation in Jesus Christ as the constitution of true freedom, and both point out the significance of the Church as the fellowship of believers for the actualization of individual freedom in the priesthood of all believers. In view of such convergence between the theological programs and the denominational profiles portrayed in them, we understand why the church-dividing differences between the denominations of the Reformation could be overcome under modern circumstances in the Leuenberg Concord. Thinking about these differences may seem a theoretical business. But if we dispense with such theological reflection, we run the risk that one single aspect or particular exploration of Christian freedom is given absolute status in theological reasoning and also in church practice. And that would be the end of the practice of Christian freedom, because it would be the end of the ongoing discourse on freedom that should take place in a church that tries to be a "church of freedom."

Bibliography

Barth, Karl. *The Church Dogmatics*. Vols. I–II. Edited by G. W. Bromiley and T. F. Torrance. Translated by Geoffrey W. Bromiley et. al. Edinburgh: T. & T. Clark, 1975, 1956 and 1957.
Habermas, Jürgen. *Zwischen Naturalismus und Religion: Philosophische Aufsätze*. Social Theory. Frankfurt: Suhrkamp, 2006.
Luther, Martin. "De captivitate Babylonica ecclesiae praeludium (1520)." In *D. Martin Luthers Werke* 6. Edited by D. Knaake. Weimar: Böhlaus, 1888.
Pannenberg, Wolfhart. *Systematic Theology*. Vols. 1–3. Translated by Geoffrey W. Bromiley. London: T. & T. Clark, 2004.
Rat der Evangelische Kirche Deutschland. *Kirche der Freiheit*. http://www.ekd.de/download/kirche-der-freiheit.pdf.

Part 3

Freedom as Given and Shaped by God

Introduction

LARRY W. HURTADO

The essays in this section of this volume focus in varying ways on biblical emphases on freedom as based in God and as shaped and modelled in God's own redemptive actions. This book is intended to stimulate reflections on freedom, with a particular concern to promote a full realization of freedom in the life of churches and through churches into wider society. These essays explore some of the resources provided by biblical texts to encourage seeing freedom as truly a central and worthy aspiration. But also these essays show that biblical texts present true freedom as having a divine basis, and so not simply a commodity to be acquired and contended for, and freedom as having a divinely-modelled pattern or shape. That is, the freedom advocated in biblical texts takes its specific contours and purposes from God's actions, which are themselves typically portrayed as freely performed.

Patrick Miller focuses on the biblical tradition of the exodus of the people that became ancient Israel, this event typically characterized in biblical references as a liberation from servitude in Egypt. Miller contends, "There is no event in the Old Testament that is more central to the story of God's way with Israel than the exodus," and he shows that the numerous biblical references to the Lord who delivered the people from Egyptian slavery made this event "definitive of Israel's God in a large way."

As Miller shows, this liberation story is echoed, celebrated and appropriated variously through the biblical canon, including the New Testament. Jesus' redemptive death is linked with exodus traditions, and these traditions are also appropriated in New Testament visions of the consummation of redemption, which involves even liberation from the power of death.

Hans-Joachim Eckstein's discussion of "The Innovative Concept of Freedom in Paul" emphasizes the central influence of "the way of the Lord, Jesus Christ" in shaping how Paul presents true freedom. Eckstein insists that in Paul the realization of freedom by believers is to be modelled in

Jesus' "voluntary self-sacrifice and serving care." So, Paul refers to being set free by God (from sin), not for selfish indulgence, but for caring about others. In Pauline teaching, God's liberation is not to lead to autonomy but to "a life of *relationship*" involving community and mutual acceptance.

Beverly Roberts Gaventa focuses on Paul's epistle to the Romans, insisting that Paul's references to freedom in this epistle must be viewed in the context of his "apocalyptic theology." By this she means that "What Paul sees on the horizon is nothing less than the redemption of the entire cosmos." Paul's is a radical view, both in scope (the entire cosmos) and in depth, involving the complete transformation of the creation, which is to include obtaining what he calls "the freedom of the glory of the children of God" (Rom 8:21). Gaventa also insists that Paul's understanding of freedom was based in his firm sense of "the freedom of God." That is, for Paul, the fulfilment of divine promise rests in God's own character, and the form of God's fulfilment "is not subject to human judgment or expectation, since God's faithfulness does not constrain or compromise God's freedom."

Noting Paul's daring references to freedom from sin as "becoming God's slave," she observes that this servitude is to have practical and powerful consequences in the way that believers treat one another. She boldly declares, "This is what slavery to God looks like: it looks like being adopted in the family."

My own essay resonates very much with what these colleagues say. My own contributions are two. First, I consider NT references to freedom in the historical context of the Roman world, and specifically the widespread practice of slavery. The NT texts do not call for the abolition of slavery, but I contend that in various ways they do reflect a concern to ameliorate the condition of Christian slaves, at the very least offering them a new sense of identity, worth, and in the *ekklesia* new relationships that make slaves and free(d) brothers and sisters in Christ.

I also propose that the NT texts present a distinctive vision of true freedom as based in God's redeeming love and as directed toward an answering love for others. In contrast to notions of freedom as *autarchy* dominant in the Roman era, the NT texts advocate a freedom-for-others, a liberation-for-love. In making both of these points, I join with these colleagues in seeking to stimulate and resource Christian promotion and expression of freedom, a freedom whose validity rests in God.

10

God's Work for Human Freedom

Patrick D. Miller

The realm of God's activity in Scripture is a large and complex subject. No single rubric, theme, or category exhausts the fullness of God's intention and work for the creature God made in God's own image. Yet it is clear that the claim that God wills and works for human freedom from perceived and actual dehumanizing bondage is a major axis across Scripture and a fundamental definition of divine activity in the midst of humanity. Three features of that intention need to be recognized or underscored. One is that it is presented in Scripture not only as a human reflection on what will or has happened but is a self-articulated claim on the part of the one who is Lord. Second, the story of God's way with Israel and the larger human community is wrapped around the large and many modes of resistance to this divinely intended goal for human life. Third, the experience of human bondage is so manifold in the biblical story that the understanding and experience of being freed and of freedom is likewise complex and varied, though generally not something peculiar to a particular individual or community. At the same time, the foundational experience of the exodus deliverance becomes a kind of lens through which the experience of being set free is perceived and spoken of.

Setting Free as the Purpose and Work of God for Human Life: The Exodus

There is no event in the Old Testament that is more central to the story of God's way with Israel than the exodus. Not only does the account of Israel's life as a people have a new beginning in that experience, but it becomes programmatic for Israel's relationship with its Lord. The description of the Lord as the one who brought Israel out of Egypt and out of slavery becomes definitive of Israel's God in a large way. Pre-eminently, the prologue to the Decalogue provides the self-identification or self-presentation of God as the one "who brought you out of the land of Egypt out of the house of bondage." This description or epithet, however, occurs many other times and often as a self-identification (see below). Both texts that tell of the revelation of the divine name are set in the context of the exodus and in different ways associate the meaning of the name or the revelation of the name with the act of setting the Israelite slaves free from Egyptian slavery. So in Exod 6:6 we read: "Say therefore to the Israelites, 'I am the Lord, and I will free you (lit. 'bring you out') from the burdens of the Egyptians and deliver you from slavery to them.'" In Exod 3:7-17 the connection is not as direct, but it runs throughout the whole passage as the name is connected with the Lord's companioning presence with Moses when he goes into Pharaoh and, to the Israelites, as the one who has sent Moses to the people to deliver them.

This act of freeing the Israelites is described in various ways, but the many references are dominated by the use of three verbs: 'ālâ, "to go up" yāṣā', "to go out" and nāṣal "to snatch away, deliver." The primary forms of the verbs are causative, respectively "to bring up," "to bring out," and "to deliver."[1] The verbs are used interchangeably and often together.[2] The verb "to bring out" dominates — over 90 times according to some counts — and the verb "to bring up" is second in frequency of usage — over 40 times — with reference to God's action in the exodus.[3] Several observations may be made

1. The verb nāṣal does not occur in the Qal or basic stem and is primarily in the causative or Hiphil stem.

2. For the use of all three verbs with reference to the exodus, see Exod 3:8-10: "I have come down to snatch them away (nāṣal) from the hand of the Egyptians and to bring them up ('ālâ) out of that land to a good and broad land, a land flowing with milk and honey, to the country of the Canaanites ... So come I will send you to Pharaoh to bring (yāṣā') my people, the Israelites, out of Egypt" and Judg 6:8-9: "Thus says the Lord, the God of Israel: I brought you up ('ālâ) from Egypt, and I brought you out (yāṣā'), of the house of bondage, and I delivered you (nāṣal) from the hand of the Egyptians and from the hand of all your oppressors, and I drove them out before you and gave you their land."

3. There are, of course, a number of other verbs that are used with reference to God's activity in the exodus, e.g., pādâ, "to ransom, redeem," and gā'al, "to redeem." These are terms that refer more to commercial redemption of persons, real estate and things (see the discussion in Barth, *Errettung vom Tode*). These verbs are also important for thinking about the character of the divine activity in the exodus. It is not surprising that the first of these occurs in the two places in the Deuteronomic Code where the exodus is mentioned because in both cases, the reference to the Lord's redemption of Israel is a motivation first for freeing bonded servants in the seventh year and rewarding them

about these many references to the Lord's freeing Israel from Egypt and bondage.

1. Already alluded to is the *frequency of formulation in the first person*. The sentence "I brought you/them out (*hôṣî'*) of the land of Egypt" occurs a number of times (e.g., Exod 20:2//Deut 5:6; 29:46; Lev 19:36; 25:38, 42, 55; 26:13, 45; Num 15:41), and there are numerous variants of this formula. So also the verb *'ālâ*, in first person expressions, such as "I brought up Israel out of Egypt" (1 Sam 10:18) occurs a number of times (e.g., Exod 3:8, 17; Judg 6:8; Amos 2:10; 9:7; Mic 6:4). The verb *nāṣal* is less common in these first person divine speeches but does occur there as well (Exod 3:8; 6:6; Judg 6:8-9). To this could be added the many instances where the expression is in the formula of self-presentation, "I am the LORD your God who brought you out (or "up out") of the land of Egypt" (e.g., Lev 19:36; 25:38; cf. 22:33; 23:43; 26:45). This frequent first person usage is, of course, followed by many instances in the third person, for example, when Moses is speaking in Deuteronomy. When one adds to these uses, instances of a kind of creedal or catechetical formulation, such as Deut 6:21; 26:8; Josh 24:5-6), it becomes clear how definitive this event of freeing Israel from Egypt and slavery was, both for the people and for the God they worshipped.

2. As others have noted, the language that is used in these many references is especially *spatial* in character. That is, it speaks of freeing the people in terms of getting them out of a place and situation in which they are caught. The language is realistic and figurative, realistic in the sense that they are "down" in Egypt, figurative as it portrays the people as imprisoned and needing to be brought out, down in a pit and needing to be extricated, in the hands of the Egyptians and needing to be snatched away. The point is reinforced by the combination of expressions: "out of Egypt" and "out of the house of slavery."

3. The frequent addition of the clarifying phrase "out of the house of slavery" makes it clear that what takes place is genuinely an act of freeing from a real bondage and not simply a movement from one place to another. While what happens may fulfill the promise of God to bring Jacob's children home (Gen 46:4; 50:24), it is not simply that. The freeing work of God is thus a *political* act, one of complex strategy and planning, recruitment and preparation of human agents, and open conflict between super powers to bring about for one party strict control of a growing immigrant population (Exod 1:9-10) and for the other release from physical slavery, characterized

---

liberally (Deut 15:15) and then for not subverting the rights of the widow, orphan, and stranger (Deut 24:18; cf. v. 22 and 16:12). For uses of *gā'al* in reference to the exodus, see Exod 6:6; 15:13; (note the use here also of *qānāh*, which may mean "purchase" in this context); Pss 74:2; 77:16 [ET 15]; 106:10.

by forced or slave labor (Exod 1:11, 14; 2:23; 5:9, 11; 6:9), often called hard or cruel labor (Exod 1:14; 6:9) under ruthless taskmasters (Exod 1:13–14), in the fields and in construction (Exod 1:13), and finally partial genocide to keep the slave population under control (Exod 1:22).

4. The spatial character of God's freeing act is further identified in that the "bringing out of" carries with it "a bringing into," a point made at the very beginning. So the freeing is indeed a release, an extrication, a removal, but not simply that. It is also a *provision of freedom's enjoyment, for freedom's actualization*. The significance of the act of freeing is not to be underplayed, but it is not complete in itself. The story indeed makes that very clear as the people find themselves set free only to be lost in a wilderness, constantly complaining, and even willing to go back into the pit and bondage of slavery because there at least they had bread and water. The large amount of story devoted to the wilderness is not accidental. It is indicative of the fact that in itself the release may not be all it is cut out to be.[4] From the beginning, therefore, the Lord's promise to bring the people up or out is accompanied by the promise to bring them into a new place, a place of freedom, described not only geographically ("the land of the Canaanites, the Hittites, the Amorites, the Perizzites, the Hivites, and the Jebusites," e.g., Exod 3:8, 17) but more often and more specifically qualitatively as "a land flowing with milk and honey" (Exod 3:8, 17) or "a good and broad land" (Exod 3:8) In several instances a combination of two or three of these descriptions of the place of freedom is given. Or a more extended description of the land of freedom is laid out as, for example, in Deut 8:7–10, where the goodness of the land and its provision are elaborated at some length. The structure of freedom as defined by the exodus experience thus is seen to be the provision of space for freedom, a space that has several features:

a.) It is "good," the most general term for a positive valuation of the space, a reflection of the Lord's own goodness,[5] the term that represents God's repeated judgment about the world God created (Gen 1:4, 10, 18, 21, 25, 31).

b.) It is spacious, one of the key notions of freedom in Scripture (see below). Being free from imprisonment and constraint is found when there is room to move and live. The land is both good and broad and

---

4. Clearly there is a dimension of testing the people that is involved, but that testing has very much to do with their comprehension of what is involved in their freedom (see Deut 8).

5. See the characteristic and most common form of the song or prayer of thanksgiving: "O give thanks to the Lord; for he is good, for his steadfast love endures forever" (2 Chr 5:13, etc.). See Miller, *Interpreting the Psalms*, chap. 5.

the elbowroom is as important as the quality of the space into which God brings those now free.

c.) The space of freedom into which the people are brought is abundant in its provisions for life. This is implied in the "good" land but it becomes more explicit in the "land flowing with milk and honey" as well as in the extended description in Deut 8:7–10.

d.) The land has a prior ownership. It belongs to others, so that for the freed people to enjoy the space of freedom there is displacement of others.

This last is a critical feature in comprehending the structure of freedom manifest in the exodus experience. Israel's realm of freedom necessarily impinges upon the freedom of others. As the experience of bondage is characteristically one of oppression by the other, so the realization of freedom inevitably impinges also upon the other. The space of freedom is on the one hand the broad open place, room to live and move about and not be constrained. On the other hand, however, the space of freedom is limited by the existence of others with whom the freed ones now must contend. Much of the biblical story, beginning with the mixed account of the entry into the land—conquest (Joshua) and uneasy co-existence (Judges), illustrates how the space of freedom works on the continuum between complete and uninhibited or uninhibiting room and total control of the room of the other (so non-freedom). Bringing the people in is as much a political act as bringing them out. (For complete understanding of this as a political act, see below.)[6]

5. The paradigmatic or normative character of the exodus experience of bringing out/up and bringing in is demonstrated by the appropriation of the same language to speak about Israel's later experience of spatial confinement and restriction and the Lord's bringing out or up, that is, the exile. In Ezek 20:33–44 the divine voice speaks through the prophet to announce a new bringing of the peoples out of the countries where they are scattered (Ezek 20:34, 41; see also Ezek 34:13). Furthermore, the exodus is recapitulated in that they are to be brought into the wilderness once more as an act and place of judgment, seen as a repeat of what happened the first time in the wilderness. This connection between exodus freeing and bringing out of exile is perhaps taken to its farthest point in Jer 16:14–15, where, as Fuhs has put it: "He [the postexilic redactor of Jeremiah] finds the new demonstration of Yahweh's power so extraordinary that it causes the foundational

---

6. There is a further dimension to what bringing into freedom involves—Israel acknowledging the Lord as their God—on which see below. The space of freedom is also, and by definition, a space of worship.

event of the exodus to be forgotten": "it shall no longer be said, 'As the Lord lives who brought the people of Israel up out of the land of Egypt,' but 'As the Lord lives who brought the people of Israel up out of the land of the north and out of all the lands where he had driven them.'"[7] H. D. Preuss has seen the great majority of the uses of the verb "to bring out" (*hôṣî'*) in reference to the exodus as exilic or post-exilic and suggesting that this period was the fruitful growth of the focus on the Lord as the liberating God.[8] Whether or not that is the case, the political character of God's liberating act is mirrored in the release from exile, once again through human agent (Cyrus) and involving bringing the people out of their exilic confinement to enjoy God's good place again.

If bringing Israel out is a political act, so also is bringing them in. The credos of Deut 6 and 26 and Josh 24 are perhaps among the most elaborated formulations of God's freeing work in bringing the people out of slavery and into the good land. In Deut 6:21, the brief recitation has a powerful and emphatic opening: "Slaves were we in Egypt, but the Lord brought us out of Egypt with a mighty hand . . ." Here, as well as in Deut 26, the affirmation of God's freeing Israel from slavery is articulated most strongly. In both instances, the context is the practice or the interpretation of the law.[9] That is, the emphasis on God's bringing Israel up out of slavery is in the context of understanding the proper servitude that is Israel's, the service of the Lord who sets Israel free to serve him. This is central to the exodus story itself, where the request to Pharaoh is regularly "Let my people go that they may serve me." Note that in the beginning, the rationale is "that they celebrate a festival to me in the wilderness (Exod 5:1), then "that they may serve (*'ābad*) me in the wilderness" (Exod 7:16). Finally, in Exod 8:1 and following, it is simply "let my people go so that they may serve me" (*'ābad*; cf. 8:20; 9:1, 13 ; 10:3). Indeed, that God's intention from the beginning is to bring Israel out of Egyptian slavery into the Lord's service is evident from God's response to Moses' request for a sign when he is called to lead the people out: "This shall be the sign for you that it is I who sent you: when you have brought the people out of Egypt, you shall serve God on this mountain" (Exod 3:12).

---

7. Fuhs, "עלה, *'āl*," 88.

8. "Deliverance from Egypt stands transparently for deliverance from the house of bondage of the exile in Babylon. There the new deliverance, the new exodus, is hoped for and promised through reference to the former act of liberation and its emphatic interpretation as such. The postexilic texts exhibit the effective history of this primarily exilic idea; the few pre-exilic texts lead up to it. Liberating "bringing out" from exile was the newly established accent demanded by the ancient faith in Yahweh, who had been Israel's God since Egypt (Hos. 12:10[9]; 13:4)" (Preuss, "יצא, *yāṣā*," 248).

9. Cf. Exod 13:3–16.

Freeing Israel from servitude in Egypt is tied from the beginning in every way to a freedom for serving the Lord.[10] The classic formulation of the connection between freedom and service is, of course, the Decalogue and especially its opening, which identifies the deity as the one who brought Israel out of the land of Egypt, more specifically out of the house of slavery, followed by the commandments that describe the way of serving the Lord. The connection to the first commandment is especially acute: "I am the Lord your God who brought you out of the land of Egypt, out of the house of slavery; therefore you shall have no other gods before me" (Exod 20:2-3).[11] This close connection is carried through in many places, for example, the statute in Lev 25:39-42: "If any who are dependent on you become so impoverished that they sell themselves to you, you shall not make them serve as slaves. They shall remain with you as hired or bound laborers. They shall serve with you until the year of the jubilee. Then they and their children with them shall be free from your authority; they shall go back to their own family and return to their ancestral property. For they are my servants, whom I brought out of the land of Egypt; they shall not be sold as slaves are sold." And again in v. 55: "For to me the people of Israel are servants; they are my servants whom I brought out from the land of Egypt: I am the Lord your God." The connection seen here between freeing Israel from slavery and the treatment of servants in the statutes concerning the jubilee year in Leviticus 25 is reflected also in the references to the deliverance from Egypt in the Deuteronomic Code, several of which are to be found in connection with how the weak (widow, orphan, stranger, poor, bonded servants) are to be treated (Deut 5:14-15; 15:12-18; 16:11-12; 24:17-22).

Into the Psalter

What has been noted above about the Lord's intention in setting Israel free from slavery should not cause one to lose awareness of what it is that evokes the intention of God to set Israel free. That is evident most clearly in Exod 2:23-24 and 3:7-12. It is the cry of the suffering people that moves the heart of God to free them from their cruel oppression: "The Israelites groaned under their slavery, and cried out. Out of the slavery their cry for help rose up to God" (Exod 2:23). And in the conversation with Moses: "Then the Lord said, 'I have observed the misery of my people who are in Egypt; I

---

10. The association between God's freeing of the people and their service of God is also found in the prophetic words about the delivery from exile, e.g., Ezek 20:40-41.

11. On the political character of the First Commandment, see Miller, *The God You Have*.

have heard their cry on account of their taskmasters. Indeed, I know their sufferings, and I have come down to deliver them from the Egyptians, and to bring them up out of that land to a good and broad land, a land flowing with milk and honey, to the country of the Canaanites . . . The cry of the Israelites has now come to me; I have also seen how the Egyptians oppress them. So come, I will send you to Pharaoh to bring my people, the Israelites, out of Egypt" (Exod 3:7-10). The affirmation of the bringer of first fruits to the altar makes this dimension a part of the liturgical or creedal affirmation: "When the Egyptians treated us harshly and afflicted us, by imposing hard labor on us, we cried to the Lord, the God of our ancestors; the Lord heard our voice and saw our affliction, our toil, and our oppression" (Deut 26:6-7). So there is a move from both ends—the cry of the people on the front end (Exod 2-3) and the proper service of God on the other end (Exod 19-24).

This is then a direct connection to the Psalter, where the crying voice is articulated in great detail. One does not hear Israel's cry of lament and complaint in Exod 1-15, but that cry is heard again and again in the Psalms. There, of course, it is not simply the voice of the people in their original slavery but is the crying out that regularly comes up to God from those in slavery and bondage, under oppression and suffering.[12] The psalms become the paradigmatic (and actual) voice of those who are in that situation and so again and again describe the experience of bondage and the hope of freedom.

It is also in the Psalms that two things happen. The experience of bondage and oppression is opened up to include a broad range of things, both individual and communal and not just the bondage of political slavery. Further, it is in the Psalter that such bondage is most clearly described with the language of and the experience of death. It is from that bondage or prison that the psalmic voice again and again seeks God's freeing power.[13]

Among the concepts and images of freedom in the Psalter are the following:

- The exodus story of freedom and service is sung in the Psalms, particularly in the historical psalms, 78, 105, 106, and 136. Several things especially should be noted: a.) The exodus event is the central feature of the history that is remembered in these psalms; b.) The poetic account of this story puts as much or more weight on the issue of the

---

12. For elaboration of the character of this cry in the psalms and elsewhere in the Old Testament, see Miller, *They Cried to the Lord*, chap. 3.

13. For a detailed discussion of this aspect of the Psalms, see Barth, *Die Errettung vom Tode*.

service of God as it does on freeing from slavery, but particularly in the framework of the failed service; c) The rooting of God's freeing Israel in the cry of the people is recalled (Ps 106:44-45); d.) The retelling of the story in these psalms is probably rooted in the experience of exile and so once again the experience of political bondage and the hope of being brought out is to the fore;[14] e.) God's freeing Israel from slavery is central but it is also seen as part of the whole of God's work as these psalms also place that act in relation to creation, both by the beginning verses of Ps 136 and by the redaction of the Psalter that has Ps 104 leading into the narrative psalms 105 and 106;[15] and f.) The paradigmatic character of God's freeing activity in the exodus is carried over into a wider and complex depiction of God's freeing work in many kinds of human experiences of bondage and oppression in Ps 107, such as homelessness and hunger, imprisonment, sickness, and hurricane storms.

- There are various images of bondage and oppression in the Psalms. Among those are the net/snare (e.g., Pss 25:15; 31:5 [Eng. 4]), the mighty waters (e.g., Pss 18:17 [Eng. 16]; 69:15-16 [Eng. 14-15], and the pit/Sheol (Pss 30:4, 10 [Eng. 3, 9]; 40:3 [Eng. 2]). Clearly the language of death is related to the last of these as well as to the others (e.g., Pss 16:9-11; 116:3-4, 8). It connotes a realm of imprisonment, a spatial notion, appropriate to the numerous verbs that speak of freeing in spatial terms.[16] The psalms thus represent an important move in their bringing in death as a form of bondage and a way of speaking about all sorts of experiences in human life. The large difficulty is precisely at the point of trying to identify the phenomena behind such references, which are often figurative but may be literal. The same is true for the many references to sickness. Once again, the openness of the language of the Psalms is a hindrance to discerning specific phenomena but a plus for the appropriation of the Psalms in many different circumstances.[17]

- Once again there is a bringing to as well as a bringing out. This is best represented in the imagery of the broad place, a figure that is related both to the language of bondage as well as to the exodus experience of

---

14. The language of "bringing out" or "bringing up from" occurs in these psalms but is confined to the references to the exodus, not to the future return from exile.

15. This important connection between creation and freeing is carried over elsewhere in the Psalms, e.g., Pss 33:4-7 and 146:5-9. Cf. Isa 45:11-13.

16. Cf. Barth, *Errettung vom Tode*, 98-106.

17. On this openness, see Miller, *Interpreting the Psalms*, chap. 2.

freedom. So in Ps 4:1 [ET 2], the psalmist says: "You gave me room in my distress."[18] And in Ps 18:20 [ET 19], we hear: "He brought me into a broad place; he delivered me, because he delighted in me." The act of salvation and deliverance, of setting free is found in the Lord bringing the psalmist into a spacious place, where there was room and the one in trouble no longer hemmed in and beset but now having room to live (cf. Ps 118:5).

- Several of the psalms place the freeing activity of the Lord in relation to other sorts of deliverances, such as opening the eyes of the blind, upholding the widow and the orphan, lifting up the downtrodden. This is especially characteristic of the final coda of the Psalter, Pss 145–149. It is important to observe the way in which acts of freeing are central to the deeds of the Lord that evoke praise but also are part of a much larger complexity. The connection between the freeing work of God and the care of the weak and the poor that is seen elsewhere in the Old Testament comes to the fore here (e.g., Pss 145:14; 146:7–9; 147:3, 6; cf. Isa 58:6–7, on which see below).

On to the New Testament

While the New Testament is not the primary focus of this paper, it is not finally possible to talk about God's will to freedom without taking account of it. The relevance is immediately indicated by two features of the New Testament that resonate with the matters above. One is the second point on the axis of God's freeing work that is mentioned in the opening paragraph. It is the Lucan programmatic interpretation of Jesus' mission in Luke 4:16–21 when Jesus reads from Isa 58 and 61 in the synagogue at Nazareth:

> The Spirit of the Lord is upon me,
> > because he has anointed me
> > > to bring good news to the poor.
> He has sent me to proclaim release to the captives
> and recovery of sight to the blind,
> > to let the oppressed go free,
> > > to proclaim the year of the Lord's favor.

Several things need to be noted:

---

18. The NJPS translation here is "You freed me from distress."

1. The reading joins Isa 58:6 and 61:1–2 generally by subject matter but more specifically by catchword principle, in this case the repetition of the Greek word *aphesis*, which occurs in the Septuagint of both passages, translating respectively "release" in Isa 61:2 and "go free" in Isa 58:6. The emphasis of the text is thus on the work of freeing and release.

2. The Greek word translates two Hebrew words (*děrôr* and *ḥopšim*), both words that have to do with manumission and release of slaves or of land. The sabbatical year and the jubilee year are in the background and the context for these words. Their usage in Isaiah, however, opens them up in two ways: a.) The release is of "captives" or "prisoners," the bound ones, and the oppressed or suffering ones. So the horizon includes the specific concrete release of slaves or bonded servants. Like the Psalms, however, the text uses language that is broader in its reference and may be understood both literally and figuratively. b.) The release and setting free is once again bound up with other types of delivery as indicated by the reference to the poor and the blind, a broadening that is evident as one moves from Isa 58:6 into v. 7 (sharing bread with the hungry, hospitality to the poor, clothing the naked). This broadening is evident elsewhere, for example, Luke 7:22, which is a reflex of this passage in its testimony to the work of Jesus, or Matt 25:31ff.

3. The customary translation of the Greek *aphesis* in the New Testament is "forgiveness." So the freeing activity of Jesus is seen to be comprehensive in that it includes all kinds of human, physical, social, and economic forms of bondage and release but it also recognizes the bondage of sin and guilt and the need for "release" from their power over human life.

4. Once again, the intention to set free in a broad way is a matter of self-identification and self-understanding for Jesus as it was for the Lord in the exodus story. The matter is not presented as a narrative reflection on the work and ministry of Jesus but as his articulation of his mission. If there were any question about this, the final words would confirm the matter: "Today, this Scripture is fulfilled in your hearing" (Luke 4:21). In other words, God's purpose to provide release is underway in Jesus and it is a comprehensive and multi-faceted divine activity. It is as much what Jesus was about as it is what the Lord was about in the exodus.

That God's intention to set the bound free—whether from sin, oppression, poverty, or whatever has ensnared them—is both self-understanding and the practice of Jesus is well-indicated by other texts, such as Luke 13:10–17 and 14:1–6. While both of these texts are controversy stories involving dispute over sabbath observance, in both instances Jesus engages in an act of healing, first for a woman crippled for eighteen years and unable to stand up straight (Luke 13:11) and secondly for a man with dropsy (Luke 14:2). In the latter case, we are told that Jesus took the man and healed him

(Luke 14:4). With regard to the crippled woman, Jesus twice refers to the woman being set free, first in direct address to the woman: "Woman, you are set free from your ailment" (v. 12). Then, he turns to those who are challenging his actions as violation of the sabbath and says: "And ought not this woman, a daughter of Abraham whom Satan bound for eighteen long years, be set free from this bondage on the sabbath day." (v. 16). In both cases, we are confronted with instances of sickness and healing, but in the first instance such activity on Jesus' part is described as an act of freeing—from sickness and from the power of Satan. As Robert Tannehill observes, "it fits Jesus' proclamation of 'release to the captives' in his inaugural sermon (Luke 4:18)."[19]

An important dimension of both stories is their connection to the sabbath, that is, acts of healing that are viewed by the Jewish leaders as a violation of the sabbath. One of them, referring to the sabbath commandment in the Exodus version of the Decalogue, says to Jesus "There are six days on which work ought to be done; come on those days and be cured, and not on the sabbath day" (Luke 13:14). While Jesus argues against this protest by noting that any of his hearers would certainly free their domestic animals from trouble or take them to get water on the sabbath, implicit in the story is the Deuteronomic form of the sabbath commandment, where its purpose is seen as providing for release for male and female servants: "so that your male and female slave may rest as well as you" (Deut 5:14). That is, the sabbath whether on the seventh day or the fiftieth/Jubilee day is an occasion when those who are bound are regularly given freedom.[20] Jesus act of healing is thus a reflection of his own self-identification, God's act of setting free from bondage, and a strict adherence to the Commandments.

The second feature of the New Testament that connects back to the Old Testament is its focus on the release from death and the climax of the gospel in the resurrection of Jesus. While there are many places where God's overcoming of death through the death and resurrection of Jesus is referred to, one of the strongest proclamations is closely tied to the Old Testament. The resurrection is the focus of 1 Cor 15 and in vv. 24–27, Paul cites Pss 110 and 8:

> Then comes the end, when he hands over the kingdom to God the Father, after he has destroyed every ruler and every authority

---

19. Tannehill, *Luke*, 219. Tannehill comments further with regard to the Satan reference: "One of the kinds of captivity from which Jesus frees people is Satanic oppression in the form of physical ailments, but this may be accompanied by social oppression through being stigmatized."

20. Cf. Miller, "The Human Sabbath."

and power. For he must reign until he has put all his enemies under his feet [cf. Ps 110:1]. The last enemy to be destroyed is death. For "God has put all things in subjection under his feet" [cf. Ps 8:6].

Paul's point in the citation of Ps 110 is to identify death as one of the enemies, much like the enemies of the Psalms. Only this is the final enemy. Richard Hays aptly describes the connections between the Psalms and the release from death in the defeat of death:

> The personification of Death (see also 15:54–55) is characteristic of Paul's understanding of salvation as a great narrative drama in which the protagonist Jesus Christ delivers God's people from bondage to Sin and Death through his obedience in going to death on a cross (cf. Rom 5:12–21; Phil 2:5–11). This interpretation of Death as one of the defeated eschatological enemies is in turn justified by appeal to Ps 8:7, which shows that God has put all things (including death) under Christ's feet. Thus according to Paul's reading, these Psalm texts prove that Christ will finally overcome death.[21]

The emphasis on the defeat of the enemy death is then reinforced when Paul moves to discuss the resurrected body and alludes to Isa 25: "When this perishable body puts on imperishability, and this mortal body puts on immortality, then the saying that is written will be fulfilled: 'Death has been swallowed up in victory'" (v. 54). The enemy death is overcome in God's victory manifest in raising Jesus from the dead. God's work for human freedom, rooted deeply in Israel's story, as these texts make clear, reaches its climax in the final deliverance, the resurrection of the body.

Bibliography

Barth, Christoph. *Errettung vom Tode: Leben und Tod in den Klage- und Dankliedern des Alten Testaments*. Newly edited by Bernd Janowski. Stuttgart: Kohlhammer, 1997.
Fuhs, H. F. "עלה, 'al." In *TDOT* 11 (2000) 88.
Hays, Richard B. *First Corinthians*. Interpretation. Louisville: Westminster John Knox, 1997.
Miller, Patrick D. *The God You Have: Politics and the First Commandment*. Facets. Minneapolis: Fortress, 2004.
———. "The Human Sabbath: A Study in Deuteronomic Theology." *Princeton Seminary Bulletin* 6 (1985) 81–97.
———. *Interpreting the Psalms*. Philadelphia: Fortress, 1986.

---

21. Hays, *First Corinthians*, 266.

———. *They Cried to the Lord: The Form and Theology of Biblical Prayer*. Minneapolis: Fortress, 1994.

Preuss, Hans Dieter. "יצא, *yāṣā*." In *TDOT* 6 (1990) 248.

Tannehill, Robert C. *Luke*. Abingdon New Testament Commentaries. Nashville: Abingdon, 1996.

11

Freedom in Apocalyptic Perspective
A Reflection on Paul's Letter to the Romans

BEVERLY ROBERTS GAVENTA

Paradoxically, Paul's letter to the Romans is instructive for reflection on freedom precisely because much of the first half of the letter so relentlessly depicts not the freedom of humanity but its subjugation. Among the several features that make this letter distinctive in the Pauline corpus is its preoccupation with the enslaving character of Sin, which receives more attention here than in any of Paul's other letters.[1] As Paul offers his apocalyptic interpretation of God's deliverance of the entire cosmos from the anti-God powers, including most especially the powers of Sin and Death, he develops (sometimes explicitly, at other times implicitly) an understanding of human freedom.[2] This human freedom is not to be identified with independence

---

1. The noun ἁμαρτία and related words occur 81 times in the undisputed letters of Paul; 60 of those times are in Romans. The noun appears 42 times in Rom 5–8 alone, where it is very often the subject of an active verb, as in "Sin entered" (5:12 [twice]), "Sin increased" (5:20), "Sin ruled as a king" (5:21; see also 6:12, 14), "Sin set up a ground of operation to produce" desire (7:8), "Sin sprang to life" (7:9), "Sin set up a ground of operation to deceive" and "to kill" (7:11), "Sin brought about" death (7:13), "Sin dwells in me" (7:17, 20).

2. The ἐλευθερ– word group appears at 6:18, 20, 22; 7:3; 8:2, 21. See the discussion of vocabulary in Hans-Joachim Eckstein, "The Innovative Concept of Freedom in Paul," and the literature cited therein; in addition, see Coppins, *Interpretation of Freedom in*

or autonomy, by contrast with many contemporary notions of freedom (particularly in the West). For Paul, genuine human freedom results from the freedom of God. There is also need to distinguish in Romans between false human freedom, one that is both self-deceptive in its actions and disastrous in its consequences, and genuine human freedom that contributes to the upbuilding of the body of Christ and the glorification of God. This treatment of freedom in Romans thus echoes Larry Hurtado's pithy phrase, "freed by love and for love,"[3] although locating both those "loves" in the context of Paul's apocalyptic theology.

Romans and Apocalyptic Theology

Understanding how notions of human freedom are reflected in Paul's letter to the Romans involves recognizing Paul's apocalyptic theology. Space precludes a full discussion of Romans and apocalyptic theology, but an explanatory note may be helpful as background to what follows, especially given the vigorous scholarly debate about Romans[4] as well as some contemporary objections to the use of the term "apocalyptic theology" for Paul.[5]

To say that Romans is characterized by apocalyptic theology means not simply that Paul draws on a specific word group (ἀποκάλυψις and its cognates) or that the letter contains passages that reflect an apocalyptic eschatology. Instead it means that Romans reflects Paul's conviction that the death and resurrection of Jesus Christ constitutes God's invasion of the world, an invasion that reveals the world's captivity to anti-God powers (especially the powers of Sin and Death) and begins the liberation of all creation from those powers.[6]

---

the Letters of Paul.

3. As in the title of his paper for this project, "Freed by Love and for Love: Freedom in the New Testament."

4. Some of the major positions are represented in the essays collected in Donfried, ed., *The Romans Debate*. See also the review of literature by Miller, "The Romans Debate: 1991–2001."

5. See especially Matlock, *Unveiling the Apocalyptic Paul*.

6. This avenue of interpretation is influenced by the work of Ernst Käsemann, J. Christiaan Beker, J. Louis Martyn, and Martinus de Boer. Some of my own preliminary work along these lines is available in *Our Mother Saint Paul*. The word "invasion" is a strong one, but it seems required to do justice to the extensive conflict language in Romans (e.g., "weapons" in 6:13; 13:12; "enemies" in 5:10; "ground of operation" at 7:11; "peace" and "reconciliation" at 5:1 and 11); it is important to understand that the "invasion" is God's action on behalf of humankind, not an action by one human group against another (see Rom 16:20).

This approach to Romans stands in considerable tension with recent work, especially work in North America and the U.K. A. Katherine Grieb has argued, for example, that Romans is primarily Paul's attempt to extend the history of God's faithfulness to Israel. Romans is "Paul's sustained argument for the righteousness of God," and this argument should be understood as a "great story" that begins with Adam and Abraham and now includes the Gentiles as well.[7] Central to this developing story is God's faithfulness to Israel, so that chapters 9–11 are understood as "the very center" of the letter. Other scholars emphasize the social dimension of the letter, drawing attention to Paul's attempt to reconcile Jew and Gentile. Philip Esler, for example, contends that "central" to Paul's purpose in this letter is the "social identity that his addressees in Rome gain from belonging to the Christ-movement." Throughout the letter, Paul emphasizes the "supremacy" of belonging to this movement over against other identities, particularly ethnic identities.[8] Still other scholars argue that the letter promises God's salvation in distinction from the salvation (and peace and honor) proclaimed by the Roman empire. That argument constitutes a major theme in the important new commentary by Robert Jewett in the Hermeneia series.[9]

Some of the points being made in these other approaches can be granted. The letter does demonstrate Paul's passionate concern about God's dealings with Israel. This concern is announced explicitly at the beginning of chapter 3 and becomes a major feature of the letter in 9–11. At least one way of reading the conflicts about dietary observance and other practices in chapters 14–15 is that they derive, perhaps indirectly, from conflicts between (some) Jews and (some) Gentiles. I have more difficulty seeing the anti-imperial thrust of Romans, although I would freely concede that Paul's understanding of the gospel implicitly constitutes a threat to any human empire.[10] Nevertheless, while acknowledging that some of these points are indeed reflected in the letter, I want to insist that none of these proposals sees as far as does Paul in this letter. What Paul sees on the horizon is not simply the redemption of the individual (whether a lot of individuals or a select few). Nor is Paul interpreting the gospel as the reconciliation of ethnic groups, the extension of God's covenant history with Israel, or even the overthrow of the Roman empire. What Paul sees on the horizon is nothing less than the redemption of the entire cosmos (understanding κτίσις in

---

7. Griebe, *The Story of Romans*, 87.
8. Esler, *Conflict and Identity in Romans*.
9. Jewett, *Romans*.
10. On this point, see the instructive essay of Barclay, "Why the Roman Empire Was Insignificant for Paul."

8:19-21 as including the whole of the created order). And this redemption has begun already in God's invasion in the cross and resurrection of Jesus Christ of a world that is under the control of Sin and Death. That is to say, it is an apocalyptic redemption. M. Eugene Boring wrote that the controlling question of Romans 5 is: "Who is in charge? Who is in control of the world and humanity?"[11] My contention is that this is not the controlling question of Romans 5 alone, but of the whole of the letter.

The Freedom of God[12]

Paul's answer to that question carries us into the most important understanding of freedom in Romans, namely, the freedom of God. Paul does not, to be sure, refer to God explicitly as a "free" agent or attribute the standing of "freedom" to God.[13] Nevertheless, the important actions Paul does attribute to God all assume God's freedom,[14] and identifying that freedom of God offers an important corrective to the recent and understandable emphasis in the scholarly literature on God's faithfulness, an emphasis that can appear to imply that for Paul God's actions are merely predictable. J. D. G. Dunn, for example, regards Paul's understanding of God as "taken for granted": nothing in Paul's understanding about God changes as a result of the Christ event.[15] And various features of Romans foster the notion that in the gospel God is doing nothing more than what was promised. The letter opens with a reference to the gospel having been promised "through God's prophets, in holy Scriptures" (1:3-4; and see also 3:21). The discussion of Abraham features the promise that he would be the inheritor of the cosmos (4:13). The long discussion of God's relationship with Israel (and the Gentiles) in

11. Boring, "The Language of Universal Salvation in Paul," 283.

12. This section draws on Gaventa, "The God Who Will Not Be Taken For Granted," in *Our Mother Saint Paul*, 149-60. That essay was originally written for a Festschrift in memory of Donald H. Juel, and it reflects a conversation with Juel's reading of the role of God in the Gospel of Mark.

13. Notice, however, the use of the passive forms of ἐλευθερόω at 6:18, 22; 8:21 certainly referring to divine actions of liberation, which could scarcely be carried out apart from the freedom of the divine agent (and see 8:2; Gal 5:1).

14. See in this volume the discussion of God's freedom by Gertz, "Concepts of Freedom in Deuteronomy?"; and by van Oorschot, "Potentials for Freedom in Concepts of Order." In addition, see Friederike Nüssel's discussion of divine freedom in Barth's doctrine of revelation in this volume ("Protestant Concepts of Freedom and Their Foundations in Biblical Traditions"); not surprisingly, Barth's position seems to be derived from Paul.

15. Dunn, *The Theology of Paul the Apostle*, esp. 29. See the trenchant critique by Francis Watson in "The Triune Divine Identity."

chapters 9-11 opens with a list of God's gifts to Israel, included in which are "the promises" (9:4). These references to the promises, coupled with Paul's complex and intense engagement with Scripture, give rise to the notion that the letter understands the gospel as a promise fulfilled, and nothing more than a promise fulfilled. Yet alongside that emphasis on the divine promise is a recognition that God's way of fulfilling promises is not subject to human judgment or expectation, since God's faithfulness does not constrain or compromise God's freedom.

Paul's understanding of God's freedom comes to expression in several ways. First, God is radically free in the liberating act of the cross. The relentless argument of 1:18—3:20 regarding humanity's captivity to Sin leads logically to the conclusion that there is no hope for humankind, that humanity as a whole deserves only condemnation. The lengthy depiction of Gentile behavior in 1:18-32 ushers in the conclusion that "they" are "worthy of death" (1:32). As Paul expands his discussion in chapter 2 to include Jews, he writes that those who do what is right will be rewarded and those who do not will be punished (2:6-11). Yet the category of those who do what is right turns out to be null and void by the time Paul reaches the declaration of 3:9 that all, Jew and Greek alike, are under the power of Sin. The relentless accusation made in 3:10-18 is that no one does what is right, which logically ushers in the conclusion that for humankind there can be only condemnation (3:19-20).

Yet this condemnation is followed immediately by the claim, not just that there are some few who will be rescued or that a minority have learned to avoid sinning (as in 4 Ezra 7:45-61), but that God has acted in Christ Jesus to redeem all.[16] That point is reinforced when Paul later claims that Christ died for the "ungodly" (5:6), died while "we" were sinners (5:8), while "we" were God's "enemies" (5:10). The Adam-Christ typology in 5:12-21 furthers this point, as Paul claims that the actions of both Adam and Christ involve all of humanity. There is no question here of rewarding the good and punishing the evil, but of grace for all.

Second, God is radically free in the historic election of Israel and also now in the salvation of the Gentiles. As Wayne Meeks has argued, one of the burdens of Rom 9-11 is to show that God is not fickle, that God can be trusted; if God has abandoned Israel, then Gentiles must wonder whether God will also abandon them.[17] What is sometimes neglected in

---

16. To be sure, 3:22 qualifies the "all" with "who believe" (and see 3:26), which is often read as a limitation; that is, only those who believe in Jesus Christ are the recipients of God's action, but the universal language of 5:12-21 at least stands in tension with that qualification (as does 11:32).

17. Meeks, "On Trusting an Unpredictable God," 213.

contemporary discussion, however, is that Paul's argument in Rom 9–11 depends both on the notion that God can be trusted and on the notion that God is free. This point is especially clear in 9:6–30, where Paul reviews the history of God's calling-into-being of Israel. The category of "Abraham's offspring" exists because God called it into being (9:7, and see the important antecedent in 4:17, "the one who calls into being the things that do not exist"). The calling of Jacob results from God's free act, not from anything that Jacob had done to warrant selection.[18] Reinforcing the argument is the comment in vv. 11–12: "so that God's purpose of election might continue, not by works but by his call." The phrase "purpose of election" joins two nouns (ἐκλογὴν and πρόθεσις) that do not appear together elsewhere in the New Testament. Either of them might have served to make the point of God's initiative, but together they underscore God's role, a role reinforced by the additional statement, "not by works but by his call."[19] Only God's act of creation accounts for Israel's status with God, just as God's act accounts for the hardening of Pharaoh's heart (9:17) and for the temporary stumbling of Israel (9:30–33). Indeed, God elects also "from the Gentiles" (11:24), a point Paul paradoxically reinforces by quoting Hosea's words about the restoration of Israel and applying them to Gentiles instead of to Israel (9:25–26).

God's freedom again comes into view in chapter 11. As Paul interprets what has happened and looks toward the future, he contends that Israel's unbelief has led to salvation for the Gentiles, which will in turn prompt Israel's jealousy (11:11–12). A number of scholars connect Romans 11 with the eschatological pilgrimage tradition, in which Israel's restoration in the last days will prompt the Gentiles to stream into Jerusalem. Yet it is actually a complex inversion of that tradition that is at work here, as it is not Israel's triumph (its restoration) but Israel's failure (its rejection of the gospel) that invites the Gentiles to recognize God. Indeed, through God's actions, the Gentiles lead Israel to its redemption rather than the other way around.[20] Without ever asserting God's freedom explicitly, Romans 11 repeatedly demonstrates God's freedom to select (11:1–6), to harden (11:7–10), to engraft (11:21–24), to confine and to show mercy (11:32). The closing lines, which praise God's wisdom, a wisdom not navigable by mere human

---

18. Gaventa, "On the Calling-Into-Being of Israel: Romans 9:6–29."

19. Importantly, Paul does not here contrast "works" and "faith," as in 3:28; 4:5; 9:32, but "works" and "call," making it clear that this is God's action.

20. In Romans, then, God's freedom is not to be understood in isolation from humanity, since God's free acts are found in the liberation of humanity through the cross and resurrection and through the free election of Israel and the Gentiles. This point is explicated especially well in Karl Barth, "The Gift of Freedom."

intelligence, might be summarized: God is free, unconstrained by humanity's flawed understanding of what God may and may not do."

False Human Freedom

When we turn from God's freedom to ask about the freedom of human beings, the answers yielded by the letter are complex. The letter does eventually attribute to human beings a startling degree of freedom, but this development follows on an extended discussion of the consequences of a false freedom, a freedom that takes the form of rebellion against God and thereby produces disaster.

As Paul takes up the apocalyptic revelation of both God's rectification and God's wrath, he asserts that humanity chose—apparently acting on its own volition—not to acknowledge God as God (1:18–32). Following the opening claim about God's wrath against "all human impiety and wrong," Paul charges that God has made Godself known to humanity, that since the time of creation God has been known, so that humanity is without excuse (i.e., there can be no plea of ignorance). Verses 21–23 then take up the "free" act of humanity in rejecting God:

> Now although they knew God, they did not glorify or give thanks as if to God, but their thoughts grew vain and their senseless heart was darkened. While they claimed to be wise, they became foolish, and they exchanged the glory of the immortal God for the likeness of an image of a mortal human—even of birds and of four-footed animals and of reptiles.

Paul returns to reiterate this point in v. 28: "They did not see fit to recognize God...."

The underlying logic is emphatic. The major act of this false human "freedom" that Paul adduces is the "free" act of refusing to honor God as God, and it is this "free" act that produces the disaster that follows. Because of this refusal of worship and glory to God, God "handed them over." Three times Paul makes this charge (1:24, 26, 28). Humanity is handed over to "the devices and desires of their hearts, to impurity" (v. 24), to "dishonorable passions" (v. 26), to "an unfit way of thinking" (v. 28).[21] Elsewhere

---

21. Discussion of this passage generally understates the importance of this repeated statement that God "handed them over." The verb παραδίδωμι frequently refers to the turning over of persons into the custody of a third party, and often that turning over is actually surrender in contexts involving conflict, both in the LXX (e.g., Deut 2:24; 7:2; Josh 2:14; Jer 21:20; Ezek 7:21) and in extra-biblical literature (e.g., P.Hib. 92.11; P.Lille 3.59; Herodotus, *Histories* 1.45.1; see also the discussions in LSJ, MM, and BDAG).

I have argued that the things to which humanity is handed over here are metonyms for Sin itself (see 6:19; 7:5; 8:6–7).

Because of human refusal to acknowledge God, God hands humanity over to the powers of Sin and Death. The considerable scholarly argument concerning whether this text pertains to Gentiles only or to both Jews and Gentiles does not alter this observation. Even if Paul has in mind only Gentiles at this point, by the time he reaches 3:9, it is clear that all humanity is involved, Jew and Gentile alike: all are under the power of Sin.

Although one might expect that this captivity to Sin has been left behind with the discussion at the end of chapter 3 about rectification through the death of Jesus Christ, it returns again in chapter 5, where Paul contrasts Adam's act of free disobedience with Christ's act of obedience. The somewhat cryptic conclusion of 3:9 that all are under sin here becomes explicit and expansive: Adam's free disobedience renders all captive to the rule of Sin. Even in chapter 6, as Paul takes up the newness of life, he returns again to reiterate that "you" were "slaves of Sin" (6:17, 19, 20). This false human freedom expresses itself in rebellion against God and eventuates in enslavement to the powers of Sin and Death.

It may be objected, of course, that the refusal of humanity to acknowledge God is not rightly characterized as "freedom." Perhaps the use of the term risks a certain confusion, but it does appear that Paul understands human unwillingness to recognize its own created state as an attempt at autonomy, at independence even from God. He does later speak of the former state of humans–prior to the gospel–as that of being "free" with respect to rectification (6:20). This particular (false) form of freedom results in enslavement since, in Paul's thought, genuine human freedom exists only in relation to God's freedom; it is only possible as a result of God's actions in Jesus Christ.[22]

Freedom in Christ: Present and Future

On closer examination, what emerges from Romans is evidence that God has brought about in the gospel a genuine and radical human freedom that is both present and proleptic, a freedom that includes humanity but extends to include all of creation.[23] The first hint of this human freedom comes in

For the full argumentation in support of this point, consult Gaventa, *Our Mother Saint Paul*, 113–23.

22. Note the conclusion of van Oorschot re: Isa 40-66: "In consequence human beings do not have freedom by themselves . . . For them freedom is just a derived entity."

23. On human freedom as God's gift, see Schnelle, *Apostle Paul*, 539, 544.

6:1–11: if "we" are "dead to Sin" and experience the "newness that is life," the implication is that this new life is freed from the constraints of Sin and Death. This freedom becomes explicit in 8:2, when Paul writes that "the Law as controlled by the Spirit of life in Christ Jesus freed you from the Law as controlled by Sin and Death."[24] The Spirit of Christ brings about life even in the midst of physical death (8:10).

Slaves of Christ

Romans 5 depicts the overturning of the reign of Sin and contrasts Sin's defeated power with the surpassing reign of righteousness and grace (that is, the reign of God). Here Paul does explicitly refer to freedom, yet he does not initially identify the redemption of humankind as freedom. Despite the language of grace and gift in 5:15–21 and the "newness of life" in 6:4, Paul later forthrightly says, "You became the slaves of rectification" (6:18), and "Present your members to rectification as slaves for the purpose of holiness" (6:19, see also 6:22). Freedom from the grasp of Sin does not mean that humanity belongs to itself; instead, freedom from Sin means becoming God's slave (6:22; see also 1 Cor 7:22–23).[25]

Commentators work to muffle this logic in the text,[26] but other strands of Romans make that difficult. The discussion about conflicts over food practices and other observances in chapter 14 analogizes the believer (regardless of eating practices) with the household slave (οἰκέτης). Paul's logic at this point seems clear: believers have no right to criticize one another since they are both functionaries in God's household. No one belongs to the self, as everyone belongs to the Lord (14:7–9). But one need not reach all the way into chapter 14 for this point, since as early as the second word of the letter, Paul identifies himself as the slave (δοῦλος) of Jesus Christ.

24. This translation reflects the treatment of Romans 7 in Meyer, "The Worm at the Core of the Apple," as well as Martyn's "*Nomos* Plus Genitive Noun in Paul."

25. Udo Schnelle puts it well: "Paradoxically, the only true freedom comes by being tied down to God" (*Apostle Paul*, 545). Bob Dylan's "Gotta Serve Somebody" serves as an apt paraphrase: "Well, it may be the devil or it may be the Lord / But you're gonna have to serve somebody."

26. See, for example, the discussion of Rom 6 in Engberg-Pedersen, *Paul and the Stoics*, 225–39, which concludes that at most Paul has in view the notion that believers "voluntarily" enslave themselves to righteousness (239). Engberg-Pedersen takes the statement, "I am speaking in a human way because of the weakness of your flesh" (6:19) to mean that Paul is apologizing for having to use the analogy of slavery (235–36). More on target is Käsemann's explanation that "it was necessary to speak thus because the flesh desires autonomy and thus rejects the idea of slavery as too much to demand" (*Commentary on Romans*, 182).

As he expands on the implications of the Spirit's activity, Paul returns again to the language of slavery, but here in a startlingly different way. After identifying those who are led by God's Spirit as God's children, he insists, "You did not receive a spirit of slavery again to fear but you received a spirit of adoption by which we cry out, 'Abba, Father'" (8:15). The language of mutually exclusive slaveries that threads through Romans 6 gives way to a different form of mutual exclusion, in that one is either a "slave" again to fear or a child of God. This is what slavery to God looks like: it looks like being adopted into the family.[27]

Freedom in the Present

Adoption into the family carries with it certain specific consequences that bear on human freedom, including freedom from fear, freedom of discernment, freedom for upbuilding, and freedom for praise and thanksgiving.

Spirit-mediated Freedom from Fear (8:1–39)

At the outset of chapter 8, as Paul moves from discussion of Sin's ability to twist even the Law of God to its own purposes, he declares that the "Law as controlled by the Spirit of life in Christ Jesus freed you from the law as controlled by Sin and Death."[28] Unlike earlier statements that involve simultaneous freedom (from rectification or from Sin) and enslavement (to Sin or to rectification), this declaration carries no qualification or stipulation, and in the lines that follow Paul can characterize "you" (his addressees) as "in the Spirit" (8:9), as people in whom Christ dwells (8:10), as God's children and fellow-heirs of Christ (8:17).

This Spirit-granted freedom is simply the "first fruit" (v. 23), but it has the consequence already of rendering "us" free from fear. Given the earlier discussion of God's wrath, this reference to fear might be understood as fear of God's justice, but the context suggests otherwise. What follows in the remainder of the chapter suggests that fear is generated by the "sufferings"

---

27. This shift from the language of slavery to that of adoption into the household resembles other places in Romans where Paul shifts his argumentation. For example, having undermined the distinction between circumcision and uncircumcision in 2:25–29, in 3:1–2 he insists that there is an advantage to circumcision ("much in every way"); at 15:1, when he finally introduces the word "strong" (δύνατοι) into the discussion about eating practices, the "strength" he identifies is that of Jesus who "did not please himself."

28. On freedom from the Mosaic law in Romans and elsewhere in the Pauline corpus, see Eckstein, "The Innovative Concept of Freedom in Paul."

of the present time (vv. 17-18), sufferings produced by circumstances such as those itemized in 8:35 and generated by the powers named in vv. 38-39. Nothing here suggests that "we" are immune to these circumstances as a result of individual choice or virtue,[29] but rather that the Spirit's presence grants freedom from the crippling fear of their results.

Paul does not venture to detail what this freedom from fear looks like in daily life, although his later admonitions may offer some clues. One of the prominent threads in the instructions of chapter 12 is that urging the audience to pursue the good, even with those who stand over against them. Not only does the chapter end with an extended argument against giving way to anger and evil, but it includes earlier admonitions, "Bless those who persecute" (12:14), "Repay no one evil in exchange for evil" (12:17), and "If possible for you, be at peace with all people" (12:18).[30] Among the signs of freedom from fear, then, would be conduct that pursues the good for others, even in situations that provoke the urge toward hostility.

Freedom of Discernment (12:1-2)

The explicit vocabulary of freedom ends with 8:21; nevertheless, much in the so-called "ethical" section of the letter is predicated on a notion of freedom in Christ. Those who have been freed for new life, freed for rectification, are the recipients of a new life; they are now and only now capable of genuinely free acts.[31] Freedom here is not to be equated with independence or autonomy, but instead derives from life in Christ that makes possible what was previously impossible (see 8:7-8).

The opening lines of chapter 12 tell the story. At the outset of his depiction of life "in Christ" (see especially v. 5) Paul calls for the presentation of the entire person, the σῶμα. This presentation takes place "through the mercies of God," which already suggests that it is not the result of an individual's decision apart from God. And it has the result of making it possible that "you might discern what is God's will, what is good and acceptable and complete" (v. 2). Those who were previously incapable of seeking God or doing what is good (see 3:10-18), who were so captive to Sin that even

---

29. By contrast with Epictetus (see the discussion in Lampe, "Freedom in Antiquity," in this volume).

30. These admonitions may be regarded as traditional, given that numerous parallels to individual statements can be located elsewhere. Yet the fact that Paul has included several of them here suggests that this strand of admonition is especially important for him, perhaps by way of anticipating what he will argue in 13:1-7.

31. On this point, see Martyn, "Epilogue"; and Martyn, "The Newly Created Moral Agent in Paul's Letters."

the desire to do the Law was ineffective (as in 7:7–25), are here for the first time admonished as people who are actually capable of making a decision about the disposition of their persons, who are able to perceive God's will for them.

That assumption about the capacity of the addressees is reflected in the discussion that follows, as Paul draws on a variety of traditional exhortations. The nature of these exhortations (e.g., generosity, sharing in the needs of the saints, pursuing good for all) provides a corrective to any premature conclusion that the admonition to "present your bodies" pertains only to individual acts or that "discerning God's will" is an individual matter.

Freedom for Upbuilding (14:1—15:6)

The discussion in 14:1—15:6 offers perhaps the best vantage point for understanding the complex character of Paul's notion of Christian freedom. The discussion begins with an even-handed declaration that both those who eat everything (the omnivores) and those who eat only vegetables (the lettuce eaters) act on the basis of their gratitude to God (14:6). The implication is that both groups are free to hold these judgments and to act accordingly because they are God's servants. They may not be condemned by others because they answer only to God (14:1–13).

Yet when Paul moves forward from that initial statement, he urges the omnivores to compromise their convictions so as not to do harm to those who may be led to act against their own conscience. Freedom is not absolute here, and the importance of the issue is evidenced in the number of admonitions in this passage (vv. 13, 15, 16, 19, 20, 22). Genuine freedom is not consistent with destroying the "brother" or "sister," the one for whom Christ died (v. 15, 20–21). Upbuilding of the community is more important than holding on to private convictions (v. 19; and see also 15:2; 1 Cor 8:1, 10; 10:23; 14:4, 17).[32] Genuine freedom, like genuine strength (15:1), involves action on behalf of the other.

This nuanced understanding of freedom within the Christian community stands out more sharply when compared with the vice list of 1:29–31, which prominently features actions and attitudes that are destructive of community life (e.g., covetousness, envy, gossip). In its previous state of having been "handed over" to Sin, humanity is incapable of the free actions admonished in Romans 14.

---

32. Even as Paul admonishes the omnivores to restrain themselves for the sake of upbuilding, however, he in fact sides with them, saying that "all things are clean," a statement that would have seemed highly suspicious to Jews who followed kosher law. On this point, see Barclay, "Do We Undermine the Law?"

Freedom for Praise and Thanksgiving (15:7-13)

In addition to this delicately crafted statement about freedom of practice and freedom for upbuilding, Romans depicts freedom for praise and thanksgiving. That statement will seem of little importance, until the place of praise and thanksgiving is traced through the argument of the letter. Paul's diagnosis of human enslavement to Sin focuses on the refusal of humanity to acknowledge God as God (especially 1:21, 28) and on the corrupt worship that ensues from that refusal (1:23, 25). This is not a problem for Gentiles alone, as becomes clear in the catena of 3:10-18, with its claims about the corruption of human speech (especially vv. 13-15) and its conclusion that "every mouth" is shut (v. 19).[33] Among the pivotal signs of the new life granted by the death and resurrection of Jesus is that the Holy Spirit enables human beings to cry out to God (8:15). And, when Paul concludes his discussion of the conflicts over food and calendar observance, he does so with the prayer that "you might together with one voice glorify God" (15:6). In what many regard as the culmination of the body of the letter, Paul celebrates the fact that all who have been called into faith, Jew and Gentile alike, join together in praising God and God's Messiah.[34] Humanity's enslavement to Sin stemmed from its refusal to offer God thanks and praise, but by means of God's redemption, human beings can cry out to God (8:15), can together engage in praise and thanksgiving (15:7-13). The free praise of God is further reinforced by the several expressions of doxology and thanksgiving (e.g., 1:25; 6:17; 7:25a; 9:5; 11:33-36; 15:33), as well as the frequent use of "Amen" (1:25; 9:5; 11:36; 15:33; [16:27?]).[35]

Eschatological Freedom

The freedom created in the Christ event is not the entire story; indeed, it is only the beginning. The praise offered by genuinely free human beings—Jew and Gentile together—anticipates the eschatological freedom of all creation. Along with many interpreters of Romans, I regard the κτίσις of Rom 8 as a reference to all of creation, human and non-human.[36] Here Paul

33. For this reason, it is important that in 4:20, Abraham is said to have given God glory.

34. Note the use of πάντες in 15:11, reinforcing the use of "all" earlier in the letter (as in, e.g, 1:5, 7, 8; 3:9, 19-20, 23; 5:18).

35. The argumentation behind this paragraph appears in Gaventa, "From Toxic Speech"; and Gaventa, "For the Glory of God."

36. The debated questions include whether κτίσις includes both human and non-human creation and whether (assuming humanity is included), it includes both

looks forward to the final liberation of creation (8:21). Importantly, while all creation is together in the pains of birth (8:22), what Paul anticipates is not that creation itself will give birth, but that there will be "adoption" and "redemption." This full eschatological freedom comes, not as the natural product of something creation itself does or humanity does on behalf of creation, but as God's act of liberation.

Conclusion

Paul's analysis of the human situation contains much that challenges and instructs contemporary understandings of freedom, at least as those understandings come to expression in North America. There is here an unmasking of the assumption that freedom is always and everywhere good, that freedom is inherently and automatically beneficial. Paul's contention that humanity's choice to withhold honor from God results in nothing less than enslavement is not only surprising but probably offensive in a context where religious "affiliation" is regarded as nothing more than personal choice. More important, Paul's notion that freedom exists for something outside the self (for the larger community, for the praise and glory of God) provides a significant corrective to a narcissistic understanding of freedom as a "right" of the individual for self alone.

Finally, Romans is a forceful argument that talk of human freedom is rightly located in a robust understanding of the freedom of God; indeed, for Paul there is no human freedom apart from God's freedom.

Bibliography

Barclay, John M. G. "'Do We Undermine the Law?' A Study of Romans 14.1—15.6." In *Paul and the Mosaic Law*, edited by James D. G. Dunn, 287–308. Grand Rapids: Eerdmans, 1996.

———. "Why the Roman Empire Was Insignificant for Paul." In *Pauline Churches and Diaspora Jews*, 363–87. 2011. Reprint, Grand Rapids: Eerdmans, 2016.

Barth, Karl. "The Gift of Freedom: Foundation of Evangelical Ethics." In *The Humanity of God*, 69–96. Translated by John Newton Thomas and Thomas Wieser. Richmond, VA: John Knox, 1960.

Boring, M. Eugene. "The Language of Universal Salvation in Paul." *Journal of Biblical Literature* 105 (1986) 269–92.

Coppins, Wayne. *The Interpretation of Freedom in the Letters of Paul with Special Reference to the 'German' Tradition*. WUNT 2/261. Tübingen: Mohr/Siebeck, 2009.

Donfried, Karl P. *The Romans Debate*. 2nd ed. Peabody, MA: Hendrickson, 1991.

---

believers and non-believers.

Dunn, James D. G. *The Theology of Paul the Apostle*. Grand Rapids: Eerdmans, 1998.
Engberg-Pedersen, Troels. *Paul and the Stoics*. Louisville: Westminster John Knox, 2000.
Esler, Philip F. *Conflict and Identity in Romans: The Social Setting of Paul's Letter*. Minneapolis: Fortress, 2003.
Gaventa, Beverly Roberts. "'For the Glory of God': Theology and Experience in Paul's Letter to the Romans." In *Between Experience and Interpretation: Engaging the Writings of the New Testament*, edited by Mary F. Foskett and O. Wesley Allen, Jr., 53–65. Nashville: Abingdon, 2008.

———. "From Toxic Speech to the Redemption of Doxology in Paul's Letter to the Romans." In *"The Word Leaps the Gap": Essays in Scripture and Theology in Honor of Richard Hays*, edited by A. Katherine Grieb et al., 392–408. Grand Rapids: Eerdmans, 2008.

———. "On the Calling-Into-Being of Israel: Romans 9:6–29." In *Between Gospel and Election: Explorations in the Interpretation of Romans 9–11*, edited by Florian Wilk and J. Ross Wagner, 255–69. WUNT 257. Tübingen: Mohr/Siebeck, 2010.

———. *Our Mother Saint Paul*. Louisville: Westminster John Knox, 2007.
Grieb, A. Katherine. *The Story of Romans: A Narrative Defense of God's Righteousness*. Louisville: Westminster John Knox, 2002.
Jewett, Robert. *Romans*. Hermeneia. Philadelphia: Fortress, 2005.
Käsemann, Ernst. *Commentary on Romans*. Translated and edited by Geoffrey W. Bromiley. Grand Rapids: Eerdmans, 1980.
Martyn, J. Louis. "Epilogue: An Essay in Pauline Meta-Ethics." In *Divine and Human Agency in Paul and His Cultural Environment*, edited by John M. G. Barclay and Simon J. Gathercole, 173–83. Library of New Testament Studies 335. London: T. & T. Clark, 2007.

———. "The Newly Created Moral Agent in Paul's Letters." Unpublished paper delivered at the Society of Biblical Literature, San Diego, November, 2007.

———. "*Nomos* Plus Genitive Noun in Paul: The History of God's Law." In *Early Christianity and Classical Culture: Comparative Studies in Honor of Abraham J. Malherbe*, edited by John T. Fitzgerald et al., 575–87. Novum Testamentum Supplements 110. Leiden: Brill, 2004.

Matlock, R. Barry. *Unveiling the Apocalyptic Paul: Paul's Interpreters and the Rhetoric of Criticism*. JSNTSup 127. Sheffield: Sheffield Academic Press, 1996.
Meeks, Wayne A. "On Trusting an Unpredictable God: A Hermeneutical Meditation on Romans 9–11." In *In Search of the Early Christians: Selected Essays*, edited by Allen R. Hilton and H. Gregory Snyder, 210–19. New Haven: Yale University Press, 2002.
Meyer, Paul W. "The Worm at the Core of the Apple: Exegetical Reflections on Romans 7." In *The Word in This World: Essays in New Testament Exegesis and Theology*, edited by John T. Carroll, 57–77. Louisville: Westminster John Knox, 2004.
Miller, James. "The Romans Debate: 1991–2001." *Currents in Research* 9 (2001) 306–49.
Schnelle, Udo. *Apostle Paul: His Life and Theology*. Translated by M. Eugene Boring. Grand Rapids: Baker, 2005.
Watson, Francis. "The Triune Divine Identity: Reflections on Pauline God-Language, in Disagreement with J. D. G. Dunn." *Journal for the Study of New Testament* 80 (2000) 99–124.

12

Freed by Love and for Love
Freedom in the New Testament

Larry W. Hurtado

Freedom unquestionably continues to be a major theme of modern life and thought. Whether it is the political freedom of nations and groups within nations, or greater social freedom of individuals and/or groups within given societies, the topic figures large in current discourse. For Christians, and for others as well who may be affected by what Christians think and do, it is worthwhile to note how freedom is treated in the New Testament (NT), as this body of texts has a central significance in shaping Christian thought and behavior. Freedom was in fact also a major topic in the ancient Roman period of the NT writers, and so it is not an anachronistic question to ask how the topic is handled in these texts.[1]

---

1. A word on assumptions and objectives: In what follows, I do not take the NT texts as fully reflective of the actual lives of all first-century Christians. Although these texts (and other early Christian writings) are historical evidence of early Christianity, and can be mined for "social-description" of the movement, they are also expressions of early Christian aspirations and of voices *advocating and maintaining particular points of view*. I focus on the NT here mainly because of the importance of these texts as resources for Christian thought and action, and because of their potential consequences for wider exploration of "freedom." That is, my emphasis is more on the values explicitly or tacitly advocated in the NT, and I do not stake a claim here as to how widely or consistently early Christian behavior actually reflected these values.

In what follows, I have two main aims: (1) to survey briefly references to the freedom in the NT (particularly as manifested in social life) with a view to the historical context in which they appeared, and (2) to show that the NT is notable in its emphasis on love, both as the basis and the purpose of freedom.[2] I contend that this NT emphasis is radically distinguishable from dominant treatments of freedom in the Roman era, and in our era as well. Indeed this idea of freedom-for-love is so distinctive that perhaps it may be almost unrecognizable as freedom in the eyes of those for whom freedom means primarily being liberated from any sense of responsibility to others. But I further propose that this NT emphasis also provides a potentially productive and noteworthy line of thought for Christian participation in, and discussions about, freedom in the current scene. The freedom advocated in the NT is based in powerful spiritual realities, but is intended to have outward and very material manifestations in new social relationships, to be exhibited especially within the circle of the *ekklēsia*. In the final paragraphs of this essay, I offer some brief reflections on how the treatment of freedom in the NT might suggest directions of thought and action by Christians today.

Freedom in the Historical Context

In order to appreciate what we find in the NT, it is important first to give some attention very briefly to ideas and practices of "freedom" in the larger intellectual and cultural environment of earliest Christianity. In view of previous studies (including Peter Lampe's essay in this volume), it is sufficient for me simply to underscore key points.[3]

In the Roman-era setting of the NT there is scant discussion about national freedom. By the first century CE, Roman military adventures and expansion had produced conquest and colonization of many peoples and territories. The conquered and colonized peoples generally were well aware

---

2. This is a radically shortened version of the paper I prepared for the research project. I have omitted discussion of several matters in view of them being addressed by other contributors to this volume, in particular, Peter Lampe's discussion of ideas of freedom in the Roman cultural setting, Hans-Joachim Eckstein's essay on Pauline notions of freedom, and Beverly Roberts Gaventa's essay emphasizing the theo-centric basis of human freedom in Paul's thought. At some points, I also engage Elisabeth Schüssler Fiorenza's provocative essay.

3. In addition to Peter Lampe's essay in this volume, the following studies are especially important: Nestle, *Eleutheria*; Nestle, "Freiheit"; Niederwimmer, *Der Begriff der Freiheit im Neuen Testament*, esp. 1–68; Grigon, "Der Begriff der Freiheit in der Antike,"; Schlier, "ἐλεύθερος κτλ."; Blunck, "Freedom."

of their status as such, and aware also that any collective ethnic or national freedom eluded them under the weight of Roman force. To my knowledge, the only salient expressions of the ideal of national freedom (from Rome), and the expressions that clearly proved the greatest worry to Roman authorities as well, were those from Jewish resistance movements.[4]

There were a few Roman voices raised in support of traditional ideas of the rights and freedoms of Roman citizens, and in lament over the erosion of these rights and freedoms in the transition from the Republic to Empire. Among these voices, Cicero is perhaps the best known, but a somewhat similar standpoint is also reflected in Tacitus.[5] However, it does not really appear that this sort of discourse involved more than some among the traditional social-elite of Rome who objected to the negative effects upon their own privileges that resulted from the growth imperial structures, replacing earlier republican ones.

There was also the philosophical development of the idea of freedom (e.g., Stoic tradition) as an inner state in which, by diligent cultivation of the right frame of mind, one regarded oneself as free and sovereign within, whatever one's outward situation. In this notion, one disregarded in varying ways the outer world and focused on the internal, subjective realm.

By far, however, the most common notion of freedom in the Roman period was to designate a social/legal status, especially the pervasive distinction between free(d) persons and slaves. In Roman-era societies, slavery was a common and familiar social and legal category, its often ugly and always demeaning effects well known. Indeed, slaves comprised a major part of the human population of the Empire, and particularly in wealthier agrarian estates and urban households easily outnumbered those who owned them.[6] In this ironic situation of ubiquitous slavery and universal abhorrence of being a slave, to be "free" meant, most commonly and explicitly, not to be a slave. It is not going too far to judge that the ubiquitous place of slavery and its well-known features likely help account for the considerable place given to the discussion of personal freedom in Roman-era texts.[7] In short, slavery is the key cultural factor that defined "freedom" in the Roman world.

---

4. Hengel, *Zealots*, esp. 110–22. Hengel has argued (persuasively to my view) that the "freedom" sought was not only what we would today call "political" but also fundamentally involved a strong eschatological and religious hope and outlook.

5. I depend gratefully upon the discussion by Harris, "'Libertas' in Cicero and Tacitus." For a fuller treatment, see Wirszubski, *Libertas as a Political Idea at Rome*.

6. See, e.g., Raaflaub, "Freedom in the Ancient World." Bradley, *Slaves and Masters in the Roman Empire*, represents somewhat recent changes in scholarly views of Roman-era slavery.

7. Note, for instance, Epictetus, *Discourses as Reported by Arrian*, 1:244–304;

I wish to emphasize that in all these preceding types of freedom as treated in Roman-era texts, the dominant emphasis is on autarchy, the ability of a people or an individual to be master of choices and actions, not dictated to by, or bound to regard, anyone else. To cite again one of the most generous thinkers of the Roman period, Epictetus, "He is free who lives as he wills, who is subject neither to compulsion, nor hindrance, nor force, whose choices are unhampered, whose desires attain their end."[8] Or, to cite an old Greek saying, "The free man is one who lives as he chooses."[9] We may also note Philo's characterization of freedom as obeying no orders and working no will but one's own.[10]

I underscore the point that in the dominant view of freedom of the time, others (whether other nations, social groups, or individuals) are always a real or potential threat to one's freedom, or at best are an unavoidable constraint upon the scope of one's freedom. As I shall demonstrate shortly, this makes for interesting comparison with the religious notions of "freedom" that we encounter in the NT, in which other people play an important but very different role, and are, in fact, positively constitutive to true freedom.

Freedom in the New Testament[11]

We may begin our analysis of freedom in the NT with a brief assessment of how much of a place notions of freedom have in these texts. If, as in some previous studies, this question is addressed simply on the basis of occurrences of the Greek words which are translated directly as "freedom" (*eleutheria*), "free" (*eleutheros*), and "set free" (*eleutheroun*), then one could conclude that the idea of freedom is heavily (almost exclusively) Pauline, and not all that important in the rest of the NT.[12]

Philo, "Every Good Man Is Free."

8. Epictetus, *Discourses as Reported by Arrian* 4.1.1. For further discussion of freedom in Epictetus and Cynic-Stoic circles, see Galloway, *Freedom in the Gospel*, 57–102.

9. Cited in Schlier, "ἐλεύθερος κτλ.," 490 [ET].

10. Philo, "Every Good Man Is Free," 22.

11. Among major studies, the following are particularly important to note: Niederwimmer, *Der Begriff der Freiheit*, esp. 69–234; Jones, *"Freiheit" in den Briefen des Apostels Paulus*; Vollenweider, *Freiheit als neue Schöpfung*. However, Niederwimmer focuses almost entirely on the theological idea of freedom from sin and the Law, his discussion obviously shaped much by Lutheran traditions of bondage/freedom of the will. Jones's study is unduly restricted both in approach and data (as indicated in notes later in this essay). Like Niederwimmer, Vollenweider concentrates almost entirely on traditional theological issues and, like Jones, makes debatable comparisons of Pauline with Stoic and Cynic ideas of freedom.

12. So, e.g., Niederwimmer (*Der Begriff der Freiheit*, 69) commences his discussion

But to restrict attention to these three terms narrows unduly the scope of data relevant for an analysis of what we may characterize as the "discourse concept" of "freedom" in the NT.[13] A "discourse concept" may be comprised of a number of words ("lexemes"), and not only words that are etymologically related. For example, "upward" and "downward," "left" and "right" are obvious (in this case, contrasting) components in a discourse concept of "direction," just as "affection," "endearment," and "fondness" are among the components in a discourse concept of "love." So, a concept of "freedom" may be reflected in sentences that do not even use the words "freedom" or "free."

To illustrate this point, the terms *lutroō*, *lutron*, *antilutron*, *antilutrōsis*, *lutrōsis*, and *lutrōtēs* all have associations with the liberation of captives and slaves by payment of some fee or ransom. Likewise, the words *exousia* and *exestin* can be used to refer to the right/freedom of action characteristic of a "free" person, as distinguished from the captive will of a slave. The term *parrēsia* can denote the boldness and freedom to speak that pertains to a free person. So, clearly, if we wish to grasp the full discourse concept of "freedom" in Greek texts of that era, we simply must take account of these terms as well as those more customarily considered.

Although space does not permit here a detailed discussion, it is clear that references to ideas and images of "freedom" are actually more frequent, more important, and more widely distributed in the NT than might at first appear.[14] For example, if we simply take account of the Greek word *lutron* and cognate words (all of which were used to refer to the redemption of captives and slaves), the great majority of uses of this word-group lie outside the Pauline corpus, and are scattered among several NT authors.[15] Furthermore,

---

of the idea freedom in the NT with an analysis of occurrences of these words, concluding that, judged by their usage, freedom was essentially a Pauline idea (69). Similarly, Jones (*"Freiheit" in den Briefen des Apostels Paulus*) makes the deployment of these words in Paul the totality of the evidence to be considered.

13. For an explanation of "discourse concept" and the distinction between it and the lexical sense of words, see Peter Cotterell and Max Turner, *Linguistics & Biblical Interpretation*, 180-81.

14. Jones's study (*"Freiheit" in den Briefen des Apostels Paulus*) is, unfortunately, a prime example of an unhelpful narrowing of the evidence and questions. Three criticisms can be lodged: (1) He restricts the context of Pauline references almost entirely to Greek and Roman philosophical texts, failing to take adequate account of the significance and meanings of "freedom" in Jewish tradition; (2) he restricts the data solely to uses of the three Greek words *eleutheria*, *eleutheros*, *eleutheroun*; and (3) in his concern simply to show some Pauline acquaintance with common philosophical usage, he does not do adequate justice to the distinctive ways that Paul deploys and adapts the theme of freedom.

15. *lutrōsis* (redemption): Luke 1:68; 2:38; Heb 9:12. *lutrōtēs* (redeemer): Acts 7:35.

the uses of these terms in these texts to refer to God's "redemption" of Israel and/or Christian believers indicates how the idea of "freedom" quickly assumed a major place in articulating soteriological hopes and beliefs.

Political and Social Freedom

It will be disappointing to many moderns, however, that there is scant overt reference to the political idea of freedom in the NT. That is, it is very difficult to find any direct reference in the NT to aspirations for political enfranchisement and political rights as we know them today. There is, e.g., no encouragement to mount overt resistance to the regnant Roman regime or to organize to secure change of the political system. Of course, this probably reflects the Roman historical situation previously noted, in which Roman rule was widely deemed sufficiently tolerable (or at least was unavoidable), serious change in political structures was in any case judged completely unfeasible, and revolt was deemed unlikely to succeed or (for religious reasons specific to early Christian faith) inappropriate to contemplate. On the other hand, in some NT texts (most explicitly in Revelation), we certainly have indications of a longing for a "regime change," and even the expectation that it was certainly to come. But, the perception of the endemic nature of evil in political structures and more broadly in society meant that any genuine change for the better could come in reality only through divine intervention. So, for many early Christians, the prayer-petition, "Your kingdom come," appears to have expressed a sincere longing for radical change from the often dismal experience of human rule. But there was scant confidence that this longing could be answered by human political action. Instead, God's kingdom would require divine action to establish it.

In short, one factor accounting for the apparent lack of interest in attempting to promote greater political freedom through some sort of social or political movement was, obviously, the strong eschatological outlook characteristic in the NT.[16] Paul, for example, seems to have looked fervently for Jesus' return in power and glory (e.g., 1 Thess 4:13—5:11), which would also involve divine "wrath" upon all evil; and it is apparently this hope that Paul alludes to in his passing reference to the transitory nature of the "rulers

---

lutron (ransom price): Matt 20:28; Mark 10:45. *lutroomai* (to ransom/redeem): Luke 24:21; Titus 2:14; 1 Pet 1:18. Of this word-group, only *apolutrōsis* (redemption/ransom) appears in the Pauline corpus, comprising seven of its ten NT uses: Luke 21:28; Rom 3:24; 8:23; 1 Cor 1:30; Eph 1:7, 14; 4:30; Col 1:14; Heb 9:15; 11:35.

16. See Gaventa's discussion of "Freedom in Apocalyptic Perspective," in this volume.

of this age" (1 Cor 2:8). Nevertheless, and although he could also express a certain disdain for the civil courts and urged Corinthian believers to handle their differences with one another without recourse to "the unrighteous," Paul does not provide any hint of a program of wider action intended, for example, to achieve greater political power for believers, or anyone else for that matter.

So it would also be mistaken to ascribe this lack of a political program of change in the NT simply to a socially conservative mindset of the authors of these texts.[17] Paul, for example, should not be confused with Seneca! Granted, Paul accepts the political structures of his time as simply the reality of the day, and can even appreciate some of the potential benefits (and so, e.g., he can advise respect for authorities and the paying of taxes, Rom 13:1-7). Moreover, as a consistent monotheist he had to see everything as in one way or another ordained or at least permitted by God, and also answerable to God. But his advice hardly sprang from a political conservatism allergic to change in social structures. Instead, he clearly longed for the radical change that he associates with Jesus' parousia. Indeed, Paul's eschatological outlook represents a far more significant qualification of earthly political and social structures than is sometimes realized today, perhaps because for most modern readers of Paul (whether Christian or not) his futurist eschatology is foreign and embarrassing, and thus difficult to engage with the necessary critical sympathy.

Slavery and the New Testament

Likewise, in my view, the treatment of slaves/slavery in the NT, which has received focused attention in some recent studies, requires some clarification. We are the beneficiaries of a renewed scholarly interest in, and also significant revisions of scholarly views about, slavery in the Roman world.[18] The net effect of this work includes a wider scholarly recognition that, how-

---

17. Here I take a view somewhat different from that expressed by Elisabeth Schüssler Fiorenza in her contribution to this volume. I also do not share her enthusiasm for Greek ideas of a "democratic" civic *ekklēsia*, which was typically restricted to free, Greek males, excluding all women, foreigners and slaves (which collectively made up the vast majority of the population of Greek society).

18. In particular, note Harrill, *Manumission of Slaves in Early Christianity*; Harrill, *Slaves in the New Testament*; D. B. Martin, *Slavery as Salvation*; and Glancy, *Slavery in Early Christianity*. Also, Callahan, et al., eds., *Semeia 83/84: Slavery in Text and Interpretation*, comprises twelve essays on various topics connected with slavery in the ancient world and the NT, and on the engagement with NT texts in American slavery controversies.

ever diverse the experience of slavery, it was ubiquitous and always, though in various ways and degrees, a demeaning, and often quite a degrading and monstrous, violation of those enslaved.[19] As noted earlier, it is therefore all the more important to observe with care what attitudes toward slaves and slavery may be reflected in the NT.[20]

My first observation is that, indisputably, there is no NT text directly condemning slavery or openly urging Christians against holding slaves. But the question is what to make of this. That is, does this lack of an explicit condemnation of slavery adequately represent all that the NT offers on the subject?[21] Slavery was enshrined in the legal system of the Roman period, and it would have amounted to an open attack upon that whole system to seek to abolish slavery. Indeed, there was no mechanism or precedent for such an objective, and I know of no such effort anywhere in the time of the

---

19. See, e.g., the survey of the shift in scholarly studies of slavery by Horsley, "The Slave Systems of Classical Antiquity." See also Harrill, *Manumission of Slaves in Early Christianity*, 11–67, who refers to "an enormous growth of research" on ancient and modern slavery in the fifty years preceding his book, and acknowledges also that the "furious debates over ideologies, Marxist or otherwise, have made this subject more controversial than any other in the study of ancient literature, society, and culture" (195). Curiously, however, these analyses do not take account of ancient Jewish slave law and practice. See further reference to this later in this essay.

20. In *Semeia* 83/84 (1998), see the critical responses, especially to Horsley, by Wire ("Reading Our Heritage: A Response") and Stowers ("Paul and Slavery: A Response"). Harrill's volume, *Slaves in the New Testament*, rather clearly seems intended mainly to sideline the NT as having any authority in moral issues, particularly with reference to current controversies about same-sex relationships, as readily apparent in his final chapter (165–96). Glancy often seems to me to draw curious conclusions that approach interpretative violence upon texts, e.g., accusing Paul of contradicting his own egalitarian-sounding statement in Gal. 3:28 by using metaphors of slavery and heirs in the same epistle (*Slavery in Early Christianity*, 34–38). I hardly see that Paul's use of these metaphors "reinscribes" or "insists upon" the validity of social distinctions of slaves and free. Instead, seen in its setting, Paul's rhetoric actually subverts in various ways the rhetorical and cultural categories of his time, e.g., in referring to all, even elite males, as slaves of God/Christ. Likewise, her discussion of 1 Thess 4:3–8 (pp. 59–63) involves contradictory interpretative moves, a confusion of questions addressed, and also a failure to take account of Paul's Jewish background in understanding his statements here. In textual interpretation as well as other areas of life, it is well to "do to others as you would have them do to you"! See now also Byron, *Slavery Metaphors in Early Judaism and Pauline Christianity*, arguing that the primary background to Paul's references to himself and believers as slaves of God/Christ is the Jewish exodus-tradition, and that his rhetoric worked against reading him as invoking Roman-era institutional slavery.

21. In *Semeia* 83/84 (1998), several essays illustrate the conflicting ways that NT texts, especially in the Pauline corpus, were appropriated in the American controversies over slavery: C. J. Martin, "Somebody Done Hoodoo'd the Hoodoo Man"; Callahan, "Brother Saul"; Smith, "Putting 'Paul' Back Together Again."

NT authors. Orlando Patterson's observation about Paul and his cultural setting is applicable generally to the NT:

> The truth of the matter is that Paul neither defended nor condemned the system of slavery, for the simple reason that in the first-century Roman imperial world in which he lived the abolition of slavery was intellectually inconceivable, and socially, politically and economically impossible.[22]

Yet, here again, we should also take seriously the eschatological stance everywhere reflected in the NT. The full manifestation of God's kingdom which was fervently hoped for surely meant the abolition of slavery and all other distinctions used to make inferior, to oppress and to exploit others. The entire body of elect were to enjoy fully "the freedom of the glory of the children [*teknōn*] of God" (Rom 8:21), and in Revelation believers are all to be "a kingdom and priests to God" (Rev 1:6).[23] So, although Patterson is correct that abolition of slavery by social/political action was "intellectually inconceivable" in that time, the ending of slavery was certainly anticipated as one happy feature of the eagerly expected eschatological redemption to be consummated with Christ's return.

Moreover, although slavery is not challenged as a legal institution in the NT, these texts do reflect attitudes and values that, if acted upon, made at least for the amelioration of slave-status. Most significantly, of course, was the acceptance of slaves along with the free(d) as full co-religionists, one's "brothers" and "sisters," in the *ekklēsiai*. Certainly, there were also some other voluntary associations in which slaves could be included, although slaves were usually required to obtain the permission of their owners to be enrolled in these groups.[24] But the evidence suggests that churches typically included slaves. This regular inclusion of slaves in itself represents an

---

22. Patterson, "Paul, Slavery and Freedom," 266. Patterson's essay offers numerous reality-checks, such as his observation that "In the West, until the emergence of agrarian capitalism in the seventeenth century, almost every attempt to escape from primitive agrarian production and to develop more productive economies entailed a return to large scale slavery . . ." (268). Also worth noting is his forthright and level-headed estimate of Paul's views about slavery and freedom (266–71) and his corrective estimate of the impact of the NT in Western ideas of freedom (271–76). Note also D. B. Martin's comments: "The institution of slavery itself was never really questioned. Slaves may have resented their bondage, but given the chance they acquired slaves themselves. When free, they simply moved up a notch in the system, becoming themselves masters and mistresses and pulling their dependents along with them. Almost no one, slaves included, thought to organize society any other way" (*Slavery as Salvation*, 42).

23. Paul's uses of "sons" (*huioi*) and "children" (*tekna*) appear to be deliberate and conditioned by the particular point he seeks to make in each passage.

24. Harrill, *Manumission of Slaves in Early Christianity*, 147–52.

important and tangible expression of acceptance of those who were slaves as full co-religionists, fellow members of God's family, joint recipients of God's mercy and of Christ's redemptive work.[25]

Furthermore, a number of texts reflect a view that believers' status as slave or free was not to exercise the usual social consequences, especially in their relationship with other believers in the church and in how they regarded themselves. This is surely the intended import of Paul's comments in 1 Cor 7:21-24, which do not represent a callous indifference or a naive view of what slavery could mean. Instead, Paul expresses here a profound, new basis for one's identity and outlook toward others. These statements directed to slaves and free persons are part of a larger body of exhortation in 1 Cor 7:17-31 (indeed, perhaps to the end of 1 Cor 7) that urges believers not to define themselves or others by social conditions (circumcised/uncircumcised, vv. 17-20; slave/free, vv. 21-24; married/unmarried, vv. 25-31), whatever their own particular situation. Both the slave and the free person are exhorted to transcend the powerful effects of the Roman honor-shame culture, and take up a new stance toward themselves and others, a stance that is defined in their mutual calling by/to God. That God has called both slaves and free(d) to comprise the elect signals a divine refusal to observe the ordinary function of these legal/social categories; and so believers are to shape their own attitudes and behavior accordingly. Thus, I contend that Paul's encouragement to Christian slaves to think of themselves as free in the Lord, and his exhortation to the free that they are Christ's slaves (v. 22) do not to validate and "reinscribe" the slave/free structures of Roman society. Instead, Paul's words here manifest a bold and potentially powerful subversion of the normal meaning of "slave" and "free," and the honor-shame categories that the terms typically represented.[26]

In this light, we can take seriously the well-known statements in Gal 3:28 and Col 3:11, in which various polarities of nation, gender and social/legal status that were so central in defining people and their relationships in the wider society are not to exercise these effects within the churches. Of course, first-century Christians did not cease to be Jew or Gentile, male or

---

25. In an earlier publication, I have very briefly discussed the presence of slaves in early Christian assemblies, and the social costs that may have been incurred by slaves of pagan masters/mistresses: Hurtado, *How on Earth Did Jesus Become a God?*, 65-67.

26. McKeown, *Invention of Ancient Slavery?*, shows how various historical depictions of Roman slavery are all shaped by the dispositions of the historian, and I am no exception. But accusations against people, even dead and ancient such as Paul, carry with them a serious moral burden of proof, and we are entitled (perhaps even required) to give the benefit of doubt until we have sufficient ground for condemnation. See, e.g., McKeown's hesitation about Sandra Joshel's effort to recover the voice of silenced slaves (26-29).

female, slave or free; yet believers were to see themselves and one another first and foremost as "one in Christ Jesus," and as all belonging to Christ. However imperfectly this outlook was actualized in early Christian circles and subsequently (and there is no denying a regrettably frequent failure to exhibit this outlook), I contend that the nature of these exhortations should not be discounted.[27] They provide a potentially powerful body of teaching that can be drawn upon in churches to re-awaken the vision of them as circles that model and prefigure eschatological freedom.

To be sure, the NT exhortations to slaves to obey their masters with diligence (e.g., Eph 6:5-8; Col 3:22-25; 1 Pet 2:18-25) show an acquiescence to the social and legal realities of slavery. But in each of these passages we also have efforts to re-define radically for Christian slaves their situation, and to give them their own new sense of who they were and how they could deal with a condition that could not otherwise be changed by them. So, although in Roman law they were the possession of their human owners, Christian slaves were to re-orient themselves, rendering their service as to Christ, their true Kyrios, in the sure hope that their efforts will receive Christ's reward, however their earthly owners might react (Eph 6:6-8; Col 3:23-24). We should note that this sort of exhortation effectively treats slaves as moral agents, and offers them at least a conceptual means to re-signify for themselves a social status that they could not change.

In 1 Pet 2:18-25, Christian slaves who may suffer unjustly at the hands of their masters (which in the context appears to mean suffering related in some way to their faith) are to see themselves as aligned with Christ's sufferings.[28] This association with Christ was obviously intended to give Christian slaves an ennobled sense of themselves, and to strengthen their resolve to "do right and suffer for it" (v. 20). That is, the passage gives Christian slaves a new self-understanding (the significance of which should not be underestimated), and also an implicit authorization to act as moral agents, to identify for themselves what is "right" and to stand by their moral judgment courageously.

We should also take account of the equally striking exhortations to Christian owners of slaves (Eph 6:9; Col 4:1; and similarly in *Did.* 4.10;

27. Note Patterson's pithy statement, "without slavery, no genesis of freedom; without the slavery-freedom dialectic, no understanding of Pauline Christianity; without Pauline Christianity, no tradition of freedom in the West" ("Paul, Slavery and Freedom," 266).

28. The unjust sufferings in this passage may well include harsh responses of masters against Christian slaves who refused certain demands that were incompatible with the ethical teachings of their faith. For instance, we know that masters/mistresses commonly regarded their slaves as freely their property for sexual gratification, as discussed by Bradley, *Slaves and Masters*, 116-19.

Barn. 19.7). On the one hand, these statements obviously show that some Christians continued to hold slaves, and that there was no Christian program of emancipation in that time. On the other hand, the tone of these exhortations is significant. The dominant view in Roman society was that fear and intimidation (overt or subtle, depending on the circumstances) was the best means of handling slaves and ensuring their obedience. But the author of Ephesians urges Christian slave-owners to break with this practice and to treat their slaves as fellow-servants of the same heavenly Master, who shows no partiality to social status (Eph 6:9).[29] Also, in Col 4:1, Christian slave-owners are ordered to treat their slaves "justly and fairly", for slave-owners as well as slaves will answer for their conduct to the same heavenly Master.

To invoke shared standards of justice and fairness in the treatment of slaves was, in the Roman setting, simply remarkable, even something that many non-Christians may have regarded as nonsensical. The more common view in that time was that slaves were one's property, to use or dispose of as one pleased. Recognizing this helps us to perceive the true force of these exhortations. To cite also a couple of early extra-canonical texts, in *Did.* 4.10 and *Barn.* 19.7 Christian masters are specifically warned not to give orders to their slaves when angry, lest this cause the slaves to turn from their faith in God.[30]

Of course, probably the most familiar NT text in discussions of slavery and freedom is Philemon. The traditional view, that Onesimus was Philemon's slave, whom Paul sends back as courier of this letter, asking Philemon to receive him now as a Christian brother, has come in for vigorous disputation in some recent studies.[31] Although it is not clear that Onesimus was a fugitive slave, I remain persuaded that he was likely Philemon's slave, which makes the epistle an important text for us to consider, albeit briefly.[32]

29. On Roman advocacy of fear and intimidation of slaves, see Bradley, *Slaves and Masters*, 113-37. The phrase "desist from threats" clearly calls for Christian slave owners to break with the common attitude toward slave management. Granted, there were also a few pagan voices urging moderation in treatment of slaves, e.g., Seneca, *On Mercy*, 1.18.

30. Perhaps the concern was that harsh words and actions would easily be taken by household slaves as contradicting the Christian profession of the masters, i.e., hypocrisy, which could lead slaves (whose profession of faith may well have been prompted by their owners') to respond negatively to Christian faith. Bradley (*Slaves and Masters*, 114) notes only the exhortations to slaves, and seriously misrepresents matters in claiming that they simply show "how Christian leaders absorbed and indirectly supported the ideology of the slave-owning classes in Roman society at large."

31. See the review of studies by Horsley, "Paul and Slavery," 178-82. The most serious challenge has come from Callahan, "Paul's Epistle to Philemon"; Callahan, *Embassy of Onesimus*.

32. For an effective challenge to the traditional view that Onesimus was a fugitive,

The first thing to note is that Paul treats Onesimus as a full co-religionist, even referring to him tenderly as "my own child" (v. 10) and "my own heart [*splanchna*]" (v. 12). Moreover, Paul urges Philemon to receive Onesimus as "a beloved brother" (v. 16) and as Paul himself (v. 17). Other than requesting that any debt be charged to him instead of Onesimus (v. 18), Paul does not spell out what precisely all this should mean in Philemon's conduct toward his slave.[33]

As numerous others have judged, however, it seems very likely that one of Paul's particular hopes in this situation was that Philemon would send Onesimus back to Paul, to serve Paul on behalf of Philemon (v. 13). This request is never formally made, but the coy expression of confidence that Philemon will do "even more than the things I have said" (v. 21) is probably a further hint of Paul's wish. Whether this would have involved Onesimus being manumitted or simply seconded to Paul, we cannot say with confidence. But there is certainly no reason to exclude Onesimus' manumission from Paul's hopes, and, in my view, this is at least as likely as the alternative.[34]

In any case, this carefully-crafted epistle radiates attitudes that worked against ordinary Roman notions of slavery, and that at least implicitly, and within the constraints of the legal system of that day, promote the dignity and freedom of action of all concerned, including the slave Onesimus. Granted, he has no voice in this letter, because as a slave he had no legal standing from which to speak. But Paul's intercession on his behalf gives Onesimus a new status, as Paul's dear child, and as a beloved brother to Paul and Philemon, a status that derives from and invokes the Christian faith that unites him with Paul and with his owner. Certainly, this new status seems intended to have profound effects upon Onesimus' former status as slave.

Moreover, by making his intercession to Philemon an open and public matter, Paul effectively disregards the legal status of Onesimus as the private property of Philemon. Timothy is included as co-sender, and five others are

---

see esp. Lampe, "Keine Sklavenflucht des Onesimus."

33. But, of course, Paul says that he did not wish to command Philemon directly, preferring instead that Philemon have the opportunity to act out of his own volition (vv. 8, 14). If Onesimus had been sent to Paul by Philemon, Paul may be referring to any extra expenses incurred by Onesimus in v. 18, perhaps through over-staying his original mission. In any case, contra Harrill (*Slaves in the New Testament*, 13), who strangely represents the verbs in this verse as subjunctive (!) and claims that the debt is only a theoretical possibility, the phrasing (εἰ δέ τι ἠδίκησέν σε) suggests some real cost or debt that has somehow been incurred.

34. E.g., had Paul simply wanted Onesimus consigned to him, he might have requested this without sending Onesimus back; but this would make more sense if Paul hoped for his manumission. See also Patterson's forthright comments on the matter ("Paul, Slavery and Freedom," 270–71).

named as sending greetings (vv. 23-24, and thus aware that Paul is writing to Philemon). Also, Apphia (Philemon's "sister" or wife?), Archippus, and all the house-church are included as recipients of the letter, which likely means that it was expected to be read out in the gathered church. In making the treatment of Onesimus an ecclesial matter, Paul thus effectively overrides the Roman legal system with a new ethos and set of values.

In sum, the NT does not provide us with a program or precedent for achieving liberation by collective social or political action; but this should not blind us to the other ways in which these texts reflect a concern for real freedom of persons. There are notable expressions of a desire to transcend within the *ekklēsia* the negative social categories of the time, particularly the ways that slave/free distinctions operated in the larger Roman environment. Also, the strong eschatological vision reflected in the NT, which includes a relativization of the Roman imperial structures, and the hope of their replacement with God's beneficent and ennobling kingdom, comprises a radical alternative allegiance and value-system in which "freedom" for all the elect can feature as an important aspiration.[35]

Freedom and Love

I come at last to my most important point, which is the distinctive connection of freedom and love in the NT. The freedom celebrated and anticipated in the NT is entirely a divine gift, and it flows from redemptive actions by God and Christ that are typically portrayed in the NT as motivated by "love" (*agapē*). It is patently clear that "love" is an important component in the NT

---

35. Moreover, in assessing how earliest Christians may have regarded and treated slaves, scholars commonly overlook the question of the influence of the commandments in the Torah on the matter, which significantly restricted the powers of owners over slaves in comparison with Roman legal tradition: e.g., killing and wounding (Exod 21:20-27), sexual relations (Deut 21:10-14), and returning fugitive slaves (Deut 23:15-16). Both NT references and manuscript artifacts show that the Pentateuch was read and treasured as Scripture in many/most early Christian circles. Also, studies of Roman-era slavery regularly ignore the question of how Jewish practice may have been affected by Torah. On this, see Urbach, "The Laws Regarding Slavery"; cf. Flesher, *Oxen, Women, or Citizens?*, and Hezser, *Jewish Slavery in Antiquity*. D. B. Martin, "Slavery and the Ancient Jewish Family," claims no significant difference between ancient Jewish and pagan slave practice, but the evidence he offers does not really speak to his claim. Gibson, *Jewish Manumission Inscriptions*, however, reaches somewhat similar conclusions. The question is important in so far as Paul's own attitudes and those of his Gentile converts who included those who had previously associated themselves with synagogues would likely have been influenced to some degree by Jewish slave-laws/practices, not merely by general Roman law on the matter. Tomson, *Paul and the Jewish Law*, shows that Paul employed Torah positively in shaping Christian behavior.

vocabulary. As a concordance will readily show, both the noun and the verb are used frequently and across the entire NT (*agapē* 116 uses, *agapaō* 143 uses).[36] Moreover, the *specific behavioral import* of these terms in the NT derives from the redemptive acts of love that form the heart of the faith proclaimed in these texts. Love for a deity is not without parallel in the Roman setting, but the strong emphasis on God's love for humans is highly unusual in the wider religious discourse of the time.[37] For us, however, the idea of God's love for humans has become so common a notion that we may miss how striking it must have seemed to those who first heard it announced.

A selection of NT references will suffice to make the basic point. In Rev 1:5, Jesus is referred to as the one "who loved us and loosed us from our sins through his blood," the term "loosed" an obvious image of freedom. Similarly, in Gal 2:20, Paul movingly declares his life of faith "in the Son of God, who loved me and gave himself for me," the latter phrase obviously referring to Jesus' redemptive death. Romans 5:8 refers to God's love manifested toward sinners in Christ's redemptive death. In Eph 2:4-7, out of God's great love, believers have been raised from death in sin to new life with Christ, with still more glorious gifts to come.

This gives to the freedom celebrated in the NT a distinctive flavor. It is the gift of *divine* love. But the still more radical distinction characterizing NT freedom is that it is intended to promote in those liberated by this love an answering love, for God and Christ, and also, just as emphatically, for others as well. This latter emphasis on the expression of freedom in love for others is particularly unusual in the Roman world. NT freedom involves being emboldened and liberated from past habits and all other deflecting and constraining forces, so that one is able to relate to others on the basis of a giving, empowering, caring love that is to be patterned after God's love (and empowered by God's Spirit).

In addition to his appeal to the Galatians not to sacrifice their freedom in Christ and enslave themselves through a misguided notion that they must supplement their faith in Christ with a further conversion to Torah-obedience (Gal 5:1-6), Paul also warns them not to use their freedom simply for self-gratification (5:13-15). Instead, he urges in bold terms "through love

---

36. The overwhelming preference for these terms over other Greek words for "love" may derive from several factors, including their frequent use in the LXX. See, e.g., discussions of the terms by Schneider, "ἀγάπη"; Günther and Link, "Love," (and the copious bibliography in the latter article).

37. Human love for god(s) was usually referred to as an *eros* that involved a desire for association with the divine/beautiful. See, e.g., Bierwaltes, "The Love of Beauty and the Love of God." I have not found references in Roman-era pagan texts to the gods *loving* humankind.

become slaves to one another" (5:13), declaring that love of others fulfils the whole Torah (v. 14). Moreover, in 1 Cor 8, Paul exhorts the Corinthians to avoid their God-given freedom becoming a cause of discouragement and weakening of faith in other believers, and in the following chapter he lays out his own behavior as an example. Here, he declares that he has chosen to forego his special rights as apostle (e.g., to claim financial support, for himself and a wife, from his churches), making himself "a slave to all" for their sake, to win them to faith and salvation, and thereby share in the blessings of the Gospel (esp. 9:19-23). In 1 Cor 10:23—11:1, Paul contrasts a selfist notion of freedom ("All things are lawful," 10:23) with seeking the welfare of others (10:24). Thereafter, in an extended discussion of differences over eating meat that might have come to the market from pagan altars, and about eating with unbelievers (10:25-33), Paul warns against exercising one's personal freedom in the matter without regard for others. Instead, he advocates a concern to avoid offence "to Jews or to Greeks or to the church of God" (v. 32).

In a somewhat similar tone, 1 Pet 2:16 urges believers to "live as free people, yet do not use your freedom as a pretext for evil." In the immediate context, this freedom is to comprise doing God's will (v. 15), which includes due honor to everyone, love for other believers (*tēn adelphotēta*), a proper fear of God, and honoring the Emperor (v. 17).

In this NT emphasis upon *agapē* as the central responsibility that believers owe to others, we see the profoundly new and *social* dimension to NT freedom. There simply is no extended attention given to freedom in NT writings as the exercise of power on one's own behalf and without having to consider others. The only freedom that we see advocated in the NT is one that requires others for it to be exercised. To make the point emphatically, *one cannot exhibit this distinctive freedom except in relationship to others.*

By contrast, the common form of freedom sought in the Roman era likewise required others (especially slaves) in order for it to be to be exercised, indeed, even for it to be defined. But this kind of freedom was always actually at the expense of others, their labor and service enabling one to enjoy a freedom from labor and service. Moreover, as noted briefly already, in all the typical notions of freedom in the Roman era (and in our day as well), whether national, social/political, or inward-philosophical, to take account of others (other peoples/nations, groups, or persons), to allow one's actions to be shaped by others, represents either a real or potential threat to one's freedom, or, at best a necessary constraint upon one's freedom (e.g., in the interests of social peace). In short, there is no positive role of others in this sort of idea of freedom, except perhaps, for example, that one's freedom from manual labor or other objectionable tasks required others to perform these tasks. One's leisure was typically enabled directly by the labor of others, especially slaves.

In the NT, however, freedom is not to be exercised at the expense of others but with their interests and needs in mind. It is precisely the freedom to be "for others." That is, the freedom advocated in the NT requires others, not to relieve one from labor, but as objects of the love that comprises this freedom. This definition of freedom is, to my knowledge, unprecedented in the Roman world. Indeed, most people, then and now, for whom freedom consists in autarchy would likely not recognize as freedom what the NT advocates. This radically different view of freedom simply has to be faced seriously in considering what kind of contribution the NT might make to our concerns today. In any case, this idea of freedom-for-love/others is perhaps the most notable and distinctive feature of freedom in the NT.

It is conspicuous that the NT exhortations about the loving exercise of freedom are directed particularly to those in socially advantaged positions.[38] Loving service may more naturally be thought to be the duty urged on those in subservient positions in patriarchal and hierarchical societies, such as slaves, wives, and children. It is all the more important, thus, to note that those urged to loving regard for others in the NT are the entire body of believers, with specific exhortations in the "household codes" notably directed to husbands (Eph 5:25–33; Col 5:19). This suggests that the love-exhortations were not intended primarily to promote or reinforce a traditional hierarchical/patriarchal social-structure, and were not directed simply to promote the subservience of those in more vulnerable social relationships. Instead, however imperfectly it was conceived or actualized, the NT articulation of freedom as love for others represents a genuinely novel, even counter-cultural vision in which those who enjoy comparatively greater social status are to invest themselves in the interests of others.[39]

Concluding Reflections

Those who require an explicit scriptural text to authorize any thought or action will find the absence of NT statements on political liberation either frustrating or a (dubious) justification for conservatism. Those whose vision of liberation is essentially a hastily baptized version of Greek traditions of

---

38. It seems to me that this is a point not sufficiently noticed by Elisabeth Schüssler Fiorenza in her contribution to this volume.

39. One of the more vivid indications of how some early believers lived out this commitment to others is the reference to those who sold themselves into debt-slavery to ransom or feed others (e.g., *1 Clement* 55:2).

autarchy will find the NT vision of freedom incomprehensible and repugnant. I suggest, however, that neither represents an adequate engagement with the NT.

As we have noted earlier, the NT does not teach about political liberation, largely because the sorts of actions open today (especially political organization) were not available or even conceived then. But the strong affirmation and enhancement of personal moral agency in the NT are most compatible with social and political environments that make ample room for freedom of conscience and action. The *agapē* urged in the NT requires a real measure of personal freedom in order to be exercised authentically. It is not possible to render the love advocated in the NT under compulsion and coercion. So, e.g., freedom of religion and conscience, and freedom from intimidation and oppressive social relationships are essential for the cultivation of opportunities for true faith and loving freedom to be exercised.

The eschatological vision that fuels NT teaching on freedom and other matters has been effectively lost in most versions of Christianity, along with the concomitant radical view of evil, with unfortunate results. Conservative Christianity has tended to identify too readily the Kingdom of God with this or that political regime (from Constantine onward), whereas liberal Christianity has tended to under-estimate the depth of evil and in its own ways has tended to assume that radical change for the better can be achieved by well-intentioned people. But the eschatological outlook of the NT reflects a profound, if jarring, view of the human predicament, which, in view of daily news reports, at least seems more realistic. Moreover, that same eschatological hope also requires a stubborn refusal to confuse any human regime with God's Kingdom, which should allow scope for critique of all regimes, even those established in the name of freedom.

The NT emphasis on freedom for the love of others may be instructive as well. There are plenty of indications that modern liberal democracies are good at promoting individualism, and a culture of self-attainment. But these societies are not very successful in promoting a productive and free social cohesion, and common values, or in getting individuals to use their wealth and other advantages for the good of other people. Perhaps, then, the remarkable version of freedom in the NT is worth a second look. One implication of the NT treatment of freedom is that a "free" society cannot be measured simply in the degree of autocracy exercised by individuals. In today's political climate, choice is a major commodity offered by politicians to a public coached to prize enjoyment of maximum personal opportunities. But the NT idea of freedom rejects acquisitive choice in favor of serious and productive inter-personal involvement. This dynamic freedom involves a greater realization of one's own moral agency and an enlargement of one's vision to take in others. The expression of this sort of freedom promotes inter-personal relationships that nurture and enhance others, freely loving others in the power of God's freely given redemptive love.

Bibliography

Bierwaltes, Werner. "The Love of Beauty and the Love of God." In *Classical Mediterranean Spirituality: Egyptian, Greek, Roman*, edited by A. H. Armstrong, 293–313. World Spirituality 15. New York: Crossroad, 1986.

Blunck, J. "Freedom." In *New International Dictionary of New Testament Theology*, edited by Colin Brown 2:715–21. 4 vols. Grand Rapids: Zondervan, 1975–1978.

Bradley, Keith R. *Slaves and Masters in the Roman Empire: A Study in Social Control*. 1984. Reprint, New York: Oxford University Press, 1987.

Byron, John. *Slavery Metaphors in Early Judaism and Pauline Christianity*. WUNT 2/162. Tübingen: Mohr/Siebeck, 2003.

Callahan, Allen Dwight. "Brother Saul: An Ambivalent Witness to Freedom." *Semeia* 83/84 (1998) 235–50.

———. *Embassy of Onesimus: The Letter of Paul to Philemon*. Valley Forge, PA: Trinity, 1997.

———. "Paul's Epistle to Philemon: Toward an Alternative *Argumentum*." *Harvard Theological Review* 86 (1993) 357–76.

Callahan, Allen Dwight et al., eds. *Semeia 83/84: Slavery in Text and Interpretation*. Atlanta: Society of Biblical Literature, 1998.

Cotterell, Peter, and Max Turner. *Linguistics & Biblical Interpretation*. Downers Grove, IL: InterVarsity, 1989.

Epictetus. *Discourses as Reported by Arrian*. Translated by W. A. Oldfather. 2 vols. Loeb Classical Library. Cambridge: Harvard University Press, 1925–1928.

Flesher, Paul V. M. *Oxen, Women, or Citizens? Slaves in the System of the Mishnah*. Brown Judaic Studies 43. Atlanta: Scholars, 1988.

Galloway, Lincoln E. *Freedom in the Gospel: Paul's Exemplum in 1 Cor 9 in Conversation with the Discourses of Epictetus and Philo*. Contributions to Biblical Exegesis and Theology 38. Leuven: Peeters, 2004.

Gibson, E. Leigh. *The Jewish Manumission Inscriptions of the Bosporus Kingdom*. Texte und Studien zum antiken Judentum 75. Tübingen: Mohr/Siebeck, 1999.

Glancy, Jennifer A. *Slavery in Early Christianity*. New York: Oxford University Press, 2002.

Grigon, Olof. "Der Begriff der Freiheit in der Antike." *Gymnasium* 80 (1973) 8–56.

Günther, Walther, and Hans-Georg Link. "Love." In *New International Dictionary of New Testament Theology* 2 (1975) 538–47.

Harrill, J. Albert. *The Manumission of Slaves in Early Christianity*. HUT 32. Tübingen: Mohr/Siebeck, 1995.

———. *Slaves in the New Testament: Literary, Social, and Moral Dimensions*. Minneapolis: Fortress, 2006.

Harris, B. F. "'Libertas' in Cicero and Tacitus." In *Freedom as a Political Ideal: A Series of Five Lectures*, edited by B. F. Harris, 13–24. Auckland: University of Auckland, 1964.

Hengel, Martin. *The Zealots: Investigations into the Jewish Freedom Movement in the Period from Herod I until 70 A.D.* Translated by David Smith. Edinburgh: T. & T. Clark, 1997.
Hezser, Catherine. *Jewish Slavery in Antiquity.* Oxford: Oxford University Press, 2005.
Horsley, Richard A. "The Slave Systems of Classical Antiquity and Their Reluctant Recognition by Modern Scholars." *Semeia* 83/84 (1998) 19–66.
———. "Paul and Slavery: A Critical Alternative to Recent Readings." *Semeia* 83/84 (1998) 153–200.
Hurtado, Larry W. *How on Earth Did Jesus Become a God?* Grand Rapids: Eerdmans, 2005.
Jones, F. Stanley. *"Freiheit" in den Briefen des Apostels Paulus: Eine histororische, exegetische und religionsgeschichtliche Studie.* Göttinger theologische Arbeiten 34. Göttingen: Vandenhoeck & Ruprecht, 1987.
Lampe, Peter. "Keine Sklavenflucht des Onesimus." *ZNW* 76 (1985) 135–37.
Martin, Clarice J. "'Somebody Done Hoodoo'd the Hoodoo Man': Language, Power, Resistance, and the Effective History of Pauline Texts in American Slavery." *Semeia* 83/84 (1998) 203–33.
Martin, Dale B. "Slavery and the Ancient Jewish Family." In *The Jewish Family in Antiquity,* edited by Shaye J. D. Cohen, 113–29. Brown Judaic Studies 289. Atlanta: Scholars, 1993.
———. *Slavery as Salvation: The Metaphor of Slavery in Pauline Christianity.* New Haven: Yale University Press, 1990.
McKeown, Niall. *The Invention of Ancient Slavery?* Duckworth Classical Essays. London: Duckworth, 2007.
Nestle, Dieter. *Eleutheria: Studien zum Wesen der Freiheit bei den Griechen und im Neuen Testament.* Hermeneutische Untersuchungen zur Theologie 6. Tübingen: Mohr/Siebeck, 1967.
———. "Freiheit." In *Reallexikon für Antike und Christentum,* edited by Theodor Klauser, 8:269–306. Stuttgart: Hiersemann, 1972.
Niederwimmer, Kurt. *Der Begriff der Freiheit im Neuen Testament.* Theologische Bibliothek Töpelmann 11. Berlin: Töpelmann, 1966.
Patterson, Orlando. "Paul, Slavery and Freedom: Personal and Socio-Historical Reflections." *Semeia* 83/84 (1998) 263–79.
Philo. "Every Good Man Is Free (*Quod Omnis Probus Liber Sit*)." In *Philo IX,* 10–101. Translated by F. H. Colson. LCL. Cambridge: Harvard University Press, 1941.
Raaflaub, Kurt. "Freedom in the Ancient World." In *Oxford Classical Dictionary,* edited by Simon Hornblower and Anthony Spawforth, 609–11. 3rd ed. Oxford: Oxford University Press, 2003.
Schlier, H. "ἐλεύθερος κτλ." In *TWNT,* 2 (1935) 484–500.
———. "ἐλεύθερος κτλ." In *TDNT* 2 (1964) 487–502.
Schneider, Gerhard. "ἀγάπη." In *Exegetical Dictionary of the New Testament,* edited by Horst Balz and Gerhard Schneider, 1:8–12. Grand Rapids: Eerdmans, 1990.
Smith, Abraham. "Putting 'Paul' Back Together Again." *Semeia* 83/84 (1998) 251–62.
Stowers, Stanley K. "Paul and Slavery: A Response." *Semeia* 83/84 (1998) 295–311.
Tomson, Peter J. *Paul and the Jewish Law: Halakha in the Letters of the Apostle to the Gentiles.* Compendia Rerum Iudaicarum ad Novum Testamentum 3/1. Minneapolis: Fortress, 1990.

Urbach, E. E. "The Laws Regarding Slavery as a Source for Social History of the Period of the Second Temple, the Mishnah and the Talmud." In *Papers of the Institute of Jewish Studies, London*, edited J. G. Weiss, vol. 1, 1–94. Lanham, MD: University Press of America, 1989.

Vollenweider, Samuel. *Freiheit als neue Schopfung: Eine Untersuchung zur Eleutheria bei Paulus und in seiner Umwelt*. FRLANT 147. Göttingen: Vandenhoeck & Ruprecht, 1989.

Wirszubski, Chaim. *Libertas as a Political Ideal at Rome during the Late Republic and Early Principate*. Cambridge: Cambridge: University Press, 1960.

13

The Innovative Concept of Freedom in Paul

Hans-Joachim Eckstein

NOWHERE IN THE NEW Testament are "freedom" and "liberation" spoken of so frequently and centrally as in Paul. Seven of the eleven New Testament occurrences of ἐλευθερία/"freedom"[1] are in Paul, fourteen of the twenty-three occurrences of ἐλεύθερος/"free,"[2] five of the seven occurrences of ἐλευθερόω/"to free," "set free,"[3] and the sole occurance in 1 Cor 7:22, of ἀπελεύθερος/"freed person."[4] Apart from this, regarding the fateful claim to power by death, sin, and the law, Paul can say that the believers have "died" in Christ.[5] They have been "purchased," that is, legally acquired,[6] and they have been ransomed out of slavery through Christ.[7] Through belonging to

---

1. ἐλευθερία: Rom 8:21; 1 Cor 10:29; 2 Cor 3:17; Gal 2:4; 5:1.13 (2x). Cf. Jas 1:25; 2:12; 1 Pet 2:16; 2 Pet 2:19. Accordingly, the term "freedom" does not occur in the Gospels, in Acts or in any other of the longer non-Pauline scriptures.

2. ἐλεύθερος: Rom 6:20; 7:3; 1 Cor 7:21, 22, 39; 9:1, 19; 12:13; Gal 3:28; 4:22, 23, 26, 30, 31.

3. ἐλευθερόω: Rom 6:18, 22; 8:2, 21; Gal 5:1.

4. For the discussion see above all Niederwimmer, *Der Begriff der Freiheit im Neuen Testament*; Niederwimmer, "ἐλεύθερος κτλ."; Nestle, *Eleutheria*; Nestle, "Freiheit"; Schlier, "ἐλεύθερος κτλ." (cf. vol. 10/2, 1073–76); Vollenweider, *Freiheit als neue Schöpfung*; Vollenweider, "ἐλεύθερος κτλ."; Dunn, *Christian Liberty*.

5. ἀποθνήσκω with *dat. incommodi*, cf. Rom 6:1–11; 7:4, 6; Gal 2:19.

6. 1 Cor 6:20; 7:23: ἀγοράζω with absolute τιμῆς [*gen. pretii*].

7. ἐξαγοράζω: Gal 3:13; 4:4–5; cf. Eckstein, *Verheissung und Gesetz*, 55ff., 153ff., 237ff.; Eckstein, "Auferstehung und gegenwärtiges Leben nach Rom 6:1–11."

Christ believers are removed from the deadly reign of sin[8] and its absolute power.[9]

In addition to the concept of "freedom" itself, when one considers the various instances of the motifs "to free," "to redeem,"[10] "to save,"[11] "to die," "to justify from,"[12] it becomes increasingly clear how central in Pauline theology the motif "freedom," "to set free" is. This is true of Galatians, the "Magna Carta of Christian freedom," as well as of Rom 5–8, the triumphal unfolding of the "glorious liberty of the children of God." And it is even more true of the various discussions in the earlier letters to the Corinthians.[13]

In this connection, Paul undoubtedly takes up Greco-Roman social, political and philosophical conceptions of "freedom" and "slavery." As in general linguistic usage, the adjective ἐλεύθερος / "free" refers first of all to the social status of the "free person" as opposed to the δοῦλος / "slave" (1 Cor 7:21b, 22a; 12:13; Gal 3:28; 4:22). When one thinks of the comprehensive rights of the free person as societal member and fellow citizen[14] (in contrast to slaves or aliens), or when one considers the freedom of the Polis,[15] or has in view the freedom to exercise one's own will in everything he does,[16] or the inner freedom of the individual as regards social conventions, or freedom from one's own passions, it is no wonder that Paul assumes not only the

---

8. βασιλεύω, Rom 5:14, 17, 21; 6:12.

9. κυριεύω, Rom 6:9, 14.

10. "Redemption"/ἀπολύτρωσις; Rom 3:24: δικαιούμενοι δωρεὰν τῇ αὐτοῦ χάριτι διὰ τῆς ἀπολυτρώσεως τῆς ἐν Χριστῷ Ἰησοῦ. Rom 8:23: υἱοθεσίαν ἀπεκδεχόμενοι, τὴν ἀπολύτρωσιν τοῦ σώματος ἡμῶν. 1 Cor 1:30: ὃς ἐγενήθη σοφία ἡμῖν ἀπὸ θεοῦ, δικαιοσύνη τε καὶ ἁγιασμὸς καὶ ἀπολύτρωσις.

11. ῥύομαι—The risen Son of God is awaited as the final savior from godlessness and its consequences. 1 Thess 1:10: ὃν ἤγειρεν ἐκ [τῶν] νεκρῶν, Ἰησοῦν τὸν ῥυόμενον ἡμᾶς ἐκ τῆς ὀργῆς τῆς ἐρχομένης. Rom 11:26: ἥξει ἐκ Σιὼν ὁ ῥυόμενος, ἀποστρέψει ἀσεβείας ἀπὸ Ἰακώβ. Cf. as an expression of desperation Rom 7:24: τίς με ῥύσεται ἐκ τοῦ σώματος τοῦ θανάτου τούτου;

12. δεδικαίωμαι ἀπό, "to be free from," "to receive the final verdict of acquittal." Rom 6:7: ὁ γὰρ ἀποθανὼν δεδικαίωται ἀπὸ τῆς ἁμαρτίας.

13. Cf. 1 Cor 7:17–24; 1 Cor 8–10 [esp. 9] and 2 Cor 3.

14. In this sense Paul speaks in Phil 3:20 and 1:27 of πολίτευμα—"rights as citizen," "community," "home"—and of πολιτεύομαι—"to live as a citizen."

15. Cf. Gal 4:26 the introduction of the "heavenly Jerusalem above" as description of "the free," in contrast to "the present Jerusalem, for she is in slavery with her children" (v. 25): ἡ δὲ ἄνω Ἰερουσαλὴμ ἐλευθέρα ἐστίν, ἥτις ἐστὶν μήτηρ ἡμῶν (v. 26).

16. Paul also uses as an expression of bondage and dominated status, the inability to do what one wills, as well as the compulsion to act against one's own will—Rom 7:15–16: οὐ γὰρ ὃ θέλω τοῦτο πράσσω, ἀλλ' ὃ μισῶ τοῦτο ποιῶ. εἰ δὲ ὃ οὐ θέλω τοῦτο ποιῶ (cf. 7:19–20); Gal 5:17: ἵνα μὴ ἃ ἐὰν θέλητε ταῦτα ποιῆτε.

denotation of the Greek concept of freedom, but at the same time also the connotations of his own Greco-Roman environment.

However, the "apostle of freedom" did not need to adopt these concepts from the slogans of his opponents at Corinth; rather, he had already embraced them before his calling, in the context of the Greek-speaking synagogues of the Diaspora. Here, and due to his Jewish upbringing, Paul also got to know the Old Testament-Jewish tradition which understood the designation "servant of God" / δοῦλος θεοῦ as a title of honour of the prophets and of the people of Israel. In taking up this tradition, Paul too is able to understand himself proudly as δοῦλος Ἰησοῦ Χριστοῦ, as "servant of Jesus Christ" (Rom 1:1; Gal 1:10; Phil 1:1). Accordingly, in 1 Cor 7:22 Paul calls every believer a "slave of Jesus Christ" even if his social status is that of a "free person."

The decisive mark of Paul's ideal of freedom, however, is primarily the orientation toward the Person and the way of the Lord, Jesus Christ—beginning with his incarnation and commission, continuing through his life of loving obedience right up to his death on the cross: "who, though he was in the form of God, did not regard equality with God as something to be exploited, but emptied himself, taking the form of a slave, being born in human likeness. And being found in human form, he humbled himself and became obedient to the point of death—even death on a cross" (Phil 2:6-8). With reference to Christ as the "servant of the circumcision," in Rom 15:3, 7-8, Paul can challenge his congregation to mutual consideration and acceptance, "just as Christ has received, accepted and welcomed you, for the glory of God" (v. 7)—"for Christ did not please himself" (v. 3).

This specific realization of one's own sovereignty and freedom in voluntary self-sacrifice and serving care may have seemed particularly foolish or even offensive for the ancient thinking that maintained contrasts between God and humankind, freeman and slave, and freedom to decide and obedience: "but we proclaim Christ crucified (Χριστὸν ἐσταυρωμένον), a stumbling block (σκάνδαλον) to Jews and foolishness (μωρίαν) to Gentiles" (1 Cor 1:23). However, for the apostle himself, as well as for his churches, the binding model of how to live before God and with one another is the Son of God who out of love has become a slave and servant.[17]

Presupposing Hellenistic usage and perception, Paul contrasts the social status of the "freeman" / ἐλεύθερος with that of the slave / δοῦλος (cf. 1 Cor 7:21, 22; 12:13; Gal 3:28; 4:22; cf. Phlm 16). Galatians 3:28: "there is no longer slave or free . . . for all of you are one in Christ Jesus." On the basis of this new equality and unity in Christ, however, the "slave" is comprehended

---

17. 1 Cor 9; cf. Rom 15:1ff., 7-8; 1 Cor 8:9-11; 2 Cor 8:7ff.; 9:6ff.; Phil 2:1ff.

precisely as "freedman of the Lord" / ἀπελεύθερος κυρίου (1 Cor 7:22) who should no longer be concerned about his social status (v. 21). The addition ἀλλ' εἰ καὶ δύνασαι ἐλεύθερος γενέσθαι, μᾶλλον χρῆσαι in 1 Cor 7:21b may be best understood as an encouragement to seize social freedom if possible, rather than remain in slavery.[18] In as much as Paul, in the face of the present political circumstances, is not in a position to request the social-political implementation of the fundamental equality in Christ, he nonetheless expects his churches to welcome one another in mutual love as "brothers and sisters" (Phlm 16: οὐκέτι ὡς δοῦλον ἀλλ' ὑπὲρ δοῦλον ἀδελφὸν ἀγαπητόν, cf. Gal 3:28; 1 Cor 12:13). Paul's respectful but firm pleading for the slave Onesimus with his Lord Philemon (Phlm 8ff.) aims at the favourable reception of the offender as well as his commissioning as co-worker of Paul. For the social differences between "slaves" and "free persons"—in the same way as those between "Jew" and "Greek" and "man" and "woman"—are no longer a decisive factor owing to the reconciliation given by the cross of Christ and the life opened up by his resurrection (Gal 3:28).[19]

It is also in accordance with Greek usage when Paul in a transferred sense describes the "slavery" of humankind under sin and death as "being unable to do what one wants" (Rom 7:15: οὐ γὰρ ὃ θέλω τοῦτο πράσσω; Gal 5:17: ἵνα μὴ ἃ ἐὰν θέλητε ταῦτα ποιῆτε. However, for the apostle the reverse of this does not mean that the liberated person now "owns himself" and "can do whatever he wants." Rather, he should now belong to Christ as his Lord (Rom 7:4),[20] be led by his Spirit (Rom 7:6)[21] and thus live for God (Gal 2:19). Consequently, for Paul, liberation from sin, from the condemnation by the law[22] and from the impending death is not aimed at the absolute "autonomy" and "self-sufficiency" of the person. On the contrary, it is intended as an enabling for a life of relationship, that is of community and mutual acceptance.

At the same time, in the context of Old Testament-Jewish tradition it is highly remarkable that Paul applies the liberation in Christ not only to sin, but also to the law.[23] With regard to the Jewish and Gentile Christians of the Roman congregations, Paul offers this highly provocative formulation:

---

18. Cf. Schrage, *Der erste Brief an die Korinther*, 138-40; Stuhlmacher, *Der Brief an Philemon*, 44-49; Lampe, *Der Brief an Philemon*, 222.

19. Cf. 1 Cor 12:13; Col 3:11.

20. Cf. Rom 14:7-8; 2 Cor 5:15; Gal 2:19-20.

21. Cf. Rom 8:2, 14; Gal 5:16-18.

22. On this topic, see further Eckstein, *Verheissung und Gesetz*; Eckstein, *Der aus Glauben Gerechte wird leben*, 3ff.36ff.55ff; Eckstein, "Gott ist es, der rechtfertigt."

23. Cf. Rom 6:14; 7:1-6; 10:4; 1 Cor 9:20-21; 2 Cor 3:6; Gal 2:4, 19; 3:25; 4:5; 5:1-4, 18.

"Sin will have no dominion over you, since you are not under law but under grace" (Rom 6:14). "You have died to the law through the body of Christ, so that you may belong to another, to him who has been raised from the dead in order that we may bear fruit for God" (Rom 7:4). Or to use Paul's most pregnant and—for his Jewish hearers, his most provocative—formulation: "For through the law I died to the law (ἐγὼ γὰρ διὰ νόμου νόμῳ ἀπέθανον), so that I might live to God. I have been crucified with Christ" (Gal 2:19).

For Paul as the apostle to the Gentiles[24] this is relevant with regard (1) to the legitimacy of the mission to the Gentiles (Gal 2:1-21), (2) to the justification of Jews and Gentiles by faith in Christ (Rom 3:21—4:25; Gal 2:15—4:31) and (3) to the ethical conduct of believers. As a Jewish Christian Paul naturally takes the divine origin of the law as his starting point (even in Gal 3:19) and finds within it as Scripture the Gospel already promised (Rom 1:2).[25] However, as an ἔννομος Χριστοῦ (1 Cor 9:21) the final binding authority is for Paul the orientation toward "God's Gospel of his Son" (Rom 1:1ff.)[26] and the "law of Christ" (Gal 6:2).

In order to categorize correctly the significance, relevance, and limits of the law according to Paul, we doubtless require a clearer differentiation of the various uses of the term Law (νόμος) Torah. First, Paul uses the concept "law" as *prima pars pro toto* in the broad sense of "Scripture" (γραφή), and under this rubric can include citations from the prophets and the Psalms.[27] Regarding the law as *Scripture*, the self-evident principle applies for him— as for all the authors of the New Testament writings: "Do we then overthrow and nullify the law (νόμον οὖν καταργοῦμεν) by this faith? By no means! On the contrary, we uphold the law (ἀλλὰ νόμον ἱστάνομεν)" (Rom 3:31). In this connection the apostle develops in detail from the scripture (γραφή) the fact that Abraham and David were not justified on the basis of their Torah observance, but because of the promise and by grace through faith (Rom 4:1-25). Paul begins from the same continuity of promise and gospel when in the phrase "Law and Prophets" he identifies the first part of the scripture, the Pentateuch, as "Law."[28] Thus he can use the paradoxical formulation in Rom 3:21: "But now apart from the Law (χωρὶς νόμου) the righteousness of God has been manifested, being witnessed by the Law and the Prophets (μαρτυρουμένη ὑπὸ τοῦ νόμου καὶ τῶν προφητῶν)."

24. Cf. Rom 1:5; 15:6; Gal 1:6; 2:7-9.
25. Cf. Rom 3:21, 31; and 4:1ff; Gal 3:8.
26. Cf. Rom 1:9, 16ff.; Gal 1:6ff.
27. Cf. Rom 3:19a (citations from the Prophets and Psalms); 3:31 (see the following evidence in 4:1ff., above all 4:3a: γραφή); 1 Cor 14:21 (citing Isa 28:11-12); 14:34 (Gen 3:16); Gal 4:21b (Gen 16 and 21); cf. John 10:34; 12:34; 15:25.
28. Cf. Matt 5:17; 7:12; 11:13; 22:40; Luke 16:29-31; 24:27.

When Paul speaks critically of the law he means the "Law of Moses," the "Sinai Torah" in the specifically theological sense of the legal requirement and the legal decree of God.²⁹ These meanings are articulated, for example, in Lev 18:5 (Gal 3:12; Rom 10:5) and Deut 27:26 (Gal 3:10): "He who does them shall live by them." — "Cursed is everyone who does not continue to do everything written in the Book of the Law." As a result of his encounter with the crucified and risen Lord, the former Pharisee Paul came to the realization that, apart from faith in the Son of God there is no eschatological justification before God and therefore—apart from this faith—there can be no eternal life, not even for the Jews, and not through Torah observance. — Gal 2:16: "Yet knowing that a man is not justified by the works of the law (οὐ δικαιοῦται ἄνθρωπος ἐξ ἔργων νόμου) but through faith in Jesus Christ, even we [as Jews by birth, v. 15] believed on Christ Jesus, that we might be justified by faith in Christ, and not by the works of the law: because by the works of the law shall no flesh be justified (ὅτι ἐξ ἔργων νόμου οὐ δικαιωθήσεται πᾶσα σάρξ)" (Gal 2:16).³⁰

With ἔργα νόμου the apostle indicates neither only "legalistic works," that is depraved and perverted performance of the law,³¹ nor merely the so-called "identity marker" resp. "boundary marker"³²—like circumcision, food laws or Sabbath—of Diaspora Judaism, but in a broad and neutral sense, he means the fundamental affirmation and extensive obedience to the Torah which is made concrete by attitude and deed—"Torah observance."³³

---

29. So in Rom 2:12-15, 17-18, 20, 23, 25-27; 3:19b, 20-21, 27a, 28; 4:13-16; 5:13, 20; 6:14-15; 7:1-9, 12, 14, 16, 22, 23b, 25; 8:3-4, 7; 9:31; 10:4-5; 13:8, 10; 1 Cor 9:8-9, 20; 15:56; Gal 2:16, 19, 21; apos 3:2, 5, 10-13, 17-19, 21, 23-24; 4:4-5, 21a; 5:3-4, 14, 18, 23; Phil 3:5-6, 9 (Paul's writings contain 120 [118] of the 195 New Testament references).

30. On Paul's assertion of the impossibility of justification based on Torah observance, see Rom 3:20 (Ps 143:2); 3:28; 4:13-14; 8:3a; Gal 2:16 (Ps 143:2); 2:21; 3:11-12, 21.

31. See Klein, "Gesetz III," 67-71 ("das Gesetz in dieser Perversionsform," 67); cf. Bultmann, "Rom 7 und die Anthropologie des Paulus," 200: "Schon die Absicht, durch Gesetzeserfüllung vor Gott gerecht zu werden, ist die Sünde, die an den Übertretungen nur zu Tage kommt"; Bultmann, "Christus ist des Gesetzes Ende," in *Glauben und Verstehen*, 37ff.; Hübner, *Das Gesetz bei Paulus: Ein Beitrag zum Werden der paulinischen Theologie*, 28ff.

32. Cf. Dunn, *Romans 1-8*, LXXI, 153-54, 185-86; Dunn, "The New Perspective on Paul." On this topic, see further Strecker, "Paulus aus einer 'neuen Perspektive'"; Bachmann, "J. D. G. Dunn und die Neue Paulusperspektive"; Landmesser, "Umstrittener Paulus."

33. See note 22 above. On "Torah observance" in the broad sense (Heb. מעשי תורה cf. 4QFlor I,7; II,2) as the way to justification, that is, to salvation, see Gal 5:4: οἵτινες ἐν

In the retrospective of faith the apostle realizes that, in truth, the law was not given by God as the way to life, but—in agreement with the court prophets of Israel—as the way to document, to unmask, and to condemn sin: "For through the law comes the knowledge of sin" (διὰ γὰρ νόμου ἐπίγνωσις ἁμαρτίας, Rom 3:20). — "For the law brings wrath" (ὁ γὰρ νόμος ὀργὴν κατεργάζεται, Rom 4:15).—"In order that sin might be shown to be sin, and through the commandment might become sinful beyond measure" (ἵνα φανῇ ἁμαρτία, διὰ τοῦ ἀγαθοῦ μοι κατεργαζομένη θάνατον, ἵνα γένηται καθ' ὑπερβολὴν ἁμαρτωλὸς ἡ ἁμαρτία διὰ τῆς ἐντολῆς, Rom 7:13).

With this assumption it becomes clear why those who wish to live by Torah observance—according to Paul—stand fundamentally under the legitimate indictment and condemnation of the law—that is, under the "curse" (Ὅσοι γὰρ ἐξ ἔργων νόμου εἰσίν, ὑπὸ κατάραν εἰσίν, Gal 3:10).[34] According to the gospel, it is only the Spirit of the Lord—that is, of Jesus Christ (2 Cor 3:14, 16, 17)—which frees from the dominion of sin and death. Because of this, Paul can use an extremely provocative and pointed emphasis in his description of the ministry of the God-given law as a ministry of condemnation (ἡ διακονία τῆς δικαιοσύνης, 2 Cor 3:9), and even as the ministry of death (ἡ διακονία τοῦ θανάτου, 2 Cor 3:7): τὸ γὰρ γράμμα ἀποκτέννει, τὸ δὲ πνεῦμα ζῳοποιεῖ . . . ὁ δὲ κύριος τὸ πνεῦμά ἐστιν· οὗ δὲ τὸ πνεῦμα κυρίου, ἐλευθερία (2 Cor 3:6, 17). In fact, enslavement under the dominion of sin (ὑφ' ἁμαρτίαν εἶναι, Gal 3:22; Rom 3:9; cf. 5:12; 7:14) corresponds to the existence under the inescapable condemnation of the law (ὑπὸ νόμον εἶναι): "Now before faith came, we were imprisoned and guarded under the law (ὑπὸ νόμον ἐφρουρούμεθα συγκλειόμενοι) until faith would be revealed ... But now that faith has come, we are no longer under a custodian (οὐκέτι ὑπὸ παιδαγωγόν ἐσμεν)," Gal 3:23-26.

Finally, Paul can use the concept of "law"—in addition to (1) "scripture"/Pentateuch and (2) "Law of Moses"/"Sinai Torah"—also (3) in the figurative sense of "binding instruction" (*bestimmende Weisung*) as well as "standard," "lawfulness"/"regularity" (*Gesetzmässigkeit*), "principle": "On what kind of law / principle [is boasting excluded]? On the law / principle of works? No, but on the law / principle of faith" (διὰ ποίου νόμου; τῶν ἔργων; οὐχί, ἀλλὰ διὰ νόμου πίστεως, Rom 3:27). According to Wis 2:11, in this figurative sense the godless can elevate themselves above the righteousness of

---

νόμῳ δικαιοῦσθε. Also in the expressions ἐξ ἔργων νόμου (Rom 3:20; Gal 2:16 [3x]; 3:2, 5, 10), in short: ἐξ ἔργων (Rom 4:2; 9:12, 32; 11:6); χωρὶς ἔργων νόμου (Rom 3:28), in short: χωρὶς ἔργων (Rom 4:6); ἐν νόμῳ (Gal 3:11; 5:4; Phil 3:6); ἐκ [τοῦ] νόμου (Rom 10:5; Gal 3:21; Phil 3:9); διὰ νόμου (Gal 2:21).

34. On ὑπὸ νόμον εἶναι see also Gal 4:4-5, 21; 5:18; Rom 6:14-15; cf. 1 Cor 9:20; Gal 3:23.

God, with the words: "Let our might / strength be our law / our norm (NAB) / our yardstick (NJB) of right, for what is weak proves itself to be useless."

In Rom 7:7–25 Paul describes the inability of human beings, of themselves, to fulfill God's good and just commandment and his holy law (Rom 7:12, 14). This is because in connection with Genesis 2 and 3, the human being reflects the situation of Adam, that is, "of humankind." In so doing Paul exposes the situation of humankind without Christ—*remoto Christo*. Paul himself only realized this situation in retrospect, that is in Christo, from the vantage point of faith. Accordingly, from the beginning "humankind" has in fact not belonged to the life-fostering instruction of God according to Gen 2:17 / Rom 7:10, 12, but has allowed itself to be seduced and deceived by the serpent's "instruction," which brings death (Gen 3:13 / Rom 7:11: ἐξηπάτησέν με). Because of its disastrous effect Paul describes this "instruction" of the serpent, as well as that of sin (Gen 3:1–5; Rom 7:8, 11), as the "law of sin" (Rom 7:23) and the "law of sin and of death" (τῆς ἁμαρτίας καὶ τοῦ θανάτου, Rom 8:2).

According to Paul, while God's good commandment is not itself sin nor does it bring about death (Rom 7:7, 13), neither is the Law of Moses able to free humankind from the dominion of sin which brings death (τὸ γὰρ ἀδύνατον τοῦ νόμου, Rom 8:3). For since Adam there is found in the human being "another law" (ἕτερος νόμος) which is in conflict with the law of God (ἀντιστρατευόμενον τῷ νόμῳ τοῦ νοός μου) and takes human beings prisoner under the dictate of sin (καὶ αἰχμαλωτίζοντά με ἐν τῷ νόμῳ τῆς ἁμαρτίας τῷ ὄντι ἐν τοῖς μέλεσίν μου, Rom 7:23). On the basis of Gen 3:6 and Exod 20:17, Paul defines this "other law"—binding instruction / standard / principle—as "sinful passions" (τὰ παθήματα τῶν ἁμαρτιῶν, Rom 7:5), as "covetousness" (ἐπιθυμία, Rom 7:8) and as the human principle of the flesh (σάρξ, Rom 7:25; 8:1–13).

Since his encounter with Christ, the apostle no longer finds in the mosaic law the answer to this desperate situation of fundamental bondage, imprisonment and enslavement of the human being, but rather he finds it in the "law of the spirit that makes alive" which is effective in Christ Jesus (ὁ γὰρ νόμος τοῦ πνεύματος τῆς ζωῆς ἐν Χριστῷ Ἰησοῦ, Rom 8:2) and the "instruction," the "standard," and the "principle" of faith (νόμος πίστεως, Rom 3:27). Faith in Christ—that is "faith expressing itself in love" (πίστις δι' ἀγάπης ἐνεργουμένη, Gal 5:6)—and the Fruit of the Spirit (ὁ καρπὸς τοῦ πνεύματός, Gal 5:22) confirm and do not refute the good demand for righteousness by the law of God (τὸ δικαίωμα τοῦ νόμου, Rom 8:4), the Ten Commandments (Rom 13:8–10) or the commandment to Love Thy Neighbor (Gal 5:14; Rom 13:8, 9)—"against such there is no law" (κατὰ τῶν τοιούτων οὐκ ἔστιν νόμος, Gal 5:23b). But should these conflict, it is not the Law of Moses, but the instruction and Torah of Christ (τὸν νόμον τοῦ Χριστοῦ, Gal 6:2) that is ultimately binding for the Apostle of the Gentiles (ἐθνῶν ἀπόστολος, Rom 11:13). According to 1 Cor 9:20, 21, the apostle no longer sees himself "under the law" (μὴ ὢν αὐτὸς ὑπὸ νόμον), but "under the law of Christ" (ἔννομος Χριστοῦ)—and precisely for this reason he is no longer "lawless" in relation to God (μὴ ὢν ἄνομος θεοῦ). Correspondingly, in each case Paul succeeds in basing the standards for his ethical instructions altogether concretely in the person, the way, and the instruction of the crucified and risen Lord.[35]

Or, with Paul's own words from Rom 8:1–4, to summarize the entire theology of freedom from the powers that enslave human beings:

> There is therefore now no condemnation for those who are in Christ Jesus. For the law of the Spirit of life in Christ Jesus has set you free from the law of sin and of death (ὁ γὰρ νόμος τοῦ πνεύματος τῆς ζωῆς ἐν Χριστῷ Ἰησοῦ ἠλευθέρωσέν σε ἀπὸ τοῦ νόμου τῆς ἁμαρτίας καὶ τοῦ θανάτου). For God has done what the law, weakened by the flesh, could not do and was powerless to do (τὸ γὰρ ἀδύνατον τοῦ νόμου): by sending his own Son in the likeness of sinful flesh, and to deal with sin, he condemned sin in the flesh (ἐν ὁμοιώματι σαρκὸς ἁμαρτίας καὶ περὶ ἁμαρτίας κατέκρινεν τὴν ἁμαρτίαν ἐν τῇ σαρκί), so that the just requirement of the law (τὸ δικαίωμα τοῦ νόμου) might be fulfilled in us, who walk not according to the flesh but according to the Spirit.

As we have seen above, such a liberation from sin, from the condemnation by the law and from impending death—such a liberation does not merely lead to an absolute "autonomy" and "self-sufficiency" of the person. On the contrary, it is intended to enable the believer for a life of relationship and mutual acceptance. However, it is possible to go a step further and state that the freedom of the "liberated one" (Rom 6:18, 22: ἐλευθερωθέντες, cf. Rom 7:3: ἐλευθέρα ἐστίν; 8:2: ἠλευθέρωσέν σε) exists precisely in belonging to Christ who, as the crucified and risen one, is himself free from sin and death (Rom 6:9–10). Believers are not "crucified" per se, but "crucified" with Christ and hence "dead" to sin and the law, i.e. liberated from their dominion (Rom 6:6–7). Only "in Christ"—i.e. on the basis of his substitution and in communion with him—are they set free from the dominance of the life-destroying separation from God (Rom 6:1ff.; 8:1ff.). The believer is not free and alive as an independent "self" but only because—and insofar—the risen Christ "lives in him" by his life-giving Spirit (Rom 8:9–11; Gal 2:19–20).

For Paul, Christian freedom is not only focused on "relationship" with regard to ethics, but it is also grounded in it soteriologically. This

---

35. See Rom 14:15; 15:1–3, 7; 1 Cor 8:11; 2 Cor 8:7–9; Phil 1:27—2:18.

relationship is not experienced as a limitation and boundary of freedom but as the realm of its unfolding and development (*Entfaltungsbereich*). Nor is it experienced as a contrast to freedom but as its realization. Propositionally speaking therefore, we can say that for Paul, freedom from sin and law does not exist in and of itself, but only as freedom for God. "Freedom from" only exists as "freedom for." Autonomy over against God and his righteousness would inevitably lead to slavery under the life-denying forces. In accordance with the Old Testament–Jewish tradition, for Paul human beings never exist in and of themselves and without belonging. For him they always exist in relation to entities that govern and affect them.

Being created by God, human beings are always dependent on the loving care of their God and thus never live autonomously but always "in relationship." If a human being *is*, he is *in relationship*. If he turns away from his creator he inevitably makes himself a "slave" to other influences which put himself, his life and his relationships in danger. It is only logical that the liberation from this slavery needs to be understood as a *change of lordship*. Romans 6:16–18:

> Do you not know that if you present yourselves to anyone as obedient slaves, you are slaves of the one whom you obey, either of sin, which leads to death, or of obedience, which leads to righteousness? But thanks be to God that you, having once been slaves of sin, have become obedient from the heart to the form of teaching to which you were entrusted, and that you, having been set *free from sin*, have become *slaves of righteousness*.

Nonetheless, it was the accusations of his opponents that prompted Paul to formulate this formal contrast of "slaves of sin" vs. "slaves or servants of righteousness." His opponents insinuated that his proclamation of the surpassing grace and of the freedom from sin and the law would in effect advance the sway of sin (Rom 6:1, 15; cf. 3:8; Gal 2:17: ἆρα Χριστὸς ἁμαρτίας διάκονος; μὴ γένοιτο). By way of contrast, Paul employs in his own, positive exposition of the Spirit-determined life in Rom 8:1–39 the contrast of "*slavery*" vs. "*sonship*"/"*adoption*": "For you did not receive a spirit of slavery (δουλεία) to fall back into fear, but you have received a spirit of adoption (υἱοθεσία). When we cry, 'Abba! Father!' it is that very Spirit bearing witness with our spirit that we are children of God (τέκνα θεοῦ)" (Rom 8:15–16).

The relationship of the believers to God is fundamentally different from the former dependencies. Faith in the Father of Jesus Christ is not just a "relationship of lordship" (*Herrschaftsbeziehung*) but a *positive, holistic*, and *personal* relationship that is based on unconditional affection and unlimited care. For the mission of Christ, even to the point of giving his life on the cross, is seen as the unambiguous proof of the unconditional love of both the Father (Rom 5:8; 8:31–32, 38–39; cf. Eph 2:4ff) and the Son (Rom 8:35; Gal 2:20; cf. Eph 5:2, 25b). This *christologically* motivated combination of a *relational concept of freedom* with a thus positively determined *concept of God and man* surely is a fundamental characteristic of the innovative concept of freedom in Paul.

The "glorious freedom of the children of God" (ἡ ἐλευθερία τῆς δόξης [*gen. qual.*], Rom 8:21) may still be limited with regard to physical salvation from persecution, decay and suffering (Rom 8:21–25). And those already appointed as children and heirs (Rom 8:17) may presently together with the suffering creation still long for their salvation from the "bondage to decay" (ἀπὸ τῆς δουλείας τῆς φθορᾶς, Rom 8:21). However, they are already now empowered to unfold their freedom in relation to God (Rom 8:28; 1 Cor 8:3) and to other people (Rom 12:9ff.; 13:8–10; 14:1—15:7) as love.

In every situation—no matter whether it regards mutually accepting one another when debating the renunciation of meat and wine (Rom 14), or making allowances for former pagans in the context of eating "idol meat" (1 Cor 8–10)—Paul expects that believers will not insist on their own freedom (ἡ ἐξουσία, 1 Cor 8:9; 9:4ff.) and knowledge (γνῶσις, 1 Cor 8:1ff.) but demonstrate their freedom precisely in love and mutual consideration. For Paul, what applies in one's relationship to God also applies in one's interpersonal relationships: "freedom from" always realizes itself as "freedom for"; and on the basis of love this relationship is not experienced as limitation but as the realm of the unfolding (*Entfaltungsbereich*) of freedom: "For though I am free with respect to all (ἐλεύθερος γὰρ ὢν ἐκ πάντων), I have made myself a slave to all (πᾶσιν ἐμαυτὸν ἐδούλωσα), so that I might win more of them" (1 Cor 9:19). — "For you were called to freedom, brothers and sisters; only do not use your freedom as an opportunity for self-indulgence, but through love become slaves to one another (ἀλλὰ διὰ τῆς ἀγάπης δουλεύετε ἀλλήλοις)" (Gal 5:13).

In view of the Greco-Roman environment, the Innovative Concept of Freedom in Paul consists precisely in the definition of freedom as the ability for community and for service in reciprocal awareness and personal acceptance. Compared with its Jewish environment, the innovation and unprecedented nature lies in the fact that this freedom and redemption bear the name of a person and are identical with that name—the name of the crucified and risen Lord, Jesus Christ. For both groups—Greeks as well as Jews—it appears highly provocative and "innovative" that the one who was in the form of God (ὃς ἐν μορφῇ θεοῦ ὑπάρχων, Phil 2:6), did not just speak to humankind or dwell above them, but he humbled and emptied himself and took the form of a slave (ἀλλ᾽ ἑαυτὸν ἐκένωσεν μορφὴν δούλου λαβών).

He himself became a human being—that is, capable of suffering, mortal and obedient—in order that in this he might show himself sovereign, free, and worthy of honor: ἐταπείνωσεν ἑαυτὸν γενόμενος ὑπήκοος μέχρι θανάτου, θανάτου δὲ σταυροῦ. διὸ καὶ ὁ θεὸς αὐτὸν ὑπερύψωσεν καὶ ἐχαρίσατο αὐτῷ τὸ ὄνομα τὸ ὑπὲρ πᾶν ὄνομα . . . (Phil 2:7ff.).

Bibliography

Bachmann, Michael. "J. D. G. Dunn und die Neue Paulusperspektive." *Theologische Zeitschrift* 63 (2007) 25–43.
Bultmann, Rudolf. "Christus ist des Gesetzes Ende." In *Glauben und Verstehen*, vol. 2, 32–58. 5th ed. Tübingen: Mohr/Siebeck, 1968.
———. "Röm 7 und die Anthropologie des Paulus." In *Exegetica: Aufsätze zur Erforschung des Neuen Testaments*, 198–209. Tübingen: Mohr/Siebeck, 1967.
Dunn, James D. G. *Christian Liberty: A New Testament Perspective*. Grand Rapids: Eerdmans, 1993.
———. "The New Perspective on Paul." *Bulletin of the John Rylands Library* 65 (1983) 95–122.
———. *Romans 1–8*. Word Biblical Commentary 38A. Dallas: Word, 1988.
Eckstein, Hans-Joachim. "Auferstehung und gegenwärtiges Leben nach Rom 6:1–11: Präsentische Eschatologie bei Paulus?" In *Der aus Glauben Gerechte wird leben: Beiträge zur Theologie des Neuen Testaments*, 36–54. 2nd ed. Beiträge zum Verstehen der Bibel 5. Münster: Lit, 2007.
———. *Der aus Glauben Gerechte wird leben: Beiträge zur Theologie des Neuen Testaments*. 2nd ed. Beiträge zum Verstehen der Bibel 5. Münster: Lit, 2007.
———. "Gott ist es, der rechtfertigt: Rechtfertigungslehre als Zentrum paulinischer Theologie?" *Zeitschrift für Neues Testament* 14 (2004) 41–48.
———. *Verheissung und Gesetz: Eine exegetische Untersuchung zu Gal 2,15—4,7*. WUNT 86. Tübingen: Mohr/Siebeck, 1996.
Hübner, Hans. *Das Gesetz bei Paulus: Ein Beitrag zum Werden der paulinischen Theologie*. 2nd ed. FRLANT 119. Göttingen: Vandenhoeck & Ruprecht, 1980.
Klein, G. "Gesetz III." In *TRE* 13 (1984) 58–75.
Lampe, Peter. *Der Brief an Philemon*. Neue Testament Deutsch 8/2. Göttingen: Vandenhoeck & Ruprecht, 1998.
Landmesser, C. "Umstrittener Paulus: Die gegenwärtige Diskussion um die paulinische Theologie." *Zeitschrift für Theologie und Kirche* 105 (2008) 387–410.
Nestle, Dieter. *Eleutheria: Studien zum Wesen der Freiheit bei den Griechen und im Neuen Testament*. HUT 6. Tübingen: Mohr/Siebeck, 1967.
———. "Freiheit." In *Reallexikon für Antike und Christentum*, edited by Theodor Klauser, 8:269–306. Stuttgart: Hiersemann, 1972.
Niederwimmer, Kurt. *Der Begriff der Freiheit im Neuen Testament*. Theologische Bibliothek Töpelmann 11. Berlin: Töpelmann, 1966.
———. "ἐλεύθερος κτλ." In *Exegetisches Wörterbuch zum Neuen Testament*, edited by Horst Balz and Gerhard Schneider, 1:1052–58. Stuttgart: Kohlhammer, 1980.
Schlier, H. "ἐλεύθερος κτλ." In *TWNT* 2 (1935) 484–500
———. "ἐλεύθερος κτλ." In *TDNT* 2 (1964) 487–502.

Schrage, Wolfgang. *Der erste Brief an die Korinther (1 Kor 6,12—11,16)*. Evangelisch-katholischer Kommentar zum Neuen Testament 7/2. Neukirchen-Vluyn: Neukirchener, 1995.

Strecker, Christian. "Paulus aus einer 'neuen Perspektive': Der Paradigmenwechsel in der jüngeren Paulusforschung." *Kirche und Israel* 11 (1996) 3–18.

Stuhlmacher, Peter. *Der Brief an Philemon*. 3rd ed. Evangelisch-katholischer Kommentar zum Neuen Testament 18. Neukirchen-Vluyn: Neukirchener, 2004.

Vollenweider, Samuel. *Freiheit als neue Schöpfung: Eine Untersuchung zur Eleutheria bei Paulus und in seiner Umwelt*. FRLANT 147. Göttingen: Vandenhoeck & Ruprecht, 1989.

———. "ἐλεύθερος κτλ." In *Theologisches Begriffslexikon zum Neuen Testament*, 499–505. Rev. ed. Wuppertal: Brockhaus, 2005.

Part 4

Freedom as Ethos of Belonging

Introduction

Dirk J. Smit

The fourth section deals with different traditions in which freedom has been understood as integral to forms of belonging, to life in community. The first two essays focus on Biblical periods and documents. In the first contribution, Jan Christian Gertz shows that, although there are considerable differences between the Ancient Greek concept of freedom and the concept found in Deuteronomy, the latter introduces essential perspectives to the idea of freedom: The exclusiveness of the deity limits all national and royal power and leads to the equality of the king and full citizens before the (divine) law (cf. the Greek idea of *isonomia*). Moreover, the idea of fraternal ethic—which is characteristic of Deuteronomy—obligates those involved to extend inner-familial solidarity to the whole people of Yahweh. Thus, in Deuteronomy the rights of the free are joined to an ethos of freedom.

In a second essay, Jürgen van Oorschot investigates whether it makes sense to speak of concepts of freedom under Persian Rule and focuses on prophetic literature in Isa 40–66. He argues that freedom as a concept was unknown, also in the Hebrew Bible, both in political and individual sense. Freedom was much rather combined with concepts of regularity and order. Together, they form the basis for potentials of freedom, which should be understood as the potential to act, based on regularity and order which make prosperous and wise living possible. He illustrates these functions in the book of Qohelet and then analyzes a special transformation of this understanding in Isa 40–66. There, regularity and order take the form of the ways in which Persian kings use policy and political strategies to wield their power. Concrete experiences of the potential to act in freedom may be the unintended results, but it would be anachronistic to interpret those policies as religious or political tolerance. When similar policies are then attributed to God as King in the prophetic literature, the same consequences follow. Therefore political freedom as the potential to act in the Old Testament texts is not the function of political and military power, but the result of the one and only acting God, according to theocentric and eschatological thinking. Human beings gain the potential to act because God's power and sovereignty ensure a scope for acting in situations no longer dominated by chaos. Ambivalent historical events can now be interpreted religiously and politically as opportunities for acts of freedom, individually or collectively. In Isa 40-66, God is portrayed as free subject and because of the salutary relationship between God and God's people they too receive the potential to act.

The other two contributions deal with Reformation history. In a third contribution, Jindřich Halama discusses notions of freedom from the Czech Reformation. He argues that an urgent need to liberate the church from the "snares of the Antichrist" and to restore true Christian freedom was the original and primary aim of the Czech Reformation. From the early fifteenth to the early seventeenth century, there was more than one attempt to achieve this aim. The radical Hussite emphasis on liberating the entire Czech Christian society and establishing a kingdom of freedom and justice throughout the Czech lands led to revolutionary violence that ended in fratricidal conflict and in a less than equal compromise with the ruling ideology. The attempt of the Czech Brethren, which was based on voluntary choice, exclusivity, and a moral strictness that rejected the ways of the "fallen world," fell into legalism and internal contradictions within two generations. However, he claims, as a result of the struggles of the Czech Reformation during the sixteenth century, concepts of toleration, freedom of conscience, and freedom of belief and religion developed. Christian freedom was recognized as being something that could not be attained by human effort, but could only be gratefully accepted as God's gracious gift. The only way to promote it was to not deny it to those who believed differently, but to respect them and to witness to true Christian freedom through a faithful life. Such a fragile concept was doomed to be suppressed in the political arena of the time, but it helped pave way for the modern concepts of freedom of conscience and freedom of religion.

In the fourth and final essay, Dirk Smit takes his point of departure in the widespread claim that major Reformers, including Luther and Calvin, regarded service as the highest form of freedom. He illustrates this controversial position by using John Calvin. Calvin's views on human freedom were situated within the context of his understanding of the Christian life, which he saw as a life of not belonging to oneself, but to God. In an attempt to understand this paradoxical, even contradictory claim, Smit closely follows the interpretation of Calvin's thought by the political scientist William Stevenson, who argued that Calvin defended a threefold concept of freedom, namely individual, corporate and historical freedom, however, each of them self-critically qualified in important ways. Against this background, Smit concludes with a recent South African case-study, in which notions of freedom (and in fact the direct influence of Calvin) played a central role in public struggles for freedom (corporate over against individual) and (historical) liberation.

Together, these essays investigate understandings of freedom—not theoretical concepts of freedom, but rather historical practices developed in particular Biblical and historical contexts—where freedom was seen as intimately related to life in community and forms of belonging, whether to the people, groups, communities or to God as giver of freedom.

14

Concepts of Freedom in Deuteronomy?

Jan Christian Gertz

The Problem[1]

In the European tradition, freedom is commonly understood as the autonomy of the individual or the state. The origins of this understanding may be sought in the Greek polis. The polis understood itself to be independent from other states and powers, and its citizens understood themselves to depend solely on the law and the will of the gods. The foundational myth for this understanding of autonomy of both the individual and the state is the Persian Wars in which the Greeks defended their freedom, ἐλευθερία, and democracy and thus protected it for Europe against the much different concept of oriental despotism embodied by the Persians. Viewed historically, this myth—colorfully depicted especially by neo-humanistic Philhellenism—is "true" insofar as the victory against the Persians brought about a constitution in Athens founded upon three basic democratic freedoms that go back to Cleisthenes in the sixth century BCE:[2] ἰσονομία, or the equality of all before the law; ἰσομορία, or the equality of polis leadership; and ἰσηγορία, or the freedom of speech in the assembly. There is however an

---

1. For more on the (political) understanding of freedom by the Greeks and in the Old Testament, which is only touched upon in what follows, see Kaiser, "Freiheit im Alten Testament."

2. See Herodotus, *The Persian Wars* VI, 131. Welwei, *Die griechische Polis*. For the Persian wars as the founding myth of Greek freedom, see the tragedy "The Persians" by Aeschylus.

essential restriction to these fundamental democratic freedoms which must be remembered: These freedoms are privileges of free citizens; they were denied to women, slaves and other men who did not belong to the polis as well as metics.

The Old Testament, and with it the book of Deuteronomy, belong more or less to the cultural circle whose politically dominant representatives, in terms of the myth presented above, existentially threatened the freedom of Greece and thus the European concept of freedom at the Thermopylae, in Marathon and before Salamis. Whether the biblical authors would have accepted this identification is of course more than questionable. The time of Persian dominance was intellectually and theologically formative for Judaism, and the biblical texts present this developing Judaism as the beneficent contribution of their God and the Persian kings. The biblical reactions to the rise and fall of the Persian Empire correspond to this view: The first Persian ruler Cyrus is celebrated by Second Isaiah as a liberator (see Isa 44:28; 45:1; 2 Chr 36:22–23 par. Ezra 1:1–2). On the other hand, the sudden downfall of the Persian Empire after the victory of Alexander the Great at Gaugamela evoked a series of prophetical texts depicting a global cataclysm that was seen as already present or at least as very imminent (see Joel 3 [Heb. 4; Isa 24–27). Here it should be noted, however, that the praise for the granted freedom is found for the most part in texts of elites who were loyal to the Persians and whose own rise to power was directly influenced by the imperial rulers.

In any case, the view from Athens—as the home of Cleisthenes or Pericles—eastwards reveals differences and—more often from the Greek perspective—deficits. The view from the Ancient Near East westwards reminds the world that the Greek perspective is not the only one.[3]

The Dearth of Conceptual Parallels in Deuteronomy

I will start with the differences and deficits, focusing on the book of Deuteronomy and the search for a concept of freedom, thus intentionally leaving aside the pre-theoretical desire for "freedom" that indubitably already existed in ancient Israel. It is striking that this book, as the Old Testament in general, does not contain an exact conceptual equivalent to the Greek term ἐλευθερία or the Mishnaic Hebrew term ḥêrût, which appears for the

---

3. For an comparative study on "freedom" in the Ancient Near East, see Snell, *Flight and Freedom in the Ancient Near East*.

first time on coinage from the Jewish War and the Bar Kokhba Revolt. In addition one can say that even the adjective "free" is rarely used.⁴

Thus, the Hebrew term חפשי which is rendered as "free," following the LXX, has primarily the passive meaning of discharge from indebtedness. Most relevant is Deut 15:12–18. This regulation, which incidentally is the only witness for חפשי "free" in Deuteronomy, pre scribes the modalities of the treatment and liberation of Hebrew (i.e., Judean) slaves. Outside the book of Deuteronomy, the act of discharge is designated as חפשה "manumission" (Lev 19:20) or דרור "(return of) freedom of movement" (Lev 25:10 and Jer 34:8–22). Similarly, חפשי + עשה (lit. "to make free") in 1 Sam 17:25 refers to the exemption of servants from compulsory labour and tribute vis-a-vis the king. The term חפשי, which the LXX translates as ἐλεύθερος "free," has accordingly an explicit legal and economic connotation. From a Greek perspective, this appears to be an inappropriate limitation. However, one should remember that also the Greek concept of freedom represents a generalization and abstraction of the idea of independence, specifically that of the indigenous population and aristocracy in contrast to the dependents or the δοῦλοι. A corresponding potential is also conceivable for the Hebrew adjective חפשי and related terms such as the verb פדה "ransom." Thus, חפשי refers in Isa 58:6 to an emancipation from oppression and captivity. In Job 3:19 this term is even used metaphorically for the freedom of the deceased (see MT Ps 88:5 [Heb. 6]). Also פדה, which in Deut 15:15 is still used in the context of slave laws, appears in Ps 49:15 (Heb. 16) without a concrete reference. However, these developments take place outside Deuteronomy and they are rather marginal in Old Testament traditions.

The Law of Freedom

Now, in terms of method, it would certainly be inappropriate to conclude from negative terminological findings that a certain conception is entirely lacking. However, the results presented above are not accidental, as can be demonstrated by an examination of the exodus credo, which has repeatedly been pointed out to be central to the biblical concept of freedom. The most prominent passage for the credo in Deuteronomy is the preamble to the Decalogue:

אנכי יהוה אלהיך אשר הוצאתיך מארץ מצרים מבית עבדים

---

4. See Lohfink, "חפש, ḥpš."

"I am the Lord your God, who brought you out of the land of Egypt, out of the house of slavery." (Deut 5:6)

This preamble is followed by the prohibition of worship of other Gods and of idolatry, the prohibition against misusing the divine name, and the command to keep the Sabbath. And following these laws related to the deity are the rules which insure social unity. Thus, in the perspective of the one responsible for this arrangement, the social regulations of the second tablet unfold the meaning of the laws related to the deity on the first tablet. Read as a unity and as a whole, the Decalogue formulates the entire divine will. In its structure, everything depends upon both the first commandment of worshipping Yahweh alone and the preamble recalling Yahweh's act of liberating Israel from Egypt.[5] Together they formulate the insoluble connection between Yahweh's acts of salvation and—following from it—his claim and promise to be the God of Israel. This connection also describes the foundational structure of Old Testament law.

Highlighting this connection between Yahweh's salvific act and his command, the Decalogue is often described as a law to preserve (social) freedom.[6] The God who speaks now has already proven his salvific will; now it is a matter of ensuring the future of the freedom granted in the salvific act. This may be conceptually correct, yet it requires differentiation in light of our present questions. It should be remembered that the preamble does not explicitly refer to "liberation." Deut 5:6 simply speaks of "bringing out." Nevertheless the usual counterpart to freedom—בית עבדים "house of slavery"—is mentioned here and Deut 7:8 uses the term פדה "ransom" stated above:

ויפדך מבית עבדים מיד פרעה מלך־מצרים

He [the Lord] ransomed you from the house of slavery, from the hand of Pharaoh king of Egypt.

In all this, one must hear the entire story of Israel's exodus from Egypt and its redemption. It is not just a matter of ending the corvée labor in Egypt. It is also about the military victory over the despots, which represents, as in the Greek myth of origin, winning and maintaining one's freedom.

However, decisive for this understanding is the connection between liberation and the requirement to worship Yahweh alone:

לא יהיה־לך אלהים אחרים על־פני . . . לא־תשתחוה להם ולא תעבדם

---

5. Concerning the Decalogue, see the introduction by Köckert, *Die Zehn Gebote*.
6. See Crüsemann, *Bewahrung der Freiheit*.

> ...you shall have no other gods before me...you shall not bow down to them or worship them. (Deut 5:7*, 9*)

This connection clearly shows that political liberation or the autonomy of the individual and the state is not the central interest of the text. Rather, the text treats a change in loyalty. Corresponding to this perspective is the number of texts in which the root עבד "serve/to be a servant," only just before used in a negative sense, refers to Yahweh (Deut 6:13; 10:12; 11:13, etc.). The alternative is not slavery or autonomy of the individual and the state, but rather to serve Yahweh or other gods. The fulfillment of the promise of land and peace—both national and individual (Deut 3:20; Josh 1:13, etc.)—which can be understood as an expression of political autonomy, is clearly subordinated to this alternative. Thus, Norbert Lohfink speaks pointedly but still adequately of a "divine enslavement" (*Gottessklaventum*).[7]

This "divine enslavement" has little to do with the common European Enlightenment concept of freedom, as can be seen from a glance at the texts in Deuteronomy that mainly focus on loyalty to Yahweh. An example can be found in Deut 13. It treats lawful revenge for the case of disloyalty to Yahweh in the closest circle of friends and family. The passage is framed by similar stipulations for the treatment of religious experts that entice people to commit apostasy or a city that rebels against Yahweh:

> **6** If anyone secretly entices you—even if it is your brother, your father's son or your mother's son, or your own son or daughter, or the wife you embrace, or your most intimate friend—saying, "Let us go worship other gods," whom neither you nor your ancestors have known, **7** any of the gods of the peoples that are around you, whether near you or far away from you, from one end of the earth to the other, **8** you must not yield to or heed any such persons. Show them no pity or compassion and do not shield them. **9** But you shall surely kill them; your own hand shall be first against them to execute them, and afterwards the hand of all the people. **10** Stone them to death for trying to turn you away from the LORD your God, who brought you out of the land of Egypt, out of the house of slavery. **11** Then all Israel shall hear and be afraid, and never again do any such wickedness. (Deut 13:6–11 [Heb. 7–12])

It is not surprising that Deut 13 is usually not associated with the concept "freedom." Bernard Lang assesses the situation boldly but correctly in the

---

7. Lohfink, "חפש, *ḥpš*," 118.

title of an article from 1984: "Georg Orwell im gelobten Land: Das Buch Deuteronomium und der Geist kirchlicher Kontrolle."[8]

In fact, no one can deny the intolerant, inhumane, and illiberal formulation of Deut 13. But even a negative assessment should account for the conditions of the text's origins. The text mirrors an exilic-post exilic conflict situation in which the Yahweh-religion of Deuteronomic provenance attempted to survive. In order to inculcate loyalty to Yahweh, the authors drew on a model of loyalty that was known to them from Ancient Near Eastern treaties:[9] The loyalty to the suzerain demanded in Ancient Near Eastern sources is transferred in Deut 13 to Yahweh without the intermediate institution of the state. The consequences of this transfer are immense. The demand of absolute loyalty to the deity means a reduction in the loyalty demanded by every state. The boundaries of political authority are demarcated. In this way, Deut 13 contains an aspect of freedom—even though this is difficult to recognize amidst the violent language adopted from the Ancient Near Eastern treaties.

Another point deserves to be mentioned here. The formulation of the alternative of following Yahweh or other gods presupposes freedom of choice—both for the people and the individual. On the assumption that the sanctions in Deut 13 did not have a state institution to enforce them, one could perhaps even recognize in the formulation of the alternatives the first, although fully unintended, beginnings of religious freedom—or more accurately the freedom to choose one's religion.

If this interpretation of Deut 13 seems too radical, one should examine the final chapters of Deuteronomic teaching. Deuteronomy 28–29 and 30 treat basically just one subject: blessings in the case of obedience to Yahweh's commandment and curses in the case of disobedience. Doing so, the chapters offer a concise summary of the Deuteronomic ethics of choice and responsibility. Concerning our question, two observations are important. First, obedience to Yahweh's commandment explicitly includes the demand of absolute loyalty to the deity:

> **15** See, I have set before you today life and prosperity, death and adversity. **16** If you obey the commandments of the LORD your God that I am commanding you today, by loving the LORD your God, walking in his ways, and observing his commandments, decrees, and ordinances, then you shall live and become

8. Lang, "George Orwell im gelobten Land."
9. For the debate on the literary history of Deut 13 and the interpretation of the chapter in the context of Ancient Near Eastern treaties cf. Veijola, "Wahrheit und Intoleranz nach Deuteronomium 13"; Otto, *Das Deuteronomium*; and Koch, *Vertrag, Treueid und Bund*.

numerous, and the LORD your God will bless you in the land that you are entering to possess. (Deut 30:15-16)

Second, Israel and the individual Israelite—the use of the address in the 2nd pers. sing. masc. changes in its meaning—are presented with the option, Heb. בחר, to choose the good:

> **19** I call heaven and earth to witness against you today that I have set before you life and death, blessings and curses. Choose life so that you and your descendants may live, **20** loving the LORD your God, obeying him, and holding fast to him . . . (Deut 30:19-20*)

The Deuteronomistic authors of these chapters already look back on the Judean catastrophe. They interpret the downfall of Jerusalem and the loss of autonomy and the land as the result of a false choice on the part of Israel (see Deut 30:17-18). Hence, it is beyond doubt that in the view of these authors the alternative presented by Yahweh truly gave Israel a free choice.

God's Freedom

It is hardly possible to speak about the free choice between good and evil as well as the law of freedom in Deuteronomy without saying at least a few words about the underlying view of God. This theology can be described in loose reference[10] to Max Weber as follows: For the authors of Deuteronomy Yahweh was an elective god (*Wahlgott*) and not a functional or local god.[11] What does this mean? Already in the older Exodus story the god assisting Israel is not the god of a clan, a dynasty, or a nation.[12] Thus, Yahweh,

---

10. This is described as "loose" because the conception that Weber calls "Mosaic" does not belong to the early period of Yahweh-religion but rather formed itself after the fall of the Northern Kingdom in 722 BCE before reaching its mature form in Deuteronomism. See Gertz, "Mose und die Anfänge der jüdischen Religion."

11. See Weber, *Die Wirtschaftsethik der Weltreligionen. Das antike Judentum*; ET = *Ancient Judaism*; Weber, *Gesamtausgabe* I/21: *Die Wirtschaftsethik der Weltreligionen: Das antike Judentum: Schriften und Reden 1911-1920*. For Yahweh's character as a "Wahlgott," see *Das antike Judentum*, 140 (ET = 130). Weber takes up thoughts and formulations by Valeton, "Die Israeliten," 403, and Budde, *Die altisraelitische Religion*, 19-20. See Weber, *Gesamtausgabe*, 424. My interpretation of Weber's thesis on ancient Israelite religion is presented in Gertz, "Der fremde und ferne Gott."

12. For the dating of the older Moses-Exodus-Conquest story to the end of the eighth and beginning of the seventh century BCE as well as for an analysis of its conception of God, see Gertz, "Mose und die Anfänge der jüdischen Religion." For a more detailed analysis of Exod 1-15, see Gertz, *Tradition und Redaktion in der Exoduserzählung*.

Moses, and the Israelites do not have a common history before the exodus, the memory of which could construct identity. The relationship to god is also not based on the harmony between a kingdom given by god, on the one hand, and a dynastic or national god, on the other. According to the exodus story Israel did not exist in a natural relationship to its deity, who is known for a long time and dwells in the midst of his people. Rather the relationship between the Israelite people and their god Yahweh is a matter of choice; it is founded solely on the primordial act of the exodus, ascribed to a deity that was previously unknown to Moses. In Deuteronomy this concept of God is expressed by the idea of covenant and election, while the former is understood as a reciprocal relationship of covenant faithfulness. The central text in this respect is Deut 7. I quote those passages concerning our question:

> **7** It was not because you were more numerous than any other people that the Lord set his heart on you and chose you—for you were the fewest of all peoples. **8** It was because the Lord loved you and kept the oath that he swore to your ancestors, that the Lord has brought you out with a mighty hand, and redeemed you from the house of slavery, from the hand of Pharaoh king of Egypt. **9** Know therefore that the Lord your God is God, the faithful God who maintains covenant loyalty with those who love him and keep his commandments, to a thousand generations, **10** and who repays in their own person those who reject him. He does not delay but repays in their own person those who reject him. **11** Therefore, observe diligently the commandment—the statutes, and the ordinances—that I am commanding you today. (Deut 7:7–11)

The expressions "choose" and "covenant" characterize the special relationship between Yahweh and Israel. The expression "covenant" is more oriented to the inner perspective, whereas "choose" emphasizes the external perspective. Choosing always presupposes a plurality. That Israel is chosen from all peoples means that Yahweh is in control of the entire earth and all its peoples and thus has power to choose from these peoples. Put simply: it is the aim of the text to express the connection between the universality of god and the particularity of his relationship to Israel. This is especially clear in the parallel of Deut 10:14–15:

> **14** Although heaven and the heaven of heavens belong to the Lord your God, the earth with all that is in it, **15** yet the Lord set his heart in love on your ancestors alone and chose you, their descendants after them, out of all the peoples, as it is today.

Deuteronomy 7 and 10 formulate the connection between the universal God and the particularity of the divine relationship in the language of election. The reason for the election remains hidden, however. It is not prompted by any special qualities of Israel (Deut 7:7-8) but rather by the free and gracious decision of God. Election in its essence is no reason for self-praise insofar as it is solely founded on Yahweh's freedom, manifested in the love to the patriarchs (Deut 10:14-15; 4:37) or the sons (Deut 7:7). Deuteronomy 7 emphasizes that the act of election consists in the liberation of the exodus and the gift of the land. In terms of "salvation history," election is not an abstract conception but a concrete historical act. The external perspective of election and the inner perspective of the covenant concur: the liberating and electing God is the faithful "keeper of the covenant," who also demands adherence to the divine commandments and laws necessary to Israel's welfare. It is thus up to Israel to accept this call and choose life.

To summarize these ideas with reference to our question: It is the relationship of the covenant, which is founded on a mutual choice and formed through reciprocal promises, that makes possible the freedom of choice for Israel and individual Israelites.

Deuteronomy and Democratic Fundamental Freedoms

Returning to the political concept of freedom, I will now examine what should be added to the Greek perspective in the light of Deuteronomy. A political concept of freedom, founded on the principle of the equality of all citizens, did obviously not correspond to the conditions of ancient Near Eastern monarchies. Also in Judah the king was considered to be the terrestrial representative of the divine or the son of God (Ps 2:7), who was responsible for law and justice in his kingdom (Ps 72:1-2) and ensured the divinely promised welfare of the land. Yet the imperilment and downfall of the monarchy initiated a process of reflection in Deuteronomy in which something like a concept of freedom indeed began to emerge. I will discuss three of the most important points:

1. By means of the covenant, the claims of the Assyrian and Babylonian suzerains were countered with "Yahweh alone!" Thus, the claim of exclusiveness of the suzerains is replaced by the exclusive relationship between Israel and its god. In this way, the divine relationship to Israel was

formulated according to a national-constitutional analogy. The "covenantal theology" delivered the comprehensive interpretational key for the newly won—or better: hoped for—political autonomy.[13] Whether newly won or hoped for, in Deuteronomy this autonomy is defined by conditions of confined national power, which is an essential basis for individual rights of freedom. The way Deuteronomy confines national power is concretized in the next point.

2. Since according to Deuteronomy, the basis for the law as well as its formulation and execution were not tied to a monarchic power but rather legitimated by means of divine revelation, it can be placed over the monarchy. This becomes especially clear in the law of the king in Deut 17:14-20. Although formulated after the demise of the state, it fundamentally departs from the ancient Near Eastern royal ideology.[14] According to Deut 17:14-20, the king has no authority in the judiciary or legislature. Although the text allows him to rule over the people (v. 15a), his rule is restricted by means of legal specifications, which dictate that he belongs to the people (v. 15b) and limit his fiscal budget (vv. 16-17). Above all the rule of the king is limited by obedience to the law (vv. 18-19): In the formulation "neither exalting himself above other members of the community nor turning aside from the commandment, either to the right or to the left" (v. 20), one observes, in addition to the warning about hubris, the idea that both the king and (full) citizens are equal under the law. This idea has analogies in the somewhat contemporary Greek constitutional debate, and it promotes the law almost to the position of the sovereign of the state.[15] Stated differently: Insofar as

---

13. For the current debate on the dating of Deuteronomy either into the time of the Exile or into the last years of the Judean monarchy, cf. the articles by Pakkala, "The Date of the Oldest Edition of Deuteronomy"; and MacDonald, "Issues in the Dating of Deuteronomy."

14. For a detailed analysis cf. Hagedorn, *Between Moses and Plato*, 140-56 (with n.193: further literature concerning the debate on the literary history of Deut 17:14-20).

15. Cf. Herodotus, *Persian Wars* III, 80-83. See also Rüterswörden, *Von der politischen Gemeinschaft zur Gemeinde*, 102. However, Rüterswörden limits the comparison with Herodotus to the reconstructed pre-Deuteronomistic *Grundschicht* of Deut 17:14-20, in which the prohibitives of v. 16-17 are directly followed by the final clause of v. 20. Thus only the one aspect is stressed, that wealth leads to the elevation of the king in relation to the fellow citizens. On the other hand, the aspect of equality of all before the law (ἰσονομία), that in the law of the king results from the succession of vv. 18-19 and vv. 20 and that is brought up by Herodotus as well, is not mentioned: "But I have yet worse to say of him than that; he (the absolute ruler) turns the laws of the land upside down, he rapes women, he puts high and low to death. But the virtue of a multitude's rule lies first in its excellent name, which signifies equality before the law . . ." (*Persian Wars* III, 80; text and translation in Godley, trans., *Herodotus: Books III-IV*, 106-107.). For a detailed comparison between the law of the king in Deut 17:14-20 and the position of the king in Ancient Greece, see Hagedorn, *Between Moses and Plato*,

the Torah is binding for all Israel without exception, Deuteronomy also has an ἰσονομία, an equality of all before the law.

3. Deuteronomy is almost solely addressed to a second person singular object. Ever since the foundational study of Deuteronomy's concept of nation by Gerhard von Rad, scholarship has identified this "you" as free men who owned land, were required to serve in war and therefore were capable of holding rights and were equal before a court of law. In view of the exclusion of women, foreigners and strangers, this concept of nation almost exactly corresponds to the constellation of the Athenian ἐκκλησία as an assembly of free citizens.[16] More important than this concept of a free and equal citizen, defined by sex, origin and wealth, which maintained itself even after the French Revolution, is the connection of the second person singular with the so-called fraternal ethic of Deuteronomy.[17] The Judean slave, whose manumission we considered at the outset, is emphatically identified as the brother of the person addressed as "you." The expansion of the designation "brother" beyond the limits of familial relations is typical for Deuteronomy: the indebted slave remains a brother (15:12–18), the brother is to be protected in legal proceedings (19:15–21; 25:1–3), just as his cattle are to be cared for (22:1–4) and interest is not to be charged from him (23:19 [Heb. 20]). It is characteristic of the texts employing this expression to emphasize the solidarity of the directly addressed community (= "you") with members who are caught in crises. In this way the so-called fraternal ethic transfers the obligation of inner-familial solidarity to the people as a whole. In Deuteronomy and in the Old Testament in general, this expansion of the familial ethos has its limits. It applies only to the people of Yahweh. The absolute universalization of "fraternal ethic" is not yet completed in the Old Testament. The brother is the fellow person, but not (yet) the person as such.

The absolute universalization of this "fraternal ethic" is problematic as goes without saying.[18] For our purposes a different point is more important: the rights of the free are joined to the ethos of freedom. Thus, the concept of the free citizen defined by sex, origin and wealth receives an ethical significance which is not restricted to the social conditions of ancient Israel. And this is perhaps the most important contribution of Deuteronomy to

140–56.

16. Von Rad, "Das Gottesvolk im Deuteronomium (1929)"; ET = "The People of God in Deuteronomy."

17. Perlitt, "'Ein einzig Volk von Brüdern.'"

18. See Gehlen's criticism of the extension of the familial ethos and the relinquishing of the differentiation essential to a clan ethos in so-called "humanitarianism" ("Humanitarismus"); Gehlen, *Moral und Hypermoral*.

the discussion of concepts of freedom. Political freedom does not just mean the majority principle but also basic freedoms, which need to be filled with content and can be injured by actual or self-proclaimed majorities.

Bibliography

Budde, Karl. *Die altisraelitische Religion*. 3rd ed. Giessen: Töpelmann, 1912.
Crüsemann, Frank. *Bewahrung der Freiheit: Das Thema des Dekalogs in sozialgeschichtlicher Perspektive*. Kaiser Traktate 78. Munich: Kaiser, 1983.
Gehlen, Arnold. *Moral und Hypermoral: Eine pluralistische Ethik*. 6th ed. Frankfurt: Aula, 2004.
Gertz, J. C. "Der fremde und ferne Gott: Max Webers Sicht der altisraelitischen Religion." *Journal for the History of Modern Theology* 6 (1999) 246–63.
———. "Mose und die Anfänge der jüdischen Religion." *Zeitschrift für Theologie und Kirche* 99 (2002) 3–20.
———. *Tradition und Redaktion in der Exoduserzählung: Untersuchungen zur Endredaktion des Pentateuch*. FRLANT 186. Göttingen: Vandenhoeck & Ruprecht, 2000.
Godley, A. D., trans. *Herodotus: Books III–IV*. LCL. Cambridge: Harvard University Press, 2000.
Hagedorn, Anselm C. *Between Moses and Plato: Individual and Society in Deuteronomy and Ancient Greek Law*. FRLANT 204. Göttingen: Vandenhoeck & Ruprecht, 2004.
Kaiser, Otto. "Freiheit im Alten Testament." In *Zwischen Athen und Jerusalem: Studien zur griechischen und biblischen Theologie, ihrer Eigenart und ihrem Verhältnis*, 179–198. BZAW 320. Berlin: de Gruyter, 2003.
Koch, Christoph. *Vertrag, Treueid und Bund: Studien zur Rezeption des altorientalischen Vertragsrechts im Deuteronomium und zur Ausbildung der Bundestheologie im Alten Testament*. BZAW 383. Berlin: de Gruyter, 2008.
Köckert, M. *Die Zehn Gebote*. Munich: Beck, 2007.
Lang, Bernhard. "George Orwell im gelobten Land: Das Buch Deuteronomium und der Geist kirchlicher Kontrolle." In *Kirche und Visitation: Beiträge zur Erforschung des frühneuzeitlichen Visitationswesens in Europa*, edited by Ernst Walter Zeeden and Peter Thaddäus Lang, 21–35. Stuttgart: Klett-Cotta, 1984.
Lohfink, Norbert. "חפש, ḥpš." In *TDOT* 5 (1986) 114–18.
MacDonald, Nathan. "Issues in the Dating of Deuteronomy: A Response to Juha Pakkala." *ZAW* 122 (2010) 431–35.
Otto, Eckart. *Das Deuteronomium: Politische Theologie und Rechtsform in Juda und Assyrien*. BZAW 284. Berlin: de Gruyter, 1999.
Pakkala, Juha. "The Date of the Oldest Edition of Deuteronomy." *ZAW* 121 (2009) 388–401.
Perlitt, Lothar. "'Ein einzig Volk von Brüdern': Zur deuteronomischen Herkunft der biblischen Bezeichnung 'Bruder' (1980)." In *Deuteronomium-Studien*, 50–73. Forschungen zum Alten Testament 8. Tübingen: Mohr/Siebeck, 1994.
Rad, Gerhard von. "Das Gottesvolk im Deuteronomium (1929)." In *Gesammelte Studien zum Alten Testament II*, 9–108. Theologische Bücherei 48. Munich: Kaiser, 1973.

——— . "The People of God in Deuteronomy." In *Studies in Deuteronomy*. Studies in Biblical Theology 1/9. London: SCM, 1971.

Rüterswörden, Udo. *Von der politischen Gemeinschaft zur Gemeinde: Studien zu Dtn 16,18—18,22*. Bonner Biblische Beiträge 65. Frankfurt: Athenäum, 1987.

Snell, Daniel C. *Flight and Freedom in the Ancient Near East*. Culture and History of the Ancient Near East 8. Leiden: Brill, 2001.

Valeton, J. J. P. "Die Israeliten." In *Lehrbuch der Religionsgeschichte*, edited by P. D. Chantipe de la Saussaye, vol. 1, 384–467. 3rd ed. Tübingen: Mohr/Siebeck, 1905.

Veijola, Timo. "Wahrheit und Intoleranz nach Deuteronomium 13." *Zeitschrift für Theologie und Kirche* 92 (1995) 287–314

Weber, Max. *Ancient Judaism*. Translated and edited by Hans H. Gerth and Don Martindale. Social Theory. Glencoe: Free Press, 1952.

——— . *Gesamtausgabe I/21: Die Wirtschaftsethik der Weltreligionen: Das antike Judentum: Schriften und Reden 1911-1920*, edited by Eckart Otto, 210–757. Tübingen: Mohr/Siebeck, 2005.

——— . *Die Wirtschaftsethik der Weltreligionen: Das antike Judentum*. Gesammelte Aufsätze zur Religionssoziologie 3. 8th ed. Tübingen: Mohr/Sieck, 1988.

Welwei, Karl-Wilhelm. *Die griechische Polis: Verfassung und Gesellschaft in archaischer und klassischer Zeit*. 2nd ed. Stuttgart: Kohlhammer, 1998.

15

Potentials for Freedom in Concepts of Order

Transformations of Wisdom and Political Theology in the Hebrew Bible

Jürgen van Oorschot

Freedom as a Concept or as Implicit Element of Acting

Freedom as a normative concept[1] is unknown in the Ancient Near Eastern World and in the Hebrew Bible. We do not find a normative idea or ethical standard combined with freedom. Freedom is solely known as part of concrete action and as a special option to act.[2] Accordingly we detect in the West-European and Greek view to the Near East the notation of a deficit. The Ancient Middle Eastern or in our historical context called Near Eastern political and religious systems neither generate concepts of political nor of individual freedom. Under the keyword "Freiheit," in the encyclopaedia of the Ancient World, the so called *Der neue Pauly*, defines freedom as:

---

1. Cf. Foppa, "Konzept, konzeptibel," who describes the use of *conceptus* and *conceptibile* from the late antiquity (fourth century) to the modern age.

2. Besides concrete acting the matter of freedom does also play a role, describing options of wise and therefore beneficial attitudes and thinking. This is one of the main targets of wisdom, documented, for example, in the book of Proverbs.

> Die Unterscheidung zwischen "frei" und "unfrei" im Sinne der Befreiung von Abgaben oder Leistungen findet sich bereits im Alten Orient. Einem Konzept polit. F. auf der Basis einer polit. berechtigten Bürgerschaft steht jedoch ein autokratisches und göttlich legitimiertes Königtum entgegen sowie ein abgestuftes Statussystem, das die Gesellschaft in Gruppen unterschiedlicher Abhngigkeit 'zwischen F. und Sklaverei' (Pollux) gliedert.[3]

Ἐλευθερία arose as a special concept in consequence of the Persian wars in 480/479 B.C. Pindar (frg. 77 [83 Snell]; *Pyth.* 1,61; *Ol.* 12,1) and others understand freedom as liberty of despotic rule, first in confrontation with the Persians and later on with Athens. In this regard it is not a surprising coincidence that the cult of Zeus ἐλεύθερος was established past to the war against and the victory over the Persians at Plataiai. Among this political connotation freedom means that the citizens have the chance to govern themselves, which is combined with the *isegoria*, the equal right to speak, and the *parrhesia*, the freedom of speech. Later on, we find different variations of these concepts in Greek history and philosophy that became vivid on the background of an anti-Near-East and anti-Persian myth. Thus freedom belongs to the Greek and to the later European identity, clearly marked-off from traditions of the Ancient Near East, and it has—if necessary—to be defended against political or ideological despotism.

The Old Testament in General: A Wisdom-Based *Ordnungsdenken* and Political Theology in Transformation

In contrast, the inside perspective of the Old Testament texts is remarkable different. It is indeed true that in the Old Testament's literature we don't find an equivalent to a concept of individual freedom. As often demonstrated,[4] the Hebrew texts on freedom concentrate rather on legal subjects concerning laws for slaves and imprisonment, than speaking of freedom as a political category. Freedom in that sense first emerged in Hellenistic times—evidently inspired by Greek ideas (1 Macc 10:25-45; 15:7; 1 Macc 2:11; [3 Esdr 4:49-52]).

But implicitly the matter of freedom is combined with concepts of regularity and order leading in the Persian period to a very positive view on the Persian Power. Regularity and order are the basis for potentials of

---

3. Raaflaub, "Freiheit I. Politisch," 650.

4. Kaiser, "Freiheit. I. Altes Testament," 304-6; Bartsch, "Freiheit. I. Altes Testament," 497-98; and Becker, *Freiheit*.

freedom. To understand the relating concepts one has first of all to mention the Near Eastern and Old Testament's literature on wisdom. Wisdom here is commonly understood as based on experience, as *Erfahrungsweisheit*; experiences gained in families and clans or as a part of education and formation. The wisdom thinking is a thinking in order and regularity, as Hans Heinrich Schmid has underlined in his publication *Gerechtigkeit als Weltordnung*.[5] and as we find it often in modified presentations until today.[6] To describe and teach the recurrent events and generate an empirically based prediction—this all should create possibilities of acting and thinking. Knowing and taking into account the orders and regularities should diminish the chaotic complexity that according to the Near Eastern and Old Testament's wisdom endangers a successful life. Order should render possibilities for a prosperous and wise living. The aim is to gain options to act. Therefore the Old Testament's sages do not design any concepts of freedom. In their thinking freedom is just thinkable as potentials of acting (*Handlung*) and speaking of freedom means to describe concrete potentials of freedom.

These coherences are very obvious in an Old Testament book, which reflects the limits of this *Ordnungsdenken*, the book of Qohelet. Here we have a skeptical wise man on stage in the role of an Israelite king. He confronts the reader with the absurdness searching

בחכמה על כל־אשר נעשה תחת השמים

by wisdom all that is done under heaven. (Qoh 1:13)

This is like snatching the wind. Again and again the human is confronted with the limits of his or her knowledge and ability. He or she knows neither the future nor the past (Qoh 3:12–13; 6:12b; 9:11–12a). And death restricts him definitely (Qoh 9:4b, 5*). The advice of the sceptic wise man reminds the reader that there is just one place and time to act: *carpe diem*:

כל אשר תמצא ידך לעשות בכחך עשה
כי אין מעשה וחשבון ודעת וחכמה בשאול
אשר אתה הלך שמה

Whatever your hand finds to do, do with your might;
for there is no work or thought or knowledge or wisdom in Sheol,
to which you are going. (Qoh 9:10)

To act here and now, when your hand finds something to do—that's the chance. In chap. 3 of the book Qohelet this belief is combined with the

5. Schmid, *Gerechtigkeit als Weltordnung*.
6. Perdue et al., eds., *Scribes, Sages, and Seers*.

conception of the *zufallenden Zeit*. The wise can only find out, that there exists "a time to be born, and a time to die; a time to plant, and a time to pluck up what is planted; a time to kill, and a time to heal; a time to break down, and a time to build up . . ." (Qoh 3:2-3). The long meditation about the different qualities of time ends in a dialectic conclusion: "He (God) has made everything suitable for its time; moreover, he has put a sense of past and future into their minds, yet they cannot find out what God has done from the beginning to the end" (Qoh 3:11). There is an existing order behind the whole world. God as the faraway creator is the guarantor for this order. But the humankind, living in this world order, neither can understand nor control it. Speaking about the limits of this *Ordnungsdenken*, the book of Qohelet leads back to the center of wisdom. The challenge of the carpe diem, which is the consequence of Qoehelet's wisdom,[7] includes also a thesis on freedom: freedom for humans can just be found in the possibilities to act.

Isaiah 40-66: Pro-Persian Political Theology and a Theocentric Transformation

In the prophetic literature of Isa 40-66, the since Bernhard Duhm distinguished Deutero- and Trito-Isaiah, we are confronted with a special transformation of this concept. There we can find a theology of order in the shape of a pro-Persian political theology with Cyrus as liberator of the exiled Israel; Cyrus, the Persian king, re-establishes God's salutary order and becomes the personification of the new hope. As liberator he is legitimized by God as we can read in Isa 45: "Thus says the Lord to his anointed, to Cyrus, whose right hand I have grasped to subdue nations before him and strip kings of their robes, to open doors before him—and the gates shall not be closed" (Isa 45:1).

Until today the historiography reflects this pro-Persian qualification. Cyrus is shown as an exponent of a tolerant regime seen on the background of the predominant power of Babylon and Assyria. Especially three elements are often cited to distinguish between the Persian Rule and their predecessors. First, the Persians have not displaced the conquered peoples, so that they could live in their ancestral territories. And if a displacement took place in former times, they allow and partly support a returning of the peoples into their original settlement areas. Second, the conquered peoples got the permission for a local self-administration, which led to a great diversity in the different parts of the Persian Empire. The language-in-use reflects this

---

7. On the *carpe diem* motif in Qoheleth, see Schwienhorst-Schönberger, "E. Die Bücher der Weisheit. V. Das Buch Kohelet," 343.

diversity. For the communication in the West Semitic parts of the Empire the Aramaic became more and more a sort of lingua franca. And even the official inscriptions of the Persian kings, like the Behistun Inscription, were formulated in three languages: the Elamite, the Babylonian and the Persian. And third, the Persians did not dominate the religious affairs in the territories under their rule. They respected the religious traditions and, as far as we can see, they supported the establishing or re-establishing of the local cults.

This last point can clarify the rationale of the Persian policy. Terms like tolerance are not useful to understand this policy. Even speculations on the piety of Cyrus II are misleading. The Persian kings are simply using other strategies to wield their power. The intention to establish a robust hegemonic regime is evident and is the consequent focus. That is the reason why Cyrus worships Marduk as the supreme God in Babylon and his successor, Cambyses, does this too, becoming Pharaoh by the grace of Re in Egypt. And also Darius I (522–486), who gained power in 521 BC after the revolt of Gaumata, aimed at dominance and political stability by establishing the new system of twenty-three administration units, called satrapies, and by replacing the different currencies in the Persian Empire by a standard one, the *dareikos*. These actions are combined with an ideology connecting two elements: the dominance of the Persians and the individuality of nations. To interpret this policy in terms of more or less political or religious tolerance, as it's often done in modern historiography,[8] tends to be a misunderstanding. That is the same by using concepts of freedom as leading thoughts. The rationality is one of power and the stability of the regime. What we can find, are concrete potentials of freedom as unintended consequences. Remigration of few Judeans to Jerusalem and the surrounding areas and support for the poor countryside by the Persians can stabilize the Persian Rule at the border to Egypt. Judeans may understand this as a concrete form of freedom, which leads to Pro-Persian images.

One of these ancient Pro-Persian images can be found in Isaiah 40–66. The military and political rise of the Persians under Cyrus since 547 BCE as the dominant power in the whole Near Eastern region is not solely presented as an act done by the God of Israel. In addition, the global change is understood—by the elites loyal to the Persians—as the work of salvation by the unique God: "For the sake of my servant Jacob, and Israel my chosen, I call you by your name, I surname you, though you do not know me. I am the

---

8. Recent studies have shown in many cases that the pro-Persian presentation in a lot of ancient texts do not fit with the historical realities. For example, the generous treatment of Croisos by Cyrus, told by Herodotus, is part of a late Cyrus presentation and is entirely ahistorical; see Wiesehöfer, *Das antike Persien*, 81–84.

Lord, and there is no other; besides me there is no God. I arm you, though you do not know me" (Isa 45:4–5).

In analogy to the former exodus from Egypt, YHWH intends to liberate the "robbed and plundered" people, "all of them . . . trapped in holes and hidden away in prisons" (Isa 42:22) and finds a way for that people back from Babylon to Zion. With astonishment we can read a few sentences later about the same God of Israel as the origin of Israel's suppression: "Who gave up Jacob to the spoiler, and Israel to the robbers? Was it not the Lord, against whom we have sinned, in whose ways they would not walk, and whose law they would not obey?" (Isa 42:24).

The God of Israel is presented as a sovereign entity that is the only one that possesses the power and knowledge—both skills are necessary to act as a free subject. And God's freedom can be seen as an act on the one hand against and on the other in favor of Israel. Right in the same manner he handles the power using it as instrument to fulfil his plans. This role of the deity is part of the Near Eastern concept of Kingship with the sovereign God as King in heaven and his representative in the shape of the king on earth. Life and death, salvation and judgement—the whole spectrum of reality is dominated by the free God. God is free in the sense of having the potential to act in history.

This concept of kingship, found in different types in Egypt and the Near East, supplies the background for the prophecies in Isa 40–66. In these prophecies we find a parallel concept of political theology and history to pro-Persian texts deriving from the Marduk-priesthood in Babylon. The inscription on the so-called Cyrus-cylinder reports about the activities of the main city-god of Babylon, Marduk, in similar manner: "(Then) he pronounced the name of Cyrus, king of Anshan, declared him to be(come) the ruler of all the world . . . Marduk . . . ordered him to march against the city Babylon. He made him set out on the road to Babylon going at his side like a real friend . . . Without any battle, he made him enter his town Babylon."[9]

The field of activity, on which the highest god Marduk or the one God YHWH create new political realities, is history. On the background of a Marduk-theology, the prophecies of the so-called book of Deutero-Isaiah try to formulate an anti-Marduk statement and a one-god theology, accumulating all dominant power and knowledge in the one and only God, YHWH. The contour of this so-called monotheistic religious concept since the seventeenth century, also implies a new conceptualization of freedom. Both we can find *in nuce* in the texts of Isa 40 and following. Based on that text I will summarize elements of this specific concept of freedom.

---

9. From the so-called Cyrus Cylinder; see Cogan, "Cyrus Cylinder."

Conclusion

1. *Regularity and order are the basis for potentials of freedom.* Order should render possibilities for a prosperous and wise living. The aim is to gain options to act. Potentials to act are therefore the concrete form of freedom. Speaking of freedom means to describe concrete potentials of freedom.

2. *Political freedom as potential to act is in the Old Testament texts not a function of political and military power, but a result of the one and only acting God.* According to the biblical texts in Isa 40–66 liberation from despotism is therefore not the consequence of Israel's new power or other things changed but of YHWH himself. In search for freedom Israel referred neither to a new powerful king, nor to its own power or to other putative deities, but to the universal and exclusive God YHWH. Freedom is a consequence of the relationship to this god and of God's relation to the people of Israel. Prophetic-theological proclamation establishes a forum behind the forum of politics and religious legitimized political power. The central aspect on this forum is the relation between God and the people of Israel. Religious and ethic commandments express this relations. These commandments are directly or indirectly expressed in the prophetic book of Isa 40–66 in two ways: speaking about confidence in the God of Israel, in his will and power of salvation and speaking about justice to others (Isa 56 or 59) or authenticity in the cult (Isa 58). Here we detect a change of traditions and theology, which can be linked with the establishing of a Torah-concept in the Deuteronomic and Deuteronomistic Texts of the Old Testament. (cf. the contribution of J. C. Gertz).

3. Seen as development of religious history these prophetic texts in Isa 40–66 deliver an insight to *the change from a traditional Near Eastern-like concept of kingship to a theocentric and eschatological thinking.* Still these texts are used as a basic element of affirmation and stabilizing for the political power. Still the texts reserve a role for a king, but the king does not belong to the own folk. Instead of the former kings of Israel and Judah we find now the foreign king Cyrus. Since the Assyrian times the real historic circumstances have already not allowed seeing the king of Judah in a none-dialectical way as representative of an universal kingship of YHWH. At least the conquests of Jerusalem in 597 and 587 BCE have made this evident. But now also the new top-down political theology with Cyrus as liberator, represented in the oldest stratum of the book of Deutero-Isaiah, failed. Cyrus re-established a Marduk cult in Babylon and did not really worship YHWH. And as far as we can see, the first repatriation occurred under Darius I and not in the time of Cyrus. In the prophetic book, as consequence of these experiences YHWH more and more took over the role of the one and only

king, as we can see in Isa 40–52* and its theocentric composition.[10] Looking beyond this prophetic book we can find in the early Jewish literature of the Persian period a theological transformation of the concept of Near Eastern kingship with anthropological implications. Central texts like Gen 1:27–28, part of the priestly creation account,[11] or Ps 8[12] do present us now what is often called democratization or a demotic concept of kingship. The role to represent God on earth is transmitted to humankind, which means to every single human being. It became an anthropological designation and in consequence the question of order and regularity against the chaos, which is the specific sort of speaking of freedom in the Near East, has to be faced anew. In the Old Testament context this designation has the function to legitimize the ruling of humans over animals and earth. Once again this concept is linked to the topic of power. In short, the political, theological, and anthropological shapes, which are important for the Old Testament thinking of freedom, are concepts of order and regularity, concepts to ensure a scope for acting by power and sovereignty that is otherwise dominated by chaos. In this way the individual or the people could gain opportunities to act, potentials of freedom.

Another interesting religious and theological transformation has been presented by Jan C. Gertz in his lecture on Deuteronomy. There we find the codified law as relativizing dimension, best to see in Deut 17:14–20, the law for the king under the Torah.

4. What kind of *consequences* will these transformations have for a concept of freedom? Two of them I like to mention here. *First, we have to realize a distinction between political and religious rule, or between political and religious authority.* Distinctions and differences occur, so that we always have to ask: What kind of freedom do we mean? How can this freedom be established? By whom or by which structures may this freedom be brought forward and protected? In Isa 40–66 and in the different distinguishable editorial levels[13] it is more and more a concept of a *Gegenwelt* or better described by using a term of Michel Foucault a concept of *heterotopia*. Heterotopia means not just utopia—places, that are not real but have effects. Heterotopia means places that are real and have effects. To illustrate that, Foucault uses the metaphor of the mirror. "In the mirror you can see the exact copy of a thing you can look at. But the crux is that this thing appears

---

10. See Ehring, *Die Rückkehr JHWHs*.

11. Schmitt, *Abeitsbuch zum Alten Testament*, 197–98 (on Gen 1:26ff.); and 189–200 (on Ps 8).

12. Hossfeld and Zenger, *Die Psalmen*, vol. 1, 77–80.

13. Albertz, *Die Exilszeit*, 283–301, 319–23.

in the mirror, at a place, where it cannot really be. The simultaneity of presence—that means, the mirror and the image are real—and absence—that means, the thing that appears in the mirror only exists outside of that mirror—is characteristic for a heterotopia."[14] So, there are . . . , probably in every culture, in every civilization, real places—places that do exist and that are formed in the very founding of society—which are something like counter-sites, a kind of effectively enacted utopia in which the real sites, all the other real sites that can be found within the culture, are simultaneously represented, contested, and inverted. Places of this kind are outside of all places, even though it may be possible to indicate their location in reality. Because these places are absolutely different from all the sites that they reflect and speak about, I shall call them, by way of contrast to utopias, heterotopias."[15] In this sense the mentioned Old Testament literature of the Persian time presents the mighty God, his actions and in Gen 1 or Ps 8 the human being as a mirror, where we have the chance to see how to create potentials of freedom, respectively how the human being should act along an order of creation. The prophetic book concretely has in mind the ending of exile, the return of the Judeans to their country and the re-establishing of the city of Jerusalem and its temple.

5. The second consequence is that historical events are ambivalent and are open to either different political or religious interpretations. This deconstructs both a Greek historiography of the Persians as well as a Judean prophetical. Looking at the *Redaktionsgeschichte* of Isa 40–66[16] we become witnesses of this deconstruction. In this literary process the concrete religious and theological interpretation of the political event, the rise of the Persians under Cyrus to become the dominant power in this region, took a back seat. The prophetic writer began to speak in mythological terms, as we can see in Isa 51 and 52. The prophetic author stages the return of YHWH to Zion and God's mighty power with the phrase that his arm has cut up the monstrous Rahab (Isa 51:9). The hope for freedom is no longer linked with political powers or historical shifts. In consequence the role of a theocentric viewpoint is intensified.

6. In our prophetic texts freedom is in the first instance linked to the people of Israel and has therefore a collective dimension. But in regard to a theological "heterotopia" we find elements of individualization in the prophecies too, like we can read in Isa 56:4–5: "For thus says the Lord: To

---

14. Keitel und Allolio-Näcke, *Erfahrungen der Transdifferenz*, 111. ET by Jürgen van Oorshot.

15. Foucault, "Of Other Spaces," 24–25.

16. See, for example, Ehring, *Die Rückkehr JHWHs*, 1–18.

the eunuchs who keep my sabbaths, who choose the things that please me and hold fast my covenant, I will give, in my house and within my walls, a monument and a name better than sons and daughters; I will give them an everlasting name that shall not be cut off." Because the relation of the human being to God is superior even in the world of a dominant collective thinking there is the possibility to get known as individual and not as "foreigner" or as "eunuch" (Isa 56:2). Here the definition of the relation to God through commandments creates new possibilities for the non-Judean. It opens the way to a universal understanding of the Israelite religion.

7. Speaking of individual persons based on a lack of justice was established by a minority in the Persian Judah. A collectively understood salvation, i.e. salvation for the whole "Israel," does not fit with the unjust behavior of major parts in Judah. Texts like Isa 56 indicate by this way a schism within "Israel." *Freedom understood as a salutary relation between God and his people is now restricted to a minor group.* Salvation for the minor group in "Israel" is opposed to salvation for the majority. Criterion is justice revealed by God.

8. As outlined in Isa 40–66 God is presented as a free subject, because of his power and knowledge. This means that power and knowledge are the exclusive criteria for each definition of a real deity (Isa 41:21–29*). *In consequence human beings do not have freedom as their own potential*, i.e. on the basis of their own ability or knowledge. For them freedom is just a derived entity. Like the category "subject," freedom also belongs—strictly speaking—first and foremost to God. We find here a theocentric concept emerged as counterpoint to the mainstream political and religious implicitness of the Ancient Near East. In consequence freedom on the human level can only be understood as potentials to act.

Bibliography

Albertz, Rainer. *Die Exilszeit: 6. Jahrhundert v. Chr*. Biblische Enzyklopädie 7. Stuttgart: Kaiser, 2001. [ET = *Israel in Exile: The History and Literature of the Sixth Century B.C.E*. Studies in Biblical Literature 3. Atlanta: Society of Biblical Literature, 2003.

Bartsch, Hans-Werner. "Freiheit. I. Altes Testament." In *TRE* 11:497–98.

Becker, U. *Freiheit: Altestamentliche Perspektiven*. Tübingen: Mohr/Siebeck, 2011.

Cogan, Michael. "Cyrus Cylinder." In *The Context of Scripture*, vol. 2, *Monumental Inscriptions from the Biblical World*, edited by William W. Hallo et al., 314–16. Leiden: Brill, 2000.

Ehring, C. *Die Rückkehr JHWHs: Traditions- und religionsgeschichtliche Untersuchungen zu Jesaja 40,1-11, Jesaja 52,7-10 und verwandten Texten*. Wissenschaftliche Monographien zum Alten und Neuen Testament 116. Neukirchen-Vluyn: Neukirchener, 2007.

Foppa, K. "Konzept, konzeptibel." In *Handwörterbuch zur Philosophie*, 4:1082–86.

Foucault, Michel. "Of Other Spaces." *Diacritics* 16/1 (1986) 22–27.

Hossfeld, Frank-Lothar, and Erich Zenger. *Die Psalmen*. Vol. 1, *Psalmen 1–50*. Herders Theologischer Kommentar zum Alten Testament 25. Freiburg: Herder, 2004.

Kaiser, Otto. "Freiheit. I. Altes Testament." In *Die Religion in Geschichte und Gegenwart*[4], 3:304–6.

Keitel, Christoph, and Lars Allolio-Näcke. "Erfahrungen der Transdifferenz." In *Differenzen anders Denken: Bausteine zu einer Kulturtheorie der Transdifferenz*, edited by Lars Allolio-Näcke, et al., 104–17. Frankfurt: Campus, 2005. (translation by JvOo).

Perdue, Leo G., ed. *Scribes, Sages, and Seers: The Sage in the Eastern Mediterranean World*. FRLANT 219. Göttingen: Vandenhoeck & Ruprecht, 2008.

Raaflaub, Kurt. "Freiheit I. Politisch." In *Der neue Pauly: Enzyklopädie der Antike*, 4:650.

Schmid, Hans Heinrich. *Gerechtigkeit als Weltordnung: Hintergrund und Geschichte der alttestamentlichen Gerechtigkeitsbegriffes*. Beiträge zur Historischen Theologie 40. Tübingen: Mohr/Siebeck, 1968.

Schmitt, Hans-Christoph. *Arbeitsbuch zum Alten Testament: Grundzüge der Geschichte Israels und der alttestamentliche Schriften*. Rev ed. UTB 2146. Göttingen: Vandenhoeck & Ruprecht, 2007.

Schwienhorst-Schönberger, Ludger. "E. Die Bücher der Weisheit. V. Das Buch Kohelet." In *Einleitung in das Alte Testament*, edited by Erich Zenger, 336–44. 4th ed. Kohlhammer Studienbücher Theologie 1/1. Stuttgart: Kohlhammer, 2001.

Wiesehöfer, Josef. *Das antike Persien: Von 550 v. Chr. Bis 650 n. Chr.* Zurich: Artemis & Winkler, 1993.

16

Freedom in Community

"Surprising Discovery" and *"Paradoxical Connection"?*

Dirk J. Smit

Connecting Freedom and Community— Surprising, Paradoxical, Controversial?

Die weltgeschichtliche Bedeutung der Reformation hängt an der Radikalität, mit der die Reformatoren ein einziges Thema ins Zentrum der christlichen Existenz wie des theologischen Nachdenkens rückten. Reformation heisst insgesamt nichts anderes als die Wiederentdeckung der christlichen Freiheit. Dass es sich dabei um *eine überraschende Entdeckung* handelt, hat Luther durch den provozierenden Widerspruch deutlich gemacht, mit dem er die christliche Freiheit beschrieb . . . Die *paradox klingende Verknüpfung* von Freiheit und Dienst findet man noch kürzer bei einem anderen grossen Theologen der Reformation, bei Johannes Calvin: "Gott zu dienen ist die höchste Freiheit" (my italics).

With these words Wolfgang Huber summarizes the lasting historical impact of the Reformation on modern developments, including discourses and practices of freedom[1]—as the impact from both a surprising discovery (Luther) and a paradoxical connection (Calvin). As social ethicist, public intellectual, church leader, and ecumenical theologian, Huber has indeed made influential contributions concerning contemporary notions of freedom over many years, drawing on sources from the Christian and particularly the Protestant tradition, as well as on key insights of present-day philosophical, legal and social theories.

In all these aspects of Huber's own life and thought, freedom has indeed been a central category, whether in the fields of ethics, critical theories of justice, notions of humanity and human dignity, Protestant and ecumenical ecclesiology, and public life in pluralist societies.[2]

Of particular interest, therefore, is the explicit way in which he combines freedom and service, following this Protestant rediscovery. In fact, he claims that the impact of the Reformation on the history of the world was

1. Huber, *Protestantismus und Protest*, 53. It is instructive that Huber so deliberately links Luther and Calvin as sharing the more common convictions of the Reformation regarding freedom. These words in fact appear in a chapter on "Theologie der Befreiung—ein Anstoss Martin Luthers" in his small monograph on Protestantism and protest.

In the long process of six consultations between 1989 and 1994 and the many papers and documents produced by the ethical study group of the Leuenberg Church Fellowship, leading to the report The Christian Witness on Freedom, the same fundamental conviction can be seen, namely that the Reformation shares a common witness regarding freedom, however complex and controversial that witness may have become today, under new conditions.

The same conviction was of course also shared by Ernst Troeltsch. In his several essays and major studies on the impact of Protestantism during the formation of the modern world, he would always first emphasize the fact that Calvin and Luther shared the same basic assumptions, before he would then demonstrate the differences brought about by Calvin's own emphases: see, for example, "Luther und die moderne Welt," "Calvinismus und Luthertum," "Die Genfer Kalvinfeier," "Calvin and Calvinism," "Die Kulturbedeutung des Calvinismus," and "Die Bedeutung des Protestantismus für die Entstehung der modernen Welt" (translated as *Protestantism and Progress*), all reprinted with annotation in Troeltsch, *Kritische Gesamtausgabe*, vol. 8, as well as his influential *Die Soziallehren der christlichen Kirchen und Gruppen* (also translated, as *The Social Teaching of the Christian Churches*).

2. His discussions of notions of freedom are central to his own thought. See for example his collection, Huber, *Das Netz ist zerrissen und wir sind frei*; but also *Folgen christlicher Freiheit*; *Zur Freiheit berufen: Biblische Einsichten*. Over the years, he dealt with freedom in many essays, including "Verantwortete Freiheit als Lebensform." For a study of Huber's understanding of freedom, see Fourie, *Communicative Freedom*. The volume dedicated to him on his sixtieth birthday also dealt with the theme of freedom, Reuter et al., eds., *Freiheit verantworten*. It is obvious from the many ways in which Huber combined freedom with expressions like institution, solidarity, binding force, challenges, community, task, responsibility, and others that his thoughts move in exactly the same directions as Calvin's, although he does not appeal to this tradition.

related to precisely this radical insight — or rather conviction, seeing that it is so controversial. He refers to this combination as "radical," as "a surprising discovery," as "a thought-provoking contradiction," as "a paradoxical combination." According to this "paradoxical sounding connection," freedom and service belong together, freedom and belonging, freedom and relationship, freedom and community.

Huber is of course not the only ethicist and theologian to underline the importance of this surprising and controversial link. Many other Protestant authors have recently developed similar views of freedom and belonging. Well-known examples include voices from the Reformed tradition, like Karl Barth and the Barth scholars Clifford Green, John Macken, and Michael Weinrich,[3] the Dutch theologians Gerrit C. Berkouwer and Martien Brinkman as well as Bram van de Beek,[4] the British systematician Colin Gunton,[5] and the North American Daniel Migliore,[6] but also scholars from other traditions, for example the Methodist ethicist from Chicago, William Schweiker,[7] as well as several Bonhoeffer scholars, including the British ecumenical theologian Keith Clements[8] and the German Lutheran ethicist Heinrich Bedford-Strohm.[9]

Not all of them use the expression "service." Perhaps the more general description would rather be that all these contributions argue that freedom should not be construed without an integral link to concrete forms and practices of belonging. They stress, for example, the integral link between freedom and love, they emphasize freedom in community, they argue for freedom and sociality, they combine freedom and solidarity, they take freedom and responsibility together. They point out, for example, that not only freedom-from, but also freedom-for constitutes true freedom. They seriously consider, for example, freedom in embodiment, freedom and structure, freedom and order, even freedom and discipline.

---

3. Green, *Karl Barth*; Macken, *The Autonomy Theme in the Church Dogmatics*; Weinrich, "Zur Freiheit befreit," with a concluding section reflecting this same spirit, called "Die Freiheit ist konkret: Verwirklichung von Gemeinschaft."

4. Berkouwer, *De mens het beeld Gods*; Brinkman, *The Tragedy of Human Freedom*; van de Beek, "A Life in Freedom."

5. Gunton, "God, Grace and Freedom," in *God and Freedom*, 119-34, 1-12.

6. Migliore, *Called to Freedom*.

7. Schweiker, "We Are not Our Own."

8. Clements, *What Freedom?*

9. Bedford-Strohm, "Geschenkte Freiheit."

In general, in the words of Gunton, they would agree that, "It is community that enables us to be what we each particularly are, and that is what is meant by *freedom*."[10]

Notions like belonging (or community, love, solidarity, responsibility) are, of course, also ambiguous and very problematic, and should therefore also be used carefully and critically.[11] Recent discourses about social capital (an umbrella term for connections among individuals, including social networks and the norms of reciprocity and trustworthiness that arise from them) often distinguish between bonding social capital and bridging social capital.[12] Bonding refers to forms of community that are more inward-looking, often reinforcing exclusive identities and homogeneous groups. Bridging refers to forms of community that are more outward-looking, often encompassing people from across different social divides.

Precisely for these reasons, this link between freedom and community has always been not only surprising, but explicitly problematic, controversial, contested and fiercely critiqued and rejected. During the group discussions within this project there has also been strong resistance against this form of link, from the side of philosophers who found such notions of freedom, involving self-limitation and service, logically contradictory, confusing and meaningless, but also from the side of feminist and ideologically-critical thinkers, who are very much aware of the oppressive role that such notions have played and still play in history and in many communities, traditions and societies.

In this regard, the contribution of John Calvin may be instructive. His own views and practices regarding freedom have been notoriously controversial, already in his own time—and also in the course of this project. The link between freedom and service—which Huber also uses as summary of the Protestant legacy—has worked both liberating and world-formative as well as totalitarian and oppressive. In the South African history and experience, this has been dramatically illustrated. The ambiguity of the Calvinist tradition in the colonial and apartheid history has been well captured and described in John W. de Gruchy's study with the deliberately ambiguous title, *Liberating Reformed theology*.[13] Precisely for that reason, it may be

---

10. Gunton, "Introduction," in *God and Freedom*, 11.

11. One instructive example of an attempt to think seriously about the complex nature of forms of belonging, focused on the nature of being "in relationship," is for example available in Welker, "Beziehung—menschlich und göttlich." He suggests distinguishing between different forms of reciprocal, interactive, and personal relationships, in order to understand diverse forms of love, and—in Calvin's terms—forms of belonging, and of freedom in these relationships.

12. Putnam, *Bowling Alone*, but especially his later work.

13. De Gruchy, *Liberating Reformed Theology*.

instructive to consider Calvin's own views of freedom and this ambiguous potential more closely.

Broader Background: Situating Calvin's Thought on Freedom

It is not without reason that Huber specifically refers to the specific contribution of John Calvin's complex and paradoxical understanding of human freedom. Freedom was indeed of central importance to John Calvin—contrary to what many critics have claimed and to what has become almost common wisdom amongst many.[14] Something of this importance can still be heard in his own words from the *Institutes*, "Unless this freedom be comprehended, neither Christ nor gospel truth, nor inner peace of soul, can be rightly known."[15] This is however also heard in Barth's remarkable claim already early in the *Church Dogmatics* that "Calvin has done more for the sake of freedom than all predecessors of modern doctrine of freedom in his time together."[16]

In her well-known Warfield Lectures on *Women, Freedom, and Calvin*, the Princeton historian Jane Dempsey Douglass also points to the lasting importance of Calvin's views on freedom, claiming that Calvin's "theology of freedom has proved enduring, giving rise to new generations of 'freedom fighters' in the following centuries."[17] She is, however, very careful to underline the fact that Calvin himself did not already see and draw the same practical implications in his own theology that later generations would see and draw.

Protestantism in general has of course been called "the religion of freedom" in Hegel's well-known description.[18] It is certainly also not without significance that Luther chose to succinctly summarize his whole understanding of the gospel under the theme of the freedom of a Christian person.[19] Still, it

14. Even scholars, including historians, have accused Calvin of being an enemy of freedom. Famous examples include the British liberal politician and Roman Catholic historian Lord Acton, in his influential *History of Freedom and Other Essays*, and the church historian from Yale, Roland Bainton, who actually followed Lord Acton in his Protestant persecutors. According to Acton, Calvin's theology was actually a theology of persecution and therefore radical opposition to freedom. For a critical discussion of some of these accusations, see Balke, *Calvijn en de Bijbel*, 15–38.

15. Calvin, *Institutes of the Christian Religion*, Book 3, 19, 1 (1559).

16. Barth, *Church Dogmatics* I/2, 748.

17. Douglass, Women, *Freedom, and Calvin*.

18. See, e.g., the popular overview of Moltmann, "Protestantismus als 'Religion der Freiheit.'"

19. For the background and Luther's early developments see e.g. Jacobi *'Christen*

is possible to distinguish Calvin's particular contribution from that of Protestantism in general, in particular the implications of his thought for later, typically modern notions and practices of political freedom.

Much of Calvin's influence and impact in real historical Calvinism, of course, seems to contradict the claim that freedom, particularly political freedom, was indeed central to his thought and work.[20] It is therefore also important to distinguish his own work from many later forms of Calvinism.[21] This seeming contradiction and obvious tension led the authoritative Calvin scholar from the Netherlands Willem Balke to claim that "In spite of later developments in Calvinism, we may therefore honor Calvin as one of the best advocates of freedom in the sixteenth century."[22]

The fact remains, of course, that the *Wirkungsgeschichte* of Calvin's own legacy within historical Calvinism worldwide, particularly also with regard to his understanding of freedom, has given rise to a long tradition of conflictual interpretations, amongst historians and biographers,[23] amongst legal scholars,[24] amongst political scientists[25] and amongst theologians,[26]

heissen Freie'; and for the pamphlet itself the helpful analysis and commentary in Jüngel, *The Freedom of a Christian*.

20. The ambiguous legacy of Calvinism in the history of apartheid South Africa provides a classic case study in this regard. The theological justification of apartheid and the theological and church struggle against apartheid both appealed to the legacy of Calvin—and in fact to ideals of freedom embedded in this legacy; see Smit, "Views on Calvin's Ethics from a South African Perspective."

21. Making and applying this distinction is of course extremely problematic and controversial. For three positions on the methodology involved, see Trueman, "Calvin and Calvinism"; Strohm, "Methodology in Discussion of 'Calvin and Calvinism'"; as well as the polemical Muller, *The Unaccommodated Calvin*.

22. Balke, "Calvin's Concept of Freedom." For a general introduction to the development of Calvin's views in this regard in distinction from the so-called radicals, see his translated doctoral study, *Calvin and the Anabaptist Radicals*.

23. For example, Bouwsma, *John Calvin*; Douglass, *Women, Freedom, and Calvin*; McNeill, *The History and Character of Calvinism*; and Walzer, *The Revolution of the Saints*.

24. For example L. M. du Plessis, "Calvin on State and Politics according to the Institutes"; Little, "Reformed Faith and Religious Liberty"; Witte, "Moderate Religious Liberty in the Theology of John Calvin." Particularly instructive is the study by Witte, *The Reformation of Rights*. He tells the story how "moderate liberty" in Calvin led to a tradition of increasing claims on freedoms and rights, from French-speaking societies, to the Netherlands, to England and Puritan New England. His concluding reflections are called "The Biography and Biology of Liberty in Early Modern Calvinism," 321–33. For Calvin's views on tolerance, Strohm, "Calvin und die religiöse Toleranz."

25. For example, Hancock, *Calvin and the Foundations of Modern Politics*; Höpfl, *The Christian Polity of John Calvin*; Stevenson, *Sovereign Grace*. Interesting, for example, is Davies, *Foundation of American Freedom*.

26. For example, the South African John W. de Gruchy in his well-known Warfield

even amongst scholars specifically concerned with studying Calvin's own views of politics and social life.[27]

Calvin famously dealt with freedom in an essay called "On freedom." It already formed part of the first edition of his *Institutes of the Christian Religion* (1536). In this very early edition it introduced the explicitly political final chapter. As separate section it remained unchanged until the very last edition of the *Institutes* (1559), where it was moved to form the conclusion of the explicitly theological chapter on faith and justification, in Book III.[28] This move is of course very significant in itself. The larger context (after the new placement in the final edition) is now his description of the Christian life. In itself the fact that this description forms an integral part of his exposition of the faith is already very significant, demonstrating the way in which ethics—of which human freedom forms the concluding pinnacle[29]—is integrated into doctrine or faith, according to Calvin.[30] Indeed, "Calvin's particular transfer of this essay suggests that in his mind the idea of Christian freedom constituted an important link between his theological and political understandings."[31]

He also dealt extensively with the notion of freedom in several other writings, including the informative preface to the *Institutes*,[32] many

Lectures published as *Liberating Reformed Theology*; also Jonker, "The Gospel and Political Freedom."

27. For example, Biéler, *Calvin's Economic and Social Thought*; Graham, *The Constructive Revolutionary*; Wolterstorff, *Until Justice and Peace Embrace*.

28. Calvin, *Institutes of the Christian Religion*, Book 3, 19, par. 1–16. In the first edition (1536) it was still joined with two other sections on the polity of the church and on political government in the sixth and final chapter, under the rubric *De libertate Christiana, potestate ecclesiastica, et politica administratione*. In the final edition (1559) these sections were separated from one another. While the essay on freedom was moved to Book III as part of the theological description of Christian life, the essay on church polity was moved to Book IV, chapters 8–12, and the essay "On Civil Government" became Book IV, chapter 20, still the last section of the monumental work.

29. "Der Leitbegriff dieser Ethik ist die neu gewonnene christliche Freiheit," 53.

30. On Calvin's views on the Christian life, see, for example, Gerrish, *Grace and Gratitude*; Leith, *John Calvin's Doctrine of the Christian Life*; and Wallace, *Calvin's Doctrine of the Christian Life*.

31. Stevenson, *Sovereign Grace*, 4.

32. See Jones, *Calvin and the Rhetoric of Piety*. She creatively analyzes three of the "prefatory letters" to the *Institutes* in order to reimagine some of the rhetorical audiences whom Calvin had in mind when he constructed his arguments over the decades with such obvious rhetorical awareness and skill. The best known and indeed very important prefatory letter is the original one in the 1536 edition addressed to King Francis I of France, and retained in all the other editions, even when other prefaces were also added and the King had in the meanwhile died, *Praefatio ad Regem Gall* ("The Prefatory Address to King Francis I of France").

monographs, a large number of personal letters, often addressed to people in positions of authority and often addressed to people in prison and under threat, and also in his many sermons and commentaries.[33] Commentators however agree that the short essay "On freedom" may indeed be read as a representative summary of his main ideas on human freedom. He never changed his mind on this and it always served a crucial role in his systematic work. His view on human freedom is integrally related to his very fundamental but complex view on divine freedom, sometimes (deliberately ambiguously) summarized as "sovereign grace."[34] In these brief comments, however, the focus is deliberately limited only to his understanding of human freedom, or rather freedom as integral to the Christian life, and its crucial social and political implications.[35]

Specific Background: Calvin's View of the Christian Life as not Belonging to Ourselves

The section on human freedom functions—in Book III, 19 of the 1559 edition of the *Institutes*—as an integral part of Calvin's description of the Christian life. This description already begins in Book III, 6. The section on freedom serves as bridge between his discussions of justification (Book III, 11–18) and of prayer (Book III, 20). The key to his vision of the Christian life is his conviction that we do not belong to ourselves, but to God in Jesus Christ and through the Spirit and therefore to one another. This is the sum of the Christian life, expressed as refrain, as motto.

> Now the great thing is this: we are consecrated and dedicated to God in order that we may thereafter think, speak, meditate, and do, nothing except to his glory. If we, then, are not our own [1 Cor 6:19] but the Lord's, it is clear what error we must flee, and whither we must direct all the acts of our life. We are not our

---

33. See the collection of Calvin's political writings by McNeill, *On God and Political Duty*; for secondary discussions, also Olson, "Calvin and Social-Ethical Issues"; and Stevenson, "Calvin and Political Issues."

34. Stevenson combines these words in the title of his major study (*Sovereign Grace*), but the combination of "sovereign" with "grace" expresses a tension in Calvin's thought that has intrigued many interpreters through the centuries and that characterizes his position on almost every doctrine.

35. For a discussion of the different issue of Calvin's treatment of the freedom of the will, see, for example, Brümmer, "Bernard, Calvin and the Freedom of the Will." For a popular discussion of the controversial issue of Calvin on freedom and church discipline, see, for example, Birnstein, *Der Reformator*.

own: let not our reason nor our will therefore sway our plans and deeds. We are not our own: let us therefore not set it as our goal to seek what is expedient for us according to the flesh. We are not our own: in so far as we can, let us therefore forget ourselves and all that is ours. Conversely, we are God's: let us therefore live for him and die for him. We are God's: let his wisdom and will therefore rule all our actions. We are God's: let all the parts of our life accordingly strive toward him as our only goal. (C)onsulting our self-interest is the pestilence that most effectively leads to our destruction. Let this therefore be the first step, that we depart from ourselves in order that we may apply the whole force of our ability in the service of the Lord.[36]

It is based on this motto that Calvin then deals with the Christian life in the different chapters to follow. Together, they build a neat and logical argument. Believers are called to lives of self-denial, searching for justice and righteousness in relation with others and godliness in relation with God (Book III, 7). For that reason, they are called to take up their cross, as followers of Jesus Christ, accepting their sufferings and cross and trusting in God's power, learning patience and experiencing God's comfort and consolation (Book III, 8). For that reason, they are called to meditate on the future life, not in order to escape the present, but precisely to come to proper estimation of the present life, and to receive orientation, perspective and proper priorities (Book III, 9). For that reason, they are called to enjoy and appreciate the wonderful gifts of God, so that these can delight, sustain and support them, and enable and empower them for daily lives of service, love and well-doing (Book III, 10). All of this flows from the knowledge and trust that they indeed are not their own, but belong to God in Jesus Christ and thereby to one another.

Major studies of Calvin's thought and work endorse the centrality of this perspective for understanding his life and work, his theology and biography, as preacher, teacher, and social and economic reformer. In his ministry to congregations of refugees, exiles and strangers,[37] deeply aware of the hardships, suffering and daily cares of widows, orphans, poor people, refugees, exiles and aliens, he comforted them with the good news that they

---

36. Calvin, *Institutes of the Christian Religion*, Book 3, 7,1, 1559. It is precisely this link between "belonging to" and "not belonging to ourselves" which seemed particularly problematic and unacceptable to some participants, including Rüdiger Bittner, who finds Calvin's argument that believers should therefore "not let our reason nor our will" ultimately determine their own priorities and life-style untenable.

37. For the nature of this social ministry, see for example McKee, *Diakonia in the Classical Reformed Tradition and Today*.

belonged to "the Living God and his Christ" and were safe, protected, their lives hidden in Christ sitting at God's right hand.

All major themes of Calvin's theology are related to this fundamental conviction that we belong to God in Jesus Christ and accordingly to one another.[38] This is the sum, the heart and the thrust, of the Christian life—according to Calvin. Belonging to God in Jesus Christ means—for Calvin—that we also belong to one another. The glory of God depends on how we practice this mutual belonging, unity, solidarity, inter-connectedness, sharing with one another. Major aspects of his personal life, ministry, preaching and teaching, his involvement in social welfare and economic justice, and his treatment of major theological themes make no sense if not understood as motivated by this deep awareness of our belonging together.[39]

This conviction found major resonance in the Reformed tradition, from confessional documents to doctrinal discussions, from ecclesial decisions to sermons and popular publications.[40] During the twentieth century this theme would find powerful expression in the Theological Declaration of Barmen (1934).[41] The church belonging to Jesus Christ is not free to exclude

---

38. In Oberman, *Two Reformations*, this authoritative Reformation scholar argues very convincingly how Calvin's main theological concerns can only be appreciated properly within their historical context and his own local congregations and his pastoral and public ministry. This would include themes like election by grace, not depending on us but seen in the mirror of Jesus Christ; God's providential care, covering the whole of creation, actions and decisions of free and responsible human beings, and the smallest eventualities threatening the poor and suffering; God's faithful, covenantal dealings with the work of God's hands as a living, involved, compassionate, personal God; the ministry of the resurrected and ascended Jesus Christ as prophet, priest and king; but also other characteristic teachings.

39. See the joint declaration of a conference on "The Impact of Calvin's Economic and Social Thought on Reformed Witness," in October 2004, the John Knox Center, the Theology Faculty of the University of Geneva, and the WARC, *Reformed World*.

40. One well-known example remains the *Heidelberg Catechism* (1563). The first question and answer powerfully restate this central conviction. What is your only comfort in life and death? That I, with body and soul, both in life and death, am not my own, but belong unto my faithful Savior Jesus Christ. Our deepest comfort in life and death is that we are not our own, but that we belong to Jesus Christ. He has fully satisfied for our sins, delivered us from evil power, preserves us, assures us, and through his Holy Spirit makes us heartily willing to live unto Him, to whom we belong. The whole Catechism builds on this central conviction, as a deeply personal, comforting exposition of what it involves that we belong to Jesus Christ, in life and death, with all we are and all we do. On freedom as theme of the *Heidelberg Catechism*, see, for example, Busch, *Der Freiheit zugetan*.

41. In words directly from the *Heidelberg Catechism* Barmen claims that the church that belongs to Jesus Christ may not proclaim one message, yet practice another, different message, whether by its structure, obedience, ministries, public witness or mission. See Burgsmüller and Weth, eds., *Die Barmer Theologische Erklärung*; Barth, *Texte zur*

others at will. Other Reformed churches and bodies would also confess this fundamental conviction.[42]

The challenging yet fascinating question is how such a strong emphasis on not belonging to ourselves could form the framework for an emphasis on human freedom, to the extent that this view on freedom provides sources of orientation for contemporary social and political views? Should not-belonging-to-ourselves not fundamentally exclude human freedom, not rather contradict the very idea of freedom, in Calvin, and also in Pauline and other Biblical traditions?

A Complex Notion: Calvin's View of Human Freedom

Calvin discusses human freedom under three aspects that, when taken together, lead to a complex, even paradoxical understanding of human freedom. The first aspect is that "the consciences of believers in seeking assurance of their justification before God should rise above and beyond the law, forgetting all law righteousness"—in other words, the freedom of being saved by grace alone. The second aspect is that "consciences observe the law, not as if constrained by the necessity of the law, but that freed from the law's yoke they willingly obey God's will"—in other words, the freedom of eager and cheerful gratitude and service. The third aspect is that "we are not bound before God by any religious obligation preventing us from sometimes using them and other times not using them, indifferently"—in other words, the freedom to be indifferent towards human, cultural, ecclesial and religious obligations. The first two correspond with the two fundamental yet paradoxical claims of Luther on Christian freedom. It is clear that Calvin followed Luther in this regard. In the third aspect, he takes the discussion further and makes the understanding of freedom even more complex—and radical, with regard to its concrete political and public implications.

In his study called *Sovereign grace. The place and significance of Christian freedom in John Calvin's political thought*, political scientist William R. Stevenson Jr. argues that all three these aspects have major political

---

Barmer Theologischen Erklärung; Busch, *Die Barmer Thesen 1934-2004*; specifically on freedom, Welker, "Die freie Gnade Gottes in Jesus Christus und der Auftrag der Kirche: Die VI Barmer These: 1934-1984-2004."

42. It structures the opening statement of the *Brief Statement of Faith* (1993) of the Presbyterian Church of the United States (PCUSA), see the official *The Book of Confessions of the Presbyterian Church (USA)*, Volume 1; also Placher and Willis-Watkins, *Belonging to God*. See also the litany by the WARC in Debrecen (1997), presented to member churches for liturgical use in the face of global injustice and ecological destruction see M. Opocenský, *Debrecen 1997*.

implications. According to him, Calvin's complex concept of freedom serves as bridge between theology and politics, providing the foundation for participation in the public arena, in such a way that it both anticipates and critiques the primary modern ideas of freedom.[43]

His study is an attempt to show how each of the three aspects of Calvin's description of human freedom serves simultaneously both as positive and foundational "anticipation" as well as negative and critical "antidote" for what could be regarded as the dominant modern notions of freedom, each represented by major modern political philosophers. He distinguishes three main modern ideas, namely freedom as a matter of individual fulfillment in individual identity and distinctiveness (Hobbes, Locke); freedom as individual and communal fulfillment but only within the context of communal identity and sacrifice (Machiavelli; Rousseau); and freedom as historical development and thus dialectical fulfillment, within the context of changing political and economic institutions and relationships, and culminating in a particular post-historical epoch (Hegel; Marx)—or, briefly put, respectively individual, communal and historical notions of freedom.[44] Most people, speaking about freedom in modern discourses, stand in one of these three traditions and use the term in one of these three senses.

For Stevenson, what is most problematic about these various dominant modern notions of freedom is "their fragmented and thus superficial, even illusionary, character." Diverse and partial notions of freedom, he argues, vie with one another for supremacy as in themselves comprehensive and complete, without being complemented by other emphases, leading to more complex understandings. Over against these, he believes, Calvin's notion of freedom offers "a much more intricate and comprehensive conception of human freedom." In fact, Calvin anticipates these dominant modern ideas. His systematic description of three parts of freedom corresponds quite well to the three primary modern ideas, but, in demonstrating their interdependence, even their coherence within a larger framework, Stevenson argues, Calvin's description already warns "against just the sort of superficiality and fragmentation of freedom the modern age appears to have bequeathed to us."[45] Attempting to demonstrate this claim, Stevenson's overall argument is so clear, neatly constructed and informative that it could be heuristically worthwhile to follow his analysis more closely, perhaps to appreciate better

---

43. In the following section his instructive argument is therefore followed very closely and quoted in detail, from Stevenson, *Sovereign Grace*.

44. Stevenson, *Sovereign Grace*, 6.

45. Stevenson, *Sovereign Grace*, 7.

some of the implicit political and public consequences of Calvin's fairly dense portrayal.

Individual Freedom to Judge— but not Alone and on Our Own

Calvin's first aspect deals with freedom from righteousness based on works. It presents classic reformation teaching of salvation by grace alone, and builds on Luther's description of Christian freedom, particularly the first thesis in his Freedom of a Christian. Christian freedom invites the consciences of believers, Calvin follows Luther in saying, to rise above and advance beyond the law.

According to Stevenson, this first aspect of Calvin's understanding of freedom constitutes the individual as an irreducible person. It anticipates liberal individualist notions of political freedom, he says. Calvin indeed appears to subscribe to a number of liberalism's tenets. "The idea of human institutions resting on an explicit 'contract,' the so-called privatization of religious concerns, the idea of political equality, the capacity of ordinary individuals to distinguish legitimate from tyrannical governments—all these liberal principles can be found, at least in a superficial way, in Calvin's writings"[46]—and it seems plausible to discern their foundation in this first aspect of Calvin's understanding of human freedom as the freedom of the individual person and the individual's conscience. In his words, "Calvin understands conscience to be the key operating component of each human being, and so the principal source of political maturity."[47] In the personal freedom to resist tyrannical forms of government, both the power and the problems of this fundamental form of individual freedom would be particularly demonstrated in history and in the *Wirkungsgeschichte* of this legacy. However, this is not all that should be said. Although Calvin sees the individual as free in this sense—as "basic, integral, unshrinkable, irreducible"[48]—he simultaneously insists that it is important to hold the

---

46. Stevenson, *Sovereign Grace*, 11–12, for more in-depth discussion, for example of Troeltsch's suggestions that Calvin's notion of public covenant underlies modern social contract theories, or Hancock's ideas that Calvin's notion led to a private sphere for religious beliefs and to modern political secularization, or the question how Calvin understood personal and political equality, or the theme of democratic resistance against tyrannical regimes, 21–36.

47. Stevenson, *Sovereign Grace*, 15.

48. Stevenson, *Sovereign Grace*, 12.

irreducibility of the individual conscience in continuous tension with human partiality and finitude.[49]

> Calvin's individual, in other words, while potentially independent of human social structures, is far from autonomous ... Calvin thus manages to hold in creative tension an elemental individual, as the primary building block in the world's moral order, with a partial and incomplete individual, dependent for the very working of his or her conscience on a moral order reflected in but transcending the world (his italics).[50]

These social and political convictions have deep theological roots, in Calvin. Christian freedom liberates from guilt, but not from spiritual and emotional need, and indeed for the consciously needy individual it does not even fully liberate from guilt either, Stevenson claims. This is the important consequence from the fact that Calvin in the later edition of the *Institutes* deliberately moves this political essay into the broader theological context of justification and specifically of his thoughts on Christian life.

> Journeying through the stages of mortification, vivification, and sanctification, believers grow even more deeply in the awareness of their personal inadequacy and their consequent need for divine guidance and support. The major part of faith, after all, is

---

49. Describing the message of the Reformation for today and commenting on Luther's words at Worms, Welker makes a similar point about the conscience of the individual believer being free yet theologically bound at the same time. "Es ist richtig, dass sich der freie evangelische Christenmensch in letzter Instanz nur Gott gegenüber verantwortlich und gebunden wei ... Falsch aber ist, dass sich der freie evangelische Mensch damit nur in sein eigenes und ganz persönliches religiöses Bewusstsein versenkt ... (Er) bleibt in seinem Glauben gerade nicht bei sich selbst stehen," "Die Botschaft der Reformation—heute," 68-69.

50. Stevenson, *Sovereign Grace*, 12, 37ff. Perhaps it is fair to say—by way of illustration—that it is this same tension between primary and partial, between elemental and incomplete, that would later occupy the thought of the French Reformed philosopher Paul Ricoeur. Right through his long career, he was fascinated by questions of anthropology, and in particular the tensions between what human beings are able to do and not able to do, are capable of and not capable of, are free to do and not free to do, from his earliest writings like *Freedom and Nature: The Voluntary and the Involuntary* and the two volumes of *Finitude and Culpability*, namely *Fallible Man* and *The Symbolism of Evil*, through his major writings like the three volume *Time and Narrative*, and the systematic treatment in his Gifford Lectures, *Oneself as Another*, but still also in his last major publications, like *Memory, History, Forgetting*, as well as *The Course of Recognition*—the theme of the human freedom and ability to act (specifically, to speak; to do; to narrate; to take responsibility; and later then also to recognize, and to remember, forget, and ask for forgiveness) remains central. In a famous interview, he acknowledged that his upbringing—in the Reformed community and tradition—had a lasting influence on his questions and all his work.

> the recognition of one's need for something or someone outside oneself ... Thus when Calvin discusses the 'life of the Christian' ... he concentrates on virtues such as humility, gratitude, self-renunciation, prudence, and recognition of one's status as only one member of the larger body of Christ.[51]

Individual freedom and belonging to God and to the body of Christ therefore go together, and do not contradict one another.[52] Being part of the body of Christ however calls for institutional forms of belonging, including law.

> In this way, Christian freedom ... links human beings even more tightly to the specific detail of God's now revealed law. For Calvin, law is as much a help as a warning and a barrier. His so-called third use of the law ... drives his emphasis on the close connection between living the Christian life and acknowledging the legitimacy of the institutional reflections of God's law. Church, family, polity: All are ordained institutional manifestations of the law by which God desires sinful human beings to live and thrive. Even Christian conscience requires the aid of sound and supportive human institutions. Hence the legitimacy of those institutions and their superiority to individual conscience should in the vast majority of cases be plain.[53]

This means that the Christian person is both a free individual and someone belonging to God and others at the same time, both whole and part, both self-sufficient and dependent on sociality.

> The individual Christian believer, Calvin insists paradoxically, is both a whole and a part, both sufficient and insufficient, both complete and incomplete, and both adequate and inadequate.[54]

---

51. Stevenson, *Sovereign Grace*, 12–13.

52. "The baseline Christian teaching, after all, spotlights both human dignity and human inadequacy in the face of God's explicit call ... Human beings must be both respected and upheld as God's special creatures and restrained and redirected as the recalcitrant rebels they tend to become, Stevenson, *Sovereign Grace*, 26.

53. Stevenson, *Sovereign Grace*, 13, 45ff. "(F)or Calvin, there exists no inherent conflict between law and gospel ... (F)or Calvin love is the law ... The first part of Christian freedom for Calvin, then, is nothing like freedom from the law, it is freedom within the law, even freedom as a result of the law" (his italics), 46-47. For the notion of "institutional help," including ecclesiastical organization and church discipline, 49ff.

54. Stevenson, *Sovereign Grace*, 12. "Because of Calvin's emphasis on the disciplinary role of institutional helps, many scholars argue persuasively that Calvinist societies ... developed both strong church polities and vigorous civil polities ... (F)or Calvin, the individual believer is never in a position either to dispense with the instruction of church, civil government, or individual fellow believers or, therefore, to take God's mercy for granted. Sanctification, effectuated by the Holy Spirit through

Stevenson acknowledges that this picture of the free person is one of paradox and seeming tension and contradiction.

> One can easily turn Calvin's Christian individual into a caricature of what Calvin understood the person to be. No doubt Calvin found himself tempted to oversimplify the Christian individual's character and makeup. What appears to have driven him to hold to the truth of human tension, however, was his determination to be faithful to Scripture, to God's revealed Word ... Drawing out the political implications of Calvin's first part of Christian freedom will thus always be a dangerous business, for Calvin's determination to be faithful trumped his desire to be philosophically coherent or systematic.[55]

In short, for him Calvin hereby anticipates modern notions of individuality as a matter of individual fulfillment in particularity and distinctiveness—known from the work and impact of Hobbes and Locke. At the same time, however, Calvin views this irreducible individual as "part of the whole," as integrally embedded in and dependent on community and on forms of belonging. Thereby, his views already, albeit implicitly, prepare potential sources of critique of modern notions of radical autonomy.[56] In several complex and creative tensions, Calvin wants to keep together what modern notions of freedom are willing to divide and fragment.

Corporate Freedom to Act—but Always under Critique from the Others and Outsiders

The second aspect of human freedom, according to Calvin, describes the eager, ready and cheerful obedience that Christians gladly offer to God when they realize that their works are no longer measured by the standards of the law. This takes the form of acts of love to others. Here, Calvin clearly follows the second thesis of Luther's depiction of the Christian life, but in Calvin

---

the instrumentalities of spiritual and political communities remains a constant task and a lifelong process ... (E)ach individual can hardly fail to appreciate not only their radical insufficiency and incompleteness but also their blessedness in the face of a community's love and care. Rather than the proud and spiritually self-sufficient (effectively autonomous) individual of modern liberalism, ... 'the beginning of piety is willingness to be taught,'" 52–53.

55. Stevenson, *Sovereign Grace*, 13.

56. The first part discussing this first aspect is called "The irreducible, yet partial, individual," 11–58.

this becomes the so-called third use of the law, in the form of very concrete obedience in everyday social, economic and political realities.

For Stevenson, there is an element of truth in those well-known interpretations—including Weber's famous thesis—that the roots of some form of active materialism can be found in Calvin's thought. In Calvin's description of the second part of human freedom, he says, is a description of the societal of corporate response to the conscience's individual vision. Now, the rejuvenated conscience moves through a grateful soul towards concrete and embodied social action. Calvin promotes not only the individual freedom to judge, but indeed also the corporate freedom to act, together.[57] Since they do not belong to themselves, but to God and to one another, they are being freed to love God and one another, together and concretely, and indeed confidently.

> Understanding themselves bound to each other by means of God's sovereign grace, not to mention guided by God's loving rule, frees them for positive service in God's developing kingdom . . . (It) engenders a kind of corporate confidence. Assured of God's love and care, and so renewed and reborn, believers can leave behind petty worries over their deservedness of God's mercy, relish the warmth of God's fatherly gaze, and concentrate their energies on social renewal.[58]

57. Stevenson, *Sovereign Grace*, 59. In his brief description of the Reformed tradition in his *Der Protestantismus*, Graf also stresses this second characteristic, although motivated in a slightly different way: "Die Betonung der Autonomie der einzelnen Gemeinden, deren Selbstregierung . . . und die Bildung . . . Synoden trugen dazu bei, da. in den reformierten Kirchen intensiv auch Ideale republikanischer Bürgerfreiheit entwickelt wurden. Die Freiheit eines Christenmenschen wurde kommunitär, von der umfassenden Einbindung des einzelnen in die christliche Gemeinde her und mit Blick auf das gemeine Wohl aller gedacht" (my italics), 43. Graf is obviously very critical of the consequences, "Die reformierte Sozialethik tendiert daher zu einer radikalen Moralisierung der öffentlichen Ordnung," which often combines itself with "Moralterror gegenüber Andersdenkenden, Laxeren," 43-44.

58. Stevenson, *Sovereign Grace*, 59-60, for the importance of this freedom from anxiety in Calvin's thought, 64-69. For Troeltsch, this lack of anxiety, which he regards as a major difference from Lutheranism, is key to understand the Calvinist practice of freedom, for example: "With Luther it was at bottom always a question only of the certainty of salvation and blessedness of the individual, produced by the certainty of forgiveness of sins . . . In Calvinism all this is different . . . (A)s it is not the salvation of the creature's soul but God's honor, which is, for him, the central idea, so, too, it is the glorification of God in action which is the real test of a genuine personal religion . . . (H)erein lies the sharpest difference in the two-sided interpretation of religious individualism, the Protestant religion of faith and character . . . Of this possibility of falling away from grace, and, by implication, of this anxiety, Calvinism knows nothing . . . The Calvinist knows that God's election cannot be lost, and will therefore have to direct his efforts, not to himself, but to the task of fashioning the world and the community

They are being freed to gratefully and willingly obey God's will. They are being freed to perform all the duties of love. Summarized in Stevenson's words, they are freed to embrace and build up what social institutions they confront, they are freed to practice piety by serving the material and spiritual interests of others, they are freed to attend to the poor and strengthen the body of believers.[59] In short, they are freed and called toward concrete social action on the world.

According to Stevenson, "two primary implications of Christian freedom's second part should now be apparent." The first one is that "Christian freedom implies, to a significant degree, losing oneself in the bonds of corporate, social life." The second implication is that such freedom "obliges believers to serve the material interests of other human beings and their societal institutions."[60]

Again, however, Calvin's notion remains complex and paradoxical. This promotion of social involvement and activity remains again only one dimension in his analysis of the second part of human freedom, as Stevenson shows. Once again it is important to see the subtleties and creative tension intrinsic to Calvin's description. The corporate action and social service of the freed community is namely put under continuous critique, it remains subject to ongoing judgment.[61]

---

after God's will. His obligation is not to hold to God, but, on the contrary, to be himself upheld by God. The reformed individualism therefore contains on all sides impulses to activity, to a full co-operation of the person with the tasks of the world and the community, to work of unceasing strenuousness and utility," "Calvin and Calvinism," 130–31. His descriptions are of course controversial, but in these words the same paradox that Stevenson points out is clearly described, a form of individualism that leads to communal activity and belonging.

59. Stevenson, *Sovereign Grace*, 60, for the nature and role of such "social duties" in Calvin, including "embracing and edifying social institutions," 70–76.

60. "(F)or Calvin social bonds are both natural and necessary . . . Corporate links require . . . institutional mechanisms sufficient to reinforce such links. Responding to God's call to follow his law willingly, eagerly, and freely means immersing ourselves in the practice of piety . . . The practical effect of this call is to engage believers in building up those social institutions that tend to be the most reliable helps for encouraging them in the resignation to do God's will . . . The second key implication of freedom's second part thus points to believers' obligations to serve the material interests of other human beings and their communal institutions . . . Calvin is no contemplative. His concerns are ever in the world: in the physical health and strength of the visible church and in the physical and psychic condition of its present and potential members . . . In emphasizing the ministry of material aid and institutional change, Calvin was clearly no ascetic," Stevenson, *Sovereign Grace*, 72–75 (his italics).

61. Stevenson, *Sovereign Grace*, 60. "(A)ll human beings ought to understand themselves as primarily reflective of God's judgment. This fact clearly implies several theological points relevant to politics . . . First, God's judgment and his justice are real

> Christian freedom not only liberates the Christian actor; it liberates the Christian prophet. Hence, while it frees the Christian community for service in the world, it simultaneously puts that service under God's omniscient and continuing judgment.[62]

In other words, exactly like the experience of the first part of human freedom, the experience of the second part of freedom again "works both to loosen and to bind." Believers demonstrate their gratitude "in the midst of a delicate and creative tension ... They must act for the good without understanding themselves to be the real actors." Always acting in the presence of an the all-seeing and all-judging God presents believers "with as many grounds for hesitation as for action."[63] Always being aware of the reality of God's judgment confronts believers with "the limits inhering in their institutional aspirations."[64]

In a flood of scholarly literature, this tension between social involvement on the one hand and self-critical limitation on the other hand, between moral activism and so-called prophetic criticism and self-criticism would of course characterize the Reformed tradition and community, under the influence of Calvin. For this tradition, Christian freedom indeed liberates not only the Christian actor, but also the (self-)critical Christian prophet. It would be expressed and described in many different ways, for example in H. Richard Niebuhr's depiction of the Christ-transforming-culture type in his influential typology of Christian positions towards culture. According to him, this type, amongst others represented by the Reformed tradition, always simultaneously acts and hesitates—it acts, because it affirms reality, culture and everyday-life as the sphere of God's calling, and it hesitates, because it remains continuously aware of the limitations and flaws of whatever corporate action may achieve.[65] According to Stevenson, this characteristic

---

and tangible. Second, human beings can see only so far with regard to God's ultimate plan for them; hence to be under God's judgment means to be neither overly curious in thought nor overly presumptuous in deed. Third, due to the attitude of humility necessary in the face of God's judgment, human accountability to God's judgment ought to breed a tolerance for human opinions regarding specific aspects of that judgment and therefore a plea for peace as a primary duty of governments" (his italics), 84.

62. Stevenson, *Sovereign Grace*, 60.

63. Stevenson, *Sovereign Grace*, 60–61. This self-critical tension between action and hesitation, between what many would see as social activism and at the same time self-critical relativization would characterize the position of many Reformed theologians in the tradition of Calvin. One well-known illustration would be the ethics of Barth, see for example the analysis in Bigger, *The Hastening That Waits*.

64. Stevenson, *Sovereign Grace*, 61.

65. Niebuhr, *Christ and Culture*.

habitus is already at work in Calvin's views on the second aspect of human freedom.

For Calvin, the practical implications of God's establishment of explicit limitations on human action are of extreme importance. Human beings are therefore called to responsible freedom, which includes the responsible use of power, including social, political and institutional power. Calvin is interested in these forms of power, because they contribute to form the world in which human beings live and can therefore serve the purposes of the kingdom, of love and justice and mercy and peace and mutual service. There is, however, no guarantee that such social, political and institutional power is exercised in ways that actually do serve God's will and the well-being of others, and therefore their exercise always stands in the need of critical scrutiny. Power is necessary but not necessarily good. He therefore pleads for gifted, attentive and responsive rulers, in other words for good governance, his position calls for all kinds of restraint on exercises of power, for governmental modesty in both style and substance, for the duty of government to protect the church and serve the poor and dispossessed.[66] Later, this habitus would of course also be expressed in the formula *ecclesia reformata semper reformanda secundum Verbum Dei*, an attempt to capture this ongoing yet creative tension between affirmation and critique.[67]

In short, according to Stevenson, this second aspect of Calvin's understanding of freedom liberates people to constructive, corporate action and especially service in the world. It thereby anticipates modern notions of freedom involving communal identity and sacrifice—represented for example by Machiavelli and Rousseau. At the same time, however, Calvin regards these corporate actions of freedom as always being under judgment. With this element of criticism and judgment, says Stevenson, Calvin's views already offer a potential critique of modern notions of both suffocating community as well as over-confident activism.[68]

---

66. Stevenson, *Sovereign Grace*, 61, for good governance, see especially 94–100; for the fact that service better describes Calvin's views than action, 103.

67. See for example Smit, "Can We Still Be Reformed?"; for the formula and the expression, Pelikan, *Reformation of Church and Dogma (1300–1700)*, 217ff.; Frey, "Ecclesia semper reformanda—ex fide scripturae sacrae"; also Obderdorfer, "'Ecclesia semper reformanda'—eine Tradition der Traditionsverzehrung?" The title of this last volume of essays, which deals with the Lutheran tradition, again shows the close resemblences between these mainline Protestant communities regarding their understanding of freedom.

68. The second part in which he discusses this aspect is called "Corporate action, but under judgment," 59–104.

Historical Freedom as Liberation—but within the Boundaries of Wisdom, Community, and Justice

The third aspect of human freedom, according to Calvin, is the freedom from adiaphora, the freedom of conscience from all kinds of outward things which are in themselves indifferent, the freedom to be indifferent about the indifferent. This aspect can take the concrete form of human liberation in specific historical situations from the power and influence of culture and tradition—and can therefore be experienced as very dramatic, radical and even revolutionary. With this third aspect, Calvin emancipates the Christian conscience from both particular cultures and particular traditions. In principle, they are all declared indifferent, and thereby Calvin liberates believers from "the stranglehold of cultural superstitions."[69]

Many commentators find this third aspect Calvin's most radical and even revolutionary contribution.[70] In a European society bound in both its ecclesiastical and its secular aspects by tradition and cultural authority, Stevenson remarks, this could indeed be regarded as Calvin's most revolutionary teaching.[71] Christians are free to dissociate themselves from whatever cultural and time-bound context in which they may live, whereby they are liberated both from cultural traditions and customs and liberated for the following of God's truth and God's call.[72] If the existing social order is ultimately only temporary and superficial, then its reconstruction and even if needed even destruction may indeed be called for, especially if in some crucial way it perverts and subverts the purposes of the reign of God.[73]

---

69. Stevenson, *Sovereign Grace*, 105.

70. See also Schützeichel, "Calvins Verständnis der christlichen Freiheit."

71. Stevenson, *Sovereign Grace*, 105. He also correctly points out that this conviction was already present in Calvin's work from early on, albeit formulated in different ways. This was for example underlying his position in the Prefatory Address in the *Institutes* since 1536, namely that the truth of God deserves more respect than mere human custom. God's eternal truth liberates believers from being bound to any form of historical event, cultural artefact or time-bound claim or custom, 105ff.

72. Stevenson, *Sovereign Grace*, 105.

73. Stevenson, *Sovereign Grace*, 106. Particularly interesting, although controversial, is what Stevenson discusses as Calvin's views on "change as progress," 121ff. He is however careful not to claim explicitly that Calvin held such a view. "Perhaps the key significance of Calvin's vision of providential hope ... concerns the sense in which hope of historical judgment and providential redemption imply a 'progressive' view of history ... (Calvin) inspires a new appreciation for the political implications of such hope within historical time, and he does so at a time that a recognition of the full significance of historical change was beginning to germinate and sprout. Perhaps most important, Calvin challenged head on the transhistorical 'antispeculation' of the medieval/Augustinian vision. As a result, we can with little trouble see in Calvin's doctrine

Not only in theory, but indeed also in historical practice this would lead to radical and sometimes revolutionary social and historical action. Calvin himself already assumed that the first two aspects would be more readily understood, since they represented basic evangelical teaching, but admitted that the third aspect introduced a "weighty controversy." This was the point where the spirits parted.[74]

The argument of Jane Dempsey Douglass in *Women, Freedom and Calvin*, on contemporary implications of Calvin's views for women in church and society, is largely based on this third aspect of human freedom. "Calvin is the only sixteenth-century theologian who views women's silence in church as an 'indifferent matter,' i.e. one determined by human rather than divine law." She situates this viewpoint, remarkable for his time, within his overall project. Her reading strategy is to read Calvin against his own practices and against major parts of his own *Wirkungsgeschichte*, arguing that at the heart of his theology and in some of his pastoral practices one may discern a liberating potential that neither he nor his contemporaries fully understood and embodied, namely in this aspect of his teaching on freedom.

Again, however, this third aspect is also more complex. Again it contains complex internal tension. The freedom to be indifferent towards what is indifferent after all suggests that there are indeed aspects which are not indifferent, and towards which believers may therefore not stand in indifference. Put differently, the freedom to disengage from specific cultural customs and traditions does not disengage believers from history life itself, from the wisdom of tradition and community as such, from all custom and tradition, as if it were possible to live without them, from the need to live in community with others, or in his own words, to belong not to oneself. If culture, custom and tradition are all truly indifferent, merely outward things, then getting rid of them is of course also indifferent, merely outward, and not ultimately necessary. This argument already presents a very strong counter-weight. If believers are truly liberated from these outward things, then they should for that very same reason "not put any more emphasis on the avoidance of such things as on their attachment."[75]

---

of providence the theme of historical progress," 122–23.

74. Perhaps one could also say that this is one of the points of difference between Calvin and much of Lutheranism that intrigued many observers, including Ernst Troeltsch, who often described the differences between the two traditions in ways that focus on this social or historical element in Calvin, see for example his essay "Calvin and Calvinism," 126–42.

75. Stevenson, *Sovereign Grace*, 106.

The complex tension raised here is however even stronger. Creation after all—in spite of all darkness, hiddenness and threat, of which Calvin is only too aware[76]—also remains "good," it remains the arena of God's wisdom, power and glory, history remains the arena of God's providential love, care and purposes, human institutions and social life remain the form in which believers serve God and neighbor, practicing their knowledge that they do not belong to themselves. Accordingly, although all specific cultural forms within history are radically undermined in their authority, since their outward form is declared as in principle indifferent, culture, history and tradition as such remain of crucial importance. In the mystery of God's grace, God confronts believers within history, culture and tradition. This is the point that people like H. Richard Niebuhr wanted to make with their description of a "Christ transforming culture" position. Stevenson describes this aspect as "historical pedagogy," as "the tutelage of history" and even as "the grace of tradition."[77] History is not only there to be changed, but also as source of instruction. "Hence, each particular set of historical circumstances—that is, the cultural matrix of institutions, needs to be seen as a significant part of God's plan for salvation and the believers response to such constraints, one of patience, forbearance, and eagerness to learn the lesson that God's direction of historical events is teaching."[78]

This clearly means that hidden within Calvin's radical and even revolutionary teaching—that every cultural form is indifferent and subjected to change, if necessary—there is a deep respected for the importance of world,

76. His whole ministry was a ministry to refugees and exiles and his faith and theology can only be understood as a ministry deeply aware of such harsh realities. Herman Selderhuis therefore exemplifies Calvin's reading of the Bible by discussing his deeply existential understanding of the Psalms and of the songs of lament and suffering, *Calvin's Theology of the Psalms*. Susan Schreiner writes movingly about Calvin's no less than 159 sermons on Job, showing how deeply aware he was of the darkness of creation and the hiddenness of God: Schreiner, *Where Shall Wisdom Be Found?*; Schreiner, *The Theater of His Glory*; and Schreiner, "Calvin as an Interpreter of Job."

77. Stevenson, *Sovereign Grace*, 106, 131ff, see specifically 138ff.

78. Stevenson, *Sovereign Grace*, 131–32. "(T)his third part reminds (believers) that history unfolds not as their story but as God's story. And God's specific purposes and directions are not always manifest. The other side of freedom as indifference to cultural forms, therefore, tells believers that every particular culture or tradition ... signifies a clear and potentially crucial stage in God's unfolding providential design. As much as Christian freedom emancipates believers from their cultural, historical contexts, it grounds them even more firmly in the workings of God by means of such contexts ... Clearly God is active in history, according to Calvin. Yet God is active not only in possible future restoration and change but also in past institutional hedges, restraints and guides. God's providential pedagogy commands as much (if nor more) attention as God's providential "ideology": What God is immediately teaching becomes as critical as where God is ultimately leading."

history, society and culture and therefore simultaneously also "a strongly conservative bent."[79]

> The Christian believer is thus free both to change such structures through God's inspiration and to accept such structures as signs of God's care and love. Christian humility can mean both a raucous charge into the fray, riding the Lord's will, and a quiet acceptance of one's place and time in recognition of one's deep ignorance of the particular details of God's plan. Ultimately, Christian freedom's indifference can imply both cool scepticism and warm acceptance of one's historical circumstances.[80]

The intrinsic tension therefore leads to a complex experience of world and history and an almost ambiguous attitude towards society and culture.

> (The believers') call is as much to seek God's will in their present surroundings as to follow God's call to renew and restore those surroundings. God seeks their attentiveness, their patience, and their perseverance as such as God seeks their hope, their zeal for progressive change.[81]

It is therefore with good reasons possible to question whether Calvin's own position and intentions may in fact be describes as radical and revolutionary, as so many scholars have done. The ambiguities and the complex tensions within this third aspect of human freedom calls for some reservation and restraint in this regard, at least according to Stevenson.

> Attempting to be faithful to Scripture, Calvin saw in God's providence both liberation from cultural context and an obligation

---

79. Stevenson, *Sovereign Grace*, 106–7. It is of course this "conservative bent" that would sometimes in the legacy of Calvin's teachings in Calvinist circles lead to a very strong emphasis on nature and even natural law, on the status quo, on obedience, on respect for authority. In apartheid theology in South Africa, this would be expressed in the motto that recreation does not destroy creation, but perfects creation, interpreted to mean that what could be observed with natural reason "in creation," namely that human beings are created "differently", according to race and nation, language and culture, should be respected, conserved and obeyed in recreation, which means the church and its outward form, with the result that separate and exclusive churches could be seen as the will of God.

80. Stevenson, *Sovereign Grace*, 132. With different vocabulary, this reminds one of Bonhoeffer's personal struggle in prison with the question of *Widerstand und Ergebung*, the personal difficulty to discern when to submit and when to resist, see Letters and papers from prison, for example aptly translated in Dutch as *Verzet en overgave*, where he often contrasts these two attitudes by referring to Don Quixote (always eager to resist and fight) and Sancho Panza (always submissive and willing to endure).

81. Stevenson, *Sovereign Grace*, 107.

to recognize the presence of God's will within that context. The conservative dimension to Calvin's doctrine of providence is thus real and, although superficially paradoxical, not at all incongruous with his theology as a whole. Attempting faithfulness to Scripture, Calvin simply desires politically minded believers to carry in their minds an appreciation of their very human temptations to identify their purposes with God's purposes rather than the reverse.[82]

For Calvin himself, this third part of human freedom was the most significant part of all. "For within the third part lay the church's sense of its destiny within history ... Christian believers must inevitably see themselves as both providentially embedded in historical context and providentially destined to emancipation from that context. If they misunderstand this part of freedom, they mistake their status and fall prey to either a debasement of historical order or an idolization of mere culture."[83]

In short, according to Stevenson, this third aspect of Calvin's understanding of freedom frees people from the pressures and restrictions of custom and culture. Through this historical liberation, his view anticipates modern notions of freedom as historical progress and dialectical fulfillment[84]—represented for example by the dominant understandings of Hegel and Marx. At the same time, however, Calvin binds such forms of historical liberation them to the wisdom of history and tradition, thereby

---

82. Stevenson, *Sovereign Grace*, 143.

83. Stevenson, *Sovereign Grace*, 147.

84. Again, Graf in *Der Protestantismus*, also describes this third aspect of Calvin's understanding of freedom and its historical impact: "Die unmittelbare Rückbindung politischer Autorität an den souveränen Gesetzeswillen Gottes hatte langfristig ambivalente Folgen. Die Tendenz zur religiösen *Übermoralisierung* des Politischen eröffnete den einzelnen Gemeinden und Christen auch bestimmte Freiheitschancen im Verhältnis zur Obrigkeit. Stärker als viele lutherische Theologen erkannten die führenden reformierten Theologen den Bürgern ein Recht auf Widerstand gegen eine Obrigkeit zu, die Gottes Gesetz missachtete ... Nach der Bartholomäusnacht von 1572 entwickelte (Beza) eine Theorie politischer Autorität, die später für demokratischen Partizipationsansprüche der Regierten in Anspruch genommen wurde ... Auch mit dieser Lehre vom Recht auf Widerstand entfaltete der reformierte Protestantismus indirekt modernisierende Wirkungen, weil nun die unmittelbare Autorität der Obrigkeit reflexiv gebrochen und der fromme Bürger als eine eigene normative Instanz der Gestaltung des Politischen anerkannt war" (my italics), 44–45. For a detailed historical study of the impact of confessional, particularly Reformed, legal thinkers on the formation of public justice and legal traditions in early modern times, see Strohm, *Calvinismus und Recht*.

already offering potential sources of criticism regarding modern notions of progressive ideological enslavement.[85]

The South African Case Study: Freedom with Paradox and Constructive Tension?

Recent South African history, including the reception of Calvin within South Africa, can serve as one dramatic example of the potential tensions between these three aspects of human freedom, according to Calvin, in other words, between what Stevenson describes as Calvin's understanding as "a three-dimensional liberation, even emancipation," namely calling for forms of individual, communal and historical freedom.

One could argue that all three aspects have been emphasized in South Africa, in different social groups and discourses, often in direct conflict with one another.[86]

An Afrikaner Calvinism developed, and in fact became the dominant social and political tradition in the country, that emphasized communal freedom, the freedom of the *volk*—appealing to Calvin and Calvinism. This Afrikaner Calvinism regarded liberalism, emphasizing individual freedom and freedoms and eventually individual rights and liberties—often also appealing to Calvin and Calvinism as sources of inspiration[87]—as the main opponent in public life in South Africa.[88]

---

85. The third part discussing this aspect is called "Cultural Dissociation and the Tutelage of History," 105–48.

86. For an overview of viewpoints and literature, see Smit, "Morality and Politics—Secular or Sacred?"

87. In English-speaking settler circles quite different developments took place, but again not without controversy and conflict. Mainly because of the Evangelical Revival in Britain and elsewhere in Europe many Protestant missionaries came to the (Cape) Colony, including for example figures like Johannes van der Kemp (of the London Missionary Society), a convinced Calvinist, James Read (also from the LMS), founder of the Calvinist Society in Cape Town, and John Philip (the Superintendent of the LMS in the Colony). All of them were Calvinist evangelicals and founders of the Congregational Church in South Africa. At the same time, they were outspoken liberals. Van der Kemp married an indigenous woman, Philip was the leader of the anti-slavery abolitionist movement, Read had strong liberal views—and all of them based on their understanding of their Calvinist heritage. In English-speaking churches this was again not at all the only tradition. There were for example controversies between the sentiments and practices of respectively the (often more liberal) missionary initiatives and the (often more conservative) settler churches of the colonists themselves. By way of over-simplification one could therefore say that two dominant versions of Calvinism developed over several centuries and directly opposed one another, an exclusivist Afrikaner Calvinism and a liberal evangelical and missionary Calvinism.

88. In 1948 an important study was published, in many ways representative of

In the self-understanding of Afrikaner Calvinism and its apartheid theology, the main alternative and the real enemy was liberalism. Again and again this was the way in which the alternatives for South African society were construed in these circles—although the term liberalism was of course used rhetorically, for propaganda and political impact, and therefore often without conceptual clarity and as synonym for all other social evils, like humanism, individualism, later secularism, even communism, and of course the dreaded one-person-one-vote and human rights, all lumped together as threats to true freedom (understood and protected by true Afrikaner Calvinists), namely the *vryheid* of the *volk*.

As far as Afrikaner Calvinism was concerned, the choice was construed as a radical alternative between the mutually exclusive freedom of the group and the freedom of the individual.[89] Finally, a more historical

---

perhaps the most enduring debate in Dutch Reformed circles in South Africa during the nineteenth and twentieth centuries. It was called *Die liberale rigting in Suid-Afrika: 'n Kerkhistoriese studie* (The Liberal School of Thought in South Africa. A Church-Historical Study). Its author was the respected historian T. N. Hanekom, at the time a minister in Stellenbosch, but for some time also assistant editor of *Die Kerkbode*, the official journal of the DRChurch, and later Professor of Church History in Stellenbosch. Later in 1948, when the Nationalist Party came to power for the first time, with apartheid as its policy and popular slogan and with D. F. Malan, a former DRC minister as first Prime Minister, Hanekom wrote as assistant editor in *Die Kerkbode* that finally the church polity of the DRChurch (of racial separation) had become the official policy of the government and public life. A few years later he defended the deepest logic of this tradition in a monograph called *Kerk en Volk: Die Verhouding tussen Afrikaanse Lewenskringe*, 1957 [Church and Folk: The Relationship between the Spheres of Life in Afrikanerdom]; at stake was the relationship between the two spheres of on the one hand the *volk*, not to be translated as nation, since that is too inclusive and loses the cultural and ethnic connotations of *volk*, and on the other hand the church, two spheres that should be kept separate yet at the same time closely related, according to this understanding). The study on *Die Liberale Rigting* was his doctoral dissertation at Potchefstroom, under the supervision of J. D. du Toit (Totius), the almost iconic theologian and Afrikaans poet, who translated and rhymed the Biblical Psalms into moving Afrikaans songs and prayers. Totius again studied under Kuyper at the Vrije Universiteit in Amsterdam and was the first theologian to justify apartheid on biblical grounds. *Die Liberale Rigting* argues that the characteristic feature of the liberal position is not to be found in its longing for freedom, but in its rejection of authority. The religious foundation of liberalism is to be found in its slogan "God and my right(s)"—understood as natural rights and equal rights, not God-given and communal. According to Hanekom—representative of a dominant tradition within Afrikaner Calvinism—all of this contradicts the Calvinist understanding of freedom.

89. There were two major splits in the governing National Party during the 1970s and 1980s, both leading to the formation of right-wing political parties, opposing the (apartheid) government vehemently from the right. In both cases, those who broke away construed the differences in terms of a conflict between their own Calvinist nationalism and the too liberal attitude of the (apartheid) Nationalist government. At stake were different understandings of freedom—and always with direct appeal to

understanding developed in the circles of struggle against apartheid, and once again this black liberationist tradition also often appealed to Calvin.

In April 1969 the respected cultural figure Albert Hertzog (son of a former prime minister) resigned as minister from the cabinet. His first speech in Parliament after his resignation became known as his "Calvinism-speech" (14 April 1969). In this speech, he describes Afrikaners (he meant white Afrikaans-speaking South Africans) as Calvinist and the English (he meant white English-speaking South Africans) as liberal—and for him this is an insurmountable difference. Calvinists, according to him, take the diversity in creation seriously and therefore also their own ethnicity and whiteness; they love freedom, both of the person and of the *volk*, and no one, not even the state, may infringe on that freedom; they respect authority and they therefore maintain authority, without hesitation. Liberalists, according to him, fail in these respects, and therefore they are unable to resist the onslaught from Communism and from the left, always using (so-called) freedom to fight against (true) freedom. In the public media and in politics major debates ensued. The Nationalist government fiercely rejected this position—coming from their own ranks—since it could alienate any potential support from white English-speaking South Africans, which the ruling party could not afford. Hertzog and his followers were forced, with their Calvinist rejection of liberalism, into irrelevant right-wing politics, at the time.

In March 1982 a second split to the right took place with the formation of the Conservative Party in Pretoria. Its leader was A. P. (Andries) Treurnicht, another respected cultural figure in Afrikanerdom, another former DRC minister, another former editor of *Die Kerkbode*, another former Minister in the cabinet of the Nationalist Party—and another outspoken and articulate Calvinist and fierce critic of liberal ideas, whether in theology, public life and morality, or politics. One illustration can suffice. Treurnicht was a popular speaker and author, also editor of an influential newspaper in Pretoria. In 1974 he published a collection of his popular radio talks, called *Waar die soeklig val* [Where the Searchlight Shines]. In an instructive essay called "Verdra of nie verdra nie?" [To Tolerate or not to Tolerate?], he offers a powerful argument against toleration and for intolerance. Tolerance sounds so nice, he says, as a slogan, but in history it has led, in a foolish and godless world, to terrible evil and destruction. He therefore pleads for intolerance—and complains that many people are unwilling to tolerate intolerance—in church and in society. Slogans like "peaceful co-existence" come from the most intolerant ideologies of our world, like Communism, he explains. For that reason liberalism and its unqualified tolerance is so dangerous, as one can clearly see in "the typical slogans from the liberal camp," including freedom of religion and freedom of conscience, freedom of speech and of propaganda, freedom of a lecturer in front of a class, freedom of the press, freedom of information, no discrimination on the basis of faith, race or color, and many others. It can be life-threatening, he concludes, not to resist the powers of destruction. Within a year, he also published his major statement of his own convictions, called *Credo van 'n Afrikaner*, 1975 [An Afrikaner's Creed], in which he writes extensively about Calvinism and self-critically inquires how Calvinist the Afrikaner people still are, after all? A few years later, he broke away from the (apartheid) government to form his Conservative Party to the right, shortly before the government itself increasingly developed in the direction of a security state, portraying the South African society as facing a "total onslaught," and dramatically denying citizens even further personal freedoms, justified by the declaration of a state of emergency.

Calvin[90]—for example in the person of Allan Boesak, the well-known "black and Reformed" theologian and activist.[91] Boesak is in fact still appealing to the same Calvinist tradition—building on Reformed thinkers like Abraham Kuyper and Paul Lehmann—in his public and political writings pleading for "a spirituality of politics" in the new democratic South Africa.[92]

Not only between the three aspects, however, but, understood in Calvin's way, already within all three aspects themselves, as Stevenson argues, there is "a paradox, a constructive tension." In history, this tension would remarkably contribute both to the formation of modern understandings of freedom and to radical critique of one-sided notions, both inspiring and informing modern strivings and struggles for freedom and serving as critical antidote to "shallow and seemingly truncated ideas of freedom found in major modern thinkers."

For Calvin, his view of this paradoxical freedom was based on Biblical traditions.[93] Jane Dempsey Douglass helpfully summarizes that "Calvin depends in substance first of all on Paul, especially in Galatians, then on Luther."[94] However, it is important to recognize that Calvin's paradoxical view of freedom is not merely dependent on specific pericopes or particular historical figures and insights, but in fact deeply embedded in and dependent on his overall theological approach, on his understanding of the Christian God of the biblical traditions.[95] Stevenson captures this broader

---

90. For an instructive dialogue between Calvin's legacy and liberation theology, with explicit discussions of the understanding of freedom in this tradition, see de Gruchy, *Liberating Reformed Theology*, as well as his *John Calvin*.

91. See for example Boesak, *Farewell to Innocence*; and Boesak, *Black and Reformed*.

92. For his more recent works, see for example Boesak, *The Tenderness of Conscience*; and Boesak, *Running with Horses*.

93. He quotes from both the Old and New Testaments, but in the three points of this discussion primarily from some New Testament letters. He claims about the first aspect of human freedom that "almost the whole subject of the Epistle to the Galatians hinges" on this notion of freedom. For the second aspect he refers to Deuteronomy, again to Galatians, to Hebrews, and to Rom 6. For the third aspect he explicitly refers to especially Rom 14, but also to 1 Timothy. Calvin's understanding of freedom, like that of Luther, and in fact depending on that of Luther, was therefore closely connected with the Pauline description of believers as new creatures. For a comparison of Calvin's views on freedom with those of Luther against their historical backdrop, see therefore the contribution to this consultation by Nüssel. For contemporary discussions of the Pauline material that Calvin also used, see the contributions by Lampe, Hurtado, Eckstein, Gaventa and Schüssler Fiorenza.

94. Douglas, *Women, Freedom and Calvin*, 15ff., where she however also indicates that for the structure of these points Calvin was heavily dependent on Melanchton.

95. This applies not only to his understanding of ethics, but in fact to the whole of his ethics. In a very instructive essay called "The Wounds of God," the Reformed philosopher Nicholas Wolterstorff argues that Calvin's ethics is not based in the first

theological background when he argues that it is "the biblically inspired notion of God's sovereign grace which weaves (the different elements of this creative tension) all together." In this short essay on freedom in the *Institutes* readers of Calvin should always find "the whole behind those parts," namely his theology itself. "Between and among the parts, there is tension, even paradox, in Calvin's thinking, but it is the authentic, constructive tension of living the Christian life in the face of a sovereign yet loving divine Creator, Ruler, and Redeemer."[96]

Critical Reflection: Is Freedom in Community Possible?

This paradox, this constructive tension is obviously based on the emphasis in Calvin's theological and political thought on both freedom and belonging. For him, it is not possible to fully understand freedom—whether individual, communal, or historical—without appreciating its integral link to belonging. Without any reference to Calvin, Michael Welker offers a similar description of evangelical freedom, which also includes all three aspects of Calvin's depiction in a rich, complex contemporary portrayal.

> Was ist evangelische Freiheit? Evangelische Freiheit ist die Freiheit des Lebens in Gottes Wort. In Gottes Wort ist den Menschen eine reiche Orientierungsgrundlage gegeben. In und durch Gottes Wort werden die Menschen befreit und gefestigt, erfreut und getröstet, sensibilisiert und gestärkt, *individuell erbaut und miteinander verbunden*, belebt und beruhigt, herausgefordert und geleitet, *sie gewinnen Gewissheit und Hoffnung, sie werden aber auch in Frage gestellt* und über sich selbst hinausgeführt. In dieser Freiheit werden Menschen *befreit von Bindungen* an menschliche Satzungen und Systeme, vom Eingebundensein in menschliche Traditionen und Institutionen, vom Lechzen nach Trendkompatibilität, nach Resonanz überhaupt und nach Übereinstimmung mit dem Zeitgeist. Ihre Füsse werden auf weiten Raum gestellt.[97]

---

place—as is often thought—on notions of obligation, duty, and obedience, but rather on "something deeper," namely being grasped by the love and compassionate justice of God.

96. Stevenson, *Sovereign Grace*, 4. Amongst the flood of secondary literature available on Calvin's theology, a particularly instructive statement of his Trinitarian understanding of God and the implications thereof for Christian life in church and society is available in Butin, *Revelation, Redemption, and Response*.

97. Welker, "Die evangelische Freiheit."

It is immediately clear how Calvin's notions of personal freedom (individuality in community), communal freedom (active lives of calling and hope) and historical freedom (critical distance from customs, powers and zeitgeist) are here interwoven with one another. Like Calvin, Welker further develops this understanding of evangelical freedom by reference to the fullness, complexities and paradoxes of the Biblical drama of freedom—freedom in Christ, as member of the body of Christ; freedom in the knowledge of the cross of Christ; freedom in the creative power of the resurrection; freedom in the presence of God's coming reign.

In conclusion, there is no doubt that Calvin's notion of belonging—of the embodiment and practices of Christian community in which the threefold liberation is experienced and the threefold freedom truly practiced—calls for forms of community in which realities of exclusion, marginalization, alienation, and oppression are continuously opposed and hopefully overcome. It calls for qualitative forms of community,[98] community of radical bridging,[99] visible in actual liberation, living unity, real reconciliation, and compassionate justice[100]—as the crucial role in Calvin's thought, including his discussion of freedom, of the weak, the poor, the suffering, of widows and exiles reminds us. It calls for forms of freedom in which tyranny and oppression are indeed overcome, not strengthened and justified.

Whether the controversial notion of freedom in community, freedom in belonging, could indeed be useful for this purpose, or whether it will prove to be too confusing and potentially distortive, will have to be determined again and again in the ongoing history of the reception of this "surprising discovery" and this "paradoxical connection," in the words of Wolfgang Huber.

---

98. Albrecht, *The Character of Our Communities*; also Bedford-Strohm, *Gemeinschaft aus kommunikativer Freiheit*.

99. It is probably the fact that Calvinist communities and churches so often through the centuries became bonding rather than bridging communities, that they were seen and experienced by outsiders as exclusive and, when they were powerful, dominating and oppressive. It is no wonder that with such experiences outsiders would often find it difficult to recognize in these Calvinist groups the liberating understanding of freedom that Calvin proclaimed.

100. It comes as no surprise that the three themes described as challenges of Calvin's legacy today in the brochure by the WARC to celebrate his 500th anniversary are these three, namely to foster unity and community, to serve justice and to strengthen reconciliation and peace in the world, see *The Legacy of John Calvin*, Geneva: WARC, 2009.

Bibliography

Acton, John Emerich Edward Dalberg. *History of Freedom and Other Essays*. London: Macmillan, 1907.
Albrecht, G. H. *The Character of Our Communities: Toward an Ethic of Liberation for the Church*, Nashville: Abingdon, 1995.
Balke, Willem. *Calvijn en de Bijbel*. Kampen: Kok, 2003.
―――. *Calvin and the Anabaptist Radicals*. Translated by Willem Heyner. Grand Rapids: Eerdmans, 1981.
―――. "Calvin's Concept of Freedom." In *Freedom*, edited by A. van Egmond and D. van Keulen, 25–54. Studies in Reformed Theology 1. Baarn: Callenbach, 1996.
Barth, Karl. *Church Dogmatics I/2, The Doctrine of God, Part 2*. Edited by G. W. Bromiley and T. F. Torrance. Translated by G. W. Bromiley. Edinburgh: T. & T. Clark, 1957.
―――. *Texte zur Barmer Theologischen Erklärung*. Introduction by Eberhard Jüngel. Zurich: TVZ, 1984.
Bedford-Strohm, Heinrich. *Gemeinschaft aus kommunikativer Freiheit: Sozialer Zusammenhalt in der modernen Gesellschaft: Ein theologischer Beitrag*. Öffentliche Theologie 11. Gütersloh: Gütersloher, 1999.
―――. "Geschenkte Freiheit: Von welchen Voraussetzungen lebt der demokratische Staat?" *Zeitschrift für Evangelische Ethik* 49 (2005) 248–65.
Beek, Bram van de. "A Life in Freedom." In *Freedom*, edited by A. van Egmond and D. van Keulen, 11–24. Studies in Reformed Theology 1. Baarn: Callenbach, 1996.
Berkouwer, G. C. *De mens het beeld Gods*. Dogmatische Studien 10. Kampen: Kok, 1957.
Biéler, André. *Calvin's Economic and Social Thought*. Translated by James Greig. Geneva: World Alliance of Reformed Churches, 2006.
Bigger, Nigel. *The Hastening That Waits: Karl Barth's Ethics*. Oxford Studies in Christian Ethics. Oxford: Clarendon, 1993.
Birnstein, Uwe. *Der Reformator: Wie Johannes Calvin Zucht und Freiheit lehrte*. Wichern Porträts. 2nd ed. Berlin: Wichern, 2009.
Boesak, Allan. *Black and Reformed: Apartheid, Liberation and the Calvinist Tradition*. Maryknoll, NY: Orbis, 1984.
―――. *Farewell to Innocence: A Socio-Ethical Study on Black Theology and Black Power*. Maryknoll, NY: Orbis, 1976.
―――. *Running with Horses: Reflections of an Accidental Politician*. Cape Town: Joho, 2009.
―――. *The Tenderness of Conscience: African Renaissance and the Spirituality of Politics*. Stellenbosch: Sun Media, 2005.
Bouwsma, William J. *John Calvin: A Sixteenth-Century Portrait*. New York: Oxford University Press, 1988.
Brinkman, M. E. *The Tragedy of Human Freedom: The Failure and Promise of the Christian Concept of Freedom in Western Culture*. Currents of Encounter 20. Amsterdam: Rodopi, 2003.
Brümmer, Vincent. "Bernard, Calvin and the Freedom of the Will." In *Brümmer on Meaning and the Christian Faith: Collected Writings of Vincent Brümmer*, 333–49. Ashgate Contemporary Thinkers on Religion. Aldershot, UK: Ashgate, 2006.
Burgsmüller Alfred, and Rudolf Weth, eds. *Die Barmer Theologische Erklärung: Einführung und Dokumentation*. Neukirchen-Vluyn: Neukirchener, 1983

Busch, Eberhard. *Die Barmer Thesen 1934–2004*. Göttingen: Vandenhoeck & Ruprecht, 2004.

———. *Drawn to Freedom: Christian Faith Today in Conversation with the Heidelberg Catechism*. Translated by William H. Rader. Grand Rapids: Eerdmans, 2010.

———. *Der Freiheit zugetan: Christliche Glaube heute—im Gespräch mit dem Heidelberg Katechismus*. Neukirchen-Vluyn: Neukirchener, 1998.

Butin, Philip Walker. *Revelation, Redemption, and Response: Calvin's Trinitarian Understanding of the Divine–Human Relation*. New York: Oxford University Press, 1995.

Calvin, John. *Institutes of the Christian Religion*.

———. "Der Leitbegriff dieser Ethik ist die neu gewonnene christliche Freiheit." In Christian Link, *Johannes Calvin: Humanist, Reformator, Lehrer der Kirche*. Zurich: TVZ, 2009.

Clements, Keith W. *What Freedom? The Persistent Challenge of Dietrich Bonhoeffer*. Bristol: Bristol Baptist College, 1990.

Davies, A. Mervyn. *Foundation of American Freedom*. New York: Abingdon, 1955.

de Gruchy, John W. *John Calvin: Christian Humanist, Evangelical Reformer*. Eugene, OR: Cascade Books, 2013.

———. *Liberating Reformed Theology: A South African Contribution to an Ecumenical Debate*. Grand Rapids: Eerdmans, 1991.

Douglass, Jane Dempsey. *Women, Freedom and Calvin*. Annie Kinkead Warfield Lectures 1983. Philadelphia: Westminster, 1985.

Fourie, Willem. *Communicative Freedom: Wolfgang Huber's Theological Proposal*. Theology in the Public Square 5. Münster: Lit, 2012.

Frey, J. "Ecclesia semper reformanda—ex fide scripturae sacrae." *Herausgeforderte Kirche: Anstösse, Wege, Perspektiven: Eberhard Busch zum 60. Geburtstag*, edited by Christoph Dahling-Sander et al., 365–72. Wuppertal: Foedus, 1997.

Gerrish, B. A. *Grace and Gratitude: The Eucharist in John Calvin's Theology*. 1993. Reprint, Eugene: Wipf & Stock, 2002.

Graf, Friedrich Wilhelm. *Der Protestantismus: Geschichte und Gegenwart*. Beck'sche Reihe: Wissen 2108. Munich: Beck, 2006.

Graham, W. Fred. *The Constructive Revolutionary: John Calvin & His Socio-Economic Impact*. Atlanta: John Knox, 1971.

Green, Clifford J. *Karl Barth: Theologian of Freedom*. The Making of Modern Theology. San Francisco: Collins, 1989.

Gunton, Colin E. *God and Freedom: Essays in Historical and Systematic Theology*. Edinburgh: T. & T. Clark, 1995.

Hancock, Ralph C. *Calvin and the Foundations of Modern Politics*. Ithaca, NY: Cornell University Press, 1989.

Hanekom, T. N. *Kerk en Volk: Die Verhouding tussen Afrikaanse Lewenskringe*. Kaapstad: Kerkuitgewers, 1957.

———. *Die liberale rigting in Suid-Afrika: 'n Kerkhistoriese studie*. Stellenbosch: Christen-Studentevereniging van Suid-Afrika, 1951.

Höpfl, Harro. *The Christian Polity of John Calvin*. Cambridge Studies in the History and Theory of Politics. Cambridge: Cambridge University Press, 1982.

Huber, Wolfgang. *Folgen christlicher Freiheit: Ethik und Theorie der Kirche im Horizont der Barmer Theologischen Erklärung*. Neukirchener Beiträge zur systematischen Theologie 4. Neukirchen-Vluyn: Neukirchener, 1983.

———. *Das Netz ist zerrissen und wir sind frei: Reden*. Frankfurt: Hanisches, 2010.

———. *Protestantismus und Protest: Zum Verhälnis von Ethik und Politik*. Rororo Aktuell Essay. Reinbeck bei Hamburg: Rowohlt, 1987.

———. "Verantwortete Freiheit als Lebensform." In *Verantwortlichkeit—nur eine Illusion?*, edited by Thomas Fuchs and Grit Schwarzkopf, 319-40. Schriften des Marsilius-Kollegs 3. Heidelberg: Winter, 2010.

———. *Zur Freiheit berufen: Biblische Einsichten*. Kaiser-Taschenbücher 146. Gütersloh: Gütersloher, 1996.

Jacobi, Thorsten. *"Christen heissen Freie": Luthers Freiheitsaussagen in den Jahren 1515-1519*. Beiträge zur historischen Theologie 101. Tübingen: Mohr/Siebeck, 1997.

Jones, Serene. *Calvin and the Rhetoric of Piety*. Louisville: Westminster John Knox, 1995.

Jonker, W. D. "The Gospel and Political Freedom." In *Freedom*, edited by A. van Egmond and D. van Keulen, 243-62. Studies in Reformed Theology 1. Baarn: Callenbach, 1996.

Jüngel, Eberhard. *The Freedom of a Christian: Luther's Significance for Contemporary Theology*. Translated by Roy A. Harrisville. Minneapolis: Augsburg, 1988.

Leith, John H. *John Calvin's Doctrine of the Christian Life*. Louisville: Westminster John Knox, 1989.

Little, David. "Reformed Faith and Religious Liberty." In *Major Themes in the Reformed Tradition*, edited by Donald K. McKim, 196-213. 1992. Reprint, Eugene, OR: Wipf & Stock, 1998.

Macken, John. *The Autonomy Theme in the Church Dogmatics: Karl Barth and His Critics*. New York: Cambridge University Press, 1990.

McKee, Elsie Anne. *Diakonia in the Classical Reformed Tradition and Today*. Grand Rapids: Eerdmans, 1989.

McNeill, John T. *The History and Character of Calvinism*. New York: Oxford University Press, 1954.

———. *On God and Political Duty*. New York: Macmillan, 1950.

Migliore, Daniel L. *Called to Freedom: Liberation Theology and the Future of Christian Doctrine*. Philadelphia: Westminster, 1980.

Moltmann, Jürgen. "Protestantismus als 'Religion der Freiheit.'" In *Religion der Freiheit: Protestantismus in der Moderne*, edited by Jürgen Moltmann, 11-28. Kaiser Taschenbücher 74. Munich: Kaiser, 1990.

Muller, Richard A. *The Unaccommodated Calvin: Studies in the Foundation of a Theological Tradition*. New York: Oxford University Press, 2000.

Niebuhr, H. Richard. *Christ and Culture*. New York: Harper & Row, 1951.

Oberdorfer, Bernd. "'Ecclesia semper reformanda'—eine Tradition der Traditionsverzehrung?" In *Gebundene Freiheit?: Bekenntnisbildung und theologische Lehre im Luthertum*, edited by Peter Gemeinhardt and Bernd Oberdorfer, 108-21. Lutherische Kirche, Geschichte und Gestalten 25. Gütersloh: Gütersloher, 2008.

Oberman, Heiko A. *Two Reformations: The Journey from the Last Days to the New World*. Edited by Donald Weinstein. New Haven: Yale University Press, 2003.

Olson, J. E. "Calvin and Social-Ethical Issues," in *The Cambridge Companion to John Calvin*, edited by Donald K. McKim, 153-72. Cambridge: Cambridge University Press, 2004.

Opocenský, M. *Debrecen 1997: Proceedings of the 23rd General Council of the World Alliance of Reformed Churches (Presbyterian and Congregational)*. Geneva: World Alliance of Reformed Churches, 1997.

Pelikan, Jaroslav. *Reformation of Church and Dogma (1300–1700)*. The Christian Tradition 4. Chicago: Chicago University Press, 1984.

Placher, William C., and David Willis-Watkins. *Belonging to God: A Commentary on A Brief Statement of Faith*. Louisville: Westminster John Knox, 1992.

Plessis, L. M., du. "Calvin on State and Politics according to the *Institutes*." In *J. Calvin's Institutes*, 174–83. Potch: IRS, 1986.

Putnam, Robert D. *Bowling Alone: The Collapse and Revival of American Community*. New York: Schuster & Schuster, 2000.

Reuter, Hans-Richard et al., eds. *Freiheit verantworten: Festschrift für Wolfgang Huber zum 60. Geburtstag*. Gütersloh: Gütersloher, 2002.

Ricoeur, Paul. *The Course of Recognition*. Vienna Lecture Series. Cambridge: Harvard University Press, 2005.

———. *Fallible Man*. Rev. ed. Translation by Charles A. Kelbley. New York: Fordham University Press, 1986.

———. *Freedom and Nature: The Voluntary and the Involuntary*. Translated by Erazim V. Kohák. Northwestern University Studies in Phenomenology & Existential Philosophy. Evanston, IL: Northwestern University Press, 2007.

———. *Memory, History, Forgetting*. Translated by Kathleen Blamey and David Pellauer. Chicago: University of Chicago Press, 2004.

———. *Oneself as Another*. Translated by Kathleen Blamey. Chicago: University of Chicago Press, 1992.

———. *The Symbolism of Evil*. Translated by Emerson Buchanan. New York: Harper & Row, 1967.

Schreiner, S. E. "Calvin as an Interpreter of Job." In *Calvin and the Bible*, edited by Donald K. McKim, 53–84. Cambridge: Cambridge University Press, 2006.

———. *The Theater of His Glory: Nature and the Natural Order in the Thought of John Calvin*. Grand Rapids: Baker Academic, 1991.

———. *Where Shall Wisdom Be Found? Calvin's Exegesis of Job from Medieval and Modern Perspectives*. Chicago: Chicago University Press, 1994.

Schützeichel, Heribert. "Calvins Verständnis der christlichen Freiheit." *Catholica* 37 (1983) 323–50.

Schweiker, William. "We Are not Our Own." In *Loving God with Our Minds: The Pastor as Theologian. Essays in Honor of Wallace M. Alston*, edited by Michael Welker and Cynthia A. Jarvis, 31–49. Grand Rapids: Eerdmans, 2004.

Selderhuis, Herman. *Calvin's Theology of the Psalms*. Grand Rapids: Baker, 2006.

Smit, Dirk J. "Can We Still Be Reformed? Questions from a South African Perspective." In *Reformed Theology: Identity and Ecumenicity*, edited by Wallace M. Alston Jr. and Michael Welker, 233–53. Grand Rapids: Eerdmans, 2003.

———. "Morality and Politics—Secular or Sacred? Calvinist Traditions and Resources in Conflict in Recent South African Experiences." In *Essays on Being Reformed: Collected Essays* 3, edited by R. R. Vosloo, 513–49. Stellenbosch: SunMedia, 2009.

———. "Views on Calvin's Ethics from a South African Perspective." *Reformed World* 57/4 (2007) 306–44.

Stevenson, William R., Jr. "Calvin and Political Issues." In *The Cambridge Companion to John Calvin*, edited by Donald K. McKim, 173–87. Cambridge Companions to Religion. Cambridge: Cambridge University Press, 2004.

———. *Sovereign Grace: The Place and Significance of Christian Freedom in John Calvin's Political Thought*. New York: Oxford University Press, 1999.

Strohm, Christoph. "Calvin und die religiöse Toleranz." In *Johannes Calvin 1509–2009: Würdigung aus Berner Perspektive*, edited by Martin Sallmann et al., 219–36. Zurich: TVZ, 2012.

———. *Calvinismus und Recht: Weltanschaulich-konfessionelle Aspekte im Werk reformierter Juristen in der Frühen Neuzeit*. Spätmittelalter, Humanismus, Reformation 42. Tübingen: Mohr/Siebeck, 2008.

———. "Methodology in Discussion of 'Calvin and Calvinism.'" In *Calvinus Praeceptor Ecclesiae: Papers of the International Congress on Calvin Research, Princeton, August 20–24, 2002*, edited by Herman J. Selderhuis, 65–105. Travaux d'humanisme et renaissance 388. Geneva: Droz, 2004.

Troeltsch, Ernst. "Calvin and Calvinism." In *Kritische Gesamtausgabe*. Vol. 8, *Schriften zur Bedeutung des Protestantismus für die moderne Welt (1906–1913)*, edited by Trutz Rendtorff, 126–42. Berlin: de Gruyter, 2001.

———. *Kritische Gesamtausgabe*. Vol. 8, *Schriften zur Bedeutung des Protestantismus für die moderne Welt (1906–1913)*. Edited by Trutz Rendtorff. Berlin: de Gruyter, 2001.

———. *Protestantism and Progress: The Significance of Protestantism for the Rise of the Modern World*. Translated by W. Montgomery. 1958. Reprint, Fortress Texts in Modern Theology. Philadelphia: Fortress, 1986.

———. *The Social Teaching of the Christian Church*. 2 vols. Translated by Olive Wyon. 1931. Reprint, Library of Theological Ethics. Louisville: Westminster John Knox, 1992.

———. *Die Soziallehren der christlichen Kirchen und Gruppen*. Gesammelte Schriften 1. Tübingen: Mohr/Siebeck, 1922.

Trueman, Carl R. "Calvin and Calvinism." In *The Cambridge Companion to John Calvin*, edited by Donald K. McKim, 225–44. Cambridge Companions to Religion. Cambridge: Cambridge University Press, 2004.

Treurnicht, A. P. *Waar die soeklig val*. 1974.

Wallace, Ronald S. *Calvin's Doctrine of the Christian Life*. Edinburgh: Oliver & Boyd, 1959.

Walzer, Michael. *The Revolution of the Saints: A Study in the Origins of Radical Politics*. Cambridge: Harvard University Press, 1965.

Weinrich, Michael. "Zur Freiheit befreit: Vorüberlegungen zum systematisch-theologischen Orientierungshorizont eines christlichen Freiheitsverständnisses." In *Freiheit verantworten: Festschrift für Wolfgang Huber zum 60. Geburtstag*, edited by Hans-Richard Reuter et al., 90–101. Gütersloh: Gütersloher, 2002.

Welker, Michael. "Beziehung—mensch und göttlich." In *Was ist der Mensch, dass du seiner gedenkst? (Psalm 8,5). Aspekte einer theologischen Anthropologie: Festschrift für Bernd Janowski zum 65. Geburtstag*, edited by Michaela Bauks et al., 541–51. Neukirchen-Vluyn: Neukirchener, 2008.

———. "Die Botschaft der Reformation—heute." In *Die Reformation: Potentiale der Freiheit*, edited by Berndt Hamm and Michael Welker, 68–69. Tübingen: Mohr/Siebeck, 2008.

———. "Die evangelische Freiheit." *Evangelische Theologie* 57 (1997) 68–73.

———. "Die freie Gnade Gottes in Jesus Christus und der Auftrag der Kirche: Die VI Barmer These: 1934–1984–2004." *epd-Dokumentation* 29 (2004) 9–18.

Witte, John, Jr. "Moderate Religious Liberty in the Theology of John Calvin." *Calvin Theological Journal* 31 (1996) 359–403.

———. *The Reformation of Rights: Law, Religion, and Human Rights in Early Modern Calvinism*. Cambridge: Cambridge University Press, 2007.

Wolterstorff, Nicholas. *Until Justice and Peace Embrace: The Kuyper Lectures for 1981 Delivered at the Free University of Amsterdam*. Grand Rapids: Eerdmans, 1983.

———. "The Wounds of God: Calvin's Theology of Social Injustice." *Reformed World* 37 (1987) 14–22.

17

Concepts of Freedom in the Czech Reformation

JINDŘICH HALAMA

An urgent need to liberate the church from the "snares of the Antichrist" and to restore true Christian freedom was the original and primary aim of the Czech Reformation. From the early fifteenth to the early seventeenth century, there was more than one attempt to achieve this aim. The radical Hussite emphasis on liberating the entire Czech Christian society and establishing a kingdom of freedom and justice throughout the Czech lands led to revolutionary violence that ended in fratricidal conflict and in a less than equal compromise with the ruling ideology. The attempt of the Czech Brethren, which was based on voluntary choice, exclusivity, and a moral strictness that rejected the ways of the "fallen world," fell into legalism and internal contradictions within two generations.

However, as a result of the struggles of the Czech Reformation during the sixteenth century, concepts of toleration, freedom of conscience, and freedom of belief and religion developed. Christian freedom was recognized as being something that could not be attained by human effort, but could only be gratefully accepted as God's gracious gift. The only way to promote it was to not deny it to those who believed differently, but to respect them and to witness to true Christian freedom through a faithful life. Such a fragile concept was doomed to be suppressed in the political arena of the time, but it helped pave way for the modern concepts of freedom of conscience and freedom of religion.

When we try to take a broad view of the history of the Czech Reformation in its most significant manifestations and ask about the role played by its concept (or concepts) of freedom, the primary image we meet up with is the liberation of the Christian church from "Babylonian captivity" or the "snares of the Antichrist." The conviction shared by all of the reform movements of the time was that the late medieval church lacked true Christian freedom, and that a profound change in its structure and way of life was needed. The restoration of the true Christian church was the main requirement and source of hope for Czech reformers in the second half of the fourteenth century. Their views were especially informed by the Waldensians[1] and later by the followers of John Wycliffe. These influences, together with pronounced eschatological expectations, were formative agents in the birth of the Hussite movement and an important source of the theology that it developed during the first half of the fifteenth century.

The way freedom was envisaged in the thought of the Czech Reformation underwent several changes and shifts in emphasis during the two centuries of its existence. However, in spite of these shifts, the central emphasis of the Reformation, which focused on the Word of God and its liberating activity in human lives, remained at the core of Czech Reformation theology. On the following pages, we will attempt to analyze the aspects (or concepts) of freedom that appear in the writings of Hussite theologians and the Czech Brethren during the fifteenth and sixteenth centuries. We will also seek to pay attention to the social and political consequences of these works.

The Word of God as the Source of Human Freedom

The most frequent, and most significant, use of the word "freedom" in the documents of the Czech Reformation during its early period is to be found in the phrase, "the freedom of the Word of God." Based on a statement in the Pastoral Epistles, which declares that "the word of God is not bound" (2 Tim 2:9), this was a profession of faith in the supreme power of the Word of God and an expression of the requirement that no hindrances would be placed in the way of its operation.

Various reform preachers—and consequently, the whole reform movement—viewed the final decades of the fourteenth century, as well as a large part of the fifteenth, as the age of the Antichrist. They were persuaded

---

1. Regarding the Waldensians and their influence on the Czech Reformation, see Gonnet and Molnar, *Les Vaudois au moyen âge*; Molnar, *Die Waldenser*.

that the Antichrist had taken most of Christendom into captivity and was striving to prevent the work of the Holy Spirit and in particular to obfuscate the hearing of God's word. Reform preachers were "convinced that when it was faithful to the gospel of Christ, their preaching had a unique historic mission; . . . it could hold back the rise of forces opposed to God . . ."[2]

That is why the requirement of the free preaching of the Word of God (*predicatio libera*),[3] which was especially advocated and practiced by the Waldensians and later, by followers of John Wycliffe, became one of the crucial items on the agenda of the Hussite movement in Bohemia. The first generations of the Czech Reformation—including John Hus—viewed this requirement as he first precondition for the renewal of the Christian Church. This concern found expression in the words of the Four Articles of the Hussite program. One of these articles declares: "First of all, the Word of God should be preached and annunciated by Christian priests freely and without obstacle in the Czech kingdom . . ."[4]

This requirement, which was so important to the Hussite program, was supported by faith in the renewing power of God's word through preaching. This was closely associated with the eschatological idea of the end times and the belief that God sends his word to save all those who accept it from the coming judgment. In the interpretation of Militius de Chremsir (Milíč z Kroměříže), who was a forerunner of John Hus and his contemporaries, the preacher has a key role and great responsibility in this process: "the preacher is a representative of the eschatological age . . . , who has to convert sinners and distinguish between good and evil."[5] A hierarchical view of church is still operative for Militius, and the role of clergy is particularly irreplaceable in mediating the word of God: "Therefore, a preacher is a liberator, freeing his people from captivity . . . He sets the people free from the power of evil."[6]

Such high expectations regarding the task of preachers or priests could be voiced by a prophetic figure like Militius, but it did not represent a viable concept for the larger community of believers. As soon as Hussite

---

2. Opočienský, ed., *The Message for the Last Days*, 13.

3. For more on the principle of the free preaching of God's word, see Morée, *Preaching in Fourteenth-Century Bohemia*, 76–99.

4. "Čtyři pražské články" [The Four Articles of Prague] (1420), in *Čtyři vyznání* [The Four Confessions], 39. "Verbum dei, exemplo Christi et apostolorum, a sacerdotibus domini libere ac sine impedimento fideliter et veraciter debet predicari et annuciari." in Bartoš, ed., *Orationes, quibus Nicolaus de Pelhřimov*, 86–113. Quotation on 88. The order of the Four Articles was changeable. The article on free preaching, which traditionally is considered to be the first, was defended as the third article at the Council of Basel.

5. Morée, *Preaching in Fourteenth-Century Bohemia*, 176–77.

6. Morée, *Preaching in Fourteenth-Century Bohemia*, 165.

theologians turned their attention from critiquing the medieval church to a constructive project of reform, they attributed liberating power solely to God's activity. "Above all, their concern was to constantly make room for the sovereign freedom of God's activity until it could manifest itself positively by liberating the faithful."[7]

The liberating power of God's word, which works through faithful preaching of the Gospel, should be accessible to all people. This idea stood behind the founding of Bethlehem Chapel in Prague in 1392. This chapel was established, not as a parish church, but solely for the preaching of the Gospel. (During the first decade of the fifteenth century, John Hus was the preacher at this chapel). The word of God was understood to have the power to liberate human lives from captivity to the Antichrist. It was God's free and gracious gift which brought freedom to the lives of the faithful. This was a theological break-through that could not be omitted from the defense of Hussite theology at the Council of Basel.

Freedom of Preaching and Freedom of Grace

At the Council of Basel in 1433, the Hussites were given an opportunity to defend their theological views. This occurred after a tumultuous period of revolutionary clashes in Bohemia and the Hussites' successful military defense against the crusades that took place between 1420 and 1431. The Hussites defended their primary document, The Four Articles of Prague. The article on the free preaching of God's word was defended by Ulricus of Znojmo.[8] In his address to the Council, Ulricus tried to explain the concept of freedom using categories that were current at that time. He presented three different understandings of freedom that were supposed to be commonly accepted; i.e., freedom of guilt (*libertas culpae*), freedom of grace (*libertas gratiae*), and freedom of glory (*libertas gloriae*).[9]

Freedom of Guilt

The first type of freedom, freedom of guilt, is a negative freedom. In fact, it is no freedom at all, but an audacity that enables people to commit any crime.

7. Wernisch, *Husitství*, 63.
8. Bartoš, ed., *Orationes, quibus Nicolaus de Pelhřimov*, 86–113.
9. Bartoš, ed., *Orationes, quibus Nicolaus de Pelhřimov*, 100. The threefold concept of freedom that we find in patristic literature speaks of *libertas naturae*, instead of *libertas culpae* when referring to the original state of human beings before the fall. See Migne, *Patrologia Latina*, vol. 171, 356 or 791.

Ulricus argues that this is what the Apostle means when he says: "When you were slaves of sin, you were free in regard to righteousness" (Rom 6:20). Unfortunately, this is the kind of freedom that most people—and even most Christians—have. They commit injustice with pleasure and do not recognize the sinfulness of their actions. Paul's admonition, "you were called to liberty; only do not use your freedom as an opportunity for the flesh" (Gal 5:13), and these words from 1 Pet 2:16, "[live as free people, not] using your freedom as a pretext for evil," speak against this false view of freedom. It is our natural inclination to exercise this false freedom, and we do so whenever we have an opportunity, even if we act under some pretense. We may believe that we are doing the right things, or at least, things that are not contrary to our Christian commitment. However, our sinful nature inclines us to seek our own interests and to prefer our selfish aims.

This emphasis on the negative potential of our free choice and its misuse under the pretense of freedom illustrates the line of reasoning along which the Czech Reformation developed its anthropology. From its earliest stage, this included a recognition of the depth and inevitability of human sinfulness and of the need for liberation, although the scriptural basis for this recognition was found in the Gospel of John (8:31–36), rather than in the Pauline writings. Several generations later when the Czech Brethren evaluated their situation following a period of persecution in 1508, they said, in a pastoral letter, that the church itself was partly to blame for the persecution: "for we have liberated ourselves too much, have made ourselves too comfortable in the world, and have quietly fallen asleep; and some of us have gotten involved in worldly affairs."[10] In other words, whenever the circumstances offer us an opportunity, we tend to "liberate ourselves too much," to misuse our freedom, and to turn it into "freedom of guilt."

Freedom of Grace

The second type of freedom, the freedom of grace, is genuine Christian freedom. It is freedom that is brought about by the Holy Spirit and revealed by God's word. Ulricus characterized it as the "courage to do good without fear," and connected it with the biblical assurance that "where the Spirit of the Lord is, there is freedom" (2 Cor 3:17). The concept of the freedom of grace, which is understood as freedom from sin, can be traced back to the

---

10. "List Bratří Starších 1510" [A Letter of the Elders from 1510], in Říčan, *Zprávy, naučení a napomenutí Jednoty bratrské* [Instructions, Morals, and Admonitions of the Unitas Fratrum], 114.

patristic period,[11] and we can follow its development throughout the era of the Reformation.

This aspect of freedom had become central in the theology of the Czech Brethren by the beginning of the sixteenth century. When one of the Brethren, Prokop from Neuhaus, wrote a tract rejecting the use of force in matters of faith, he described Christian freedom as liberation from sin and from the power of the devil which is given to us by the grace of God.[12]

For him, the key text for understanding Christian freedom was also John 8:31–36, and in particular, its final verse: "So if the Son makes you free, you will be free indeed." Christ came to overcome the devil and his works, and to liberate people from his power. Liberation from the power of the devil occurs when people, through the grace and power of Christ's merits, overcome and abandon sin. In their natural state, human beings are not free and cannot be free. Our natural state is slavery to sin, while freedom is Christ's gift to those who follow him. The freedom of grace is "the liberation from bondage to sin and eternal damnation"[13] that is given to us by the Holy Spirit, who is the Lord of freedom.

Freedom of Glory

Finally, the third type of freedom, the freedom of glory, is understood as eternal rest in God without any pain. Hope for this kind of freedom is expressed by Paul in the epistle to the Romans, when he writes: "The creation itself will be set free from its bondage to decay and obtain the glorious liberty of the children of God" (8:21). This is the eschatological freedom that all of the faithful hope to enter.

After sketching these three types of freedom, Ulricus returns to defending freedom of preaching. He asks what concept of freedom should be applied to preaching: "In this matter, we talk of freedom . . . as a capacity

---

11. "Libertas gratiae dicitur libertas a peccato, quia per ipsam consequimur remissionem peccatorum, sum quorum jugo quasi servi tenebamur." Hildebertus Cenomanensis, Migne, *Patrologia Latina*, vol. 171, 356. Among the Greek fathers, Gregory of Nazianzus uses the expression, *eleutheria tes charitos*, in his *Epistulae*. See the work of Serhiy Hovorun.

12. Prokop from Neuhaus, *Proč lidé k víře mocí nuceni býti nemají* [Why People Should not Be Forced to Believe through Coercion] Litomyšl 1508. The writing was published by Molnár, "Neznámý spis Prokopa z Jindřichova Hradce." Quotation fol. D3.

13. This characterization is found in comments on 2 Cor 3:17 in the Bible of the Czech Reformation.

given and authorized by the Lord himself, which is received by everyone who is legitimately admitted into the office of deacon or priest."[14]

In presenting this matter to the Council, Ulricus naturally emphasized the Church's role. The task of preaching is reserved for priests. The Church's authority to scrutinize the candidates for priesthood and to decide if they are eligible for that office is not questioned. However, their freedom is "given and authorized by the Lord himself," which means they should have the freedom to proclaim the word of God without being restricted by any authority except the Scriptures.

The year before the Council, representatives of both sides met in Cheb (Eger) to prepare for the hearing and establish the rules. They agreed to the statement that the decisive yardstick should be "the law of God and the practices of Christ, the apostles, and the early church."[15] The law of God, as found in the Scriptures, was thus declared to be the supreme authority over the church and its affairs. Freedom of preaching was to be determined by the limits set by the Scriptures in every respect and those limits should not be expanded arbitrarily.

In spite of the importance of this article for the Hussites, freedom of preaching was just an auxiliary tool. It was meant to help people find and accept the true Christian freedom, the freedom of grace.

Freedom and the Law of God

For Hussite theology, the law of God was the principle that gave shape to true freedom. It was a "manifestation of God's free love, which was willing to share with human beings, and thereby, to show the way back from slavery to sin and from the destruction to which this slavery leads."[16] As Peter Lampe shows in his study, the concept of law (*nomos*)—as a necessary tool designed to protect the freedom of those who participate in the legal

---

14. Bartoš, ed., *Orationes, quibus Nicolaus de Pelhřimov*, 100. "Sed in presenti loquimur striccius de libertate . . . ut dicit facultatem ab ipso Domino concessam et approbatam, quam quis suscipere dicitur, quando ad ordinem diaconatus aut presbiteratus legitime est susceptus."

15. The document known as "iudex Egranus" or "iudex compactatus in Egra" was signed on May 18, 1432: "in causa quatuor articulorum, quam ut praefertur prosequuntur, lex divina, praxis Christi, apostolica et ecclesiae primitivae, una cum conciliis doctoribusque fundatibus se veraciter in eadem, pro veracissimo et evidenti judice in hoc Basiliensi concilio admittentur." In Palacký, ed., *Urkundliche Beiträge zur Geschichte des Hussitenkrieges II*, 282.

16. Wernisch, *Husitství*, 62.

community—goes back to classical Greek era.[17] The Hussites found a type of authority in the law of God that protected them from the claims of human (church) authorities and kept them from falling into lawlessness. In the first years after John Hus was burned at the stake, his adherents organized gatherings to listen to the preaching of the Gospel at various public places outside of the towns. In a manifesto explaining this practice, they declared that their gatherings "take place for nothing other than an opportunity to freely listen to true salvific instruction based on the law of God."[18] They also stated that they come together "to form a divine unity for the sake of the freedom of the law of God."[19]

If it is accepted and obeyed, the law of God has the power to renew society and the whole human world. The Hussites believed this, and free preaching should have helped this vision become reality. This hope, which was connected with the expectation of the Second Coming of Christ, was very vivid during the first years of the Hussite movement. However, the practice of preaching met with decided opposition on the part of the established church and the secular authorities. The "end time" was not drawing to a close, and the activities of the enemies of the reform movement were intensifying in violence and cruelty. Under these circumstances, the Hussites succumbed to the temptation to assist the law of God with human effort and to fight their opponents with force. The liberating power of the law of God was to be defended and supported by the power of arms, which should help bring the expected kingdom of freedom, justice, and peace into existence.

Like all similar attempts in history, such efforts had to fail. When the Hussite theologians, supported by the success of their arms, went to Basel to defend their theological program, the decisive military defeat of the radical wing of the movement was only a few months away. Subsequently, the conservative branch of the Hussite movement formed the Utraquist church, which futilely sought recognition from Rome for several generations. The broader, social aspect of Christian freedom was dropped, and preaching the law of God was deprived of the dangerous dimension of social critique. From around 1440 on, the preaching of the Utraquist Church demonstrated a strong emphasis on morals, while fully respecting and supporting existing social structures.

For subsequent generations of Utraquists, Christian freedom mainly became a spiritual freedom. It was interpreted as freedom from sin, which had some consequences for just personal behavior within the social

17. See the work of Lampe in chap. 6 above.
18. Molnár, *Husitské manifesty*, 61.
19. Molnár, *Husitské manifesty*, 63.

structure. However, the Utraquists had no intention of challenging that structure. Once again, the law of the rulers became more authoritative than the law of God.

Yet, simultaneously in the middle of the fifteenth century, the radical claim of the law of God, which had been revealed by Christ, characterized the thought of Petr Chelčický whose views profoundly influenced the theology of the Czech Brethren.[20] He insisted on the radical Hussite belief that the word of God (as revealed in the law of Christ) has the power, not only to renew human lives, but—when people submit to Christ's demands—to even rectify the whole society: "If the whole world would believe the law of God and surrender to it, everyone could be one in Christ, . . . and such a thing could make one multitude, one heart, and one soul of a thousand worlds."[21] The power of the law of God (or law of Christ—for Chelčický, both expressions are interchangeable) is indisputable. Obedience to that law brings a true freedom, which is completely different than the freedom of the world. However, even if this is possible for human beings, most people do not choose to be obedient to the law of God. That is why a so-called Christian society inevitably manifests a number of signs, which show that it is governed by the Evil One. True Christians, who want to live in the freedom of the law of Christ, can do so only in strict separation from the sinful world. The Christian church cannot be anything other than a minority, seeking the "freedom of grace" in the life of a community that is detached from worldly things.

Significantly, the attempt that the first generation of the Czech Brethren made to implement this vision, was carried out under the designation "better righteousness," rather than "freedom." What the Czech Brethren sought was individual perfection instead of the freedom of grace, and what they learned within one generation was that in many respects, even a small, exclusive community separated from society was unable to achieve a perfect life through obedience to the law of Christ.[22]

Hope for a new form of societal life, liberated from the consequences of sin and consequently, characterized by true freedom, was the driving force behind the radical parts of the Czech Reformation. However, it failed, both when attempted on a large scale—to transform the whole society with

---

20. Chelčický was a yeoman from southern Bohemia who was in close contact with radical Hussite theologians, but who disagreed with them profoundly regarding the use of violence. He wrote a piercing critique of the social structure of medieval society and the church. See Wagner, *Petr Chelčický*.

21. Chelčický, *Síť víry*, fol. 29a.

22. For a discussion of this matter, see Peschke, *Kirche und Welt in der Theologie der Böhmischen Brüder*.

the use of force (the Hussites)—and on a small scale—to create a perfect community of believers detached from the evil world (the Brethren). In both cases, the human capacity for freedom, i.e., the capacity to free ourselves from sin, was assessed too optimistically.

Nevertheless, in their own way, both of these failures have contributed to the recognition that Christian freedom is a matter of faith, which cannot be ordered or demanded; rather, it is a free gift of God's grace. This realization led to the awareness that another aspect of freedom needs to be acknowledged and protected by society, i.e., freedom of conscience.

Freedom of Conscience

"I recognize no authority on earth that could judge my conscience."[23] These words are ascribed to the Czech king, George of Poděbrady during a dispute with a papal legate in 1462. The legate accused the king of having broken his coronation oath. The king denied this charge, and declared that where the coronation oath was concerned, his conscience was clear. He responded to the legate's next argument—that he had no right to interpret the oath according to his own understanding—with the words quoted above.

It was not only in the king's eyes that the authority of conscience was highly valued. A few years later, some Czech Brethren, who were among his subjects, wrote a letter to the Utraquist archbishop, Jan Rokycana, in which they explained that they would flee from the bailiffs of the same King George when they came to recruit soldiers "so that we will not be forced to do or say something that is against our conscience and hence, against God."[24]

In both cases, conscience is presented as a capacity that no human authority can judge. It tells us what views and values we should hold and compels us to maintain this orientation even if it brings disadvantage or danger. Conscience obliges us to hold onto what we believe to be true and seems to be free from any external influences. And even more than that, it is directly connected to God's law. The worldview of the fifteenth century was based on the idea that there is a universal order in God's creation in which the law of the Creator has unquestioned authority. In this framework, the claim that something might be "against conscience and hence, against God" is fully understandable.

---

23. Palacký, *Dějiny národu českého* V, 171. See also Trojan, *Idea lidských práv v české duchovní tradici*, 147ff.

24. "Čtvrtý list Rokycanovi" (1468) [The Fourth Letter to Rokycana], *Acta unitatis fratrum* I, 17b.

On the other hand, because in medieval thought, human conscience was understood to be a capacity subject to the universal authority of God's law, freedom of conscience could not involve a purely subjective attitude. Human conscience was considered to be free only within the limits of the law of God. No freedom to transgress these limits was conceivable, or, to use Ulricus'classification, only "freedom of guilt," i.e., the slavery of sin, was possible beyond these limits. The prevailing medieval view of conscience held that a believing Christian conscience should direct persons to Christian freedom, i.e., to the freedom of grace. However, experience showed that the natural state of the human mind and conscience was chiefly inclined toward "freedom of guilt." This necessarily created a tension. Could a person take responsibility for his/her state of conscience? Is it possible to require conformity between faith and conscience? When there was one Christian Church that included the whole society, these questions were answered positively, but they became more and more difficult to resolve with the growing complexity of competing influences.

Two different types of Christianity not only developed in the Czech kingdom; they continued to exist side by side for half a century after the Hussite wars. However critical the Catholics and Utraquist were of each other, they had to accept co-existence with one another because there was no reasonable hope that either of the sides could defeat and eliminate the other in the foreseeable future. It was under these conditions that a concession to "freedom of conscience" was made at the general diet in Kutná Hora (Kuttenberg) in 1485.

After a complicated discussion and under strong pressure from the king who wanted to have peace in the Czech lands, the two sides reached a compromise resolution "that everyone should preach the Word of God without vituperation and seek salvation according to their own belief and practice." The first article of the Hussite theological program, freedom of preaching, was thus affirmed. This declaration was followed by another resolution concerning the Eucharist: "Each of us will retain our own faith and be permitted to receive the Eucharist according to our belief and conscience . . ." What was even more important was the inclusion of all people in the agreement regardless of their social status. Both sides promised "to leave the subjects who live in our towns and villages in peace concerning their faith, and neither we nor our priests will use any force against them. Let all people seek salvation according to their belief . . ."[25]

This can justifiably be viewed as an act that recognizes freedom of conscience. When people were granted the freedom to choose their own

25. Palacký, ed., *Archiv český čili staré písemné památky české i moravské*, Díl IV, 512–16.

religion as early as 1485, it was a unique occurrence in the Christian world, which surely surpassed the much later principle of *cuius regio, eius religio*.

No matter how positive this may seem, we should note that the freedom which was granted was far from being universal. It was given only to people who had a sufficient power-base. Toleration was declared between Catholics (who had strong international support) and Utraquists (who constituted the overwhelming majority of Christians in the Czech lands.) The principle that enjoined people "to not persecute others because of their faith and to live peacefully together" did not apply to anyone else. Other Christians living in the Czech lands, such as the Waldensians and the Czech Brethren, were persecuted with equal fervor by both sides. In his History, when Palacký speaks of the "glorious freedom of conscience that was established in the land,"[26] we should take his words for what they are, i.e., a romantic view of history. To a certain extent, the decreed toleration was a strategic measure produced by an effect to establish and maintain a balance of power, rather than by an appreciation for the dignity of human conscience.

No matter what reasons lay behind of the "religious peace of Kuttenberg," the fact that two different strains of the Christian Church existed side by side in the Czech lands for several generations gradually led more and more people to realize that the Christian faith can be brought to life in different ways—and can take different forms—without ceasing to be Christian. The discovery that there can be different ways of believing must have led to an additional conclusion; namely, that there may also be different ways of shaping the believing conscience. These circumstances contributed to an increased "respect for conscience, governed by the law of God."[27]

As a small, persecuted minority, the Unity of Brethren quite understandably advocated toleration and freedom of belief from the very beginning of its existence.[28] The Brethren repeatedly reflected on the use of power and violence in matters of faith and emphatically rejected such practices. Almost half a century before the famous treatise by Sebastian Castellio,[29] who was a member of the Unity of Brethren, Bachelor Prokop from Neuhaus published a treatise titled "Why people should not be pressured into faith by coercion."[30]

26. Palacký, *Dějiny národu českého* V, 667.

27. Říčan, *Zprávy, naučení a napomenutí Jednoty bratrské*, 84.

28. The beginnings of the Unity are traditionally traced back to 1457. See Müller, *Geschichte der Böhmischen Brüder*.

29. Castellio, *De haereticis an sint persequendi*.

30. Prokop z Jindřichova Hradce (from Neuhaus). *Proč lidé k víře mocí nuceni býti nemají* 1508. See n12 above. The following citations include the pages of the original in parentheses.

Prokop pits the example of Christ and the apostles—and especially Jesus' statement: "If any man would come after me" (Luke 9:23)—against the traditional argument for coercion, which included an unfortunate interpretation of the words, "compel people to come in" (Luke 14:23). According to Prokop, the statement, "if any man would," means that Christ gives everyone the freedom to choose. Freedom of choice is based on the fact that faith is understood to be a gracious gift from God: "For they generally have living faith, love, and true hope in God's salvific gifts . . . , which are granted freely by God's grace. Therefore, if God does not bestow such faith, who can do that?" (D4a)

The idea that human conscience must be respected in matters of faith is a natural consequence of this view. Prokop's emphasis on conscience is very strong. We even find a statement that places conscience above the "objective" correctness of a belief:

> A weak person can be driven by fear to confess something different than what he believes and to say he believes what his heart is against. But even if he is forced to accept something that is right, he sins if he acts against his conscience. "For whatever does not proceed from faith is sin" (Rom 14:23), and God will not accept it. (G1a)

In other words, if a person acts against his/her inner convictions, his/her act is worthless even if it is right. Deciding and acting in faith requires the free consent of one's conscience; otherwise, it cannot be called acting in faith. Our conscience must voluntarily recognize and accept what is true. This observation, which is relatively psychological, is supported by a theological argument:

> By itself, worldly power is unable to help anyone to salvation. Only the power, wisdom, and goodness of God the Father, the Son, and the Holy Spirit; only the power of faith in the inner man; only the power of the holy Gospel in the witness of faith; only the power of good works to fulfill the new covenant; only the power of staying with in it to the end can help people reach salvation. And this spiritual power never takes away one's freedom of will or the voluntary nature of reason . . . (G2b)[31]

---

31. When we compare this view with the writings of the European Reformers we find that to a large extent, these two traditions are congruent. Luther maintains (at least after the diet of Worms) that worldly power is not permitted to intervene in human conscience. Outward obedience may be obtained by force, but inner consent cannot be coerced, and even if conscience can be manipulated, it is unwise to act against it. McKim, ed., *The Cambridge Companion to Martin Luther*, 266.

Calvin's position is similar. See Wendel, *Calvin*, 177. When freed by God's word, our

God's gracious way of treating human beings not only does not need, it will not tolerate, any use of pressure or violence. It is freely offered, and must be freely accepted. God's power is spiritual power, which works through persuasion, rather than coercion. Here, Christian freedom is described as an inner freedom, as the state of the inner person. This often is the perspective of persecuted minorities. The weakness of this view is that it takes no note of the social dimension and of the responsibility that is associated with Christian freedom. It took another generation and contact with the European Reformation for this feature of the radical Hussite legacy to be redeveloped.

Freedom of Religion

During the sixteenth century, the Czech Brethren developed their teachings in dialogue with the European Reformation. They received a lot of theological inspiration and changed their views on a number of topics. However, their insistence on the need for religious toleration remained unchanged, and gained an even broader social horizon. In 1575, they were able to work with the Utraquists to prepare the Czech Confession (Confessio Bohemica). That statement was intended to represent all of the Protestants in the Czech lands. In 1604, almost a hundred years after Prokop, the Brethren published another treatise in which the concept of religious toleration occupies an important place.[32] This writing represents an elaborate "defense of freedom of conscience against religious persecution."[33] Its author argues in favor of religious toleration, using examples from Poland, Switzerland, and even Turkey:

> Where there is no oppression and persecution of some people by others, even if they are of different religions, all things happen in peace. In Constantinople, there are three religious groups and three peoples, Turks, Jews, and Christians, who are very different from each other when it comes to religion. Yet, they live in peace and concord, and no one interferes with another person's religion or defames the other. In Poland, everyone is Christian, but they are also different from each other. That is, there are people who follow the Pope; the new Arians and Trinitarians; and those who claim that they belong to the reformed

conscience accepts the will of God with the consent of its innermost convictions.

32. The treatise, titled *Poznamenání, jakým původem mandatové královšti . . . na Bratří . . . vycházeji*, [An Observation as to the Origin of the Royal Mandates against the Brethren . . .], was published by Slizilński, *Rękopisy Braci Czeskich*, 203–85.

33. Bartoš, "Budovcova obrana Jednoty bratrské a svobody svědom. z r. 1604," 91.

religion and are called Lutherans, Calvinists, and Brethren by their adversaries. All of these people get along well with each other; no one oppresses or disturbs another's conscience. The Swiss have great concord because Catholics and Protestants live in peace and are forbidden to oppress each other because of religion under the pain of death.[34]

The last example reveals more about the wisdom of Switzerland's rulers than about the willingness of Christians to live peacefully with each other. However, the other two examples are important for understanding the concept of religious freedom that the Brethren held. They extend toleration to non-orthodox groups (i.e., the Anti-Trinitarians) and to non-Christians. Theologically, this seems to be a consequence of viewing faith as a free gift of God's grace that cannot be ordered, mediated, or imposed by any human effort. If God is the only authority who can give faith, we humans can only witness, pray, and hopefully, provide an example of a life lived in faith. We must remain tolerant of other faiths and religions.

Needless to say, such a view was far from being popular, and even in the Unity of Brethren,, not everyone shared this view. For example, one of the Brethren's outstanding noblemen, Václav Budovec, who was the spokesman for the Unity on many occasions during the years leading up to the Thirty Years War, held that there must be severe punishment for heretics.[35] Being a nobleman, he undoubtedly saw the political aspect of the problem—religion still was an important—and frequently was the decisive—binding agent in society. Extending toleration to those who disturbed the unity of religion might bring political problems. This was even more the case in the early seventeenth century when Protestantism became a political force in Europe, and tried to draw a clear line between Protestant orthodoxy and various types of heretical movements.

Budovec's perspective agreed with what we find elsewhere starting from the time of Augustine's struggle against the Manicheans and spanning the entire medieval period. God's truth was believed to have been revealed in such a way that anyone who did not recognize it was to blame for not trying hard enough. Faith was more a matter of rational recognition and persuasion than of personal trust and faithfulness to God. However, Budovec's writing from 1604 reveals a different perspective from which the nature of

---

34. Slizilński, *Rękopisy Braci Czeskich*, 242.

35. Budovec (who was executed in 1621 for being one of the leaders of the uprising against the king) wrote about "deserved punishment" (by means of fire and sword) for Anti-Trinitarians. See Rejchrtov, *Václav Budovec z Budova*, 169–70.

faith may be understood. Its passage on freedom of faith is worth quoting because of its theological sagacity:

> Because no one can judge human conscience but God alone; and St. Augustine said that no one should be forced to believe because God wants to have free, voluntary, and willing hearts; ... and Christians are called free because their work and acts do not stem from an enforced law, but from the free inspiration of God's Spirit—who is the source of our faith, who teaches us to believe, and who enflames our hearts with love.
>
> Therefore, people, who intervene in the conscience of others, who judge them and try to perturb them, and who force them to accept a certain belief, oppose the will and power of God. They try to do what is not within their power, and they oppress others because of their own presuppositions. Yet, even according to a popular saying, our thought is free of all taxes and fees.[36]

This citation very clearly states that Christian freedom is a responsibility before God that is voluntarily and willingly chosen and is inspired by the Holy Spirit. It is a state of mind—a state of conscience—that cannot be initiated by any human tradition, law, or authority, nor even by our own efforts. It is purely a gift of God that is to be joyfully accepted (and developed through a personal relationship with its Giver). Thus, no one can be blamed for not having it. This interpretation even opens up the possibility of acknowledging the freedom to not believe. Human thought is fundamentally free before any human authority. God is the only authority who can hold us responsible for what we think and believe. Therefore, we must grant other people the freedom to believe or to not believe, and leave judgment to God.

In the midst of a general increase in confessionalism and intolerance as the political situation in Europe ripened for violent conflict, the anomaly of religious toleration in the Czech kingdom became a law for a short time (by order of the Imperial Charter of 1609), only to come to naught a few years later (1620) in the tumult of the Thirty Years War. The Pope, who was horrified to hear that some daring people had tried to introduce "the ill-fated freedom of conscience" in the kingdom, could be at peace again.[37]

---

36. Slizilński, *Rękopisy Braci Czeskich*, 232.

37. Hrejsa, *Česká konfesse, její vznik, podstata a dějiny*, 427–28. The relevant words in the pope's letter to Emperor Rudolf II (which was written in July 1605) are: "nuper cum ingenti animi nostri dolore intelleximus eo nonnullorum audaciam, vel ut verius dicamus, impietatem pervenisse, ut non erubuerint piam mentem Maiestatis Tuae tentare, si quo pacto, auctoritate et permissu Tuo, detestabilem (quam ipsi vocant) conscientiae libertatem in regnis Tuis inducere possint..." Quoted in Hrejsa, 427 n8.

The Frailty of Freedom

In the sixteenth century, the Czech kingdom was generally regarded as a place of unusual religious freedom. We have mentioned some of the influences that contributed to the fact that religious toleration found a place—at least among a notable segment of Czech Christianity.

This development began with the revolutionary impetus of the Hussites, who believed that the "captivity" of the medieval church (which was viewed as captivity to the snares of the Antichrist) could be broken by the free preaching of God's Word. They anticipated the transformation of the whole church and society through the power of the Word. Christian freedom was considered to be attainable by the entire society. It was thought that God's law would bring about a new justice, which would include both the personal (moral) and social aspects of life. An attempt at communal ownership, which was undertaken in Tábor around 1420 by a radical branch of the Hussite movement may be seen as evidence that the social aspect of Christian freedom was also viewed in a radical way.

However, this project of renewal through God's Word met with decided opposition from those who held power and from the established church. Thus, the Hussite movement turned to violent means and to methods of coercion which ended with fratricidal conflict within a single generation. Radical liberation of the whole society through one universal pattern, even if that was based on the law of God, proved to be an illusion. The "freedom to sin," which should have been overcome, manifested itself by dividing the movement into different interest groups, to such an extent that the original hope was abandoned and preferential advantages were sought.

The first generation of the Brethren was aware of the failure of the movement and was convinced that the Hussites' critical mistake was accepting the ways of this world. Thus, they took a different course. Abhorred by the disastrous consequences of violent revolution and military conflicts, their concept of freedom focused on a community of believers that would be detached from the "evil world." Their vision of freedom was to be implemented by a small community of believers that would live strictly according to the "law of Christ," rejecting responsibility for the broader society and focusing on moral perfection with little interest in the surrounding world.

Within a single generation, the Brethren came to the realization that this course resulted in legalism and the danger of self-righteousness, rather than bringing real freedom to their communities. Eventually, they discovered that "freedom of grace" is a gift from God, not the result of moral effort. The consequence of this recognition was accepting life in society as a place of Christian witness. In addition, the ideas of toleration, freedom of conscience, and freedom of belief and religion were emphasized. A gift can be gratefully accepted, but it cannot be required.

Nevertheless, it is likely that the Czech Brethren's plea for tolerance across the borders of confessions and other religions was greatly influenced by the fact that they themselves were a minority that was constantly persecuted. When they were in a position to have a choice, they had difficulties remaining tolerant. In the second half of the sixteenth century, we find some Brethren priests serving as parish pastors at various estates in Poland who considered asking the authorities to ban the "religion of the Antichrist" (Catholicism). This request was rejected by the Elders of the Unity with the admonition that faith is a gift of God which must not be controlled by force.[38] However, the suspicion that the level of tolerance tends to decrease with increasing social power remains plausible.

The Brethren welcomed reformation teachings and their emphasis on freedom, but they retained a strong church discipline. They saw a morally upright life as being a necessary sign of the "freedom of grace." Even if Christian freedom is a gift of God's free grace, it involves an obligation: it must be implemented in our lives. The tension between the concept of Christian freedom as a free gift and the task that it poses for believers can be found in the Brethren's teachings from the beginning of the Reformation until the Thirty Years War. This tension is especially apparent in the work of the Brethren's last bishop, John Amos Comenius.

Comenius was deeply convinced that all people should be free in what they believe and that no one has the right to rule over another person's conscience. Concerning freedom of conscience, Comenius—more than anyone else—stressed that this was connected with an awareness of God's grace. We are free only when we learn to know the gracious and loving God. An inattentive, uneducated, and godless conscience cannot be free; thus, no one should be left in a state of ignorance. For Comenius, this was a challenge for education. Like most of the Christian humanists of his age, he believed that our human world could be perfected to a substantial degree if we manage to improve our humanity. He, like many others, was persuaded that such a project is feasible, and should be even easy. All we need to do is "remove any obstacles that stand in the way of [our] natural tendency."[39]

As people created in God's image, we human beings are naturally directed to higher things, Comenius says; all we need is wise leadership. If we succeed in opening the way to true knowledge for all people, if we can teach them how to use their abilities, senses, and reason in accordance with

---

38. Halama, *Sociální učení Českých bratří 1464–1618*, 113.
39. Comenius, *Comenius's Pampaedia*, 2.22.

the natural harmony of creation, a new age will begin on earth: "See that all men read God's books and understand them and put them into practice, and they will all be wise, everyone according to the measure of the gift of Christ."[40] The belief that everything that we have is a gift of God was central for Comenius. However, at the same time, he believed that we all have the capacities required to learn how to use God's gifts properly, and to thereby attain the freedom intended for God's children. His faith in education as a tool for liberating humankind was extraordinary.

On the one hand, this pedagogical optimism can be justifiably seen as having roots in renaissance humanism, which revived the classical tradition and its optimistic view of human potential.[41] Yet, on the other hand, we should take into consideration the fact that Comenius was educated at Calvinist universities where he learned to see history "as the arena of God's action in wisdom and providential love."[42] No matter how these influences may have been combined, they enabled Comenius to preserve and broaden the Brethren's understanding of Christian freedom—as a deep personal relationship with the loving God who sets human beings free from all other authorities but at the same time, as the freedom to rely on God's promises and to seek the transformation of the whole society. Comenius agrees that true freedom is a gift of God; yet, it is also something we can learn to recognize. Comenius believes that we have been given all of the necessary tools and gifts through which true freedom may be attained. Thus, since it is God's purpose that we learn to know the truth and achieve freedom, he will assist us so that one day, we will succeed.

Each of the concepts of freedom that we find in the Czech Reformation is fragile or even deficient. The social and political freedom under the authority of God's law which should have given rise to universal justice ended up in a political revolt and fratricidal violence. The attempt to find true freedom through separation from the world and by engaging in a moral struggle to overcome sinfulness by fulfilling the law of Christ led to disappointment and conflict in the community of believers.

Even the third way—which consisted of an attempt to find a socially relevant freedom by combining personal freedom of belief with social toleration for "otherness"—is not without problems. The possibility of toleration—of respecting the freedom to believe differently from the majority or even to not believe—grows out of a humble recognition that we cannot

40. Comenius, *Comenius's Pampaedia*, 2.27. Here, Comenius is reflecting on Eph 4:7.

41. Regarding this feature of Comenius' thought, see Lampe.

42. For more on this matter, see the work of Dirkie Smit. The reference to "historical pedagogy" is especially pertinent (Stevenson).

define the moral and legal status of Christian freedom. Christian freedom is something we can only accept, and the only way we can promote this freedom is to not deny it to anyone. However, this is a position that is usually defended by minorities. The majority, even a Christian majority, which bears responsibility for shaping the life of society, always tends to set narrower limits for freedom and toleration.

That was the case with the Utraquists who constituted the official church in Bohemia. Having been part of the establishment, they felt responsible for the social and political situation in the Czech lands. Striving for as much religious unity as possible within the region was an understandable consequence of this situation. Church and society were still firmly intertwined, and any diversification of religion was politically dangerous. Having reached a certain balance of power with the Catholics, the Utraquists were interested in keeping this balance and had no understanding for any experiments that might broaden the scope of toleration. In fact, that could endanger the existing state of "religious peace." This view was supported theologically by the widespread medieval belief that the truth of Christianity was obvious enough to be accepted by every reasonable person. Thus, some degree of coercion was justifiable.

The perspective represented by the Brethren, who understood the Christian faith to be a free gift that no one can attain by virtue of human capabilities, led to a broader view of freedom of conscience and religious toleration. Their experience of marginalization and persecution helped the Brethren realize that unity of faith could not be enforced without freedom of conscience and faith being suppressed.

Theologically, the Brethren understood Christian freedom in a way that was in line with the mainstream European Reformation. However, with regard to its social consequences, they followed the course of the radical reform movements, insisting that broad religious toleration and high social sensitivity were legitimate Christian values. In spite of the fact that their community was destroyed during the tumult of the Thirty Years War, they were among the movements that helped pave way for the modern rights of freedom of conscience and freedom of religion.

Bibliography

Bartoš, F. M. "Budovcova obrana Jednoty bratrské a svobody svědom. z r. 1604" [The Defense of the Unity of Brethren and Freedom of Conscience from 1604, by Budovec]. *Theologia Evangelica* 4 (1951) 88–101.

———, ed. *Orationes, quibus Nicolaus de Pelhřimov, taboritarum episcopus, et Ulricus de Znojmo, orphanorum sacerdos, articulos de peccatis publicis puniendis et libertate verbi dei in concilio basiliensi anno 1433 ineunte defenderunt.* Tábor, 1935.

Castellio, S. *De haereticis an sint persequendi.* Basel, 1554.

Chelčický, Petr. *Sít' víry* [Net of Faith]. Edited by E. Melantrich Smetánka. Prague, 1929.

Comenius. *Comenius's Pampaedia or Universal Education.* Translated by A. M. O. Dobbie. London: Buckland, 1986.

Čtyři vyznání [The Four Confessions]. Prague, 1951.

Gonnet, Jean, and Amedeo Molnár. *Les Vaudois au moyen âge.* Torino: Claudiana 1974.

Halama, Jindřich. *Sociální učení Českých bratří 1464–1618.* Brno: Centrum pro studium demokracie a kultury, 2003.

Hrejsa, Ferdinand. *Česká konfesse, její vznik, podstata a dějiny* [Czech Confession, Its Origin, Substance, and History]. Prague, 1912.

McKim, Donald K., ed. *The Cambridge Companion to Martin Luther.* Cambridge Companions to Religion. Cambridge University Press 2003.

Morée, Peter C. A. "Preaching in Fourteenth-Century Bohemia." 1999.

Molnár, Amedeo. *Husitské manifesty.* Prague: Odeon, 1980.

———. "Neznámý spis Prokopa z Jindřichova Hradce." [An Unknown Writing by Prokop from Neuhaus]. *Husitský tábor* 6–7 (1983–1984) 423–48.

———. *Die Waldenser: Geschichte und europäisches Ausmass. Einer Ketzerbewegung.* Göttingen: Vandenhoeck & Ruprecht, 1973.

Müller, Joseph Th. *Geschichte der Böhmischen Brüder.* 3 vols. Herrnhut: Winter, 1922–1931.

Opočienský, M., ed. *The Message for the Last Days: Three Essays from the Year 1367. Milič of Kroměříž.* [Militius de Chremsir]. Studies from the WARC 39. Geneva: WCC, 1998.

Palacký, František, ed. *Archiv český čili staré písemné památky české i moravské.* Díl IV. Praha, 1846.

———. *Dějiny národu českého V.*

———, ed. *Urkundliche Beiträge zur Geschichte des Hussitenkrieges II.* Prague: Tempsky, 1873.

Peschke, Erhard. *Kirche und Welt in der Theologie der Böhmischen Brüder.* Berlin: Evangelische Verlaganstalt, 1981.

Rejchrtov, N. *Václav Budovec z Budova.* Prague: Melantrich, 1984.

Říčan, R. *Zprávy, naučení a napomenutí Jednoty bratrské* [Instructions, Morals, and Admonitions of the Unitas Fratrum]. Unpublished manuscript. Praha, 1957.

Slizilński, Jerzy. *Rękopisy Braci Czeskich.* Warsaw: Zakład Narodowy im Ossolińskich, 1958.

Trojan, J. S. *Idea lidských práv v české duchovní tradici* [The Idea of Human Rights in the Czech Spiritual Tradition]. Prague, 2002.

Wagner, Murray L. *Petr Chelčický: A Radical Separatist in Hussite Bohemia.* Scottdale, PA: Herald, 1983.

Wendel, François. *Calvin: Origins and Development of His Religious Thought.* 1963. Reprint, Durham, NC: Labyrinth, 1987.

———. *Calvin: Ursprung und Entwicklung seiner Theologie.* Translated by Walter Kickel. Vivimus ex uno. Neukirchen: Neukirchener, 1968.

Wernisch, M. *Husitství: Raně reformační příběh* [The Hussites: An Early Reformation Story]. Brno, 2003.

Part 5

The Dialectics of Freedom and Modernity

Introduction

MICHAEL WELKER

The last part of the book starts with perspectives on the topic of freedom by Asian scholars, respectively scholars with Asian roots, engaging Western classics in the contexts of economic and ecological brutalism and the (post) colonial climate. Carver Yu ("Freedom and Commitment: Christian Tradition and Liberal Humanism") engages what he takes as "the two most powerful essays in shaping the idea of freedom in our contemporary culture," namely Isaiah Berlin's Oxford inaugural address "Two Concepts of Liberty" and John Rawls' "A Theory of Justice."

He first investigates Berlin's option for "negative freedom" and his rejection of any notion of freedom as "freedom for." He sees the rejection of any idea of the common good as a result of bitter experiences of totalitarian regimes. But he questions whether a vision of negative freedom alone can be practically implemented without the support of moral commitments, particularly in the context of contemporary economic and ecological threats.

Rawls' vision of a society upholding "justice as fairness" and the attempt to direct moral and legal orientation toward "the greatest benefits of the least advantaged" offers in his view a more convincing approach toward individual and communal freedom. But one should acknowledge that it is loaded by a latent ethos of empathy, mercy and love. In Rawls' anthropological and epistemological presuppositions, he sees himself abstracting human existence from the natural and biological needs of self-sustenance and from the "life-supporting system that nurtures . . . (and educates concrete individuals) into a full human person."

He argues that a Christian ethos of good neighborhood in covenantal partnership, ultimately conditioned by love, can confront the challenges of natural limitations and the sinful distortions in social and economic life that generate pretenses of human freedom. He argues for an appreciation of the divine and human freedom in the form of free self-limitation in favor of others.

The cosmopolitan and postcolonial visions of Gayatri Chakravorty Spivak and Pheng Cheah are reconstructed and presented in Susan Abraham's contribution ("Freedom in Postcolonial Perspective"). Arguing for the need to relate freedom to liberation and questioning the "assumption that there is already a positive reality called 'postcolonial freedom,'" she presents two critical readings of the modern classic ethics of Kant. Spivak ("A Critique of Postcolonial Reason") shows how much most national liberation movements and their results ("citizenship, sovereignty and nationhood") are grounded in the eighteenth-century European Enlightenment. She uncovers Kant's ethnocentric and classist (against the "raw man"), patriarchal, and even racist assumptions. Like already Hegel, she sees that in Kant freedom sadly becomes a mere desire.

Cheah (*Spectral Nationality: Passages of Freedom from Kant to Postcolonial Literatures of Liberation*) explores the framework of "European arguments for organismic vitalism" as a basis for Kant's ideal of a cosmopolitan federation. He identifies "three matrices of freedom in Kant—the transcendental idea of freedom, the concept of culture and the idea of organism." How fruitful or how dangerous is the organismic metaphor, particularly in connection with the nationalist spirit? Cheah shows that Kant does not develop a consistent attitude toward organic life. His own thought and all forms of political organicism suffer from "irreducible hetoronomy." They threaten to turn well-meant projects of instantiated freedom into ambivalent and even dangerous specters.

Susan Abraham offers a subtle reconstruction that differentiates respect for Kant's genius and the philosophical merits of his transcendental framework and the shortcomings in his practical and political visions and even ideological blockages. She argues that a consistent resistance against old and new forms of colonial violence and constructive work for participatory and representative democracies must be directed concretely. The poor women of the South should not be "subsumed into a general category of freedom." And the critique of ideological and colonial nationalism should not lead to a dismissal of "the living nation people" and territorialized approaches to liberation. "Freedom is not an escape from one's historical and cultural conditions." And these include not only political but also the religious and theological narratives of freedom and practices of liberation.

The last two contributions to the book—by an American Roman Catholic and a German Protestant theologian—turn to such narratives and reflect their orienting potentials. Francis Schüssler Fiorenza ("Freedom and Human Rights: The Cosmopolitan Context of the Justification of Human

Rights in Roman Catholicism") investigates the affirmation of human rights in Roman Catholic teaching (papal teaching and Vatican II) after World War II. He illuminates as a background of the new view "an emerging cosmopolitan understanding of human rights" and the growing respect for their "social dimensions." Already in his 1942 Christmas message, Pope Pius XII connects the affirmation of human rights and his critique of totalitarian societies. He not only affirms respect for human dignity-connected fundamental personal rights, but also the rehabilitation of the juridical order. This leads in the following papal messages and statements to a growing explicit respect for international organizations that care for the juridical and political ordering of the global community. Schüssler Fiorenza shows how also the following popes and the Vatican Council respect the United Nations and the declarations for human dignity, freedom and peace.

A growing concern becomes the increasing disparity between the rich and the poor nations of the world and the call for economic justice and ethics of solidarity. This concern has parallels in the evolution of the declarations and documents of the United Nations, which developed lists of social rights and later environmental rights. At the same time, the long shadow of the atrocities of the Third Reich and other totalitarian regimes remained present and conditioned precautions against political appeals to emergency, exception and pre-emption.

Schüssler Fiorenza reconstructs the complex global history of the second half of the twentieth century and the shifting political and ideological moods. He argues that the voices and documents of the Catholic teaching, particularly on the disparity between the rich and the poor nations, became a very strong moral and political factor in the international discourse on justice and freedom. Cosmopolitan multicentric perspectives and a thorough balance between the appeal to efficient leadership on the one hand and the warning against dangers of emergency legislation on the other have been developed. Definite needs for further development in Roman Catholic teaching on human dignity and freedom are finally diagnosed at the frontiers of equality of gender within the church and the legitimacy of a plurality of religious viewpoints in contemporary societies.

The contribution by Michael Welker ("Divine Spirit and Human Freedom") enters the contemporary academic and media discourse on concepts of freedom in Euro-American environments. It encourages facing the future discourse on the most important difference between dominant notions of the spirit—both human and divine—in the occidental philosophical and metaphysical traditions and the common sense shaped by them, and in biblical traditions, which offer a much more nuanced and multidimensional view. In both anthropology and theology an organismic pluralism should be discovered and treasured, which could provide great potential for promoting liberation and freedom.

The challenging figure of the "pouring out of the Spirit" offers a direct critique of thinking in binary or only triadic "relational constellations." In an explicitly subversive mode, it focuses in biblical Spirit-Classics on constellations in which male and female, old and young, even male and female slaves become ennobled and empowered—and this in definitely patriarchal, gerontocratic, and slaveholder societies. Tribalistic and ethnocentric perspectives become relativized and critiqued by the pouring of the Spirit of God upon human beings from different nations, cultures, histories, and languages. This doesn't lead to the promotion of spiritual fantasies, but to the discovery of different capacities and gifts, different deficiencies and needs, and the constitution of an organismic pluralism on all levels of individual, communal, and social life.

Complex anthropologies, complex forms of social and societal order, and a strong appreciation of pluralistic forms of organization in social and political, in religious and cultural, in academic and civil societal environments can be discovered, envisioned, organized, and institutionalized in the light of the spirit of freedom. In Spirit-Christologically oriented contexts, the differentiated dynamics of a strong culture of mutual diaconal support and help, the differentiated dynamics of prophetic engagement in moral and political critique, based on the working of truth- and justice-seeking communities, and the differentiated dynamics of appreciating venerable liturgical practices and deep spiritual forms of communication can generate an ethos and many practices of freedom in local associations, in civil societal contexts, but also in broad international and ecumenical cooperation and orientation.

18

Freedom and Commitment
Christian Tradition and Liberal Humanism

Carver T. Yu

For both the Christian and liberal humanist traditions, freedom is the core of our being human. However it is the concept of freedom that divides the two in the most fundamental way, revealing also a radical difference in the understanding of authentic humanity. The liberal humanist concept of freedom poses a forceful challenge to the Christian understanding of life as it should be. In terms of who is defining the core value of our culture, the Christian tradition seems to be fighting a losing battle. Christian theologians have no choice but to confront the fundamental anthropological assumptions of liberal humanists. Since Isaiah Berlin's "Two Concepts of Liberty" and John Rawls' *A Theory of Justice* are the two most powerful essays in shaping the idea of freedom in our contemporary culture, we therefore take them as our interlocutors representing the liberal humanist tradition.

Negative Freedom and Its Predicaments

In his essay "Two Concepts of Liberty," Berlin investigates two fundamental notions of freedom—the notion of negative freedom and the notion of positive freedom.[1] Negative freedom can be defined in the simplest way

---
1. Berlin, "Two Concepts of Liberty," 118–72.

as freedom from constraints or interference imposed on an individual, whether by society or private persons. Positive freedom is "freedom for" the realization of the good, be it the entelechy intrinsic to one's being human, or values fundamental for the well-being of communal life. Berlin rejects the notion of freedom as "freedom for," be it freedom for realization of the autonomous self guided solely by rational self-direction, or a rational society guided by rational laws instituted for justice and equality, or freedom for authentic identity through communion or participation. Any counsel of perfection or ideal anthropological vision has to be shunned, for they would turn out to be despotic. Even Kant's "severe individualism," which defines "freedom as self-mastery" under the guiding light of reason, can be turned into something close to a pure totalitarian doctrine by disciples like Fichte in the name of "Objective Reason."[2] Berlin points to the belief of a unified theory of what life should be as the greatest menace to humanity. As he puts it, "One belief, more than any other, is responsible for the slaughter of individuals on the altar of great historical ideals . . . even liberty itself, which demands the sacrifice of individuals for the freedom of society. This is the belief that somewhere, in the past or in the future, in divine revelation or in the mind of an individual thinker . . . , there is a final solution."[3] With no final solution in sight, pluralism of values seems to be a truer reflection of life. "Pluralism, with the measure of 'negative' liberty that it entails, seems to me a truer and more humane ideal than the goals of those who seek in the great, disciplined, authoritarian structures the ideal of 'positive' self-mastery by classes, or peoples, or the whole of mankind. It is truer, because it does, at least, recognize the fact that human goals are many, not all of them commensurable . . . To assume that all values can be graded on one scale . . . seems to me to falsify our knowledge that men are free agents . . ."[4] Here, the freedom that Berlin considers to be worthy of "free agents" stands over-against freedom as self-mastery, which is dependent on certain understanding of the self. The concept of self-mastery can pose as interference to the true freedom of a free agent. A free agent as Berlin understands her, is one who makes choices freely, with no need of guidance or directive of any kind other than what the free agent individually conceives to be the good for her. What she chooses is simply to her the good. With this, one begins to wonder whether the concept of the good is needed here, for the free choice implies the good. Freedom borders on the willfulness of individuals.

2. Ibid., 150–52.
3. Ibid., 167.
4. Ibid., 171.

Berlin presented this essay as his inaugural address in 1958 for his professorship at Oxford, when the world had barely recovered from the Second World War only to be confronted with the menace of communist totalitarianism. His idea of freedom was most probably formulated with the terror of totalitarian states in mind. To avoid any possible encroachment of the state or collective ideology, ideal humanity or the idea of the common good has to be shunned. Liberty was taken to be "the last ditch," to use Charles Taylor's expression, to defend the individual from any sort of collective control for the sake of Utopian ideals or realization of preconceived human nature. Liberty conceived in such a way confines itself to liberty as sufficient conditions for something, and that something is in principle left undefined or indeterminate. Liberty conceived in such way is liberty with no definite moral discrimination; it is a liberty of indifference.

However, can the absence of external interference be the sufficient condition for freedom? Berlin rejects any idealization of the human person. Yet, if his notion of negative freedom is to work at all, it has to rest on one idealization, that we are all "free agents." That is, if left all to ourselves without external interference, we would be able to exercise our free agency. However, is this a true picture of the human condition? External interference may all be eliminated, but what about inner inhibitions preventing the "free" agent to exercise her freedom, even as she is aware of it but finds herself incapable of transcending it, thus finds herself not even able to make a choice or to realize that choice? What about "false consciousness" that may have already been so embedded in the so-called "free agent" that it has become an integral part of her, leading her to willingly, in an exercise of her "free" choice, relinquish what our liberal humanists regard as genuine freedom in exchange for something ideologically constructed as the good? The Grand Inquisitor in Dostoevsky's *Brothers Karamzov* points to a hard fact in life, i.e. the majority of the people would willingly bring give up their freedom in exchange for bread or peace of mind. How are we to distinguish the "true self" from the "self" infused with fears, inhibitions of all kinds, and "false consciousness"? What would they say to a Confucianist who genuinely believes that the self can only find freedom in participation with the Way of Heaven, and thus make free choices in the Confucian way? What are the criteria for differentiating "false consciousness" and "pure consciousness" of the "authentic self." Without a concept of "authentic self," can a "free agent" confidently identifies her "free choice" to be genuinely free? It seems that the "metaphysical blanket"[5] that Berlin tries so hard to get rid of simply refuses to go away.

5. Ibid.

Perhaps there is something more serious than psychology or metaphysics. Let us idealize a bit along Berlin's line and visualize a pluralistic society where free agents pursue their ends without interference, where conflicts among them are reduced to a minimum, and even as they exist, they are resolved in a civil manner. However, it is conceivable that after a considerable period of free and fair exercise of choices, a small group of free agents have amassed much of the resources in fair competition, whereas the majority of free agents have found themselves in utter scarcity. Wherever they move they run into non-possibility due to extreme scarcity. As a formal principle, the majority remain free agents by virtue of non-existence of external interference. However, the formal principle is empty, for choices left to them are mere phantoms. If Berlin's principle of freedom is to be consistent, there is no justification why the process is to be reversed so that the "have not" may be given back some of the resources they have somehow lost through a series of free choices. Indeed, we may of course do so out of benevolence, but if benevolence is to be incorporated into our system, interference to the freedom of choice of the successful minority is to be anticipated. There is however no justification why the system of free choice be tempered with for the sake of benevolence. If we believe that there is such justification, then we are in effect introducing a vision of humanity into our system of non-interfered free choices. However, if some form of redistribution of resources is not introduced, it is highly conceivable that the majority may be driven further to poverty, until they willingly sell themselves into slavery. Is such a society that upholds non-interference at all cost be worthy of the name of a "free society"? Is not the term "free agent" a mockery to the majority in a society where they lead an actual life of slavery?

There is still a bigger concern. It has to do with the survival of the whole human race. The concern is more than pragmatism. It confronts directly the meaning of freedom, if freedom so conceived turns out to negate the existence of free agents. Due to the principle of non-interference, rejecting the idea of the common good, there is no way to guarantee that our society would not fall into a free-for-all situation. Such a situation can be socially and ecologically devastating. In fact, right before our eyes, due to human selfishness, Mother Earth is being so abused that she is fast becoming uninhabitable, as the biosphere is being destroyed in our free pursuit of personal ends. There may come a day when all "free agents" would be totally wiped out from the face of Mother Earth. Such would be the cost of their freedom individualistically conceived. What is more, our freedom is determining the condition in which the future generation may live as "free agents." When resources are so depleted by our free choices, our children may not have the luxury of free choice at all.

Berlin of course does not preclude the possibility that each and every individual may act morally out of her personal choice. If indeed enough individuals make personal choices with certain moral orientation without being coerced, there may be a chance that our ecological crisis may be resolved. However, is this not wishful thinking? When any form of socially promoted moral principle is rejected at all cost, and society has to be vigilantly sanitized of any form of moral vision, which is supposed to pose as a threat to individual freedom, how can we assume that individuals may have certain moral principles in their characters? When the Self is socially promoted as the ultimate value, how can we expect the Self to see beyond itself, and expect it to submit itself for something "bigger"? The future of Mother Earth or our future generation can only be left to the hope that somewhere somehow there is a mysterious harmonization of arbitrary exercises of free wills that would bring result in the health of everything. Indeed, we may like to bring back the idea of "pre-established harmony" for our consolation.

Should certain interference with our freedom be entertained for the sake of the vision of a society which ensures some sharing of resources despite inequality of capability? Is there a limit to non-interference? Should we not interfere with individuals' pursuit of good life for the sake of saving Mother Earth? But how can such a vision of society be justified? Is not the "metaphysical blanket" being smuggled back? Can negative freedom work all by itself without the support of moral commitment? Should moral conviction be in principle excluded to ensure the individual as the sole supreme value? Can positive freedom be completely obliterated if our society is to remain sane?

Freedom and the Common Vision of a Just Society

Rawls follows Berlin's line of thought, articulating it in contractual principles as guidance for social arrangement and social change.[6] Rawls attempts at the same time to bring back the ideal of an autonomous self guided by practical reason, so as to allow some imaginative space for positive freedom. Rawls tries also to address the problem of inequality resulted from free and fair competition, a problem haunting Berlin's concept of negative freedom. To him, mere negative freedom is not enough. A common vision of society has to be found and made the foundation of our social contract. The common vision is found by Rawls to be the vision of a society upholding justice

---

6. "Thus we are able to derive a conception of a just basic structure, and an ideal of the person compatible with it, that can serve as a standard for appraising institutions and for guiding the direction of social change." Rawls, *A Theory of Justice*, 263.

as fairness. It is a society which takes justice as prior to all moral values, and constitutes it in such a way that equal individual rights are safe-guarded for pluralistic pursuit of values. It is only within such a society that freedom can be truly guaranteed. Defending justice is synonymous to defending freedom, for justice as fairness means equal rights to liberty for all. Justice is formulated in terms of two principles. The first principle stipulates that "each person is to have equal right to the most extensive total system of equal basic liberties compatible with a similar system of liberty for all."[7] The comprehensive rights of one person can only be defended when the rights for all are defended.

Rawls intends to defend the vision of a just society without metaphysics or utilitarianism. The starting point is human autonomy founded on practical reason, that each person, as a rational agent is an end in itself, and as such is inviolable. Rawls translates this into the public realm and phrases it thus: "Each person possesses an inviolability founded on justice that even the welfare of society as a whole cannot override."[8] Such a simple statement expresses Rawls' project in deriving a conception of justice based on principles of rights and putting forward an ideal of the human person compatible with it.[9] In the public realm, it is the inviolability of the human person that is founded on justice, and not the other way round. "Justice," for Rawls, "is the first virtue of social institutions, as truth is of systems of thought."[10] It is the good that is prior to all goods, even prior to the inviolability of the human person. We may however take justice and the inviolability of the human person as the two sides of the same coin. The inviolability of the human person expressed as virtue of social institutions is justice. Without justice, there can be no guarantee for the inviolability of the human person; without the inviolability of the human person, justice is empty and aimless. Right here one may ask in one breath: on what ground is the inviolability of the human person founded? And on what is justice grounded?

As justice cannot be "contingent upon existing desires and present social conditions," on what should justice as the supreme good be founded? It seems that justice is grounded on shared presumptions, something that Rawls himself assumes. Rawls indicates his assumption when he says, "I assume, for one thing, that there is a broad measure of agreement that principles of justice should be chosen under certain conditions (i.e. under the veil of ignorance). To justify a particular description of the initial situation one

7. Ibid., 302.
8. Ibid., 3.
9. Ibid., 263.
10. Ibid., 3.

shows that it incorporates these commonly shared presumptions."[11] Relying on such commonly shared presumptions is crucial, for Rawls intends to avoid appealing to a priori or any sort of perfectionist principle. He makes this quite clear, "In order to find an Archimedean point it is not necessary to appeal to a priori or perfectionist principles. By assuming certain general desires, such as the desire for primary social goods, and by taking as a basis the agreements that would be made in a suitably defined situation, we can achieve the requisite independence from existing circumstances."[12] Perhaps the most common presumption and general desire is that each and every human person is concerned with her own inviolability. Fundamentally, it is self-interest that is most general and unshakable. "The veil of ignorance" is a contractarian strategy for impartiality, so that a sensible person, in order to guarantee her own rights, has to guarantee the same rights for all. In the "Original Position," as Rawls terms it in his thought experiment, all parties are situated behind a veil of ignorance. "They do not know how the various alternatives will affect their own particular case and they are obliged to evaluate principles solely on the basis of general considerations. First of all no one knows his place in society, his class position or social status; nor does he know his fortune in the distribution of natural assets and abilities . . . Nor again, does anyone know his conception of the good, the particulars of his rational plan of life, or even the special features of his psychology . . ."[13] One's social status, ability, fortune or psychological state are contingent conditions, but the desire for one's inviolable rights can safely be assumed to be most commonly shared. Justice is the social articulation of such fundamental self-interest. For the sake of self-interest to all parties, "justice should be chosen." Justice is a matter of sensible choice, it is grounded on free choice.

While it is not easy to deny that the guarantee for one's inviolable rights is the most general desire, but how do we know the desire of safe-guarding one's inviolable rights does not come from the truly most general desire of safe-guarding the inviolable rights of oneself as well as that of others? That is, this general desire does not come merely from self-interest, but also from an inner urge to love one's neighbor as much as one loves oneself. Is it not possible that love as much as self-interest is the substance of this most general desire? Is it not possible that the desire of self-interest and the desire both to love and to be loved are so intertwined that there is no such thing as pure self-interest and pure unconditional love without any reference back

11. Ibid., 18.
12. Ibid., 263.
13. Ibid., 136–37.

to the self? That is, the desire for justice as fairness may have come from self-interest intertwined with a deep empathy for others.

Just imagine a society which is perfectly just, armed with the most impeccable defense of individual rights based purely on self-interest, where love is subsumed under self-interest as one of its function, what sort of society would that be? Within the highly market driven capitalist context, where the market logic turns everything into a marketable function or commodity, the human person can be reduced to an item in transactions. A clear example is provided by Richard Posner, a believer of the Chicago School of economics, who attempts to reduce marriage into some kind of economic arrangement, in which each party pays the other party by granting sexual favors, among the broader set of exchange arrangements. From a purely functional perspective, marriage is a voluntary economic transaction for mutual benefit, and as such, it is in essence not so different from the exchange involved in prostitution.[14]

Of course, it is understandable that the concept of love can hardly be articulated in a contractual situation, and the society envisioned by Rawls is basically a contractual society.[15] As he puts it, "The intuitive idea of justice as fairness is to think of the first principles of justice as themselves the object of an original agreement in a suitably defined initial situation. These principles are those which rational persons concerned to advance their interests would accept in this position of equality to settle the basic terms of their association."[16] However, in a contractual situation where fairness is the only principle at work, utter inequality is bound to be resulted. Thus Rawls' formulation of the principle of justice stipulates a second principle, the "Principle of Difference," to restrain liberty in order to ensure it. It requires that "social and economical inequalities are to be arranged so that they are . . . to the greatest benefit of the least advantaged, consistent with the just savings principles . . ."[17] Here, Rawls' idea of "mutual disinterest" takes a positive turn. "Disinterest" does not actually rules out benevolent response to others. However, the benevolent response is less than moral. It is a calculated measure to ensure that should oneself fall into a disadvantaged position, one will have the benefit from the "Principle of Difference." It is very much like a social insurance.

However, right here, Rawls's inconsistency becomes obvious. While it can be assumed that in the "original position" all would choose to be

14. Nelson, "Economic Religion versus Christian Values."
15. Rawls, *A Theory of Justice*, 175.
16. Ibid., 102–3.
17. Ibid., 302.

treated fairly, and thus justice as fairness seems to be most generally desired. However, can we be sure that the "Principle of Difference" is also generally desired? On what basis can we establish the principle? There may in fact be a considerable number of people in our society who genuinely believe in fair competition and nothing else. For one to be genuinely free, one has to bear the consequence of one's choice. They see themselves as having the freedom to throw themselves completely into competition without reservation and bear the consequence, rather than having their freedom held back in exchange of some form of social insurance. To them, "the greatest benefit to the least advantaged" is an interference that will eventually jeopardize freedom, not only the freedom of choice, but also the freedom to live with the consequence of free choices and drink the cup to the last drop. On what basis do we require them to accept the "Principle of Difference"? Why should we not let fairness as equality of rights prevail and run its own course? Sure enough, the allotment of fortune is arbitrary, and it may appear to be "unfair." But what is "fairness" other than fairness of competition or fairness as equal opportunities? There are of course differences in fortune's allotments. But who is to decide which allotment is judged to be disadvantaged or which is advantaged? A person allotted great financial resources may lament the severe deprivation of emotional, spiritual and aesthetic resources. On the other hand, a person judged to be disadvantaged financially may be lavished with joy of other forms of fulfillment achieved at the expense of financial effort. How are we to discern who are the least advantaged? On what criteria, and why? Even if financial condition is used as the main criteria, there are considerable number of people who believe that any form of social arrangement that deviates from the principle of fair competition will in the long run jeopardize free economy and thus hampers economic development for all.

If pragmatism proves to be problematic, should we not appeal to something which has been hitherto suppressed? Is it not possible that the principle of love is truly the most generally desired, as something that is intrinsic to being human? It is not true that the desire for fairness comes from the love for others as much as the love for oneself? Love thus takes fairness beyond "fairness in competition"? Is it not possible that love—the love for the self and the love of others going hand in hand—is in fact the ground of justice as fairness? It would be easier to understand that love as the ground of justice as fairness is at the same time the ground for preference for the least advantaged? Is not sharing of life resources, whether material or spiritual, part of authentic humanity? Is not commitment to others integral to one's being free? Right here, we may be accused of infringing on the principle of "bare essentials," we may be considered to be expanding our anthropological vision. However, only in so doing do we make better sense of ourselves as social being.

Freedom in Abstraction

To Rawls, the theory of the good used in arguing for the principles of justice has to be restricted to the bare essentials. Not only is strong anthropological or moral vision to be avoided, one has to assume as little as possible.[18] The bare essential of anthropological premise is simply this: what really defines a human person is her capability to exercise free choices, and not the teleological ends intrinsic to her being, and not even the ends she chooses. "[T]he self is prior to the ends which are affirmed by it; even a dominant end must be chosen from among possibilities."[19] To uphold the priority of the self over ends, the contractual agreement in the Original Position has to stipulate a mutual disinterest among contracting parties, to ensure that all are left to themselves to decide what their own ends are to be.

With this vision of a just society, freedom is defined as freedom for each and every free agent to exercise her rights to define the good for herself within the boundary of justice, which also means the categorical defense of such freedom for all. Freedom here can no longer be accused as empty, for it is no longer merely "freedom from," it is also "freedom for," i.e. freedom for realizing the ends, not pre-given, but chosen out of the individual's autonomy at the core of her being. Nothing is pre-given as the authentic nature of being human except one's autonomy to define the ends for oneself. "The self is prior to the ends which are affirmed by it." What is the self? That in itself is a wrong question, for the self cannot be presumed to have a "what" that defines itself as a self. The self with its autonomous will is the "given," it is "given" in such a way as to define the "what" of itself. The good cannot therefore have existence prior to the choice of the autonomous will. The autonomous self is therefore the Alfa and the Omega of all values. Rawls gives absolute primacy to justice among all moral values, in fact out of free choice in the Original Position for instituting the social contract. One's rights, which means one's unobstructed freedom to choose, as a moral category, is taken to be prior to the good and independent of it. Given its independent status, one's rights constrain the good and set its bounds. The priority of rights is of course derived from the concept of the assumption of the priority of the self's radical autonomy.

18. Ibid., 126.
19. Ibid., 560.

Right here, Rawls may run into two problems. First, he brings us back to a metaphysic of human existence. How does the claim of foundational autonomy be established other than an act of faith or simply by choice in a rather arbitrary way? Just how real is one's autonomy? To ensure genuine autonomy, the concept of natural law or naturalism of all kind has to be avoided in the understanding of the self. In order to be truly independent, the autonomous self has to be made independent of the laws of nature so that she can act according to the laws she gives herself. As the human body is subjected to the laws of nature through and through, the legislating autonomous subject cannot therefore include the body. Only the will remains at the center of choice making. However, it has to exist in abstraction from bodily existence. We may then ask, what is the "will"? Why do we believe that there is such a thing as the "will" and that it is capable of free choices? Is not the "will" an abstraction, constructed ideologically to be unquestionable? It is one thing to have desire for the capability of making free choices, but another thing to actually have that capability. It is indeed the most general desire that each and everyone of us can make free choices out of nothing else but purely her own will, but it is another thing that the human race most generally have that capability of making choices purely out of pure will.

Secondly, Rawls not only postulates in the human self the capability to make free choices, he also postulates the fact that the self can do so in abstraction not merely from natural laws but also from the life-supporting system that nurtures her into a full human person. She is in effect assumed to be able to make choices with no precondition or preunderstanding of any kind, or even if there is such thing as preunderstanding, it would not in any way hamper her free choices. That is, her choices remain free even as the system of values which nurtures her may have infused into her life and constituted part of her identity. This leads us to ask, what constitutes the identity of the autonomous person? When the person makes choices, does she make those choices out of the identity of her being this unique self? If so, what constitutes her identity? Is her identity made purely out of her past choices? Are life-supporting systems of values count as nothing in the shaping of one's identity? Would not the network of interpersonal relations count in the person's making choices? Given the fact that we are all embedded in a life supporting system of values, how is the concept of autonomy to be understood? This question is more than academic and is in fact becoming more and more serious. We have to face the fact that our modern society is very much shaped by huge corporations which have no interest other than making profits. To do so, they will not refrain from marketing strategies which involve channeling our choices by drumming into our consciousness desires for their products. They have become so powerful that in conditioning our consciousness that many of our so-called "free choices" are in fact preconditioned.

The "self" as Rawls envisions is very much a self in a vacuum. Not only is it disembodied, but also disfranchised of cultural traditions, interpersonal relations and "social engineering" by market-capitalists. Such a self's identity conceived ideally depends solely on the making of choices. "I choose, therefore I am." Dostoevsky knows this radical liberalism very well. He pushes it to the logical conclusion by depicting his anti-hero in The Possessed, Kirilov, who, in proving that he had absolute freedom, exercised his freedom to annihilate it. He shot himself. However, our modern world does not allow such a character of intense free will as Kirilov to exist. Rather the "self" that we encounter are dissolved personalities like Leopold Bloom of James Joyce's *Ulysses*, or Ulrich of Robert Musil's *Der Mann Ohne Eigenschaften*, or Moses Herzog of Saul Bellow's *Herzog*. We see in our world a parade of hollow human persons whose consciousness run full and wide through the will-less. "It is the Mover that is moved. Whichever we turn, we see the measurable taking charge of him who measures" (Auden).

Perhaps, the bigger concern is in the implication of the actual exercise of freedom as rights. Given the reality of infinite possibilities of ends imaginable by individuals who, within the boundary of fairness, under the principle of mutual disinterest, is not supposed to be accountable to anyone except herself, moral laws are rendered irrelevant so long as the principle of fairness is upheld. To have rights is "to have something which society ought to defend me in the possession of it." In fact, so strong is society's obligation that one's claim of rights assumes the character of absolutism. Society here is nothing other than an aggregate of individuals who make arrangement to be mutually disinterested in order not to interfere with one another. Such a society is reduced to a mechanism for maintaining contractual arrangements. It would be divested of common moral assets other than legislation based on rights. There is nothing to stop the game of fairness from becoming the game in the jungle.

There is yet another problematic stipulation: the stipulation of mutual disinterest to one another in their autonomous choice of ends or the good. How realistic is such stipulation? How often do we encounter in real life a person who can genuinely be disinterested in other's well-being, and expects no genuine interest from others in her well-being? Is this not in fact an idealized situation ideologically concocted? If we assume that individuals are "by nature" capable of doing this, we need to explain how have we come to such an assumption. Is it not true that the assumption of disinterest puts an individual in a surreal and abstract mode of existence? What would become of any individual in a society where fathers and mothers take an indifferent approach to their children as autonomous individuals? When do we regard a child to be truly autonomous? Is there an inception point? If there is, there would be prior conditions in which the autonomy of a child emerges. If there is not, it would mean that a child is autonomous from birth, and she should be treated with disinterest as far as determining by herself the good or virtues for her existence are concerned. This would have tremendous implications for education. It would be doubtful whether one should inculcate values in a child or to develop in him a sense of identification with common values in a tradition.

The stipulation of mutual disinterest depends on a totally optimistic assessment of human nature. It envisions a rosy picture of each and every individual founding her paradise in arriving at the ends she chooses for herself. There are occasions where we see individuals making choices which eventually lead to immense suffering or even destruction, leaving others to pay heavy prices for them. There are individuals who can play the game of fairness to enslave others. The reality of evil is as real as freedom. The reality of evil is not easy to explain philosophically. Kant, a strong believer in human reason and in human autonomy, finds evil to be too real to ignore, and as he attempts to locate its origin within the human person, he finds two opposing disposition of the will, one tending to act in accordance with reason, the other inclined to act in the opposite direction. Again, Dostoevsky knows the inner contradictions of the human heart all too well. The Underground Man points to the fact that, more often than not, human persons would act in contradiction to the guidance of reason or self-interest, as if trying to show that one can rebel even against oneself (Notes From Underground). Mitya in Brothers Karamazov knows too well that as soon as he yearns for the purity of Madonna, without warning, without any prompt from outside, without any explicable reason, he would plunge into the vilest wickedness. When other moral values are marginalized and reduced to an appendage to justice, society virtually disarms itself of moral forces to constrain evil forces. All have to be left to legislation.

Indeed, both Berlin and Rawls have made tremendous contribution in formulating a concept of freedom to legitimate a form of society where the threat of totalitarianism is reduced to the minimal. What we need to ask is: for that defense, is the price we are paying too high? Such a society would be a radically contractual association (*Gesellschaft*). What have been valued as virtues within a society as community (*Gemeinschaft*) would have to be held suspect in principle. Justice, no matter how valuable it may be, is inadequate as an institutional arrangement if it stands alone in abstraction from the reality of love in human life. A more holistic society can be visualized when justice and love interlock with one another, even as the two sides of the same coin. Here the Christian tradition has a lot to contribute.

Freedom and Commitment

The Christian tradition knows the menace of tyranny too well. In First Samuel chapter 8, when the elders of Israel demand, "Give us a king to govern us," God's answer is a clear warning: "These will be the ways of the king who will reign over you: he will take your sons and appoint them to his chariots and to be his horsemen . . . he will take your daughters to be perfumers and cooks and bakers . . . he will take the best of your fields . . . and in that day you will cry out because of your king . . ."

There was no king in Israel. God was her king. What does that mean? It means that no one in Israel can be regarded as higher than others, and no one can rule over others. All are equal, equally but relatively absolute before God. One has to treat her neighbor as inviolable because God is in her, over her and beside her. When one sees her neighbor, she sees a covenantal partner of God, with God's absolute commitment to her. Any violation of her dignity and right is a violation of God's dignity. Seeing the other as absolute is not a contractual decision but an ontological understanding. This is the meaning of theocracy. Theocracy in the Bible indeed affirms the absoluteness of God, yet God exercises His absolute freedom in a responsive way as a covenantal partner. His freedom is not freedom to aggrandize Himself, but freedom to realize His covenantal partnership. So, when the demand for a king came, He gave the warning, and respected the wish of the people. Something amounting to the first "universal franchise" (taken in a metaphorical way) in human history was granted. Israel as a people elected their king. God's freedom as manifested in this incident is freedom in commitment. God is committed to Israel's right to her own path even though it means strife and deterioration along the way, yet God is also committed at the same time to accompany them in their hardship and struggle. He is committed in such a way that He would not take a disinterested posture, but would chide them for going astray, for self-abuse, self-alienation, and would not refrain from showing them the right way.

The possibility to sin should be contemplated as one of the most fascinating components in God's grand design. It opens up a hole in God's absoluteness. God, by His own freedom, refuses to eradicate all possible rejection, opposition and even revolt against Him. God in effect suspends the absoluteness of His freedom to accommodate the genuine freedom of His covenantal partner, not because of indifference and disinterest, but because of commitment to make room for the other to exercise her freedom so as to become a genuine covenantal partner. In becoming a covenantal partner, God puts Himself in a vulnerable position at the mercy of His partner. His absolute autonomy is compromised by the covenantal law binding Him and His partner together. As an absolute subject in absolute possession of Himself, He is the law to Himself. Yet, in covenantal relation, His action becomes contingent on the action of the other. The covenant requires Him to be responsive to the condition of the covenantal partner. He is responsible for ensuring that the other realizes herself as covenantal partner, while ensuring at the same time that the other remains genuinely free in covenantal commitment.

As the covenantal law is written into God's absolute autonomy, so is the covenantal law written into human autonomy. Human autonomy is intrinsic to the human person as the image of God. Yet, being the image of God means being God's covenantal partner. The covenantal law is therefore intrinsic to human autonomy. The autonomy that a human person has is autonomy with responsiveness and responsibility. All self-legislation has an orientation that transcends the autonomy of the self-legislator. As a genuine covenantal partner, the human person is ensured of a genuine selfhood. She is truly a self that can decide even to rebel against God. As such she can genuinely make covenantal response and commitment out of herself. Yet, the self is a covenantal self. She by nature seeks to transcend herself in order to realize herself. The self has an existential center to herself. Yet the existential center goes beyond itself in order to affirm itself. That is to say, human autonomy is self-legislation and self-transcendence at the same time. There is another principle at work alongside what we generally understand as autonomy as self-determination and self-legislation. This principle is love. Love without autonomy is not genuine. Autonomy without love is empty and aimless.

God's freedom, as Barth points out, is the freedom to love. It is love that is the substance of God's freedom. It gives direction in His exercise of freedom. Both are from the very being of God, and both are prior to all moral attributes. There is in God no freedom or autonomy without love, and there is no love without freedom.

The problem with liberal humanists like Rawls is that he takes autonomy as an isolated category, pure in itself, being the foundational singularity point. Any association with another principle is regarded as a compromise. The Christian tradition, however, brings autonomy and love together. In the exercise of freedom, love is being exercised at the same time. The combination of the two makes each of the two different from what it would be in isolation.

The Incarnation and the Cross express the togetherness of freedom and love in God. God exercises His freedom as freedom to love. Freedom by itself as the absolute power of determination and control becomes a freedom in self-limitation in the Incarnation, which is God's being in His act of love given freely to sinful humanity. Love on the cross reveals the absoluteness of God's freedom in that He gives His only Son, something that nothing can compel God to do. In fact, it reveals God giving up Himself in confrontation with the utter rejection by mankind. Such love is God's being in His act, acting on His own accord.

Freedom to love creates communion between that which are originally ontologically distinct. Communion as a value acquires a teleological status. However, communion as a value cannot be separated from the autonomous individual. For communion is not achieved out of instinctual acts, but become realized in acts of freedom by free agents who choose to come into covenant. So the communion realized is a communion that preserves distinction, while distinctive individuals find their fulfillment as truly individual in and through the act of covenanting, creating a covenantal structure. The Trinitarian structure of God's being holds communion and distinction together. Thus individuality, in conjunction with communion, also has the teleological status as a value.

Concluding Remarks

Having a much deeper understanding of human sinfulness than liberal humanists, the Christian tradition takes negative liberty seriously. But negative liberty at the expense of positive liberty is simply too costly for humanity. What has been given to humanity as gifts from God are a whole range of values, which are meant to be realized, and humankind are also given the freedom to make them real in life. So, positive liberty as the capacity for the realization of wonderful gifts from God and for the fulfillment of communion with God is indeed regarded by the Christian tradition as much more important than the defense of our rights. The Christian tradition has not paid as much attention to individual rights as liberal humanists. That does not mean the tradition is not aware of such moral category. However, rights are always put in the covenantal context, and in such a way, rights are fused into righteousness and become meaningful in a relationship of mutuality, reciprocity and responsibility.

Bibliography

Berlin, Isaiah. "Two Concepts of Liberty." In *Four Essays on Liberty*, 118–72. Oxford: Oxford University Press, 1969.

Nelson, Robert N. "Economic Religion versus Christian Values." *Journal of Markets and Morality* 1 (1998) 142–57.

Rawls, John. *A Theory of Justice*. Oxford: Oxford Universality Press, 1971.

19

Freedom in Postcolonial Perspective

Susan Abraham

How do we construe the relationship between freedom and postcoloniality? This is the question I explore below. At an intuitive level postcolonial "freedom" refers to political and national independence and liberation from colonial power. The nation then, becomes the site and concretion of freedom in the postcolonial context. Nevertheless, as a number of postcolonial theorists have argued, independence from a colonial power did not mark the end of oppression. Instead, domestic forms of tyranny or neocolonial oppressions replaced the departing colonial authority. Since oppression continues in a transmuted form, how can we still talk of "freedom?" Despite the temptation to imagine postcolonial freedom as a positive reality that awaits our (re)imagining, the decolonizing instinct of contemporary postcolonial theory alerts us to the dangers of neocolonial domestication and co-optation of freedom in economic, cultural and academic frameworks. In light of these theoretical complications, it is critical to develop a way to do postcolonial theory by enacting in its performance the (im)possibility of producing an affirmative discourse of freedom.

Since postcolonial theory negotiates its Western provenance and its political interests in Marxism, feminism, political theory and political aesthetics, any attempt to do it (as opposed to an ungainly application methodology) must be reflected in its performance as an instantiation of a decolonizing project. Thus, a decolonizing project on freedom interrupts the expectation of an answer to the question what is freedom in a postcolonial context by challenging the presumptions foundational to the framing of the question. In so doing it permits an interpretive reading of how freedom relates to liberation while also attempting to challenge the discursive frameworks structuring contemporary academic discussions. It challenges the assumption that there is a positive reality called "postcolonial freedom."

Consequently, I present below two differing interpretations of Kant's philosophy of freedom, refracted through the postcolonial lens of Gayatri Chakravorty Spivak and Pheng Cheah. Spivak and Cheah teach in the US—Spivak is the Avalon Foundation Professor in the Humanities at Columbia University and Cheah is Professor of Rhetoric at the University of California, Berkeley. Both are prolific and extremely influential thinkers, deeply embedded in Western philosophy and theory. Their suspicion of particular forms of knowledge production which they share with postmodern thinkers leads them to deconstruct and decolonize modern notions of freedom while asking how best freedom may be realized under the conditions of postcoloniality. The essay proceeds as a reading of two readings in particular. That is, even as I read Spivak and Cheah reading Kant, I discuss only a few political problems highlighted by Spivak and Cheah in their analysis of Kant and how best to complicate his discussion of freedom through postcolonial materials. As is well known, the postcolonial "context" is not simply a reference to the historical context of the aftermath of colonialism and its departure in the mid twentieth century for former colonies. While the experience of colonialism has led in multiple ways to a global climate of intertwined cultural, political, social and economic systems presently, Spivak and Cheah among a host of other thinkers, seek to clarify the ever more complex systems of exploitation and devastation oppressing the most vulnerable human beings on the planet.

Neither Spivak nor Cheah will claim that they are providing an authoritative reading of Kant by presenting a "Kantian notion of freedom for a postcolonial context." Both would consider such an attempt to be contradictory to the fundamental enterprise of decolonizing thinking under the conditions of postcoloniality where "authoritative" readings, particularly from the recently arrived postcolonial intellectual in the West are heralded as authoritative only because it comes from a newly ordained and sanctioned cultural identity. That is, they wish to avoid social inscription as the basis of any decolonizing project. Both, however, seek to illuminate the aporias presented by Kant's thinking on freedom and engage Kant in terms of ethics and politics. Each is acutely aware that any postcolonial reading of a seminal figure such as Kant will be taken to be a "newer" and therefore commodifiable reading of Western philosophy. Further, both present their reading of Kant as a criticism of postcolonial reason (Spivak) and cultural studies (Cheah). Thus, their critique of modernity, or, in this case, the critique of Kantian freedom is not another instance of postcolonial self-righteousness.

Decolonization as the urgent task of ethics requires reading in a different key.

While both thinkers are involved with exposing the aporias of modern thought, each is also committed to thinking constructively within their analyses of the discourse of power. Consequently, each crafts an argument with a slightly different emphasis. Spivak, for example, presents us with the epistemic limits of modern theories of freedom and subjectivity in view of liberation for the "poorest woman of the South," while Cheah argues that the link between modernity and coloniality is not just epistemic in character, but may be the site of a national haunting. At first blush therefore, it looks as if the two thinkers share nothing in common. Yet both thinkers demonstrate striking similarities in their presentations, permitting their readings of Kantian freedom to complexify the (postcolonial) conversations we may undertake in the name of freedom. For example, both agree that the postcolonial condition exacerbates a complicitous relationship with the very powers that seek to define and exclude. Spivak, for example, speaks of the foreclosure of the subaltern in modern theory and in the nation, a phenomenon she identifies originally in Kant. Cheah, on the other hand, reading Derrida's *Specters of Marx* against Kant, speaks of the haunting of the subaltern in the space of the nation, caused by a "constitutive finitude" and the possibility of alienation always already inscribed within freedom. Both, therefore, speak to the failure of multiculturalist projects in the West and nationalist projects in domestic contexts and thus the failure of postcolonial theory and imagination to deliver freedom to its constituents.

Deconstruction and Foreclosure: The Rhetorical Matrix of Freedom

For Gayatri Chakravorty Spivak, freedom in both its modern and postcolonial version cannot be explored apart from what she calls the "axiomatic of imperialism."[1] That is, freedom in its material form and its abstract conceptual form is bound up in the logic of imperialism. Unmasking the limited situation of modern knowledges and their links to older and newer forms of colonialism is critical to decolonizing the idea of freedom. Her deconstructive reading of Kant's notion of freedom consequently does not establish a simple overturning of Kant. It argues instead that the rhetorical framework in which Kant articulates his notion of freedom is a performance of deconstruction against the preceding modern view of freedom.[2] But, she points

---

1. Spivak, *A Critique of Postcolonial Reason*, 4, (henceforth CPR).
2. Spivak writes: "Kant is careful to fix the limits of reason, to see it as free yet

out, even as Kant is infusing the idea of freedom with a more responsible ethics and a different ontology, he elides and forecloses the figure of the native subject. That move in Kant is worthy of note for a postcolonial analysis of freedom. In situating her discussion of the Kantian notion of freedom in a rhetorical frame, Spivak distances herself from the implications of Kant for freedom in terms of human subjectivity. Instead, her rhetorical investigation pushes forms of secularized democracies, including academic contexts, to examine their fundamental assumptions about freedom.

It is her conviction that contemporary forms of critique is too "thoroughly determined by Kant, Hegel and Marx"[3] to reject them as simple imperialists. Reading these critics of modernity however, in a postcolonial context leads to a layered criticism of the manner in which these thinkers capitulated to the demands of imperial logic as well as the manner in which Kant and the others are read contemporaneously in view of political liberation. Thus we note in her work a critique of postcolonial freedom. Her work is a critical evaluation not just of the genealogy of the concept in modern philosophy, but also its counterpart in much contemporary theoretical analyses: "I concentrate more on mainstream texts even as I try to probe what subaltern is strategically excluded from organized resistance."[4] The book therefore, stands in line with the kind of Kantian critique well established in Western philosophy. In establishing the determinate and necessary limits of reason, Kant forwarded a way to critically examine reason and its universal principles. Spivak suggests that this critical work was necessary in laying the foundations of future critical methodologies, including the philosophies and politics of freedom from cultural or political standpoints other than the European. Consequently, Spivak is fiercely critical of academic postcolonial theory, deeming it an "alibi,"[5] because its critical analysis only asserts nationalist and identitarian politics. This is a problem in two ways. Firstly, for Spivak, national liberation movements and their effects—citizenship, sovereignty and nationhood—are all products of 18th century European enlightenment. Any notion of "postcolonial" freedom therefore is complicit with the Western philosophical tradition. Complicity, however, does not simply mean an opportunity to dismiss this tradition; complicity entails a

---

bound, determined to supplement what must always remain a lack. The human being is moral insofar as he cannot cognize himself. Kant does not give cognitive power to the subject of reason, and indeed he makes his own text susceptible to the system of determined yet sometimes wholesome illusions he seeks to expose. This may be called a tropological deconstruction of the concept of freedom" (CPR, 22–23).

3. Ibid., 7.
4. CPR, Preface, xi.
5. Ibid., 1.

moment of responsibility in which elements of the Western philosophical tradition need to be constructively used to advance participative democracy. Contemporary postcolonial academic theory fails in this regard. Secondly, postcolonial studies, "unwittingly commemorating a lost object," produce not postcolonial knowledge, but neocolonial knowledge. Colonialism did not create a loss of simple identity (for identity was always complex and negotiated before modern colonialism). If postcolonial studies only raises up social inscription in the colonial aftermath it runs to risk of being reduced to "becoming a substantial subdisciplinary ghetto." Instead, in spite of the potential for cooptation, postcolonial studies must resolutely perform "a persistent dredging operation" of the "crystalline disciplinary mainstream" while interrogating its "alibi" in the general frame of academic endeavors. Deconstruction therefore, is the method that reveals the complicitous nature of postcolonial studies and Western philosophy.

Acknowledging complicity allows Spivak's interpretation of Kant to move in the direction of decolonizing freedom. She is less interested in pointing out Kant's obvious class, race, and gender privilege through which he develops his idea of transcendental freedom. To do so would only create a "reversal" of the Kantian model. Instead, as she demonstrates in her analysis, the great modern conceptualizations of freedom performed the violence of "foreclosure" of the native subject and repeated in contemporary proposals of freedom. Foreclosure, a term borrowed from Lacanian psychoanalysis is the "rejection of an affect."[6] That is, Lacan, drawing on Freud, notes a particular defense mechanism of the ego that rejects not only an incompatible idea to that held by the ego, but also its accompanying affect. Spivak hones in on the displacement of affect as the site of ethical responsibility. A disciplined empathy for the foreclosed figure reveals that it is the foreclosure of the subaltern which inaugurates speaking of human in the name "Man." "Man," a concept in which the native subject only functions as an absent foil. In order to preempt any form of identity politics, however, Spivak is careful not to name the subaltern as representing any particular race, culture or ethnic identity. The absent foil is repeated in the newly sanctioned subjectivity of the "Native informant" in postcolonial theory. Western philosophy takes it for granted that the "European" is the human norm while using the native informant in a specific way. In Kant, asserts Spivak, the native informant is "needed as the example for the heteronomy of the determinant, to set off the autonomy of the reflexive judgment, which allows freedom for the rational will."[7] As always for Spivak, the "typecase" of the foreclosed

6. CPR, 4.
7. Ibid.

native is the poorest woman of the South and it is this figure which remains absent in academic political theory.

Stephen Morton in his presentation on Spivak's critical retrieval of Kant lucidly argues that Spivak's emphasis on the rhetorical undergirds her argument that Kant's critical philosophy provides the basis of ongoing critique.[8] As Morton argues, Spivak's title *A Critique of Postcolonial Reason* aligns her project within the philosophical mainstream.[9] However, in critically scrutinizing Kant's universal principles, Spivak excavates Kant's ethnocentric assumptions. Kant's anthropomorphism, for example, explains the problems of epistemology using the experience of the white, masculine bourgeois European subject. A postcolonial reading of Kant's freedom, utilizing the method of deconstruction, seeks not to construct a positivist notion of postcolonial freedom. Instead it asks how these modern "fabrications"[10] of the self and world are new and subtle forms of domination, exploitation and epistemic violence and the role of these fabrications in contemporary discursive traditions attempting to achieve freedom for the poorest and most invisible. Morton underscores the idea that what Spivak's layered deconstructive analysis achieves is to incite the postcolonial intellectual into a more critical relationship with the western philosophical tradition.

Deconstruction, therefore, serves two purposes. The hoary figure anchoring Kant's autonomous and reflexive subject is really a foreclosed figure without freedom. The self-styled postcolonial discursivist, insofar as she or he draws on the Western canon to ground a culturally specific idea of the ethico-political subject also performs an erasure of freedom. Methodologically, deconstruction emphasizes that only a political reading strategy can bring these issues to light. In this her "mistaken" reading of Kant, Spivak goes on to argue that "[the] exercise may be called a scrupulous travesty in the interest of producing a counter-narrative that will make visible the foreclosure of the subject whose lack of access to the position of narrator is the condition of possibility of the consolidation of Kant's position."[11] The "bungling" of the reading, she asserts, is a necessary intervention in the context of postcolonial politics. Stephen Morton in another[12] explanatory note on Spivak argues that her rhetorical emphasis on texts reveals her reading strategy which seeks to "highlight instances where ideas, concepts, or metaphors are

---

8. Morton, *Gayatri Spivak*, 2007.
9. Ibid., 140.
10. CPR, 7.
11. Ibid., 9.
12. Morton *Gayatri Chakravorty Spivak*, 2003.

deployed as truth within the broader historical and geographical context of imperial expansion."[13] The deconstructive stance, realized in the "bungled" reading argues that all texts perform figuratively and invite bunglings and misreadings. In the case of Kant for example, reading thus demonstrates that culture itself is a form of rhetoric if we are able to prise the text away from the rigidly narrow philosophical questions that Kant addresses.[14]

Thus, in her "mistaken" reading, there comes to light, a "programmed"[15] access to the concept of freedom in Kant's The Critique of Judgment. She points out that in his consideration of the Beautiful and the Sublime, Kant posits that reason, or rational will is an inescapable obligation exercised in the experience of the Sublime. In other words, the rational is always superior to the sensible. Thus, while the concept being discussed is freedom, Kant's insists that the determination of the affect of the Sublime is obligatory. This assertion creates a conundrum for Spivak. The programmed access to the concept of reason, in her reading, implicitly presupposes that the concrete expression of freedom is troped within a rhetorical framework. The feeling of the Sublime in nature is the "clandestine metalepsis" which Spivak defines as "the substitution of effect for cause."[16] Such a substitution is the result of a subreption (the suppression of truth) exists as a trope in Kant, for the sublime is everything that excites a feeling of superiority to nature within and without us.[17] Thus morality and freedom operate in a rhetorical context, which is "clandestine" or obscured. Hence, the rational will escapes cognitive control while being grounded in the cognitive.

Spivak also zeroes in on how the category "culture" is understood by Kant. Spivak points out that in The Critique of Judgment, culture for Kant is a rational faculty—a receptivity which is a natural possibility of the "programming of determinate humanity."[18] She argues that while Kant emphasizes that judgment is programmed in nature and that it needs culture, there is a resulting subtle argument to exclude those who are "naturally alien" to culture.[19] Thus, it is primarily cultivated and educated men who are able to make rational judgments. Moral ideas are developed in the crucible of culture even though the receptivity to ideas and moral feeling are available to all human beings. But the uncultured man, or in Kant's words, "the raw

13. Ibid., 114.
14. Ibid., 113–16.
15. CPR, 11.
16. Ibid.
17. Ibid., 12.
18. Ibid.
19. Ibid., 13.

man," in the absence of the development of moral feeling or ideas, simply experiences the sublime as "terrible." It has been pointed out by many thinkers[20] that for Kant, the term "raw" has generally meant "uneducated." The uneducated of course are children, the poor and women. The exclusion functions in a manner that is different to the foreclosure of the native informant. In other words, Spivak is taking pains to nuance her criticism of Kant. Her point is not that Kant performs exclusions of the native informant through a simplistic erasure. Her point is that Kant uses the native informant in such a manner as to determine the nature of the native informant in relation to his ideal, "cultured" man.

In fact, it is a complex deconstructive moment which reveals the rhetorical framework in which Kant's notion of freedom operates. She writes:

> Kant calls the source of our sense of *duty* "a commanded *effect*" (CJ 321; emphasis mine)—*eine gebotene Wirkung*—rather than a mere command or a commanding cause. I have been at pains to trace the supplementary production of the concepts of practical reason as *effects* of a structuring, an *Anlage*. If we keep that necessarily-groundless-yet—necessarily—supplemental structure in mind, Kant's own description of exposing the supplementary production of the concept of freedom becomes interpretable as itself a supplementing of the abyss . . .[21]

Freedom, in this view exists as a desire, viz., the desire to account for the existence of things, commensurate with a final purpose, which presupposes the presence of the purposiveness of nature and the presence of an intelligent author of the world. Judgment therefore belongs to the transcendent realm, which Spivak asserts is *Kant's* deconstructive move on the concept of modern freedom. Freedom in Kant is thus exercised in a context of contingency—freedom and its final purpose cannot be discerned by us. Consequently, Kant's philosophical presentation of freedom in the context of a moral author of the world is a significant departure from "physicotheology" (the theological understanding of freedom as a gift given to human nature by God, as I understand her to say) and "ethicopolitical theology" (political theology in my understanding) in Spivak's reading.[22] For Spivak, Kant's move of situating an argument for the transcendence of freedom in a supplement called God is a better way to frame the issue of the relationship between human beings and the thing called God—an immanent argument

---

20. See also Morton's analysis in *Gayatri Spivak* (2007), 146.
21. CPR, 21, emphases in the original.
22. Ibid., 23.

for transcendence rather than the other way around, Kant's deconstructive move.

Nevertheless, the immanent source of transcendence also poses a problem in the manner in which the category "culture" operates in Kant. Spivak points to the two kinds of judgment in which Kant grounds his discussion of rationality and free will. Her reading here is in itself not new, but sets up her argument about the foreclosing mechanism in Kant. Thus, reflective judgment is different and autonomous than determinant judgment which is heteronomous and contextual. Determinant judgment seeks to make determinations of the final purpose of objects or of nature in view of a pre-understanding of a final purpose. Reflective judgment, on the other hand, understands the purposive laws operating in nature. Determinant judgment is "suprasensible" because it depends on conditions for understanding outside of immediate experience.

This suprasensible referent is the context in which we must think the final purpose of "Man," except in one stunning counterexample. Spivak shines a laser beam on Kant's invocation of the "natural man" in his allusion to "the New Hollanders or the inhabitants of Tierra del Fuego."[23] Here, argues Spivak, the raw man of the Analytic of the Sublime is named as a "casual object of thought," not a paradigmatic example. He is "not only not the subject as such; he also does not quite make it as an example of the thing or its species as natural product."[24] Why does Kant refer to these "geopolitically differentiated" people? Stephen Morton argues that these figures are "invoked to support Kant's broader philosophical view that it makes no sense to think of man as a part of nature if we wish to account for the supersensible origin of nature."[25] The relegation of the *aboriginal* to the natural reveals for Spivak that the aboriginal "*cannot* be the subject of speech or judgment in the world of the Critique"[26] even as the aboriginal is "the representative example" of the kind of determinant judgment which

---

23. Ibid., 26. Spivak quotes a passage from the *Critique of Teleological Judgment* (225), interspersed with her comments in square brackets: "Grass is needful for the ox, which again is needful for man as a means of existence; but then we do not see why it is necessary that men should exist (a question which is not so easy to answer if we cast our thoughts by chance [*wenn man etwa ... in Gedanken hat*] on the New Hollanders or the inhabitants of Tierra del Fuego). Such a thing is then [*alsdem ist ein solches Ding*] not even a natural purpose; for it (or its entire species [*Gattung*—the connotation of "race" as in "human race" cannot be disregarded here]) is not to be regarded as a natural product."

24. Ibid.

25. Morton, *Gayatri Spivak* (2007), 147.

26. CPR, 26, emphasis in the original.

Kant's reflective judgment corrects.[27] This is the foreclosure, the legible trace of the native informant whose self-determination or freedom has no part to play in the late 18th century's philosophical notions of freedom. The deconstructive move therefore discerns both the limits Kant places on the modern notion of freedom through the category of culture, but also deconstructs his racial anthropology which undergirds his philosophical project. It also hints at the (im)possibility of using Kant to develop decolonizing discourses on freedom in its relation to culture.

While it is true that the foreclosed native informant, on whom is built a "relationship without a relationship," inserts an interruption of Kantian universalism, Spivak's criticism is not merely the criticism of classism, racism or sexism. As she writes: "Quite apart from Kant's expressed opinion on race and colonization, I am noting here the mysterious working of the savage and the named savage in the central text on the subject's access to the rational will and its consolidation as the transcendental subject."[28] It is this aporia in Kant's philosophy which ought to make his philosophy "unreadable." Postcolonial discourses on freedom cannot draw on Kant because Kant's system which only makes sense within the "axiomatic of imperialism," excludes any consideration of the framing of the globally differentiated subject. Further, as Spivak points out, Kant cannot be read simplistically in order to perform "mere reversals."[29] The axiomatics of imperialism are also clearly discernible in domestic contexts: "there is something Eurocentric about assuming that imperialism began with Europe."[30] Hence, the excavation of the Eurocentric frame cannot result in its replacement by nativist ideologies resting on the reversal.

Foreclosure is explicitly not erasure or exclusion. What Spivak means by the "geopolitical differentiation" of the subject is that the "cultured" subject who is able to make judgments about the sublime or about nature is not the same as the raw man to whom the sublime simply appears as terrible. Nevertheless, the anthropological strand of Kant's philosophical system needs the raw man for its argument. The technique of foreclosure comes to view when deconstruction is utilized in a more strategic way than simply engaging in the politics of inclusion or exclusion. For Spivak, the strategic use of deconstruction points to the folly of the politics of inclusion which in the Western academy has taken the form of privileging the migrant as an

---

27. Ibid., 28.
28. See fn. 36, CPR, 32. Emphases in the original.
29. Ibid., 37.
30. Ibid.

exemplar of freedom, liberation and self-determination.[31] A political philosophy employing deconstruction cannot simplistically perform reversals of Kant as a mode of settling the dispute. But it can throw light on how freedom functions within a rhetorical framework safeguarding particular forms of racial, class, and gender privilege and also how it functions within nationalist rhetorics attempting to secure cultural, race and class privilege. It also throws light on the manner in which the contemporary academy privileges the "underclass" by exoticizing and commodifying particular identities, a strategy which repeats Kant's foreclosure.

Specters of Freedom: Beyond an Ontopology[32] of Freedom

Whereas for Spivak freedom in Kant and Kantian freedom is to be traced in a rhetorical framework, Pheng Cheah tracks the organismic nature of freedom in Western philosophy and its association with the postcolonial nationalist imperative. His explicit stance is that the organismic foundation for freedom is inadequate for postcolonial contexts even though as the basis of ontopology, it has provided foundational ways to narrate identity, nation, race and ethnicities. Cheah is critical of contemporary cultural theory (and much postcolonial theory) because of its refusal to engage political theory and philosophy. Consequently, the book's aim is to present a philosophical analysis that will complicate cultural studies, much of which has laid responsibility for postcolonial failures at the door of nationalism. Freedom, culture and the organic life are "philosophemes" which ought to be studied in relation both to their European provenance as well as their "displacement outside of the North Atlantic."[33] That is, philosophy and culture are not oppositional, though he is also critical of contemporary philosophy's "retreat into the insular space of specialized exegesis." Cultural studies and postcolonial theory are also at fault. "Nation" is not an obsolete term. Its ontopological foundations are to be interrogated as he demonstrates by breaching the borders between theory/philosophy and area/cultural studies.

What comes to view in such a refusal to honor disciplinary conventions and bounds is the "exemplary performance and undoing" of European arguments for organismic vitalism, an idea that played a great role in the

---

31. Ibid., 18

32. Cheah, *Spectral Nationality*. Cheah quotes Derrida: "By ontopology we mean an axiomatics linking indissociably the ontological value of present-being to its situation, to the stable and presentable determination of a locality, the topos of territory, native soil, city, body in general," 392.

33. Ibid., 12.

framing of national identities as homogenous and unified. Organismic vitalism is the idea undergirding the notion that freedom is self-actualizing behavior intended to transcend finitude. It is the idea of freedom as self-actualization (at the level of nation) that provokes Cheah: "is organismic vitalism an adequate framework for understanding postcolonial nationalism's persistence in the contemporary global order and its future as an emancipatory project? If not, how should we rethink the ideas of freedom and emancipation?"[34] Consequently, he proposes that freedom as self-actualization is inadequate to the task of postcolonial nation. Instead, freedom is contaminated from within and haunted from without.

Organismic vitalism is a feature of Kant's transcendental freedom. Indeed, asserts Cheah, freedom was characterized through metaphors of organic life from the late eighteenth century on.[35] As is known, transcendental freedom in Kant is a power of causality which is opposed to the arational mechanism of nature. The actualization of freedom in the empirical world gives rise to the particularity of culture and to the formation of political bodies based in such a particularity. Culture and the organic life were analogues for Kant. These individual political bodies however, were not Kant's ideal. For Kant, the ideal political body was a cosmopolitan federation.[36] He writes:

> What Kant calls "a universal cosmopolitan existence" is nothing less than the regulative idea of "a perfect civil union of mankind." ... Individual states would retain their sovereignty but would be held accountable by a universal citizenry—humanity—with regard to issues such as disarmament and imperialist expansion. Kant's world federation would therefore fall somewhere between the political community of the state in its lawful relations with other states and a world state. Yet, Kant's cosmopolitanism is not opposed to the organic political community of the nation. His world federation is clearly an association of sovereign territorial states. His vision, articulated in 1795, prior to the age of nationalism in Europe, is a prenationalist attempt to reform absolutist statism. It is also irrigated by an organismic discourse.[37]

Kant's cosmopolitanism depends on a teleological view of nature, a system of ends, in which the political body is understood as an organism. The organism is the basis for realizing ideal communities because nature

34. Ibid., 7.
35. Ibid., 10.
36. Ibid.
37. Ibid., 61–62.

gives to natural beings an "auto-causality" that enables individual organisms to overcome finitude and preserve the species. For Cheah, it is this auto-causality means that the organism is a "phenomenal analogue of transcendental freedom."[38] Nevertheless, he moves beyond Kant's organismic metaphor for nations and republics. As we shall see, the postcolonial nation cannot simplistically argue that it is already constituted as an organism. To do so would create a new order of oppression: the postcolonial state and its particular vision of (hegemonic) organismic vitalism. Kant is important to Cheah's analysis for two reasons he asserts. First, Kant was the first to link the realization of freedom to organic life and second, the *Critique of Judgment* contains the first modern formulation of the organismic metaphor of the political body.[39]

Like Spivak, Cheah develops a nuanced argument for the nature of freedom by reading the philosophical tradition attentively. Spivak had drawn attention to the "suprasensible" ground of determinant judgment, which is heterogeneous to itself. For Cheah, the critical question is why freedom is understood in terms of an organic model and the scope and limits of such a suggestion. His analysis demonstrates the problem with the organicist idea of freedom: "although Kant inaugurates a sharp distinction between organism and artifice and forbids the association of the former with instrumentality, his elucidation of organized natural beings in terms of a technic of nature also implies an aporetic interplay between *physis* and *techne*, the inhuman and the human, that complicates the realization of freedom at various levels."[40] While both Spivak and Cheah would be in agreement that freedom's becoming in Kant is not related to mechanical causation, Cheah unearths a slippage in Kant's limiting of instrumentality. This becomes visible only when we examine the concrete conditions of for freedom's becoming, that is when it is "incarnated" in specific spatio-temporal contexts. Hence, there is much potential, in his view, to examine the interaction of these three matrices of freedom in Kant—the transcendental idea of freedom, the concept of culture and the idea of organism[41]—philosophically and politically. Thus, Cheah's attempt to decolonize freedom in Kant and in cultural studies, seeks to intensify its heterogeneity. At stake in the analysis of freedom in relation to nationalism, then, is a "philosophical idea of the concrete, of how universal freedom can be actualized in a concrete proper body."[42] Such an "implicit philosophy" (quoting Derrida),

38. Ibid., 63.
39. Ibid., 64.
40. Ibid.
41. Ibid., 34.
42. Ibid., 4; emphases in the original.

is the condition for nationalism. The constellation of philosophical concepts inhabiting the implicit philosophy of nationalism is freedom, culture and organic life.[43]

Freedom as it relates to organic life in a person or in the nation is not a novel concept. The organismic idea is the Kantian ontological thread linking the philosophical and political projects of Frantz Fanon, Marx and Fichte. He writes:

> It is also part of a philosophical history that sees organic life qua organized matter as an analogue of freedom and, therefore, as the paradigmatic metaphor for social organization and political life. This organismic vitalism is the thread linking Frantz Fanon's assertion that "each man or woman brings the nation to life by his or her action," to Marx's idea of living labor as the source of proletarian revolution, and Fichte's characterization of the German nation as a self-originating and self-organizing living whole.[44]

The organismic metaphor, which hinges on German idealism as behind the nationalist spirit, is distinguished from the concrete reality of the state. Such a provenance for nationalism permits a clearer understanding of how freedom functions in postcolonial nationalism. Further, the organismic metaphor and its dimension of personal and social freedom informs progressive philosophies of cosmopolitanism and other forms of belonging wider than tribe and nation. Thirdly, the organismic metaphor points to the failure of postcolonial nationalisms and its inability to actualize and concretize freedom for its people. Finally, the metaphor clarifies the connection between culture and politics which seem to be absent in most academic analyses of politics. For Cheah, the interdisciplinary method of bridging culture and politics through a Marxist lens is not adequate. The organismic metaphor, instead, understands the cultural articulation of political perspectives as an analogue of freedom and less related to class inequalities. Thus, "culture is the ontological paradigm of the political."[45]

Freedom conceived in terms of an organic life implies a sharp distinction from the blind mechanical causality of nature. Cheah argues, however, that the turn to the organic model is gradual in Kant. For example, before the Third Critique, Kant is resolute in demarcating a non-mechanical frame for freedom. Our ontological constitution as beings with a rational will means that for Kant "moral freedom is essentially a will that is determined

43. Ibid.
44. Ibid., 5.
45. Ibid., 7.

by itself, from the inside of itself as reason rather than by what is outside itself, the necessitation of external nature or natural inclinations within us as sensible beings."[46] Reason, as an original condition, is "intractable," existing outside of temporal sequence and spatial limits. Here Cheah traces the Kantian argument of the universality of reason (that is, as outside of time and space), as a key feature of transcendental freedom. Initially, the "explicit antimechanism" of Kant's moral philosophy construed freedom as a causality independent of all alien influences. Moral freedom is of "so exacting"[47] a nature that it cannot be compared to any causality in the sensible world. He expounds on the matter thus:

> Kant's moral antimechanism can be summarized as follows: the existence of nature as a whole and any nonrational beings within it is fundamentally heteronomous. Because the self-moving machine is the clearest case of nature's other-directedness, Kant figures any alien influence as an alien hand that is instrumental in the making of automata. Thus, *techne*, the sum of all artificial objects that bear the mark of this alien hand, is the paradigm of nature's heteronomy.[48]

But then, how do we establish the objective presence of freedom? Since the moral law is both an "ought" as well as a "would do," there is a basis for thinking that moral actions can have real effects in the sensible world. It is justifiable to think in this way when we understand that the moral action takes place in the backdrop of "teleological time."[49] Thus, where morality can only think of a "possible purposive order," teleology provides the "actuality of a purposive order."[50] In this view, a moral community is a community of moral ends, the actuality of the moral impulse. Moral freedom's teleological nature and its affirmation of moral freedom's end has an analogue in the constitutions of living organisms. Thus Kant's idea of a moral community of rational beings is, in Cheah's estimation, "implicitly organismic."[51]

In Kant's historical writings, culture as freedom demonstrates the features of moral freedom[52] and therefore is not to be understood as ahistorical or abstract. Culture as a form of human power to transform the sensible world both originates and incarnates ends. Since these ends are not lim-

---

46. Ibid., 65.
47. Ibid., 68.
48. Ibid., 69.
49. Ibid., 73.
50. Ibid.; emphases in the original.
51. Ibid., 74.
52. Ibid., 76.

ited to individual human desire, but to the species as a whole, culture is the historical medium for the development of our rational capacities. Secondly, the power to develop within the historical frame of culture means that freedom in this view is not simply a given, but a development of a natural capacity. As such, culture is the development of the predispositions given to us by nature. Finally, culture is the transcendence of finitude as both the evidence of and the effect of an inner worldly transcendence. In this sense, "culture itself is a form of freedom."[53]

Implicit in such a view of culture is the idea that an organismic vitalism undergirds its workings. Culture, like organisms, demonstrates auto-causality. The political organism similarly demonstrates auto-causality in that Kant imagines the political state to exhibit "the same purposive auto-causality of an organism because it is a self-organizing whole in which there is reciprocity between parts and whole, means and end."[54] But, the political state must be distinguished from the political body. By itself the political state cannot achieve moral freedom. It belongs to the realm of external freedom and consequently, to the realm of mechanical nature. But through cultural education, a moral culture could evolve in the political state. It is consequently through its relation to culture that the state becomes "organicized."[55] For Cheah, the organismic connection between culture and freedom constitutes Kant's unique contribution. Kant's gift to moral and political thought has to be acknowledged in the organismic metaphor of culture and political thought which privileges culture as the site of transcendence and the actualization of freedom.[56]

Kant does not, however, finesse his notion of freedom in a manner suited to the history and context of postcolonialism. In developing a postcolonial critique of Kant's notion of freedom, Cheah argues that Kant fails to provide a stable framework for the continuity of cultural progress, moral purposiveness and natural purposiveness. Organic life is itself invaded by heteronomy, an idea that Kant does not consider. Organic life, for example, is invaded by human *techne* because nature in Kant's argument is an instrument of practical reason. Cheah explains:

> By insisting on the organism's irreducibility to human artifice, Kant breaks with the Aristotelian view of a mimetic continuity between *physis* and *techne*. However, the technic of nature makes organic nature dependent on us because it is a principle

53. Ibid., 77.
54. Ibid., 90.
55. Ibid., 94.
56. Ibid., 99.

that we anthropomorphically project onto nature so that we can view it as an instrument of practical reason. Mimeticism returns. Only this time, it is *physis* that mimes *techne*! ... We need the existence of organisms so that we can postulate purposive nature as ground for actualizing our freedom from the mechanism of nature. But such a ground is thereby also a means towards a higher end that lies beyond it. Paradoxically, we need nature to be independent of us so that it can finally be subjected to us via the technic of judgment![57]

In Cheah's argument, therefore, Kant's organicist foundation for political organization alone does *not* imply the priority and originality of organic life. *Techne* creeps back in, that is, Kant seems to be asserting that we can only understand organismic causality through technical causality. Secondly, even as Kant seems to be foregrounding the projection of human purposiveness onto nature, there are also a number of instances where Kant seems to concede that it is nature that prods and prompts us to experience. In other words, nature already seems to provide the conditions for judgment. These promptings may surpass our understanding; we are finite beings and require nature's favor to actualize moral freedom. In pointing out this aporetic slippage, Cheah argues that Kant repeatedly effaces and obscures nature, effectively choking nature's radical alterity. It is not that Kant wants to deliberately efface the impulse of nature. Rather, Kant seems to prefer to conceptualize the impulse of nature in epistemological terms. Hence Kant anthropomorphizes the impulse and limits it. Cheah in contrast argues that the impulse is beyond the human—it is in inhuman (in a manner of speaking). It possesses a radical alterity which cannot be grasped by human thought.

Organic life consequently is "contaminated" in its very origins by a radical alterity. There is always an excess, a "more" to the organismic vitalism of the nation and the people. Cheah's organismic model, which reveals the incarnation of rational ideals, reveals that all talk of freedom is always and already susceptible to distortion from within. The organismic model never truly embraces the whole life of all the people. Such a move is explicitly not to herald "the people's punctual death,"[58] that is, the failure of democratic national identities. What Cheah wants to underscore, rather, is that the Kantian model for nation succeeds insofar as its grounding in organic freedom demonstrates that the nation is not simply a Marxist ideological construct. Deterritorialization in the time of globalization is absent (as the

---

57. Ibid., 106.
58. Ibid., 382.

limits on transnational labor are to be easily observed in the xenophobic and racist backlash against foreign workers in the West). Since global capital organizes labor unevenly and capriciously, popular nationalist movements are on the rise around the world. The "nation" clearly is not an obsolete category. Cultural theorists and postcolonial theorists are wrong to dismiss nation. Kant's model of transcendental freedom for nation fails insofar as it does not chart the excess of nature and the other as the deepest impulse of transcendental freedom. Thus, the postcolonial state cannot depend solely on the organismic vitalism of Kant's argument in asserting an ontology of the people and culture. Kant or Kant's model does not provide for the distortion within freedom and the excess of nature from without freedom. The instability of the Kantian model however, permits another and more "apposite" and imaginative figure of freedom in a postcolonial context—the incarnation of alterity within freedom, the excess of nature haunting ontopology and its assertions. It hovers as a specter over the attempts to account for life in the postcolonial context.

Developing Derrida's philosophical hauntology for the postcolonial context, the haunting bespeaks the failure of organismic vitalism and the nation, a "gestative spectrality."[59] Prime among these systems being haunted is the postcolonial state, which channels the nation into state-sponsored, official national culture. But precisely because the nation is constantly attempting to decolonize, the instrumental logic of the state must be undone by the imaginative exercise for freedom and community in the nation. A national sense of its life and its people is a vision that always escapes the control of the postcolonial state. The organicist vitalism of the nation is present, albeit only as a specter. Cheah labors throughout the book to illuminate the "irreducible heteronomy" intrinsic to all forms of political organicisms. The spectral nation is an example of the heteronomy of organic life. Incarnational freedom is always and everywhere touched by a radical contamination of externality, which means that it is not just freedom's organic vitalism that political theories ought to take into account, but also the excess of life and being that forever escapes programmatic control by state sponsored national apparatuses.

"Hauntology" indicates for Cheah the contamination already and always inscribed within incarnational freedom and the necessary postcolonial task arising as the result of acknowledging the productive spectrality. The specter of postcolonial freedom is not a ghostly presence. It is rather the "incarnation of autonomized spirit in an aphysical body that is then

---

59. Ibid., 303.

taken on as the living subject's real body."⁶⁰ The specter is not a "nonactual phantom" but a result of the process of spectrality which arises out of our freedom enacted in space and time. Spectrality is "coextensive with our radical finitude" which also grounds the radical alterity that makes all presence possible without being a presence itself. Cheah writes:

> What Derrida points to is the original exposure of any body to alterity, not only in the maintenance of its already constituted form, in the process of its self-identity, its being proper to itself. This other is not a secondary reflection a living body generates to reproduce and transform itself. It precedes and constitutes the body even though it does not belong to it as its other. This alterity is so radical that it is not a thing or another present being, not even an infinite, absolute, self-causing presence called God. It is absolutely contingent, but it is, at the same time, the absolutely necessary condition of our existence.⁶¹

Since spectrality occurs in time, it offers not only the hope that freedom can be actualized but also the (im)possible conditions of its incarnation. Spectrality is not an occasion for the abdication of ethics and responsibility; indeed, it radicalizes both. It is in the here and now, in this time and place, that an (im)possible incarnational freedom must be actualized. In the context of the nation-state, it is the specter of the nation which haunts the state. Cheah forthwith argues that the spectral nation must necessarily seek to incarnate as freedom those life giving visions of nation which are in contrast to the bourgeois state produced by its relation to global capital. In other words, the vision of nation articulated by the critics of the state is precisely the "apposite figure of freedom today."⁶²

Cheah, as has been demonstrated, is far from the Kantian paradigm of thinking freedom as the radical transcendence of finitude in the organism. Yet, he has drawn for us a complex genealogy of freedom, based as it was in European philosophy and incarnating itself in concrete contexts far removed from Europe. The organicist metaphor of freedom, so foundational for philosophy and cultural studies is breached by the (in)human vision of the spectral nation. The breaching is not a thorough repudiation of the organicist model; it is a radicalization of the model devoid of presence. Only as specter can the nation form unburden itself of nationalist ideology and only as specter can it haunt both the bourgeois state as well as global capital

---

60. Ibid., 385.
61. Ibid., 387; emphases in the original.
62. Ibid., 395.

processes. Hauntology reveals the ghost within the ontopolitical nature of postcolonial freedom. Cheah concludes his book with these words:

> The postcolonial nation must be seen as a specter of global capital (double genitive): it is originally infected by the prosthesis of the bourgeois state as the terminal of capital. But it is also specter that haunts global capital and awaits reincarnation, the undecidable neuralgic point that refuses to be exorcised. That is why it is the most apposite figure of freedom today.[63]

Performing Postcolonial Freedom

What do Spivak and Cheah contribute to the postcolonial conversations on freedom? Right away it can be noted that talk about freedom in a postcolonial context is not unmoored from its historical and philosophical development in eighteenth century Europe. Freedom in postcolonial contexts has to do also with the manner in which community or democratic living is imagined and organized. Neither Spivak nor Cheah is interested in the now bankrupt method of postcolonial theory underscoring simple cultural identity or social inscription as the basis of liberation and freedom. Both, however, drive home the need to examine critically the modern and philosophical notion of freedom for the hoary figure discernible in the margins of those narratives. Their methods intensify and clarify each other. For example, it might look as if Spivak's method of deconstruction only examines the epistemological limits of Kant's notion of freedom. Yet, she identifies the mechanism of violence towards the "raw man" in Kant only to assert that the poorest woman of the South "invaginates" the pages of her book. Invagination highlights the presence of the part which contains the whole, "a chiastic relationship,"[64] and the outlines the contours of a political feminist anthropology. Recall also that Spivak argues that the transcendental framework of freedom, Kant's own deconstructive move, seemed to her to provide a positive source for thinking about transcendence. Freedom as transcendence is located in concrete immanent reality, a positive resource for feminist politics. Kant cannot be condemned simplistically as an European privileged male; rather, since feminist politics is able to utilize the transcendental framework, care must be taken to read Kant strategically. Conversely, Cheah's proposal asserts that moving beyond modern philosophy and Kant's organismic vitalism is a critical necessity for postcolonial contexts. Thus Cheah, in contrast to Spivak

---

63. Ibid.
64. Spivak, CPR, 70. See also n88.

traces the limits of Kant's ontology of freedom. A close reading, however, has shown that that neither is allergic to Kant's transcendental framework. Cheah for example needs the Kantian idea of organic life to complicate the idea of nation in relation to teleological time. The arguments indicate the aporias in the transcendental framework by emphasizing Kant's rhetorical choices on the one hand and on the other the excess of transcendence that always and already contaminates transcendental freedom in teleological time. Freedom in both proposals is haunted by a hoary alterity lurking in the margins, always seeking to be incarnated and enfleshed. Consequently, a postcolonial framing for freedom performs a strategic reading in view of radical critical politics which traces its genealogy to Western and modern philosophy and moves beyond it.

Freedom in both also escapes a Marxist deterritorialization, while simultaneously using Marx to reveal class privilege. Both Cheah and Spivak argue that decolonization must be territorialized, that is, speaking from particular perspectives of gender or racial identity, mobilized in view of a strategic attempt to counter violence. Indeed, participative and representative democracy is for both the key to resisting newer forms of colonial violence. Thus both perform readings of influential European thinkers but in contexts unimagined by these thinkers. The difference between the two is also critical. Both, like Derrida, abhor ontopology. They are disparaging of it in different ways which throws light on their differing agendas. For Spivak, it is critical theory, specifically feminist in its orientation, which challenges "ontopology and identitarian culturalisms."[65] That is, a feminist critique, (rather than a postcolonial reconstruction) of those systems configuring freedom must be directed in view of the poorest woman of the South. For her, the global context of capitalist exploitation and its disproportionate effect on poor women from the South is the critical task at hand. In a more recent assessment of her now famous query "Can the subaltern speak?" Spivak decries the rise of hauntology employed by masculinist critics.[66] Capitalism's mode of exploitation undercuts those agendas which construe haunting as an ethical strategy. "Woman" inscribed within nationalist and global projects sustained by modern capitalism is doubly silenced if her structured

---

65. Ibid., 404.

66. See Spivak, "Can the Subaltern Speak?," 21. She writes: "Women outside of the mode of production narrative mark the points of fadeout in the writing of disciplinary history even as they mime "writing as such," footprints of the trace (of someone? something? we are obliged mistakenly to ask) that efface as they disclose. If . . . the mode of production narrative is the final reference, these women are insufficiently represented or representable in that narration. We can docket them, but we cannot grasp them at all. The possibility of possession, of being haunted, is *cut* by the imposition of the tough reasonableness of capital's mode of production" (emphasis added).

subjectivity and imposed silence is the source for liberation and freedom. Thus hauntology is limited in her view. What hauntology is possible for ethics when the transglobal coding of "woman" is ignored? A feminist perspective on freedom is strongly critical of masculinist political theory which can afford these occlusions in which the freedom for "woman" is subsumed into a general category of freedom. Woman as the subject and object of ethics infinitely complicates philosophy, politics and cultural theory and the trope of "haunting woman" is meaningless.

Cheah goes after ontopology in view of his desire to excavate the dependence on the organicist ideal for nationalism. Drawing on Derrida he asserts that ontopologies, only present an "outmoded doctrine of self-present place."[67] Such ontopologies result in the death of the nation; it simply plays into a mechanism of social ascription. This is not however, to herald the death of the people. For Cheah, such a dismissal of nation is hasty and ill-advised. The nation is dead if one reads it ideologically instead of spectrally. Political theory can assert a reterritorialized ontopology because it invigorates a statist decolonization precisely as an "organismic persuasion."[68] But one may not forget that as organismic persuasion, the postcolonial state "stands between the living nation-people and dead global capital, pulling on both even as it is pulled by both."[69] It is the specter of nation that haunts the postcolonial state and strikes at the heart of any vitalist ontology. Freedom's incarnation is (im)possible and makes the homeland *unheimlich*. Nation is uncanny.

Further, the vitalist strand remains important as a critical necessity precisely in the face of deterritorialized global finance. Freedom is not an escape from one's historical and cultural conditions; freedom is a way of being in specific contexts which then generates forms of knowledge and action necessary for neutralizing the axiomatic of imperialism, but attentive always to the spectral possibilities that haunt the national narratives of cultural and political particularity. For Cheah, the cultural and historical context is able to imagine forms of engagement with global capital that may be radical interventions for freedom and liberation. Thus political ontologies, attempting to speak of human agency in ways that are non-modern and inclusive of ghosts and specters; spiritual work is key for liberation agendas. As ongoing work in view of freedom, such a non-modern and (post) colonial[70] work

---

67. Cheah, *Spectral Nationality*, 392.

68. Ibid., 225.

69. Ibid., 394.

70. In saying (post) colonial, I want to signal the unease with which Cheah approaches the canon of postcolonial literature.

"makes nationalism neither the political telos of modernity's unfinished project nor its betrayal, as its defenders and opponents want to believe, but instead the political aporia of modern freedom."[71] A spirituality of nation re-members the hovering specters of the more-than-the-people and more-than-the-state into its present narrative.

What, then, has this performance of reading Spivak and Cheah reading Kant yielded? It seems to me that postcolonial freedom is realized in a dialectical movement between cultural studies and philosophy in view of decolonization. The reading of the two together underscores the idea that it is not simply cultural critique that has valence for political liberation or philosophical precision that clarifies freedom in the postcolonial context. Their reading of Kant and the two readings of Kant presented together in this essay argue that Kant cannot be ignored in the context of postcolonial politics. For example, modern democracies will draw on Kant positively for agency. However, only a critical strategy of reading, that is freedom as deconstruction, will show that the Kantian ideal freedom is least visible in the muted women of the South, who even when they speak and act, are inscribed within a narrative organized by global capital. Revealing this form of oppression requires Spivak's attention to the rhetorical matrix of freedom. On the other hand, it is Cheah's proposal which actually concretizes Kant's transcendental freedom in the assertion that culture ought to be understood as an analogue of freedom. Postcolonial thinkers such as Talal Asad and Saba Mahmood have argued variously that Western liberal notions of freedom and agency necessarily need to be complicated by narratives of freedom and agency that are culturally and religiously inscribed. Ontopologies therefore, confound liberal Western notions of nation as multicultural, if the underlying argument for multicultural is assimilation managed by global capitalism. Freedom here is countering the liberal West's idea of individualist autonomy usually unmoored from its religious and cultural roots.

Finally, in my reading, it is clear that neither thinker is inimical to the political investments of theology and religion though I have not presented any such analysis. Freedom's complex trajectory in the modern West has its roots in the Christian tradition. Neither Spivak nor Cheah follows this strand; they do not present any subjectivist grounding for freedom. Nevertheless, freedom is complexly related to nationalist discourses grounded as they are in a symbolic and ideational religious repertoire. It is evident that further constructive work thinking through the lens of Spivak's feminist politics and Cheah's (post) colonial political theory will invigorate postcolonial religious, theological and political narratives of freedom. A feminist

---

71. Ibid., 304.

deconstruction of theological proposals universalizing freedom without an adequate analysis of gender relations as organized by globalized capitalism can sharpen the call to justice and care in Christian ethics. An ontopology such as Cheah's goes far in suggesting a critical evaluation of nationalist policies constraining the freedom of all of a nation's inhabitants and a criticism of ordinary categories of citizenship. As a Christian theologian, it occurs to me that Spivak's suggestion that freedom is the immanent source of transcendence necessarily challenges those forms of secularized political theory that sidelines both woman and religion. Cheah's proposal that nationalism is a spirituality of the people, on the way to becoming by developing an ontopology, intensifies the feminist impulse though he does not present such an option. His development of hauntology also signals the space of excess and radical alterity which has always been the site of the holy in Christian theology. Both proposals advance the continuing potential of deconstructing theology at both its conceptual and discursive levels, resulting in an invaginating haunting of the more-than. In my view, performing such a deconstruction and dialectics is freedom's relationship to postcoloniality.

Bibliography

Cheah, Pheng. *Spectral Nationality: Passages of Freedom from Kant to Postcolonial Literatures of Liberation*. New York: Columbia University Press, 2003.
Derrida, Jacques. *Specters of Marx: The State of the Debt, the Work of Mourning, and the New International*. Translated by Peggy Kamuf. New York: Routledge, 1994.
Kant, Immanuel. *Critique of Teleological Judgment*.
Morton, Stephen. *Gayatri Chakravorty Spivak*. London: Routledge, 2003.
———. *Gayatri Spivak*. Cambridge, UK: Polity, 2007.
Spivak, Gayatri Chakravorty. "Can the Subaltern Speak?" In *Can the Subaltern Speak? Reflections on the History of an Idea*, edited by Rosalind C. Morris, 21–80. New York, Columbia University Press, 2010.
———. *A Critique of Postcolonial Reason: Toward a History of the Vanishing Present*. Cambridge: Harvard University Press, 1999.

20

Freedom and Human Rights
The Cosmopolitan Context of the Justification of Rights in Roman Catholicism

Francis Schüssler Fiorenza

The relationship between Roman Catholic theology and human rights has a very complex and long history. Unfortunately, a couple of assumptions are commonly accepted as true. There is the widespread claim that human rights are an invention of modernity in that the notion of subjective rights can be traced only to the modern European Enlightenment. There is the claim that Roman Catholic theology has been historically critical and hostile to the notion of human rights and only recently revised its view. The historical reality is much more complex and nuanced.

On the one hand, medieval canonists have shown that one can trace a pre-history of modern rights and one can discover elements of even of subjective human rights within the medieval period, indeed, as far back as the twelfth and thirteenth century.[1] In addition, the discovery of the new worlds and the brutal Spanish conquest with its "wholesale slaughter" of the indigenous people—as Bartholomé de las Casas labeled it—was a

---

1. Tierney, *The Idea of Natural Rights*. Reid, "The Canonistic Contribution to the Western Rights Tradition; and Coleman, "Medieval Discussions of Human Rights"; Mäkinen and Korkman, *Transformations in Medieval and Early-Modern Rights Discourse.*

decisive turning in Catholic theology.[2] It led in sixteenth-century Spain to a new understanding of human rights and freedom that saw the need for international standards that could be applied to the new world.[3] Though this understanding was not accepted without debate and contestation, an ecclesiastical court came down on the side of the critics of the barbarous treatment of the native Americans and the defenders of their rights.

On the other hand, as is well-known, Pope Pius VI objected to the "French Declaration of the Rights of Man." He contested its assertion of the freedom, equality, and fraternity of all males (clearly limited to males as French indicates). In his view the equality of all was a preposterous idea--contrary to common sense and evidence. Pope Gregory XVI's encyclical *Mirari vos* (1832) condemned the right of freedom of conscience as a madness (*deliramentum*) along with the freedoms of opinion and of press and it objected to the separation of church and state. Similar rejections of religious freedom can be found in Pope Pius IX's encyclical *Quanta Cura* (1864) and its appendix listing errors. (*Syllabus Errorum*). A much more positive, though limited, conception of rights emerges in Leo XIII's affirmation of the right to a living wage in his social encyclical *Rerum Novarum* (1891).

Instead of tracing the varied debates about freedom and human rights throughout Roman Catholic theological tradition, this essay focuses primarily on the affirmation of human rights in Roman Catholic Teaching after World War II as it developed in papal teaching and in Vatican II. I shall attempt to show that the emergence of a new understanding of human rights and human freedom within official Roman Catholic teaching parallels the developing conception human rights in the various documents of the United Nations in the same time period. In distinction to an earlier bourgeois understanding of human freedom and human rights, this new understanding of human rights resulted from an attempt to deal with the atrocities of World War II in both Europe and Asia. Both developments show an emerging cosmopolitan of understanding of human rights that was elaborated that in ways that highlighted the internation cooperation necessary for peace as well as the relationship between human rights of freedom and social rights. These two aspects: the cosmopolitan and social dimension of human rights have consequences for a political theology and for the relation between human freedom and human rights. This relation becomes increasingly important in view of the current postmodern contestations of

---

2. De las Casas, *A Short Account of the Destruction of the Indies*, 14.

3. Cavallar, *The Rights of Strangers*. See especially chapter 2 on "Vitoria and the Second Scholastic"; and Ruston, *Human Rights and the Image of God*.

human rights as bourgeois and Western despite claims of universality.⁴ It also provides a context to view the deconstructive unveilings of the ambiguous relationship between justice and law.⁵ This essay attempts to show that recent Catholic teaching on human rights as well as recent developments with the documents of the United Nations have a special significance in view of the experience of World War II and the issues facing us today.

The Affirmation of Human Rights in Catholic Teaching after World War II

Although the Second Vatican Council with its Constitution on the Church and the World Today (*Gaudium et spes*) and its Declaration on Religious Freedom (*Dignitatis humanae*) are decisive to any interpretation of Roman Catholic teaching about human freedom and human rights, they should be seen within the context of the development in papal teaching that took place during and after World War II. This development took place not only in the writings of Pope John XXIII, especially in his encyclical *Pacem in Terris*, but also in Pope Pius XII's papal messages and encyclicals. Pope Pius XII was pope during the period of World War II and its aftermath—the period in which the United Nation's Declaration about Humans Rights came into existence. Pope John XXIII's papacy and teaching on human rights took place during the expansion in the international and social understanding of human rights. Moreover, his invocation of Vatican II led to further affirmation and codification of this understanding of human freedom and rights.

Papal Statements on Human Rights in the Context of World War II

In his 1942 Christmas message, "The Internal Order of States and People," Pope Pius XII denounces Hitler and National Socialism.⁶ The Pope links the affirmation of human rights and the critique of totalitarian societies. He looks ahead toward a time of peace, admitting that "the road from night to full day will be long." As decisive first steps along this long path, the Pope sees the affirmation of the dignity of the human person that necessarily

---

4. See for example, Donnelly, *Universal Human Rights in Theory and Practice*; Douzinas, *The End of Human Rights*); and more recently Baudrillard's critique in *The Agony of Power*.

5. Derrida. "The Force of Law."

6. See http://papalencycilicals.net/Pius12/P12CH42.HTM.

entails "fundamental personal rights: rights to maintain one's corporeal, intellectual, and moral life, rights to religious formation and education, rights to conjugal and domestic society, right to work."[7] Pius XII also advocates the rehabilitation of the juridical order as another decisive step. Such an order should not be subject to special groups, classes, and programs. Instead, it should be juridical order, resting on the supreme domination of God that is "safeguarded from all human whims: a consciousness of an order over the unforgettable rights of man." Pius XII's defense of the human person's "inalienable right to juridical security, and by this very fact to a definite sphere of rights immune from all arbitrary attack" was clearly directed against the National Socialistic overturning of the juridical order. He outlines the importance of these rights for the state and for the post war renovation of society.

Two years later, in his Christmas message of 1944, "Democracy and a Lasting Peace," Pope Pius XII re-affirms the critique of the absolutism of the state, but underscores much more the needs for the unity of humankind and the family of all peoples.[8] He proposes that "an essential to peace is the establishment of international organization." It is quite clear that Pius XII's strong affirmation of human rights as a protest to totalitarian societies and his equally strong support for the legitimating and preventing role that international organization has for peace finds its correlation in the later development of the United Nations and its initial declaration of human rights. Pius XII explicitly counters the reliance on a balance power for security and peace with a legal system of collective security based on international institutions and respect for human rights.

Pope Pius XII's advocacy of human rights and the significance of international legitimacy and organizations for peace is further developed by Pope John XXIII in *Pacem and Terris*.[9] This encyclical more than any remains a significant marker for the Roman Catholic teaching on human rights. Pope John XXIII explicitly refers to Pius XII's affirmation in the 1942 Christmas message that human rights are "universal and inviolable and therefore altogether inalienable" (PT #9). The encyclical *Pacem in Terris* is decisive. It not only affirms Pius XII's advocacy of human rights, but also

---

7. Ibid.

8. See http://papalencycilicals.net/Pius12/P12XMAS.HTM.

9. See John XXIII, *Pacem in Terris: Encyclical of Pope John XXIII on Establishing Universal Peace in Truth, Justice, Charity, and Liberty*." April 11, 1963. http://w2.vatican.va/content/john-xxiii/en/encyclicals/documents/hf_j-xxiii_enc_11041963_pacem.html.

sets the way for the Second in Vatican Council, especially *Gaudium et spes*, and for future papal teaching.[10]

Pope John XXIII not only praises the establishment of the United Nations but argues that "a clear proof of the farsightedness of this organization is provided by the Universal Declaration of Human Rights."[11] He acknowledges these modern developments as "Signs of the Time." He is aware that some criticisms exist of the declaration. Nevertheless, the Pope asserts that the "declaration should be considered a step in the right direction of an approach toward the establishment of a juridical and political ordering of the world community."[12] In sections 11–27 of *Pacem and Terris*, Pope John XXIII gives a list of human rights that is very close to the list in the United Nation's Declaration. He not only refers rights to the political space of individuals within the state, but he also affirms the existence of moral, cultural, economic, and participatory rights.[13] In affirming human rights, Pope John XXIII underscores a correlation between rights and duties, thereby complementing the treatment of human rights with an analysis of human duties (sections 28–45).

Pope John XXIII's encyclical is significant for its cosmopolitanism. The traditional and classic principle about the "common good" is interpreted not so much in relation to the national state or to ethnic societies, but globally and internationally. The principles of nationalism and state sovereignty that had ruled Europe since the Peace of Westphalia in 1648 are now limited with an appeal to human rights and to international legitimacy. Human rights are not simply favors granted by national states, understood with certain absolutism of power or legitimacy. Instead the legitimacy of a nation state is limited both externally and internally: Internally in relation to the rights and the good of its citizens, and externally in relation to the solidarity and peace of human race. In short, the step that Pius XII took toward a cosmopolitan view of responsibility involving human rights and international legitimacy is further re-affirmed and advanced by Pope John XXIII.[14] The context of the statements of Pope Pius XII and Pope John XXIII is very similar to that of the declaration and conventions issued by the United Nations. Both reflect an overwhelming concern for international peace. Both correlate human rights with the limitation of national sovereignty not only

---

10. Utz, "Was heist 'Entwicklung' der päpstlichen Sozialdokrin?"

11. *Pacem in Terris*, especially, #142–145.

12. *Pacem in Terris*, especially, #144.

13. *Pacem in Terris*, especially, #18–22.

14. This cosmopolitanism of Pope John XXIII has, of course, been criticised from a more nationalist or "realist" or "power political" position; see Niebuhr, "*Pacem in Terris*: Two Views."

for the sake of safeguarding of citizens, but also for restricting the resort to war. Human rights limit national sovereignty for the sake of peace.

Affirmation of Freedom and Human Rights in Vatican II

Human rights is a topic for treatment within the Second Vatican Council in its Declaration on Christian Education (*Gravissimum educationis*), its Declaration on Religious Freedom (*Dignitatis humanae*) as well as in its Constitution the Church in the World Today (*Gaudium et spes*). The Declaration on Religious Freedom deals with one of the most controversial issues within the Council, that of freedom of religion. Its teaching represents a significant development beyond the teaching of Pope Leo XIII. It shifts the perspective on freedom of religion from an epistemological view of religious truth to a civic and legal perspective. It grounds the right to religion freedom upon the dignity of the human person and locates this freedom in relation to the civic juridical order. By distinguishing between the moral and the civic, the declaration makes possible two distinct affirmations. All individuals are obligated to seek the truth (religious and moral), but this obligation takes place within a civil context that does not contest the juridical and civic right to religious freedom.[15] Moreover, it locates religious freedom within a dynamic relationship: the freedom of the individual within contemporary society is related to the freedom of the Catholic Church within that same society. The Declaration also uses language similar to that of the documents of the United Nations insofar as it underscores the necessity of protecting human rights and human freedom of conscience.

Gaudium et spes has the character of a pastoral constitution in that it seeks to address the contemporary situation of the world.[16] The text of *Gaudium et spes* itself begins and ends with a careful description of the situation of the modern world. Any accusation that *Gaudium et spes* has an overly optimistic view of the world overlooks the Council's description of the modern world. On the one hand, there is an increased amount of technological resources and an increase in wealth. Yet, on the other hand, the contrast between the rich and the poor grows; the contrast between the well-off and impoverished becomes starker and starker. This contrast is one of the signs of the times that *Gaudium et spes* underscores in its interpretation of the signs of the time.

The text describes the growth of both scientific knowledge and technology along with the ensuing increase in the abundance of wealth,

---

15. See Böckenförde, "Die Bedeutung der Konzilserklärung über Religionsfreiheit."
16. See my treatment in "Vatican II."

resources and economic power, on the one hand. These are then correlated with the disproportionate increase in poverty, hunger, and illiteracy, on the other hand. The acceleration of the tempo of change results in an acceleration of the pressing imbalances of the modern world. The scientific spirit has impacted the cultural, psychological, and biological spheres and yet has led to an increased hunger for a dignified life and for spiritual meaning. Vatican II sees these imbalances as reflecting and stemming from the basic imbalance in the root of the human person. It is important to note that the Council affirms human dignity, human freedom, and freedom not abstractly, but concretely in relationship to disapportionate increase in poverty and in relation the political, economic, and international dimensions of the cause of poverty and of the threats to human dignity and peace. In addition, by referring to the rights of individuals and groups against totalitarianism, *Gaudium et spes* makes a cosmopolitican understanding of human rights central to its argument.

Such a procedure illustrates how the Council approaches dialogue with the modern world. It takes over a central concept and acknowledges the importance of that concept as a limit upon national sovereignty and totalitarian governments. In addition, it supports the transcendence of human rights over national interests through a theological foundation, namely, that understands the transcendence of human dignity in relation to divine transcendence. Moreover, *Gaudium et spes* display a significant historical consciousness in relation to previous church documents and its affirmation of human dignity and human rights displays its historical awareness of changing conditions.[17] *Gaudium et spes* notes the changes that the emphasis on human rights has for the life of the political community. This change is one of the signs of the times. In its very words, "Such changes have a great influence on the life of the political community, especially regarding the rights and duties of all in the exercise of civil freedom and in the attainment of the common good, and in organizing the relations of citizens among themselves and with respect to public authority."[18] The text notes that any dialogue and conversation between the church and world takes place with affirmations that range from the more universalistic to the more contingent and historical. Rather than simply appeal to the common good as if the common good were a-historical, *Gaudium et spes* argues that the common good should be interpreted in relation to the changing conditions of the time.

In this text, the Council acknowledges that there is in the "present a keener sense of human dignity" and it "attempts to bring about a

17. Forster, "Die Menschenrechte—aus katholischer Sicht."
18. *Gaudium et spes* #73.

politico-juridical order which will give better protection to the rights of the person in public life." At the same time, the document notes that in acknowledging the rights of groups, persons must not neglect their obligations or "duties toward political community."[19] *Gaudium et spes* sees in the protection of human rights, the condition for persons to participate in the political life and it condemns all political systems that denigrate civil and religious communities.[20]

In defending human rights *Gaudium et spes* clearly affirms human rights as decisive for resisting totalitarian developments within the nations and states of the twentieth century. It strongly affirms the need for international organizations to promote peace. These affirmations display a parallel development between the various human rights declarations of the United Nations and the statements from Pius XII through John XXIII to *Gaudium et spes*. The historical and political context of initial Declaration of Human rights in the United Nations' was World War II, the emergency legislation during the Nazi period, and the ensuing need for the multilateral justification. The later covenants of the United Nations increasingly bring to the fore social rights. To the extent that Third world countries were involved in the formulation of these covenants, they pointed to the need for social and welfare rights, whereas the United States was opposed. The U.S. not only refused to ratify some of these conventions, but they were not even submitted by the President to the U.S. Senate for ratification out of fear they would be rejected.

Gaudium et spes was promulgated in 1965. The European Social Charter, signed in Turin on October 18, 1961, sought to protect economic, social, and cultural rights.[21] The United Nations Covenant on Social and Economic rights was promulgated three years after *Gaudium et spes* in 1968. Obviously, similar developments and currents were under reflection at the same time in the decades of the 1950s and 1960s. Consequently, one sees similar emphases and developments in *Gaudium et spes* not only in its advocacy of peace and its affirmation of the necessity of human rights and international legitimacy for peace, but also in its concern for the economy and with the family. The imbalance in the modern world is not only present in the contrast between the advances of technology and science and human spiritual needs, but also in the contrast between the increase of wealth in some nations and areas and the poverty in others. In this context, *Gaudium*

19. Ibid.
20. *Gaudium et spes*, #73–76.
21. Nevertheless the states did not have to commit themselves to all the enumerated rights and avoided entitlements, as its appendix demonstrates, see Tomuschat, *Human Rights*, 30–31.

et spes points to social injustices and deprivations between the rich and the poor not only in terms of social rights but also in terms of peace and the unity of humankind.

Gaudium et spes concludes with a cosmopolitan vision of the world and the role of the church in regard to peace and solidarity among all humans. *Gaudium et spes* frames the dignity of the human person within a social and religious context. Although it points to human freedom in relation to human dignity, it defines human dignity and human nature relationally. The human person is understood not simply as an individual standing alone with freedom of choice. Instead, the human person exists socially in relation to other humans and to God. Hence, *Gaudium et spes* interprets the dignity of humans precisely by affirming that human persons have their dignity in their relation to one another and in their relation to God. One could say that *Gaudium et spes* brings anthropocentricism in relation to theocentricism.[22] Consequently, human persons have their dignity to the extent that they mirror and have their solidarity with God and express their dignity in peace and solidarity with their fellow humans.

Human Rights in Papal Teaching after *Gaudium et spes*

The teaching in *Gaudium et spes* concerning human rights has been continued and expanded by Paul VI, John Paul II, and Benedict XVI. After the death of Pope John XXIII at Pope Paul VI took over and continued the Council, but in a more cautious manner. His interventions withdrew some controversial issues from the Council and he sought that Council's conception of collegiality be clarified and interpreted within the context of papal authority. During the Council, he visited the United Nations and addressing it in French, "I proclaim to you that there are fundamental human rights and duties, dignity, freedom, and above all religious freedom."[23] His first social encyclical, *Populorum progresso* (1967) issued after the Council, follows the emphasis of *Gaudium et spes* on the increasing disparity between the rich and poor nations of world. The Pope underscores the importance of economic rights within the context of this contrast among the rich and poor nations.

---

22. Schrofer, "Kirche unterwegs zum Menschen."

23. (My own translation) "Ce que vous proclamez ici, ce sont les droits et les devoirs fondamentaux de l'homme, sa dignité, sa liberté, et avant tout la liberté religieuse." See Paul VI, "Discourse to the Organization of the United Nations on the Occasion of Its Twentieth Anniversary."

His successor, Pope John Paul II continues to affirm human rights within his specific philosophical and theological perspective.[24] In his October 1979 speech before the United Nations, John Paul II characterizes the 1948 declaration of human rights as a milestone on the long and difficult path of humanity.[25] He expresses concern that human rights are now endangered by utopianism and by a myth of progress. Both can lessen the safeguard of human rights to a diminution of human dignity. Twenty-five years later, the Pope again addresses the United Nations on the importance of freedom. He notes that violations of national and individual freedom that led to the United Nations and its charter continue today and so its importance remains today. Underscoring the economic injustices and the lack of democracy in totalitarian states, the Pope points to the necessity of economic justice as well as democracy. This leads him to call for an ethics of solidarity. Four years later in his "1999 World Day of Peace Message: Respect for Human Rights—The Secret of True Peace," he correlates respect for human rights with peace, as indicated by the very title of his address.[26] John Paul II's encyclical, *Redemptor Hominis* develops some of the same points in a different context. He emphasizes that human rights are based on the dignity of each human person and as such they provide the essential criterion for all political programs and regimes.[27] These rights should form the basis and standard of social justice within all political institutions.[28] In other words, they are stallwarts against totalitarianism.

In the course of his long papacy, some shifts take place in Pope John Paul II's approach. Though he continues to affirm human rights and religious freedom, he modifies his perspective and the grounding of these rights. Three shifts are significant: First, coming to the Papacy from his immediate experience in Poland, the Pope at first affirmed religious freedom as integral to the Catholic Church's opposition to atheistic communism. Although this perspective remains, he comes to see religious freedom in the modern world increasingly threatened by modern secularism. It is not just the totalitarianism of the communist world that he experienced, but the pervading influence of secularism within modern culture. He views this secularism entails a relativism and denial of the possibility of ascertaining religious truth. Consequently, a connection exists between his

24. See the essays Höffe, "Papst Johannes Paul II. und die Menschenrechte"; and Macheret, "Johannes Paul II. und die Menschenrechte."

25. John Paul II, "Address to the Fiftieth General Assembly of the United Nations Organization."

26. *Origins* 28 (1998) 240.

27. John Paul II, *Redemptor Hominis*, #17.

28. See his General Audience of August 11, 1978.

social encyclicals *Laborem exercens* (1981), *Sollicitudo rei socialis* (1987), *Centesimus annus* (1991), and his encyclicals on religious epistemology and truth, *Veritatis splendor* (1993), and *Evangelium vitae* (1995) that combat the relativism of modern culture.

Second, the Pope develops the contrast between secular culture as a "culture of death" and Christian faith as entailing a "culture of life" in detail in *Evangelium vitae*. The four roots of the culture of death are located in sin. They entail an exaggerated autonomous individualism, a skepticism toward truth, a lack of a sense of God, and inadequate understanding of the human person. He develops a phenomenological personalism that is ordered to the common good as a vision that counters a too individualistic conception of human freedom and dignity. Third, in line with the first two shifts, there is another change. Whereas his earlier statements follow the emphasis on the dignity of the human person as the ground of human rights, his later writings, especially his encyclical *Veritatis Splendor* bring much more into consideration a natural law argumentation. It is a very specific conception of natural law that is developed.[29]

Nevertheless, it is important to observe that just as Pope Pius XII and Pope John XXIII did, so too does Pope John Paul II underscore the importance of a juridification of human rights. It does not suffice merely to proclaim or declare that human rights exist, but they have to be given concrete form within positive civil legislation. In a message to the general secretary of the United Nations, on the thirtieth anniversary of the United Nation's Declaration of Human Rights, Pope John Paul II praised the declaration as a decisive and extraordinary step in support of the ideals of human rights. He points to the growing disregard for human dignity in all areas: not only is there an increase in non-governmental violence, but also in institutional, systemic, and state violence. In *Dives in misercorida* (November 30, 1980), John Paul II emphasizes the necessity of bringing the anthropocentric and the theocentric together, and he points out that the church does this through its focus on Jesus Christ. In his second social encyclical, *Sollicitudo rei socialis*, issued to commemorate the twentieth anniversary of Paul VI's *Populorum Progressio*, John Paul II highlights that human rights should not be understood in an isolated or as individualistic fashion, but rather within a societal and economic context. Societal and economic structures decisively impact human life. What is needed therefore is an ethic of solidarity. Such an ethic entails not only a dedication to the common good, but solidarity for the poor and for those suffering from the violations of human rights as a result of sinful structures, When John Paul II links the anthropocentric and

---

29. For an analysis of Pope John Paul II's interpretation of natural law, see Curran, *The Moral Theology of Pope John Paul II*.

the theocentric with one another, he does so through Christology and most often quotes the theological principle of section 22 of *Gaudium et spes*: it is in the mystery of the Incarnate word that the mystery of man takes on light.

His successor, Pope Benedict XVI, follows in the tradition established by his immediate predecessors, Pope Paul VI and Pope John XXIII. In 2008 he addresses the General Assembly of the United Nations at the sixtieth anniversary of the universal declaration and defends the Universal Declaration of Human Rights of the United Nations. He underscores the importance of the international character of human rights and the importance of the United Nation's role and responsibility to promote human rights. As *Gaudium et spes* did, he underscores the contrast between rich and poor nations and to the increasing inequality among social groups. He addresses the need for international intervention, when it is in accordance with international law. The failure to intervene in cases of horrendous violations of human s nation allows harm to increase.

Pope Benedict XVI's address to the United Nations re-affirms the United Nation's Universal Declaration of Human Rights.[30] His affirmation of international responsibility and his specific interpretation of the question of legitimacy of international intervention correlates with the framework of the original historical context of the Charter of the United Nations and declaration of human rights that sought to contravene the experiences of World War II. Pope Benedict XVI's own context was the events of 9/11 and the destruction of the World Trade Center Towers in New York that led to the invasion of Iraq by the United States. An invasion that had limited international approval. Both as Cardinal and as Pope he was critical of this military intervention in Iraq.

In his social encyclical *Caritas in veritate* (2009) that deals with social justice, Pope Benedict XVI emphasizes the role of charity in guiding justice and the importance of avoiding a culture of secularism and relativism. This critique of relativism echoes the cultural criticism that Pope John II had developed. It also mirrors his own theological writings as Prefect of the Congregation of the Christian Faith. In his writings both prior and after his election to the papacy, the Pope argues for an intrinsic relation between an affirmation of human dignity and a philosophical view that eschews relativism. His critique of pluralism (understood as religious indifferentism) and relativism (understood as a skepticism toward the truth) have been a constant theme of his writings. The affirmation of religious truth and a transcendent God correlates in his view with the affirmation of human rights and human dignity. This religious and metaphysical affirmation stands at

---

30. See Benedict XVI, Address to the United Nations.

the basis of his conception of human rights and the common good. His social encyclical contrasts such pluralism and relativism with the affirmation of human rights. Religious freedom should not be understood in a relativistic manner as religious indifferentism, but rather as the freedom and responsibility for what is true and good.

Therefore, he is able to defend the teaching of the Council's "Declaration on Religious Freedom" insofar as he carefully distinguishes between religious freedom as an expression of religious relativism and religious freedom as a concrete societal condition in modern society. In this regard, he follows Ernst-Wolfgang Böckenförde's interpretation of the significance of the Council's statement on religious freedom as a shift from a moral to a legal and societal point of view.[31] He also takes over Böckenförde's criticism of liberal society as being incapable of providing the basis for its own foundation. By following Böckenförde, he can interpret the council's document on religious freedom not so much as a rejection of the epistemological point of the previous Popes, but rather as the practical attempt to live in a pluralistic state. As a theologian and prefect of the Congregation he has cautiously interpreted *Gaudium et spes*. Though accepting it major points, he has been critical of its attempt to dialogue with the modern world and has viewed its vision as more optimistic.[32]

In summary, both Pope John Paul II and Pope Benedict acknowledge the significance of the human rights that *Gaudium et spes* has underscored. However, they argue that it is important to give these rights theological and philosophical basis that avoids the individualism and relativism which they see as dominant in modern culture. One can view their attempts to give this theological and philosophical grounding not only as a re-affirmation of human rights, but also as done in a way that counters what they see as negative not only within the modern economic situation, but also within modern Western culture.

Human Rights as a Cosmopolitan Response to World War II

The notion, foundation, and application of human rights are all contested. One controversial issue concerns the relation between human rights and the distinctiveness of religious beliefs; another is the relation of human rights to diverse cultures; another is whether rights represent the bourgeois culture

31. Böckenförde, "Die Bedeutung der Konzilserklärung über Religionsfreiheit."
32. See Ratzinger, *Theological Highlights of Vatican II*; and his commentary on *Gaudium et spes*, "Part I The Church and Man's Calling."

of the modern European West and therefore are colonial or imperialistic. An examination of the development of human rights in the post-World War II area, and in particular in the various declarations, protocols, and covenants of the United Nations can help resolves some of these debates.[33] After World War II, one sought to implement world peace in several ways. One was international institutionalization of human rights in order to prevent nations from genocidal actions toward its own citizens; another was the establishment and threat of multilateral sanctions in order to prevent nations from using force to achieve their ends. Both had the effect of relativizing national sovereignty. Both sought to integrate the actions of nations into the goal of peace for which the U. N. as world organization was established. Today as then these goals retain their utmost importance as recent political events and debates at the United Nations clearly indicates.

Human Rights in the Face of Atrocities and Emergency Legislation

The establishment of human rights in the United Nations Charter and in the Universal Declaration of the Human Rights is much more closely related to the crises of World War II than the critics of human rights often assume. The relation is vital for both understanding and for evaluating the cultural critique of rights. It also provides a context for the papal teaching that emerged after World War II and led to *Gaudium et spes*. When the United Nations General Assembly accepted the Universal Declaration of Human Rights in December 10, 1948, it was the beginning of decades of declarations and covenants concerning rights. The immediate and driving context of the development of human rights after World War II was both the memory of and the reaction to the atrocities before and during World War II. These took place worldwide, not only in Auschwitz, but also in Asia.

It is important to understand that the Universal Declaration of Human Rights was a specific response to a particular challenge for several reasons. First of all, the Declaration represents a significant and very specific understanding of human rights. Often, when contemporary critics of modernity and modern human rights criticize rights, they often refer to a specific interpretation of John Locke's philosophy or they claim that rights express nothing more than the possessive individualism of the Western bourgeoisie.[34] For these critics, rights are the epitome of Western individualism and possessivism. Therefore, in their criticism of rights, these critics appeal to

33. Lauren, *The Evolution of International Human Rights*.
34. See Macpherson, *The Political Theory of Possessive Individualism*.

non-Western conceptions of community or to pre-modern conceptions of ethics in order to criticize such a modern Western conception of rights. Such a view overlooks that how in the various declarations and covenants concerning Human Rights of the United Nations the social and environmental conventions became part and parcel of the understanding of rights. The later development in the following decades represents both a further and a distinct development of this initial reaction. The various covenants, elaborating a list of social rights, were urged by third world countries and the socialist nations. The United States has regrettably refused to sign many of these covenants—some were not even submitted to the United States Senate for ratification—lest it be obligated to alleviate the misery and poverty within poor nations. These rights have, over the years, been expanded to include environmental rights especially insofar as the environment represents a global challenge.

Likewise, it is obvious that a "bourgeois" understanding of human rights and freedom can be found in Roman Catholic teaching about right. In the treatment of human rights in *Gaudium et spes* and in the ensuing papal documents, there is the constant attempt to interrelate an understanding of rights with a commitment to the disparity between nations, to correlate rights and duties, individuals and communities. Pope John Paul II places human rights within the context of an ethics of solidarity and Pope Benedict XVI emphasizes the importance of environmental rights.

Secondly, the immediate post-World War II context for the development of rights is important for the interpretation of these rights. There is in the immediate formulation of rights the specific memory of suffering that resulted from the rise of National Socialism and the atrocities in Asia. The United Nations Charter itself and the various documents that constitute the International Bill of Rights responded to the atrocities of World War II by setting limits on "emergency" or "exception" legislation. The United Nations sought to prevent the future use of emergency legislation in the way that Hitler and the National Socialists had done prior to World War II. The Weimar Constitution (August 11, 1919) had Article 48 "If public safety and order in Germany are materially disturbed or endangered, the President may take the necessary measures to restore public safety and order, and, if necessary, to intervene with the help of the armed forces. To this end he may temporarily suspend, in whole or in part, the fundamental rights established in Articles 114, 115, 117, 118, 123, 124, and 153 paragraph 23." Under Hitler's encouragement, specific legislation was passed, namely, the *Reichstagsbrandverordnung und das Ermächtigungsgesetz*, that gave Hitler emergency powers. Hitler could appeal to the emergency clause of the Weimar Constitution itself on the occasion of the "emergency" of the burning of the

Reichstag to suspend basic rights. In addition, it gave Hitler a juridical basis for a foreign policy that justified pre-emptive wars against alleged threats to security. Consequently, Hitler could claim a juridical and constitutional basis for abolishing rights and for engaging in the pre-emptive invasions of France, Poland, Norway, and Denmark. Such actions had been envisioned even earlier. The last chapter of *Mein Kampf* was almost prescient when it was entitled "Notwehr als Recht."

The United Nations, therefore sought to contravene such unilateral appeals to exceptional emergencies by stipulating that collective and multilateral consensus was necessary for legitimacy.[35] It has been suggested that the United Nation's documents can be seen as "Hitler's Epitaph."[36] Article 51 of the United Nations Charter "internationalizes" the right of self-defense and so does article 39 for collective security. The international and collective nature of legitimacy should prevent individual nations from declaring on their own that a situation was an exceptional emergency situation that warranted the suspension of rights and pre-emptive attacks. The United Nations reinforced these safeguards through the fourth article of the International Covenant of Civil Rights and through the Genocide Treaty because these limited what could be done in such exceptional cases of responses for the sake of national security.

Hitler had appealed to the singularity of an emergency to justify his action. It would be wrong to think of Hitler's actions as if they were just the criminal acts of a mentally deranged dictator. One fails to understand Hitler unless one takes into account the theoretical convictions and the philosophical climate that justified Hitler's action. A very influential thinker at the time was the jurist, Carl Schmitt, a legal and political philosopher, known for his criticisms of liberalism, especially the bourgeois liberal political philosophy, expressed in the Weimar Republic. Against this contemporary liberalism, Carl Schmitt had appealed to the political theology of the French Restoration in order to argue that a sovereign's very power, that is, the nature of sovereignty itself, comes to the fore in emergency situations and in exceptional crises. Carl Schmitt had written *Gutachten on Notverordnungen* before 1933 and later developed a theoretical basis for Hitler's actions in his political theology. In addition to his defense of the sovereign on the basis of the divine power, he developed a political and ethical theory that challenged universal norms because of the paradox of legislation. Schmitt developed

---

35. Morsink, *The Universal Declaration of Human Rights*; and Glendon, *A World Made New*.

36. David Little has argued that Hitler's use of emergency can be seen as the background to the emergency legislation in the United Nations Charter and Documents. See Little, "Liberalism and World Order."

a "critique of normativism" that was a critique of universal norms based on the consideration that all legislation involves the exercise of power. The enactment of legal rights entails an exercise of sovereign power so that the very act of including also excludes. His critique of normativism had two elements. One was a critique of the existence of universal values that came to be expressed in diverse positions, such as early liberal conceptions of natural law, modern legal positivism, and the universalistic moral ideal that undergirds the liberal aspiration requiring politics to be subject to universal moral norms.[37] The other was the chasm or gap that exists between any norm, ideal, or principle, and any application, realization, and legislative enactment.

When, therefore, the United Nations affirmed the universality of human rights and insisted that appeals to emergency, exception, and pre-emption needed collective legitimation, it was affirming a position that stood in stark contrast to the Nazi appeal to exception. In formulating the universality of human rights, it starkly contrasts with contemporary appeals to exceptionalism. Today, in the face of the collapse of the World Trade Center, the President of the United States and the Attorney General of the Justice Department have appealed to a similar rationale of "exception" and "emergency" and have sought and are seeking similar "exception legislation." There is a certain parallelism to their defense of the power of the President to act in such exceptional cases and Schmitt's theoretical and theological defense of a sovereign's exceptionalism. Hitler used the burning of the Reichstag in 1933, just as now, seventy years later, in the wake of September 11, the curtailing of basic rights is taking place in the name of an exceptional emergency. The US Patriot's Act allows the detention of prisoners without warrants, public trials, or lawyers.[38] It curtails a host of political and civil rights. Likewise, appealing to national security, President Bush has announced a policy of pre-emptive military attacks, even in the absence of an immediate threat.[39] In addition to the enactment of "The Homeland Security Act of 2002," the controversial "Domestic Security Enhancement

---

37. See Scheuerman, "Carl Schmitt's Critique of Liberal Constitutionalism," where Scheuerman revises his earlier interpretation of Schmitt's view of "Normativism" as well as that of Matthias Kaufmann; Scheuerman, *Between the Norm and the Exception*. See also, Kaufmann, *Recht ohne Regel?* For Scheuerman's fuller development, see his *Carl Schmitt*; and Dyzenhaus, *Law as Politics*; Dyzenhaus, *Legality and Legitimacy*; and Dyzenhaus, *Recrafting the Rule of Law*.

38. The official title is: "Uniting and Strengthening America by Providing Appropriate Tools Required to Intercept and Obstruct Terrorism Act (Oct. 25, 2001)" HR 3162 RDS.

39. In this context, Pope Benedict XVI's talk to the United Nations is especially relevant.

Act of 2003" (sometimes referred to as "Patriot Act II") further increases the powers of the Executive Branch, especially the Justice Department and the FBI and abridges political rights. The declarations by the Secretary of Defense that the prisoners in Guantanamo are not subject to the Geneva Conventions has led to the abuse of enemy combatants and other prisoners. Such declarations and actions violate the third convention of the Geneva Conventions which was enacted to protect the rights of prisoners of war as well as the fourth convention which was intended for the sake of civilians in the war-time.

These events show that Carl Schmitt's political theology advocated positions that need to be critically examined because of the present parallelism, if not link, between the contemporary political argument connecting the exercise of Presidential sovereignty with emergency situations.[40] The use of sovereign power in exceptional situations was a focal point that distinguished a sovereign from an administrator. The opening sentence of Schmitt's Political Theology reads, "The sovereign is the one who decides about the state of exception."[41] In cases of emergency, the sovereign has the "explicit power to suspend basic rights, the basic rights are no longer an obstacle to his measures."[42] At the center of his political theology stands not only an emphasis on the state of exception, but also on a sharp separation between friend and enemy. Schmitt's political and constitutional theory rests on the substitution of ethnos for demos, an ethnic group for a people. He underscored the cultural oneness of the ethnos in the face of the enemy.[43] Emergencies and exceptional situation are used as the justification for the denial of basic human freedoms and rights. Such a viewpoint places his political theology, with its emphasis upon the importance of ethnos, in sharp contrast to any political theology that has a cosmopolitan view of the world of nations.

Human Rights and Social Problems of Third World

The United Nations Declaration of Human Rights should not be seen just as the end of a development; it is also the beginning of a development. In contemporary discussions of human rights, it is customary to refer to

---

40. For accounts of the English reception of Schmitt, see Drury, *Leo Strauss and the American Right*; see also McCormick, *Carl Schmitt's Critique of Liberalism*; and Manemann, *Carl Schmitt und die Politische Theologie*, 201–21.

41. Schmitt, *Political Theology*.

42. Schmitt, *Legality and Legitimacy*, 73.

43. See Preuss, "Constitutional Powermaking for the New Polity," 650.

three distinct stages of the development of rights, with each of the stages involving a distinct set or type of rights. The first type involves what is often known as negative rights or rights that entail certain civil liberties. Such rights prohibit states from interfering with an individual's personal freedom, such as the freedom of speech, or from violating the personal bodily integrity of persons through torture. A second stage, usually referred to as positive social or economic rights, entitles groups or individuals to certain social services or goods that the state provides. Examples of such social and economic rights include the right to work or the right to social security. More recently, a third stage or dimension of rights, much more complex, has been elucidated, such as the right to peace or the right to a healthy environment. Although these rights have been sometimes enumerated in terms of "generations" because historically and chronically their articulation and establishment have succeeded one another, such an historical division of rights should not over look mutual interdependence of rights.[44] Economic rights often provide necessary conditions for the exercise of civil liberties and environmental rights or peace provide the necessary conditions for economic and social rights.

The horrors and atrocities of World War II formed the background to the establishment of the 1945 Charter of the United Nations and the 1948 Universal Declaration of Human Rights. In this sense the rights in the original declaration sought to protect individuals from the abuses of sovereign state power. The two decades following saw the further development of rights. There was the 1951 convention relating to the status of Refugees; the 1952 convention affirming the political rights of women, the 1954 recognition of the status of stateless persons, and the 1956 convention on the abolition of slavery, slave trade, and practices of similar slavery. These conventions and treatises cited the Universal Declaration of Human Rights in their documents and sought to implement and expand the scope of the Declaration. 1966 began another set of covenants and rights. These covenants on civil and political rights included the covenant on economic social, and cultural rights, and on the elimination of all forms of social of racial discrimination. These were followed in 1967 with the convention against discrimination against women, and in 1968 with the protocol on the status of refuges. The adoption by the United Nation's General Assembly in 1966 of the International Covenant on Economic, Social, and Cultural Rights along with the International Covenant on Civil and Political Rights marked a significant step forward in the development of human rights.

---

44. For the critique of the language of "generations of rights," see Wellman, "Solidarity, the Individual and Human Rights."

Both treatises built upon and extended the Universal Declaration of Human Rights.

In the period following World War II, a distinctive understanding of human rights resulted from complex and diverse struggles. This development occurs much more as a winding path rather than as multi-lane highway moving in one clear direction. The Western powers were reluctant to have their sovereignty limited by international human rights. However, the atrocities of World War II and the demands its victims led them to acknowledge the importance of rights that limited the ability of sovereign states to harm their people and to affirm the necessity of collective legitimation for claims of self-defense. Elements of this history are often neglected by critics of human rights who see rights as nothing but expressions of Western imperialism. It was China, victimized by the war, that insisted on rights affirming the equality of all. Eleanor Roosevelt, who had been at the forefront of the advocacy of rights, was asked to resign. In fact, in 1953 not only was Eleanor Roosevelt asked to resign, but John Foster Dulles enunciated a major shift. The United States would stop cooperating in the Human Rights Commission's work on a binding convent or covenants. Dulles praises the critics for having pointed out that these treatises would impose "socialistic conception," and he notes that the critics had, therefore, "performed a genuine service in bringing the situation to the attention of the American public."[45] In the context of this reaction within the United States to the social conventions of the United Nations, the Catholic teaching in Vatican II and in the various papal documents precisely on the disparity between the rich and poor nations receives its acute relevance.

Contestability of Cosmopolitan Human Rights as a Challenge to Political Theology

Although the support for human rights and human freedom is widespread, there is at the same time an increasing critique of human rights in postmodern and postcolonial theory.[46] It is one the signs of our times that, on the one hand, the advocacy of human rights language is seen as essential for human freedom, while, on the other hand, such language is questioned as a specifically modern Western and European heritage that should not be imposed upon others or should be suspended in terms of national security or in terms of integrity of cultural and ethnic identity. The current political critique of rights relies in no small degree on the criticisms of constitutionalism, liberal

45. Glendon, *A World Made New*, 205.
46. See Souillac, *Human Rights in Crisis*.

democracy, and of "normativism" that were advanced by Carl Schmitt during the Nazi period. This critique has been taken up in part by Schmitt's student Leo Strauss, a person whose political philosophy, as the popular newspapers have also noted, has had considerable influence upon the Neo-Conservatives within the Pentagon.[47] Consequently, the current cultural and philosophical critique of human and political rights poses a challenge to political theology that raises anew the problem of the relation between political theology and political practice, between interpretation and action, between theology and human rights.[48]

The "contestability" of human law and rights comes to the fore in the following challenges. First, the ambivalence of the de facto invocation of legal rights is evident from many historical examples. Although human rights were invoked to protest the exploitation and massacre of the American Indians, they were equally appealed to in order to legitimate the property rights of the colonialist countries. Likewise, there is the post World War II emphasis on highlighting the atrocities perpetuated by the Germans (against which Carl Schmitt protested) and the Japanese, whereas the atrocities of the allies in firebombing of cities, so well documented by Jörg Friedrich in *Der Brand*, were overlooked.[49] Similarly, powerful capitalist countries often place a greater emphasis on property rights, copyrights, and patent rights than on social rights as conditions for membership in international trade and banking organizations. Today, the struggle against AIDS is hampered because the profit-bearing patent rights of pharmaceutical companies often take priority over the rights of the gravely ill to life-saving medicines. The invocation of human rights has historically been one-sided: exercised by the powerful and victors rather than by the weak and the victims. An element of indecidability and of contingency exists that cannot be fully incorporated into such universal principles. Bonnie Honig underscores this point in her comparison of Derrida and Arendt's analysis of the American Declaration of Independence and Constitution. She brings Derrida and Schmitt close together by suggesting: "Derrida's point like Nietzsche's is that in every system

47. See Atlas, "The Nation: Leo-Cons: A Classicist's Legacy: New Empire Builders." Frachon and Vernet, "The Strategist and the Philosopher."

48. Attorney General of the United States John Ashcroft responded as follows during a Senate hearing in December 2001: "To those who scare peace-loving people with phantoms of lost liberty, my message is this: 'Your tactics only aid terrorists, for they erode our national unity and diminish our resolve. They give ammunition to America's enemies.'" Similarly, President Bush divided the world into friends and enemies: those who are with us and those who are against us. It is Bush's voice, but Schmitt's understanding of political sovereignty, his contrast between friend and enemy, and his advocacy of a homogeneous culture and people.

49. Friedrich, *Der Brand*.

(every practice), whether linguistic, cultural, or political, there is a moment or place that the system cannot account for. Every system is secured by placeholders that are irrevocably, structurally arbitrary, and prelegitimate."[50]

Schmitt's *Political Theology* highlights the importance of what is an exception, an interruption, or an extreme situation by alluding to Kierkegaard's suspension of the ethical. Schmitt writes: "The exception can be more important to it than the rule, not because of the romantic irony for the paradox, but because the seriousness of an insight goes deeper than the clear generalizations inferred from what ordinarily repeats itself. The exception is more interesting than the rule. The rule provides nothing; the exception proves everything."[51] A similar emphasis upon exception not only pervades much of the contemporary political response to the terrorist acts of September 11, but also pervades the critique of liberal political philosophy and an ethics based upon transcendental principles. Schmitt overcomes the distance between norms, ideals, and principles through a pure decisionism.

Today, many critics of the culture of liberalism and many critics of human rights approximate Schmitt's decisionism. The appeal to Schmitt's political theology as a critique of a more rationalistic conception of consensus may have a point, but the question remains whether his conception of the normative aspects of politics suffices.[52] The contemporary emphasis on the absolute singularity of the ethical experience in some critics and on the emphasis that rules and regulations need to be conceived ex nihilo in order to effect the transition from ethics to politics comes close to Schmitt's decisionism. Such a decisionism, almost like a leap of faith, is echoed by Derrida: "That far from ensuring responsibility, the generality of ethics incites to irresponsibility. It impels me to speak, to reply, to account for something, and thus to dissolve my singularity in the medium of the concept."[53]

One cannot evaluate Schmitt's conception of political theology without examining the role that his political theology served in the 1930s and

50. Honig, "Declarations of Independence"; Derrida, "Declarations of Independence." See also Mouffe, *The Return of the Political*; and Mouffe, *The Democratic Paradox*. For an analysis of Arendt and Schmitt, see Kalyvas, *Democracy and the Politics of the Extraordinary*.

51. Schmitt, *Political Theology*, 15.

52. See the recent essay by Bernstein, "The Aporias of Carl Schmitt," with the judicious judgment: "Perhaps the most fundamental aporia in Carl Schmitt is that he leads us with clarity and brilliance to an appreciation of the normative-moral issues that must be confronted if we are to avoid unrestrained and unlimited violence. Yet at the same time, he dismisses—and undermines—the very possibility of seriously confronting these urgent issues" (424). On the issue of pluralism, see Sluga, "The Pluralism of the Political."

53. Derrida, *The Gift of Death*, 61.

without ask—now eighty years later--how does one deal with today's political challenges and problems?[54] Does it call for apocalyptic interruption or does it call for a link between Christian hope and human rights?[55] Does it call for "undecidability" as Jacques Derrida's political philosophy emphasizes? Does it ridicule the "assumed universalism" of rights with the label of "Esperanto" as George Lindbeck and Michael Walzer do, when they prioritize the local and particular over the universal? Do today's international challenges and crises allow one to belittle international rights as an Esperanto?[56] Does not, instead, the international aspect of the challenge call for a more cosmopolitan vision? The destruction of the World Trade Center is indeed a quite different event from the burning down of the German parliament building (*Reichstag*). Nevertheless, the use of "exception" legislation to weaken basic rights and to justify "pre-emptive" wars without imminent danger is formally very similar.

Such an emphasis upon singularity should be countered by the memory that rights legislation arose in response to the suffering during the World War II and in reaction to the political and theological justifications that national emergencies of self-defense require the suspension of basic rights. To eliminate such exceptions and interruptions, the United Nations affirmed a cosmopolitan view of legitimacy and an international view of human and political rights. Similarly, the post World War II papal teaching on right underscored the need for international institutions, cooperation, and legitimacy. Although the exercise and practice of rights is often deficient, the way to overcome these deficiencies is to keep constantly present the suffering that these rights seek to prevent.

The question remains: what are the implications of my interpretation of Declaration of Human Rights by the United Nations, the affirmation of human rights in *Gaudium et spes*, and the papal documents preceding and following it? In my view, it shows us something important about the nature of a religious and political theological engagement with modernity and the modern world. *Gaudium et spes* is clearly not a capitulation to the modern world, as some critics today would maintain. It exhibits an engagement with the modern world that takes seriously the technological and communicative developments that have in some ways brought all parts of the globe in

54. For a fuller development of a theological response to this question, see my essay, "Prospects for Political Theology in the Face of Contemporary Challenges."

55. See the helpful analysis of Jürgen Moltmann's understanding of human rights: Henley, "Theology and the Basis of Human Rights."

56. Walzer, *Thick and Thin*, 9. Walzer has later clarified (if not modified) his earlier critique of the universal nature of human rights; see Walzer, "Beyond Humanitarian Intervention."

relationship to with one another. At the same time, it argues that despite these development (and perhaps in part because) the inequalities between the rich and poor both within nations and between nations and parts of the globe have intensified. Therefore, *Gaudium et spes* as well as the papal teaching since World War II spell out the need for international cooperation and even authority.

What should a political theology spell out in regard to the relationship between Christian churches and this globalized world? It should not stand for the act of eliminating basic civil rights by appealing to emergency legislation (as was unfortunately done in World War II or now); it should support the attempts of the United Nations to outlaw genocide and to subject emergency legislation to multilateral and multinational legitimation? It should resist the recent claims made by the United States government that its treatment of prisoners of war (alleged terrorists) stands outside of the Geneva Conventions and that cruel behavior is legitimate. It should support the International Covenant on Economic, Social, and Cultural Rights with its emphasis on social and economic rights or bring a critical awareness to the refusal of rich countries, especially the United States, to resist the acknowledgement of any obligation to societies and peoples in dire need, especially many argue that the poverty and hunger of the world is in no small part due to the exploitation of the powerful rich nations.

The development of human rights provides a crucial example in which one can see the significance of Pope John XXIII and his invocation of Vatican II.[57] One can clearly see how in his support of peace and the need for cosmopolitan laws and institutions how Pope John XIII initatiated the Vatican II the transition of the Catholic church away from a church focused mainly on Europe to one reflecting the global task as Karl Rahner's interpretation of the Council highlights. Nevertheless, in its analysis of the failures and deficiencies of the modern world it highlights dimensions that Cardinal Joseph Ratzinger's interpretation of the Council brings to the fore. In entering into dialogue with the modern World, *Gaudium et spes* not only points to an absence of spiritual meaning in a world dominated by science and technology, but also it strives to give a religious foundation to human dignity and a transcendent foundation to human rights.

This analysis suggests that it would be erroneous to view human rights primarily or exclusively as a reflection of the bourgeois "modern West."[58]

---

57. On a comparison between Karl Rahner and Joseph Ratzinger's interpretation of *Gaudium et spes*, see my essay on *Gaudium et spes* in Weaver, ed., *The Church and Human Freedom*. Rahner is noted for his interpretation of the Council as a transition point from a Western European Church toward one that goes beyond it.

58. See MacIntyre, *After Virtue*, 70; and Lindbeck, "The Gospel's Uniqueness,"

The post World War II development of human rights has its basic historical context the basic suspending of human rights under the National Socialistic regime. Yet its response was not only the affirmation of the human rights, but the emphasis that only international collective judgments can provide legitimacy for exceptional situations. At the same time, we can see today a resistance to the implementation of human rights because they limit national sovereignty and impose social obligations. Just as United States in the 1950s and following opposed such limitations and such obligations. Moreover, the post World War II development of the various covenants that extended the scope and breath of the Universal Declaration of Human Rights often came from non-Western countries. These underscored the social obligations and issues of social welfare and the duties of richer countries over against poorer countries. Freedom and obligation were linked together.

However, at the same time the attempt at the United Nation in securing of rights over against national totalitarianism went hand-in-hand with an attempt not to appeal to a specific historical cultural and religious heritage. Hence there was no appeal to a specifically religious interpretation or foundation of rights in a transcendent belief. In going beyond the notion of rights formed within the modern Western bourgeois period, the Declaration of Universal Rights of the United Nations sought to underscore that peace and security required not only rights but also multi-national juridification and legitimation. It was concerned with gathering international support for human rights, from all countries and cultures. Therefore, it was cosmopolitan in the sense that it sought to embrace diverse cultures, non-theistic as well as atheist.

Gaudium et spes stands in the same historical context. It takes up as a sign of the times, not only the distance between the technological and scientific world and the spiritual hunger of human person, but also the striving for peace on an international scale. It is within this context that *Gaudium et spes* enters into dialogue with the world. On the one hand, it sees this striving for peace and it acknowledges the importance of human dignity that underlies the language about rights.[59] On the other hand, it seeks to give a transcendent foundation for human rights in the Christian religious belief in God and in Christ. It seeks to bring together a theocentric and anthropocentric viewpoint with reference to international and global needs: not just social and economic, but also in regard to peace. It is on this point that one sees further development in the papal teaching after Vatican II.

especially 427.

59. For a survey of the teaching about peace, see Nagel, *Die Friedenslehre der katholischen Kirche*.

From Paul VI to John Paul II and to Pope Benedict XVI, human right and human freedom on placed within the context of global peace. As Roman Catholic Christians they seek to develop a religious justification for human rights that includes global solidarity with the poor, oppressed and exploited. This religious justification underscores the ambiguities of the technological and scientific progress of modernity and highlights the spiritual hunger of human nature. In acknowledging the importance of cosmopolitan solidarity and unity for peace, Vatican II and papal teaching attempts to show how Christian traditions and beliefs can contribute to peace.

Today, the issues of globalization and peace remain as central to our concerns as they were at the end of World War II and at the time of Vatican II. Therefore, the need for the religious engagement with a religious support for cosmopolitan justification of human freedom and human rights remains urgent and important. However, one must also concede there aspects of this development within official Roman Catholic teaching is clearly deficient. Although this teaching in papal documents clearly emphasizes the equality of male and female within society, yet because of an "Romantic nineteenth-century understanding of the duality of gender (with the world as proper locus for the male, and the home for woman), it has refused to acknowledge the equality of gender within the church, especially in regard to sacramental orders and church governance. In addition, the acknowledgment of religious freedom as a civil and legal issue cannot be as sharply separated from a legitimate theoretical plurality of religious viewpoints, not only among Christians, but also among the other religions of the world.

The Catholic teaching since World War II has moved within the issue of freedom and human rights. In the face of totalitarianism, it has come to understand religious freedom requires a freedom of the church from the state, but that also requires the freedom of religion within the state. The papal teaching during this period of time has consistently attempted to show human rights in correlation to human duties. In addition, it has placed much more emphasis on the importance of legal structure and international organization to deal with the crises facing the West. In face of some criticisms, this teaching has significance, especially if one examines the historical context out of which it developed and the political challenges that face us today.

Bibliography

Atlas, James. "The Nation: Leo-Cons: A Classicist's Legacy: New Empire Builders." *New York Times*, May 4, 2003. https://www.nytimes.com/2003/05/04/weekinreview/the-nation-leo-cons-a-classicist-s-legacy-new-empire-builders.html.

Baudrillard, Jean. *The Agony of Power*. Cambridge: MIT Press, 2010.
Benedict XVI, Pope. Address to the United Nations. http://www.vatican.va/holy_father/benedict_xvi/speeches/2008/april/documents/hf_ben-xvi_spe_20080418_un-visit_en.html.
Bernstein, Richard J. "The Aporias of Carl Schmitt." *Constellations* 18 (2011) 403–30.
Böckenförde, Ernst-Wolfgang. "Die Bedeutung der Konzilserklärung über Religionsfreiheit. Überlegungen 20 Jahre danach." In *Religionsfreiheit: Die Kirche in der modernen Welt*, 59–70. Freiberg: Herder, 1990.
Casas, Bartolomé de las. *A Short Account of the Destruction of the Indies*. London: Penquin, 1992.
Cavallar, George. *The Rights of Strangers: Theories of International Hospitality, the Global Community, and Political Justice since Vitoria*. Burlington, VT: Ashgate, 2002.
Coleman, Janet. "Medieval Discussions of Human Rights." In *Human Rights and Cultural Diversity*, edited by Wolfgang Schmale, 103–20. Goldbach: Keip: 1993.
Curran, Charles E. *The Moral Theology of Pope John Paul II*. Washington, DC: Georgetown University Press, 2005.
Derrida, Jacques. "Declarations of Independence." *New Political Science* 15 (1985) 1–32.
———. *The Gift of Death*. Translated by David Wills. Religion and Postmodernism. Chicago: University of Chicago Press, 1995.
Drury, Shadia B. *Leo Strauss and the American Right*. New York: St. Martin's, 1997.
Dyzenhaus, David. *Law as Politics: Carl Schmitt's Critique of Liberalism*. Durham: Duke University Press, 1998.
———. *Legality and Legitimacy: Carl Schmitt, Hans Kelson, and Hermann Heller in Weimar*. New York: Clarendon, 1997.
———. *Recrafting the Rule of Law: The Limits of Legal Order*. Portland, OR: Hart, 1999.
Fiorenza, Francis Schüssler. "*Gaudium et spes* and Human Rights: The Challenge of a Cosmopolitan World." In *The Church and Human Freedom: Forty Years after Gaudium et spes*, edited by Darlene Weaver, 38–65. Villanova, PA: Villanova University Press, 2006.
———. "Prospects for Political Theology in the Face of Contemporary Challenges." In *Politische Theologie: Neuere Geschichte und Potenziale*, edited by Michael Welker, 41–63. Neukirchen-Vluyn: Nuekirchener, 2011.
———. "Vatican II." In *The Routledge Companion to Modern Christian Thought*, edited by Chad Meister and James Beilby, 364–76. Boston: Routledge, 2013.
Forster, Karl. "Die Menschenrechte—aus katholischer Sicht." In *Glaube und Kirche im Dialog mit der Welt von heute*, vol. 2, 538–48. Würzburg: Echter, 1982.
Frachon, Alain, and Daniel Vernet. "The Strategist and the Philosopher: Leo Strauss and Albert Wohlstetter." *Le Monde*, April 16, 2003; *Counterpunch*, June 2, 2003.
Friedrich, Jörg. *Der Brand: Deutschland im Bombenkrieg 1940–1945*. Munich: Propyläen, 2002.
Glendon, Mary Ann. *A World Made New: Eleanor Roosevelt and the Universal Declaration of Human Rights*. 1st ed. New York: Random House, 2001.
Henley, John. "Theology and the Basis of Human Rights." *Scottish Journal of Theology* 39 (1987) 361–78.
Höffe, Otfried. "Papst Johannes Paul II. und die Menschenrechte—Philosophische Überlegunen." In *Johannes Paul II und die Menschenrechte*, edited by Otfried Höffe et al., 15–35. Friburg: Universitätsverlag, 1981.

Honig, Bonnie. "Declarations of Independence: Arendt and Derrida on the Problem of Founding a Republic." *American Political Science Review* 85 (March 1991) 97–113.
John Paul II, Pope. "Address to the Fiftieth General Assembly of the United Nations Organization." New York, October 5, 1995. http://www.vatican.va/holy_father/john_paul_ii/speeches/1995/october/documents/hf_jp-ii_spe_05101995_address-to-uno_en.html.
Kalyvas, Andreas. *Democracy and the Politics of the Extraordinary: Max Weber, Carl Schmitt, and Hannah Arendt*. Cambridge: Cambridge University Press, 2008.
Kaufmann, Matthias. *Recht ohne Regel? Die Philosophischen Prinzipien in Carl Schmitts Staats- und Rechtslehre*. Freiburg: Alber, 1988.
———. "Carl Schmitt's Critique of Liberal Constitutionalism." *Review of Politics* 58 (1996) 299–322.
Lauren, Paul Gordon. *The Evolution of International Human Rights: Visions Seen*. 2nd ed. Pennsylvania Studies in Human Rights. Philadelphia: University of Pennsylvania Press, 2003.
Lindbeck, George. "The Gospel's Uniqueness: Election and Untranslatability." *Modern Theology* 134 (1997) 423–50.
Little, David. "Liberalism and World Order: The Thought of James Luther Adams." *Harvard Divinity School Bulletin* 31.3 (2003) 7–9.
Macheret, Augustin. "Johannes Paul II. und die Menschenrechte." In *Johannes Paul II. und die Menschenrechte*, edited by Otfried Höffe et al. Friburg: Universitätsverlag, 1981.
MacIntyre, Alisdair. *After Virtue: A Study in Moral Theory*. 2nd ed. Notre Dame: University of Notre Dame Press, 1984.
Macpherson, C. B. *The Political Theory of Possessive Individualism: Hobbes to Locke*. Oxford: Clarendon, 1962.
Mäkinen, Virpi, and Petter Korkman. *Transformations in Medieval and Early-Modern Rights Discourse*. New Synthese Historical Library 59. Dordrecht: Springer 2006.
Manemann, Jürgen. *Carl Schmitt und die Politische Theologie : Politischer Anti-Monotheismus*. Munsterische Beitrage zur Theologie 61. Münster: Aschendorff, 2002.
McCormick, John P. *Carl Schmitt's Critique of Liberalism: Against Politics as Technology*. New York: Cambridge University Press, 1997.
Morsink, Johanne. *The Universal Declaration of Human Rights: Origins, Drafting and Intent*. Philadelphia: University of Pennsylvania Press, 1999.
Mouffe, Chantal. *The Democratic Paradox*. New York: Verso, 2000.
———. *The Return of the Political*. New York: Verso, 1993.
Nagel, Ernst Josef. *Die Friedenslehre der katholischen Kirche: Eine Konkordanz kirchenamtlicher Dokumente*. 2nd ed. Stuttgart: Kohlhammer, 1997.
Niebuhr, Reinhold. "*Pacem in Terris*: Two Views." *Christianity and Crisis* 13 (May 1963) 81, 83.
Paul VI, Pope. "Discourse to the Organization of the United Nations on the Occasion of its Twentieth Anniversary." http://www.vatican.va/holy_father/paul_vi/speeches/1965/documents/hf_p-vi_spe_19651004_united-nations_fr.html.
Preuss, Ulrich K. "Constitutional Powermaking for the New Polity: Some Deliberations on the Relations between Constituent Power and the Constitution." *Cardozo Law Review* 14 (1993) 639–50.

Ratzinger, Joseph. "Part I The Church and Man's Calling Introductory Article and Chapter 1: The Dignity of the Human Person." In *English Commentary on the Documents of Vatican II*, 3 vols., edited by Herbert Vorgrimler, 115–63. New York: Herder & Herder, 1967–1969.

———. *Theological Highlights of Vatican II*. New York: Paulist, 1966.

Reid, Charles J., Jr. "The Canonistic Contribution to the Western Rights Tradition: An Historical Inquiry." *Boston College Law Review* 33 (1991) 37–92.

Ruston, Roger. *Human Rights and the Image of God*. London: SCM, 2004.

Scheuerman, William E. *Between the Norm and the Exception: The Frankfurt School and the Rule of Law*. Cambridge, MA: MIT Press, 1994.

———. *Carl Schmitt: The End of the Law*. Lanham, MD: Rowman & Littlefield, 1999.

Schmitt, Carl. *Legality and Legitimacy*. Durham: Duke University Press, 2004.

———. *Political Theology: Four Chapters on the Concept of Sovereignty*. Cambridge, MA: MIT Press, 1985.

Schrofer, Erick. "Kirche unterwegs zum Menschen. Katholische Theologie nach dem II. Vatikanum." *Geist und Leben* 4 (1984) 267–78.

Sluga, Hans. "The Pluralism of the Political: From Carl Schmitt to Hannah Arendt." *Telos* 142 (2008) 91–109.

Souillac, Geneviève. *Human Rights in Crisis: The Sacred and the Secular in Contemporary French Thought*. Lanham, MD: Rowman & Littlefield, 2005.

Tierney, Brian. *The Idea of Natural Rights: Studies on Natural Rights, Natural Law, and Church Law, 1150–1625*. Emory University Studies in Law and Religion 5. Atlanta: Scholars, 1997.

Tomuschat, Christian. *Human Rights: Between Idealism and Realism*. Oxford: Oxford University Press, 2003.

Utz, Arthur-Fridolin. "Was heist 'Entwicklung' der päpstlichen Sozialdokrin." In *Die Friedensenzyklika Papst Johannes XXIII. Pacem in Terris*, 13–78. Freiburg: Herder, 1963.

Walzer, Michael. "Beyond Humanitarian Intervention: Human Rights in Global Society." In *Thinking Politically: Essays in Political Theory*, 253–63. New Haven: Yale University Press, 2007.

———. *Thick and Thin: Moral Argument at Home and Abroad*. Notre Dame: University of Notre Dame, 1994.

Weaver, Darlene, ed. *The Church and Human Freedom: Forty Years after Gaudium et spes*. Villanova, PA: Villanova University Press, 2006.

Wellman, Carl. "Solidarity, the Individual and Human Rights." *Human Rights Quarterly* 22 (2000) 639–57.

21

Divine Spirit and Human Freedom

MICHAEL WELKER

The plasticity of the human brain and the versatility of the human mind are extremely impressive. The capacity of the human spirit to host huge realms of memory and imagination, to keep memories and imaginations latent or to activate them, to share and to communicate them, can evoke strong impressions of individual freedom. The ability to communicate emotional, rational, cognitive, and voluntative powers, to connect and to intensify them, and to shape natural and social environments generates feelings of shared and communal freedom. But the many experiences of limits to transforming imaginations and thoughts into action, the many experiences of disagreements and conflicts in social life, experiences of self-jeopardy and self-endangerment require the complicated discernment between illusions of freedom and reliable experiences of freedom.

Freedom-Discourse in the West

The last decades have seen several areas of discourse in the academic orbit in the West, in education systems and civil societies that have tried to rise to this challenge. A dominant discourse was marked by the debate between liberalism and communitarianism.[1] At the center of the discussion we found the question: "Freedom or community?" and a (readily expected)

---

1. The following observations have been inspired by Wolfgang Huber's perspective on the recent Euro-American academic and public discourse about the topic: "Verantwortete Freiheit als Lebensform," 319–20. The following parts refer partly to Welker, "Where the Spirit of God Is, There Is Freedom!"

search for all possible compromises and syntheses. "Not only 'freedom from' but also 'freedom to' and 'freedom for'" had become the standard topics of the debate.[2] Up for consideration were, on the one hand, self-determination, freedom of action and "self-causality" and, on the other, the limitation of our spheres of freedom.[3] Concerted efforts were made to distinguish between the true spirits of liberation in justice-oriented struggles and deceptive, indeed often dissembling and deceitful activities performed in its name. And of course, theology continually expressed the insight that, at least with respect to issues of healing and salvation, freedom is always a gift granted by God.[4] Discussions about human dignity attempted to illuminate the foundations and scope of human and creaturely freedom.[5] In reflections on responsibility, law and love, attempts were made to shape and direct the use of freedom into life-promoting forms. All these attempts stood up bravely against naturalistic and scientistic ideologies, which, given the supposedly indisputable insight that all human desires and actions are naturally determined, sought to abandon thought about freedom or toss the quest for freedom onto the scrapheap of history.[6]

Since the time of Aristotle and the Stoa, discourses on freedom throughout Western history were often latently characterized by an understanding of freedom and the human spirit that focused on the cognitively steered self-referentiality of persons, societies and cultures. Spirit and freedom became tangible and effective in self-determinative thought. In the famous Book XII of his *Metaphysics*, Aristotle defines the spirit as the driving force that thinks itself, insofar as it participates in what is thought, and becomes part of it.[7] The spirit is the power that does not lose itself in relationships with the other, but rather receives and maintains itself in the thinking relationship. Our understanding of the world and our understanding of ourselves are mediated through this spirit. The quality of all thought and understanding comes from the heightening of self-understanding together with a simultaneous recognition and understanding of external reality. Aristotle connects this spiritual activity with self-actualization, freedom and one's own wellbeing. He even calls it "divine," for it is the perfect actualization of all knowledge about all reality together with the absolute

---

2. Cf. the contribution of Carver Yu in this volume.
3. Huber, "Verantwortete Freiheit als Lebensform," 321ff.
4. Ibid., 328ff.
5. Cf. the contribution of Francis Schüssler Fiorenza in this book.
6. Huber, "Verantwortete Freiheit als Lebensform," 337.
7. Cf. Aristotle, *Metaphysics X-IX*, XII, 1072b, esp. 19-32; Welker, *God the Spirit*, 283ff.

self-knowledge that characterizes divinity. The best and eternal life comes to it, and it does so in perfect freedom.[8]

This brilliant philosophical theory of the spirit and its correlated view of freedom have had an incredible influence on Western cultural history. They have provided societies and cultures with an often extremely individualistic and intellectual understanding of freedom based in theoretical subjectivism. It is impossible to hold this great achievement in too high regard, although one has to address its problems and limitations. Greek political thought further developed the theory of freedom by connecting the intellectual freedom of ideas with forms of oligarchical equality in the public sphere. The freedom to speak in public assemblies (*parrhesia*), the equal right to express oneself publicly (*isegoria*), equality before the law (*isonomia*) and equal entitlements with regard to exercising political leadership (*isokratia*) were all important elements in the empowerment of free men, both individually and communally, and in the direction of their paths through society (*eleutheria*).[9] Today, when we study Jürgen Habermas's description of the so-called "democratic process,"[10] we must ask ourselves whether philosophical thought on the concept of freedom has really made any significant advances over the last 2,000 years.

According to Habermas, members of society [*Gesellschaftsbürger*]—who are the recipients and beneficiaries of civil rights and liberties, and who stand as the addressees of the law—should qualify and understand themselves as citizens of the state [*Staatsbürger*] and as the "authors of the law."[11] Habermas presents us with a vision of a "democratic process" in which more and more members of society become citizens of the state, citizens who consciously understand themselves as tasked with authoring the laws via civil societal discursive and institutionally legal means to secure increasingly better and clearer principles of justice within the interwoven network of a society's cultural value orientations. Here we see the propagation of an elitism within civil society:[12] one that establishes an essentially appellative-moral relationship to the power structures of pluralistic societies, with their systemic political, media-based, economic, legal, academic, educational and even religious forms of organization.

---

8. Cf. Aristotle, *Metaphysics* XII, 1072b, 19–32.

9. Cf. the contributions of Peter Lampe, Jan Gertz, and Jürgen van Oorschot in this volume.

10. Habermas and Ratzinger, *Dialektik der Säkularisierung*.

11. Ibid. 18ff.

12. Cf. the contribution of Susan Abraham in this volume and her references to the work of Gayatri Chakravorty Spivak.

In this situation, what can genuine theological thought about the Spirit and about the freedom that comes from the Spirit contribute? The following comments will concentrate on a biblically oriented relativization of what is essentially a self-reflective, intellectual understanding of the spirit. Though I will not offer a detailed discussion of Paul's thinking here, my comments are significantly shaped by his anthropology and by his distinction between the human and divine spirits.[13]

The Subversive "Outpouring" of God's Spirit

A biblically oriented alternative to Aristotelian thought about the spirit has to start from a different perspective than self-referential cognitive and mental power. It should start with the great biblical image of the "outpouring of the Spirit." The talk about the outpouring of the Spirit forces us to focus on a wealth and plenitude of relations, on the constitution of a spiritual community with many interrelations, mutual impacts and radiations. This is a very different starting point over against the reflexive, mentalistic and often individualistic anthropomorphic concepts of the spirit, which have resulted from the influence of Aristotelian metaphysics and related theories.

However, the wealth of relations captured with the notion of the outpouring of the Spirit is not easily perceived as helpful exactly because the generated diversity and plenitude are not easy to control in imagination. This approach then leads many people to assume that we cannot really know anything about the Holy Spirit at all, that the Spirit is just a numinous power. And it seems to follow that we had rather remain piously silent in the face of the divine apophatic mystery when we want to focus on the divine Spirit. Over against an intellectualistic reductionism in the Aristotelian vein on the one side and over against the—only seemingly pious—will to intransparency and vagueness on the other side, the biblical classics about the pouring of the Spirit provide us with illuminating insights. The topmost classic, the prophet Joel 2:28–29, tells us that God's Spirit will be poured out on men and women, on the old and the young, and on male and female slaves. The other great classic, the Pentecost narrative in Acts 2, quotes Joel and adds that the Spirit of God comes down on human beings of different nations, cultures and languages.[14]

The consequences of this outpouring of the Spirit are indeed seen to be salvific. The human beings who are gifted and filled by the Spirit gain cognition of God, they gain the power of proclamation and spiritual

---

13. Cf. Welker, "Flesh–Body–Heart–Soul–Spirit."
14. Cf. Welker, *God the Spirit*, 134–58, 228–48.

communication, and they gain the related orienting ethical powers for their lives.[15] At this point it should be emphasized that the biblical traditions do not regard each and every pouring of the spirit as salvific. Rather, God can pour out a "spirit of distortion" (Isa 19:14) or a negative "spirit of deep sleep" that blinds even the prophets (Isa 29:10). Over against this negative impact, the salvific pouring of the spirit, of which not only Joel and Acts, but also Isaiah (32:15), Ezekiel (39:29), Zechariah (12:10) and Paul's letter to the Romans (5:5) speak, constitutes a lively spiritual plural and polyphonic communality and community.

In the light of the biblical classics, this polyphony appears to be loaded. It can be regarded as subversive and even as revolutionary. According to the prophet Joel, not only the men, but also the women are overcome by the spirit—and this is said in patriarchal environments. The young people are overcome by the spirit—and this is said in gerontocratic contexts. And even the "menservants and maidservants," and these were most likely slaves, are overcome and gifted by the spirit of God—and this is said in slaveholder societies. Finally, the account of Acts challenges all ethnocentric, tribalist, and exclusivist perspectives on the work of the Spirit by its emphasis on the fact that people from many nations, many cultures and many languages are overcome by the Spirit of God.

The idea of such a polyphony and of the multitude of interrelations in the community of the Spirit easily raises the fear that we have nothing but chaos. To be sure, the emergent reality of the working of the Spirit and the emergent reality of the coming of the reign of God that the biblical traditions envision present multifarious cognitive difficulties to grasping this process and event.[16] However, the pouring of the divine Spirit gains clarity by its connection with the gifts of the Spirit (*charismata*), which are especially emphasized by Paul (1 Cor 12:4ff; 7:7; 13:1-3 and 14:4ff; Rom 12:4ff). According to Paul, the Spirit and the gifts of the Spirit serve the edification, enlivenment and vivification of a multidimensional and polyphonic community, of the "body of Christ" (1 Cor 12 and Rom 12). The church as the body of Christ has to be seen as a pluralistic and organismic unity of a distinct number of members. These members are all related to Jesus Christ as their head, but among themselves they live in only relative and functional hierarchical relations. Sometimes the eyes are particularly important, sometimes the hands, sometimes the feet . . . (cf. 1 Cor 12:12ff.). The lively

---

15. Cf. Welker, ed., *The Work of the Spirit*; and Macchia, *Baptized in the Spirit*.

16. Cf. Welker and Wolter, "Die Unscheinbarkeit des Reiches Gottes"; and Welker, *God the Revealed*, 223ff.

polyphonic "unity of the body" is constituted and maintained by the pouring of the Spirit and by the multitude of the gifts of the Spirit.[17]

Since many established monohierarchical, patriarchal, ageist, classist, nationalistic and culture-chauvinistic guidelines are thus questioned and challenged by the outpouring of the Spirit, we should ask again: How is it that Paul can claim that the "Spirit of freedom" is not actually a Spirit of disorder, even of chaos (cf. 1 Cor 14:33)?

Spirit, Freedom, and the Law of Justice and Mercy

The first response, dealing with the form and efficacy of the Spirit, helps us to address the concerns that the Spirit of God is just a "numinous being" and that the outpouring of the Spirit leads to simple religious and cultural "confusions"—yet it is also vital for the discourse between different religions and other worldviews. This answer is that the efficacy of the Spirit of God stands in continuity and discontinuity with the law traditions, with the Torah. In several messianic promises in the Book of Isaiah (Isa 11; 42; and 61), which the New Testament expressly and explicitly associates with the person and work of Jesus of Nazareth, we find mention of "the Chosen One of God" upon whom the *Spirit of God rests*. It is said that he will bring justice among the nations, protection for the weak and knowledge of God. Justice, compassion and the knowledge of God—here we have the fundamental goals of the biblical law. Matthew 23:23 identifies "the most important matters of the law [as] justice, mercy, and faith." One can hardly overestimate the incredible influence on Western culture of the normative connection between these concepts.

Even today, the connection between justice and the protection of the weak continues to shape the dynamics behind the evolution of a just and humane law. Conversely, the connection between the protection of the weak and the law has led to the institutionalization of a "culture of aid," not only in the social work of the church but also in the form of a legal, societal and national interest in general education, in basic economic welfare for all people and in a dependable healthcare system. It was hardly coincidental that after the fall of the Nazi regime, Germany sought to regain international trust and recognition by portraying itself as a "state under the rule of law" and as a "welfare state." There is no room in this context to examine the complex normative dynamics of the biblical law traditions, which have been

---

17. Cf. Zizioulas, *Being as Communion*, 110ff.; and Welker, *The Work of the Spirit*, 221ff.

powerfully effective down into our modern era.[18] Yet we must recognize that the creation of the dichotomies "law and Spirit" and "law and gospel" has been fatal in both theology and the church: for even God's good law, as with the human spirit, can fall under the power of sin. The law can indeed take on highly dangerous forms, even degenerating into a "law of sin" (Rom 8:2). But if Paul was operating with some primitive dichotomy between law and Spirit, then he could never have spoken of a "law of the Spirit" (Rom 8:2), a "law of faith" (Rom 3:27) or a "law of Christ" (Gal 6:2). Rather what is characteristic for the work of the Spirit of God is the further development of the ethos of the law into an ethos of love, hope and faith. But the intentions of the law—to promote justice, mercy and the knowledge of God (or perceptions of the truth)—remain intact. In a positive sense they have been "elevated."

This elevation also applies to the Spirit of Christ. For many people, even within the churches, the "Spirit of the Lord" is still connected with the model of a monarchical "royal rule of Christ" or a "Christocratic brotherhood" in the sense of Barmen III,[19] the hierarchical-patriarchal tones of which are not easily associated with a very heartening understanding of freedom today. The Spirit of Christ can also be connected with the Spirit of kenosis, of sacrificial surrender and co-suffering—yet in which we easily lose all clear perspectives on the liberation and elevation of creation.

The Spirit of Christ as a Spirit of Freedom

We can find a helpful alternative when, with Calvin, we reclaim the biblical and original understandings: that Jesus Christ, upon whom the Spirit of God (the Spirit of justice, mercy and knowledge of God) rests, pours out this Spirit upon all "those who are his."[20] In his work the *Institutes of the Christian Religion*,[21] Calvin emphatically notes that: Christ the Messiah was not anointed with oil but with the Holy Spirit so that those who belong to him might have a share in his power:

> Therefore the anointing of the king is not with oil or aromatic unguents. Rather he is called "Anointed" [*Christus*] of God

---

18. Cf. Welker, "Justice—Mercy—Worship"; and Welker, "The Power of Mercy in Biblical Law."

19. While the Barmen Declaration was in its own time, and is still today, a highly laudable and in many respects exemplary theological text, it does display significant pneumatological deficits; cf. Welker, "Barmen III."

20. Dunn, "Towards the Spirit of Christ."

21. Calvin, *Institutes*, Vol I., chap. II, 15.

> because "the spirit of wisdom and understanding, the spirit of counsel and might ... and of the fear of the Lord have rested upon him" [Isa 11:2p.] ... he did not enrich himself for his own sake [*privatim*], but that he might pour out his abundance upon the hungry and thirsty.[22]

Here Calvin stresses the so-called "baptism of the Spirit" through the "Anointed by the Spirit," which became a groundbreaking spiritual experience for the early church, and which the global Pentecostal movement and twentieth-century charismatic renewal have made the center of their piety.[23]

In this re-orientation toward the resurrected and exalted Christ, Calvin also offers a second key insight that links us back into the Old Testament traditions and their broad spheres of remembrance and horizons of expectation:

> To know *the purpose* for which Christ was sent by the Father, and *what* he conferred upon us, we must look above all at *three things* in Him: the *prophetic office, kingship,* and *priesthood*.[24]

The doctrine of the "threefold office" of Christ (*munus triplex Christi*) helps us to understand the public and eschatological work of Jesus Christ in all its differentiated richness. It incorporates links to the Old Testament traditions—continuities in the work of the pre-Easter and post-Easter Christ with the actions of anointed kings, priests and prophets, constantly alluded to by the witnesses of the New Testament. Schleiermacher, Bath and other leading theologians of Reformed traditions have taken up and developed this doctrine of the *munus triplex Christi*. Through the work of Johann Gerhard, it found a point of entry into Lutheran theology,[25] and it was also adopted by the Roman Catholic[26] and Orthodox Churches.[27] Edmund Schlink notes that: "In the spread of the doctrine of the *munus triplex Christi* we can witness a unique ecumenical phenomenon. For this point of doctrine did not achieve its dogmatic form before, but rather after the division of the

---

22. Ibid. II, 15.5 499–500; cf. II, 15.2; Calvin continues: The Father is said "not to measure to have given the Spirit to his Son" [John 3:34p.]. The reason is expressed as follows: "That from his fullness we might all receive grace upon grace" [John 1:16p.] (II, 15.5, 500).

23. Macchia, *Baptized in the Spirit*. The following part takes up a part of Welker, *God the Revealed: Christology*, 209–313.

24. Calvin, *Institutes*, II, 15, 494.

25. *Loci theologici* 1610–22 Loc. IV, chp. 15.

26. Scheeben, *Handbuch der katholischen Dogmatik*, 226–305.

27. Trempela, *Dogmatike tes orthodoxu katholikes ekklesias*, vol. 2, 143–203.

churches. With its views on the salvific work of Jesus Christ, it established itself as common teaching across church divisions."[28]

If we take the doctrine of the threefold office seriously from a pneumatological perspective, then we must develop it further into an understanding of the *threefold Gestalt of Christ's reign*. Since the doctrine of the threefold office can often seem contrived or cobbled together, we should take care to orient these three dimensions toward the pre-Easter life, cross and resurrection of Jesus Christ. Due to the characteristics of Jesus' life and his charisma, the work of the pre-Easter Jesus is often attributed to the "prophetic office," with the cross signifying the "high-priestly office" (touching on sacrifice and the one who brings it) and the resurrection ushering in the "kingly office." *But if we begin with the presence of the resurrected Christ in the Spirit and then look back upon Jesus' formative life, we discover quite a different order.*

In the light of the pre-Easter life of Jesus, we suddenly see a brighter image of the *kingly rule of Christ* and of those who belong to him, an image that displays a clear message of realistic freedom. In the light of the outpouring of the Spirit, this royal rule revolutionizes hierarchical and monarchical forms of order, in both the church and the state, for this king is a brother and friend, indeed even one who is poor and outcast. With its radical democratic and post-patriarchal concepts of order, this royal rule, for some contemporaries, can take on an uncomfortable and chaotic appearance; yet on the other hand, it becomes exemplary for all those seeking to orient themselves toward the promotion of freedom in their environments.

This reign is marked by the praxis of loving and forgiving acceptance, by healing, and by liberating teaching and education. In continuity and discontinuity with the Torah traditions, love and forgiveness are defined through one's *free and creative self-withdrawal*[29] for the benefit of others. The freedom-promoting power that arises from this type of free, creative and (in the case of love) also joyous self-withdrawal for the benefit of one's neighbor is tremendous. The goal of love—which can be defined only unsatisfactorily through *eros, agape and philia*[30]—is that "all things work together for the good" of the one who is loved; to set his or her feet "in a broad place." When it comes to the reign of God, it is vital to realize that we are not primarily aiming to propagate in ourselves a responsibility toward freedom-promoting action or behavior, but rather to promote a joyous and thankful recognition of the *experience of free self-withdrawal that is done for our own*

---

28. Schlink, *Ökumenische Dogmatik. Grundzüge*, 414.

29. Huber, *Gerechtigkeit und Recht*, 316–17; Bedford-Strohm, *Vorrang für die Armen*.

30. Welker, "Romantic Love, Covenantal Love, Kenotic Love."

good. For this reason is it said that children express a particular closeness to the reign of God.³¹ Yet an ethos of liberating joy and thankfulness is also fundamental for an ethos of benevolent social care in the church.

A thankful sensitivity to the enormous potential behind free and creative self-withdrawal in our family contexts, among friends, and in our civil and societal organizations, together with a sensitivity to today's tremendous global welfare, educational, therapeutic, constitutional, ecclesiastical and intercultural challenges, can truly open our eyes to the incredibly formative and freedom-promoting forces of the *munus regium Christi*. The reign of God and the reign of Christ take on form through many, often seemingly insignificant acts of love and forgiveness. And it is not only the direct witnesses who receive a share in this often inconspicuous yet incredibly powerful reign. "Christian humanism"[32] also shines upon other religious and secular forms of practiced love and compassion, while also receiving strong impulses from them. The boundaries of the freedom-promoting reign of Christ are broader than all churches of all times and all regions. "Whatever you did to one of the least of these who are members of my family, you did for me," whether you recognized me in them or not.[33] Those who limit the reign of Christ to "word and sacrament" alone fail to recognize the breadth of Christ's liberating presence in the power of the Spirit.

Understandings of the *priestly dimension* of the rule and reign of Jesus Christ are often linked with the Book of Hebrews, where the focus falls upon the difficult themes of "sacrifice and atonement." In contrast to this narrow view,[34] when understanding the priestly office we should rather focus on the biblical witnesses to the appearances of the post-Easter presence of the resurrected Jesus Christ. Francis Fiorenza has helped us to see that the appearances of the risen Christ—which tell of greetings of peace, the breaking of bread, the expounding of Scripture, the command to baptize and the sending of disciples into the world—all outline the fundamental forms of the life of the early church and its charismatic powers [*Ausstrahlungskräfte*].[35] A polyphony of church life and existence is bound together with the priestly office, and it is this priestly office in which the "priesthood of all believers" shares and in which it finds its concretization.

---

31. Matt 10:14; Welker, "The 'Reign' of God."

32. Cf. Klemm and Schweiker, *Religion and the Human Future*; Schweiker, "Flesh and Folly."

33. Cf. Matt 25:40 or 25:34ff; Hoffmeyer, "Christology and Diakonia."

34. Cf. Brandt, *Opfer als Gedächtnis*.

35. Fiorenza, "The Resurrection of Jesus and Roman Catholic Fundamental Theology," 238ff; cf. also Eckstein and Welker, eds., *Die Wirklichkeit der Auferstehung*, esp. 318ff.

A continuous concentration on worship services and the celebration of the sacraments can already bring about extraordinary experiences of the liberating power of the Spirit. In baptism we bear witness to a change of lordship. The baptized person—whose life stands under constant threat of sickness and need, violence and mortality—now receives the promise of an enduring life of community together with God. The biblical texts describe this new life given to us in baptism with words that are hard to understand: liberation from the powers of sin and death, community with Christ, endowment with the power of the Holy Spirit, protection into eternal life. In these ways they describe a life that, on the one hand, has already materialized and been realized in the kingly rule of Christ; yet, on the other hand, it extends far beyond mere earthly existence. In the celebration of the Lord's Supper, the participating believers find themselves surrounded by the exalted Jesus Christ and his life. They celebrate that meal "in remembrance of him;" they remember his life and his work; they especially remember "the night in which he was betrayed;" they proclaim his death on the cross; they celebrate his resurrection and his presence; they look toward the *parousia* ("you proclaim the Lord's death until he comes").

The entire fullness of the life of Jesus Christ is present in this celebration—indeed we encounter there the entire presence of the Trinitarian God. The *eucharistia*, the expression of thanksgiving to the Creator God and the creative Holy Spirit for the created gifts of bread and wine, is followed by the *anamnesis*, when we remember Jesus Christ and his salvific work in the events of the cross and resurrection. These in turn are followed by the *epiclesis*, the thankful and joyous invocation of the Holy Spirit, who elevates believers, forming them into members of the body of Christ and giving them a share in the new creation.[36]

It is in this celebration of the presence of the sustaining, saving and exalting Trinitarian God that *a liberation of liturgical and spiritual life, a liberation of spiritual imagination, feeling and thought* occurs. The celebration of the sacraments and a biblically oriented proclamation and teaching repeatedly call into question all banal, artificial and oppressive concepts of God, as well as banal and oppressive religious and moral practices. This moment of table fellowship, symbolized by peace and justice, refers to the royal rule of Christ and to the church's actions of love. In our remembrance of the night of Jesus' betrayal and the events of the cross, we are pointed to the prophetic office and to the richness of its radiant blessings.

The nature of the *prophetic office,* or the prophetic dimension of the reign of Christ, becomes particularly clear in the light of the cross. In order

---

36. Welker, *What Happens in Holy Communion?*

to recognize this, we must avoid reducing the message of the cross simply to the revelation of a "suffering God." God's benevolent nearness in the poverty, weakness and powerlessness of the Crucified One is vitally important.[37] However, a concentration upon this "crucified God" should never obscure God's mighty confrontation against the powers and forces of this world—a confrontation that takes shape in the cross and resurrection. Jesus Christ, who brought us the message of the coming reign of God, who gave us the power to heal, the power to care for children, for the weak, the outcast, the sick and the suffering; this Jesus Christ was condemned, unanimously, by the "principalities and powers" of this world.

Religion, law, politics, public morality and opinion all like to present themselves as "forces for good," which are here to "marvelously protect" us; yet in the event of the cross they all conspire together to work against God's presence in Jesus Christ. The cross reveals the world "under the power of sin," a dark "night of God-forsakenness," not just for Jesus himself but rather as a constant threat for all humankind. It shows us that all of our public and powerful protective mechanisms—such as the law, politics, religion, morality and public opinion—can fail us and our communities.[38] The great liberating importance of the Christian proclamation, the great importance of theological teaching, the indispensable, liberating mission of truth and justice-seeking communities—and here we mean not only the church but also the sciences and the legal system—all become clear in the dimension of the prophetic office. As truth and justice-seeking communities,[39] the church of Jesus Christ allows itself to be filled with Christ's Spirit of freedom.

Actions ranging from the needful analysis and critique of current distorted social and global conditions to passive resistance against corrupt and perverted politics, media influence, economics, and even corrupt morality and religion—actions of critique and resistance grounded in the responsible search for truth, justice and care and respect for the weak—all become newly visible in the context of the prophetic office. In the confrontations with the powers of sin, we need spiritual and moral depth as well as analytical clarity. An opposition politics superficially flavored with religiosity and focused simply on making moral appeals on trending hot-button issues hardly does justice to the tasks of the prophetic office. The boundaries of this office also extend far beyond the walls of the church and may even turn today against

---

37. Luther, "Heidelberg Disputation 1518"; Bonhoeffer, *Letters and Papers from Prison*, 131–37; Moltmann, *Crucified God*.

38. Cf. Smit, "'. . . Under Pontius Pilate' (n.16); Smit also offers a most insightful and consolidated overview and evaluation of my various publications and comments on the theology of the cross.

39. Cf. Polkinghorne and Welker, *Faith in the Living God*, esp. chap. 9.

a self-glorifying, self-justifying or ideologically blinded church and forms of ecclesiasticism.

Bibliography

Aristotle. *Metaphysics I–IX*. Translated and edited by Hugh Tredennick. Loeb Classibal Library. Cambridge: Harvard University Press, 1935.
Bedford-Strohm, Heinrich. *Vorrang für die Armen: Auf dem Weg zu einer theologischen Theorie der Gerechtigkeit*. Öffentliche Theologie 4. Gütersloh: Gütersloher, 1993.
Bonhoeffer, Dietrich. *Letters and Papers from Prison*. Edited by John Bowden and Eberhard Bethge. London: SCM, 2001.
Brandt, Sigrid. *Opfer als Gedächtnis: Auf dem Weg zu einer befreienden Rede von Opfer*. Altes Testament und Moderne 2. Münster: Lit, 2001.
Calvin, John. *Institutes of the Christian Religion*. Edited by John T. McNeill. Translated and indexed by Ford L. Battles. Louisville: Westminster John Knox, 2006.
Dunn, James D. G. "Towards the Spirit of Christ: The Emergence of the Distinctive Features of Christian Pneumatology." In *The Work of the Spirit: Pneumatology and Pentecostalism*, edited by Michael Welker, 3–26. Grand Rapids: Eerdmans, 2006.
Eckstein, Hans-Joachim, and Michael Welker, eds. *Die Wirklichkeit der Auferstehung*. 4th ed. Neukirchen-Vluyn: Neukirchener, 2010.
Fiorenza, Francis. "The Resurrection of Jesus and Roman Catholic Fundamental Theology." In *The Resurrection: An Interdisciplinary Symposium on the Resurrection of Jesus*, edited by Stephen T. Davis et al., 213–48. Oxford: Oxford University Press, 1997.
Habermas, Jürgen, and Joseph Kardinal Ratzinger. *Dialektik der Säkularisierung: Über Vernunft und Religion*. Edited by Florian Schuller. Freiburg: Herder, 2005.
Hoffmeyer, John F. "Christology and Diakonia." In *Who Is Jesus Christ for Us Today? Pathways to Contemporary Christology*, edited by Andreas Schuele and Günter Thomas, 150–66. Louisville: Westminster John Knox, 2009.
Huber, Wolfgang. *Gerechtigkeit und Recht: Grundlinien christlicher Rechtsethik*. 3rd ed. Gütersloh: Gütersloher, 2006.
———. "Verantwortete Freiheit als Lebensform." In *Verantwortlichkeit—nur eine Illusion?*, edited by Thomas Fuchs and Grit Schwarzkopf, 319–40. Heidelberg: Winter, 2010.
Klemm, David E., and William Schweiker. *Religion and the Human Future: An Essay on Theological Humanism*. Oxford: Blackwell, 2008.
Luther, Martin. "Heidelberg Disputation 1518." In *Luther's Works*, vol. 31, edited by Harold J. Grimm and Helmut T. Lehmann, 35–70. Philadelphia: Muhlenberg, 1957.
Macchia, Frank. *Baptized in the Spirit: A Global Pentecostal Theology*. Grand Rapids: Zondervan, 2006.
Moltmann, Jürgen. *The Crucified God: The Cross of Christ as the Foundation and Criticism of Christian Theology*. Translated by R. A. Wilson and John Bowden. 1974. Reprint, Minneapolis: Fortress, 1993.
Polkinghorne, John, and Michael Welker. *Faith in the Living God: A Dialogue*. 2nd ed. Eugene, OR: Cascade Books, 2019.

Scheeben, Matthias Josef. *Handbuch der katholischen Dogmatik.* Vol. 5.2. Freiburg: Herder, 1954.
Schlink, Edmund. *Ökumenische Dogmatik. Grundzüge.* 2nd ed. Göttingen: Vandenhoeck & Ruprecht, 1985.
Schweiker, William. "Flesh and Folly: The Christ of Christian Humanism." In *Who Is Jesus Christ for Us Today? Pathways to Contemporary Christology,* edited by Andreas Schuele and Günter Thomas, 85–102. Louisville: Westminster, 2009.
Smit, Dirk. "'. . . Under Pontius Pilate': On Living Cultural Memory and Christian Confession." In *Who Is Jesus Christ for Us Today? Pathways to Contemporary Christology,* edited by Andreas Schuele and Günter Thomas, 19–49, Westminster John Knox, Louisville.
Trempela, Panagiotes. *Dogmatike tes orthodoxu katholikes ekklesias.* Vol. 2. Athens, 1959. [Greek]
Welker, Michael. "Barmen III: Woran orientieren? Die Gestalt der Kirche in gesellschaftlichen Umbrüchen." In *Begründete Freiheit—Die Aktualität der Barmer Theologischen Erklärung: Vortragsreihe zum 75. Jahrestag im Berliner Dom,* 59–75. Evangelische Impulse 1. Neukirchen-Vluyn: Neukirchener, 2009.
———. "Flesh–Body–Heart–Soul–Spirit: Paul's Anthropology as an Interdisciplinary Bridge Theory." In *The Depth of the Human Person: A Multidisciplinary Approach,* edited by Michael Welker, 45–57. Eerdmans: Grand Rapids 2014.
———. *God the Revealed: Christology.* Eerdmans: Grand Rapids 2013.
———. *God the Spirit.* 1994. Reprint, Eugene, OR: Wipf & Stock, 2014.
———. "Justice—Mercy—Worship: The 'Weighty Matters' of the Biblical Law." In *Concepts of Law in the Sciences, Legal Studies, and Theology,* edited by Michael Welker and Gregor Etzelmüller, 205–24. Religion in Philosophy and Theology 72. Tübingen: Mohr/Siebeck, 2013.
———. "The Power of Mercy in Biblical Law." *Journal of Law and Religion* 29 (2014) 225–35.
———. "The 'Reign' of God." *Theology Today* 49 (1992) 500–515.
———. "Romantic Love, Covenantal Love, Kenotic Love." In *The Work of Love: Creation as Kenosis,* edited by John Polkinghorne, 127–36. Eerdmans: Grand Rapids, 2001.
———. *What Happens in Holy Communion?* Grand Rapids: Eerdmans, 2000.
———. "Where the Spirit of God Is, There Is Freedom!" In *Living Theology: Essays Presented to Dirk J. Smit on His 60th Birthday,* edited by Len Hanse et al., 73–90. Wellington, South Africa: Bible Media, 2011.
———, ed. *The Work of the Spirit: Pneumatology and Pentecostalism.* Grand Rapids: Eerdmans, 2006.
Welker, Michael, and Michael Wolter. "Die Unscheinbarkeit des Reiches Gottes." In *Reich Gottes.* Marburger Jahrbuch Theologie 11 (1999) 103–16.
Zizioulas, John. *Being as Communion: Studies in Personhood and the Church.* New York: St. Vladimir's Seminary Press, 1997.

Scripture Index

HEBREW BIBLE

Genesis

	77
1	275
1:4	188n
1:10	188n
1:18	188n
1:21	188n
1:25	188n
1:26ff.	274
1:27–28	274
1:31	188n
2	242
2:17	242
2:23	76
3	242
3:1–5	242
3:6	242
3:13	242
3:16	239
12	29
12:17	29
16	239
16:1–2	33
17:12	31
18	85
18:14	87
21	239
28:21	84
30:3–12	33
32:22	84
38	88
46:4	187
50:24	187

Exodus

1–15	192, 260n
1:9–10	187
1:11	188
1:13–14	188
1:13	188
1:14	188
1:22	188
2–3	192
2:23–24	191
2:23	188, 192
3:7–17	186
3:7–12	191
3:7–10	192
3:8–10	186
3:8	187, 188
3:12	191
3:13–14	169
3:17	187, 188
5:1	190
5:9	188
5:11	188
6–7	85
6:6	186, 187n
6:9	188
7:16	190
8:1	190
8:20	190
9:1	190
9:13	190

10:3	190
12	31
13:3–16	190n
13:3–10	32
15:13	187n
19–24	192
20:2–3	191
20:2	187
20:17	242
21:1–12	34
21:2–11	35
21:2	143
21:5	143
21:7–11	33
21:20–27	227
21:23–25	35
21:26–27	143
21:32	32
22:3	33
34:6	175

Leviticus

	74
18:5	240
19:20	143, 256
19:36	187
22:33	187
23:43	187
24:20	35
25	191
25:10	256
25:38	187
25:39–54	33
25:39–42	191
25:42	187
25:55	187
26:13	187
26:45	187
27:3–8	33

Numbers

	27
11:15	87
11:23	87
15:41	187
21:26ff.	33

Deuteronomy

	34, 187, 251, 254–65
2:24	205n
3:20	258
4:37	262
5:6	187, 257
5:7	258
5:9	258
5:12–15	30–31
5:14–15	191
5:14	196
6	190
6:13	258
6:21	187, 190
7	261–62
7:2	205n
7:7–11	261
7:7–8	262
7:7	262
7:8	257
8:7–10	188–89
10:12	258
10:14–15	261–62
11:13	258
13	258–59
13:6–11	258
15:12–18	191, 256
15:12–13	39, 143
15:12	34
15:15	187n, 256
15:18	143
16:11–12	191
16:12	187n
17:14–20	263, 263nn, 274
19:21	35
21:10–14	227n
21:14	143
23:15–16	227n
24:7	33
24:17–22	191
24:18	187n
24:22	187n
26	190
26:6–7	192
27:26	240
28–29	259

29:46	187
30	259
30:15–16	259–60
30:17–18	260
30:19–20	260

Joshua

	189
1:13	258
2:14	205n
6:17	88
24	190
24:5–6	187

Judges

	189
5:30	33
6:8–9	186n, 187
6:8	187

Ruth

	89, 89n
3:9	88

1 Samuel

4:9	33
8	33, 356
10:18	187
17:25	256

2 Samuel

11	88

1 Kings

9:15–21	33
20:8	143
20:11	143

2 Kings

4:1	33
5	33
23:21ff.	32
24	40

1 Chronicles

1–11	28

2 Chronicles

28	11, 35, 40–41
28:9–11	41
28:14–15	41
36:22–23	255

Ezra

1:1–2	255

Nehemiah

	37n
5	33, 35–37
13	36n
13:17	143

Esther

	89, 89n

Job

	85, 300n
3	34
3:19	256
31:13–15	35
39:5	143
42:2–3	87

Psalms

2:7	262
4:1	194
8	196, 274
8:6	197
8:7	197
16:9–11	193
18:17	193
18:20	194
25:15	193
30:4	193
30:10	193
31:5	193
33:4–7	193n
40:3	193

49:15	256
69:15–16	193
72:1–2	262
74:2	187n
77:16	187n
78	192
87:5	143
88:5	256s
103:8	175
104	193
105	192, 193
106	192, 193
106:10	187n
106:44–45	193
107	193
110	196–97
110:1	197
116:3–4	193
116:8	193
118:5	194
127:3–5	78n, 79
136	192, 193
143:2	240n
145–149	194
145:8	175
145:14	194
146:5–9	193n
146:7–9	194
147:3	194
147:6	194

Proverbs

	267n
25:10	143

Ecclesiastes/Qoheleth

	251, 269–70
1:13	269
3	269–70
3:2–3	270
3:11	270
3:12–13	269
6:12b	269
9:4b	269
9:5	269
9:10	269

9:11–12a	269
10:17	143

Isaiah

	418
11	418
11:2	420
24–27	255
25	197
28:11–12	239n
32:15	417
40–66	206, 251–52, 270–76
40–52	274
40	272
41:21–29	276
42	418
42:22	272
42:24	272
44:28	255
45	270
45:1	255, 270
45:4–5	272
45:11–13	193n
51	275
51:9	275
52	275
56	276, 273, 276
56:2	276
56:4–5	275–76
58	194, 273
58:6–7	194
58:6	195, 256
58:7	195
59	273
61	194, 418
61:1–2	195
61:2	195

Jeremiah

1:5–6	85
1:8	85
16:14–15	189
21:20	205n
22:3	33
34	11, 34–35, 37–41

34:8–22	256	10:25	143
34:16–20	42	33:26	143

Ezekiel

7:21	205n		
20:33–34	189		
20:34	189		
20:40–41	191n		
20:41	189		
34:13	189		
39:29	417		

Wisdom of Solomon

2:11	241

Judith

16:23	143

1 Esdras

4:49	143
4:53	143

Hosea

9:9	41
10:9	41
12:10	190n
13:4	190n

3 Ezra

4:49–52	268

4 Ezra

3:22	203n
3:26	203n
5:6	203
5:8	203
5:10	203
5:12–21	203n
7:45–61	203
11:32	203n

Joel

	417
2:28–29	416
3	255
3:3ff.	33

Amos

2:10	187
9:7	187

Jonah

4:1–11	85

1 Maccabees

2:11	143, 268
10:25–45	268
10:33	143
12:30	143
14:26	143
15:7	143, 268

Micah

6:4	187

Zechariah

12:10	417

2 Maccabees

1:27	143
2:22	143
9:14	143

APOCRYPHA

Sirach

7:21	143

PSEUDEPIGRAPHA

3 Maccabees
3:28	143
7:20	143

4 Maccabees
14:2	143

∾

NEW TESTAMENT

Matthew
	88–89
5:17	239n
7:12	239n
10:14	422n
11:13	239n
20:28	219
22:40	239n
23:23	418
25:31ff.	195
25:34ff.	422n
25:40	422n

Mark
	202n
10:45	219n

Luke
	12, 72, 83
1:34	87
1:37	87
1:48	91
1:68	218n
2	82
2:19	87
2:38	82, 218n
2:51	87
4:16–21	194
4:18	196
4:21	195
7	74
7:22	195
9:23	327
10	41
13:10–17	195
13:11	195
13:14	196
14:1–6	195
14:2	195
14:4	196
14:23	327
16:29–31	239n
21:28	219n
22:42	87
24:21	219n
24:27	239n

John
1:16	420n
3:8	175
3:34	420
4:8	175
4:16	175
4:17	74
4:42	177
5–8	199n
7:35	
8	74
8:31–36	319–20
10:34	239n
12:34	239n
15:25	239n

Acts
2	416
7:35	218n

Romans
	59, 184, 199–212
1:1ff.	239
1:1	237
1:2	239
1:5	211n, 239n
1:7	211n
1:8	211n
1:16ff.	239n

1:21	211	5:17	236n
1:23	211	5:18	211n
1:25	211	5:20	199n, 240n
1:28	211	5:21	199n, 236n
2:12–15	240n	6	130, 306
2:17–18	240n	6:1ff.	243
2:20	240n	6:1–11	235n
2:23	240n	6:1	244
2:25–29	208n	6:4	207
2:25–27	240n	6:6–7	243
3:1–2	208n	6:7	236n
3:8	244	6:9–10	243
3:9	211n, 241	6:9	236n
3:10–18	211	6:12	199n, 236n
3:13–15	211	6:13	200n
3:19–20	211n	6:14–15	240n, 241n
3:19a	239n	6:14	199n, 236n, 238n, 239
3:19b	240n		
3:20–21	240n	6:15	244
3:20	240n, 241	6:16–18	244
3:21—4:25	239	6:16	84
3:21	239	6:17	84, 211
3:23	211n	6:18	199n, 207, 235n, 243
3:24	219n, 236n		
3:27	241	6:19	84, 207
3:27a	240n	6:20–23	59
3:28	240n	6:20	199n, 235n, 319
3:31	239	6:22	199n, 207, 235n, 243
4:1ff.	239n		
4:1–25	239	6:23	83
4:2	241n	7–8	155–56
4:3a	239n	7	150–51, 155
4:6	241	7:1–9	240n
4:13–16	240	7:1–6	238
4:13–14	240n	7:3	199n, 235n, 243
4:15	241	7:4	235n, 238, 239
5–8	236	7:5	242
5	207	7:6	238
5:1	200n	7:7–25	209, 242
5:5	417	7:7	242
5:8	228, 245	7:8	199n, 242
5:10	200n	7:9	199n
5:11	200n	7:10	242
5:12–21	197	7:11	199n, 200n, 242
5:12	199n, 241	7:12	240n, 242
5:13	240n	7:13	199n, 241, 242
5:14	236n	7:14	240n, 241, 242
5:15–21	207	7:15–16	236n

7:15	142, 238	9:31	240n
7:16	240n	9:32	241n
7:17–18	155	10:4–5	240n
7:17	155	10:4	238n
7:18–20	142	10:5	240, 241n
7:18	155	11:6	241n
7:19–20	236n	11:13	243
7:22	240n	11:26	236n
7:23	242	11:33–36	211
7:23b	240n	11:36	211
7:24	236n	12	209, 417
7:25	240n, 242	12:1–2	209–10
7:25a	211	12:2	209
8	155, 208	12:4ff.	417
8:1ff.	243	12:5	209
8:1–39	208–9, 244	12:9ff.	245
8:1–13	242	12:14	209
8:1–4	243	12:17	209
8:2	199n, 235n, 238n, 242, 419	12:18	209
		13	49
8:3–4	240n	13:1–7	209n, 220
8:3	242	13:8–10	242, 245
8:3a	240n	13:8	240n, 242
8:4	242	13:9	242
8:5–8	156	13:10	240n
8:6	156	13:12	200n
8:7–8	209	14:1—15:7	245
8:7	240n	14:1—15:6	210–11
8:9–11	243	14	207, 210, 245, 306n
8:9	208		
8:10	208	14:1–13	210
8:14	238n, 243	14:6	210
8:15–16	244	14:7–9	207
8:15	211	14:7–8	238n
8:17–18	208	14:13	210
8:17	208, 245	14:15	210, 243n
8:21–25	245	14:16	210
8:21	143, 184, 199n, 212, 222, 235n, 245, 320	14:19	210
		14:20–21	210
		14:20	210
8:22	212	14:22	210
8:23	208, 219n, 236n	14:23	327
8:28	245	15:1ff.	237n
8:31–32	245	15:1–3	9, 243n
8:35	208, 245	15:1	208n
8:38–39	208, 245	15:3	237
9:5	211	15:6	211, 239n
9:12	241n	15:7–13	211

15:7–8	237n	9:21	239, 243
15:7	237, 243n	10:23—11:1	229
15:11	211n	10:23	210, 229
15:33	211	10:24	229
16:20	200n	10:25–33	229
16:27	211	10:29	235n
		10:32	229
		12	417
		12:4ff.	417

1 Corinthians

1:23	237	12:7	9, 417
1:30	219, 236n	12:12ff.	417
2:8	220	12:13	235n, 236, 237, 238
3	236n		
6	57	13:1–3	417
6:19	285	14	49, 210
6:20	66, 235n	14:4ff.	417
7	57, 223	14:4	210
7:17–31	223	14:17	210
7:17–24	236n	14:21	239n
7:17–20	223	14:33	418
7:21–24	51, 223	15	196
7:21	235n, 237, 238	15:1	210
7:21b	51n, 236, 238	15:6	240n
7:22–23	207	15:24–27	196–97
7:22	117n, 235, 237, 238		

2 Corinthians

7:22a	236	3	236
7:23	66, 235n	3:6	238n, 241
7:25–31	223	3:7	241
7:37	136	3:9	241
7:39	235n	3:14	241
8–10	236n, 245	3:16	241
8	229	3:17	66, 143, 235n, 241, 319, 320n
8:1ff.	245		
8:1	210	5:15	238n
8:3	245	8:7–9	243n
8:9–11	237n	8:7ff.	237n
8:9	245	9:6ff.	237n
8:10	210		
8:11	243		

Galatians

9	236n, 237n		62, 228, 236, 306
9:1	235n	1:6ff.	239n
9:4ff.	245	1:6	239n
9:8–9	240n	1:10	237
9:19–23	229	2:1–21	239
9:19	235n, 245	2:4	235n, 238n
9:20	238n, 240n, 241n, 243		

2:15—4:31	239
2:15	240
2:16	240, 241n
2:17	244
2:19-20	238n, 243
2:19	235n, 238, 239, 240n
2:20	228, 245
2:21	240n, 241n
3:2	240n, 241n
3:5	240n, 241n
3:8	239n
3:10-13	240n
3:10	240, 241
3:11	241n
3:12	240
3:13	235n
3:17-19	240n
3:19	239
3:21	240n, 241n
3:22	241
3:23-26	241
3:23-24	240n
3:23	241n
3:25	238n
3:28	53, 54, 59, 60, 67, 121, 221n, 223, 235n, 236, 237, 238
4:4-5	235n, 240n, 241
4:5	238n
4:21-31	58
4:21	241n
4:21a	240n
4:21b	239n
4:22-26	1433
4:22	235n, 236, 237
4:23	235n
4:25	236n
4:26	235n, 236n
4:30	235n
4:31—5:1	46
4:31	143, 235n
5:1-6	228
5:1-4	238n
5:1	143, 202n, 235n
5:3-4	240n
5:4	240-41nn

5:6	242
5:13-15	228
5:13	3, 66, 245, 319
5:14	240n, 242
5:16-18	238n
5:17	236n, 238
5:18	238n, 240n, 241n
5:22	242
5:23	240n
5:23b	242
6:2	239, 243, 419

Ephesians

	49, 53
1:7	219n
1:14	219n
2:4-7	228
2:4ff.	245
4:7	333
4:30	219n
5:2	245
5:22—6:9	49
5:25-33	52
5:25b	245
5:22-24	77, 225
5:32	76
6:6-8	224
6:5-8	224
6:9	224, 225

Philippians

1:1	237
1:27—2:18	243n
1:27	236n
2:1-7	9
2:1ff.	237n
2:5-11	197
2:6-8	237
2:6	245
2:7ff.	246
3:5-6	240n
3:6	241n
3:9	240n, 241n
3:20	236n

Colossians

	49, 53
1:14	219n
3:11	223, 238
3:18—4:1	49
3:19	52
3:22–25	224
3:23–24	224
4:1	224, 225

1 Thessalonians

1:10	236n
4:3–8	221n
4:13—5:11	219

1 Timothy

	64, 306n
2:11–15	49
5:3–8	49
6:1–2	49, 63

2 Timothy

2:9	316

Titus

2:2–10	49
2:14	219n
3:1–2	49

Philemon

	51, 225–27
8ff.	238
8	226n
10	226
12	226
13	226
14	226n
16	226, 237, 238
17	226
18	226
21	226
23–24	227

Hebrews

	306, 422
9:12	218n
9:15	219n

James

1:25	143, 235
2:12	143, 235

1 Peter

1:18	219n
2:15	229
2:16	229, 235, 319
2:17	229
2:18—3:7	49
2:18–25	224

2 Peter

2:19	235

Revelation

	219, 222
1:5	228
1:6	222

Names Index

NB: numbers in **bold** indicate the essays in this volume

MODERN AUTHORS

Aasgard, Reidar, 64n, 68
Abraham, Susan, **360–83**
Achtemeier, Paul J., 68
Acton, Lord (John Emerich Edward Dahlberg), 282n, 309
Adler, Mortimer, 48, 68
Aejmelaeus, Lars, 163
Albertz, Rainer, 274n, 276
Albrecht, G. H. 308n, 309
Allen, O. Wesley, 213, 275n
Allolio-Näcke, Lars, 275n, 277
Alston, Wallace M., Jr., 312
Anshen, Ruth Nanda, 48n, 68
Arendt, Hannah, 8–9, 12, 91, 91n, 404, 405n
Armstrong, A. H., 232
Arnim, Hans von, 116n, 131
Arnold, Patrick, 41, 43
Atlas, James, 404n, 409
Augustine, Saint, 108n, 130, 134, 147, 150–52, 154, 157, 162, 329–30

Bach, Alice, 43, 68, 71, 92
Bachman, Michael, 240n, 246
Balch, David L., 48, 50, 68, 71
Bales, Kevin, 21, 47n, 68
Balke, Willem, 282n, 283, 309
Balz, Horst, 233, 246
Bar-Asher, M., 44

Barclay, John M. G., 201n, 210n, 212, 213
Barth, Christoph, 186n, 192n, 193n, 197
Barth, Karl, 96, 166–79, 202n, 204n, 212, 280, 282, 287–88n, 296n, 309, 357
Bartoš, F. M., 317n, 318n, 321n, 328n, 334–35
Bartsch, Hans-Werner, 268n, 276
Baudrillard, Jean, 386n, 410
Bauer, Gary, 78n
Bauer, Jörg, 12
Bauks, Michaela, 313
Baumann, Peter, 113n, 115
Beavis, Mary Ann, 55n, 68
Becker, U., 268n, 276
Bedford-Strohm, Heinrich, 280, 308n, 309, 421n, 425
Beek, Bram van de, 280, 309
Beilby, James, 410
Beker, J. Christiaan, 200n
Bellow, Saul, 354
Benedict XVI, Pope, 392, 395–96, 398, 400n, 409, 410; *see also* Ratzinger, Joseph Kardinal
Berkouwer, Gerrit C., 280, 309
Berlin, Isaiah, 106, 108, 111n, 115, 339, 343–47, 355, 359
Bernstein, Richard J., 405n, 410
Bethge, Eberhard, 425
Betz, Hans Dieter, 48n, 67n, 68
Bevere, Allan R., 52, 68
Biéler, André, 284n, 309
Bierwaltes, Werner, 228n, 232

NAMES INDEX

Bigger, Nigel, 296n, 309
Birnstein, Uwe, 285n, 309
Bittner, Rüdiger, 1, 95, **98-115**, 286n
Bleicken, Jochen, 116n, 131
Blunck, J., 215n, 232
Bobzien, S., 116n, 131
Böckenförde, Ernst-Wolfgang, 101n, 115, 389n, 396, 410
Boer, Dick, 32n, 43
Boer, Martinus C. de, 200n
Boesak, Allan, 306, 309
Bonhoeffer, Dietrich, 76, 280, 301n, 424n, 425
Boring, M. Eugene, 202, 212, 213
Bornkamm, Heinrich, 149n, 162
Bosse-Huber, Petra, ix
Botticelli, Sandro, 29
Bouwsma, William J., 283n, 309
Bowden, John, 425
Boyarin, Daniel, 59n
Bradley, Keith R., 48n, 55n, 68, 216n, 224n, 225n, 232
Brandt, Sigrid, 422n, 425
Brecht, Martin, 10n, 12
Briggs, Sheila, 32n, 43, 58n, 50, 68
Brinkman, Martien E., 280, 309
Brockmeyer, Norbert, 29n, 43
Bromiley, Geoffrey W., 179, 213, 309
Brooten, Bernadette, 8n, 12
Brown, Brian, 78n
Brown, Colin, 232
Brümmer, Vincent, 285n, 309
Budde, Karl, 260n, 265
Buell, Denise Kimber, 59n
Bugg, Laura Elizabeth, 49n, 68
Burgsmüller, Alfred, 287n, 309
Busch, Eberhard, 287n, 288n, 310
Butin, Philip Walker, 307n, 310
Byron, John, 221n, 232

Callahan, Allen Dwight, 51n, 55n, 68-69, 220n, 221n, 225n, 232
Calvin, John, 80, 148, 152, 162, 252-53, 278-79, 281-303, 305n, 306-8, 310, 327n, 419-20, 425

Campbell, Nancy, 79, 92
Cardellini, Innocenzo, 32n, 34n, 43
Carmichael, Calum M., 32, 43
Carpentier, Jean, 10n, 12
Carroll, John T., 213
Carroll, Robert P., 40, 43
Casas, Bartolomé de las, 384, 385n, 410
Castelli, Elizabeth, 59n, 69
Castellio, S., 326, 335
Cavallar, George, 385n, 410
Chantipe de la Saussaye, P. D., 266
Chantraine, Pierre, 142n, 146
Cheah, Pheng, 340, 361-62, 370-83
Chelčický, Petr, 323, 335
Chirichigno, G., 32n, 43
Clements, Keith W., 280, 310
Cockburn, Andrew, 47n, 69
Cogan, Michael, 272, 276
Cohen, Samuel, 26-27n
Cohen, Shaye J. D., 233
Coleman, Janet, 384, 410
Comenius, 332-33, 335
Copleston, Frederick, 155n, 162
Coppins, Wayne, 199n, 212
Cotterell, Peter, 218, 232
Crouch, James E., 48, 50n, 66n, 69
Crüsemann, Frank, 44, 257, 265
Curran, Charles E., 394, 410

Dalferth, Ingolf U., 157-58, 161, 162
Dandamayev, M. A., 34n, 43
Daube, David, 50n, 69
Davies, A. Mervyn, 283n, 310
Davis, Stephen T., 425
De Gruchy, John W., 281, 283n, 306n, 310
Denifle, Heinrich, 148
Derrida, Jacques, 362, 370n, 372, 377-78, 380-81, 386n, 404-6, 410
DeSaar, Malia Saada, 83n, 92
Deutscher, Elisabeth, ix
Dietrich, Walter, 33n, 43
Dihle, Albrecht, 124n, 131
Dixon, Suzanne, 48n, 69
Dobson, James, 78n
Donfried, Karl P., 200n, 212

Dostoyeski, Fyodor, 345, 354–55
Douglass, Jane Dempsey, 282, 283n, 299, 306, 310
Drägert, Christian, ix
Drury, Shadia B., 401n, 410
DuBois, Page, 9n, 12, 51, 69
Dunn, James D. G., 47, 48n, 69, 202, 212, 213, 235n, 240n, 246, 419n, 425
Dyzenhaus, David, 400n, 410

Eckstein, Hans-Joachim, 2–3, 73–74, 75n, 183, 199n, 208n, 215n, **235–47**, 235n, 238n, 246, 306n, 422n, 425
Edzard, D. Otto, 43
Egmond, A. von, 309, 311
Ehring, C., 274n, 275n, 276
Elliott, John H., 48, 50, 69
Enders, Christoph, 101n, 115
Engberg-Pedersen, Troels, 207n, 213
Epstein, I., 86n, 92
Escobedo, Andrew, 98n
Esler, Philip F., 201, 213
Etzelmüller, Gregor, 426

Finkelstein, Israel, 29n, 43
Fiorenza, Francis Schüssler, 4, 340–41, **384–412**, 410, 414, 422, 425
Fischer, Georg, 34n, 37n, 40, 43
Fischer, Irmtraud, 32n, 43
Fitzgerald, John T., 132, 213
Flesher, Paul V. M., 227n, 232
Foppa, K., 267n, 277
Forster, Karl, 390n, 410
Foskett, Mary F., 213
Foucault, Michel, 274, 275n, 277
Fourie, Willem, 279n, 310
Frachon, Alain, 404n, 410
Frankfurt, Harry G., 107, 108, 113n, 115
Frey, J., 297n, 310
Friedrich, Jörg, 404, 410
Frisk, Hjalmar, 142n, 146
Fuchs, Esther, 43, 68, 71, 88n, 89n, 90n, 92
Fuchs, Thomas, 311, 425

Fuhs, H. F., 189, 190n, 197

Gallagher, Maggie, 78n
Galloway, Lincoln E., 47n, 69, 217n, 232
Gardner, Jane, 48n, 69
Garnsey, Peter, 48n, 63n, 69
Gathercole, Simon J., 213
Gaventa, Beverly Roberts, 2–3, 83n, 84n, 87–88, 92, 184, **199–213**, 202n, 204n, 205n, 211n, 213, 215n, 219n, 306n
Gehlen, Arnold, 264n, 265
Gemeinhardt, Peter, 311
Gerrish, B. A., 284n, 310
Gerth, Hans H., 266
Gertz, Jan Christian, 2, 33n, 202n, 251, **254–66**, 260n, 265, 273–74, 415n
Gibson, E. Leigh, 227n, 232
Ginzberg, Louis, 86n, 92
Glancy, Jennifer A., 55n, 69, 220n, 221n, 232
Glendon, Mary Ann, 399n, 403n, 410
Godley, A. D., 263n, 265
Goethe, Johann Wolfgang, 99, 115
Gonnet, Jean, 316n, 335
Graf, Friedrich Wilhelm, 294n, 302n, 310
Graham, W. Fred, 284n, 310
Green, Clifford J., 280, 310
Gregory, Pope, 385
Grieb, A. Katherine, 200–201, 213
Grieser, Heike, 33n, 44
Grigon, Olof, 215n, 232
Grimm, Harold J., 425
Gros, J., 162
Gudorf, Christine, 81n, 92
Günther, Walther, 228n, 232
Gunton, Colin E., 280–81, 310

Habermas, Jürgen, 166n, 179, 415n, 425
Hagedorn, Anselm, 263n, 265
Hahmann, Andree, 116n, 131
Halama, Jindřich, 4, 252, **315–35**, 332n, 335

NAMES INDEX

Hallo, William W., 276
Hamm, Berndt, 313
Hancock, Ralph C., 283n, 290n, 310
Hanekom, T. N., 304n, 310
Hanse, Len, 426
Hardesty, Nancy, 49n, 71
Harrill, J. Albert, 51n, 63n, 65, 69, 220n, 221n, 222n, 226n, 232
Harris, B. F., 47n, 48n, 69, 216n, 232
Harrison, Beverly Wildung, 89, 92
Hauschild, Wolf-Dieter, 148–49, 151–52, 162
Hayek, F. A. von, 110n, 111n, 115
Hays, Richard B., 197
Heckausen, H., 131
Hederich, Benjamin, 136n, 137n, 142n, 146
Hengel, Martin, 216n, 233
Henley, John, 406n, 410
Hermann, Rudolf, 151, 162
Herrmann, C. S., 131
Hezser, Catherine, 227n, 233
Hieke, Thomas, 36n, 44
Hilpert, Konrad, 33n, 43
Hilton, Allen R., 213
Hobbes, Thomas, 99, 102, 105–6, 109n, 115, 289, 293
Hodge, Johnson, 59
Höffe, Otfried, 393n, 410, 411
Hoffmeyer, John F., 422n, 425
Holl, Karl, 149, 152, 162
Honig, Bonnie, 404, 405n, 411
Hope, Valerie, 64n, 69
Höpfl, Harro, 283n, 310
Hornblower, Simon, 233
Horsley, Richard A., 53–54, 68, 69, 221n, 225n, 233
Hossfeld, Frank-Lothar, 274n, 277
Hovorun, Cyril, 3, 97, **134–46**
Hovorun, Serhiy, 320n
Hrejsa, Ferdinand, 330n, 335
Huber, Wolfgang, 278–82, 308, 310–11, 413n, 414n, 421n, 425
Huovinen, Eero, 159, 162
Hurtado, Larry W., 2–3, 55n, **183–84**, 200, **214–34**, 223n, 233, 306n
Huskinson, Janet, 69

Imber, Naftali Herz, 26

Jacobi, Thorsten, 282–83n, 311
Japhet, Sara, 41, 44
Jarvis, Cynthia A., 312
Jefferson, Thomas, 7–8, 121
Jewett, Robert, 201, 213
John XXIII, Pope, 81n, 386–88, 391–92, 394–95, 407
John Paul II, Pope, 392–94, 396, 398, 409, 411
Jones, F. Stanley, 47n, 69, 217n, 218n, 233
Jones, Henry Stuart, 142n, 146
Jones, Serene, 284n, 311
Jonker, W. D., 284n, 311
Joshel, Sandra, 223n
Joyce, James, 354
Joyce, Kathryn, 78n, 92
Judge, E. A., 65, 69
Jüngel, Eberhard, 283n, 309, 311

Kähler, Else, 49n, 69
Kaiser, Otto, 254n, 265, 268n, 277
Kalyvas, Andreas, 405n, 411
Kant, Immanuel, 95, 101, 112–14, 115, 130, 149, 153, 156–59, 340, 344, 355, 361–80, 382, 383
Käsemann, Ernst, 200n, 207n, 213
Kaufmann, Matthias, 400n, 411
Keck, Leander E., 66n, 69
Keitel, Christoph, 275n, 277
Kellenbach, Katharina von, 1, 11–12, **72–92**, 90n, 92
Keller, I., 131
Kenkel, Hajo, ix
Kessler, Martin, 37n, 44
Keulen, D. van, 309, 311
Kierkegaard, Søren, 148–52, 405
King, Martin Luther, Jr., 76
Kittel, Gerhard, 233
Kittredge, Cynthia Briggs, 49n, 70
Klauser, Theodor, 70, 233, 246
Klein, Richard, 116n, 132
Klemm, David E., 422n, 425
Knaake, D., 179
Knuuttila, Simo, 116n, 132

Koch, Christoph, 259n, 265
Köckert, M., 257n, 265
Korkman, Petter, 384n, 411
Kratz, Reinhard G., 36n, 44
Kreutzer, Mary, 43n, 44
Kreuzer, S., 33n, 44
Kümmel, Werner Georg, 149

Lampe, Peter, 2, 51n, 70, **95–97**, **116–33**, 117n, 130n, 132n, 209n, 215, 226n, 233, 238n, 246, 306n, 321, 322n, 333n, 415n
Landmesser, C., 240n, 246
Lang, Bernhard, 259n, 265
Lang, Peter Thaddäus, 265
Lassen, Eva, 48n, 70
Lauren, Paul Gordon, 397n, 411
Laytner, Anson, 84n, 85n, 92
Lehmann, Helmut T., 425
Lehmann, Paul, 306
Leith, John H., 284n, 311
Leo, Pope, 385
Levinson, Bernard M., 32n, 44
Levy, Andrew, 121n, 132
Liddell, Henry George, 142n, 146
Lieu, Judith, 59n
Lillie, William, 49n, 70
Lindbeck, George, 406, 407n, 411
Link, Christian, 310
Link, Hans-Georg, 228n, 232, 411
Little, David, 283n, 311, 399n, 411
Lohfink, Norbert, 256n, 258, 265
Lührmann, Dieter, 49n, 50, 70
Luther, Martin, 10, 80, 96, 148–52, 154–57, 161–62, 164–66, 179, 252, 278–79, 282, 288, 290, 291n, 293, 294n, 306, 327n, 424n, 425

Macchia, Frank, 417n, 420n, 425
MacDonald, Nathan, 263n, 265
Macheret, Augustin, 393n, 411
MacIntyre, Alisdair, 407n, 411
Macken, John, 280, 311
Macpherson, C. B., 397n, 411
Mäkinen, Virpi, 384n, 411
Maier, Christl M., 37n, 44

Malherbe, Abraham, 66n, 70
Mandolfo, Carleen, 85, 92
Mannerma, Tuomo, 160, 162
Markschies, Christopher, 150n, 163
Martin, Clarice J., 49n, 70, 221n, 233
Martin, Dale B., 48n, 59n, 70, 220n, 222n, 227n, 233
Martyn, J. Louis, 200n, 207n, 209n, 213
Martindale, Don, 266
Mather, Cotton, 80
Matlock, R. Bary, 200n, 213
Mayr, Ernst, 153n, 162
Mayr, F., 116n, 132
McCormick, John P., 401n, 411
McKee, Elsie Anne, 286n, 311
McKeown, Niall, 48n, 70, 223n, 233
McKim, Donald K., 311, 312, 313, 327, 335
McNeill, John T., 283n, 285n, 311, 425
Meeks, Wayne A., 203n, 213
Meister, Chad, 410
Melanchthon, Philip, 10, 152
Mendelsohn, I., 34n, 44
Meyer, Paul W., 207n, 213
Miers, Suzanne, 47n, 70
Migliore, Daniel L., 280, 311
Milborn, Corinna, 43n, 44
Mill, John Stuart, 109n
Miller, James, 200n, 213
Miller, Patrick D., 2, 28–29, 183, **185–98**, 188n, 191n, 192n, 193n, 196n, 197
Mirguet, Françoise, 34n, 44
Mollenkott, Virginia Ramey, 49n, 70
Molnar, Amedeo, 316n, 320n, 322n, 335
Moltmann, Jürgen, 282n, 311, 406n, 424n, 425
Morée, Peter C., 317n, 335
Morsink, Johanne, 399n, 411
Morton, Stephen, 365, 367n, 368, 383
Mouffe, Chantal, 405n, 411
Müller, Joseph Th., 326n, 335
Muller, Richard A., 283n, 311
Musil, Robert, 354

Mustakallio, Antti, 163
Mützlitz, Nina, ix
Nagel, Ernst Josef, 408n, 411
Nasrallah, Laura, 57n, 70
Neff, David, 78n
Nelson, Robert N., 350n, 359
Nestle, Dieter, 47n, 70, 116n, 132, 215n, 217n, 233, 235n, 246
Niebuhr, H. Richard, 296, 300, 311
Niebuhr, Reinhold, 388n, 411
Niederwimmer, Kurt, 48, 70, 215n, 233, 235n, 246
Nisula, Timo, 150n, 163
Numbers, Ronald I., 27n, 44
Nüssel, Friederike, 3, 96, **164–79**, 202n, 306n

Oberdorfer, Bernd, 311
Oberman, Heiko A., 287n, 311
Oeming, Manfred, 1, 10–11, **26–45**, 27n, 35n, 44
Olson, J. E., 285n, 311
Oorschot, Jürgen van, 2, 202n, 206n, 251, **267–77**, 415n
Opočíenský, M., 288n, 312, 317n, 335
Osiek, Carolyn, 48n, 68, 71
Ostriker, Alicia Suskin, 85, 92
Osumi, Y., 32n, 44
Otto, Eckart, 37n, 44, 259n, 265, 266

Pakkala, Juah, 263n, 265
Paul VI, Pope, 392, 394–95, 409, 411
Palacký, František, 321n, 324n, 325n, 326, 335
Pannenberg, Wolfhart, 96, 173–79
Parijs, Philippe van, 109n, 115
Patterson, Orlando, 52–53, 59, 70, 222, 224n, 226n, 233
Pelikan, Jaroslav, 297n, 312
Perdue, Leo G., 269n, 277
Perkins, Tony, 78n
Perlitt, Lothar, 264n, 265
Peschke, Erhard, 323n, 335
Peterson, Norman, 59n, 70
Pettit, Philip, 109n, 115
Pius VI, 385
Pius IX, Pope, 385

Pius XII, Pope, 341, 386–88, 391, 394
Placher, William C., 288n, 312
Plessis, L. M. du, 283n, 312
Pohlenz, Max, 116n, 124n, 125n, 127n, 132
Polkinghorne, John, 424n, 425, 426
Preuss, Hans Dieter, 190, 198
Preuss, Ulrich K., 401n, 411
Putnam, Roert D., 281n, 312

Raaflaub, Kurt, 61, 70, 116n, 132, 216n, 233, 268n, 277
Rad, Gerhard von, 28, 264, 265
Ratzinger, Joseph Kardinal, 396n, 407, 412, 415, 425; *see also* Benedict XVI, Pope
Rawls, John, 109n, 115, 339, 343, 347–50, 352–55, 357, 359
Reid, Charles J., Jr., 384n, 412
Rejchrtov, N., 329n, 335
Rendtorff, Trutz, 313
Reuter, Hans-Richard, 279n, 312, 313
Říčan, R., 319n, 326n, 335
Ricoeur, Paul, 291n, 312
Riedinger, Rudolf, 140n, 146
Rom-Shiloni, D., 44
Rosenberg, Alfred, 128n, 132
Ruston, Roger, 385n, 412
Rüterswörden, Udo, 263n, 266

Saarinen, Risto, 3, 95, **147–63**, 150n, 152n, 161–63
Saller, Richard P., 48n, 69, 70
Sampley, J. Paul, 120n, 132
Sanders, J. O., 37n, 44
Scanzoni, Letha, 49n, 71
Schaberg, Jane, 43, 68, 71, 83, 87, 89, 92
Schäfer, Klaus, 64n, 71
Scheeben, Matthias Josef, 420n, 426
Schenker, A., 32n, 37n, 44
Scheuerman, William E., 400n, 412
Schiller, Friedrich, 114n, 115
Schlier, H., 116n, 132, 215n, 217n, 233, 235n, 246
Schlink, Edmund, 420, 421n, 426

Schmale, Wolfgang, 410
Schmid, Hans Heinrich, 269, 277
Schmitt, Carl, 399–401, 404–5, 412
Schmitt, Hans-Christoph, 274n, 277
Schmitz, Otto,
Schneider, Gerhard, 228n, 233, 246
Schneider, Nikolaus, ix
Schneider, Theodor, 147n, 148n, 162, 163
Schnelle, Udo, 206n, 207n, 213
Schopenhauer, Arthur, 124, 148, 151
Schottroff, Luise, 33n, 44
Schrage, Wolfgang, 238n, 246
Schreiner, Susan E., 300n, 312
Schroeder, David, 50n, 71
Schrofer, Erick, 392n, 412
Schuele, Andreas, 425, 426
Schuller, Florian, 425
Schüssler Fiorenza, Elisabeth, 1–3, **7–13, 46–71**, 51n, 57n, 68, 69, 70, 71, 75, 215n, 220n, 230n, 306n
Schüssler Fiorenza, Francis, *see* Fiorenza, Francis Schüssler
Schützeichel, Heribert, 298n, 312
Schwarzkopf, Grit, 311, 425
Schweiker, William, 280, 312, 422n, 425, 426
Schwienhorst-Schönberger, Ludger, 270n, 277
Scott, Robert, 142n, 146
Selderhuis, Herman J., 300n, 312, 313
Shakespeare, 102n
Shotter, D. C. A., 116n, 132
Silberman, Neil A., 29n, 43
Skinner, E. Benjamin, 8n, 12, 47n, 71
Sliziński, Jerzy, 328n, 329n, 330n, 335
Sluga, Hans, 405n, 412
Smit, Dirk J., 4, 73n, **251–53**, 252–53, **278–314**, 297n, 303n, 312, 333n, 424n, 426
Smith, Abraham, 221n, 233
Snell, Daniel C., 255n, 266, 268
Snyder, H. Gregory, 213
Snyder, R. Claire, 80–81, 92

Soodalter, Ron, 10, **14–25**, 43
Soon, C. S., 130n, 131n, 132
Sophocles, E. A., 136n, 137n, 146
Sorabji, Richard, 116n, 132
Souillac, Geneviève, 403n, 412
Spawforth, Anthony, 233
Spencer, F. Scott, 41, 44
Spivak, Gayatri Chakravorty, 340, 361–70, 372, 379–80, 382–83, 415n
Starke, Ekkehard, ix
Stendahl, Krister, 149
Stephani, Henrici, 136n, 142n, 146
Stevenson, William R., Jr., 252, 283n, 284n, 285n, 288–303, 306, 307n, 313, 333n
Stoddard, Lothrop, 128n, 132
Stoellger, Philipp, 161n, 163
Strohm, Christoph, 283n, 302n, 313
Stowers, Stanley K., 54, 71, 221n, 233
Strecker, Christian, 240n, 246
Stuhlmacher, Peter, 238n, 246
Syme, Ronald, 51n, 71

Talbott, Rick F., 9–10, 13
Tannehill, Robert C., 196, 198
Taylor, Charles, 345
Taylor, Joan E., 63n, 71
Theissen, Gerd, 27, 45, 155n, 163
Thomas Aquinas, 102n, 115
Thomas, Geoff, 77–78
Thomas, Günter, 425, 426
Thraede, Klaus, 48, 50, 71
Tierney, Brian, 384, 412
Tomuschat, Christian, 391n, 412
Tomson, Peter J., 227n, 234
Torrance, T. F., 179, 309
Tov, E., 44
Tredennick, Hugh, 425
Trempela, Panagiotes, 420n, 426
Trible, Phyllis, 89n, 92
Troeltsch, Ernst, 279n, 290n, 294n, 299n, 313
Trojan, J. S., 324n, 335
Treurnicht, A. P., 305n, 313
Trueman, Carl R., 283n, 313
Turner, Max, 218n, 232

Urbach, E. E., 227n, 234
Utz, Arthur-Fridolin, 388n, 412

Valeton, J. J. P., 260n, 266
Van Seters, John, 32n, 45
Veijola, Timoo, 32n, 45, 259n, 266
Vernet, Daniel, 404n, 410
Vogt, Joseph, 48n, 71
Vollenweider, Samuel, 47n, 71, 217n, 234, 235n, 247
Vorgrimler, Herbert, 412
Vosloo, R. R., 312

Wagner, J. Ross, 213
Wagner, Sabine, ix
Wagner, Murray L., 323n, 335
Wallace, Ronald S., 284n, 313
Walzer, Michael, 283n, 313, 406, 412
Wander, Bernd, ix
Washington, George, 121
Waskow, Arthur, 84n, 92
Watson, Francis, 202n, 213
Weaver, Darlene, 407n, 410, 412
Weber, Max, 104, 115, 260, 266, 294
Weber, Ulrich, ix
Wegner, Judith Romney, 74n, 92
Weidinger, Karl, 50n, 71
Weinrich, Michael, 280, 313
Weiss, J. G., 234
Welker, Michael, **ix**, **1–4**, 281n, 288n, 291n, 307–8, 312, 313–14, **339–42**, 410, **413–26**, 413n, 414n, 416n, 417n, 418n, 419n, 420n, 421n, 422n, 423n, 424n, 425, 426
Wellman, Carl, 402n, 412
Welwei, Karl-Wilhelm, 254n, 266
Wendel, François, 327n, 335
Wenz, Gunther, 147n, 148n, 162, 163
Wernisch, M., 318n, 321n, 335
Westerholm, Stephen, 150n, 163
Weth, Rudolf, 287n, 309
Wicker, Kathleen O'Brien, 50n, 71
Wiesehöfer, Josef, 271n, 277
Wilk, Florian, 213
Willis-Watkins, David, 288n, 312
Winfrey, Oprah, 23

Winter, Sarah C., 51n, 71
Wirszubski, Chaim, 47n, 71, 116n, 132, 216, 234
Witte, John, Jr., 283n, 314
Witte, Markus, 45
Wolter, Michael, 417n, 426
Wolterstorff, Nicholas, 284n, 306–7n, 314
Würthwein, Ernst, 37n, 45

Yoder, John Howard, 50
Yu, Carver T., 4, 339, **343–59**, 414n

Zeeden, Ernst Walter, 265
Zenger, Erich, 274n, 277
Zizioulas, John, 418n, 426
Zöller, Rainer, 124, 133

ANCIENT AUTHORS

Aelius Aristides, 129n
Aeschylus, 118n, 124, 130, 254n
Agatho, Pope, 140
Alcaeus, 129n
Alcidamas, 121n, 129
Alexander of Aphrodias, 126n, 127
Arcesilaos, 124n
Aristotle, 50–51, 67, 118n, 119n, 120n, 121, 122, 124–26, 129, 414, 415n, 425
Arius, 135
Athanasius of Alexandria, 135–36

Basil of Caesarea, 107n, 136–39

Carneades, 124
Cassius Dio, 118n
Chrysippus, 123–24, 126–27
Cicero, 124n, 216
Clement of Alexandria, 129n, 137, 140, 144
Demosthenes, 120n

Dio Chrysostom, 116–17, 119n, 121n, 122n
Diodorus Siculus, 129n, 137n
Diogenes Laertius, 121n, 122n, 124n
Diogenes Sinope, 122n, 123

Epictetus, 117, 122n, 123n, 129, 142, 209n, 216n, 217, 232
Epicurus, 122n, 124
Euripides, 110, 119n, 120n, 142, 144

Gregory of Nazianzus, 138, 144–45, 320
Gregory of Nyssa, 138–39, 144

Herodotus, 109, 118n, 119n, 120n, 205n, 254n, 263n, 271n
Hippolytos, 123n
Homer, 118n, 124, 130

Ignatius of Antioch, 49, 63–65, 143–44
Irenaeus of Lyon, 137
Isocrates, 118n, 121n

John Chrysostomos, 144
John of Damascus, 140–41
Justin, 144

Livy, 119n
Lucian, 120n, 122n, 129n
Lucretius, 122n

Martin, Pope, 140
Maximus the Confessor, 135, 140–41
Nemesius of Emessa, 138

Oinomaos, 124
Philo, 63, 70, 122n, 137, 217, 233
Pindar, 118n, 268
Plato, 117n, 118n, 119n, 120n, 121, 124–26, 127–28n
Plutarch, 120n
Polybius, 118n
Pseudo-Aristotle, 125n
Pseudo-Plato, 119n

Quintilian, 127–28

Seneca, 105n, 121n, 122n, 129, 220, 225
Socrates, 123, 125–26
Sophocles, 120

Tacitus, 116n, 120n, 216
Theophrastus, 124
Thucydides, 118n

Xenophon, 118n, 123n

Zenon, 122n, 123–24